Date d

International Financial Centres

International Financial Centres

Concepts, Development and Dynamics

Edited by

Richard Roberts

Lecturer at the School of Social Sciences
University of Sussex

INTERNATIONAL FINANCIAL CENTRES

An Elgar Reference Collection

Published by
Edward Elgar Publishing Limited
Gower House
Croft Road
Aldershot
Hants GU11 3HR
England

Edward Elgar Publishing Company
Old Post Road
Brookfield
Vermont 05036
USA

British Library Cataloguing in Publication Data
International Financial Centres
I. Roberts, Richard
332.15

Library of Congress Cataloguing in Publication Data
International financial centres / edited by Richard Roberts.
p. cm. — (An Elgar reference collection)
Includes bibliographical references and index.
Contents: v. 1. International financial centres: concepts, development, and dynamics — v. 2. Global financial centres — v. 3. International financial centres of Europe, North America, and Asia — v. 4. Offshore financial centres.
1. International finance. 2. Central places. I. Roberts, Richard, 1952– . II. Series.
HG3881.I60727 1994
332′.042—dc20 94-21487
CIP

ISBN 1 85898 152 2
1 85278 758 9 (4 volume set)

Printed in Great Britain at the University Press, Cambridge

Contents

Acknowledgements

The editor and publishers wish to thank the following who have kindly given permission for the use of copyright material.

Allen & Unwin Pty Ltd for excerpt: Herbert G. Grubel (1986), 'Trade in Financial Services: Its Nature, Causes, Growth Prospects and Social Effects' in Augustine H.H. Tan and Basant Kapur (eds), *Pacific Growth and Financial Interdependence*, 247–60, 381–2.

American Banker for figure included in excerpt: Richard McGahey, Mary Malloy, Katherine Kazanas and Michael P. Jacobs (1990), 'What Makes a Financial Center?', *Financial Services, Financial Centers: Public Policy and the Competition for Markets, Firms and Jobs*, Chapter 2, 22.

American Finance Association for article: Kenneth D. Garbade and William L. Silber (1978), 'Technology, Communication and the Performance of Financial Markets: 1840–1975', *Journal of Finance*, **XXXIII** (3), June, 819–32.

Banca Nazionale del Lavoro for articles: H.W. Arndt (1984), 'Measuring Trade in Financial Services', *Banca Nazionale del Lavoro Quarterly Review*, No. 149, June, 197–213; H.W. Arndt (1988), 'Comparative Advantage in Trade in Financial Services', *Banca Nazionale del Lavoro Quarterly Review*, **XLI**, 61–78.

Cambridge University Press for article and excerpt: Woodruff D. Smith (1984), 'The Function of Commercial Centers in the Modernization of European Capitalism: Amsterdam as an Information Exchange in the Seventeenth Century', *Journal of Economic History*, **XLIV** (4), December, 985–1005; Geoffrey Jones (1992), 'International Financial Centres in Asia, the Middle East and Australia: A Historical Perspective' in Youssef Cassis (ed.), *Finance and Financiers in European History, 1880–1960*, 405–28.

E.P. Davis for his own article: (1990), 'International Financial Centres – An Industrial Analysis', *Bank of England Discussion Paper*, No. 51, September, contents, abstract, 1–23.

International Finance Section of Princeton University for excerpt: Charles P. Kindleberger (1974), *The Formation of Financial Centers: A Study in Comparative Economic History*, Princeton Studies in International Finance No. 36, November, 1–78.

Kluwer Academic Publishers, Inc. for excerpts: Yoon S. Park (1989), 'Recent Functional Changes in International Finance and their Implications for International Financial Centers' in Yoon S. Park and Musa Essayyad (eds), *International Banking and Financial Centers*, 235–46; Howard Curtis Reed (1989), 'Financial Center Hegemony, Interest Rates, and the Global Political Economy' in Yoon S. Park and Musa Essayyad (eds), *International Banking and Financial Centers*, 247–68.

Lafferty Publications Ltd and the Economists Advisory Group for excerpts: Economists Advisory Group (1984), 'The Evolution of London as an International Financial Centre', *City 2000: The Future of London as an International Financial Centre*, Chapter 2, 7–17; Economists Advisory Group (1984), 'Regulation, Competition and Technology in the Supply of Financial Services', *City 2000: The Future of London as an International Financial Centre*, Chapter 4, 37–55.

McKinsey & Company, Inc. for article: Joel A. Bleeke and Lowell L. Bryan (1988), 'The Globalization of Financial Markets', *The McKinsey Quarterly*, Winter, 17–38.

MIT Press for excerpt: Howard Curtis Reed (1983), 'Appraising Corporate Investment Policy: A Financial Center Theory of Foreign Direct Investment' in Charles P. Kindleberger and David B. Audretsch (eds), *The Multinational Corporation in the 1980s*, 219–44.

Oxford University Press for excerpt: Roy C. Smith and Ingo Walter (1991), 'Reconfiguration of Global Financial Markets in the 1990s' in Richard O'Brien and Sarah Hewin (eds), *Finance and the International Economy 4*, Chapter 8, 143–68.

Pergamon Press Ltd for article: John Langdale (1985), 'Electronic Funds Transfer and the Internationalisation of the Banking and Finance Industry', *Geoforum*, **16** (1), 1–13.

Pinter Publishers Ltd for excerpt: Richard O'Brien (1992), 'Everybody Has To Be Somewhere: The New Determinants of Location', *Global Financial Integration: The End of Geography*, Chapter 8, 73–82.

Prentice-Hall, Inc. for excerpt: Gunter Dufey and Ian H. Giddy (1978), 'Financial Centers and External Financial Markets', *The International Money Market*, Appendix 2, 35–47.

Sage Publications Ltd for excerpt: Nigel Thrift (1987), 'The Fixers: The Urban Geography of International Commercial Capital' in Jeffrey Henderson and Manuel Castells (eds), *Global Restructuring and Territorial Development*, 203–33.

Springer-Verlag for article: Michael A. Goldberg, Robert W. Helsley and Maurice D. Levi (1988), 'On the Development of International Financial Centers', *Annals of Regional Science*, **22** (special festschrift issue), February, 81–94.

Swiss Bankers' Association for excerpt: Sir David Scholey (1987), 'Essential Features of International Financial Centres' in *International Financial Centres: Structure, Achievements and Prospects*, Proceedings of the 40th International Banking Summer School, 11–24.

Transaction Publishers for article: Mitchell L. Moss (1988), 'Telecommunications and International Financial Centers', *Information and Behaviour*, **3**, Chapter 13, 239–52.

Weltwirtschaftliches Archiv for article: Sang-Rim Choi, Adrian E. Tschoegl and Chwo-Ming Yu (1986), 'Banks and the World's Major Financial Centers, 1970–1980', *Weltwirtschaftliches Archiv*, **122** (1), 48–64.

Westview Press, Inc. for excerpt: Richard McGahey, Mary Malloy, Katherine Kazanas, and Michael P. Jacobs (1990), 'What Makes a Financial Center?', *Financial Services, Financial Centers: Public Policy and the Competition for Markets, Firms, and Jobs*, Chapter 2, 15–76.

Every effort has been made to trace all the copyright holders but if any have been inadvertently overlooked the publishers will be pleased to make the necessary arrangement at the first opportunity.

In addition the publishers wish to thank the Library of the London School of Economics for their assistance in obtaining these articles.

Introduction

International financial centres are an important subject of widespread topical interest. In Europe, the process of economic and financial integration, in particular the formation of a European central bank and its location, raises questions about the future roles not only of London and Frankfurt, but of every European financial centre. In the United States, there is concern about the international competitiveness of New York, while greater participation in the provision of international financial services has become an ambition of other North American centres. In Asia, the international dimension of Tokyo's financial service industry has grown rapidly in recent years, but there is much scope for further development, while participation of foreign firms remains a matter of controversy. Another Asian issue is the future of Hong Kong as an international financial centre when it reverts to Chinese rule in 1997. Then there are the offshore centres whose futures are clouded by uncertainty as deregulation in the world's major economies undermines their *raison d'être* as international financial centres.

The essays on international financial centres in this volume focus on key concepts, on comparative and other historical studies illustrating conceptual points, and on certain common factors (notably international financial flows, communications and information technology, and the nature of international financial services). Essays on individual centres appear in the three companion collections, *Global Financial Centres – London, New York, Tokyo*; *International Financial Centres of Europe, North America and Asia*, and *Offshore Financial Centres*.

It is generally agreed that a hierarchy exists amongst international financial centres, with several different typologies of the various types of centre being suggested in essays in this volume. The typology used in this volume and its companion collections corresponds exactly with none of the above models, though there are many common elements. It comprises four tiers which are: (1) domestic financial centres serving a national clientele; (2) regional financial centres serving a regional clientele (a region in this context being a supra-national entity not a sub-national entity); (3) offshore financial centres, financial entrepots whose activities as international financial centres have little to do with the financial system of the country in which they are located; and (4) global financial centres serving a world-wide clientele. Of course, by definition, domestic financial centres are not international financial centres and thus lie outside the scope of these volumes; they are mentioned here, however, because they form part of the hierarchy of financial centres and because the term is used occasionally in the introductions to these volumes.

Concepts and Typologies

The opening essay in this volume is a formal and rigorous theoretical treatment of the subject by Bank of England economist Philip Davis (1990). Industrial location theory forms his analytical framework. Using this theory to explain the location decisions of banks and other financial firms – the constituent components of international financial centres – he presents a set of propositions about the growth and development of financial centres. This is a particularly useful and original contribution to the literature.

In general terms, there are three factors that influence firms' decisions to locate at a given site: the supply of factors of production, the demand for output and external economies. Of course, these considerations are always relative to alternative sites. Applying this framework to financial firms, Davis identifies the availability of suitable personnel, the cost of funds, the efficiency of settlement systems, and regulatory distortions as the principal supply-side factors. For financial firms established in a particular location, an important cost consideration is unrecoverable 'sunk costs' which may be substantial. As regards demand, a distinction is made between retail activities, for which face-to-face access to clients is important, and operations in the wholesale markets that today, with modern communications technology, can be undertaken from almost anywhere. For international activities, time zone location is also an important demand-side factor. But the most important factors are external economies of scale and economies of agglomeration. Many of the external economies are related to superior information flows, providing the basis for more accurate and more competitive pricing of financial services and financial instruments. Typically for financial markets, the larger the market the greater its efficiency and liquidity. Moreover, financial markets are closely interrelated and reinforce each other when located together. Another aspect of agglomeration is the growth of related professionals and trades providing services for financial firms, such as lawyers, accountants, printers or computer programmers.

Thus the financial centres industry exhibits increasing returns to scale at all levels of activity. This means that major financial centres have a competitive advantage over lesser centres, and their growth may be to the detriment of smaller centres. A corollary is that concentration of financial services in major centres offers a global gain in terms of economic efficiency. Once established, the growth of major centres is likely to be self-sustaining. The importance of sunk costs means that a significant deterioration in market conditions is needed to stimulate the relocation of financial firms or markets. But once the process has begun it may prove cumulative, given the nature and importance of external economies. Weighing up costs and benefits of hosting a major international financial centre, Davis comes to the conclusion that its presence is likely to be of considerable advantage to the domestic economy and thus any decline would constitute a considerable cost.

Sir David Scholey's essay, the text of an address delivered to the 1987 International Banking Summer School in Basle, offers the perspectives of a major figure in international finance, the author being chairman of the leading London merchant bank S.G. Warburg Group plc. He proposes that the operations of financial centres comprise three elements: a surplus of capital (i.e. a supply of funds), a deficit of capital (i.e. a demand for funds) and an intermediation process (to match supply with demand). With this straightforward model as a framework, he analyses the historical evolution of various international financial centres through to the 1960s. Particularly noteworthy are his comments on the Genoese financiers of the 16th century and his observation of a parallel between their activities (which were based on gathering funds from other centres and not just local surpluses) and the operations of modern international financial centres. Such free flows of funds are characteristic of the euromarkets, whose development is incisively analysed. The resurgence of London as an international financial centre since the 1960s came about as a consequence of playing host to the euromarkets and the international banks that participated in them. This role, of 'attracting, welcoming, facilitating participation by firms all over the world, a true *entrepot* and market place in the fullest sense', as Scholey puts it, is that of an 'inward international financial centre'. The vulnerability of this role is that it is essentially passive, which in modern competitive conditions is no longer adequate. The successful international financial centre of the future, he argues, will be an 'outward international financial centre', that is 'the hub of a global network of trading, financing and broking businesses with tentacles reaching deep into market places of other countries'.

In an appendix to their book *The International Money Market* (1978), economists Gunter Dufey of the University of Michigan and Ian H. Giddy of Columbia University provide a helpful set of discursive definitions of various terms encountered in the literature on financial centres. These include financial centre; international financial centre; traditional capital exports; entrepot financial services; offshore banking; international entrepot financial centres, and offshore banking centres, with the two latter terms receiving closest attention. 'International entrepot financial centres' (called global financial centres in these four volumes), such as London and New York, have four characteristics according to Dufey and Giddy: economic and political stability; an efficient and experienced financial community; good communications and supportive services, and an official regulatory climate favourable to the financial industry, in the sense that it protects investors without unduly restricting financial institutions. Dufey and Giddy regard offshore banking centres as constituting a sub-group amongst the providers of entrepot financial services, offering the much narrower service of intermediation for non-resident borrowers and residents. The principal attraction for banks of location in offshore banking centres is the absence of intrusive and expensive official regulation and taxation. The authors also furnish a number of case studies: London, Luxembourg (a useful source of information on a centre about which little is available in English), Singapore and Hong Kong, and the Caribbean.

The most thorough and comprehensive empirical investigation of the development of international financial centres is Howard Curtis Reed's, *The Preeminence of International Financial Centers* (1981). This study used data for nine variables relating to 80 cities for the years 1900–1980 to explain the evolution of an hierarchical order amongst international financial centres. Reed's (1983) article in this section (Chapter 4) uses a revised data set of 16 variables covering the 36 leading centres for the year 1980. His variables are of three main types, measuring international clearing operations, global portfolio management and communications links.

The outcome of Reed's research is a three-tier classification of international financial centres: (1) host international financial centres which 'enhance their own financial infrastructures and capabilities by attracting relatively large numbers of foreign financial institutions from a large number of countries'; (2) international financial centres that 'are headquarters for large internationally active banks which influence events that pertain to global asset and liability management'; and (3) supra-national financial centres which 'are managers of large amounts of foreign financial assets and liabilities; net suppliers of foreign direct investment capital to the rest of the world; located close to a large number of large industrial corporations; active users of global communications facilities; and management meccas that attract and generate ideas and information in ways that eventually establish the organizational and operating norms that govern internationally active organizations (private and governmental)'.

Matching cities to categories, Reed suggests the following classification as of 1980. Amongst the 'supranational financial centers', New York and London are ranked as 'first order' centres, with Amsterdam, Frankfurt, Paris, Tokyo and Zurich as 'second order' centres. His 'international financial centers' are Basle, Bombay, Brussels, Chicago, Dusseldorf, Hamburg, Hong Kong, Madrid, Melbourne, Mexico City, Rio de Janeiro, Rome, San Francisco, Sao Paulo, Singapore, Sydney, Toronto and Vienna. The 'host international centers' are Bahrain, Buenos Aires, Kobe, Los Angeles, Luxembourg, Milan, Montreal, Osaka, Panama City, Seoul and Taipei.

Reed, an economist and Arkansas-based business consultant, maintains that the role of international financial centres as intermediaries has been neglected in the literature concerned with the process of foreign direct investment. Thus his essay explores the relationship between multinational corporations, 'supranational financial centers' and foreign direct investment, arguing that 'the underlying determinants of foreign direct investment activity are best explained (and understood) by determining the motives and methods of evaluation employed by the supranational financial centers as they appraise, on a continuing basis, the activity of internationally active institutions'.

Reviewing the literature for the purpose of selecting appropriate independent variables for a statistical study of international financial centres, Michael A. Goldberg, Robert W. Helsley and Maurice D. Levi (1988), of the Faculty of Commerce and Business Administration of the University of British Columbia, identify four principal factors: the level of overall economic development; the level of international trade; the extent of financial intermediation, and the stringency of financial regulation. Employing regression analysis, they investigate financial centres at three levels using 1984 data: (1) the international level, examining the determinants of the level of international banking and financial activity in 42 countries; (2) the interregional level, investigating the determinants of the level of financial activity across regions of the US; and (3) the interurban level, studying the determinants of the size of the banking sector across the 31 cities containing the world's 750 largest banks.

The models tested by Goldberg, Helsley and Levi in Chapter 5 explain to a significant extent the variation in the size of financial sectors between countries, regions and cities. The following independent variables were found to be statistically significant: income levels; hosting of corporate headquarters; the occupational and industrial structure of centres; importance within a country or time zone, and international trade. Their results suggest that the same basic economic forces underlie the development of the financial service industry at each functional level.

The nature and location of financial centres are discussed at some length by Richard McGahey, Mary Malloy, Katherine Kazanas and Michael P. Jacobs (1990) in their book *Financial Services, Financial Centers*, part of which is reproduced here as Chapter 6. They begin by defining the 'traditional' role of financial centres, drawing in particular on Kindleberger's historical study (see below), and then examine the impact of recent developments in international finance, notably globalization and improvements in communications technology, themes pursued in subsequent sections of this volume. They assess how changes in financial markets and organizational developments in financial institutions influence location decisions by firms, which in turn affect financial centres. Their examples are drawn from the US and provide insights into the competitive standing of the leading US financial centres. They identify and explore four 'dimensions of competitiveness': location costs and location advantages; the labour force and human resources; telecommunications and technology; and regulation and taxation. In the forefront of their considerations are the practical policy implications of their analysis, as befits a study which grew out of work undertaken on behalf of the New York Governor's Advisory Panel on Financial Services.

Nigel Thrift (1987), professor of geography at Bristol University, offers a Marxist perspective on the development of international financial centres, employing Marxist terminology. He attributes their growth to the expansion of the operations of 'commercial capital', which he differentiates from industrial capital, banking capital and merchant capital. He identifies four main 'clusters' of 'organisations and practices that go to make up commercial capital' (presumably referring to firms and markets), which specialize respectively in the exchange of commodities, 'mediating monetary exchange', securities, and the provision of corporate services. Financial centres form the 'natural habitat' of commercial capital, facilitating access to clients, access to markets and access to information. Thrift provides a case study of the internationalization of the activities of London-based providers of financial and commercial services, focusing in particular on accountancy firms and estate agents about which he presents a formidable body of original empirical information. He detects a tendency towards large multinational service corporations, which suggests an increasing centralization of decision making. He ends with the broad and bland pronouncement that 'the internationalisation of commercial capital poses a considerable economic, social and political challenge to a number of cities which shows no signs of abating'.

Historical Development

Part II presents four historical studies. Virtually every writer on the subject of international financial centres acknowledges a debt to Charles P. Kindleberger's pioneering essay, *The Formation of Financial Centers: A Study in Comparative Economic History*, published in 1974. Kindleberger, a distinguished Massachusetts Institute of Technology economist, identifies the operation of powerful economies of scale and centralization in financial markets, resulting in a single pre-eminent domestic financial centre in each country. The same forces, he argues, led to the emergence of a hierarchy of international financial centres that culminated in a sequence of pre-eminent world centres – London prior to 1914, then New York and, since the 1960s, the international euromarket. These propositions are derived from and applied to a series of qualitative comparative historical case studies: London, Paris, Berlin and Frankfurt, Italy, Switzerland, Canada and New York. Finally, he considers the question of the emergence of a pre-eminent financial centre for the European Economic Community, foreseeing Brussels performing this role, a prediction that has not been fulfilled.

A shortcoming of Kindleberger's historical survey was the omission of Amsterdam, the leading international financial centre of the 17th and 18th centuries. Amsterdam's pre-eminence, derived from its position at the apex of several regional and inter-continental trading systems, made it the focal point for information flows and Europe's leading 'information exchange'. So argues Woodruff D. Smith (1984), professor of history at the University of Texas, in Chapter 9. After listing the channels of information flow, he presents a six-part typology of the functions of an information exchange that provides the structure of his analysis: acquisition of information; transfer; short-term analysis; dissemination; long-term accumulation; long-term analysis. The systematic filing of quantitative commercial information was an innovation pioneered by Dutch institutions, especially the Dutch East India Company. This formed the basis for innovative market analysis; as early as 1692, for instance, an elaborate set of time-series was used to identify inventory cycles and to plot a marketing strategy. Such sophistication in the sources and uses of information explains Amsterdam's continued importance as an international financial centre even when surpassed as a port by London and Rotterdam. Moreover, the systematic collection and analysis of information for planning and investment purposes form one of the central characteristics of modern capitalism. Their emergence in Amsterdam in the 17th century thus made a significant contribution to the modernization of capitalism.

Chapter 10 by the Economists Advisory Group (1984), which forms part of its report to the City's local government authority on *The Future of London as an International Financial Centre*, identifies two types of international financial centres: 'classical centres' and 'modern financial centres'. Classical centres – based on London in the years 1870–1914 – have a unique pre-eminence amongst international financial centres, since their position is based on playing leading roles in international trade finance, being a source of international capital, and on the transaction and reserve functions of their currency. Modern financial centres, they argue, fulfil an entrepot role, collecting the savings of surplus countries and lending them to deficit countries, while the currency factor is of diminished importance. Indeed, so large have holdings of US dollars outside America become that the widespread use of the US dollar as an international means of payment and as a reserve currency has little relevance to the success of New York as a financial centre. The authors observe that 'financial centres grow only slowly but, once established, they show remarkable powers of survival'. They also provide an analysis of the role of economies of scale in relation to financial centres to explain their longevity.

The next essay by Geoffrey Jones (1992), professor of business history at Reading University, focuses on the historical development of the international financial centres of Asia, Australasia and the Middle East, locations that received little attention from Kindleberger. He formulates a typology of centres somewhat similar to that adopted for these volumes, though not classing offshore financial centres as a separate tier. 'Global financial centres' provide a broad range of financial services on a world-wide basis, a role pioneered by London in the 19th century, then assumed by New York, and recently shared between London, New York and Tokyo. 'Regional financial centres' supply financial services to a geographical region. 'Sub-regional financial centres' provide mostly domestic financial services; the international financial activities that occur in such locations usually focus on bilateral trade between the centre's domestic economy and other countries.

In the inter-war years Shanghai, Hong Kong and Singapore functioned as sub-regional financial centres. The two decades after the Second World War saw the dynamic emergence of Beirut as a regional financial centre, the continuation of Hong Kong and Singapore as sub-regional financial centres and the eclipse of Shanghai as an international financial centre because of the Communist Revolution in China. The rapid expansion of the eurocurrency markets in the years 1965–75 led to the emergence of Singapore and Hong Kong as regional financial centres. The Lebanese Civil War, which broke out in 1975, caused Beirut's demise as an international financial centre. In the late 1970s Bahrain emerged as a regional financial centre, as did Sydney. Jones excludes the Japanese international financial centres of Tokyo, Osaka and Yokohama from his analysis, though he briefly mentions their evolution.

Jones's empirical historical observations lead to an explanation of the development of 'sub-regional' and 'regional' financial centres. Their emergence rests, he argues, on the achievement of reputations for stability, integrity, impartiality and confidentiality, on their 'haven' status, and on accessibility. Once established, further growth is encouraged by external economies, by economies of scale and agglomeration. It was not a lack of competitiveness or any other strictly economic cause that led to the demise of Beirut and Shanghai as international financial centres, but political and military developments outside their control.

International Finance and International Financial Centres in the 1980s and 1990s

The function of international financial centres is to intermediate international flows of funds. Naturally, major changes in international finance have an impact on international financial centres. The essays in Part III examine developments in international finance in the 1980s and 1990s and give some consideration to their implications for international financial centres. The analyses have a number of common themes: the 'explosive growth' in the volume of international financial transactions; globalization, defined as the process by which the world's various national financial marketplaces are beginning to act as if they were one single, integrated market; deregulation or the removal of restrictions on financial markets, allowing them to become more competitive and efficient; securitization or the substitution of various kinds of negotiable instruments for bank lending; and innovation in financial products and institutional arrangements.

Chapter 12 by Roy C. Smith and Ingo Walter (1991) of the Stern School of Business at New York University, a prize-winner in the 1991 AMEX Bank Review awards, reviews financial market developments in Europe, the US and Japan and suggest that a 'seamless' international market for many securities and derivatives will exist by the end of the decade, akin to the established seamless foreign exchange market. There will be powerful capital market centres in the US, Europe and Japan functioning with extreme competitiveness – internally, with each other, and with lesser centres. The authors envisage a convergence of market governance practices in these three major 'hubs': universal banking will become the norm; commission rates will be negotiated; foreign banks and brokers will gain market access equal to locals, though slowly in some places; cross-border investment demand will be a major factor in all securities trading; and similar rules and standards will be adopted in respect of trading, disclosure requirements, settlement procedures and capital adequacy. This reconfiguration of the financial markets may provide a basis for sustained world economic growth in the 21st century by helping to lower the cost of capital.

Globalization is the theme pursued by Joel A. Bleeke and Lowell L. Bryan (1988), senior executives with international consultants McKinsey. Writing in the aftermath of the international stock market crash of October 1987, which saw simultaneous price falls across the world's capital markets, they present a careful exposition of the evolution and extent of linkages in the international foreign exchange markets, bond markets and equity markets. They foresee further strengthening of the price linkages between all types of financial assets, reflecting underlying structural forces that have significantly reduced the transaction costs of global financial operations. They identify three reasons why such linkages among financial markets are likely to increase rather than diminish: many banks and other financial firms have already made heavy investments in the infrastructure of globalization; enormous benefits from globalization are already being enjoyed by the leaders in the field; and the fact that re-regulation is not feasible given the size of existing linkages. 'We are moving rapidly to a fully integrated, global financial marketplace', they conclude. 'We are headed for a financial marketplace where the price of all financial instruments in all domestic markets is heavily affected, not just by the domestic supply and demand for that instrument, but by the supply and demand for all other financial instruments in other countries.'

Yoon S. Park (1989) of the School of Government and Business Administration, George Washington University, presents a focused summary of the forces transforming international finance in the 1980s and into the 1990s (Chapter 14). He endeavours to relate these developments directly to international financial centres. In particular, he addresses the question of the opportunities they present for the promotion of Anchorage (Alaska) as an international financial centre, his essay being written as a contribution to a conference on this subject organized by the Alaska Center for International Business in July 1987.

Deregulation and its effect on competitiveness are the main subjects of the chapter of the report by The Economists Advisory Group (1984) on London's prospects as a financial centre, included here as Chapter 15. Distinguishing between regulations that impede competition and those that protect consumers, they discuss the regulatory environment and agenda in London, New York, Tokyo and elsewhere. They also examine the likely impact of improvements in communications technology on the competitiveness of international financial centres, predicting that the chief beneficiaries will be the global centres – London, New York and Tokyo. This issue is discussed more fully in the essays in the following section.

Communications and Financial Centres

The focus of the essays in Part IV is on the impact of improvements in communications technology on financial services and on the hierarchy of international financial centres. Advances in telecommunications and computer technology have all but eliminated spatial barriers in the conduct of financial transactions, a development that Richard O'Brien (1992), senior economist at American Express, has dubbed 'the end-of-geography'. In Chapter 16, he identifies two opposite propositions concerning the impact of this development on international financial centres. On one hand, communications improvements undermine local monopolies and broaden markets, thereby facilitating the operation of economies of scale and strengthening the position of the leading centres, notably London, New York and Tokyo. On the other hand, since financial markets are now electronic and no longer confined to a physical space, the traditional concentrations of firms and practitioners that constituted financial centres are no longer necessary for the conduct of business. In fact, both processes are probably operating simultaneously, but at different levels. In the wholesale markets, the global centres will be increasingly dominant and will also continue to enjoy comparative advantages in the provision of specialist services requiring high levels of expertise, such as corporate finance. But as regards retail activities, the new technology should strengthen the position of regional and domestic financial centres. In fact, there need be no losers in this process since O'Brien foresees a dynamic increase in the aggregate demand for international financial services.

The role of cities as financial centres was traditionally based on the advantage of face-to-face contact on the part of financial market participants. Recent improvements in communications technologies, it has been argued, allow the exchange of information and ideas and the conduct of transactions without interpersonal contact, undermining the comparative advantage of cities. Mitchell L. Moss (1988) examines critical issues concerning the way in which new communications technologies are influencing the pattern of urban development and the operations of global financial centres. He argues in Chapter 17 that advances in communications technologies are not undermining the importance of an urban location but are diminishing the significance of lesser centres, thus strengthening the handful of leading 'world cities'.

A case study in the application of new communications technology in the international financial services industry is provided by John Langdale (1985), a Macquarie University geographer. His subject is the development of the electronic transmission of payments among international financial institutions – EFT (electronic funds transfer). Demand for international EFT services expanded rapidly with the growth of euromarket transactions and the proliferation of the offices of international banks. In turn, the supply of EFT services has facilitated and encouraged these developments. Langdale examines various types of EFT systems, including SWIFT and leased networks operated by transnational banks. The majority of EFT transactions are between international financial centres, the quality of the service being a significant competitive factor. The impact of this technology on the international financial centre hierarchy appears to have been simultaneously to strengthen the position of the major centres and to assist the growth of offshore centres.

New York University economists Kenneth D. Garbade and William L. Silber (1978) present the results of an empirical inquiry into the impact of major innovations in communications technology on the integration of geographically separated markets as measured by the elimination of differentials in securities prices. In Chapter 19, they report three case studies: the introduction of domestic telegraphic communications between New York and Philadelphia and New Orleans in 1846–48; the opening of the trans-Atlantic cable connecting the London and New York stock markets in 1866; and the advent of the consolidated stock market ticker tape on the New York and regional stock exchanges in 1975. The first two innovations resulted in a significant and rapid narrowing of market price differentials, though the ticker tape had little impact. The authors suggest that innovations in communications technology are better accomplished by the private sector than by public agencies.

International Financial Services and International Financial Centres

Part V features essays presenting a variety of perspectives on international financial services – the activities which take place in international financial centres. It begins with a complementary pair of articles by Australian economist H.W. Arndt. Chapter 20 concerns problems encountered in the measurement of trade in financial services, a matter of considerable consequence for the study of international financial centres. Such problems are partly conceptual and partly practical and Arndt (1984) provides guidance in both regards, with special attention devoted to Luxembourg, Singapore and Australia. Chapter 21 (1988) further explores trade in financial services using data on cross-border lending by banks in 1978, 1984 and 1986, relating the issue to international financial centres.

Sang-Rim Choi, Adrian E. Tschoegl and Chwo-Ming Yu (1986) produce data on the location of the offices of the world's major international banks in order to rank 14 international financial centres in the decade 1970 to 1980. They divine an increase in the importance of Asia Pacific centres, especially Tokyo but also Hong Kong and Singapore, over the decade and the supplanting of London by New York as the leading international banking centre, a proposition that finds little support in other studies and thus raises doubts about the significance of counting bank offices. They demonstrate that the degree of interpenetration of the major financial centres by international banks increased over the 1970s, suggesting increased interconnectedness amongst these centres.

Herbert G. Grubel (1986) presents a useful general analysis of the nature and magnitude of trade in international financial services in Chapter 23. He identifies four distinct types of activity: traditional capital flows intermediation; transactions diverted from domestic markets to international markets due to taxation and regulation; global money market business; and direct financial service and retail business. The development of Singapore and Hong Kong as international financial centres is discussed in relation to his general propositions.

Howard Reed's statistical study of international financial centres (1981) has been mentioned above in relation to Chapter 4. His essay in this section (1989) contains a brief resume of the typology and principal propositions presented there, but breaks new ground by positing a connection between interest rate behaviour and international financial centres.

Richard Roberts

Part I
Concepts and Typologies

[1]

Article from *Bank of England Discussion Paper*, No. 51, contents, abstract, 1–23

Contents

Abstract

This paper discusses the determinants of financial firms' location decisions, thus providing a framework for the analysis and evaluation of factors underlying the development of financial centres such as the City of London. It is suggested that the analysis is relevant both for policy makers and financial institutions. External economies of scale and relative conditions between centres are highlighted as key determinants of location for financial firms, which may imply the existence of a cumulative or self-sustaining process whereby financial centres grow or decline. Analysis of financial centres in the light of oligopoly theory, given the importance of sunk costs and increasing returns to scale, offers further insights into the nature and dynamics of financial centres. For example, it illustrates the difficulties minor centres have in competing with global centres as well as offering the insight that concentration of business in major centres may be economically efficient. It is suggested that the mechanisms outlined in the paper are likely to be of particular relevance in coming years, given such potential reforms as domestic deregulation in the United States and Japan and the establishment of the EC internal market as well as advances in technology, all of which may entail shifts in the location of financial activity. Given the potential for such shifts, the paper goes on briefly to discuss the net benefits of a financial centre to a domestic economy, which would be lost if business were to shift elsewhere.

1 Introduction

(1) Can the City of London survive as a major financial centre? Or will it absorb much of the business currently conducted in Paris, Frankfurt and Amsterdam? Will financial centres soon cease to be necessary, given developments in technology? Or are there structural factors which will continue to attract financial firms to such centres? And does a major financial centre benefit the domestic economy in any case? Such questions have arisen frequently in recent years in the context of more general discussions of the location of financial business, which are focussed on the possibility that business may in some way be lost to its current location due to a change in relative business conditions between the centre and other locations. However, a criticism of such discussions has been a lack of theoretical focus.

(2) As a contribution to debate on these matters, this paper sets out to provide an analytical framework for interpreting the underlying issues, namely the motivations which lead financial firms to their choice of location, (which enables one to assess the potential effects of various adverse changes in conditions), and the benefits of a financial centre to the domestic economy.[1] The paper's principal claims to originality lies in the application of industrial location theory to the location decision of the financial firm, the development from this basis of a theory of growth and decline of financial centres, and the application to these problems of the theories of oligopoly and contestable markets.

(3) It should be noted that although the thrust of the paper is largely forward-looking and focussed on *prospects* for *international* centres, the analysis can equally be used for interpretation of *past* changes in the location of financial activity (for example the recent growth of London following "Big Bang" at the expense of smaller centres), and for analysis of the development and prospects for domestic centres such as those in Paris, Frankfurt and Milan. In addition, the current level of globalisation,[2] is taken as given. Instead, the paper assesses the determinants of the location of globalised activity.

(4) The paper is structured as follows; in Section 2 the theory of the location of firms is set out in general terms. This highlights the importance of cost, demand and external economies in location decisions as well as the importance of uncertainty and sunk costs. In Sections 3 and 4 the focus is narrowed to the financial firm. It is suggested that external economies of scale are of particular importance, though the influence of the other factors should not be neglected. In Section 5 the implications of location theory for international financial centres are assessed, and the nature of the risks to such centres highlighted. Section 6 offers a contrasting view of international financial centres based on the theory of oligopoly, which offers further insights into the development of such centres. As a counterpart to concerns over the future of centres, Section 7 briefly examines the value of an international financial centre to the domestic economy. It is emphasised that summation of value-added is not an adequate measure of the contribution of finance. Background data indicating the relative size of financial centres and the contribution of a typical centre (London) to its domestic economy are given *in the Appendices*.

(5) It is concluded overall that concerns regarding the future of international financial centres should be focussed on the possibility that once a move of firms and business away from a centre begins, it can easily become cumulative, given the importance of external economies. Technological change, regulation and taxation are among the potential causes of such shifts. Given the importance of an international financial centre to the domestic economy, such a move would be at a net cost.

(1) An earlier version of this paper constituted the theoretical background for the analysis of London's status and prospects as a financial centre provided in Davis and Latter (1989).
(2) See Bank for International Settlements (1986) Chapter 7.

2 The Optimal Location of the Firm

(6) In this initial section the theory of the location of firms is set out in general terms [see Devine et al (1979), Richardson (1969), (1978)]. Although partly a paradigm for industrial firms, this provides a general framework for analysis of the location decision, while also enabling one to highlight by contrast the main determinants of location in the case of financial firms. In the absence of such a framework a discussion of concerns regarding the future of financial centres risks becoming purely taxonomical. ***A summary is provided in paragraph 22 for those wishing to omit the detailed analysis of theory.***

(a) Theories of industrial location

(7) Early studies of location theory tended to concentrate on relative *transport costs* of the factors of production and finished product [Burn (1958), Mathias (1969), Richardson (1978) Ch3]. Suppose a firm uses two factors, of which one is generally available while another is only available at one site A, and the product can only be sold at a single site B. Then optimisation will entail minimisation of total transport costs for a given level of output. If the localised factor is bulky relative to the product, the "pull" will be to site A, if the opposite for the product, site B. Such a mechanism can be generalised for more than one localised factor. The optimal location changes over time in response to the location of resources or products, and any change in the production technology which alters the combination of factor inputs.

(8) The transport cost minimisation model is rather simple and ignores the potential for factor prices to vary over space for other reasons besides transport costs (higher wages for workers in the centre of cities to compensate for commuting, lower costs of land on greenfield sites). Given these shortcomings, transport cost minimising will thus only by chance be optimal for a profit maximising firm. A more realistic objective is *production cost minimisation* [Mills (1972), Richardson (1978) Ch11]. The spatial location chosen will depend on the pattern of factor prices (including the influence of transport costs), though it will also affect the firm's production decision, to the extent that factor proportions can be varied. The simultaneously chosen location and method of production will economise on the use of the spatially expensive resource (for example land in the centre of cities).

(9) The definition of the market underlying the approaches noted above is of a single centre. Hence profits are maximised if the establishment is located so that production costs inclusive of transport are minimised. More than one market centre with different levels of demand adds a further refinement to the location decision—the gain in profit from locating at one must exceed the loss in profit from not locating at the other.

(10) These mechanisms can be combined in a generalised framework known as the *profit maximising model* [see Richardson (1969)]. The key constructs needed are the space-revenue (TR) and space-cost (TC) functions. As their names suggest, they illustrate how revenue and cost vary by location. The space revenue curve shows how (post tax) receipts vary over space given a constant ex-works cost, while the space cost curve sums the costs of factors and production processes at each allocation. The special cases of production cost minimisation and revenue maximisation as criteria for profit maximisation are given by flat space revenue and space cost curves, respectively. Plotting these functions together, as shown below, allows one to find the location which maximises profits (the maximum distance between the curves).

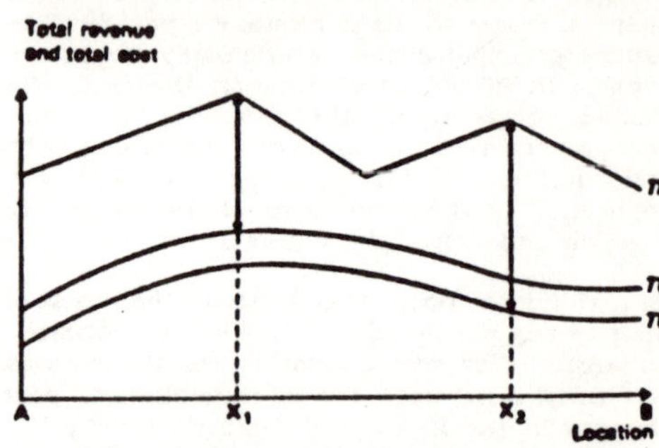

(11) The diagram also shows how a change in one of the functions TC1 and TC2 can change the optimal location. Evidently, the optimal location need not be either that of maximum revenue or minimum cost, unless they happen to coincide. In addition, the diagram illustrates how demanding the location decision may be in terms of *information*, as in reaching a fully-informed decision *all* combinations of revenue-price and cost-output at all locations must be calculated. As well as being relevant for siting of a new enterprise, these mechanisms are also relevant in the case of a branch or subsidiary, in which case costs and revenues as a function of the location of the subsidiary in relation to other establishments of the enterprise must be taken into account.

(12) The analysis can be refined by the inclusion of *scale economies* as determinants of plant location. *Internal economies* (at the level of the establishment) are relevant to choice of location of a firm which has the alternative of one large establishment or several small ones at different locations. Although locational factors as identified above may still be important and might suggest a variety of plants given constant returns to scale, significant internal economies of scale may mean that the firm maximises profit by disregarding them and concentrating production in a single plant.

(13) *External economies* of scale accrue because of the scale of the industry and not the size of its constituent firms. Once an industry exceeds a certain size in a given location, it may attract a variety of institutions that enable it to obtain factors of production more cheaply and reliably, and to sell products more effectively, than would otherwise be the case. For example, there may develop a pool of local labour experienced in the techniques of the industry, local advertising and market organisations, co-operative r & d and specialist raw material markets.[1]

(14) In each of these cases of scale economies, there may be a point at which *diseconomies* come into play, which will tend to repel rather than attract further expansion. A large establishment may become harder to manage; large scale economic activity in an area may require factors of production to be acquired at a greater distance and hence at greater expense. It may also lead to congestion on transport networks, resulting in increased transport costs to establishments.

(15) In addition to these refinements, there are various shortcomings and over-simplifications in the profit maximising model as presented here, appreciation of which are essential to understanding the motivations and constraints underlying location decisions. Perhaps the most important relate to *sunk costs*. If a firm is already established in one location, there are likely to have been considerable expenditures on factors of production which are not transferable to other sites (buildings, land improvements) or only at considerable cost (labour, machines, electronic and computer systems). Such costs entail a considerable degree of inertia in the location decision; a new location must not merely provide a greater unit profit in a comparative static sense, but must also provide sufficient profit to compensate for the discounted present value of the new investments—and losses on existing investments—that are necessitated. Conversely, if sunk costs of location are zero the industry is "contestable"[2] in a location sense and any location is vulnerable to sudden "hit and run" entry or departure. Related to sunk costs are *indivisibilities;* in many cases it is not possible to transfer marginal quantities of business to a better location in order to optimise. Instead, the new location must be profitable for a whole establishment, which particularly in the presence of internal economies of scale may be large. Together, sunk costs and indivisibilities imply that the location decision is typically not a marginal one (except in "contestable" industries as noted above). The relative disadvantage of an existing location must be sizable in order to provoke a move.

(16) Nor are these the only problems. Given positive sunk costs, the choice of a new location entails a commitment over time, which means that the choice has an *intertemporal* aspect. Not only must the new location offer advantages now, but the firm must be confident that these will remain—not always a simple decision when government policy may be one of the inputs to costs or revenues at the different locations.

(17) Intertemporal aspects introduce the more general problem of *uncertainty*. It has already been noted that gathering information on all possible sites is likely to be extremely difficult. In addition, the firm may be uncertain as to the advantages of different sites. What will be the reaction of factor suppliers or of demand for the product to a new establishment? An additional source of uncertainty in the case of oligopoly if of course the likely *strategic reaction* of rivals to a change in location, which may affect supply and demand at the new location.

(b) Empirical studies

(18) Other criticisms have originated from *empirical studies* of location decisions. These suggest that firms are rather unsystematic in choosing new sites, typically only investigating a few sites and often not performing costings or

(1) A variant of external economies is *agglomeration economies*, which vary with the total concentration of economic activity in an area.

(2) See Baumol (1982). According to the theory of contestable markets, many seeming oligopoly situations may be characterised by competitive behaviour on the part of existing firms, because of the potential for new firms to enter in a "hit and run" manner in response to excess profits. Contestable markets may thus benefit both from efficient industrial structures and competitive behaviour. In order to induce competitive behaviour there has to be an absence of significant lags between a decision to enter and entry occurring, an instant response of demand to changing prices and an absence of losses on exit due to *sunk costs* (for example capital specific to the industry that cannot be used if the firm decides to withdraw). According to this theory, economies of scale need not be a barrier to entry; firms can produce at minimum efficient scale for a short period and sell (storable) output over a long period. Contestability in terms of location is perhaps more demanding than in terms of product or market sector. For example movement of staff is unlikely to be costless.

financial evaluations [Townroe (1971), Luttrel (1962)]. While this can be rationalised as worthwhile economies in information given the costs of gathering it, (ie still potentially consistent with profit maximisation), it might equally reflect bounded rationality, (ie the firm often does not recognise the importance of the location aspect) [Hamilton (1974)]. In empirical studies, the main identified cause of movement has been *stress within the firm*, such as pressure for space caused by growth of the firm, together with inadequate supplies of local labour or existing premises [Townroe (1971), Sant (1975)]. Such repulsion factors were generally more important than attraction to other sites. This finding presents further difficulties in that it suggests growth rather than profit maximisation (in line with the managerial theory of the firm and divorce of ownership from control). The location theory developed here can be adapted, for example, to sales revenue maximisation—location would be at the peak of the space revenue curve—but the predicted location could be different from profit maximisation.

(19) The extent to which these empirical findings refute the neoclassical theory of location is open to dispute. As noted, limited search and crude evaluation technique may be consistent with profit maximisation given high costs of search and large elements of uncertainty in financial evaluations of costs of transfers. Growth maximisation may be consistent with long-run profit maximisation, and would still take account of the basic market, cost and agglomeration variables of the profit-maximising model.

(20) Other empirical studies have cast light on the relative importance of the factors identified in the neoclassical model. These emphasis the self-perpetuating nature of the success of large economically viable regions [Latham (1976), Chalmers and Beckheim (1976)]. Key underlying factors are the locational pull of market and agglomeration economies, and the reluctance to transfer existing plant or establish new branches at great distance from such regions. Government regional policies have typically had a significant influence on location, though the size of the effect is open to dispute [Keeble (1976), Sant (1975), Ashcroft and Taylor (1977), Moore and Rhodes (1976)].

(c) Theory of multinational enterprises

(21) The above discussion offers a generalised theory of firm location. However, some specialised considerations may apply in the case of *multinational enterprises* (MNEs) [for a summary see Hood and Young (1979)]. To briefly recapitulate the theory of MNEs: in imperfect market situations firms have incentives to internalise certain activities within their organisations [Coase (1937)]. By this means they can exploit ownership-specific advantages such as technology, management skill, r & d and product differentiation, and compete with firms in other countries which otherwise have inherent advantages such as familiarity with local market conditions and the legal framework. These tendencies are particularly marked for large firms with ready access to capital and oligopoly at home. However, explanation of location abroad rather than competition by exports requires analysis of locational factors related to the host country. Those found particularly relevant in statistical analyses [see Dunning (1973)] include tariff barriers of the host country, political stability, and "defensive" shifts to protect the position of the firm in an oligopoly (by setting up plant at locations where rivals have already established themselves) as well as variables identified in the analysis above such as market size and growth, relative labour costs and transport costs. However, Hood and Young concluded "it would be wrong to over-dramatise .... in reality MNEs may be only slightly less susceptible to locational inertia than other companies. Moreover, not all .... are in 'footloose' industries .... many have high fixed investment on each site" [Hood & Young (1979), p124].

(22) To summarise, the theory of the optimal location of firms suggests that the principal underlying factors are the supply (of factors of production), demand (for the product) and any external economies at a given site *in relation to alternative sites*. Sunk costs of location at a given site provide a degree of inertia, as does a high level of uncertainty over future conditions elsewhere. Information problems mean in practice that only a few sites are likely to be investigated. Empirical studies highlight particularly the supply-side factor of "stress" at the existing location in precipitating movement. In the case of Multinational Enterprises tariff barriers, political stability and strategic moves in oligopoly situations may also have a role to play. We now go on to focus on the locational choice of financial firms, examining in detail the implications for financial institutions of each of the principal factors influencing location.

3 Application to the financial firm

(23) To what extent is the general theory outlined above applicable to the financial firm? The conclusion reached in this section, after a detailed assessment of each determinant of locational choice for financial firms, is that the same basic mechanisms are likely to be operative. However some refinements and caveats are required, as discussed in Section 4 below.

(a) Supply-side influences

(24) Among the principal *factors of production* for financial institutions at a given location are rights of establishment, personnel, premises, machinery (computers, ATMs) and costs of funds—again *relative* to other locations. Rights of establishment or costs of licences require little further comment—though deregulation (for example recent reforms in Canada and France) can increase the attractiveness of a location. Personnel must not only be of low cost but also reasonable quality or training—not typically the case in ldcs, for example. Rates of personal and corporate taxation for which the firm needs to compensate should be low, unless they are compensated by better public services of benefit to financial institutions. The extent to which staff can be profitably employed (rather than regulatory form filling etc) is another important factor. Again, premises must be suitably adapted, although unlike manufacturing financial institutions can generally fit into existing buildings. For both personnel and offices, the marginal revenue product relative to cost is the appropriate decision variable, not cost itself. Cost and quality of personnel and premises obviously differ between locations.

(25) Machinery by contrast may be classified as an ubiquitous factor, ie available at the same price everywhere, though transport costs may affect this in the more remote locations (offshore centres). Some would argue that technology embodied in machinery is increasingly making location a matter of indifference, particularly for the more routine bookkeeping and clerical tasks associated with financial intermediation. Whether it could also lead to dispersion of dealing and decision making is less clear. For example, telecoms could aid concentration if one centre is a superior "hub" of a global network. It may be impossible to benefit from technology without labour skilled enough to use it—a potential problem in some offshore centres or ldcs. An assessment of the impact of technology requires gauging its relative importance vis-à-vis the other factors whose importance is likely to continue, a task which is attempted in this and the following section. Finally, the importance of political and economic stability to location (given the importance of confidence to operation of financial institutions and markets) should also be borne in mind.

(26) *Funds* defined widely are perhaps the most important supply side factor. As well as being determined by intrinsic factors related to the demand and supply for loanable funds, the cost of funds in any location is also a function of domestic regulation; if capital ratios, reserve asset ratios[1] or other regulations are more onerous in one location or for one nationality of firms than another, then the cost of funds is higher. The same arguments apply to taxes such as stamp duty and withholding taxes (for example the stamp duty has hampered growth of financial activity in Switzerland). The efficiency of payments and settlements systems will also affect the overall cost of funds.

(27) Taking a more general view of costs, *regulations* that distort or prevent competition, for example, which impose limits on the range of activities of any financial institution (such as separation of commercial from investment banking in the United States and Japan) may raise costs—risk may be higher because there is less possibility of diversification. Intertemporal aspects are also important—firms must be confident that regulation will not change adversely. A capricious regulatory authority may be one of the greatest disincentives to location in a centre. On the other hand, all regulation should not be seen as purely a cost. Strong arguments can be adduced that strong regulation which provides *consumer protection*, and hence reduces the overall risk to depositors or investors, may actually depress the cost of funds (by contrast, weak regulation may operate to the detriment of certain offshore centres). In addition, if firms expect regulations to be tightened in all centres by international agreements such as capital convergence, there will be no incentive to change

(1) These constitute a considerable discentive to international banking activity in several European countries. Indeed Grubel (1983) suggests that domestic reserve asset ratios are largely responsible for the growth of offshore banking.

location. Finally, there is a game-theoretic argument that it is *always* in firms' interests to argue regulation is too tight and to threaten to leave, even if they are unlikely to do so, in the hope of loosening regulation in the process[1] unless the regulation constitutes a restriction on entry, support of which[2] may be rational for individual incumbent firms,[3] or if regulation can reduce the risk premium firms need to pay for finance.

(b) Demand

(28) On the demand side financial firms are likely to place a premium on ease of access to customers, modified by communications and technology. The continuing importance of branch networks suggests that this is at least the case for retail intermediation. For wholesale, the case is less clear from the point of view of an individual institution. Hence there is no longer a necessary connection between concentration of manufacturing and of finance, as the growth of entrepot financial centres has illustrated. In addition, as discussed below, the importance of access to customers may differ for primary and secondary markets. However, one factor that remains important on the demand side is location in a time zone (see Hewson (1982) for the case of Singapore).

(c) Stress

(29) The "stress" factor highlighted above for manufacturing in terms of lack of physical space is probably less important for finance, given it can take over nearby buildings from other service industries at an appropriate rent. However, another type of stress may be important, namely the stress caused by such "shocks" as excess capacity in certain major centres since the equity market crash and the intensification of competitive pressures with 1992. Such abrupt changes in conditions can plausibly precipitate reassessment on the part of financial firms of their commitment to a given centre.

(d) Sunk costs and indivisibilities

(30) Sunk costs for financial institutions are sizable, particularly at the time of entry to a location or market ("start up costs") but are nonetheless perhaps less important than for manufacturing. Sunk costs are likely to include training and movement of labour, improvement or construction of premises (though it may be saleable to another institution) and costs of application for licences and establishment rights, as well as potential loss of clientele and loss of "face" from withdrawal from a site or market. Sunk costs of relationships may be the most significant—location in a new centre does not guarantee that relationships developed in the former centre will continue to operate. Relationships may be more important for primary issuing business than secondary trading, which would imply that the second is more "contestable" in terms of location—firms may enter or leave a location without concern over breaking of relationships and consequent losses. Another example of a "contestable" sector in finance may be mortgage lending [see Davies and Davies (1984)].

(31) Indivisibilities are low, given the relatively low level of *internal economies of scale*—at least to an industrial establishment—in finance.[4] This has the consequence that it is economic for a firm to have branches in many centres, so it may be relatively easy to transfer business in a response to adverse changes in conditions. Not that internal economies are entirely absent. Revell (1987) suggested that individual units such as branches within a financial firm may obtain significant scale economies. A certain size of institution in terms of capitalisation may be needed to become a "major player" in, for example, securities markets, and it is likely to be advantageous for dealers, salesman, analysts etc to be in the same place and for decision making to be centralised. Clearing and settlement may also offer economies of scale. Finally, there may be considerable *economies of scope* in finance, ie joint[5] costs and joint demands[6] between products.

(e) External economies of scale

(32) All of the factors enumerated so far suggest a somewhat greater degree of footlooseness for financial institutions than the generalised theory would suggest, although the barriers to movement should not be underestimated. In the case of *external economies of scale* very much the

(1) The recent threat by a major Swiss bank to shift its securities operations away from Switzerland if stamp duty is not abolished may fall into this category.
(2) Technically a form of DUP (directly unproductive profit seeking) behaviour.
(3) Paradoxically, such regulation also increases the attraction of a location to entrants by leading to higher profit margins (Spain was an example before the recent deregulation).
(4) It is argued below that for *financial centres* they are very high.
(5) For example, shared buildings and management.
(6) For example, for mortgages and life insurance.

opposite is the case. Many of these external economies are related to improvements in information flows—and hence more accurate and competitive pricing of financial services and instruments. For example, firms may be linked together by participation in organised markets whose liquidity (defined as entailing low dealing costs and rapid execution of large orders with minimum disturbance to prices) and efficiency (in establishing price which reflect all available information)[1] increases with the number of participants.[2] Groups of markets themselves may be so closely inter-related that is is hardly conceivable that they should operate other than in one place (for example short-term money markets). There may be joint membership facilities.

(33) Even if firms do not operate in such markets, financial firms frequently enjoy close business contacts with each other, for example in loan syndication. Documents may frequently and speedily require dispatch. A group of trades and professions is likely to grow around a group of institutions to provide services—lawyers, accounts, actuaries, computer programmers and consultants. [Lee (1986) discusses the advantage of Hong Kong over Singapore in syndicated-credits due to its legal skills.] Customers of financial institutions such as the central bank and industrial and commercial companies may have offices in such centres. A supply of skilled labour becomes readily available to newcomers (at a price). More generally, a fund of expertise is built up and innovation is stimulated among a group of people with similar occupations and interests whose work brings them into close proximity. Research institutes, of benefit to all markets, may be set up.[3]

(34) There are many other advantages of proximity. Directors of financial firms often sit on several boards, and it is an economy of their time if their various activities are located together. Links with customers, in terms of familiarity with complex and changing needs, (for example in corporate finance) may be facilitated by location together. Firms in related activities may need to be linked, for example, the lead manager and seller of bond issue. Access to professional advisers and the central bank may equally be of importance. Financial institutions often set up joint services for clearing and settlement,[4] which especially where documents are concerned will lead to external economies of scale. Finally avoidance of misunderstandings over transactions requires errors to be remedied quickly and without friction—perhaps by close contact at a junior level.

(35) Equally, there may be external diseconomies to location together—discomfort of travelling, difficulty of parking, noise and grime. Arguably, there must become acute before they offset the economies of agglomeration. More seriously, common location may lead to excess capacity in markets.[5]

(36) *Economies of agglomeration* are of some importance to finance, though perhaps less so than external economies. Commuter railways, for example, may only be economic in large conurbations. A diversified set of economic activities in an area may offer ready customers for financial services, while skills such as accountancy, law and management are useable both by finance and other sectors.

(f) Strategic interactions

(37) Given external economies of scale (together with the continued existence of protected markets, which enable cross-subsidisation) strategic interactions may be an important determinant of the location of activity in finance. For example the current level of financial activity in the City of London may be in part a product of predatory moves by firms (such as the Japanese) to capture markets—which has in turn entailed excess capacity. It may be the case that such predatory practices will also influence the

(1) Given the fundamental importance of information gathering to financial activity, this point implies that profitability for many firms will be lower or negative away from a major financial centre (in terms of the diagram in section 2, TR and TC cross).

(2) Conversely, any market fragmentation poses a threat to financial centres.

(3) As an empirical example of external economies, which supports this analysis, an empirical study by the EIU (1964) found that most financial firms locating in *London* did so for *contact with external organisations*. The types of contact which were included were categorised by Dunning and Morgan (1966) as follows. First, "knowledge in a hurry" describes the advantages in terms of information of close contact between financial firms, for example dealers in markets subject to rapid price change. One location is a trading floor—but even in a screen-based system frequent telephone calls supplemented by personal contacts are an important conduit for this type of contact. While such personal contact remains important, there is good reason for financial firms to locate together. Second, there is building of confidence. In many financial markets contracts are made by word of mouth, face to face (futures) or on telephones (other securities markets). This facilitates speed and economy in transactions but requires mutual confidence, to which close personal contact may have much to contribute, even when the principals are large firms. Observed patterns of trading location suggests that the degree to which mutual confidence is important may depend on the extent to which the product is a homogenous commodity—hence contact is less important for forex than securities, and secondary than primary trading. In non-homogeneous instruments financial trading relationships have the characteristics of a "repeated game"—where the discipline on cheating (for example, the intermediary deliberately selling a mispriced security to the investor) is loss of business in the future.

(4) Though Euroclear and Cedel (which are paperless) are not in major trading centres—because of withholding taxes and restrictions on securities lending in major centres.

(5) To the extent that all markets are not completely globalised.

equilibrium level of activity at the location, given the importance of "network" links between firms.

(g) Insights from the theory of multinational enterprises

(38) The extent to which the locational theory of multinational enterprises (MNEs) offers additional insights for finance to those outlined above is unclear [for a summary of the theories of expansion of international banking networks see Park and Zwick (1985), also Campayne (1990)]. MNE theory is clearly relevant to finance in terms of the frequent use of ownership specific advantages developed at home (such as commercial contacts with domestic head offices of MNEs, or financial innovations) to aid penetration of new markets; use of oligopoly situations at home to cross subsidise entry to new markets or centres; and the tendency of mass shifts to occur into centres or markets apparently for defensive reasons. In the discussion above of determinants of location of financial firms, political stability and relative regulatory factors have been cited, similar to those for multinationals in paragraph 21.

(39) There are also contrasts between determinants of location for multinational financial firms (for brevity, MNFs) and multinational manufacturing firms. In the absence of locational advantages to host countries such as labour costs, marketing factors and trade barriers MNEs would export and not set up plant offshore. In contrast, it can be argued that in the case of finance the need for contacts, relationships etc between financial firms as outlined above is fundamental and (lacking technological advance) is always likely to lead financial firms in certain markets to locate together[1]—although not necessarily near their customers. Largely for this reason[2] it is suggested that the theory of MNEs does not capture the unique features of finance and international financial centres, financial firms are not typical multinational enterprises, and given the global status of their markets these are best analysed in terms of a suitably adapted version of the generalised theory of firm location, as outlined in this paper [for a contrasting view see Campayne (1990)].

4 Some caveats to the analysis

(a) Technology

(40) Three caveats to the discussion in Section 3 must be borne in mind—the role of technology, the varying needs of different types of financial institution and the distinction between location of markets and firms. The key question regarding technology is whether it can completely offset the benefits of financial concentration, via audio visual links, automatic trading systems etc on a global basis, and make departure sufficiently attractive to offset the sunk costs.[3] As noted above, it has already led to a dispersal of routine functions to outlying regions. In principle, video links could also offset some of the benefits of concentration in dealing and decision making. However, it seems less likely that all of the external benefits[4] of concentration as outlined above could be offset in this way. Useful distinctions, as noted above, may be between primary and secondary trading; between "commodity" (forex, government bonds) and "specialised" (equities) secondary trading and between "advice" and trading. Given the lesser need for relationships and personal contacts for secondary trading, especially for "commodities", technology may be more able to offset the external benefits of a given location for secondary than for primary and specialised trading. Finally, as noted, the benefits of technology need to be seen in connection with the availability of labour skilled enough to use it. This may limit dispersion of finance to advanced countries.

(b) Different types of institution

(41) Different types of financial institutions differ in their needs for the external benefits of location

(1) This view contrasts with that of Giddy (1983) who suggested in the absence of regulatory barriers and other imperfections in international financial markets all international banking would be purely "arms length" (ie conducted from a home base with minimum presence offshore).

(2) Other contrasts include the fact that MNEs often create external economies, while for MNFs this is a major attraction of a financial centre. MNEs shift to avoid trade barriers in the host country, while international financial centres benefit from their absence. For an MNE the attraction of offshore location is often market size in the host country—for an MNF in an international financial centre the attraction is ability to service the global market. While an MNE often takes advantage of cheap local labour, an MNF will import its own or in any case pay the world price for local skilled labour. Finally, although MNFs do take advantage of advantages "developed internally" within the firm they also often shift to financial centres in order to *develop* such advantages (eg reputation and skills) and any technical advantages (eg new instruments) are easily copied. Advantages of "internalisation" within the firm are often partly superseded for regulatory reasons by need for "Chinese Walls" and separate capitalisation.

(3) Or alternatively, whether given its ubiquity, technology sharply increases the leverage of other factors.

(4) Such as a common pool of skills; innovation and research; confidence building; multiple directorships; personal contacts with customers; access; resolution of misunderstandings.

together. This may be seen empirically in the United Kingdom by the dispersed location of building societies, some tendencies in the same direction for (head offices of) banking and insurance, but the continuing concentration of securities firms. Such tendencies are linked to use of technology, the nature of transactions, skilled labour requirements, the importance of external economies, etc. They suggest that the degree of footlooseness of financial firms is variable. Equally, foreign firms may be more likely to move than domestic firms, given the pull of their own domestic customer bases and the lesser commitment to the country in question. Similar patterns are observable in continental European countries.

(42) More detailed suggestions regarding influences on the competitiveness of a location for the different types of financial institution are given in Economists Advisory Group (1984). Effects of these on the dispersion or concentration of world markets can be gathered from the tables in Appendix 1. For example for *banking* it was suggested that freedom from regulation is less important than external economies such as expertise developed over time; depth and breadth of money markets; close links with other financial and trading activities and the array of ancillary services available. It was also suggested that the idea that international banking has a "home" (ie that they prefer if possible to do international business from their home countries) is a fallacy. As an example, the rates for offshore dollars in the IBFs in New York are no cheaper than in eurocurrency markets in other financial centres. *Forex* is closely bound up with the presence of an international banking centre, though also the demand for forex business in the relevant time zone and the availability of forward or derivative hedging markets. *Securities* trading was thought to be attracted by turnover in the main markets, listing of international securities, clearing and settlement, consumer protection and flexibility of regulation. *Insurance* benefits from the presence of organised insurance markets (eg Lloyd's), the presence of broking firms and readily accessible banking, legal and other support services. However, information technology (IT) may be particularly able to disperse insurance, as evidenced by the dispersed nature of insurance markets in the United States. IT's development may thus reduce the need for geographically concentrated markets.

(c) Institutions and markets

(43) The discussion so far has largely been couched in terms of an individual firm's location decision. However, some of the analysis has related to markets rather than firms, and it is useful to draw these various suggestions together. Ease of access to customers may be less important for wholesale than for retail financial intermediation. Second, it was suggested that relationships may be more important for primary issuing than secondary trading. Moreover, the importance of mutual confidence in markets may vary with the homogeneity of the product: hence contact may be less important in secondary markets for forex than securities. Third, relationships may be more important for advice than trading. Multiple locations of firms may be able partly to offset the sunk cost and indivisibility problems of moving business at the margin, which would occur if the market centre shifts or becomes dispersed. Finally, technology can facilitate dispersal of the location of market trading. One can conclude there is a spectrum of footlooseness among markets, dependent on the importance of contact, availability of technology etc .(1) Markets may in general be more footloose than firms though in the long run, of course, shifts in markets' locations may be an important factor in *firms'* own location decisions. An illustration of this tendency may be the shift of eurobond and some other securities markets from European centres to London in recent years, and the later shift of intermediaries such as Deutsche Bank, BNP and Credit Lyonnais.

(44) On the other hand, it should be noted that many of the factors noted above, particularly some of the external economies, do not relate specifically to markets and would continue to attract firms to centres even if markets were totally footloose (ancillary services, the body of skilled labour and expertise, business contacts).

(45) Finally, it should be noted that the discussion above is largely set in terms of the costs and benefits of moving *away* from a location. Although considerations are similar for moving *to* a centre it should be borne in mind that given relative benefits the sunk costs (or this case "start up costs") argument then constitutes a

(1) An example of these patterns is that sales and trading of international bonds both became concentrated in major centres such as London after Big Bang. However, there is now a tendency for sales (which requires close liaison with investor customers) to be distributed back to the various countries of the investor base. Trading remains concentrated in centres such as London, as this offers benefits in terms of co-ordination and control of risk for the firm in question (*despite* the potential for technology to aid dispersion of trading).
McKinsey, reported in the Economist (1988) have put forward similar ideas in terms of "core" markets such as forex and "peripheral" ones such as corporate advice, where the importance of relationships as opposed to price increases towards the periphery.

disincentive to moving to the centre. To attract business, a centre must show greater benefits that it must to avoid losing it, though as noted above, the shifts required may be more marginal for "contestable" sectors such as trading (eg German government bonds) than primary market activity and other types of financial services.

5 Factors underlying the development of financial centres

(46) The sections above have suggested that external economies are the key influence on the location of many financial institutions, though costs and demand factors at the level of an individual establishment and the importance of the nature of markets in which firms participate should not be disregarded. External economies are precisely what international financial centres have to offer. In this section the causes of development of centres are assessed and related to the location theory noted above [see also Kindleberger (1974), Reid (1981), Scholey (1986)]. A view is developed as to the most likely threats to financial centres. Empirical data illustrating the relative size of financial centres are given in Appendix 1.

(a) Some general considerations

(47) At a most basic level, a financial market can develop where there is an agent or sector in financial surplus and an agent or sector in deficit. This allows an intermediary sector to develop, which given the various benefits of agglomeration noted above is likely to be grouped in a financial centre. Most countries have a *domestic* centre of this type. Widening the focus to an *international* level, the surplus and deficit sectors may be geographically differentiated. Although historically major financial centres have tended to develop at points of capital export (London in the 19th century; Tokyo; New York exporting captal to the West in the 19th century) the continuing importance of London and the development of offshore centres such as Hong Kong show that capital export is no longer an essential feature of a financial centre—though it may help in its development.

(48) There are several reasons why financial centres have become less dependent on the economy of their host country. Economists Advisory Group (1984) noted that since the Second World War no country has been a regular exporter of capital for decade after decade (as the United Kingdom was in the nineteenth century),[1] and hence borrowing and lending of financial institutions have become an entrepot trade, mobilising savings wherever they can be found. Second, no currency has had the dominant role in world trade that sterling once had, and there is no longer a close link between the currency in which trade is invoiced and the country in which it is financed. Third, there are no longer close links between the currency in which securities are denominated and the country in which they are issued, owned and traded. For example trading of many continental European shares owned by European investors occurs in London. These factors have entailed the development of multinational financial institutions, willing to locate in any centre rather than being tied to a domestic base.

(49) Other general factors behind the development of international financial centres can also be identified, though none are all embracing and there are generally exceptions. There would include deregulation of rights of establishment and of domestic markets, which besides encouraging entry may lead to increased competition and efficiency, thus attracting business. Of course until recently Tokyo has been a counter example. Absence of capital controls may also be important—though London thrived prior to 1979. Political stability, the prior existence of commercial trading facilities, a good local education system and liberal immigration rules for trained staff of foreign firms are also permissive factors. In addition, in order to survive, international financial centres need to develop an essential *adaptability* to change.

(b) An approach based on the theory of industrial location

(50) It may be suggested, however, that rather than relying on a similar set of determinants in each case, international financial centres have tended to evolve on the basis of diverse sets of causal factors and then (given an existing tendency towards globalisation) *grow in a self-sustaining manner on the basis of external economies of scale and economies of agglomeration.* These have already been

(1) Though international investment has been greater than at any time since World War I, thus providing business for international financial institutions.

enumerated; however, one may also divide them into *static and dynamic economies*. Static economies such as the existence of commuter railways do not tend to increase the attractiveness of a centre as it grows, though obviously only when the centre is a certain size will such services tend to develop. By contrast, the benefits arising from contacts, participation in markets etc, increase with the number of firms in the locality.[1] For example, a financial centre such as London establishing a market in a financial instrument that is bigger[2] than its rivals such as Paris and Frankfurt can, by offering the benefits of liquidity and efficiency, attract business, and secure more scale economies in a cumulative manner. In addition, beyond a certain size there will be a self perpetuating critical mass of skills and services at the disposal of firms entering financial centre. Reputation will also develop over time. It can be suggested that beyond a certain size, the growth of financial centres may become self perpetuating even if the initial motivation for growth (such as a domestic financial surplus) has disappeared. Firms will continue to be attracted given the number of firms already there; equivalently, as the number of firms increases so will the marginal benefit to new entrants, thus attracting entrants whose marginal costs were previously too high to encourage entry.[3] Business will be concentrated in such centres, smaller centres will lose business and new centres will find it hard to become established.

(51) A recent example of such tendencies for cumulative concentration relates to the fact that non-financial companies with wide-ranging financial activities—active treasury departments in particular—see an incentive in locating in well-developed centres such as London; this in turn increases the attractiveness of the place for banks and other financial institutions etc. By contrast, the lack of critical mass in the Paris financial centre operated to its disadvantage—major multinationals did not see any interest in coming to Paris due, *inter alia*, to the relative lack of sophistication of banking services, thus hindering the growth of the centre.

(52) Given such tendencies, *why should financial firms leave major centres?* Diseconomies of congestion and high factor costs (office space) could be factors,[4] though tightening of regulation is likely to be more threatening. Government subsidies (including preferential tax treatment) to other centres may make other centres more attractive. Technological factors could lead markets to shift or disperse. Put more generally, although economies of agglomeration are important to growth of financial centres and to the location decisions of individual firms, they do not override the other inputs to a firm's location decision, sufficiently adverse developments in which could lead firms to reconsider their current location.

(53) One may distinguish between *self-stabilising and self-reinforcing causes* and associated consequences of relocation. For example, high office rents or housing prices, assuming they are the *sole* disincentive factor, may be self stabilising. If firms leave due to high rents, rents will fall, thus attracting other firms previously at the margin of decision. On the other hand there are arguments that departures for any reason, for example tighter regulation/taxation relative to other centres, or political instability, may lead to further departures in a cumulative manner.[5] The dynamic benefits identified above—contacts, participation in markets, the critical mass of skills—could easily be lost in a cumulative way whereby each departure makes the centre less attractive to others already established there. On balance, the cumulative factors are perhaps more likely to be relevant than self stabilising, although there is clearly a moderate rate of departure that could be sustained without provoking large scale withdrawals. This implies that the *best way to maintain an international financial centre is to avoid provoking departures on anything but a minor scale.* The history of financial centres (Beirut, Panama) shows the relevance of this argument.

(54) Technology may, of course, change the economics of financial centres too. As well as those factors outlined above for the individual financial firm or market, it can also determine the number of centres able to exist in the world. It is often suggested that given large economies of scale, the globalisation of markets and the 8-hour

(1) Thus, in terms of the diagram in Section 2, widening the gap between space—revenue and space—cost curves at this point only, and narrowing it at other points.

(2) Or, in the recent case of German government bonds, which offers derivatives such as futures which are not available in the home market.

(3) This pattern justifies a "bandwagon" effects where numerous firms copy others' location decisions. For entry to centres, unlike entry to individual markets, such behaviour may be rational.

(4) Docklands have proved an important safety valve for the City of London.

(5) In addition, the more equal the burdens of regulation/taxation are between centres (as has been the tendency recently), the greater the leverage a single adverse measure may have.

working day enforce a maximum of three on the number of international financial centres where previously many more could subsist.[1] Three may also be a minimum, as long as it is preferred to work in daylight and the major economic regions (United States, Far East, Europe) each require a "local" centre. However, this need not be immutable. Information systems can and are increasingly used to link markets in different financial centres as well as linking participants in one market (for example, the introduction of 24-hours futures trading by Chicago Mercantile Exchange). If technology could be developed in this way sufficiently to offset the benefits of concentration, the business of the major centres could begin to be dispersed in response to any adverse cost or demand influences.

(55) To summarise, this section suggests that external economies of scale, which can lead to self-sustaining growth, may be the major factor underlying development of financial centres whatever the initial stimulus to development (history, deregulation, a centre for trade). The cumulative nature of external economies, however, also suggests that such a process of growth could go into reverse, which implies a need for caution on the part of the authorities in causing or acquiescing in a worsening of conditions.

6 An alternative approach based on oligopoly theory

(56) Using the analysis above as background, and drawing on Davis (1988), further light may be cast on the development of international financial centres and associated location of firms by pursuing an analogy between an international financial centre and a large diversified firm in an oligopoly[2] characterised by increasing returns to scale and of scope, and with large sunk costs.[3] Thus in this section, the "firm" or "agent" is the centre itself and the "market" is for location of financial activity. The diversified activities are subject to strong "synergies".[4] Obviously the analogy is imperfect; there is no strong central management of such centres (though government and central bank play a part), and centres cannot decide autonomously to raise external funds, while time zone differences may limit somewhat the degree of competition, particularly in the case of certain continuously-traded secondary markets such as forex.

(a) The importance of increasing returns to scale

(57) First, such a "market" is typically *difficult for smaller centres to penetrate*, given they lack the benefits of size and diversification in terms of average costs which result from increasing returns to scale and scope. Unless they can attain an (extremely high) minimum efficient scale, they will find that all business for which there is a free market may tend to gravitate to major centres. The advantages in terms of average costs are reinforced by intertemporal dependencies on the cost (expertise) and demand (reputation) sides, and by what are implicitly strategic investments—research by institutes or firms on the cost side and product differentiation on the demand side. The sunk costs of financial firms already established in major financial centres, as well as uncertainty, lack of information and other obstacles to movement of firms outlined in Section 2, will also tend to act as barriers to entry of new international centres.

(58) A related argument—implicitly an aspect of increasing returns to scale—is the *degree to which fixed costs are shared* between markets or institutions. This includes not merely infrastructure investment such as payments and settlements systems, but also shared research, training of the skilled labour force, and even the central bank. This reinforces the major centres' dominant positions—variable costs of markets and institutions are shared over lower fixed costs than if they stood alone. Alternatively, high fixed costs of superior technology, which increases competitiveness, may more easily be financed

(1) More than three markets may of course be sustained in certain non-homogeneous products such as oil. Sunk costs arising from historical development may also lead to multiple centres in one time zone, if they are accompanied by specialisation [eg New York (banking and securities) and Chicago (futures and options)] though the equilibrium may be unstable.

(2) Indeed, given the restrictions on competition arising from time zones, they almost qualify as "natural monopolists" given current technology (unique maxima and minima of space—revenue and space—cost, respectively).

(3) ie capital specific to the industry, the presence of which prevents other centres setting up in the industry rapidly and costlessly [the conditions for pure contestable markets, see Baumol (1982), Mayer (1985) thus do not obtain].

(4) These synergies comprise external economies of scale for the individual institutions; economies of scale (size of markets) and of scope (diversity of linked markets) for the centre as a whole.

when activity is greater. Lower fixed costs or superior technology enable penetration of new markets to be carried out more easily. The latter is also, of course, facilitated by the dominance of many financial markets by conglomerates, who can cross subsidise market penetration from earnings on other activities.

(59) In the light of these advantages to major centres, if smaller centres are to survive, government financial incentives may be required (for example lower taxes or easier regulations)—though the structural analysis suggests such "infant industry" assistance may be unavailing. More generally, it is of interest to note that increasing returns to scale imply it may be *economically efficient for financial activity to be concentrated in major centres.*[1]

(b) Limits to collusion

(60) If market penetration is difficult, it is nevertheless the case that the *major financial centres have been unable to exert strong market power*, exploiting customers by charging high mark-ups over cost. Several explanations can be offered. First, although other centres have been unable to gain a large market share they nevertheless offer a degree of actual or potential competition to global centres—a threat which has increased with the growing liberalisation of markets and improved technology.[2] Second, the customers of international financial concerns have gained stronger market power in terms of ability to switch between centres, information about different centres, and the relative importance of ongoing relationships between final users and financial centres. In general, financial intermediaries in each centre now have larger sunk costs in such relationships than the end-users, so the latter can no longer be "exploited". This has been linked to the process of institutionalisation of financial markets and the growing size and sophistication of corporate clients. Third, the major centres have not reached collusive agreements on price fixing, in contrast to industrial oligopolies where such agreements are often present (one exception may be international agreements on prudential standards).

(61) Indeed, the major centres often act in a directly non-co-operative manner. Taxation or other costs may be lowered in order to gain or avoid losing business—which may lead to a level of taxation or regulation below the social optimum. Given an interest in market penetration of other centres by their own firms, centres often apply threats and counter threats, where the threats tend to be in terms of establishment rights (reciprocity) rather than pricing as is more typical of industrial oligopolies (predatory pricing). There is, of course, a dichotomy between the interests of the financial centre itself and of national firms. The former may not be best served by reciprocity arguments but instead by openness to establishment of all comers and low costs (in terms of regulation, taxation, local costs etc).

(c) Decline of natural monopolies

(62) Oligopolies or monopolies backed by increasing returns to scale and sunk costs are typically extremely tenacious. They can often survive changes in market conditions by virtue of their reputation, expertise or by cross subsidisation from continuing profitable activities. Some, however, have fallen. The *ways in which such "natural" oligopolies have been broken* historically gives further insight into threats to financial centres. Often they have been overtaken by technical change which renders their product obsolete (trading floors) or lowers the barriers to entry arising from sunk costs (video links and other advances in telecommunications). Alternatively, well capitalised firms in other industries (countries) may cross subsidise entry. Regulatory changes in the home country or elsewhere may facilitate entry. Entry in any of these cases will be easier if the oligopolists allow costs to rise unduly (taxation, regulation) as a result of their "secure" position.

(63) Some caveats to this analysis are, of course, in order. Smaller financial centres can survive in "niches" in the market. These include activities that require a great deal of local knowledge and contacts, such as corporate finance for smaller firms, as well as locally-protected or long-established markets (domestic bond markets in European countries fall into most of these categories). Also the benefits of dominant financial centres such as increasing returns to scale do not necessarily extend to all the markets established there. Some of these may be of sub-optimal scale and hence unable to gain world status. The futures and options markets in Europe (in competition with those in the United States) may be a case in point (see Table 1.4 in Appendix 1).

(64) To summarise, analysis of financial centres as monopolists or oligopolists with increasing returns to scale and large sunk costs offers a

(1) This argument applies most strongly when there is no deviation of private from social cost—an assumption disputed in Section 7 below.
(2) Implicitly, the market for location of financial activity has become more contestable.

number of further insights into the structure and dynamics of the "market" for location of financial activity. In particular, it shows clearly why such a market is difficult for small centres to penetrate as well as pointing out the welfare benefits of concentration of financial activity. It also offers some reasons why centres have been unable to exert market paper and how they might decline—particularly technical change and willingness to allow costs to rise.

---

7 What are the net benefits of an international financial centre?

(65) The second question related to the future of international financial centres is the level of net benefits accruing to the domestic economy as a result of activity of the centre, and hence the losses should the centre cease to be of global importance. If they are low, the authorities have no reason for concern. It is thus relevant briefly to set out the main benefits and costs of an international financial centre, and suggest their likely magnitudes. Some underlying empirical evidence on the macroeconomic importance of a typical financial centre (London) is given in Appendix 2.

(a) Benefits

(66) The *benefits* include, the pecuniary benefits to the balance of payments (Table 2.3) and tax revenues. There is also a welfare gain from trade in financial services if the domestic comparative advantage leads to an improvement in the overall terms of trade. A financial centre makes a heavy contribution to employment (Table 2.2), both directly and in ancillary services, though this benefit is greatest if there was previously unemployment. One could add the benefits of a dynamic financial centre to growth, in terms of productivity, technical progress, the multiplier effect (in underemployment equilibrium) and supply of funds. Efficient capital markets should contribute to the optimal allocation of funds and hence the supply-side of the economy. On the other hand, in the absence of exchange controls it is unlikely that the presence of absence of a financial centre leads to a lower cost of capital for the corporate sector as a whole,[1] unless there is also a shift from oligopoly to competition among financial institutions.

(67) At full employment, welfare gains depend on the social productivity of finance vis-à-vis other employment. It is natural to assume they are equal; although even if social productivity is the same, *costs of adjustment* mean the decline of a financial sector cannot be viewed as a matter of indifference. On the other hand, to the extent that the analysis above, that a global centre is an oligopolist or even a natural monopoly in its own time zone, is correct, the returns to the domestic economy may partly be characterised as monopoly rent. This means that if the centre were to be dispersed, the benefits derived could not be completely replaced by redeployment of resources in a competitive industry.

(68) It is inappropriate to measure the benefits of a financial centre merely by summing value-added (the measure shown in Appendix 2 Table 2.1). For the benefits of a centre are unequal to the measured market value of services provided for at least three reasons. First, some of the benefits (and costs) constitute externalities, which are not paid for directly. Second, the benefits to users of goods or services may exceed the price paid because this is determined by the price needed to attract the marginal user (consumer surplus). Third, as noted above, the factors could be employed in other ways (opportunity costs).

(b) Costs

(69) Some of the *disadvantages* of hosting a major financial centre relate to the diseconomies of agglomeration. Congestion in transport systems may become endemic, necessitating sizable expenditures of public funds. House prices, wages and rents may be higher than desirable, (landlords or wage earners expropriate producers' surplus, which may be seen as undesirable) especially if comparability sets off inflation in the rest of the economy. Regional imbalances of poverty and prosperity may be exacerbated. Finance may cream off some able individuals, who may be more socially productive in manufacturing. More generally, there can be no presumption that the level of financial activity in a country will be socially optimal [see Mayer (1986)].

(70) Even if there is no market failure,[2] the economy may face risk due to greater

(1) There may nonetheless be distributional effects. Large firms may be indifferent to their location in respect to centres, but small firms and households may benefit from the nearby location of financial centres.

(2) In the economic sense that a system of market pricing fails to allocate resources optimally.

specialisation (in finance). There are other concerns of particular relevance to central banks. There may be undesirable macroeconomic effects from the free availability of credit (by removing liquidity constraints on consumers it reduces the leverage of macroeconomic policy—particularly fiscal policy—on consumers' expenditure). Monetary management of the economy may become more difficult. Financial instability and the danger of systemic risk may increase with a more complex financial structure. It should be noted that most of these costs are externalities, ie there is no pecuniary compensation paid. However, they must also be evaluated and set against the benefits.

(71) Some of the costs may be discounted. Diseconomies of agglomeration and regional imbalances would probably arise for any growing sector. The macroeconomic consequences could probably arise without a financial centre, given an absence of capital controls. Systemic risk does not necessarily cease to have an effect at national boundaries, either.

(72) Given these consideration, a global financial centre is likely to be of considerable benefit to the domestic economy. Nevertheless, although it can be suggested that the costs are, on balance, far below the benefits, it would be equally inappropriate for them not to be taken into account and reduced wherever possible.

8 Conclusions

(73) This paper has discussed in detail the determinants of financial firms' location decisions, thus providing a framework for the analysis and evaluation of factors thought to influence the development of international financial centres.[1] The key points may be summarised briefly. The main influences on the location of firms are factor costs and demand for the product of an individual firm, together with any external effects, sunk costs and indivisibilities. For financial firms, external economies of scale are likely to be particularly important, though regulation and technology (which affect costs and demand) are also likely to be of relevance. The importance of such external economies means growth of major financial centres may be self sustaining, to the detriment of smaller centres. Such a process may be visualised in terms of the development of an industry whose technology exhibits increasing returns to scale at all levels of activity. This analysis has the important corollary that concentration of finance in major centres offers a global gain in terms of economic efficiency.

(74) The importance of sunk costs is likely to mean that a significant deterioration in market conditions is needed to stimulate relocation, though a much smaller adverse shift may deter firms from moving *to* financial centres. In addition, markets may be more footloose than firms, though a market shift may eventually lead firms to shift. However, reversing the process of development, once a move away from a financial centre begins, it could easily become cumulative, given the nature and importance of external economies. Technological change could start and perhaps accelerate such a process, though regulatory changes or declines in political stability could equally be the spark beginning such a move. Given the net benefits of an international financial centre to the domestic economy, such a shift would be at considerable cost.

(75) This analysis offers various considerations relevant to the pattern of financial activity in EC countries after 1992. Equalisation of regulation between countries and free entry to all markets should in principal make location of financial activity more fluid. On the other hand, the importance of external economies to scale in the London market may make it hard for other centres to compete—they may even lose business, given abolition of restrictions on cross-border sale of financial services. (This raises the concern that they could become "impoverished" in terms of financial skills.) The United States may provide an illustration of the future pattern of financial activity in the absence of regulatory and fiscal differences—one global centre, with smaller "satellite" centres in each region (country).

(1) It should be noted that this subject can be approached from various angles; here we use location theory and oligopoly theory from industrial economics. Arndt (1988) has identified some of the same determining factors from the approach of international trade theory. Kindleberger (1974) discusses the development of global centres in terms of a key or reserve currency centre and lender of last resort in the international monetary system. Our argument suggests that although such factors help explain the genesis of some financial centres, they cannot account for their continuing development even when the initial stimulus has gone.

Appendix 1: Indicators of the relative size of financial centres

Table 1.1: International Banking Analysed by Centre

Gross Lending - percentage share of total market

	1978	1982	1987	1988	1989 Q1	1989 Q2	1989 Q3	1989 Q4
Belgium[(a)]	4.7	3.3	3.8	3.4	3.4	3.5	3.3	3.4
Luxembourg[(a)]	4.9	4.3	4.2	4.1	4.1	4.2	4.2	4.3
France	9.8	7.2	6.7	6.3	6.4	6.7	6.5	6.6
Germany Federal Republic	5.2	2.8	4.0	3.8	3.4	3.7	3.8	4.4
Italy	2.8	1.7	1.9	1.9	1.8	1.8	1.7	1.7
Netherlands	3.9	2.9	2.5	2.5	2.6	2.8	2.8	2.8
Switzerland	4.6	2.8	2.8	2.4	2.2	2.2	2.4	2.3
Swiss Trustee Accounts	2.7	3.9	3.4	3.2	3.3	3.5	3.5	3.6
UK	24.6	26.9	22.1	20.9	20.4	20.5	19.9	19.4
Canada	2.6	2.6	1.5	1.3	1.3	1.3	1.2	1.2
Japan	4.8	7.5	18.7	21.0	22.1	20.6	22.1	21.4
of which:								
JOM	-	-	4.0	6.8	7.1	7.1	8.1	8.0
other	-	-	14.7	14.2	15.0	13.5	14.0	13.3
US	9.7	14.5	9.9	10.1	10.1	10.0	9.7	9.7
of which:								
IBFs	-	-	5.4	5.6	5.7	5.8	5.6	5.6
other	-	-	4.5	4.5	4.4	4.2	4.0	4.2
'Offshore' banking centres[(b)]	17.5	17.7	18.0	18.5	18.2	18.4	18.2	18.4

(a) Lending by banks in Belgium to Luxembourg and vice versa is classified as lending to residents and is therefore excluded. Similarly, lending by these banks both in Belgium and Luxembourg francs is classified as domestic currency lending.

(b) Bahamas, Bahrain, Cayman Islands, Hong Kong, Netherlands Antilles and Singapore, includes also the branches of US banks in Panama.

- not available

Source: Bank for International Settlements

Table 1.2: Comparison of major stock exchanges at end-1989

Exchange	Market value of domestic equity (£ billions)	Number of listed companies Domestic	Foreign	Turnover Domestic (£ billions)	Foreign
Tokyo	2,639	1,597	119	1,436	12
New York	1,800	1,634	87	957	n/a
London	507	2,015	544	198	85
NASDAQ	241	4,026	267	249	14
German Federation of exchanges	227	628	535	218	11
Paris	227	462	223	69	3
Zurich	107	117	229	n/a	n/a
Milan	106	211	0	27	0

Source: ISE Quality of Markets Quarterly, Spring 1990

Table 1.3: Foreign exchange market turnover

$ billion per day	**1986**	**1989**
London	90	187
New York	58	129
Tokyo	48	115
Switzerland	-	57
Singapore	-	55
Hong Kong	-	49

Based on surveys conducted in March 1986 and April 1989

Source: Bank of England Quarterly Bulletin, November 1989

Table 1.4: Futures and options exchanges

Percentage share of total lots traded

Region	**Exchange**	**1984**	**1988**	**1989**
London	Baltic	0.1	0.05	0.04
	IPE	0.15	0.27	0.45
	LIFFE	0.71	2.24	2.88
	LFOX	0.87	0.57	0.51
	LME	1.13	1.12	1.21
	LTOM	0.31	1.21	1.15
	Total	**3.26**	**5.45**	**6.25**
United States	CBOE (Chicago)	33.7	16.0	14.7
	CBOT (Chicago)	18.5	20.47	16.6
	CME (Chicago)	11.8	11.22	12.59
	Total	**94.4**	**70.3**	**64.7**
Canada	**Total**	**0.55**	**1.05**	**1.09**
Europe	EOE (Amsterdam)	1.39	1.22	1.61
	MATIF (Paris)	-	2.32	3.13
	Total	**1.5**	**5.36**	**7.14**
Far East	Tokyo	-	3.01	2.71
	Total	**0.3**	**5.28**	**4.81**
Memo: World total number of contracts traded (thousands)		365,835	698,433	831,398

Source: Bank of England, based on a sample of individual exchanges.

Appendix 2: The macroeconomic benefits of a financial centre

Table 2.1: GDP at Factor Cost[a]

£ billions, percentages in italics

	1975	1985	1987	1988
Banking, finance, insurance, business services and leasing (BFIBsL) (including net interest receipts)	10.0	48.5	65.6	76.9
Rest of Economy	88.1	273.4	309.3	339.9
Total of above	**98.1**	**321.9**	**374.9**	**416.8**
Total after adjusting for net interest in financial services = GDP	94.7	305.9	355.7	394.6
BFIBsL (including net interest receipts) as a percentage of GDP	*10.6*	*15.9*	*18.4*	*19.5*
BFIBsL (excluding net interest receipts) as a percentage of GDP	*7.2*	*10.6*	*13.0*	*13.9*

Source: National Income and Expenditure (CSO)

(a) In the national accounts, the contribution of BFIBsL is measured before deducting net receipts of interest by financial companies and institutions. This is offset in the aggregate gross domestic product (where interest flows within the economy must net to zero) by a negative 'adjustment for financial services' equal (and opposite) to those net interest receipts.

Table 2.2: Employees in employment

Thousands; percentages of employees in employment in italics

		Sept(a) 1981		Sept 1984		Change	Sept 1987		Change	December 1989		Change
Banking and finance:	Great Britain	465	*2*	507	*2*	+42	574	*3*	+67	628	*3*	+54
	Greater London	162	*5*	167	*5*	+5	198	*6*	+31	...		...
Insurance:	Great Britain	224	*1*	223	*1*	-1	240	*1*	+17	273	*1*	+33
	Greater London	60	*2*	59	*2*	-1	55	*2*	-4	...		...
Business service:	Great Britain	849	*4*	1,037	*5*	+188	1,271	*6*	+234	1,532	*7*	+261
	Greater London	302	*8*	354	*10*	+52	450	*13*	+96	...		...
Other(b):	Great Britain	191	*1*	221	*1*	+30	224	*1*	+3	263	*1*	+39
	Greater London	45	*1*	52	*2*	+7	51	*1*	-1	...		...
Total BFIBsL:	Great Britain	1,729	*8*	1,988	*10*	+259	2,309	*12*	+321	2,741	*12*	+432
	Greater London	569	*16*	632	*18*	+63	753	*21*	+121	891	*24*	+138
All industries and services:	Great Britain	21,309		20,846		-463	21,271		+425	22,561		+1,290
	Greater London	3,567		3,463		-104	3,505		+42	3,720		+215

Source: Department of Employment.

(a) The breakdown of BFIBsL, is not available for earlier years.
(b) Renting of movables and owning and dealing in real estate.

Table 2.3: Net overseas earnings[(a)] of UK financial institutions

£ billions

	1975	1985	1987	1988	1989	Memorandum item: 1989 earnings from services(b)
Insurance	0.5	3.3	4.6	3.5	2.9	1.7
Banking	-	1.3	1.3	0.8	-0.7	1.5(c)
Investment trusts, unit trusts, pension funds	0.1	0.9	1.1	0.9	1.4	-
Securities dealers, brokers and leasing	0.5	1.3	1.7	2.2	2.5	2.2
Total	1.0	6.8	9.7	7.4	6.2	5.4
Memorandum items:						
Visible balance	-3.3	-3.1	-10.9	-20.8	-23.1	
Invisible balance	1.7	6.3	6.6	5.9	4.0	
Current balance	-1.5	3.2	-4.3	-15.0	-19.0	

Source: United Kingdom Balance of Payments (the Pink Book): CSO.

(a) Equals net direct contribution to UK balance of payments.
(b) Excluding net interest and other income from portfolio investment. Bank estimate based on the assumption that the contribution of investment trusts, unit trusts and pension funds to the balance of payments is entirely portfolio earnings.
(c) If income from intermediation is added, this figure rises to £3.2 billion.

References

Arndt, H W, (1988), "Comparative advantage in trade in financial services", Banca Nazionale del Lavoro.

Ashcroft, B and Taylor, J, (1977), "The movement of manufacturing industry and the effect of regional policy", Oxford Economic Papers, 29, 84-101.

Bank for International Settlements, (1986), "Recent innovations in international banking (the Cross Report)", BIS, Basle.

Baumol, W, (1982), "Contestable markets: an uprising in the theory of industrial structure", American Economic Review, 72, 1-15.

Burn, D L, (1958), "The Structure of British Industry", Cambridge University Press.

Campayne, P, (1990), "Impact of multinational banks on international location of banking activity and the global hierarchy of financial centres", unpublished PhD dissertation, University of Reading.

Chalmers, I A and Beckhelm, T L, (1976), "Shift and share and the theory of industrial location", Regional Studies, 10, 15-23.

Coase, R H, (1937), "The nature of the firm", Economica Vol 4.

Davies, G and Davies, J, (1984), "The revolution in monopoly theory", Lloyds Bank Review, July 1984, 38-52.

Davis, E P, (1988), "Industrial structure and dynamics of financial markets: the primary eurobond market", Bank of England Discussion paper No 35.

Davis, E P and Latter, A R, (1989), "London as an international financial centre", Bank of England Quarterly Bulletin, 29, 516-528.

Devine, P J et al, (1979), "An introduction to industrial economics", third ed. George Allen & Unwin.

Dunning, J H and Morgan, E V, (1966), "An economic study of the City of London", George Allen & Unwin.

Dunning, J H, (1973), "The determinants of international production", Oxford Economic Papers, 25, 289-336.

Economist, (1988), "Learning to manage: a survey of the City of London", The Economist, 25, 6.88, London.

Economists Advisory Group, (1984), "City 2000; the future of London as an international financial centre", Lafferty Publications LTd.

EIU, (1964), "A survey of factors governing the location of offices in the London area", Economist Intelligence Unit, London.

Giddy, I H, (1983), "The theory and industrial organisation of international banking", in Hawkins, R G, et al eds "The international of financial markets and national economic policy" Research in International Business and Finance Vol 3.

Grubel, H G, (1983), "The new international banking", Banca Nazionale del Lavoro.

Hamilton, F E I, (1974), "Spatial perspectives on industrial organisation and decision making ", John Wiley, London.

Hewson, J R, (1982), "Offshore banking in Singapore—a case study" in "Commissioned Studies and Selected Paeprs" Part 2, Macroeconomic Policy; External Policy, Australian Financial System Inquiry, AGPS, Canberra.

Hood, N and Young, S, (1979), "The Economics of Multinational Enterprise", Longman, London.

Keeble, D E, (1976), "Industrial location and planning in Britain", Methuen, London.

Kindleberger, C P, (1974), "The formation of financial centres; a study in comparative economic history" Princeton Studies in International Finance, No 36.

Latham, W R, (1976), "Location behaviour in manufacturing industries", Martinus Nijhoff, Leiden.

Lee, S Y, (1986), "Developing Asian Financial Centres" in Tan H H and Kapur B (eds) "Pacific Growth and Financial Interdependence", Allen and Unwin, Sydney.

Luttrell, W F, (1962), "Factory location and industrial movement", National Institute, London.

Mathias, P, (1969), "The first industrial nation", Methuen, London.

Mayer, C P, (1985), "The assessment: recent developments in industrial economics and their implications for policy", Oxford Review of Economic Policy, Vol 1, No 3, 1-24.

Mayer, C P, (1986), "The assessment; financial innovation, curse or blessing?" Oxford Review of Economic Policy, Vol 2 No 4, i-xix.

Mills, E S, (1972), "Urban economics", Scott Foresman, Glenview, Illinois.

Moore, B C and Rhodes, J, (1976), "A quantitative analysis of the effects of the regional employment premium and other regional policy instruments", in A Whiting (ed) "The economics of industrial subsidies", HMSO, London.

Park, Y H and Zwick, J, (1985), "International banking in theory and practice", Addison-Wesley Co, Reading, Mass.

Reid, H C, (1981), "The pre-eminence of international financial centres", Praeger, New York.

Revell, J, (1987), "Mergers and the role of large banks", Institute of European Finance Research Monograph No 2, (1987), Univeristy College of North Wales, Bangor.

Richardson, H W, (1969), "Regional economics", Weidenfield & Nicholson, London.

Richardson, H W, (1978), "Regional and urban economics", Penguin, Harmondsworth.

Sant, M C, (1975), "Industrial movement and regional development: the British case", Pergamon, Oxford.

Scholey, D, (1986), "Essential features of international finance centres", paper given at the International Banking Summer School, Switzerland.

Townroe, P M, (1971), "Industrial location decisions", University of Birmingham, Birmingham.

[2]

Excerpt from *International Financial Centres: Structure, Achievements and Prospects*, 11–24

Essential features of international financial centres

Sir David Scholey

I must confess that it was with considerable trepidation that I received the invitation from your President and my old and good friend Mr Rainer Gut to speak at the opening of the International Banking Summer School. To do so is a privilege indeed and to do so in Switzerland, a country synonymous with banking, heightens the compliment. On the other hand to address this audience of already experienced bankers at the commencement of such a star-studded programme on such a massive subject is a task of daunting proportions. However vanity triumphed over anxiety and here I am – and very delighted to be here too.

The matter of international financial centres which you are here to explore is, like any worthwhile subject, virtually limitless, but my knowledge is certainly not – and you have two weeks ahead of you to devote to it. So I will confine myself this evening to an overview reviewing some of the historical background to our financial communications structure, reflecting on contemporary characteristics and suggesting some possible future developments.

Over the last decade, as we all know, the international financial markets have been through a period of change of unprecedented rapidity. This is reflected in the language that has grown up to describe the characteristics of the emerging financial universe – a language peppered with new "-sations", words like "globalisation", "securitisation", "commoditisation", and even as I heard recently, "democratisation", which deal with ends rather than means, with trends rather than their causes, and which manage to imply that dynamically evolving processes are foregone conclusions.

The concept of the International Financial Centre ("IFC") forms part of this vocabulary. This is partly, no doubt, because although IFCs are not, of course, new phenomena viewed from the perspective of the historian, they may appear that way to the 1980s banker, who is used to many years of regulated, essentially national rather than international markets, whose centres – without being fully international themselves – have provided a base for financial houses to carry out certain overseas activities. More importantly, however, no one would deny their importance, at least as an idea, in a world where innovation of product and technology in every aspect of life and industry is making the financial markets simultaneously more integrated and more international.

Today, international financial institutions are formulating and implementing strategies that imply high levels of investment in establishing presences in overseas locations and in installing technology designed to minimise the inefficiencies implicit in the physical distance between those locations.

Politicians and policy makers are also directly and actively concerned; some because of a wish to attract investment into their markets and economies, others by a desire to retain it and still others by the problems of managing its presence. This last matter is, of course, also a challenge that regulators all around the world are grappling with.

In short, by putting the question "What are the essential features of IFCs?" we can hope not only to emerge with a clearer idea of what it is that banks should look for in markets in order to establish whether they are or have the potential to be on the centre or periphery of the financial world; but also to delineate what those markets should offer banks in order to attract them; and thirdly, perhaps, to shed some light on the way in which the financial world is likely to develop.

This is a pretty tall order and, as with any task that appears over-ambitious, it may be best to start by returning to basics. Although we would like to pretend otherwise (sometimes, admittedly with due cause!) the financial markets are, basically, pretty simple things. All they require are a surplus of capital (i.e. a source of supply), a roughly offsetting deficit of capital (i.e. a source of demand) and an intermediator or intermediation process (to match supply with demand). For any financial centre, market or organisation, the first of these, the surplus of capital, is, of course, most obviously important; if there is no surplus there can be no intermediation of it and those requiring capital must meet their demand via the fruits of their own efforts. However, for a financial centre to be an international one it seems reasonable to infer that there must be not only a surplus, but also a geographically differentiated deficit and an intermediator and/or intermediation process capable of bridging the physical divide. Of these ingredients it is not clear intuitively which if any is essential. Obviously there must be a means of intermediation, but this seems itself to be necessarily a response to demand rather than a precondition, and we cannot be certain without looking at specific examples whether a surplus is more likely to underpin an IFC than a deficit. Moreover, the form of intermediation, its efficiency and scope, will itself be affected by a whole variety of factors – regulatory, cultural, political, linguistic, technological, the openness of immigration policy and the very nature of the process of capital formation or the pattern of demand in the surplus or deficit areas. It is, therefore, also pertinent to ask what these factors may be and what they may need to be for an IFC to function effectively.

As is so often the case, whilst history must never be expected to repeat itself, a brief review of some historical IFCs is revealing.

The first major expansion of credit on an international scale was in the 13th century and it was centred on Florence. Florence's pre-eminent position was itself based on the surpluses generated by the activities of Italian merchants who were venturing as far afield as India and China. Florence acted as a sort of clearing house for much of this trading activity; its merchants bought and sold spices, woollens, cloth, hardware and – of course – money. Evidently, however, the credit demands of trade did not provide sufficient investment opportunities for the Florentines, who became heavily involved in the financing of the English kings. By 1345 Edward III owed 900,000 Florins to the great financial house of the Bardi and 600,000 Florins to its competitor the Peruzzi, a sum far larger than the capital of these firms, indicating that they had drawn on deposits to make the loans. By this stage the Florentines had also succeeded in gaining control of sales of English wool, vital to Europe and to the industry of Florence itself. However, in that year Edward III, illustrating dramatically the problem with sovereign risk, repudiated his debts and the power of the Florentine houses was broken.

Later the rise and fall of the Fuggers of Augsburg followed a similar pattern. They were a trading and financing house, but primarily the latter as their trading interests accumulated in relation to the loans they had made to the Habsburgs, specifically the Emperor Charles V. As with the Florentines their ties with monarchy brought wealth and then disaster. Too many of their investments represented realised security on defaulted loans and ultimately the Spanish state's finances collapsed into complete disorder at the end of the 16th century and the Fuggers suffered accordingly.

Both the Fuggers and the Florentines operated on the basis of personal ties and their lending activities embraced the trade of nations and the enterprises (and excesses) of their monarchs. Although both were based in and perhaps created what we may term international financial centres, these centres were themselves not so much intermediaries as the base from which wealthy and hierarchical families operated. Their financial empires reflect the fact that trade (the circulation of commodities) and credit (the circulation of capital) grew together and were virtually inseparable, while sovereigns represented the only major independent non-trade related source of demand with sufficient security and status to justify the risks of lending. To adopt the language of my earlier analysis the process of intermediation was basically personal; the form it took was dictated not only by the process of capital generation and the pattern of demand but also by lenders' subjective assessments of the desirability of meeting that demand; and the IFCs themselves (which might be reasonably re-named the International Financial Families), were founded on the existence of a capital surplus requiring investment opportunities.

There are of course major differences between these early IFCs and their later equivalents. The Genoese financiers of the 16th century founded their position not so much on trade as on a shrewd grasp of what may be termed, loosely, developments in the money supply of Europe. There was a new flow of silver from mines in the New World, which broke the monopoly control previously exercised by the likes of the Fuggers over European silver production. At the same time this pushed up the price of gold, which nevertheless remained the currency for settling international transactions and bills of exchange. With an eagle eye for the main chance the Genoese set about controlling both types of bullion. In the first place they offered to replace the Fuggers as financial backers of the Spanish crown; these loans were, of course, repaid in silver for the most part. Secondly they developed a system of credit based on bills of exchange that far surpassed anything that had gone before, to the extent that the Fuggers complained that doing business with the Genoese was like playing with pieces of paper – "mit Papier", whereas they themselves operated with real money – "Baargeld".

A particularly intriguing element of the Genoese system was the role played by the quarterly fairs held at Piacenza. Braudel, on whose wonderful work "Civilisation and Capitalism" I should say that I have drawn heavily for this dip into history, describes these fairs as the scenes of "decisive but discreet meetings", comparable with meetings of, for example, the Bank for International Settlements. The fair was not based on the trading of merchandise, nor of cash; rather it acted as an international clearing house for bills of exchange, a place where the Genoese financiers met with foreign exchange dealers and representatives of large merchant firms to fix the "conto" – the rate for liquidation of the bills.

This Genoese system of international finance stands alone in history up until the present day as an example of an IFC built not so much on locally based trade or primarily on a local surplus (although both elements were present), but rather on and efficient an sophisticated system for gathering the monetary surpluses of other parties, in part through a process of – to use a familiar phrase – securitisation, or the extension of paper credit. Although Amsterdam in the 18th century and London in the 19th century also based many of their financial activities on the issuance and discounting of securities, these were backed primarily by increasing volumes of trade and of surplus capital which were centred locally.

The inference, therefore, is that the existence of a local surplus is not necessarily a precondition for an IFC. This line of argument finds further support if one considers that even where a surplus did exist it was not necessarily mobilised as investment. In the France of Louis XVI, for example, unused capital abounded; in Marseilles owners of capital who offered merchants money at 5 per cent, found so few takers that when one was found he was thanked roundly for his "kindness in keeping our funds". It was not simply a matter of absence of sufficient demand, but also of a lack of investment opportunities considered to be suitable – a subjective judgement.

It would be wrong of me to leave this historical overview without commenting on the position of London in the 19th century and early 20th century. London's position as the world's financial centre was founded primarily on a massive capital surplus and the willingness to reinvest that surplus overseas, not only through the financing of trade but also to finance capital investment in industry, mining, railways and so on – the infrastructure of Empire and the new worlds of North and South America. London was not only distinguished by the range of overseas investments intermediated by it; sterling's position as the international reserve currency, backed by the Bank of England's willingness to underwrite the gold standard, added immeasurably to London's strength. Although personal ties remained important, for example in the activities of merchant banks, financial business started to become increasingly impersonal. As the range of potential investors and borrowers expanded, the intermediation process came to deal primarily with the capital of people other than the intermediators themselves. And perhaps most important of all London built up a self-perpetuating critical mass of skills and services that provided an infrastructure unique even at the time.

Now where does this all lead us? Obviously there are no easy conclusions, but a contemporary observer of 1914 might have concluded that essential features of IFCs were trade and the existence of a capital surplus. Trade created both the motor for generating a surplus and a primary source of demand for its use. If the trade was international so too would be the financial system it bore and sustained. The experience of Genoa was something of an anomaly but one might conclude from this, and the role of sterling in London's rise to prominence, that monetary systems and conditions could themselves help to shape IFCs. In addition, it would have to be accepted that a surplus did not of itself create an IFC; a surplus required a mobilising intermediation process and the success of that process depended in part on the ability to locate opportunities that investors, for a variety of reasons, were happy to take. Similarly the experience of Chicago, the gathering and departure point for North America's agricultural and extractive industries in the second part of the 19th and the first half of the 20th century, suggested that huge trade volumes and surpluses did not of themselves make IFCs; although prophetically skills were perfected here that are now very pertinent indeed to international financial markets. Finally, a lesson of history was that the world could accommodate only one IFC at any one time; there had never been two or three centres conducting a roughly equal amount of international finance, but always one predominant financial area or locality.

We have now arrived at the present, a rather roundabout way of doing so I am afraid, but one which I hope is helpful as a means of adding perspective and perhaps shedding some light on the current debate. What of modern financial centres? Which ones are really international? In what way? And why?

Unfortunately there is no time this evening to get involved in elaborate and, no doubt, contentious arguments about which modern centres are, or may be becoming, IFCs. You will not be surprised therefore, if I concentrate on what one pungent observer describes as the three best restaurants in town, London, New York and Tokyo, as I believe everyone will be agreed that these are financial centres that are to a greater or lesser extent international. Moreover, according to current wisdom they are likely to form the tripod, differentiated by time zones, for the global financial markets that are rapidly evolving. It might of course be argued that a case could be made for Switzerland, Germany and, even, Bahrain. It seems to me, however, that Switzerland's function remains primarily that of a haven for overseas investment funds – investors put money through Swiss financial markets in order to, as it were, "become Swiss" rather than to internationalise their holdings; that Germany is at too early a stage to draw any conclusions; and that Bahrain's role was specifically to consolidate the massive oil surpluses of the Middle East before passing these on to London or New York, which acted as the true centre for their international recycling.

What then are the essential features of New York, London and Tokyo as IFCs? Perhaps the best way to approach this is to ask why it is that these cities are now emerging as IFCs; what forces have internationalised them in the modern context?

Until relatively recently both the US and Japanese financial markets were heavily regulated and restricted and were essentially national in character.

The US financial markets were formulated and constrained by a series of acts passed in the first half of the century. The basic premise of these was that the forces of finance required control to be exercised both through a direct regulatory framework and by enacting various protections for investors. This was not simply a matter of prudence or good housekeeping on the part of the federal authorities; there was a widely held view that the nineteenth century had taken laissez faire capitalism too far and that its worst excesses stood to be corrected, a view perhaps most obviously expressed in the Sherman Antitrust Act and the Public Utility Holding Company Act.

By the end of Franklin D. Roosevelt's first term, in 1936, the restrictive legislative framework within which the financial services sector was to operate all the way through to the 1970s had been established. Financial institutions had been separated into functionally defined segments with a limited *domestic* range. Ceilings for interest rates on various kinds of deposits were fixed and at the same time the payment of interest on checking accounts was forbidden.

Before going on to look at developments in Japan, and then reviewing the changes in the US and Japanese markets over the last decade, I would like to pause and ask the question "why?" Why was it that the US financial sector took shape as it did? It is an important question given that the connection between circumstance and form is one of the prime concerns here. It seems to me that there are two answers. The first is that attitudes demanded that the financial sector, in common with other parts of the US capitalist economy (such as utilities, railroads, the food and drug industries), should be regulated. Secondly, things were as they were because they were able to be. In most places and most times the realms of possibility can be defined, although numerous variations may develop within them. The world economy up until the Second World War quite simply permitted and indeed complemented an essentially closed and nationalistically organised financial sector, while leaving room for occasional forays, such as that of J. P. Morgan, into the financing of First World War munitions. After 1948 for two decades of rapid growth in the world economy and international trade, the domestic structures formulated in the heyday of economic nationalism continued to be adequate. Only gradually did the seeds of their destruction germinate from the new international monetary structure created at Bretton Woods, coupled with the acceleration in technological development.

Japan, however, was quite something else, although in any description of the Japanese financial markets, many of the words used to characterise their US counterparts could be repeated – regulated, compartmentalised, organised within the boundaries of the nation state. This would however miss the point, for the rationale behind the Japanese system was quintessentially different from that of the US. Whereas the US market regulators were concerned with the concentration and abuse of capital, the Japanese faced a situation in which capital resources were scarce, so that the most urgent challenge was to build them up and while doing so ensure their efficient allocation to meet identified national goals. This was of course a challenge the Japanese faced twice within a century; once during the Meiji Restoration, and again following the end of the Second World War.

As with the US one can list the pillars on which the Japanese financial system was built and, without going into overmuch detail, the cumulative and specific effect of this regulatory framework reflected its intent; to build in incentives for the allocation of capital, the form that capital took and the means of its intermediation (witness for instance the proliferation of institutions with distinct mandates, discrete tasks to perform in the financial arena).

The system owed its existence to the managers of the Japanese political economy, it reflected their intentions and it worked because those intentions were largely unquestioned in the political arena, were vindicated by the pace of economic development and sustained by the form that development took.

I hope that it is fairly clear where this analysis is leading me to by this stage. One would expect that shifts in socio-political attitudes or changes in the economic circumstances that bore and sustained the systems described above would also lead to their demise. This, I suggest, is precisely what is happening.

The Bretton Woods Agreement and the international division of labour established between the IMF, the GATT and the World Bank were designed to ensure that the mistakes of the 1930s were not repeated. For over twenty years the system worked: fixed exchange rates based around an over-valued US dollar and the willingness, even eagerness, of America to run a balance of payments deficit in order to provide the engine for world growth, formed the necessary conditions for an unparalleled period of prosperity in the developed world.

The corollary of this economic blueprint was that a pool of dollars gradually built up outside the US, creating latent investment demand for matching assets. The catalyst that provided an outlet for this demand was not, as you might expect me to say, Sir Siegmund Warburg but the decision of the Kennedy administration to impose an interest equalisation tax on foreign borrowers in US markets. This effectively created the supply to satisfy the demand, with Sir Siegmund and others presiding as marriage brokers.

In the longer perspective it was a truly revolutionary event. Although it did not change the financial world overnight it pointed the way to a new way of doing things. The Eurodollar market was something without precedent – a supranational source of capital, unregulated (indeed, prophetically, instigated by too heavy handed an approach to regulation in the US), outside national jurisdictions; in sum an arena for unrestricted competition that was itself in competition with the domestic markets that had previously dominated the intermediation of finance.

And there were other forces at work. Within the US, double digit inflation alerted investors to the importance of assessing returns in real terms, placing irresistable pressure on the restricted interest rate environment and providing investment banks with opportunities to exploit their regulatory position by designing securities-market based packages for retail lenders.

In short the regulated interest rate environment operated by the Federal Reserve Bank and the tax imposed by the Kennedy administration presented the international markets with opportunities that are unlikely to be deliberately repeated.

Perhaps most important of all, however, was the development of technology for disseminating information, which radically altered the role of banks as financial intermediaries, as this had historically been based on monopoly control over the information on which their broking activities were based. Screen based systems allowed borrowers and their advisers to locate primary sources of capital and to present those lenders with an array of investment vehicles. The spirit of Julius Reuter was far from dead. This was a sine qua non for the Eurobond markets, which although based in London had a widely dispersed constituency. In the US it encouraged a trend towards competition and towards the securitisation of banking assets. NASDAQ, which was based on access to information that had previously been the monopoly of the New York Stock Exchange, was established as early as 1971.

However, the real boost towards disintermediation did not come until the end of the 1970s, just a few years ago. At this time American banks in particular began to feel the effect of hurriedly recycled petro-dollars with the result that concerns for the credit quality of banks, previously considered sacrosanct, grew. Banks wanted more control over the management of their balance sheets (and therefore the fine tuning of capital ratios) while investors no longer saw the need to bear the costs imputed by the banking system for intermediating the flow of funds between borrower and lender. Innovation and competition piggy-backed on the capabilities introduced by information technology to provide the means of engineering the subsequent shift to securities-based financing methods, with their far greater inherent flexibility of form and, therefore, appeal.

In sum, the US financial sector has been transformed by developments that the regulatory authorities have, quite simply, been unable to control. Underpinning this, and fostered by it, has been a shift in the political arena towards a more liberal approach to the financial markets and – perhaps in this case even more important – a growing expectation and demand on the part of investors for access to a broadly dispersed and differentiated range of investment choices. This is not to superimpose a grand inevitability. But the trends, the logic of which point inexorably towards the development of global markets, are clear.

Once again a review of the changes occurring in the Japanese markets over the last decade might use misleadingly similar terms – deregulation, internationalisation, the power of macro-economic factors – to describe a very different process. The pace of change in Japan has been far slower than in New York and has been driven by very different factors.

The forces for change in the Japanese markets have been internal, not external, and the process has been far more controlled than in the American example. Reforms have been a function of domestic requirements and successes rather than a legacy of economic mis-management or the pressure of external events. The interest rate structure of the Japanese market, for instance, has faced its biggest challenge from the level of the Japanese government's borrowings in pursuit of its historic post-war policy of generating growth through deficit finance. Over time, this has outstripped the capacity and willingness of the City banks to underwrite the bonds in the domestic markets, while simultaneously fostering the development of an active secondary market. The former resulted in government approval for the issuance of CDs as alternative financing instruments to supplement the banks' hard pressed retail base, while the two together have acted as a transmitter of market rates to investors and managers within the domestic economy. Against this background, internationalisation of the Japanese domestic markets and of outward investment by Japanese institutions has been tightly regulated, and the balance of power continues to tilt towards the technocrats of the MOF.

Nevertheless, the situation is changing. Japanese capital needs a destination and Japan by itself cannot provide it efficiently or at an acceptable rate of return. Moreover, there are good reasons of policy for liberalising the scope for outflows of capital. Japanese investors recycle a large portion of the US current account deficit into funding the US budget deficit, feeding the goose that lays the golden egg in a relationship that increasingly looks like one of mutual dependence if sometimes seeming like that between the narcotic addict and the supplier. These same investors have target rates of return to achieve and their ability to do so is an important matter of public policy, given the demographic profile of the ageing Japanese population. More insidiously perhaps the yen's growing use as a reserve and trading currency is already having some of the same repercussions as for the US dollar, as indicated by the developing Euroyen market and a far more volatile yen exchange rate. Whether it will eventually experience the same fate as other reserve currencies is a big and important question. Finally, Japan's leading financial institutions are already international in ambition and fast becoming so in practice, being numbered among the most powerful houses in the world, capable of competing in any market. In this situation a semi-closed domestic market is an anomaly.

Japan and New York are, therefore, two very different IFCs. In Japan the pressure for internationalisation comes primarily from the existence of an immense capital surplus that is increasingly proactive in seeking out overseas investment opportunities – at the end of 1986 holdings of foreign securities by Japanese institutions amounted to some Yen 32.5 trillion. By comparison the USA continues to occupy a somewhat ambiguous position. While it has large domestic surpluses it is now a net debtor on the external account. Even when the US was a net creditor, domestic capital (and, significantly, the regulatory framework which shaped the form of its intermediation) was essentially passive, even suspicious, in its attitude to overseas investments, which were largely made through governmental or multilateral institutions or directly through multinationals. This is reflected in the fact that the American capital markets have only recently begun to re-open to prime overseas names in a meaningful way; for example through ADRs, bankers' acceptances and, to a limited extent, commercial paper programmes. Similarly it took the spur of the ERISA legislation to persuade US private sector institutions to invest overseas in sizeable amounts. As we have seen, the factors that are turning New York into an IFC are essentially exogenous – they represent a challenge to its traditional way of doing things.

Although, given its massive domestic surpluses, one cannot push the analogy too far, New York is in a similar position in the international arena to London. London's development suggests that the "traditional" model for an IFC (that is that it should be built on trade and capital surpluses generated within an identifiable industrial / commercial region which acts as a defined repository for capital accumulation) may no longer hold true, although Tokyo fits the bill.

Sterling is no longer a reserve currency and the UK is neither a large capital exporter nor importer, although its net capital position is for the time being in surplus. Other financial centres can boast a similar range and sophistication in ancillary services. Moreover the domestic markets over which London presides are small by comparison with the New York and Tokyo markets.

And yet London sits at the centre of what are undoubtedly the most international markets in the world. This suggests that as long as capital flows are relatively deregulated and subject to dramatic shifts in trade imbalances it is not necessary for sterling to be a reserve currency or for the UK to be a capital exporter for London to thrive as an IFC. Similarly, simple physical proximity to sources of capital or the means of producing that capital (trade, as it used to be) is not necessary in an age of advanced telecommunications and information technology. Finally, London does retain a powerful legacy of skills, infrastructure and reputation from the days of Empire.

Nevertheless for both New York and London a note of caution is in order. There must be a recognition that the traditional definition of the role of international financial centres requires reformulating, and this has profound implications for the self-image and modus operandi of New York and London's financial communities (by which I mean the indigenous financial houses). I would suggest that the historical position of London, in particular, and to a lesser more limited extent New York, has been that of an inward International Financial Centre – attracting, welcoming, facilitating participation by firms from all over the world, a true entrepôt and market place in the fullest sense. The key point being that historically this role was essentially passive. This is no longer sufficient. London now finds itself in a position where its role as an IFC is dependent on all that is new in the financial markets. To retain this position it must continue to exploit these developments and in the process transform itself into an outward International Financial Centre – the hub of a global network of trading, financing and broking businesses with tentacles reaching deep into the market places of other countries.

New York must likewise become more proactive in competing for overseas capital to reduce its dependence on Japanese investment in the US Treasury market; in permitting a less restrictive approach to issues by overseas borrowers and in educating its investment community in overseas opportunities. The danger now for New York is that it will be blinded by its own self-sufficiency.

Having come on this journey through the past and the present I would like to end by taking a glimpse into the future. It seems reasonable to assume that financial markets will become more integrated as a result of the impact of technology, the requirements of investors and the continuing process of macro-economic and market de-restriction. Although there are some forces pushing the other way – particularly protectionist sentiment displayed both by governments and financial institutions such as the New York Stock Exchange –

these do not seem likely to reverse the trend to internationalisation, although they may affect the shape it takes. Similarly re-regulation, which must be distinguished from the process of de-restriction that the financial markets are undergoing, is likely – if handled correctly – to manage and even encourage globalisation rather than impede it.

If this is the case it seems to be implicit that, to a greater or lesser extent, all financial centres will become – if they wish – international. The distinction will be between the centre and periphery of financial markets generally rather than between international and domestic markets specifically. The ability of capital to flow freely across national boundaries and the catalytic role played by Information Technology in intermediating this flow implies that mini-centres – which may only be involved in secondary trading or may, in a more sophisticated form, provide windows onto domestic economies – may proliferate.

If there are mini-centres, there will also be macro-centres. It seems probable that three or four dominant IFCs will emerge as roughly equal partners in the international financial system, each differentiated naturally by time zone but also perhaps by function. On this last point it is interesting to speculate that already a crude division of labour is emerging, with Tokyo being the centre for the management of much of the world's internationally proactive surplus; New York being a massive source of demand (albeit also of some supply through the growing interest of investment institutions in international securities); and London fulfilling a hybrid, entrepreneurial role exploiting the unregulated environment of the Euromarkets and its position within Europe.

But perhaps this is a red herring; the clue to the future form of major IFCs could lie in the fact that whereas in the past there has been room for only one hegemonic financial centre in the world economy at any one time, in the future there may be several. Moreover, one should further consider that time zone position alone is one of the most frequently cited attributes, whether positive or negative, in evaluating financial centres.

The implication seems to be that the identity of IFCs in the future (and one can already see this today) will relate less and less to physical location and increasingly to the position of an IFC as part of a global network of sophisticated IT systems, anchored perhaps to the New York-London-Tokyo tripod, which will act as a sort of 24-hour respiratory system for the markets. While macro-centres will survive, their role in the international financial system will be that of aggregating and channelling the capital of the regions they service before delivering them into the 24-hour investment network. The implications of this are that IFCs must in future be not only open and outward-looking in a cultural and competitive sense; there must, in particular, be no anti-competitive restrictions on immigration, as the financial networks will represent the business infrastructure of institutions with heterogenous work forces. In addition it is logical that a common language – perhaps English, perhaps the mathematics of the markets, even reading in and emanating from pre-programmed computer systems – will evolve.

The consequences of this in terms of management, IT investment and supervision are, frankly, daunting but the potential benefits are immense. Provided that protectionism or political jealousies, whether generated domestically or trans-nationally, do not impede the march of progress, the international financial system has the opportunity to evolve into a truly efficient mechanism for managing, allocating and directing capital flows and for capital accumulation and investment. In this way the resources of the capitalist system can be brought together and dispersed through an arterial complex capable of sustaining its heart and fostering the health of its outer limbs.

We have now come full circle: the financiers of Genoa 300 years ago, with their international fairs for the settlement and trading of credit instruments, were way ahead of their time.

In closing, may I not only thank you but also wish you all well in the course ahead of you and in your continued progress in your banking careers. Because it is you, the leading bankers of tomorrow, who will shape the International Financial Centre of the future.

[3]

Excerpt from *The International Money Market*, 35–47

Appendix 2

Financial Centers and External Financial Markets*

The purpose of this appendix is to shed light on some of the institutional facets of the international money market. In the first part we shall attempt to clarify such widely used terms as "international financial center," "entrepôt capital market," and "offshore banking center." In the second part we shall briefly outline the characteristics of the major jurisdictions, where external financial intermediation–defined elsewhere in the book–takes place. The nature of these jurisdictions represents one important determinant of the riskiness of the financial assets (loans) and liabilities (deposits) which are the basic "instruments" of the Eurocurrency market.

A financial center is a metropolitan area that has a high concentration of financial institutions and where the financial transactions of a given country or region are centralized. It exists for the purpose of efficiency. By centralizing the major financial institutions of a country in a specific metropolis, communications are improved and a variety of cost savings through specialization and economies of scale can be realized.

Traditionally, the development of a financial center has been a cumulative process whereby the financial community expanded as a result of growth in the business sector, and vice versa. The financial industry was originally attracted to New York, for example, by the demand for financial services generated by large wholesalers who located near that city's important seaport. As more and more financial institutions located in New York, national companies began moving their central offices there in search of the benefits of improved communications, better financial services, and so on. The centralization of financial activity caused a reduction in financing costs, which in turn brought about lower interest rates on loans, thereby furthering business expansion.

International financial centers developed as an extension of domestic centers. Those domestic centers offering the greatest convenience in terms of international communications, geographic locations, financial services, and so on, became the recognized international financial centers. Although in some sense all countries must have an "international financial center," simply to effect trade with other countries, in common usage the term has come to signify only the major financial cities in the world. Although the definition of the term is somewhat subjective, the label clearly applies to a number of cities in the world, the most important being London and New York.

Only one type of transaction can occur in a domestic financial market: a domestic lender provides funds (via domestic financial intermediaries or directly through organized, regulated securities markets) to domestic borrowers. In an international financial market, however, three additional types of transactions

*David J. Donovan aided the authors in drafting this appendix. Specific sources used here are listed in the References.

may occur: (1) between foreign lenders and domestic borrowers, (2) between domestic lenders and foreign borrowers, and (3) between foreign lenders and foreign borrowers. The last of these types of transactions (i.e., between foreign lenders and foreign borrowers) are called *entrepôt* or *offshore* transactions. In this case the financial center merely provides facilitating services for foreign lending and borrowing.

Until the development of the Euromarkets in the late 1950s, international financial centers were principally net suppliers of capital to foreign borrowers. It was necessary for international financial centers to have a surplus of domestic capital available and to have ample and continuous sources of new capital to supply. Thus only the world's major and most mature economies were able to support a financial center in the traditional sense. London was clearly the leader in this traditional international market, its leadership being only occasionally challenged by Paris during the nineteenth century. With the weakening of the British economy in the aftermath of World War I, however, London became unable to compete effectively with New York for international loans. Thus London's financial community watched its business slowly disappear until the 1960s when the Euromarkets heralded a new era for the city's competitiveness in international finance.

In the post 1960-Euromarket, entrepôt-type and offshore financial transactions became increasingly predominant and the traditional nature of financial centers was altered significantly. With the effective internationalization of credit transactions, it was no longer necessary for an international financial center to be a net supplier of domestic capital. This requirement eliminated, new candidates quickly challenged the traditional centers. Small and relatively unknown parts of the world soon became important banking centers. Names such as Nassau (the Bahamas), Singapore, Luxembourg, and others took on unheard-of importance in international finance. More recently, several cities in the Middle East (e.g., Kuwait and Bahrein) have made known their ambitions of becoming international financial centers. Some of the Middle Eastern centers attempt to combine the role of traditional foreign lending with offshore financial intermediation.

The rapidly changing and complex nature of the many roles performed by financial centers in contemporary international finance makes it necessary to construct a conceptual framework for analyzing these roles separately. Although a center may specialize in one or more kinds of financial activity, the world's financial centers as a group provide three broad types of international services; (1) traditional capital exports, (2) entrepôt financial services, and (3) offshore banking.

Traditional Capital Exports

Prior to the growth of the Euromarkets, the world's major financial centers were primarily net exporters of domestic capital. Despite the subsequent rise of nany new financial centers, the traditional centers, such as New York, have continued to be net creditors to foreign borrowers over prolonged periods of time This function has been performed through foreign lending by commercial banks, the underwriting and placement of marketable securities for foreign issuers, and the purchase of notes and obligations of nonresident entities by domestic investors in secondary markets.

The concept of a traditional financial center is not be to confused, however, with *countries* that are net capital exporters (such as the oil-producing countries today). A financial center exports capital by way of its *domestic* financial institutions and organized securities markets. In addition, the traditional financial center may or may not engage in domestic borrowing of foreign capital, but the important aspect is that capital exports exceed imports.

Entrepôt Financial Services

Financial centers that offer the services of their domestic financial institutions, money markets, and securities markets to both domestic and foreign residents are called entrepôt financial centers. Such a center may or may not be a net capital exporter. Its distinguishing feature is that it permits and often encourages foreign borrowers and lenders to participate in domestic financial markets. Foreign residents are usually attracted to entrepôt centers by the extensive and sophisticated financial markets and services they provided, which may not be available elsewhere.

Offshore Banking

Offshore banking can be viewed as a special category of entrepôt financial services although its function is much narrower. Offshore banking is financial intermediation performed (primarily) for nonresident borrowers and depositors. The principal attraction of an offshore banking center (for banks as well as participants) is simply the absence of intrusive and expensive official regulation, including taxation and controls over the portfolio decisions of the banking community. Although there can occasionally be some domestic resident participation in an offshore center, typically the domestic financial market—if it exists at all—is well insulated from offshore banking activities by an array of capital and exchange controls.

A specific international financial center may offer any combination of one or more of these three services. New York, for example, continues to play a very strong role as a traditional capital exporter, despite the interruption from 1965 through January 1974, when U.S. capital controls temporarily curtailed net capital outflows. New York serves also as the largest entrepôt center, because of its huge well-organized and regulated markets for money market instruments, long term debt, and equity securities, which are very attractive to both nonresident investors and borrowers.

New York's role as an offshore banking center, on the other hand, is virtually nil. Although there are no explicit official constraints on external intermediation in New York, a number of factors combine to prevent the development of offshore banking in the United States. First, it has long been a policy of the Federal Reserve Board to discourage U.S. banks from offering time deposits denominated in foreign currencies. This policy dates from the early 1960s, when such deposits were believed to disrupt the efforts of the United States to "defend" the value of the dollar. Second, Federal Reserve regulations on reserve requirements and interest ceilings also apply to foreign-currency deposits. Third, and perhaps most importantly, U.S. banks never felt the need to offer such services, since the potential demand for offshore banking in the United States is small and there exist convenient alternative locations in which to conduct external intermediation business.[15] For example, non-U.S. depositors interested in "laying off" excess DM- or Sfr-denominated funds prefer to do business outside the United States, because of the convenience of operating in the same time zone. The same is true for non-U.S. borrowers. Finally, the U.S. banks themselves conduct many of their Eurodollar operations out of Nassau (Bahamas) branches, although most of the operating personnel are located in New York and the primary books are kept in New York, Chicago, or wherever the bank is headquartered. It is convenient, therefore, for U.S. banks to execute external intermediation business on the books of Nassau branches, especially since tax requirements are more flexible there. In short, external intermediation in New York is difficult, and convenient alternative offshore arrangements are readily available. As a result, offshore banking has never been initiated in the United States.

Offshore Banking Centers Versus Entrepôt Financial Centers

It is easy to understand why so many offshore banking centers have grown up in recent years, when we consider that the major requirements for an offshore center are low taxes and minimal government controls. Thus a government can often legislate (or better, delegislate) its country into financial prominence, if it wishes to do so. This by no means guarantees the development of a diversified, entrepôt-type financial community, however. The requirements for a well-functioning offshore banking center are far less constraining than those for a diversified entrepôt financial center.

Four conditions are necessary for the development of an international entrepôt center:

1. Economic and political stability.
2. An efficient and experienced financial community.

[15] One can argue, however, that New York could successfully challenge the Canadian banks as well as the Caribbean centers in respect to (non-U.S.) Western Hemisphere business, if the fiscal and regulatory environment were sufficiently liberal.

3. Good communications and supportive services.
4. An official regulatory climate favorable to the financial industry, in the sense that it protects investors without unduly restricting financial institutions.

An examination of each of these requirements reveals why certain cities have emerged as offshore centers only, others have played a major and diversified role in international finance (London and New York), and yet others (such as Paris, Frankfurt, and Tokyo) have failed to become dominant in international finance despite strong national economies and considerable international trade and investment activity.

The first requirement, domestic economic and political stability, is important for obvious reasons. Particularly important is the confidence that the authorities will not restrict the movement of funds by nonresidents. This requirement is not quite as important to today's offshore banking centers as it is to the traditional and entrepôt centers because of the largely intermediary nature of Euromarket offshore banking centers. Only to the extent that economic and/or political instability might threaten the smooth transfer of international capital within a financial center does this requirement become binding. In practice, the actual transfer-of-funds transactions take place outside the offshore center, and thus political risk has a relatively minor impact on interest rates offered by most of the world's leading Euromarket centers. To the extent that capital transfers are effected within an entrepôt center, on the other hand, political and economic stability is essential. A very important requirement for entrepôt financial centers is that experienced personnel operate the center's financial institutions. To a large extent London's predominance as a financial center can be attributed to its highly skilled operating personnel (e.g., traders and brokers) and widely trusted banking leaders. Conversely, the development of several promising centers elsewhere has been restricted in recent years by a lack of adequate professional resources. Although skilled personnel are also important to financial centers with activities limited to offshore banking, the much-less-sophisticated functions performed in offshore centers naturally makes this requirement less important—with the possible exception of the need for competent tax and legal counsel.

Good communications are indispensable to an industry subject to minute-by-minute changes and highly dependent on interpersonal contact and trust. Exchange brokers, for example, are instrumental in bringing together lenders and borrowers and keeping the market informed regarding exchange rate movements. This requirement is also critical for centers engaged exclusively in offshore banking.

Perhaps most important of all is the regulatory climate within which the financial center must operate. Although it is helpful to have regulations to protect depositors and investors, controls must be sufficiently lenient to permit the unhampered transfer of capital among nonresidents and to limit the cost of these transactions by minimizing taxation and reserve requirements. Furthermore, government regulation must be relatively predictable, with changes in official controls occurring infrequently and with sufficient advance warning. Last, but not least, regulations need to be administered with adequate flexibility to adjust quickly to changing conditions. It is precisely this lack of flexibility, for example, that has kept Germany, France, and Japan from realizing their full potential of developing their capitals into leading international financial centers in general, and into offshore banking centers in particular. By imposing a series of restrictive controls, these countries have somewhat discouraged the international banking community from operating within their boundaries. Instead, the actions of these governments have stimulated the development of their close neighbors, such as London, Luxembourg, and Singapore, where authorities maintain a more flexible posture regarding exchange controls and monetary restrictions.

In terms of government regulation, the requirements for an offshore banking center can be more narrowly defined than in the case of entrepôt financial centers. The requirements for a Euromarket offshore banking center are (1) freedom from reserve requirements for deposits in foreign currencies; (2) no exchange controls on nonresident transactions; (3) favorable tax treatment, especially in regard to withholding and corporate income taxes; and (4) an adequately developed socioeconomic infrastructure, with well-developed international telecommunication facilities.

The domestic income derived from international finance has been an important incentive to many governments to reduce or eliminate controls over the financial community, particularly with respect to nonresident business. In recent years a number of little-known island states have attracted hundreds of financial institutions as well as private citizens in search of a permissive tax haven. Some of these offshore centers have come under attack for allowing individuals to circumvent tax laws in other countries, but legitimate offshore banking centers are likely to thrive well into the future. The following section reviews some of the most important offshore banking centers.

IMPORTANT OFFSHORE BANKING CENTERS

London London is clearly the dominant international banking center in the world. As of 1974, 331 foreign banks were represented there, including 97 of the world's 100 largest. Hosting 170 foreign banks, New York is second to London in international representation, followed by Hong Kong and Singapore, with 130 and 100 foreign banks, respectively. The assets of the foreign banking community in London amount to roughly 53 per cent of the total U.K. banking sector, while nearly one half of all foreign transactions of U.S. banks are funneled through London branches.

London's predominance as the major international finance center in the world can be explained by three important characteristics: (1) experience, (2) communications, and (3) sensible government controls and restrictions.

"As in all games, possession of the ball is at least three-quarters of the way to victory and, in this case, possession had been a reality for almost a century."[16] Indeed, London has been carrying the ball in world banking longer than anyone else. Long before the Euromarkets were a factor in international finance, London had established itself as an important center for world trade and banking. London's experienced bankers were among the first to perceive the enormous potential of external intermediation, and it was natural that the city should assume an early leadership role in this market.

From these years of experience, an outstanding communications and brokerage network evolved which is today the envy of the banking world. Communication of correct currency rates on a minute-by-minute basis is vital to any financial center, and London brokers are reputed to be the best in the world. Although foreign exchange transactions could take place without money brokers, brokers greatly facilitate transactions by bringing market participants into instantaneous contact with one another, thereby obtaining slightly better interest and exchange rates for their clients. Today virtually every important European center has at least one London broker, while cities such as New York and Toronto host the heaviest concentrations of British brokerage firms.

London's role as the leader in world finance was further enhanced by liberal establishment provisions set forth by the Bank of England, which made entry into the London international market relatively easy for foreign banks. The business activity of foreign banks in London is oriented primarily toward Euromarket business, although they are also active in trade and investment financing as well as providing a number of customer services. Thus foreign banks are primarily involved in wholesale banking, and they engage very little in U.K. domestic commercial banking activity. Data made available periodically by the Bank of England reveal that London is not only the biggest single Eurobanking center–roughly 50 per cent of all external deposits are on the books of London-based institutions–but it is also dominant internationally in interbank lending and is thus a focal point for other international banking centers. It is not surprising, therefore, that the London interbank rate is the key rate for all Eurocurrency transactions throughout the world.

In addition to offering entrepôt services, offshore intermediation in London is performed by bank branch offices located in either the Isle of Man or the Channel Islands.

In accordance with the Exchange Control Act of 1947, specific geographical locations (which together form the sterling area) enjoy a privileged relationship with the United Kingdom in terms of exchange controls. Although once extensive, today the sterling area is composed only of Ireland, Gibraltar, the Isle of Man, and the Channel Islands. These areas are free from all exchange controls, except that transactions between U.K. residents and the rest of the world are subject to strict regulation. By locating branch offices in these (literally) offshore centers, then, banks can obtain all the advantages of a London office while

[16] Stephen O'Brien, "The Money Markets," *The Banker*, February 1973, p. 195.

avoiding the relatively high U.K. tax requirements.

Although official regulation is not necessarily lenient in the United Kingdom, there are a variety of ways in which the Bank of England permits foreign bankers to escape rigid and expensive controls. Most importantly, the Bank of England is highly supportive of the financial community and endeavors to minimize intrusive regulations. This is accomplished to a great extent by flexible administrative guidance instead of formal legalistic rules and regulations. As a result, the banking industry in London has thrived, often at the expense of other more restrictive European financial centers.

Luxembourg and Continental European centers With a population of about 350,000 people and a land area of 999 square miles, Luxembourg ranks as one of the smallest countries in the world. Its economy is undiversified, based primarily on iron and steel exports. Luxembourg has no official central bank; it does not even have a domestic capital market of any significance. Yet it is one of the major international banking centers in the world today. Hosting over 80 banks with total assets of around $25 billion, it ranks second in financial size only to London, and it even leads London in externally intermediated DM credits. It is also headquarters for both the European Investment Bank and the European Monetary Fund.

Although Luxembourg emerged as an important offshore financial center only in the mid-1960s, the foundations for Luxembourg's financial boom were laid in 1929 when the government passed legislation that exempted holding companies from all but very minimal taxation. Strict bank secrecy laws were later approved, making Luxembourg an ideal candidate for becoming a Euromarket center. The number of Luxembourg-based banks grew from 19 in 1964 to approximately 85 at the end of 1974.

Although Luxembourg's financial industry has expanded steadily during the early days of Euromarket activity, the real financial boom did not occur until after 1970. Prior to that time London had been the dominant Euromarket center, causing Luxembourg to be something of an "also-ran" in the world banking race. As banking activity flourished in the heart of London, however, property values there skyrocketed and the cost of doing business in London rose sharply. Meanwhile the cost of buying commercial space in Luxembourg was equivalent to the price of a year's rent in London. Reacting to the high cost of accommodation in London, then, many new bank offices were set up in Luxembourg. In addition, salaries for multilingual bank personnel were at times lower in Luxembourg than in London.

Another factor that stimulated the growth of Luxembourg's financial industry was the strictness of monetary regulations established in neighboring Germany and Belgium. With no minimum reserve requirements on Eurocurrency deposits and no interest withholding tax in Luxembourg, and with few restrictions on the flow of currency across Luxembourg's borders, deposits denominated in German marks and Belgian francs flowed rapidly into Luxembourg banks. By 1974, approximately 25 German banks had established branch offices in Luxembourg.

Luxembourg has long been an important center for the Eurobond market. Since 1965 dollar-denominated Eurobonds have been active on the Luxembourg stock exchange. Today, more Eurobonds are quoted on the Luxembourg stock exchange than on any other in the world.

The other important Eurocurrency centers in continental Europe are Paris, Zurich, Geneva, and Amsterdam. None of these cities, however, can compete with Luxembourg in terms of pure offshore banking business, and nowhere in continental Europe does external financial intermediation play as important a role. Frankfurt, like New York, does not participate in external financial intermediation, because of reserve requirements. In all these cities, however, traditional foreign lending and entrepôt-type securities transactions are quite important.

Singapore and Hong Kong In 1968 the Monetary Authority of Singapore decided to expand Singapore's foreign money market, a decision that marked the beginning of the Asian currency market. The purpose of this market was—and largely continues to be—to channel (non-Singapore) dollars to southeastern Pacific countries badly in need of both foreign investment funds and facilities for deposits. As the market developed, funds denominated in U.S. dollars transferred from the Euromarket (which is identical to the Asian currency market except for geographic location) began to dominate; in 1975 a full 95 per cent of the deposit transactions in the market were denominated in dollars.

Singapore was a logical spot for the birth of the Asian currency market. To begin with, the government of Singapore ensured the political stability of the island over the short run. Although the government's use of repressive measures was subject to criticism, few could deny the economic security it brought to the business community.

Furthermore, the government was intent upon setting up high technology and service industries within the republic, since Singapore has practically no economic resources but has a population of 2.2 million people. Banking naturally fit the government's development plan, and thus an open-door policy was developed with regard to the world's major banking institutions. The Monetary Authority extended a number of important incentives to foreign banks. Among these were:

1. Reduced tax rate on interest earned from offshore loans.
2. Exemption for nonresidents from the 40 per cent withholding tax on interest earned on Asia dollar deposits.
3. Abolition of stamp duties on CDs and bills of exchange.
4. Abolition of the 20 per cent liquidity-ratio requirement for Asian Currency Units (i.e., all financial institutions licensed to deal in foreign exchange).

In terms of time differentials, Singapore is well situated to deal with other

Pacific financial centers and it enjoys a time overlap with London. It also has excellent communications systems which were built up during the years of Singapore's dominance as an Asian entrepôt shipping center.

The dramatic growth of Singapore's money markets in recent years has been the cornerstone of the city-state's success in becoming a major financial center. There are two money markets in Singapore—the domestic and the international. Domestic residents are generally prohibited from participating in the international (offshore) market, and the offshore financial institutions are similarly restricted in their dealings with the domestic market.

By contrast, Hong Kong has traditionally maintained a free-market economy, with few official controls or restrictions. Among other attributes, it was this freedom from government regulation that first attracted the financial community to this tiny neighbor of China during the early 1970s. Hong Kong had no central bank to oversee the financial community, and there was minimal government interference in business generally. Thus a thriving financial center was developed there which rivaled Singapore's dominance in the Pacific. Whether Singapore or Hong Kong is the "leading" financial center in southeastern Asia has become a moot question.

Since the beginning of 1973 there have been no exchange controls in Hong Kong. Therefore, residents and nonresidents alike are able to acquire foreign currencies (most Asian currencies cost less in Hong Kong than in other countries), purchase domestic and foreign securities, transfer and invest capital overseas, maintain bank balances abroad, and deal in the gold market. Add to these advantages a strong local economy, competent business and financial leadership, and excellent communications systems, and you have the formula for Hong Kong's successful development as an entrepôt financial center.

It is only because of a 15 per cent withholding tax on interest paid on deposits in Hong Kong that more business is not wrested from Singapore's banks. Although Hong Kong banks have found some ways around this obstacle by booking loans abroad, this tax continues to be the single most important obstacle to Hong Kong's dominance within southeastern Asia's financial community.

Although many observers still view with concern the political risk of doing business in southeastern Asia's financial centers, the economic potential demonstrated by that part of the world has somewhat assuaged the fears of political turmoil. Existing financial centers have expanded and new ones have arisen to compete for the rewards of international banking, with Manila being the most recent entrant.

By January 1, 1976, the Asian currency market had grown to over $12.8 billion, up from a little over $7 billion in early 1974. Until 1971, the Asian market was a net lender of dollars to the Euromarket; since that time it has become a net borrower, a fact that is indicative of the increased demand for investment funds throughout the area.

Caribbean financial centers The lion's share of the financial activity that takes place in the Caribbean area is offshore banking. As a largely underdeveloped part of the world, the Caribbean's financial centers cannot be viewed in any sense as "natural" or traditional financial communities; rather, they have come about as the result of the active support and encouragement of their respective governments. Those places that are today well known for offshore banking (e.g., Nassau-Bahamas, the Cayman Islands, and Panama) have developed as financial centers with the support of lenient tax laws and banking regulations, not through a process of natural growth. While all of the Caribbean financial centers possess reasonable communications and transportation networks and relatively stable political environments (not to mention the famous Caribbean climate and exotic tourist attractions), the major incentive for financial institutions to operate in the Caribbean is the extremely liberal regulatory environment offered by the major Caribbean financial centers. Whereas many Latin American countries tend to impose government controls over the financial community in order to focus on domestic development needs, areas such as the Bahamas, the Cayman Islands, and Panama have liberated foreign investors and bankers from nearly all taxation and restrictive regulation.

As a result of its proximity to the United States and its well-established tourist industry, Nassau was the first Caribbean city to become a prominent financial center. With no exchange controls or taxation on foreign income, offshore banking developed rapidly in Nassau during the early years of the Euromarket. At times there has been concern about the political risk of the Bahamas, particularly when the government changed hands in 1973 and the new rulers began to demonstrate a more nationalistic and social development orientation. There have also been continuing problems in obtaining working permits for expatriate personnel. To the extent that banks are bothered by these developments—and many are not because their Nassau operations are actually run from their U.S. headquarters—foreign bankers have reacted by searching elsewhere for Caribbean branch locations, a move that contributes to the rise of the offshore banking industry elsewhere in the area.

The most obvious beneficiary of the work-permit dispute in the Bahamas has been the Cayman Islands—a small British colony with only 10,000 inhabitants and a capital city with more banks in it than anything else. Investors are attracted to the Cayman Islands by favorable tax legislation as well as by the assumed assurance of political stability—a stability that many observers felt the Bahamas might lose in the aftermath of its 1973 independence. Even after these fears about the Bahamas were diminished, however, the Caymans continued to grow as an offshore financial center. In the past few years the Caymans have received about 1,000 applications per year for new company licenses, and an average of about six banks each year have been applying for permission to join the Cayman banking community.

Panama, on the other hand, possesses a number of advantages over both Nassau and the Caymans. First and foremost, the dollar is legal tender in Panama. This, coupled with the absence of exchange controls, means that funds in Panama are free from devaluation vis-à-vis the dollar and can be moved about quickly and easily. Furthermore, the population of Panama is of diversified ethnic origin and, at least in urban areas, the people are often bilingual in Spanish and English, a significant plus for international banks serving Latin America.

Most significant of all, however, is the Panamanian dedication to becoming a financial center. The Panamanian National Banking Commission, established in July 1970, is specifically charged with both monitoring the banking system and developing Panama as an international financial center. In keeping with this responsibility the Commission has extended a number of attractive incentives to financial institutions and businesses that are considering locating an office in Panama. Fear of political upheaval over the Canal issue, however, is the one major stumbling block presently holding back Panama's continuing development as a financial center.

Although Nassau, the Caymans, and Panama are the best-known offshore banking centers in the Caribbean areas, several other Caribbean ports also have developed ambitions to play a role in international banking. Among these are the British Virgin Islands, Grenada, Curacao, and Caracas. Caracas, the capital of Venezuela, is unique in the Caribbean in that it is the center of a growing petroleum-based economy with strong domestic supply and demand for investment funds. Thus it is capable of developing beyond the stage of a purely offshore banking center. Caracas is likely to be a net exporter of capital for some time. On the other hand, the central bank of Venezuela maintains fairly stringent regulations over foreign banks and has demonstrated no inclination to loosen its grip on the international banking community. Since liberal regulation of foreign banks is a *sine qua non* for development as an offshore financial center, Caracas is unlikely to threaten the external financial intermediation business of the more established Caribbean centers in the near future. In the long run, however, as the stock exchange, capital and money markets, and the national economy as a whole develop and diversify, Caracas has the potential to become an important international entrepôt financial center.

References

Adams, Robin, "Panama and the Canal," *The Banker*, May 1974, pp. 477–520.

Arthur Anderson and Co., *Guide for Foreign Nationals to Taxation and Other Regulations in the United Kingdom*, 3rd ed., August 1975.

Baehring, Bernd, "Luxembourg–An Ally of the City," *The Banker*, June 1973, pp. 580–84.

Bell, David, "Caribbean Centres." *Financial Times*, March 3, 1975, p. 22.

Campbell, Mary, "Luxembourg–City State of Finance," *The Banker*, February 1975, pp. 189–95.

"Caracas–A Survey," *The Banker*, May 1976, pp. 485–500.

"The City of London Annual Review," *The Banker*, February 1976, pp. 155–96.

Coussement, A. M., "Luxembourg–Tighter Banking Controls," *Euromoney*, January 1975, pp. 64–65.

"Differing Strategies for Europe," *The Banker*, August 1975, pp. 951–61.

Einzig, Paul, *Foreign Dollar Loans in Europe*, New York: St. Martin's Press, 1965.

European Financial Almanac, 1974–75, New York: R. R. Bowker, 1975.

"Foreign Banks in London–Annual Review," *The Banker*, November 1975, pp. 1305–27.

"Hong Kong–A Survey," *The Banker*, July 1974, pp. 775–811.

Kindleberger, Charles P., "The Formation of Financial Centers: A Study in Comparative Economic History," *Princeton Studies in International Finance, No. 36*, Princeton, N.J.: Princeton University Press, 1974.

"Luxembourg Capital Market," *Financial Times*, October 31, 1974, pp. 15–18.

"Luxembourg's Role," *Financial Times*, March 3, 1975, p. 21.

Nathaniels, Liz, "Banking in Bahamas Continues on Upswing," *Journal of Commerce*, November 17, 1975, p. 51.

O'Brien, Stephen, "The Money Markets," *The Banker*, February 1973, p. 195.

"Offshore Investment Centers–Annual Review," *The Banker*, May 1974, pp. 477–520.

Pakshong, M. W., "Singapore–The Asian Dollar Market Now," *Euromoney*, June 1975, pp. 100–02.

Price Waterhouse, & Company, *Singapore as an International Financial Centre*, Singapore, 1976.

Sandberg, M. G. R. "Hong Kong–Rates Drop as Funds Flow in," *Euromoney*, May 1975, pp. 71–73.

Sandberg, M. G. R., "Hong Kong–Signs of Recovery," *Euromoney*, August 1975, p. 86.

Sarmet, Marcel, "Roles des diverses places financières dans les Euro-marchés," *Banque*, January 1976, pp. 17–24.

"Singapore–A Survey," *The Banker*, September 1974, pp. 1073–95.

"South East Asia: The Dragon Awakes," *Supplement to Euromoney*, May 1976

Wilson, Dick, "South East Asia's Banking Boom," *The Banker*, March 1975, pp. 253–57.

[4]

Excerpt from Charles P. Kindleberger and David B. Audretsch (eds), *The Multinational Corporation in the 1980s*, 219–44

10 Appraising Corporate Investment Policy: A Financial Center Theory of Foreign Direct Investment

Howard Curtis Reed

I. Introduction

The theory of foreign direct investment during the past twenty years has grown in its coverage and in its ability to explain why firms invest in markets alien to their decision-making centers. These theories have examined the determinants of foreign direct investment and corporate behavior by providing insight into how corporations appraise investment alternatives. Earlier studies of foreign investment activity (Behrman, 1960, Kindleberger, 1965, and others) identified interest rate differentials or capital (movement and formation) considerations as the principal determinants. In these studies, the impact of capital on foreign investment decisions centered around whether international investment took place as a result of the movement of capital from one country to another, usually from the firm's home country to the country where the investment was taking place; or as a result of capital being generated at the site where the investment was being made.

Stephen Hymer's pioneering work in 1960 used the theory of industrial organization to explain international investment behavior.[1] Hymer argued that direct investment is determined primarily by corporate organizational structure and behavior, and not by capital movement or capital formation. His central point was that if a firm is to operate in an unfamiliar political and legal jurisdiction at a long distance from its decision-making center, it will demand to be compensated with a clear operating advantage over other firms competing for a share of that market. He further argued that if capital were the principal determinant, it would move through the world's principal financial markets instead of through firms that specialize in—and seek control of—the sourcing, producing, and marketing functions.

Kindleberger in 1969 observed that multinational corporations are engaged in a wide variety of activities (i.e., managing and allocating resources, developing new products and processes, etc.), all of which are intended to enhance the firms' *growth* prospects. And in growing, these firms may invest their resources in familiar surroundings or they may choose to venture out by investing in foreign places. The investments may be the result of differences in existing levels of profits and profitability or they may be due to the plowing back into the firm of excessively large amounts of its earnings in hopes of an even larger return. The growth of the firm, it was further argued, has two dimensions. One dimension emphasizes the markets for the firm's products, and the other dimension emphasizes the firm's capacity and ability to finance a substantial percentage of its growth from profits. Businessmen, it was noted, rejected the argument that direct investment was due primarily to internally generated sources of finance. It was their contention that such investments were the results of expected levels of sales, because the firm's profit level will justify the necessary investment. Kindleberger, to a large extent, also agrees that direct investment is more closely linked to the market dimension than to the internal financing dimension. The theory offered is that "direct investment is tied to markets. If markets grow, the firm must grow. If the firm stops growing, it dies. Anything that interferes with growth of the firm, such as balance-of-payments restrictions, while the organic life of the market goes its way will kill the firm."[2]

In 1970, a paper written by Robert Aliber was published, and for the first time foreign exchange risk and currency valuation were seen as being significant determinants of foreign direct investment.[3] Aliber believed that foreign direct investment could be best explained by understanding the interrelationships between, and the behavior of, capital and foreign exchange markets. He argued that foreign direct investment is influenced significantly by the fact that the source-country firm capitalizes the same income stream of expected earnings as does the host-country firm, but at a higher rate. The difference in the capitalization comes about because the capital markets establish different capitalization rates, on debt and equity, for income streams denominated in different currencies. In his view, the difference in capitalization rates are explained by two factors. First, the market will demand a premium for accepting the exchange risk. Thus, the difference in interest rates on fixed-price securities can be expected to exceed the anticipated change in the exchange rate. Second, the market does not attach a currency premium to the foreign income of the source-country firm because the market for equities is biased against the host-country firm. The source-country firm may therefore issue securities in its market and use the proceeds to acquire the host-country firm. This argument leads Aliber to conclude that direct investment flows can, generally, be expected to flow from strong-currency areas to weak-currency areas.

In studying the movement of portfolio and direct investment capital between the United States and Western Europe during the 1960s, Ragazzi (1973) discovered that the large flow of US direct investment in Western Europe was matched by sizable purchases of US long-term portfolio assets by private European residents. He attributed the large outflow of portfolio capital to two characteristics of the European securities markets (the United Kingdom excepted). First, the European portfolio investor does not receive continually updated information. Public auditing of corporations is not as well developed in Europe as it is in the United States. This lack of information theoretically increases the risk of possible deviation from the expected rate of return for the portfolio investor. On the other hand, because the direct investor is in control of the company and therefore has immediate and direct access to all information, his risk is limited to the "industrial" risk inherent in the operations of the company. A second factor is the narrowness of the European securities market, again with the exception of the United Kingdom. This contracted state makes the fluctuations in prices of securities much larger than justified. Ragazzi concluded:

> Even if the determinants of portfolio and direct investments are different, flows of the two forms of capital are likely to be partly substitutes. Thus, an outflow of portfolio capital, for instance, will discourage direct investment abroad and might encourage an inflow of foreign direct investments. This could happen to the extent that: (a) it reduces the supply of risk capital to local firms and increases that supply to foreign firms; (b) it pushes up the market value of securities of foreign firms, increasing the cost of take-overs of foreign firms by domestic firms; and (c) it pushes up the exchange rate of the foreign country, increasing the cost of direct investment in that country.[4]

Magee (1977) combined the neoclassical theories of creation and appropriability with the theory of industrial organizations to explain why firms engage in foreign direct investments. Magee argued that industries with a high derived demand for information (technology) must continually make investments that produce five specific types of information: (1) creation; (2) development; (3) production functions;

(4) markets; and (5) appropriability. He hypothesized that multinational corporations are specialists in the production of these five specific types of information because duplication by other market participants is difficult, and as a result this information is transmitted more efficiently through the firm's internal channels as opposed to the market's mechanisms. In addition, the multinational corporation produces such information because the level of appropriability increases as the information's level of sophistication increases. This combination of actions prescribes what the firm's optimum size should be throughout its technology life cycle. As the firm's international activities grow, and it enters the mature stage of the cycle, its optimal size begins to decline in conjunction with a like decline in the generation of new information.

The foreign direct investment theories cited here are representative, to a large extent, of the evolution of ideas and the thinking that has taken place during the 1970s. All of these theories, as well as the theories that they evolved from, provide valuable insight into how and why foreign investment takes place. The focus, however, is directed primarily toward the theory of industrial organizations and microeconomics. When the macroenvironment of foreign direct investment is discussed, the focus is either on (1) arbitrage activities available in the foreign exchange and credit markets (Aliber, 1970), or (2) some form of risk reduction through diversification. The portfolio approach to foreign direct investment hypothesizes that a multinational corporation can experience a significant reduction of risk by pursuing a growth strategy of international geographic diversification. This strategy allows the multinational corporation to offset lower rates of return in some countries by simultaneously reducing the firm's risk and enlarging its markets. As a result, the firm will be attractive to investors, which will increase the supply of funds available and in turn reduce its capital costs.

Missing from these discussions and explanations is the role of the *financial center* in determining the location, magnitude, and type (direct or portfolio) of investment activity. Financial centers, in general, are important to international investment activity. Financial centers that impact on foreign investment activity can be classified and grouped into three broad categories:[5] (1) *Host International Financial Centers* enhance their financial infrastructures and capabilities by attracting relatively large numbers of foreign financial institutions from a large number of countries. (2) *International Financial Centers* are host to a large number of foreign financial institutions; headquarters for a small number of internationally active banks that tend to follow the lead of the larger international financial institutions; and they possess a limited capacity to influence events that pertain to global asset and liability management. (3) *Supranational Financial Centers* are headquarters for a large number of large internationally active banks that are well connected (directly) to other centers throughout the world; managers of large amounts of foreign financial assets and liabilities; net supplier of foreign direct investment capital to the rest of the world; located close to a large number of large (measured by assets) industrial corporations; active users of global communication facilities (airplanes, telephone, telex, etc.); and management meccas, that attract and generate ideas and information in ways that eventually establish the organizational and operating norms that govern internationally active organizations (private and governmental).

The argument put forth in this paper is that the underlying determinants of foreign direct investment activity are best explained (and understood) by determining the motives and methods of evaluation employed by the supranational financial centers as they appraise, on a continuing basis, the activity of internationally active institutions. It is presumed that institutions actively engaged in foreign investment are firms whose equity is traded on at least one major stock exchange, and whose capital structure consists of publicly held debt securities that are also traded in secondary markets. Information about the operations, policies, and strategies of these firms, their competitors, their markets, and their sources of supply are continually scrutinized and factored into the centers' evaluation of the securities of these institutions. The functional relationship between the internationally active firm and the supranational financial center is essentially one of operating efficiency and not the commonly held view of revenue maximization and cost minimization. In this context the internationally active firm seeks to maximize its operating efficiency. The operating efficiency maximum, as used here, purports that the internationally active firm continually seeks to enhance its competitive position in its product markets by maximizing its price-earnings multiple on equity, and the price paid for its publicly traded debt securities. The firm wants to maximize operating efficiency by improving its competitive status (in its product market and in the capital markets) relative to other firms in the industry(ies) in which it operates. Also, the firm desires to continually improve its competitive status relative to all other institutions and organizations that are subject to supranational financial center evaluation (i.e., all entities that utilize the center's resources or products). It is further argued that the internationally active firm's operating efficiency is evaluated by the center on the basis of the center's perception of the firm's policies and modes of operations. Corporate policies and modus operandi are represented by the firm's product portfolio, location portfolio, capital structure, and organizational structure, as well as the market structure of the industry(ies) in which it operates.

II. Financial Centers

Traditional Measures

In a recent study that classified and ranked the world's international financial centers, nine traditional variables were used to measure the relative status of these centers over time.[6] In 1980, the organizational structure of the centers was determined by the number of large internationally active commercial banks headquartered in the center, the total amount of foreign financial liabilities residing in the center, and the total amount of foreign financial assets held in the center.[7] In other time periods, direct links were important determinants of organizational structure. The linkage variable usually replaced the headquarter bank variable. There were three groups of supranational centers in 1980: Group 1 consisted only of London; Group 2 combined New York and Tokyo; and Group 3 contained eight centers—Paris, Frankfurt, Zurich, Amsterdam, San Francisco, Chicago, Hamburg, and Hong Kong.

The study concluded that not only are financial centers organized in a hierarchical structure for finance, but that they are also organized hierarchically for communications and management. As a result, the "supranational" centers are preeminent in finance, communications, and management. A finance center facilitates the flow of goods, services, and capital within its own national economy and between its national economy and the other national economies of the world. Communication centers are places where interaction occurs, ideas are exchanged, and information is gathered, analyzed, and disseminated. Management centers are locations that require and subsequently attract skilled persons to organize the sourcing, reformulation, and marketing of resources in a clearly defined manner; a manner that lends itself to standardization and eventually the adoption of these practices on a wide scale. The supranational centers, it is argued, provide the environment, the mechanism, and the competence for evaluating on a continual basis the policies and activities of the institutional components of the global political economy. These centers are important for financial sourcing and allocations; evaluating the policies, strategies, and activities of nations;[8] industrial project evaluation and pricing; monitoring the activities of the institutional components of the political economy; and providing money and capital management services. Without question, the level of efficiency with which a center can perform these functions is dependent on its astuteness in gathering, evaluating, and utilizing information from around the world. Additionally, a center's astuteness is largely dependent upon the number (and size) of its locally headquartered banks, the acumen (management) of these institutions, the collective connections (to other centers) of these institutions, and the industrial power (and reach) of the nation's corporations.

Contemporary Measures

The earlier study of financial centers using traditional variable measures was quite valuable. It provided considerable insight into what is required to build financial center infrastructure over time (institutions, connections, markets, etc.), and into the organization, distribution, and influence of these centers. On the other hand, a study using only traditional measures leaves unexplored a whole range of factors that have emerged in the past ten to fifteen years that may have a significant influence on the building of financial center infrastructure, organization, and influence. Building on the information and conclusions generated in the earlier study, and in hopes of providing additional information that could be used in developing the arguments for this paper, a sixteen variable (as opposed to nine) analysis for 1980 was performed. Thirty-six financial centers were included in the analysis. The variable measures are:

1. Capital/deposit ratio of the large internationally active banks headquartered in the center.
2. Capital/asset ratio of the large internationally active banks headquartered in the center.

3. Pre-tax earnings/capital ratio of the large internationally active banks headquartered in the center.
4. Pre-tax earnings/assets ratio of the large internationally active banks headquartered in the center.
5. Revenue/asset ratio of the large internationally active banks headquartered in the center.
6. Total international currency clearings (daily average) of the center.
7. Size (liabilities) of center's Eurocurrency market.
8. Total amount of international bonds issued in the center during the year.
9. Foreign financial assets held in the center.
10. Foreign financial liabilities residing in the center.
11. The daily average of the center's stock exchange activity (sales value).
12. The number of large internationally active commercial banks headquartered in the center.
13. The number of large internationally active foreign banks with offices (agencies, branches, or subsidiaries) in the center.
14. The number of foreign financial centers with direct links, provided by the foreign internationally active banks, to the local center.
15. The center's airline passenger traffic (yearly total).
16. The center's airmail/airfreight volume (yearly total).

The thirty-six centers were divided into five distinct groups,[9] at four hierarchical levels (figure 1). The Five-group organizational structure is determined primarily by the amount of international currency clearings, the size of the Eurocurrency market, foreign financial assets, and headquarters for the large internationally active commercial banks.

If these contemporary measures are viewed as an extension of the traditional analyses, then the supranational centers can be characterized as centers whose principal operating currency(ies) is widely used for international trade and capital transactions; and whose financial infrastructures (primarily the large commercial banks) are developed to the extent that they are entrusted with the management of the world's foreign financial liabilities and assets. The large internationally active commercial banks have the primary responsibility for facilitating international clearings (daily) which in 1980, amounted to a US dollar equivalent of $236 billion. US dollars accounted for $178 billion of

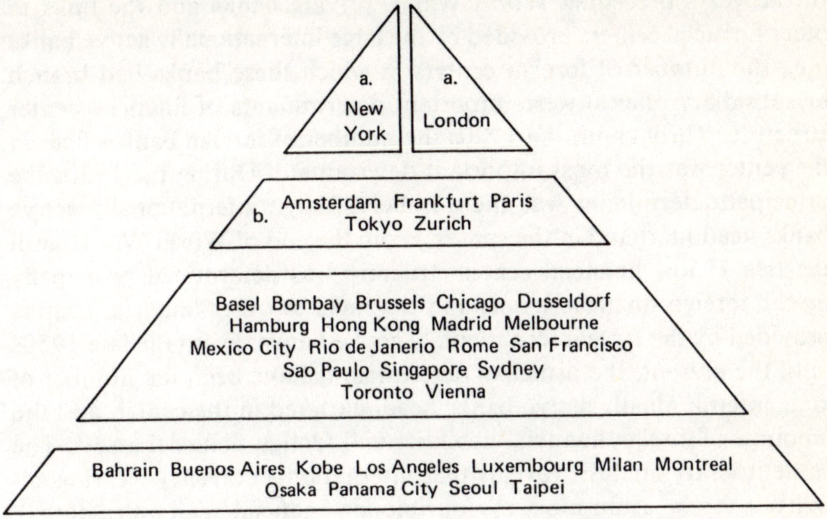

Figure 1
The hierarchy of financial centers. a, Supranational centers of the first order. New York and London differ in two variable measures: (1) total amount of international clearings (New York's dominant measure), and (2) size of the Eurocurrency market (London's dominant measure). b, Supranational centers of the second order. The magnitudes of their variable measures are less than those of the first-order centers, but their infrastructures are well-developed and well-balanced.

the total, and New York was clearing approximately 90 percent of these dollar transactions. In addition to the currency transactions, the clearing infrastructure is also used for coupon, dividend, and interest payments on securities; and it is used to facilitate the transfers and registration of securities.

It is widely believed that the large internationally active commercial banks have grown in size, reach, and scope as a result of the demands of their corporate customers. The argument is usually supported by citing examples that purportedly show that corporations establish foreign operations first, and in an effort to maintain their close ties to these corporations the banks follow this lead by establishing their own foreign offices. If this argument is accepted, then another important question must be answered: What factors explain the existence of a large number of internationally active banks (with substantial foreign office networks) during the first half of this century, when direct investment was minimal?

In the years preceding World War I, private banks and the links to other financial centers provided by the large internationally active banks (i.e., the number of foreign centers in which these banks had branch or subsidiary offices) were important determinants of financial center structure. Throughout the 1920s the number of foreign bank offices in the center was the most important determinant. During the 1930s the principal determinant was the number of large internationally active banks headquartered in the center. From the end of World War II until the late 1950s, financial center structure was determined principally by the foreign financial assets and the links to other financial centers provided by the large internationally active banks. From the late 1950s until the present, the principal determinants have been the number of large internationally active banks headquartered in the center, and the amounts of foreign financial liabilities and foreign financial assets. The contemporary analysis reveals that international currency clearing activity is the measure most responsible for financial center structure.

III. Determinants of Financial Center Structure

International Clearing Activity

It seems quite reasonable to argue that international currency clearings have throughout this century been an important determinant of financial center structure (even though comparable data for all of this period is not available). New York clears approximately $160 billion daily. Of the major centers London is next, clearing (in dollar equivalents) approximately $17 billion daily. Frankfurt and Paris follow with $12 billion each. Tokyo, Zurich, and Amsterdam clear approximately $7, $4, and $2 billion, respectively. The significance of clearing activity to the status of a financial center becomes clearer when the ancillary activities of currency clearing are examined.

In the United States, the 12 settling banks of the Clearing House Interbank Payments System (CHIPS) account for more than 70% of the annual increase in correspondent bank balances.[10] The increase in bank correspondent balances is directly attributable to increasing activity in foreign trade, foreign exchange, and capital flow activity (primarily short-term flows which include all Eurocurrency flows). The extent to which a center's principal operating currency is used in these international transactions determines the importance of that center as an international clearing center. In addition to the 12 settling banks of CHIPS, there are 87 associate member banks (an increase of 22 since January 1978).[11] These associate members, prior to 1980, were required to maintain a correspondent relationship with the 12 settling banks in order to have access to the CHIPS transaction processing mechanism.[12] Foreign bankers that have recently opened offices in New York (since 1978) readily admit that having access to CHIPS was an important consideration in deciding whether to open offices.[13] Virtually all of the Edge Act subsidiaries operating in New York are there because of the access to CHIPS.[14]

In the case of New York, there is strong evidence to indicate that international clearing activity increases the size and leveraging capacity of the banks headquartered in the clearing center by increasing the correspondent balances (deposits) of the local institutions. The level of international currency clearing in a center reflects, to a large extent, the overall importance of that center's indigenous currency in international financial transactions. Therefore it can be expected that the clearing center's large clearing banks would have foreign offices in other centers for the purpose of financial sourcing in their home currency, and for the purpose of facilitating international transactions that use their home currency. Furthermore, access to the clearing mechanism of a center is an important consideration for institutions headquartered in other centers, when deciding whether to open an office in another center, and what type of office to open in that center (e.g., a representative office or a full service banking office).[15]

Global Portfolio Management

In order for a center to be an active and influential participant in managing the world's portfolio of financial liabilities and assets, the center must be successful in attracting relatively large amounts of foreign financial liabilities. These resources can then be employed as the center sees fit, domestically or internationally. As the size, scope, and reach of the center's asset portfolio is increased, the need to enlarge its direct links to other centers is also increased. It is a natural evolution for foreign lending by the locally headquartered banks to be followed by an expansion of their overseas office network to supervise and better manage their foreign asset portfolios. The financial sourcing and allocation function demands that the center have a sufficient and well-managed infrastructure to provide liquidity and a competitive return on investments. Since there are never enough liquid reserves to cover all liabilities at any given time, the quality (risk vs. return, and maturity schedule) of a center's asset portfolio is paramount to the investor, governments of the investors, and the host nation government. Evaluating the policies, strategies, and activities of nations is necessary for several reasons. Nations (including their firms and citizens) are active users of the products and services of centers, and, as a result of the highly interdependent nature of the industrial country's markets, a shift in policy, strategy, or predicted activity could substantially alter the portfolio quality of the center, and in turn, of its investors. Accurate evaluation is also essential to evaluating and pricing industrial projects that are targeted for investment in foreign countries or projects that are dependent upon cash flow emanating from that country. Industrial project evaluation is also important for the initial pricing of the borrowed capital. Monitoring the progress of the projects is necessary so that the current value of the outstanding principal can be assessed. The quality of the money and capital management services offered by the center is largely a function of how well these other functions are managed.[16]

Communication (the Hidden Measure)

All sectors of the global political economy are heavily dependent on the medium of communication for successful performance and attainment of their operating objectives. And finance is perhaps the most dependent sector. The communication function is two-dimensional. In order to provide for a useful and continual exchange of ideas, fast and efficient communications, on a personal (face-to-face) as well as a non-personal (telephone, telex, etc.) basis, must be made available to the center.

Jet travel has made it possible to move important people and documents from one location to another, anywhere in the world, within 24 hours. This quick and relatively inexpensive means of moving highly skilled people is perhaps the single most important factor in diminishing the need for financial centers to be expert in a number of ancillary activities (i.e., accounting, advertising, law, printing, etc.). The supranational centers can export much of the needed ancillary services to other centers at substantially lower costs than would be incurred if each center had to generate these skills internally.

The nonpersonal form of communication may involve air mail or telephone, telex, or sea mail. Important documents such as letters of credit, trade bills, term loan agreements, and checks can now be moved overnight by air courier. This has improved the operating efficiency of centers and their clients in those matters that require the movement of a physical document. Telephone, telex, and other types of transmission make it possible to send and receive instructions almost instantaneously. The risk of error or misunderstanding is increased, perhaps significantly, when these nonpersonal means of communication are used. Face-to-face contact is, of course, the preferred method of communication but it is not always possible or practical. And I am told by bankers and corporate executives that the error rate of nonpersonal transmission is surprisingly low.

The importance of communications in the infrastructure of the financial center is clearly recognized, but it is difficult to measure because data on nonpersonal communications is difficult and costly to compile, and as a result most institutions make no attempt to get this data. Country data is available, but not city or center data. The absence of hard data on nonpersonal communication does not preclude the researcher from clearly seeing the connections and the relationships. The importance of direct links between centers (provided by the local and foreign banks) and the international telex activity clearly indicates that the information infrastructure is a significant determinant of financial center structure.[17] The basis for this contention is twofold. First, the greater the number of direct links, the greater the quality of unfiltered information available to the center.[18] Furthermore, unfiltered information presumably is transmitted at a greater speed and at higher levels of accuracy and quality than is filtered information. Therefore, direct links can be viewed as indicators (if not measures) of the speed with which information is transmitted between centers and the accuracy and quality of that information. Second, the volume of international telex activity is an indicator of a center's international influence as a financial and information center. Bankers, businessmen, and, to a lesser extent, international trade specialists use international telex facilities to the exclusion of nearly all other communications systems.[19]

Supranational Banks or Supranational Centers

The critical role played by the large internationally active commercial banks in the development, growth, and management of financial centers is clearly evident. The preeminent role of these banks naturally leads to an interesting question. Is it the banks or is it the centers that are the "real" preeminent actors in international finance? Or, to put it another way: Do the centers' infrastructures produce synergism? This question is perhaps best answered by examining the comprehensive character of the financial center.

Financial center eminence affects and is affected by the various commercial, monetary, industrial, and political systems of the world.[20] The centers' role in synthesizing these four systems lies in their ability to effectively gather, analyze, and disseminate information. The commercial, monetary, and industrial sectors rely on the centers' global network of offices, correspondents, customers, and suppliers for much of their information, much as political units (nation-states) rely on their diplomatic corps and intelligence agencies. The information network for commercial activities is located primarily in the major port cities of the world. Networks for industrial activities are widely dispersed, depending on the economies of location of the particular industry (should the location be nearer the supply source, the market, or somewhere in between?). Nation-states, naturally, have their information networks centered primarily in the various administrative capitals. The information network for the monetary infrastructure is located in the international financial centers.

The information generated independently by these four sectors is supplemented, in varying degrees, by the public media (the press, radio, television, and wire services). The major news (and wire) services have their international networks centered in the financial center of the nation when it is different from the administrative capital (New York instead of Washington, DC, Frankfurt instead of Bonn, and Zurich instead of Bern). The organizational structure of each individual organization (an export broker, a corporation, a bank, a nation-state, a wire service) is probably very efficient in managing information for internal purposes. With the exception of the public media, the internally generated information is usually not for horizontal distribution. As a result, there is no formal coordination and distribution of this information. The public media make a gallant attempt to perform this service. But because most of the important information must be discovered and/or uncovered, and because it requires considerable technical expertise to analyze, synthesize, and properly report, the attempt frequently falls considerably short of the objective. In an informal way the financial centers (particularly the supranational centers) perform this coordination and distribution function with considerable efficiency, a feat which seems to have been overlooked.

The centers' information systems (and networks) are important to multinational corporations, central bankers (and their governments), international organizations (i.e., the International Monetary Fund), and a number of other financial participants such as brokers, accountants, and attorneys. Multinational corporations use these information networks to assist them in their cash management activities and in transmitting information to their subsidiaries. Central bankers and international organizations find it necessary from time to time to intervene in the financial markets of the world. The questions that must be answered by these organizations are: Where should the intervention take place? Should the intervention be in more than one center? Which markets and institutions should the intervention directly affect?

The preeminence of these centers is perhaps best seen when the attributes of the large internationally active banks are examined. In Japan, the large internationally active banks headquartered in Osaka (Sumitomo, Sanwa, and Daiwa), Kobe (Taiyo), Nagoya (Tokai) have their "top" international people in Tokyo and have recently split their top domestic people between their home office and Tokyo. Similar activities have taken place in California; the Bank of America has officially split its headquarters into a northern division in San Francisco (the original headquarters), headed by the president (chief executive officer) and a southern division in Los Angeles, headed by the chairman of the board (chief operating officer). The two other large San Francisco banks—Crocker National and Wells Fargo—now have their chief executive officers spend 40 to 50% of their time in southern California. This reflects the growth of Los Angeles as a significant financial center. Also note the arguments opposing the establishment of international banking facilities in New York (see note 15).

Another action which appears to clearly favor the importance of the center over the bank is the behavior of the Organization of Arab Petroleum Exporting Countries (OAPEC) in 1973–1974. When OAPEC quadrupled oil prices in late 1973 and early 1974 its members initially chose to employ their cash reserves (billions of new dollars) in London even though comparable deposit rates in New York were 50 to 75 basis points higher in New York. The branch and subsidiary offices of the large New York banks were the principal recipients (receiving more than 70% of the total) of these funds. If the supranational banks were preeminent, then why not take advantage of the higher yields being offered in New York since the London affiliates of the New York banks were the principal depositories for these OAPEC funds? This example points to the significance of politics and confidence, in addition to the more quantifiable variables, as important determinants of financial center structure—particularly the perceived willingness of a center to use economic means to achieve a political objective. As important as the banks are, the evidence appears to clearly show that the large internationally active banks are not more important than the centers. The evidence also appears to clearly show that the reach, scope, and influence of the centers is far greater than the total reach, scope, and influence of its various institutions when measured independently.

IV. Multinational Corporations, Supranational Financial Centers, and Foreign Direct Investments

Beginning with Hymer's pioneering work in 1960, the growth of multinational activity has been well documented, and to a large extent chronologically. The "real" growth in multinational industrial activity began in the early 1950s. Between 1950 and 1965 US direct investment abroad increased nearly fivefold, from $12 billion to $55 billion. At year end 1980 the total was approximately $220 billion. Most of the early studies (prior to 1970) examined US foreign investment activity, mainly because American firms (during this period) were the dominant force in foreign investment activity. It is not surprising that Hymer found that the principal reason for foreign direct investment was monopoly power. He noted that firms operating at a distance from their decision-making center are operating at a substantial "cost" disadvantage: the cost of travel and transmitting information; the time lost in travel; and the costs associated with errors which results from misunderstandings in the absence of face-to-face communications.

Hymer's research covered the period of time when operating in foreign environments was a relatively new experience for most US firms. Most of these firms, naturally, relied on New York and its resources to assist in their overseas expansion. Even though New York emerged from World War II as the world's preeminent financial center, its direct links to other centers (its information network) never equaled or seriously challenged London's, in scope or in depth. For much of this time (prior to 1970), New York's capability in providing unfiltered information about product markets, and the legal and political environments of a large number of countries, was quite limited. It seems appropriate to argue that New York's limited knowledge about foreign places would cause it to view any substantial commitment of resources, by US-based firms, to overseas expansion in markets that did not appear to offer monopoly (or near monopoly) profits as being relatively risky. This would result in a lower price-earnings multiple for the firm's shares and a lower price for its debt.

Throughout the 1960s New York broadened and deepened its direct links to other centers. As New York's connections grew, its knowledge about foreign places grew. It was during this period that the so-called "growth" strategies and policies of the multinational corporations (MNCs) were rewarded. Some MNCs saw the price-earnings multiple for their shares soar to three-digit levels. It was during this period, when MNCs were emphasizing growth, that the so-called "two-tier" stock market developed. It was observed that the large institutional investors (i.e., bank trust departments, mutual funds, insurance companies, etc.) tend to buy and actively trade the stocks of a relatively small number of firms. These firms were usually one of the dominant firms in their respective industry, or they (and their industry) were seen as growth oriented. As a result of these activities of the institutional investors, the price-earnings multiple of the shares of these firms were far higher than the multiple for the rest of the market. Thus the firms whose shares were part of the "upper-tier" group of stocks had a substantial advantage in accessing new capital as well as in the cost they had to pay for that capital.

New York's increasing knowledge about foreign places apparently led it to conclude that it was capable of managing a much larger and more complex portfolio of activities. As the efficiency of its global information network increased, the investment opportunities available in foreign locations were more clearly seen. This understanding was made possible by having first-hand unfiltered information to corroborate, and enhance, the filtered information that had been received earlier via London. New York's view at that time was, apparently, that the product markets of the world were broad and deep enough to accommodate any market structure short of perfect competition. It therefore appears that through its appraisal machinery New York rewarded firms that retained (and reinvested in foreign locations) a large portion of their earnings. This type of foreign investment strategy meant that the MNC was also enlarging its portfolio of investments through geographic diversification. Theorists studying this phenomenon argued that geographic diversification of the MNC lowered the risk to the investor by reducing the impact of a potential loss of any single investment project. As a result, the shares of the MNC will be more attractive to the risk-averse investing public, which will increase the MNC's supply (and decrease its costs) of capital. Note that the portfolio theory of foreign direct investments places considerable emphasis on the risk of doing business within sovereign political jurisdictions, and somewhat less emphasis on the risk of competing in the marketplace.

The portfolio theory of foreign direct investment was followed by explanations based on internalization and appropriability motives. These theories argued that due to imperfect knowledge in the marketplace the MNC develops its own internal markets in intermediate products, such as marketing, personnel management and training, foreign exchange arbitrage, and capital market arbitrage. It should be noted that the emphasis at this juncture was not on capital movement, capital formation, expanding existing facilities, or building new facilities. The emphasis was on vertical integration—increasing control over all activities taking place within the firm, and particularly on activities that generated new information. As less and less of the MNC's internally generated knowledge is made available to the markets (the public), the issue then becomes appropriability of this information.

The growth of the modern MNC during the postwar period has led to the generation of hypotheses and arguments that increasingly call upon the MNC to organize and manage its resources in ways that are primarily beneficial to society. The MNC's direct concern for society must be limited, by the invisible-hand doctrine. It should presumably conduct its affairs in ways that optimize the interest of its shareholders, creditors, and management. This is best done by it maximizing its competitive position in the markets in which it operates and by maximizing its competitive position within the supranational financial center, in which it is continually being evaluated, by having the center optimally price its securities. The proposition then is to reject the arguments that have been put forth in the past, suggesting that the MNC should include as part of its objective the welfare of society.

The welfare of society is looked after by the supranational financial center (SFC). The SFC is a synthesized infrastructure of institutions and markets whose function it is to evaluate the operating efficiencies of those financial, industrial, commercial, and political organizations that utilize its capital, information, and management resources. The SFC's objective, with respect to the MNC, is to maximize the welfare of all society by optimally distributing multinational activity (i.e., sourcing, production, marketing, and information) throughout the world.

In a world divided up into developed countries (DCs) and less-developed countries (LDCs), it is the SFC's task to optimally allocate multinational activity in a way that approaches Pareto optimality. That is, if we have two multinationals, a consumer-product firm and an electronics firm, it is the SFC's responsibility to evaluate each MNC's operating efficiencies in a way that optimally distributes their resources between the LDCs and the DCs. This means that an LDC's marginal rate of substitution of the electronics MNC investment for the consumer-product MNC investment must be the same as that of the DC. That is, the ratio of the marginal utilities of the two investments must be the same. Figure 2 shows the Pareto optimal solution (curve *CC'*) to the problem of multinational resources allocation. The contract curve *CC'* represents the locus of points of tangency between the indifference curves of the DCs and the LDCs.

When the SFC evaluates the securities (operating efficiencies) of the MNC, its actions are constrained by the function it must perform. For example, if an MNC's leverage is too high (in the SFC's view) the center cannot take steps to reduce its holdings of that firm's securities because it is acting for all of society. Thus, the center's only option is to reduce the value of the firm's securities. The response of the MNC to the center's appraisal of its securities is of great interest to the SFC because if the firm does not respond to the center's signals and continues to maintain a highly leveraged structure, the center must further reduce

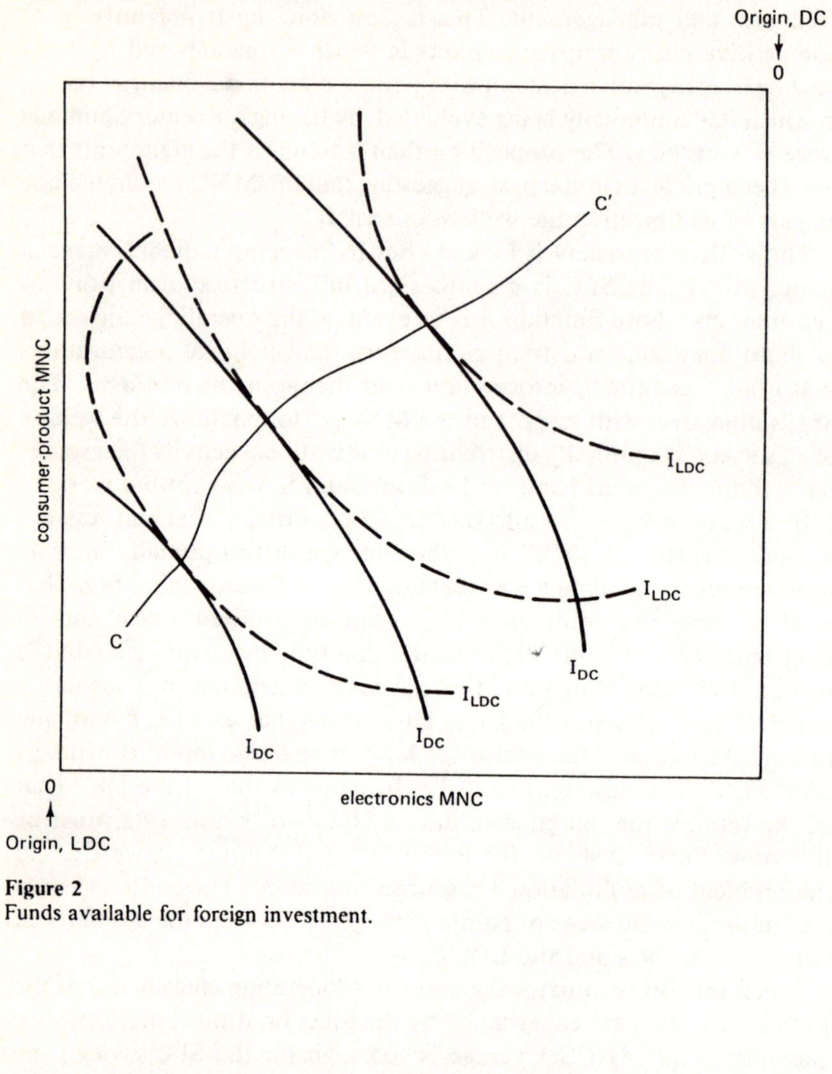

Figure 2
Funds available for foreign investment.

the value of the MNC's securities, which lowers the overall value of the center's portfolio. This means that capital is not distributed as efficiently (optimally) as it might be, which causes the cost of capital to rise for all. In addition to the issues of leverage, the SFC is continually evaluating the MNC on its other operating and performance dimensions (earnings, market share, location portfolio of investments, etc.).

When the SFC's evaluation of MNC activity suggests some adjustments be made, the center's objective is usually not to undo management's decisions but rather to alter the decision.[21] For example, when the center is continually decreasing the value of the shares of a firm, relative to its industry, the center will not be simultaneously engaging in activities that will increase the value of that firm's debt securities. The center will either take action that is designed to inform another firm, operating within that industry, that its leverage should be higher. Or, if the industry's capital structure (as determined by the center) is in balance, the SFC could purchase an amount of equity and debt securities of the other industry participants in proportions equal to their share of stocks and bonds outstanding.

When the focus is on earnings, the center must first take steps to ensure the success of its multinational clientele. This means that the SFC is concerned foremost with the earnings and overall value of the portfolio of its clients and less concerned with its own earnings and investment portfolio. The reason for this is twofold. First, the center operates as an intermediary providing capital, information, and management products and services. And second, the center's total portfolio of clients (society) represents the center's investment.[22] The financial center is unlike the corporation, in that the lower the expected risk the greater the return for the center. The center's primary concern, at all times, should be to reduce the expected risk of return on its portfolio of activities. For example, in cost-of-capital considerations and where interest rates are important, the center's behavior should be to bid down the amount it pays for funds so as to minimize what it must charge for funds. The higher the capital-servicing requirements for the borrowing firms, the greater the probability of problems occurring with the SFC's portfolio. Figure 3a shows the financial center's risk-earnings possibility curve. The center's earnings are derived principally from fees and the spreads received between bid and ask on a wide range of intermediary activities. The negative slope of the curve suggests that

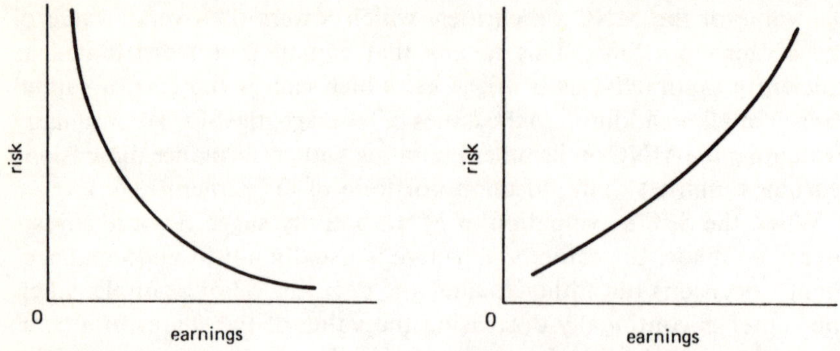

a. supranational financial centers b. multinational corporations

Figure 3
Risk-earnings possibility curves.

along with the benefits derived from an increase in the volume of activity, the center could widen the spread between bid and ask, and increase the base rate of its fee schedules without significantly increasing risk or reducing volume of activity. Figure 3b shows the MNCs' risk-earnings possibility curve. These curves depict the expected *rational* behavior of the SFC and the MNC. The SFC wants to enhance the quality of its asset portfolio by providing capital to users at a cost that minimizes the risk of capital depreciation (being unable to service debt obligations, omitting or reducing dividend payments, etc.) and capital destruction (being unable to repay the principal from debt obligations, having the value of stockholders' equity reduced, etc.). The MNC, on the other hand, seeks to increase its return on capital employed as the risk associated with employing that capital is increased. This attitude has led the MNC to pursue, at times, relatively more risky investments, in hopes of increasing revenues, or cash flow, or profits, or market share, or some combination of the four.

Developing a theoretical framework to explain behavior is not only important because it may explain the events that have already taken place, but also because it may explain future events. Theory is also important because it is useful in identifying those factors that may be impeding the more "logical" or more "rational" behavior of financial centers. Since the early 1970s financial center behavior has been at odds with the theoretical framework argued for in this paper. A case in point, since the initial quadrupling of oil prices in 1973–1974 the global economy has generated virtually no real growth, unemployment has more doubled, inflation has increased threefold, corporate bankruptcies have more than doubled, and the international financial system is precariously plodding along without a clear plan for solving the problems associated with prohibitively high capital costs.

A question that remains unanswered, in my mind at least, is: Why did interest rates not fall precipitously (perhaps as much as 300 to 400 basis points) in the weeks and months following the oil price increase of 1973–1974? At the time of the oil price increases, the international financial system was still adjusting to the consequences of the demise of the fixed exchange rate system that had been in existence since the conclusion of the Bretton Woods conference following World War II. Worries about rising unemployment and inflation, and the economic health of LDCs, were also being voiced. In early 1974 the magnitude of the shift in wealth from the industrialized Western nations to the oil-exporting countries was becoming quite clear. OPEC oil revenues were in 1973 a mere $22 billion. Early estimates of 1974 OPEC revenues ranged from $100 to $115 billion (the actual revenues were slightly less than $90 billion). Armed with this information it seems reasonable to have expected that London, the principal beneficiary of OPEC funds, would have bidded down substantially the price it was willing to pay for new deposits. New York being the only other center capable of handling such a large influx of funds was not receiving, directly, any of these new deposits from OPEC—for obvious reasons. It was clear at the time that these new liabilities accruing to London would be converted into assets by primarily increasing loans made to developing countries, which were already having difficulty meeting their financial obligations. It should have also been clear that rising interest rates have a destabilizing effect on the world's equity markets, which make it difficult for corporations to maintain the appropriate debt/equity mix in their capital structure, which is vitally important to investor confidence. London, and the American banks which dominate the Eurocurrency market, should have realized that rising interest rates increase the general level of uncertainty, which in turn tends to slow capital investments in favor of short-term cash management, which puts additional upward pressure on inflation and unemployment.

The results of London's actions to increase interest rates has led to a continual deterioration in the quality of the asset portfolios of the community of financial centers. There are at least two factors which may explain why London did not take steps to reduce the interest rate paid on deposits. First, floating interest rates were becoming the accepted practice for banks in the management of their asset portfolios. This meant that any increase in cost associated with their liabilities could be passed on to the borrower by adjusting the interest rate charged on their asset portfolios. As a result, there apparently was little or no incentive to aggressively manage the liability side—as is the case when fixed interest rates are the practice. Second, the world's principal central banks agreed to become lender of last resort for the international financial centers. This meant that any major default by a developing country, for example, would be covered by the community of central banks, and this apparently reduced the incentive of the financial centers to emphasize asset portfolio quality and prudence.

It appears that the fixed-interest-rate philosophy, policy, and practice offers some hope of a less volatile and more efficient international financial system. The practice of central banks proclaiming themselves as lenders of last resort for the community of international financial centers, particularly as it relates to LDC credits, has the disruptive effect of diverting capital away from the more efficient users such as the MNCs—which are also important contributors to the economic development process. I agree that the world financial system should in fact have a lender of last resort, but the provider of this type of insurance requires that the insurer charge a premium that must be factored into the cost of the insured credits. In most domestic financial systems reserves held against deposits act as insurance premiums; but such a system is deficient in that it is directed exclusively at the liability side and principally ignores asset quality. Perhaps a more efficient method for assessing insurance premiums for domestic as well as Eurocurrency credits, would be for the central banks to classify assets in much the same way as insurance companies classify life and casualty risks. Based on the various asset classifications, an insurance premium should be charged or a reserve requirement should be imposed. Since the primary purpose of this paper is not prescriptive, a detailed discussion of how and why these actions should be taken is inappropriate.

Notes

1. Stephen H. Hymer, *The International Operations of National Firms; A Study of Direct Investment* (Ph.D. thesis, Massachusetts Institute of Technology, 1960; published 1976, MIT Press).

2. Charles P. Kindleberger, *American Business Abroad* (New Haven: Yale University Press, 1969), p. 90.

3. Robert Z. Aliber, "A Theory of Direct Foreign Investment," in C. P. Kindleberger (ed.), *The International Corporation* (Cambridge, Mass.: MIT Press, 1970) pp. 17–34.

4. Giorgio Ragazzi, "Theories of Determinants of Foreign Direct Investments," *Staff Papers* (International Monetary Fund), July 1973, pp. 476–481.

5. Howard Curtis Reed, *The Preeminence of International Financial Centers*, (New York: Praeger, 1981), pp. 60–61.

6. Ibid., p. 10. The centers were measured in five-year intervals covering the period 1900 to 1980. The ninve variable measures were (1) the number of large internationally active commercial banks headquartered in the center; (2) the number of foreign financial centers with direct links to the local center and the links are provided by the local center's internationally active banks; (3) the number of private banks (including investment and merchant banks) located in the center; (4) the number of large internationally active foreign commercial banks with a banking office in the center (representative offices are excluded); (5) the number of foreign financial centers with direct links to the local center, with the links provided by the foreign internationally active banks; (6) the total amount of foreign financial assets held in the center; (7) the total amount of foreign financial liabilities residing in the center; (8) the number of foreign financial centers with direct links to the local center, with the links provided by the foreign internationally active banks (agency, branch, representative, and subsidiary offices); and (9) the number of large internationally active foreign commercial banks with agencies or branches, or representative or subsidiary offices in the center. In addition to these measures, another 41 variables were used to measure various dimensions of each center's country. These variables examined capital and trade flows, inflation and capital formation, industrial activity, and international communication activity.

7. Hierarchical cluster analysis was used to determine the structure of financial centers over time. Stepwise multiple discriminant analysis was then used to verify the cluster-analysis grouping (organizational structure), and determine what factors (variables) caused the particular grouping.

8. This evaluation is reflected immediately in the foreign exchange (spot and forward) market value of currencies, and later on, in the nation's collective cost of capital.

9. "Distinct" means that statistically significant separation between the groups of centers is at the .001 level of significance.

10. The 12 settling banks are all headquartered in New York and are the 12 members of the New York Clearing House Association.

11. Associate members are New York-based Edge Act subsidiaries of US banks, and New York agencies, branches, or subsidiaries of foreign banks.

12. This practice was relaxed in 1979. Today, any institution can open a CHIPS settlement account at the Federal Reserve Bank of New York, if it wants to operate independently of the New York settling banks. As of February 1982, only two banks had done so—the New York-based Edge Act subsidiaries of Bank of America and Continental Illinois. Non–NewYork settling banks with less than $250 million in capital must have their parent banks guarantee their CHIPS-related obligations.

13. Recently opened offices include foreign banks that have upgraded their representative offices to an agency or branch. This information is based on a series of wide-ranging interviews with New York-headquartered, foreign and Edge Act bankers during 1979 and 1980. Four were New York settling banks, four were Edge Act subsidiaries, and seven were foreign banks.

14. Edge Act as well as foreign bankers, while not giving exact figures, make mention that their clearing activities are one of the most profitable areas of their New York operations.

15. A group of large US banks (headquartered outside of New York), led by Bank of America and Continental Illinois, attempted to delay and perhaps prevent New York from receiving final approval from the Federal Reserve to establish International Banking Facilities (IBFs). The support of this group was contingent upon their being given direct access to the CHIPS computer from their home offices outside of New York. It was argued that with IBFs and CHIPS at their disposal, the 12 settling banks headquartered in New York will be able to obtain deposits at lower costs and make loans more profitably, thus giving the New York banks an unfair competitive advantage. Apparently, the ploy did not work. New York's IBFs began operating on December 1, 1981, and the non–New York banks do not have direct computer access to CHIPS.

16. It may also be of interest to note that large internationally active financial institutions have a tendency to assign their "best" people on the basis of a center's perceived status; see Reed, op. cit., pp. 69–74.

17. International telex emerges as the single most important determinant of financial-center structure when country variable measures are used. See Reed, op. cit., p. 48.

18. Unfiltered information refers, in this instance, to the information transmitted between centers through direct banking links; filtered information refers to the information transmitted between centers through relatively public networks. Unfiltered information is not necessarily transmitted directly from one center to another; it may be processed through an intermediary office (a regional office, or the corporate headquarters, or both), but the processing takes place within a single institution.

19. International currency clearing institutions are heavy users of personal communication facilities. CHIPS, for example, is primarily a confidence-based system where payments are made via an electronic funds transfer mechanism. The daily transactions are presently in excess of 60,000.

20. See Reed, op. cit., chapter 2.

21. The undoing of a decision would occur only in extreme cases (e.g., when, in the center's opinion, an MNC's action(s) would clearly jeopardize the future of the firm).

22. The center's portfolio of clients includes multinational corporations, nonmultinational corporations, governments, and international organizations; in other words, all of society.

[5]

ON THE DEVELOPMENT OF INTERNATIONAL FINANCIAL CENTERS*

Michael A. Goldberg, Robert W. Helsley
and Maurice D. Levi
Faculty of Commerce and Business Administration
University of British Columbia
Vancouver, B. C. V6T 1Y8 Canada

I. Introduction

As the world has shifted from the production of goods to the production of services, and as world trade has burgeoned, the international financial services sector has become increasingly important. Its role in the world economy is pivotal at present as a reading of daily headlines will show. Additionally, international financial services are increasingly being concentrated in major urban centers (international financial centers or IFCs) and the ability to attract, retain and expand these services is seen by many as a key component of future urban economic development.

However, little research has been done on the economic forces affecting the development of geographic centers of international finance. Kindleberger [1974] hypothesized that this is due to the issue falling between two areas of investigation: urban and regional economics, which is concerned with locational matters, but which concentrates on commerce, industry, and housing rather than finance, and monetary and financial economics, which has little interest in geographic location.

Research on the economic factors influencing the development of international financial centers has undoubtedly also been hindered by the diverse and complex data sets required for empirical work in this field. Kindleberger [1974, p. 68], reflecting on his comparative, historical account of the development of centers of international finance, noted that his analysis is "qualitative rather than quantitative," a characteristic which "derives from the limitations of the writer, the magnitude of the task of deriving comparable data from a wide number of countries, and an interest more in process than in detailed outcome." In a series of classic studies of financial activity in the United States, Goldsmith [1958, 1965, 1968, 1969] documented many aspects of the regional distribution of banking and financial activity. However, Goldsmith did not evaluate empirically the causes or determinants of the distribution. Recent empirical research, spawned by the renewed interest in international

---

*This paper was prepared for the Festschrift volume honoring the seventieth birthday of Michael K. Mischaikow. The outstanding research assistance of Doug McLean and the financial support of the British Columbia Ministry of Finance and Corporate Relations are gratefully acknowledged. The authors are solely responsible for all views expressed and for any errors that remain.

banking and the dramatic growth in international financial transactions, typically focuses on the experience of particular countries or particular aspects of international banking.[1] Comparative studies of the development of international financial centers are rare. The work of Howard Reed [1981], which we discuss below, is a notable exception.

This paper presents several empirical studies of the economic determinants of the "geography of finance" as it was described by Kerr [1965]. The analysis proceeds on three levels. First, on an international level, we examine the determinants of the level of international banking and financial activity across 42 countries in 1984. Second, on an interregional level, we examine the determinants of the level of financial activity across regions of the United States in 1984. Finally, on an interurban level, we examine the determinants of the size of the banking sector across the 31 cities containing the world's 750 largest banks in 1984. Our work suggests that the same basic economic forces underlie the development of the financial services industry at each of these levels.

Including this brief introduction, the paper has four parts. Section II provides historical background and describes basic characteristics of international financial centers. Section III reviews the conceptual literature on the determinants of the size of the international financial services industry. Section IV presents and discusses the results of our international, interregional, and interurban empirical studies. Section V summarizes our research and discusses ways in which it might be extended.

II. International Financial Centers.

A. Changes in the International Financial System

Recent explosive growth of the international financial system traces back to the mid-1960s in the view of most researchers, although the groundwork for this growth was laid in the immediate post-war period (Mendelsohn [1980]).[2] The system grew largely because of the accumulation of large balances of U.S. dollar denominated deposits outside the United States and the slow crumbling of the Bretton Woods agreements (Wachtel [1986]). U.S. Federal Reserve Board regulatory policies (most notably Regulation Q) fostered this growth as U.S. banks wanted to expand but were severely limited in doing so domestically within the U.S. market. London provided the ideal place for this activity to take root and grow vigorously because of relatively relaxed rules covering offshore loans and deposits, the presence of large U.S. dollar balances already held in the United Kingdom, and complementary British domestic restrictions on trade financing.

---

[1]See Brimmer and Dahl [1975], Darby [1987], Charles Freedman [1974], Goldberg and Saunders [1980, 1981a, 1981b], Ikle [1972], Kindleberger [1985], Lees [1976] and Terrell and Key [1977].

[2]For excellent background information on the rapid evolution of the international financial marketplace see: Ferris [1984], Mayer [1985], Kaufman [1986], Mendelsohn [1980], Hamilton [1986], and Wachtel [1986].

ON THE DEVELOPMENT OF INTERNATIONAL FINANCIAL CENTERS

These U.S. dollar balances and the dramatic growth in international trade during the 1970s (greatly augmented by the existence of so-called "petro-dollars" accumulated by OPEC countries in the 1970s) paved the way for the explosive development of international banking operations. This, in turn, led to the development of key urban centers to provide these international banking and related financial services. London clearly led the way, and by most reckoning is still at the top, although for certain kinds of transactions (bonds and equities most notably) it must share the lead with New York. Recently, however, staggering dollar reserve accumulations resulting from massive trade surpluses by the Japanese have combined with large Japanese government deficits to propel Tokyo into the topmost echelon of the world's financial centers. Hong Kong, Singapore, Zurich, Paris, and a host of other major comercial centers follow (Reed [1981]). Accordingly, these centers are tightly and inextricably linked to the changing world financial scene. This tight linkage being simultaneously both a cause and an effect of recent volatility in the world financial economy.

B. Characteristics of International Financial Centers

A precise definition of international financial center will probably always elude us given the enormous diversity of these centers.[3] However, a number of alternative descriptions exist in the literature that can serve the purpose of delineating what is meant by an IFC.

For example, Dufey and Giddy [1978] suggest that IFCs evolve as concomitants of leading domestic financial centers: "Those domestic centers offering the greatest convenience in terms of international communications, geographic locations, financial services, and so on, become the recognized international financial centers."[4] A much earlier definition from Nadler, et al. [1955] sketches the functions of such centers by noting, "Normally, it acts as a bank for the entire world and the services it renders facilitate the flow of goods, and services, and capital among nations. Some of its functions are unique; others are closely comparable with those performed on a national or regional scale by domestic financial centers."[5]

Finally, Kindleberger [1974, p. 57] notes that international financial centers perform "the highly specialized functions of lending abroad and serving as a clearinghouse for payments among countries. Banks, securities dealers and the like establish branches in such centers." Whichever definition is chosen though, it is clear that IFCs are major urban concentrations of financial services with a large portion of those services directed toward international financial transactions. They are also leading domestic centers for financial services in their own countries.

---

[3] Useful discussions of international financial center evolution include Kindleberger [1974, 1978, 1981, 1984, and 1985], Logan and Daly [1984], and Reed [1981].

[4] Quoted in Reed [1981], p. 3.

[5] Also quoted in Reed [1981], p. 4.

C. Reed's Study of International Financial Center Evolution

One of the most thorough studies of IFCs is that by Reed [1981]. He is careful to distinguish between international banking centers and international financial centers. After analyzing nearly 50 such centers over the period 1900-1980, Reed notes that while emergence as an international banking center often predates development as an international financial center, this is not an inviolable rule.

> A center's banking infrastructure is obviously important. However, power and influence (preeminence) is derived primarily from the center's global portfolio management activities, which usually requires that the center be successful in attracting relatively large amounts of financial liabilities. Because of the potential volatility associated with international finance,..., I believe it is reasonable to conclude that the behavior of and activities of international financial centers cannot adequately be explained or predicted by analyzing international banking centers. Therefore, analyses of international financial centers that focus only on "banking" dimensions are just as inadequate as analyses that exclude banking and focus mainly on "finance" (capital flows and foreign lending). (p. 56)

Reed also suggests that it is useful to envision international financial centers as being hierarchically ordered. Accordingly, he develops a five-level hierarchy that IFCs go through as they evolve and grow. Evolution begins when a financial center is designated or emerges

> to serve, exclusively, the lowest strata within the nation-state hierarchy (its city, its county, and its state/canton/province, and so forth). The second phase of the process envisions the center serving a geographic area larger than its immediate environs but smaller than the nation itself. In phase three, the center becomes preeminent within the nation itself. In phase four, the center is providing financial and related services to its nation and to a number of other countries that are geographically contiguous. The fifth phase of the evolutionary process places the center at the apex of the hierarchy comprising all financial centers. (p. 57)

This evolutionary picture suggests, erroneously Reed argues, that a financial center must first rise to national status before it can become an IFC. He cites a number of counter examples, and concludes that "a financial center's capacity to serve a region (domestic or international) bears little, if any, relationship to whether it is international or not." (p.67)

Reed closes his study by stressing that participants in the international economic arena (the "political economy" in Reed's words) often limit the roles of IFCs to those of "providing investment instruments and liquidity to the saver and funds to the borrower." However, he notes that his work suggests that IFCs go well beyond this perception of their traditional role and that the IFC is a key component to the global political economy "because it functions as a communication center and a management center." The ease of access to state-of-the art telecommunications is just a part of this communication system. Of

ON THE DEVELOPMENT OF INTERNATIONAL FINANCIAL CENTERS

greater importance is the presence of a dense network of airline connections to other IFCs as is typified by London, Amsterdam, New York and Zurich. Additionally, access to vital management services such as accounting, law, marketing/advertising, printing, and trade are virtually essential adjuncts of both IFC status and IFC functioning, given the ranges of autonomy granted to regional managers located in IFCs and the resulting need for many of them to have access to high quality management support services.[6] Thus, the concentration of financial services, within cities and nations and multinational regions, is a key concomitant of IFC development.

III. The Determinants of IFC Development

The development of international financial centers is dictated, in part, by factors influencing the growth of the international financial services industry. A number of explanations for the growth of international financial activity have been offered in the literature. In general terms, the factors determining the size of a country 's international financial sector can be separated into three distinct groups: international trade factors, international financial intermediation factors, and industrial organization factors.

In the traditional view of international finance, the demand for international financial services is derived from international trade. The volume of trade directly influences the activity of banks as they facilitate payments, provide letters of credit, and so on. Thus, the larger a country's participation in world export-import trade, the greater the size of its international financial sector (Lees [1976], Born [1983], Kindleberger [1984]).

The development of financial intermediation is considered a vital part of economic development process (Goldsmith [1969], Shaw [1973], McKinnon [1973]). The major determinants of financial intermediation include direct foreign investment, balance of payments surpluses or deficits and the growth of government debt. The direct foreign investment explanation of international financial activity is outlined by Brimmer and Dahl [1975], Grubel [1977], Ball and Tschoegl [1982], and Saunders and Goldberg [1980]. The essence of the argument is that banks go abroad in pursuit of the international business of their domestic customers. Kindleberger [1969], Gray and Gray [1981], and Grubel [1977] suggest that large banks use superior management techniques and experience developed through domestic operations at very low marginal costs as a competitive edge in foreign countries.

The development of international financial intermediation changed substantially during the 1970s. Two sharp rises in the price of oil and the world-wide increase in government debt had a dramatic influence on the supply and demand for international intermediation services (Llewellyn [1982], Pecchioili [1983], Monti [1982], and Aliber [1984]). In 1974-1975, the OPEC countries were running large surpluses due to the quadrupling of oil prices. They placed a large portion of these funds in Eurocurrency accounts in major international banks. These international banks then channeled the funds to non-OPEC less developed

---

[6] The recent study by Daniels [1986] covering foreign bank location in London and New York suggests that there is, in fact, an enormous range of decentralization and autonomous management from the highly independent to the almost completely subservient. Reed's comments need to be qualified in view of Daniels' current findings.

countries in order to finance the balance of payment deficits of these countries. These large payment imbalances required financial intermediation on an enormous scale. The international Eurocurrency market helps to channel funds from major financial centers to final borrowers.

The third group of factors determining the size of a country's international financial sector may be called industrial organization factors. These factors are related to banking regulation and market structure. The development of international financial activity is dependent on the degree of government regulation (Aliber [1984], Ball and Tschoegl [1982], Dean and Grubel [1979], Key [1982]). Regulation can take the form of interest rate ceilings, exchange rate controls, reserve requirements, seignorage, financial disclosure, fees, and taxes. Interest rate regulations, taxes on deposits and portfolio regulations place a wedge between interest rates paid depositors and interest rates charged borrowers (Aliber [1980], and Ho and Saunders [1981]). International banks located in less heavily regulated countries are able to offer depositors higher interest rates and charge borrowers lower interest rates than would be possible under more stringent regulations.

The cost and benefits of regulation-free banking centers are analyzed by McCarthy [1979]. The benefits appear to be only loosely related to the volume of business routed through a center but closely related to the number of banks and the types of operations carried out. McCarthy [1979] also suggests that the cost advantage for international banks increases if the country has adequate infrastructures such as telecommunications and transportation facilities.

Gray and Gray [1981] and Caves [1971] assert that the development of international banking also depends on the market structure. Multinational banks are most likely to expand into oligopolistic national markets to capture a share of the quasi-rents from barriers to entry, segmented markets, and product differentiation with institutions already in the market.

IV. Empirical Correlates of IFC Development

The discussion in the previous section suggests that the major factors influencing the level of financial development are related to:

1) the level of overall economic development;
2) the level of international trade;
3) the extent of financial intermediation; and
4) the stringency of financial regulation.

This section summarizes the results of several cross-sectional empirical studies we recently completed examining the relative importance of these factors. We examine the determinants of the size of the financial sector from international, interregional, and interurban perspectives.

A. International Results

The first part of our analysis examines the determinants of the size of the financial sector in 42 countries in 1984. These countries contained roughly 86 percent of the foreign assets held by banks in the world in 1984. We employ two proxy measures of the size of the financial sector (our dependent variable), the number of foreign assets held by domestic banks (Table 1), and the fraction of

ON THE DEVELOPMENT OF INTERNATIONAL FINANCIAL CENTERS

total employment working in the financial sector (Table 2).[7] The independent variables include: per capital GNP or GDP, a measure of the level of economic development; two international trade variables, merchandise imports and merchandise exports; variables intended to capture the extent of financial intermediation, including the national savings rate, outstanding public and private debt, and investment flows; and two proxies of the degree of financial regulation, the average reserve ratio of banks, and a dummy variable for "tax havens."[8]

TABLE 1

CROSS-SECTIONAL STUDY OF 42 COUNTRIES
Dependent Variable: Foreign Assets (all variables in logs)

Variable	Coeff.	Std. Err	T-Ratio	Std. Coeff.
GDP per capita	.583	.303	1.937*	.288
Imports	2.729	.691	3.946**	1.815
Exports	-1.587	.655	-2.442*	-1.106
Saving Rate	-.710	.906	-.784	-.091
Total debt	-.127	.224	-.570	-.110
Foreign debt	.121	.096	1.268	.159
Investment				
abroad	.015	.181	.084	.019
foreign	-.232	.197	-1.178	.159
Reserve ratio	.158	.257	.257	.075
Offshore dummy	2.328	.809	2.878*	.357
Constant	-5.846	3.858	-1.515	.0

R-Squared adjusted: .7620
Log likelihood function: -362.41

Std. Err of estimate: 1.1288
Durbin Watson: 2.1448

** Significant at the 1 percent level.
* Significant at the 5 percent level.

The regression results in Tables 1 and 2 indicate that real per capita GDP is positively and significantly related to the size of the financial sector, as expected. Also, while imports have a positive and significant effect, as expected, the level of exports is strongly and negatively related to the size of the financial sector. This seemingly counter intuitive result also appears in the interregional and interurban analyses that follow. A potential explanation can be found in the common practice of exporters to reduce the risks of adverse changes in foreign exchange rates by denominating their debt in their buyer's currency. It may well be the case that exporters utilize banks in the countries

---

[7]The complexity of the data sets used in these studies, and space limitations, prevent us from enumerating the data sources in detail. Interested readers are referred to our 1987 papers.

[8]The countries designated as "tax havens" in this study are: Bahamas, Bahrain, Panama, the Netherlands, Antilles, and Singapore.

in which they sell their products, hence reducing the size of the financial industry in their own countries (Levi [1987]). We note that a balanced expansion of imports and exports does exert a positive effect, and therefore that trade in toto is likely to stimulate financial sector growth.

TABLE 2

CROSS-SECTIONAL STUDY OF 42 COUNTRIES
Dependent Variable: Percent of labor force in financial sector (all variables in logs)

Variable	Coeff.	Std.Err	T-Ratio	Std.Coeff.
GNP per capita	.356E-05	.101E-05	3.538**	.628
Imports	.928E-06	.498E-06	1.863	2.206
Exports	-.959E-06	.469E-06	-2.048*	-1.905
Saving Rate	-.845E-01	.498E-01	-1.698	-.226
Total debt	-.124E-06	.667E-07	-1.858	-1.108
Foreign debt	.201E-06	.225E-06	.893	.265
Investment				
abroad	.131E-04	.701E-05	1.876	.801
foreign	.646E-07	.104E-05	.062	-.013
portfolio	-.892E-06	.111E-05	-.802	-.213
Reserve ratio	.817E-02	.258E-01	.317	.046
Offshore dummy	.196E-01	.947E-02	2.068*	.262
Constant	.516E-01	.124E-01	4.145**	.0

R-Squared adjusted: .5700 Std. Err of estimate: 0.01742
Log likelihood function: 99.43 Durbin Watson: 1.8448

** Significant at the 1 percent level.
* Significant at the 5 percent level.

The other significant variable in these regressions is the dummy variable identifying offshore "tax havens," which has the expected positive effect. None of the coefficients on the financial intermediation variables are significantly different from zero.

B. Interregional Results

The second part of our analysis examines the determinants of the level of financial activity across regions of the U.S. (states) in 1984. Once again, we employed two proxy measures of the size of the financial sector: total financial assets, domestic and foreign, held by banks and near-banks (Table 3); and employment in finance, insurance, real estate, and related services (Table 4). The independent variables included in the regional regressions are similar to those used in the national studies. Personal income of each state measures the level of economic activity, or economic development. Unfortunately, data on the value of imports and exports originating within each state are unavailable. The trade variables in the regional regressions are imports and exports booked through Federal Customs Offices in the 30 states containing such offices. These data allow us to investigate the effect of international trade via the point of embarkment or disembarkment, which, a priori, could be as important as the location of production or consumption of the goods.

TABLE 3

CROSS-SECTIONAL STUDY OF 30 STATES
Dependent Variable: Total Financial Assets by State
(banks and near-banks, domestic and foreign)

Variable	Coeff.	Std. Err	T-Ratio	Std.Coeff.
Personal income	423.7	133.8	3.166**	.431
Imports	6775.9	1101.1	6.154**	.864
Exports	5024.3	1497.9	-3.354**	-.405
Corporations				
multinationals	330.4	111.76	2.957**	.191
foreign	56.29	30.02	1.875*	.121
Corp.tax rate	-8271.1	32462.	-.254	-.006
Constant	-4026.4	4657.0	-.865	.0

R-Squared adjusted: .9691 Std. Err of Estimate: 19319
Log likelihood function: -571.91 Durbin Watson: 2.1459

** Significant at 1% level.
* Significant at 5% level.

TABLE 4

CROSS-SECTIONAL STUDY OF 30 STATES
Dependent Variable: Employment in the Financial Sector by State

Variable	Coeff.	Std. Err	T-Ratio	Std. Coeff.
Personal income	.900	.100	9.024**	.420
Imports	4.810	.820	5.864**	.457
Exports	-4.442	1.116	-3.981**	-.267
Corporations				
multinationals	.482	.083	5.789**	.208
foreign	.150	.022	6.710**	.240
Corp. tax rate	3.230	24.18	.134	.002
Constant	-.511	3.469	-.147	.0

R-Squared adjusted: .9905 Std. Err of Estimate: 14.39
Log likelihood function: -204.60 Durbin Watson: 2.0034

** Significant at 1% level
* Significant at 5% level.

It seems reasonable to suppose that a disproportionate share of banking will occur in those states in which large companies maintain their head offices. Thus, we included as dependent variables the number of multinational corporations headquartered in each state, and the number of employees of foreign non-bank corporations in each state. The final dependent variable is the average corporate tax rate in each state.

The results reported in Tables 3 and 4 indicate that the size of the financial sector is positively and significantly related to the level of economic activity, approximated by state personal income, as expected. Further both the import and export variables are significant, with imports having a positive effect, and exports a negative effect, as was true in the regressions reported earlier. The results also confirm the suspicion that the presence of multinational headquarters in a state contributes to the level of state financial activity: the number of multinational headquarters has a positive and significant impact on both measures of financial activity. Similarly, the level of financial activity is positively and significantly related to the scale of activity by foreign firms. The coefficient on the average corporate tax rate is not significantly different from zero in either regression.

C. Interurban Results

The third and final part of our analysis examines the determinants of the size of the financial sector in 31 major international financial centers.[9] These metropolitan areas contain the 750 largest banks in the world, and the assets (Table 5) and liabilities (Table 6) of the banks headquartered in each city serve as our proxies for the level of financial activity. This is an imperfect measure, since it omits the assets and liabilities of small banks and other financial institutions, but it should accurately represent the relative importance of the various international financial centers (Friedmann and Wolff [1982], Taylor and Thrift [1982], Semple [1977], and Thrift [1983]). Once again, the independent variables focus on the level of economic development and international trade. The level of local economic activity is approximated by the average annual income of employees in the city. Data on the value of imports and exports originating in each city are unavailable. Tonnage disembarked at the city's port divided by total tonnage shipped through the city's port is included as an independent variable to capture the relative importance of imports.

To try to control for differences between the economic structures of the cities, we included the fraction of the workforce in manufacturing as an explanatory variable. We expect manufacturing to be negatively related to the size of the financial sector, reflecting the dependence of manufacturing centers on export activity. To reflect the relative importance of cities in the national and regional economies of which they are a part, we included the fraction of total assets or liabilities for the country held by banks headquartered in a particular city and in a particular city's time zone. Finally, following Kindleberger's [1974] suspicions, we included the age of the city, and a dummy variable indicated whether or not the city is a national capital as explanatory variables.

---

[9]The cities included in the study are: Tokyo, Paris, New York, London, Osaka, Frankfurt, Toronto, San Francisco, Montreal, Munich, Amsterdam, Milan, Rome, Zurich, Chicago, Los Angeles, Madrid, Dusseldorf, Nagoya, Hong Kong, Seoul, Kobe, Sydney, Melbourne, Luxembourg, Yokohama, Hamburg, Cairo, Singapore, West Berlin, and Vancouver.

ON THE DEVELOPMENT OF INTERNATIONAL FINANCIAL CENTERS

TABLE 5

CROSS-SECTIONAL STUDY OF 31 CITIES
Dependent Variable: Total assets of large banks headquartered in each city (all variables in logs)

Variable	Coeff.	Std. Err	T-Ratio	Std. Coeff.
Avg. annual income	.229	.158	1.450	.101
% imports through port	.650	.167	3.903**	.266
% manufacturing	-.879	.266	-3.298**	-.216
Concentration				
country	.335	.068	4.939**	.375
time zone	.561	.064	8.808**	.570
Productivity	-.641	.123	-5.215**	-.324
Age	-.025	.054	-.468	-.029
Capital	-.283	.196	-1.442	-.110
Constant	14.16	1.949	7.264**	.0

R-Squared adjusted: .9113 Std. Err of Estimate: .36507
Log likelihood function: -357.00 Durbin Watson: 2.8757

** Significant at 1% level.
* Significant at 5% level.

TABLE 6

CROSS-SECTIONAL STUDY OF 31 CITIES
Dependent Variable: Total liabilities of large banks headquartered in each city (all variables in logs)

Variable	Coeff.	Std. Err	T-Ratio	Std. Coeff.
Avg. annual income	.158	.160	.984	.069
% imports through port	.628	.166	3.787**	.254
% manufacturing	-.959	.269	-3.560**	-.233
Concentration				
country	.347	.072	4.789**	.365
time zone	.557	.067	8.305**	.556
Productivity	-.589	.114	-5.144**	-.322
Age	.013	.053	-.242	-.015
Capital	-.228	.194	-1.174	-.088
Constant	14.90	1.985	7.507**	.0

R-Squared adjusted: .9135 Std. Err of Estimate: .36441
Log likelihood function: -350.02 Durbin Watson: 2.7865

** Significant at 1% level.
* Significant at 5% level.

The results in Tables 5 and 6 show that while average annual income does not have a significant effect on the size of the financial sector, the relative importance of imports in the local economy has a strong positive effect, as was true in all the empirical studies we performed. Cities with a manufacturing emphasis (and thus an orientation toward exports) have, as we expected, relatively smaller financial sectors. The national and time zone concentration ratios are also significant, and their coefficients have the anticipated positive sign. Finally, neither status as a capital, nor age of the city has a positive effect on the size of the financial sector.

V. Conclusions and Extensions

The empirical research summarized in this paper advances our knowledge of the economics of financial centers considerably. We have shown that it is possible to explain a remarkably large amount of the variation in the size of financial sectors between countries, regions, and cities with just a few variables. Our results suggest that any theory of the development of centers of financial activity should take into account the following variables all of which we found significant: income levels and the location of corporate headquarters; the nature of the centers such as their industrial structure, and their importance within a country or time zone; and measures of international trade, separated between imports and exports.

The most important determinants appear to be measures of international trade, with imports being positively associated with financial sector development, and exports being negatively associated. The level of financial activity is positively related to the overall level of economic development, and negatively related to the degree of financial regulation. Our analyses also suggest that the number and size of multinational and foreign corporations in a city is positively related with the size of its financial sector, as is the importance of the city in its country and time zone.

The research described in this paper could be refined and extended on several fronts. First, and as all previous authors in the area have complained, there is insufficient consistent data to deal with the topic in a completely satisfactory way. This is especially true at the urban and regional level, where there is a paucity of data on the financial sector and the details of international financial accounts. There are also some considerable data weaknesses surrounding imports and exports through urban regions. Second, the entire research area suffers from the absence of a strong theoretical base. We can only hope that our efforts provide a useful starting point for future theoretical and empirical study.

REFERENCES

Aliber, Robert (1984). "International Banking: A Survey," Journal of Money, Credit and Banking 16(4), 661-678.

Aliber, Robert (1980). "The Integration of Offshore and Domestic Banking Systems," Journal of Monetary Economics 6, 509-526.

Ball, Clifford and Adrian Tschoegl (1982). "The Decision to Establish and Foreign Bank Branch or Subsidiary: An Application of Binary Classification Procedures," Journal of Financial and Quantitative Analysis 17, 411-24.

Darby, Michael (1986). "The Internationalization of American Banking and

ON THE DEVELOPMENT OF INTERNATIONAL FINANCIAL CENTERS

Finance: Structure, Risk, and World Interest Rates," Journal of International Money and Finance 5, 403-28.

Dean, James and Herbert Grubel (1979). "Regulatory Issues and the Theory of Multinational Banking," in Issues in Financial Regulation, edited by Franklin R. Edwards, New York: McGraw-Hill.

Ferris, Paul (1984). The Master Bankers, New York: New American Library.

Fieleke, Norman S. (1977). "The Growth of US Banking Abroad: An Analytical Survey," in Key Issues in International Banking, Conference Series 18, Federal Reserve Bank of Boston, pp. 9-40.

Freedman, Charles (1974). "The Foreign Currency Business of Canadian Banks: An Economic Study," Ottawa: Bank of Canada Staff Research Studies.

Friedmann, John and Goetz Wolff (1982). "World city formation: an agenda for research and action," International Journal of Urban and Regional Research 6(3), 309-344.

Gart, Alan (1984). The Insider's Guide to the Financial Services Revolution, New York: McGraw-Hill.

Goldberg, Lawrence and Anthony Saunders (1981a). "The Growth and Organizational Forms of Foreign Banks in the US," Journal of Money, Credit and Banking 13, 365-74.

Goldberg, Lawrence and Anthony Saunders (1981b). "The Determinants of Foreign Banking Activity in the United States," Journal of Banking and Finance 5, 17-32.

Goldberg, Lawrence and Anthony Saunders (1980). "The Causes of US Bank Expansion Overseas: The Case of Great Britain," Journal of Money, Credit and Banking 12, 630-43.

Goldberg, Michael, Robert Helsley, and Maurice Levi (1987a). "Factors Influencing the Development of Banking and Finance: An International and Historical Evaluation," unpublished manuscript, Faculty of Commerce, The University of British Columbia.

Goldberg, Michael, Robert Helsley, and Maurice Levi (1987b). "The Location of International Financial Activity: An Interregional Analysis," unpublished manuscript, Faculty of Commerce, The University of British Columbia.

Goldsmith, Raymond (1968). Financial Institutions, New York: Random House.

Goldsmith, Raymond (1958). Financial Intermediaries in the American Economy Since 1900, Princeton: Princeton University Press.

Goldsmith, Raymond (1969). Financial Structure and Development, New Haven: Yale University Press.

Goldsmith, Raymond (1965). The Flow of Capital Funds in the Post-War Economy, New York: National Bureau of Economic Research.

Gray, Jean and H. Peter Gray (1981). "The Multinational Bank: A Financial MNC?" Journal of Banking and Finance 5, 33-63.

Grimmer, Andrew and Frederick Dahl (1975). "Growth of American International Banking: Implications for Public Policy," Journal of Finance 10, 041-03.

Grubel, Herbert (1977). "A Theory of Multinational Banking," Banca Nazionele del Lavoro Quarterly Review 1, 349-63.

Hamilton, Adrian (1986). The Financial Revolution, New York: The Free Press.

Ikle, Max (1972). Switzerland: An International Banking and Financial Center Strodsburg: Dowden, Hutchinson, and Ross.

Kaufman, Henry (1986). Interest Rates, the Markets, and the New Financial World, New York: Times Books.

Kerr, Donald (1965). "Some Aspects of the Geography of Finance in Canada," The Canadian Geographer 9, 175-192.

Kindleberger, Charles (1981). International Money, London: George Allen and Unwin.

Kindleberger, Charles (1984). Multinational Excursions, Cambridge, Mass.: MIT Press.

Kindleberger, Charles (1978). Economic Response, Cambridge, Mass.: Harvard University Press.

Kindleberger, Charles (1985). "The Functioning of Financial Centers: Britain in the 19th Century, the United States Since 1945," in International Financial Markets and Capital Movements, edited by Wilford Feaethier and Richard Marston, Princeton: Princeton University Press.

Kindleberger, Charles (1974). The Formation of Financial Centers: A Study in Comparative Economic History, Princeton Studies in International Finance, No. 36, Princeton: Princeton University Press.

Lees, Francis (1976). Foreign Banking and the Investment in the United States: Issues and Alternatives, New York: John Wiley.

Levi, Maurice (1987). "Exchange Rates and the Value of the Firm: The Theory and Evidence," Working Paper, Faculty of Commerce, University of British Columbia.

Logan, M. and Maurice Daly (1984). The International Finance System and Economic Development, Sydney: Department of Geography, University of Sydney.

Marshall, J. and J. Bachter (1984). "Spatial Perspectives and Technical Changes in the Banking Industry in the UK," Environment and Planning A 16, 437-450.

Mayer, Martin (1985). The Money Bazaars: Understanding the Banking Revolution Around Us, New York: New American Library.

Mendelsohn, M. (1980). Money on the Move: The Modern International Capital Market, New York: McGraw-Hill.

Monti, Antonio (1982). "Recent Trends in International Banking," Journal of Banking and Finance 6, 389-99.

Reed, Howard (1981). The Preeminence of International Financial Centers, New York: Praeger Publishers.

Semple, Keith (1977). "The Spatial Concentration of Domestic and Multinational Corporate Headquarters in Canada," Cahiers de Geographie due Quebec 21, 33-52.

Taylor, Michael and Nigel Thrift (eds.) (1982). The Geography of Multinationals, London: Croom Helm.

Terrell, Henry and Sydney Key (1977). "The Growth of Foreign Banking in the United States: An Analytical Survey," in Key Issues in International Banking, Conference Series 18, Federal Reserve Bank of Boston, pp. 54-86.

Wachtel, Howard (1986). The Money Mandarins: The Making of a Supranational Economic Order, New York: Pantheon Books.

[6]

Excerpt from Richard McGahey, Mary Malloy, Katherine Kazanas, and Michael P. Jacobs, *Financial Services, Financial Centers: Public Policy and the Competition for Markets, Firms, and Jobs*, 15–76

2

What Makes a Financial Center?

While financial institutions are found in towns and cities throughout the United States and around the world, much of the activity and employment of banks, insurance companies, security firms, and other financial services firms is concentrated in certain localities, or financial centers. In this chapter, we examine the factors that make for a successful financial center. While later chapters provide more specific information on the relative attractions of several locations, this chapter provides a more general discussion of financial center competition.

The first part of this chapter discusses how recent changes in financial services institutions and activities have redefined the nature and location of financial centers. The discussion then considers how organizational changes in financial institutions have affected location decisions by firms, which in turn affect financial centers. The final section highlights four key areas, or "dimensions of competitiveness," that can be addressed by public policy in order to develop and retain a concentration of financial activity in an area. While not all financial centers rate favorably on all dimensions of competitiveness, those localities which offer a sustainable combination of advantages are well positioned as centers of financial services activity.

The nature of different financial centers varies with the nature of the activities concentrated there. Centers of large-scale international corporate finance are relatively few. New York, Tokyo, and London are the three major global sites of key internationally oriented markets and institutions, with other cities, such as Hong Kong, Singapore, Paris, and Frankfurt, forming a second tier.

Other U.S. cities are regional financial centers, built largely around large commercial banking activity concentrated primarily in regional consumer markets and in regional, sometimes national, corporate middle markets. Pittsburgh, Boston, Charlotte, Atlanta, and Dallas are prime examples of such regional financial centers.

Finally, a mix of financial services activities, from some headquarters functions to back office operations such as credit card processing, characterize other financial centers. Wilmington, Delaware is one example of such a center, with a variety of financial activity drawn to it as a result of favorable state regulation complementing its low-cost attributes. Los Angeles, home to financial institutions engaged in both retail and wholesale activities, on both a domestic and international scale, is another example of a heterogeneous financial center. Chicago has strong regional attributes, along with strength derived from its innovative markets in futures and options.

The Nature and Location of Financial Centers

The recent wave of changes in financial services has influenced the nature and location of financial centers around the world. The forces of convergence, globalization, and technological development have altered financial markets and the needs of firms. The nature of long-standing financial centers has changed to the extent that some observers speak of a "redefinition" of the traditional role of a financial center. Along with new types of centers, new financial centers have emerged in diverse locations.

The Traditional Role of Financial Centers

Historically, financial centers have had two major functions. First, financial centers contribute to the efficiency of financial transactions by concentrating large financial intermediaries and large pools of capital in one place, facilitating access to both borrowers and investors. Many economic historians have documented the integration over time of local capital markets within a country into one dominant national market, viewing this integration as the key process that gives rise to that nation's financial center.[1] In their 1960 discussion of New York as a financial center, Robbins and Terleckyj viewed the money market, defined broadly as the market where a variety of both long-term and short-term financial instruments are traded, as the core feature of New York's traditional predominance.[2]

Second, financial centers also facilitate a system of interregional payments that serves the entire economy by making transactions among companies and consumers in diverse markets more efficient, and by allowing the economy to expand geographically. In this system, as Kindleberger notes, "each locality deals not with each other locality in making and receiving payments, but with a single center."[3] In Kindleberger's example, a country with ten localities only needs nine conduits of payment if there is a single financial center, whereas 45 conduits would be needed without such a center. Kindleberger also argues that "the specialized functions of international payments and foreign lending or borrowing are typically best performed at one central place that is also the specialized center for domestic interregional payments,"[4] linking a network of domestic economies to the international economy.

The concentration of financial institutions and markets in financial centers also attracts nonfinancial firms. Large companies have tended to establish offices in financial centers in order to economize financial balances through centralization, and to deal efficiently in the financial markets for their finance needs.[5] The historic concentration of these nonfinancial companies in one place further adds to the importance of financial centers by agglomerating borrowers and investors.

The concentration of financial services activity in traditional centers also creates efficiency for financial institutions themselves in two ways. First, the concentration of financial services firms and employment leads to a frequent exchange of information and ideas that can reduce the risks of financial activities. Robbins and Terleckyj point out that when participants in the financial markets cluster together, the costs of obtaining and exchanging information "can be minimized by direct and continual contact with the market."[6] Second, by locating together, financial firms "not only share common customers but also share common specialized services, which reduce the costs and difficulties of doing business."[7] Firms in the financial center have greater and cheaper access to the specialized services of law firms, printers, and public relations firms, to joint facilities and organizations that serve groups of financial firms, such as clearinghouses, organized exchanges and professional associations, and to a diverse and sophisticated labor pool.

Finally, while the historical circumstances of particular countries often play a decisive role in determining which metropolis emerges as the national financial center,[8] most traditional financial centers of North American and European countries also were commercial centers. Because of the large number and volume of payments made and received by companies operating in commercial and trading centers, these areas were well suited to become centers of both interregional and international payments. For example, the rise of New York as the largest U.S. trading center in the early 19th century was a major cause of that city's ascendance over Philadelphia as the nation's primary banking capital.[9]

The New Landscape of Financial Centers

Developments in telecommunications and computer technology, convergence, and globalization are changing the nature of financial centers. While these developments have enabled traditional financial centers to retain a large portion of the financial services activity and employment located in them, they also have fostered new types of financial centers that complement and sometimes compete with traditional leaders.

As will be discussed more fully in Chapter 3, the blurring of the traditional boundaries between financial services firms and activities, known as convergence, has a differential impact upon retail and wholesale financial services. Commercial banks and securities firms engaged in wholesale activities oriented toward large-scale borrowers and investors have sought growth through product innovation and the development and application of product-enhancing technologies.

The continual process of refining products, sometimes called a "market-deepening" strategy, relies heavily upon large numbers of highly skilled and innovative financial services professionals who have timely access to complex market information. Because the expertise, market information, infrastructure, and large-scale borrowers and investors are concentrated in relatively few locations, market-deepening strategies tend to focus wholesale activity in them. This concentration draws and strengthens the role of traditional financial centers, where increasingly important clusters of innovative professionals, market data, infrastructure, and clients can be found. The greater complexity of financial products and markets in recent years also has helped to centralize wholesale activities, because it has reinforced the need for direct contact among clients and financial services professionals.

But other factors influencing wholesale activities have encouraged the relocation of some financial activity away from traditional centers. First, as will be discussed in Chapter 4, the continuing integration of the world's financial markets has linked pools of capital funds that can be accessed more readily by investors and borrowers across borders. This has contradictory effects on the traditional landscape of financial centers. On the one hand, by facilitating greater cross-border wholesale investment and borrowing activity, globalization has heightened the importance of large pools of capital and financial expertise. To the extent that pre-existing centers have the largest concentrations of capital, this aspect of globalization reinforces traditional international financial centers.

On the other hand, globalization encourages a greater number of major economic, commercial, and financial sites. This spread of economic activity associated with internationalization fosters the growth of large capital pools, encouraging the development of financial markets, securities exchanges, and other financial activity in areas that were not previously major financial centers. As globalization facilitates and encourages cross-border access to new pools of funds, exchanges, and markets, the relative importance of secondary financial centers can be expected to increase.

Tokyo is an example of a city which has become a world financial center in large part because of the dynamic growth and positive trade balance of the postwar Japanese economy. This growth has created a large pool of funds in Japan, to which the forces of globalization are encouraging and increasingly facilitating cross-border access. Similarly, the increased integration of the European Economic Community that will occur in 1992 will create a new, huge pool of capital that will rival those of other top international financial centers. Dennis Weatherstone, former President of J.P. Morgan, speculates, "As '1992' approaches, a trend toward decentralization of wholesale financial markets may emerge, with a good deal of the business previously lost to London returning to the Continent's national financial centers."[10]

In the United States, another influence moving some wholesale activity away from traditional financial centers is the rise of regional commercial banks. While wholesale securities activities remain concentrated in traditional centers, wholesale banking activity has emerged in a larger number of locations, including Los Angeles, Pittsburgh, and Atlanta.

This growth in new, regional domestic financial centers is based in part on changes in wholesale activities. In recent years the demand for funds from small- and medium-sized corporations (the "middle market") has been growing relative to that of large corporations. While large corporations usually have access to a broader array of debt or securities instruments, smaller firms are much more dependent upon commercial and industrial loans. Given the generally weak ties of money center banks to the corporate middle market, commercial banks outside of the major financial centers have profited by serving the needs of this expanding client base.

Eroding restrictions on interstate banking have provided further opportunities for many of these regional institutions to amass greater amounts of assets, through mergers, acquisitions, and expanded deposit-taking activities. This asset growth in turn has helped position several commercial banks to meet the growing wholesale demand from the corporate middle market. And the asset bases of these regional institutions, unlike the money center banks, had not, until recently, been burdened with non-performing loans, especially those to the Third World. This contributed to their faster growth.

The increasing importance of these "superregional" banks and their bank holding companies, such as PNC and Mellon Bank in Pittsburgh, NCNB and First Union in Charlotte, Fleet/Norstar in Providence, and Bank of Boston Corporation and Bank of New England Corporation in Boston, has concentrated much financial activity in these and other U.S. cities. These regional financial centers have become important features of the new financial services landscape; see Table 2.1 for the locations of the largest superregional bank holding companies.

The rise of regional banking centers in the U.S. also has been strengthened by developments in retail financial services. In general, recent retail market strategies of financial institutions have helped to decentralize and disperse financial activity, adding new financial centers to the landscape in three ways.

First, while the growth of regional financial centers has depended upon the success of commercial banks in the corporate middle market, it is also tied to successful retail market strategies. The breakdown of regulatory restrictions on the geographic expansion of banks and bank holding companies, detailed in Chapter 3, has enabled some commercial banks to move into high growth markets through mergers, acquisitions, and extensive branching. Many major regional banks have grown through such merger and acquisition activity, including NCNB, Fleet/Norstar, First Chicago, and SunTrust. While the broadened distribution networks of commercial banks has dispersed banking activities geographically, the increased concentration of banking firms has contributed to the growth of newer regional financial centers.

Second, because the expansion of retail distribution networks through branching, acquisition, and technological networking is costly, and because competition in retail markets has put pressure on profits and earnings, the cost-sensitivity of financial institutions has greatly increased. The expansion of retail distribution networks for financial services also has been a strategy of some securities firms, such as Merrill Lynch and Dean Witter, as well as of commercial

TABLE 2.1 Locations of Largest Superregional Bank Holding Companies*

		Rank	Assets 6/30/88 ($billions)
San Francisco	BankAmerica Corp.	3	94.3
	Wells Fargo & Co.	10	45.1
Los Angeles	Security Pacific Corp.	6	75.6
	First Interstate Bancorp	8	58.1
Pittsburgh	PNC Financial Corp.	12	36.6
	Mellon Bank Corp.	15	31.2
Boston	Bank of Boston Corp.	13	34.0
	Bank of New England Corp.	17	30.0
Charlotte	NCNB Corp.	18	28.6
	First Union Corp.	19	28.4
Atlanta	Sun Trust Banks, Inc.	20	27.5
Hartford	Shawmut National Corp.	21	27.2
Buffalo	Marine Midland Banks, Inc.	22	26.9
Minneapolis	First Bank System, Inc.	24	25.9
Providence	Fleet/Norstar Financial Group	25	25.1

* *American Banker Top Numbers 1989* defines "a superregional banking firm to include any non-money center banking company that ranks among the nation's ten largest in assets plus any banking firm with $20 million or more in total assets that has merged across state lines to establish a full commercial banking presence in another state." There is no agreement as to which banks are money center and which are superregional. While *Top Numbers 1989* considers large firms in New York and Chicago to be money center banks and those in Los Angeles and San Francisco to be regional institutions, other sources consider the large California firms to be money center banks and Chicago institutions not.

Source: *American Banker Top Numbers 1989* (New York: American Banker/ Bond Buyer, 1989), p. 87. Reprinted by permission.

banks. As the costs of doing business outside of traditional financial centers are generally lower, newer financial centers are at an advantage in attracting direct retail activities and the back office and data processing operations that support those activities, in such businesses as mortgages, consumer lending, and credit card processing.

Finally, this increased cost-sensitivity combined with technological developments has encouraged organizational changes in firms that contribute both to the dispersion of financial services activity outside of traditional financial centers and to the growth of new centers. (These changes will be discussed more fully in the next section of this chapter.) In general, as financial firms have expanded the number of products and services they offer in the retail market, they have sharpened their evaluation of the relative profitability of different lines of business. By organizationally separating these lines from one another, firms can track costs more accurately and measure the incomes derived from different products and services. Advances in computer and telecommunications technology also play a role, as they enable firms to locate different organizational units far apart from one another.

As a result of firms' increased opportunity and cost-driven motivation to locate some of their operations in cost-effective sites, new locations have attracted a significant amount of financial services activity and employment in recent years, often from firms whose headquarters remain in traditional centers. In some instances, firms relocated an entire division, such as Citicorp's decision to move its entire credit card operations to South Dakota. In other cases, firms have moved back office or data processing operations to lower-cost areas away from the traditional financial centers, such as Dean Witter's relocation of its major data processing facility in Dallas. In both cases, organizational changes combined with new technological options have hastened the dispersion of financial services activity out of its traditional center in New York.

As certain cities and regions outside of traditional centers became home to dispersed financial services activities, new centers have been added to the landscape. While some of these new centers mimic the capital market and payments center functions of traditional centers, others that concentrate on back office and data processing activities do not. Furthermore, unlike traditional centers, many of the new centers are hubs of neither commercial nor industrial activity.

There are several implications of this new landscape for localities seeking to remain or become financial centers. First, while the major centers of commercial, trading, and industrial activity are likely to tap large, national pools of funds that provide the basis for financial services activity, not all financial centers today are commercial and industrial centers. This is evidenced both by the growth of smaller financial centers such as Wilmington, and by the continued international vitality of London, a traditional financial center whose strength has endured despite the decline of Great Britain as a commercial and industrial power.[11]

Because certain types of financial centers no longer need to be located in commercial centers, a firm's cost considerations and business strategy come to play a more important role in determining the location of their operations. Of course, firms do not choose a location simply on the basis of cost, but seek a cost-effective location that enables the firm to operate efficiently. Along with costs, attributes of a location such as quality and availability of the local labor force, the sophistication of the technological infrastructure, and the regulatory environment help to determine its attractiveness. As the next section discusses in more detail, organizational changes within firms and industries are complicating these decisions. A good location for credit card processing, for example, is not necessarily a good location for advising and financing complex merger and acquisition activities.

Finally, the new landscape of financial centers allows state and local governments to pursue policies that can make their localities attractive places for the location of financial services activity. Such policies can be aimed at enhancing both the cost and quality attributes of a location. This does not mean that public policy efforts alone can create a financial center in any locality. Nor does it mean that highly attractive areas can induce all financial services activities to relocate out of traditional centers. But it does mean that economic development policy, broadly defined, can and will be used to compete for financial services activities and employment, a competition that is likely to intensify as the competition in financial services intensifies.

Organizational Changes in Financial Institutions

Financial markets and the organizational structure of financial services institutions have grown and changed in tandem. Competitive pressures and telecommunications and information technology development are modifying the traditional distinctions between a firm's front and back offices. These forces and other organizational trends are influencing firms' locational considerations.

The Traditional Organization: Front and Back Offices

The traditional organizational distinction between a firm's headquarters operations and administrative support units can be stylized as the difference between the front office and the back office. For financial services firms, two criteria have been traditionally important in classifying activities as either front office or back office: the degree to which that activity involves interaction with people and offices outside the firm, especially clients, and the degree to which that activity is routine.[12] Front office activities generally are non-routine in nature, often involving face-to-face contact with people outside of the firm, especially clients. For financial firms, these activities have included sales, analysis, product development, negotiations, legal services, public relations, and central management.

In contrast, back office activities traditionally have been defined as routine and largely clerical in nature, not requiring personal interaction with people outside the firm. The processing of transactions and the compiling and supplying of information to the front office are the two main categories of financial services back office work, including accounting services, check and security transactions processing, claims processing and payment, clearinghouse operations, and basic internal management support.

Data processing centers traditionally housed large, mainframe computers and essentially were large appendices of back offices. These centers needed to be close to the paper flow generated by the back office to process transactions, as the application of computer-based technologies concentrated on large, batch processing of transactions and other highly routine operations.

In recent years, this link has loosened. Developments in telecommunications and computer-based technologies now permit greater locational decoupling of a firm's front and back offices. In combination with other organizational changes, these developments are modifying traditional definitions of back and front office work and influencing locational decisions of firms.

Prior to advanced computer and telecommunications technology, huge volumes of paper were generated by and transferred between the front and back offices of financial firms. Because of this, back offices, even if organizationally distinct from headquarters, usually were located within or near the front office. But with the development and application of advanced technology, electronic data transfers have replaced much of the paper flow, making proximity to the front office a much less important criterion for back office location. In responding to competitive pressures, firms can locate their back offices simply where operating costs are lowest.

The application of these technologies has made back office operations more efficient, cost-effective, and "footloose." In contrast, the location of front offices is less affected by pure cost considerations and more by strategic concerns such as nearness to markets, clients, and support services. However, organizational changes are blurring the traditional front and back office functions, in ways that influence location choices.

The New Structure of Financial Services Firms

While technological development has created the ability to decouple front and back offices, it also has changed the division of activities, modifying the traditional distinction. The first applications of computer-based technologies were concerned with the automation of transactions processing in the back office, without much change in overall business organization. But successive waves of innovation focused on automating management reporting systems, introducing automated systems to the front office, and using computer technology to automate simpler decision-making procedures such as policy rating, credit rating, and program trading. These later waves of applications were made possible by computer systems operating on line, in real time, or interfaced directly with users.

Microcomputers and local area networks (LANs), linking microcomputers across various business functions, are two key innovations that have altered office work organization. Improvements in computer power and operational convenience are facilitating an interactive process where greater numbers of employees are able to access and manipulate a variety of data. Microcomputers provide a powerful work station for employees, while LANs facilitate "a myriad of linkages between personal and mainframe computers, data storage banks, printers and other forms of associated information technology." LANs and other technologies, such as voice and electronic mail, also ease internal communication within a firm.[13]

Microcomputers and LANs allow firms to integrate formerly discrete back office clerical tasks into unified procedures, enabling personnel to perform all of the steps required in an entire operation, such as claims processing. The increased linking and networking of mainframe computers and microcomputers facilitated by LANs also allows integration of diverse procedures within the firm. This provides greater direct access to support service information for front as well as back office staff. This decentralized access to data and the more intensive computer use on the part of all personnel is altering the activities of back and front offices.

As computer use intensifies, many firms have developed new data processing and information centers that are organizationally distinct from both front and back offices. These new data processing centers are "the focal point for data processing and serve as the warehouse for electronically storing and disseminating vast amounts of information."[14] For many financial firms, the traditional front office/back office dichotomy is being replaced with a tripartite distinction of front office/back office/data processing.

Due to the special physical and energy requirements of much of the new computer and telecommunications equipment, data processing centers often are locationally as well as organizationally distinct.

Moss and Dunau note that the large mainframe computers of data processing centers require buildings with "a capacity for heavy floor loads and areas of 40,000 square feet or more,"[15] features not usually found in older buildings of a city's central business district.

However, in many firms the location of data processing in proximity to either the front or back office remains as much a matter of corporate culture, particular company needs, or prior planning. For example, the extent to which data processing personnel are involved in a firm's strategic planning varies by firm. The greater such involvement, the greater the likelihood that the data processing center will be located near the front office.

The need for technical support services and skilled labor constrains a firm's location choices for its data processing center. Many organizations keep their data processing operations close to headquarters so that software applications personnel are close at hand, and executives can have quick access in case of a power failure or other unexpected service disruptions.

Before considering the effects of this new tripartite organization on location decisions, it is necessary to mention an additional technological impact on back office work. Decentralized access to vast amounts of data in combination with telecommunications advances has led to a much greater telephone-based contact with customers. As Moss and Dunau point out, "Such contact can be ex-ante to a transaction — i.e., the offering of 800 numbers for those interested in purchasing a life insurance policy — or ex poste — i.e., customer account servicing, trade confirmation, or credit verification."[16]

Because telephone contact does not require face-to-face proximity with customers, these activities often can be located most profitably in back offices. So, where back offices previously housed activities that did not involve client contact, they now can be sites of employment for workers whose jobs involve frequent client contact. An example is the Salt Lake City office of American Express, which services traveler's check customers 24 hours a day via its 800 telephone number. Both the increased contact with clients and more intensive computer use by back office personnel has made labor force needs more specialized and demanding, somewhat constraining firms' ability to locate simply wherever labor and other operating costs are lowest. These human resource needs related to technology and job reconfiguration will be increasingly important in the future.

Changes in the nature of back office work made possible by technological developments are occuring along with a trend toward more decentralized organization in many firms, especially banks. Some firms have decentralized their operations by product market, in which each operating unit services a particular line of business. Within each unit, front and back office functions are more closely tied together. Such units also have substantial autonomy, with functions like strategy development for the particular product market. The most noted example of such a decentralized structure is that of Citicorp, whose operations are organized into approximately 150 distinct product and service markets.

While technological change has made this type of decentralized organization possible, the competitive pressures facing financial firms have been the main stimulus to action. With the proliferation of new financial products, some of which blur traditional distinctions between banks, securities, and insurance companies, financial services firms must make more frequent strategic decisions on whether and how to enter new markets. Decentralized organizational structures, with clearly identifiable cost centers, aid firms in making strategic decisions, enabling them to keep better track of the costs and revenues of particular lines of business, new or old. The decentralized organization helps to properly allocate shared costs of large back offices that serve a variety of operating units, allowing firms to pursue distinct cost containment strategies for each unit. Analysts at McKinsey and Company, a management consulting firm, argue that understanding the costs of operating units is key to banks' successful strategizing in the new era of deregulation and competition.[17]

A decentralized structure also enables firms to choose locations that are most cost effective for particular lines of business. For example, Citicorp's decision to locate its credit card operations in South Dakota was motivated by the removal of interest rate ceilings on credit cards by the South Dakota legislature, as well as generally lower operating costs.

It is not yet clear how the trend toward decentralized organization will affect the decoupling of back offices from front offices. Some analysts have argued that the large-scale, centralized back office, locationally separate from firm headquarters, will become a thing of the past, replaced by smaller back office units attached to particular lines of business. Others suggest that the locational separation of back office work need not follow from organizational structure, and that it often will be profitable for firms to locate back office work in less costly environments often far removed from the front office.[18]

These factors are most important for large firms. While advanced computer and telecommunications technology has played a crucial role in facilitating back office decoupling, many firms lack the scale and resources to take full advantage of such technology. According to Moss and Dunau, small- and medium-size firms without the resources to fully internalize support functions and institute computer-based processing systems "still rely on a mix of electronic data flow and paper flow," which necessitates a closer proximity of the back and front offices.[19] Large firms which have the requisite resources and economies of scale to make these changes are still in the process of routinizing the older operations of their computer-based systems, and may face difficult organizational adjustments.

The desire of firms to cut costs in the face of ongoing competition has heightened the sensitivity of back office location to operating costs. At the same time, technological advances permit greater locational leeway, and internal organizational changes also encourage dispersion. Data processing centers, like back offices, are cost-sensitive and potentially footloose, but their location often is constrained by a firm's organizational support factors, the need for technical support, and the increased interaction of data processing personnel with the front office.

In contrast, intensified competition has made firms more keenly aware of the strategic importance of locational decisions. Retail-oriented firms are more likely to pursue organizational and locational decentralization while wholesale firms, who serve large clients, tend to be more concentrated in major financial centers in order to be near major financial markets.

Variations Among Sectors: Securities, Banking, and Insurance

Although financial institutions are crossing into and blending formerly discrete lines of business, the organizational and locational considerations discussed here still vary among banks, securities firms, and insurance companies. This variation is due in large part to continuing regulatory differences, and the way that different competitive strategies emerged.

Securities. Historically, securities firms have concentrated geographically in New York City, near the stock exchanges and the clearinghouse. Firms had to be located near the clearinghouse in order to facilitate the physical delivery and transfer of paper stock certificates. With electronic processing, however, the historic rationale for this concentration has eroded. It is now technically possible for firms to clear transactions at any location, allowing them to decouple and geographically disperse back offices and data processing.

However, due to inertia and the accumulation of other critical factors such as a skilled labor force, back office and data processing centers in the securities industry generally have remained geographically closest to headquarters. Moss and Brion's survey of the 17 top New York securities firms indicates that most have retained some or all of their back offices and their data processing centers within Manhattan, usually on the periphery or just outside of the financial district in lower Manhattan. (See Table 2.2.) Some firms, such as Morgan Stanley and Goldman, Sachs, have located back offices in nearby downtown Brooklyn.

In data processing, more dispersion is taking place. This movement is driven by cost factors, but also by the need for reliable telecommunications and computer services, and the development of centers to provide backup for primary operations. Many New York firms have moved or are now moving their data processing operations to New Jersey, most just across the Hudson River (e.g., Salomon Brothers to Rutherford) but some to the center of the state (e.g., First Boston to Princeton). With the location of its main data processing center in Dallas, only Dean Witter among the securities firms surveyed

TABLE 2.2. Location of Back Offices and Data Processing Centers of Top New York Securities Firms

Firm/ Headquarters Location[1]	Back Office Location(s)[1]	Data Processing Location(s)[1]
Merrill Lynch[2] World Financial Center	One Liberty Plaza 7 others in Manhattan 330 Madison Ave. Somerset, N.J.	Lower Manhattan Staten Island Central N.J. Jersey City, N.J.
Shearson Lehman Hutton[3] World Financial Center	17 Battery Place One Western Union Plaza 12 others in Manhattan West St.	390 Greenwich St.
Dean Witter Reynolds[4] World Trade Center	World Trade Center 110 Church St. 2 Broadway 120 Broadway 75 Varrick St.	World TradeCenter Dallas, Tex.
Prudential Bache One Seaport Plaza	100 Gold St. One Seaport Plaza 199 Water St.	100 Gold St.
Paine Webber 1285 Ave. of Americas	Weehawken, N.J.	Weehawken, N.J.
Drexel Burnham Lambert 60 Broad St.	2 Broadway 25 Broadway 60 Broad St.	Weehawken, N.J.[5] 3 in Manhattan
Kidder Peabody Group 10 Hanover Square	2 Broadway	120 Broadway
Smith Barney 1345 Ave. of Americas	333 W. 34th St.	333 W. 34th St.
Thomson McKinnon Financial Square	Financial Square	Financial Square
Bear, Stearns 245 Park Ave.	2 Broadway Hanover Square	Whippany, N.J. 245 Park Ave. 131 Varrick St. 55 Water St.

(Continues)

TABLE 2.2 (Continued)

Firm/ Headquarters Location[1]	Back Office Location(s)[1]	Data Processing Location(s)[1]
Goldman, Sachs 85 Broad St.	55 Water St. 85 Broad St. Brooklyn Heights	85 Broad St.
Salomon Bros. One New York Plaza	2 New York Plaza 55 Water St.	Rutherford, N.J.
Morgan Stanley 1251 Ave. of Americas	Brooklyn Heights 55 Water St.	Brooklyn Heights
Donaldson, Lufkin & Jenrette 140 Broadway	Jersey City, N.J.	Jersey City, N.J.
First Boston Park Avenue Plaza	World Trade Center	World Trade Center Princeton, N.J.[6]
Oppenheimer World Financial Center	World Financial Center Varrick St.	World Financial Center
Gruntal 14 Wall St.	14 Wall St. 33 Water St.	14 Wall St.

[1] Street addresses are given for Manhattan locations, where known.

[2] Merrill Lynch's main back office facility is at One Liberty Plaza, and the regional center for the New York region is at 330 Madison Avenue. Thirteen other regional centers are located around the U.S. Merrill Lynch does not want the exact locations of its data processing facilities known for security reasons. The Staten Island facility is under construction, while the Jersey City facility, planned for a 1992 opening, will include both back office and data processing operations.

[3] Shearson Lehman is constructing a new facility on West Street to consolidate all back office activities, except the legal department which will remain at headquarters.

[4] Dean Witter's mainframe computer is in Dallas; data is processed nightly and sent back to the World Trade Center back office/data processing center for printing and distribution.

[5] Planned 1989-90.

[6] Planned.

Source: Adapted from Mitchell L. Moss and Joanne G. Brion, "Back Office and Data Processing Facilities of Securities Firms and Commercial Banks in New York State," Urban Research Center, New York University, New York, August 1988, Table 1.

has chosen a location far from Manhattan. The retail orientation of Dean Witter as a discount brokerage, especially in its linkage with Sears, was likely a factor in this location decision.

Moss and Brion's survey also reveals that many firms have multiple sites for back office work. Merrill Lynch and Dean Witter have nine and six back office locations, respectively,[20] reflecting organizational decentralization in some firms along with redundancy for security.

The importance of New York exchanges and markets all but ensures that securities firms will maintain important front office activities in New York, though these are likely to be complemented by front offices in other major domestic and international financial centers. Securities firms are attempting to compete in a deregulated environment that has allowed new market entrants to expand services and offer new products. Many major firms now are located in midtown Manhattan to be closer to clients.

The proliferation of new products also has been fueled by new computer and telecommunications systems that facilitate global integration of markets and 24-hour trading. Though one response to increased competition is the relocation of back office operations to lower-cost areas, firms must ensure that these functions operate smoothly to accommodate the tremendous increase in trading volume and to provide market data to brokers. The concern with the adequacy of back office and data processing functions in the securities industry has constrained removal of these facilities far from the front office. According to Moss and Dunau, concern over adequacy follows from the growth of new financial services and offerings because "with computer operations and product offerings in a dynamic state, the majority of back office operations are remaining in the same metropolitan areas as corporate headquarters."[21]

The recent slump in the securities industry, attributed largely to continuing investor caution in the wake of the 1987 stock market collapse, has heightened concerns over the industry's future. The implications for location decisions are not clear. The slump has increased firms' desires to control cost and could motivate further back office relocations to lower-cost areas. On the other hand, given the high cost of moving a financial services office, many of the weaker firms may not be in a position to undergo any costly relocations in the near future.

Banking. The organizational changes and locational decisions of commercial banks must be viewed in the context of the deregulation that has affected the industry in recent years. These changes have opened more competition by banks in traditional and new markets, with significant impact on their organizational and location strategies.

A key feature of the regulatory changes was the phased removal of interest rate ceilings, completed by April 1986, legislated by the Federal Depository Institutions Act of 1982. The Act enabled banks to offer interest rates that are competitive with high-yield money market accounts previously only offered by brokerage houses and other nonbank financial institutions. In this new competitive environment, product development and market expansion have become important ways in which banks compete with the attempts of other institutions to encroach on their market share in consumer services. Banks also have had to respond to securitization, which has posed a competitive threat to banks' commercial and industrial loan activity.

Recent merger and acquisition activity among banks has been fueled by a desire both to control costs through economies of scale and to capture new markets by expanding geographic reach. The latter goal in particular was aided by the June 1985 Supreme Court ruling that ratified interstate banking mergers within regions sanctioned by state legislatures. While money center institutions used bank holding companies to extend their reach across state lines, smaller, regionally-oriented banks have been growing and consolidating, sometimes into superregionals whose size enables them to compete with money center banks in terms of product offerings and capital base. Of course, technological developments have helped facilitate the geographic expansion of banks. They also have enabled banks to market their more sophisticated products and services outside of the main office.

The processes of consolidation, geographic expansion, and product development of commercial banks have different organizational and locational implications for money center banks than for smaller banks. Because money center banks traditionally serve national and international markets as well as local customers, their headquarters, almost by definition, have been located in large cities with national and international clientele and markets. When ranked in order of their assets, six of the ten largest U.S. commercial banks at the end of 1987 were headquartered in New York, two in San Francisco, and one each in Chicago and Los Angeles.[22]

These banks, like others, are under increased competitive pressure to exploit the possibilities of new computer and telecommunications technology, reducing costs by locating back office and data processing facilities in the least costly sites that are consistent with other strategic needs. In practice, the money center banks generally have not located these facilities far from headquarters. Moss and Dunau report that the back offices and data processing sites of money center banks generally are within a 60 mile radius of the bank's headquarters.[23] Moss and Brion's more limited survey of five large New York bank holding companies, including one British-owned bank, confirms this finding, as shown in Table 2.3.

Most money center banks have multiple back office sites. For example, Chemical Bank has a number of facilities that house both back offices and data processing operations; four of these, including the largest, are located in Manhattan, two in New Jersey, one on Long Island and one in Dutchess County (upstate), New York.[24] Manufacturers Hanover also has two back office and three data processing facilities, all of which are in Manhattan, and they are reportedly considering consolidating these into one location.[25] In contrast, Morgan Guaranty has a back office operation in Delaware, and the San Francisco-based Bank of America has facilities in southern California.

The back office functions of money center banks most subject to relocation are those related to retail operations, especially check processing and credit card operations. These operations are among the most standardized and were the first to be affected by early computerization involving batch processing. Because they are high volume and routine in nature, easily separable from other bank operations, and involve little direct client contact, these retail operations can be located away from headquarters most easily. In the past, this

TABLE 2.3 Location of Back Offices and Data Processing Centers of Top Commercial Bank Holding Companies

Firm/ Headquarters Location	Back Office Location(s)[1]	Data Processing Location(s)[1]
Citicorp		
New York	111 Wall Street	111 Wall Street
	Huntington, N.Y.[2]	20 Exchange Place
	Sioux Falls, S.D.	Multiple national locations
BankAmerica Corp.		
San Francisco	San Francisco	San Francisco
	Concord, Calif.[3]	Los Angeles
	Orange, Calif.	Concord, Calif.
	Brea, Calif.	
	West Cohena, Calif.	
Chase Manhattan Corp.		
New York	90 William Street	1 New York Plaza
	Lake Success, N.Y.[2]	Downtown Brooklyn[4]
	80 Pine Street	
	42 Trinity Place	
	59 Maiden Lane	
J.P. Morgan & Co.		
New York	New Castle, Del.	23 Wall Street
	23 Wall Street	New Castle, Del.
	30 West Broadway	
Chemical Banking Corp.		
New York	55 Water Street	Same as back offices
	Jericho, N.Y.[2]	
	95 Wall Street	
	Somerset, N.J.	
	52 Broadway	
	919 Third Avenue	
	Secaucus, N.J.	
	Pawling, N.J.	
Manufacturers Hanover		
New York	340 West Street	4 New York Plaza Corp.
	130 John Street	160 Water Street
	Hicksville, N.Y.[2]	55 Water Street
		450 W. 33rd Street
Security Pacific Corp.		
Los Angeles	Los Angeles	Brea, Calif.
	Cypress, Calif.	Glendale, Calif.
	Other So. Calif. locations	

(Continues)

TABLE 2.3 (Continued)

Firm/ Headquarters Location	Back Office Location(s)[1]	Data Processing Location(s)[1]
Bankers Trust Corp. New York	16 Wall Street 4 Albany Street	1 Bankers Trust Plaza Jersey City, N.J.
First Chicago Corp. Chicago	Elgin, Ill. Nassau Co., N.Y. [2] 1 North Dearborn 1 North State Street 1 First National Plaza	525 West Monroe 1 First National Plaza

[1] Street addresses are given for Manhattan locations, where known; street addresses for First Chicago locations are for Chicago.

[2] Long Island suburb of New York City.

[3] Suburb of San Francisco.

[4] Planned.

Sources: Adapted from Mitchell L. Moss and Andrew Dunau, "The Location of the Back Offices: Emerging Trends and Development Patterns," Sylvan Lawrence Research and Data Center, New York University, New York, 1986, Exhibit III; and Mitchell L. Moss and Joanne G. Brion, "Back Office and Data Processing Facilities of Securities Firms and Commercial Banks in New York State," Urban Research Center, New York University, New York, August 1988, Table 2.

usually has meant only a suburban location, not one very far from the front office. However, with the geographic expansion of banking nationally and improvements in technological sophistication and reliability, the location horizons of banking operations will expand in the future.

Among money center banks, Citicorp stands out in exploiting locational possibilities, reflecting the above-mentioned strategic decentralization of its operations. About half of Citicorp's square footage of U.S. operations space is outside of the New York area. As Citicorp's operations are decentralized, so too are its data processing activities. Each data processing site is the most cost-effective alternative for each business market, and such sites include Las Vegas, Nev.; Tampa, Fla.; Sioux Falls, S.D.; and Hagerstown, Md.

The organizational and locational problems facing regional commercial banks as competition intensifies differ from those facing the money center banks. Local banks often do not have the resources or scale to afford or justify the computer and data processing investments that would enable them to offer existing products and services at costs as low as those offered by large banks. Nor are they able to develop and market the range of new products and services offered by money center banks and other financial institutions. These problems become particularly acute as deregulation removes geographical constraints on money center bank expansion.

The consolidation of local banks through mergers and acquisitions has been one means by which some regional institutions have attempted to gain competitive economies of scale. Another means has been the establishment by local banks of "correspondent" relationships with larger regional banks in which the smaller local bank utilizes the back office operations and data processing services of the regional bank while remaining independent. Check clearing, wire transfers, currency dispensing, and bond coupon collection are some major functions that can be performed by larger regional banks for their correspondents. The relationship enables the local banks to offer more specialized products such as money market accounts and credit cards.

Moss and Brion's survey of back office and data processing facilities of financial services firms documents this phenomenon in New York State. As they point out, "Key Services, an affiliate of KeyCorp, handles data services for all of Key Bank's offices and branches, six New York State banks, and 15 non-bank financial service companies."[26] Additionally, Key Services serves about 60 correspondent banks, thrifts, and credit unions, all of which send data to Key Services via Key Bank facilities. Buffalo-based Merchants and Traders Bank offers services to about 40 correspondent banks at its back office and data processing site in suburban Williamsville. Norstar Data Services, an affiliate of Fleet/Norstar, has several data processing sites around the state that serve as "capture" sites for the banks in their areas. From the capture sites, information is forwarded to Albany where it is processed and then transmitted back to the local capture site for printing and microfiching. Moss and Brion describe the network of back office and data processing facilities that service the upstate and Long Island regions as a "hierarchy," and they argue that the trend is to continued centralization in the goal of achieving greater economies of scale.[27]

Insurance . The insurance industry was the first major sector of the financial services industry to exploit the technological potential for decoupling back office work from company headquarters. One reason is that, unlike banking, there were no Federal regulatory restrictions to prevent insurance companies from operating in many states. And, unlike securities, the insurance industry is not compelled to locate near a major clearinghouse or market. In fact, insurance sales and customer services activities are widely dispersed due to the nature of their markets.

The early decoupling evident in insurance also was due to the nature of much of the industry's back office work. Routine claims processing could be achieved by batch processing and other computer applications available in the 1970s.

It also was in the 1970s that changing economic conditions began to make insurance companies more sensitive to the costs of their operations. High inflation and interest rates led many life insurance policyholders to borrow against their policies at low interest rates offered through their policies' savings features, in order to reinvest the funds in money market accounts. As one report notes, policyholders also "shifted from whole life to term insurance, which offers more flexibility and higher rates of return on investment."[28] Many large companies "circumvented insurers by purchasing actuarial underwriting services from insurers and setting up so-called captive insurance firms in which funds needed to cover risks were pooled," a self-insuring approach that "allowed corporate customers to retain both the management of their funds and the returns on such funds."[29] These developments increased and/or resulted in the loss of market, and thus squeezed the insurance industry's profits.

The resulting pressures on profit margins and liquidity encouraged insurance companies to control costs by moving claims processing and other operational activities out of company headquarters into large-scale, semi-autonomous regional centers, whose locations were chosen on a least-cost basis. One company, anonymously profiled by Noyelle, established six regional centers — in Fresno, Calif.; Des

Moines, Iowa; Charlotte, N.C.; Columbus, Ohio; Colorado Springs, Colo.; and Milford, Conn. — for claims processing.[30] For insurance companies headquartered in high-cost cities, the money saved by moving many activities out of headquarters was quite substantial.

In recent years, new developments in computer and telecommunications technology plus deregulation have facilitated further locational and organizational change in the insurance industry. With deregulation breaking down many traditional barriers within financial services, banks and brokerage firms have begun offering insurance products. In this new competitive environment, insurance firms have countered by offering and aggressively marketing new and non-traditional products. For example, many insurance companies now offer products which combine savings and credit features, such as universal and variable life insurance and policy loans. Similarly, various types of hybrid savings/life protection policies have proliferated. Insurance agents have had to become highly knowledgable about a wide variety of financial products in order to compete with the insurance products offered by banks and security firms.

In recent years, advances in telecommunications and new, multi-task on-line computer technologies have been critical in allowing both independent agents and insurance carrier employees located across the country greater access to information and enhanced policy-writing capabilities. In general, much of the work formerly undertaken in insurance company front offices has been decentralized, as shown by the greater growth nationwide of employment in insurance agencies relative to direct employment by insurance carriers.

For example, Noyelle's profile of a large insurance company indicated that from 1971 to 1983, employment distribution shifted from 59 percent in the home office and 41 percent in the field to 37 percent and 63 percent, respectively.[31] In New York, Department of Labor statistics indicate that from 1965 to 1987, employment by insurance carriers declined 5 percent while employment of insurance agents increased 84 percent. If measured by direct premiums written by New York-based life and property/casualty insurers, the volume of business in real terms has risen by 167 percent in the same period.[32]

More sophisticated computer applications also are having several impacts on back office work. First, as new applications help decentralize policy marketing, data processing in most firms has become increasingly centralized. This underscores that data processing centers in many insurance firms have become increasingly important to service policies and transmit information over a wide area, especially to highly dispersed agents and officers.[33]

Second, there appears to be a trend in many firms toward consolidating field office operations. This is the case of the company profiled by Noyelle, which cut the number of its field offices in half during the early 1980s.[34] For products like medical insurance, the company employed a substantial share of processing clerks in the regional field offices, but the consolidation of field offices indicates that processing work has shifted to regional processing centers.

Third, the trend of back office dispersion from central cities where insurance companies are headquartered is likely to continue. Moss and Dunau's list of the back office and data processing centers of the ten largest life insurance companies — four are based in New York City, three in Hartford, and one each in Boston, Newark, and Milwaukee — indicates a great variance in the geographical dispersion of back offices, though in general there is greater decoupling in insurance than in banking or securities. (See Table 2.4.) For example, Teachers Insurance and Annuity Association (T.I.A.A.) conducts all its front office, back office, and data processing work in three midtown Manhattan office buildings, while Hartford-based Traveler's conducts back office work in 20 to 30 regional offices throughout the country.[35]

An extreme arrangement of decoupling, one that shows the potential for global geographic dispersion, was recently instituted by New York Life in response to high operating costs and tight labor markets in the New York area. Since July 1988, the insurer has been sending claims via overnight air freight to Ireland for processing. The processed claim information in turn is shipped back via a leased trans-Atlantic telecommunications line to a back office site in New Jersey that prints checks and/or drafts a letter explaining the benefits. New York Life anticipates a 25 percent savings on operating costs.[36]

TABLE 2.4 Location of Back Offices and Data Processing Centers of Top Life Insurance Companies

Firm/HQ Location	Back Office Location(s)*	Data Processing Location(s)*
Prudential of America		
Newark	Parsippany, N.J. Woodbridge, N.J. New Providence, N.J.	Roseland, N.J.
Metropolitan Life		
New York	Madison Avenue 2 Penn Plaza	Greenville, S.C. Scranton, Pa. Wichita, Kans.
Equitable Life		
New York	Atlanta 2 Penn Plaza 60 Hudson Street	Leonia, N.J. Ft. Worth, Tex. Easton, Pa.
Aetna Life		
Hartford, Conn.	Elmira, N.Y. Fall River, Mass. Lowell, Mass.	Hartford, Conn.
New York Life		
New York	51 Madison Avenue	Clinton, N.J.
John Hancock Mutual		
Boston	Boston	Boston Marlboro, Mass.
Travelers		
Hartford, Conn.	20 to 30 regional offices around the country	Norcross, Ga. Hartford, Conn.
Connecticut General Life		
Bloomfield, Conn.	Multiple national offices	Windsor, Conn. Vorhees, N.J. Thornton, La.
T.I.A.A.		
New York	730 & 750 Third Avenue 485 Lexington Avenue	730 Third Avenue
Northwestern Mutual Life		
Milwaukee	Milwaukee	Milwaukee

* Street addresses are for Manhattan.

Source: Mitchell L. Moss and Andrew Dunau, "The Location of the Back Offices: Emerging Trends and Development Patterns," Sylvan Lawrence Research and Data Center, New York University, New York, 1986, Exhibit IV. Reprinted by permission.

Finally, new computer applications and systems may be raising the requisite skills of clerical workers, at least in some firms. Multi-machine systems that operate on-line, in real time, and perform a variety of tasks enable skilled clerks to process claims that previously were handled only by professional examiners. The need for a skilled labor force will in turn constrain the choice of back offices or processing sites simply on the basis of minimizing operating costs.

However, some observers have stressed that the implementation of new technologies within the insurance industry varies greatly with respect to the effects on the workplace. One labor economist notes that while some firms have created multi-activity, skilled clerical jobs by integrating job tasks, others have increasingly centralized clerical operations in processing centers that employ many part-time data entry clerks.[37]

Dimensions of Competitiveness for Financial Centers

In the increasingly competitive world of financial services, the attributes that define a financial center are not limited to characteristics that make a locality attractive for business. As noted above, a historical presence of commercial activity, or of a key market, such as a major stock exchange, or the concentration of investors and borrowers for generating pools of capital, have all provided support for different financial centers. In these cases, financial firms may be compelled to locate at least part of their operations in the financial center, irrespective of the center's relative costs, labor supply, or infrastructure. Synergies that develop from the geographic concentration of many firms also are important attributes of financial centers.

Nonetheless, the location decisions of firms are greatly influenced by the relative attractiveness of different localities. Many activities of financial services firms need not be located in major financial centers. As noted before, technological and organizational developments enable firms to separate their back office and data processing operations from headquarters, making costs more important in location decisions. Also, firms with strong retail orientation are both organizationally and locationally decentralized to serve dispersed markets.

Cities and states with relatively attractive costs, a high quality labor force and infrastructure, and intelligent regulation will be well positioned to compete successfully for financial services markets, firms, and jobs. Cities and states cannot instantly develop the attributes that make a locality a major financial center. However, they can enhance their attractiveness through implementing policies in the four dimensions of competitiveness: location costs and advantages, labor force and human resources, telecommunications and technology, and regulation and taxation.

These dimensions are not the only factors that influence a firm's decision to expand or relocate operations, but they are the most important that can be influenced by public policy. Communities that effectively compete with some mixture of these factors can develop, attract, and maintain a critical mass of firms and activities. This critical mass may in turn provide the synergies that are attributes of financial centers, even if the community was not a traditional center. For their part, traditional centers must concentrate on these factors to maintain their position in an increasingly competitive environment for financial services location.

Location Costs and Advantages

A key factor figuring prominently into a company's decision-making is the costs of doing business. Office rents, real estate prices, construction costs, local wages, energy and telecommunications costs, and taxes are all aspects of an area's costs of doing business. Of course, those locations where business costs are relatively low will be preferred by a firm considering a relocation of an existing office or an expansion into a new operation, all other things being equal.

But it is important to emphasize that in most decisions, all else is rarely, if ever, equal. A commercial bank whose strategy concentrates on taking deposits from and lending to major corporations is compelled to locate front office operations in one of the handful of metropolitan areas with many corporate headquarters. Similarly, the data processing operations of a firm must be situated in an area where the local labor force has the requisite technical skills and where the telecommunications infrastructure is sophisticated and reliable. For example, a firm operating a 24-hour 800 telephone number to serve credit card users will locate this back office facility in an area in which disruptions to service due to climate are relatively infrequent. Finally, firms dependent upon timely data processing and telecommunications may choose to locate data centers in locations served by alternative power grids in order to safeguard against local power failure.

In short, it is difficult to isolate cost from non-cost considerations, especially when considering human resources and telecommunications. Those two factors, along with regulations and taxes, will be discussed later. The discussion here focuses on non-tax factors that relate solely to the costs of doing business.

Pure cost considerations often have more bearing on the relocation of existing operations than on decisions to expand into a new operation or line of business. Because expansions usually are a part of a firm's strategic plan to move into a new market and/or geographic area, considerations such as access to markets and clients, public sector responsiveness, and local technological sophistication and integrity figure prominently into the location decisions of expanding firms. However, for existing operations, cost considerations often are the key factor motivating a relocation, especially of a back office or data processing facility in which operations have been somewhat routinized.

Pure cost considerations also are less important in decisions regarding the location of front offices. Key findings from Cushman and Wakefield's 1987 survey of 400 chief executives at financial and nonfinancial firms regarding headquarters location decisions reflect this, and are presented in Table 2.5. For example, the survey found that only 9 percent of those interviewed deemed "low occupancy cost" as an "absolutely essential" criterion for a headquarters location. This compares with 36 percent and 24 percent terming "ample and functional space" and "easy access to markets, customers, or clients," respectively, as absolutely essential. Furthermore, while 53 percent considered occupancy costs at least a very important criterion, only 40 percent said it was a factor in their actual relocation decisions.[38]

With advancements in computer and telecommunications technologies allowing decoupling from front offices, and increased

TABLE 2.5 Survey of Corporate Executives

(a) Ranking of Criteria in Headquarters Location

Criterion	"Very Important" or "Absolutely Essential" (%)	"Absolutely Essential" (%)
Ample and functional space	95	36
A good quality of life for employees	74	14
Room to expand	72	19
Easy access to markets, customers, or clients	65	24
Low occupancy cost	53	9
A good business climate in terms of state and local taxes and regulation	50	12
Locating in a community that projects a favorable image on your organization	50	11
Proximity to well-trained pink or blue collar workers	40	7
A good social climate for people like yourself	38	6
Proximity to industry's best professionals	37	5
Proximity to colleges or universities for services such as business support, consulting, and continuing education	15	2
A prestigious address	14	3
Proximity to homes of senior executives	14	1

(b) Factors in Actual Relocation Decisions

Criterion	Was a Factor (%)	Was a "Crucial" Factor (%)
Larger or more functional space	90	84
More room to expand	85	72
A more favorable image	46	22
Lower occupancy costs	40	24
A better quality of life for employees	36	16
Better access to markets, customers, or clients	35	20

(Continues)

TABLE 2.5 (Continued)

(b) Factors in Actual Relocation Decisions

Criterion	Was a Factor (%)	Was a "Crucial" Factor (%)
Major change in strategic direction of organization	31	22
An organizational restructuring	21	14
Proximity to homes of senior executives	19	9
Interest in changing culture of organization	16	6
Better proximity to well-trained pink or blue collar workers	12	4
A merger or acquisition	11	8
A better social climate for people like yourself	11	3
A better business climate in terms of state and local taxes and regulation	10	5
A more prestigious address	25	7
Economic development incentives	22	11
Promotion by business development organization	10	2
Better proximity to industry's best professionals	9	2
The appointment of a new chief executive	7	3
Proximity to college or universities for services such as business support, consulting, and continuing education	6	1
Referral by executive of another company	5	3

Source: "Headquarters Relocation," *Business America Real Estate Monitor*, Study No. 871014, Cushman and Wakefield, Inc., October-November 1987, Tables 2-1 and 2-5. Reprinted by permission.

competition among firms and sectors, financial services firms now must consider relocating existing back office and data processing operations to lower-cost areas. The non-labor components of business costs — office rents, telecommunications costs, energy rates, real estate and commercial rent taxes — often are linked together into a composite measure of "occupancy costs" that is considered along with wages and other taxes when firms evaluate the costs of doing business in a particular area.

Among the components of occupancy costs, the variation in office rents within the U.S. is particularly great. For example, at $39.90 per square foot, rent of prime office space in midtown or downtown Manhattan during the second quarter of 1989 was nearly double that of Atlanta ($21.30 per square foot).[39] Also, rents in central business districts often are 20 to 50 percent higher than those of nearby suburbs. For example, second quarter 1989 rents of prime office space in Pittsburgh's central business district averaged $18.80 per square foot, compared to rents from $8.00 to $20.00 in non-central business district areas.[40]

It has been estimated that the typical back office employee occupies 150 to 160 square feet of office space while managerial and professional staff members each occupy 210 to 220 square feet.[41] On the basis of these estimates, a firm moving to a site that is $10 per square foot cheaper in office rent saves about $1,500 per back office employee and $2,100 per professional or managerial employee, annual amounts which represent a considerable portion of non-labor costs. Indeed, 58 percent of surveyed firms who moved their headquarters out of San Francisco cited "cost of space" as a factor influencing their relocation decisions, a factor cited far more often than any other.[42]

It should be noted that data on office rents in different locations is based upon current market prices. Many firms in higher-priced central business districts are currently enjoying below-market rates dictated by long-term leases. Thus, the incentive for firms to relocate is not as great in the short run as office rent differentials would suggest. But as leases come due, these costs become a major concern, and cities and states should monitor lease patterns of their major financial firms to provide "early warning" of potential relocations.

Electrical energy costs to commercial users also vary greatly in the U.S. Utility costs in New York City, 10.5 cents per kilowatt-hour, for example, are nearly double that of Dallas (5.35 cents per kilowatt-hour).[43] Differences in state and local taxes on energy contribute greatly to the variance of energy costs throughout the U.S.

The significance of energy as a percentage of total business costs in financial services has grown greatly with the increased use of computer technologies and the introduction of a 24-hour trading day. The intensive use of new computer equipment, especially in back office and data processing centers, necessitates an increased use of electricity to both operate and cool the equipment. One analyst estimated that the electrical energy requirements of computer-intensive financial firms range from 10-12 watts per square foot. Lighting accounts for only 20 percent of this energy need, while the remaining 80 percent is split between computer use and cooling requirements.[44] The growing use of LANs, private telephone systems, and other telecommunications equipment also adds to office energy loads. The 24-hour operations of many front office, back office, and data processing activities of financial services firms further increases energy costs.

The increased significance of energy costs has made financial services firms more keenly evaluate utility rates when making location decisions. Firms' greater dependence on computer services also has made the reliability of the energy source more important as a locational criterion. In many respects, reliability is more critical than cost, for firms cannot afford to be vulnerable to disruptions of service, especially in complex or risky markets or positions. The concern about energy reliability is so great that some firms now are engaging in "energy arbitrage," choosing to locate various facilities in several power grids to protect against the failure of any single energy source. Alternatively, firms may contract with independent data processing companies, located in different power grids, to serve as the backup or "data recovery" sites in case of power failure. Moss and Dunau point out that "Comdisco offers data recovery services for information intensive firms located around the country; their disaster recovery sites are presently located in Wood Dale, Ill., Lodi, Calif., Grand Prairie, Tex., Carlstadt, N.J., and Cranford, N.J."[45]

Another component of financial services firms' costs of doing business is telecommunications costs, as technological advances have intensified greatly the use of telecommunications. The telecommunications infrastructure of a firm, defined in the broadest sense, is comprised of all equipment and networks that facilitate the transfer of information, including both voice and data. In a 1988 survey of telecommunications spending by 1,500 organizations, banking and finance led the 12 industry groups surveyed with an average annual budget of over $17,600,000.[46] A recent study prepared by Coopers and Lybrand for New York State estimated that direct and indirect telecommunications costs amounted to 20 percent of non-labor inputs in the financial services sector.[47]

More detailed information on telecommunications expenditures and issues is presented below in the discussion of technology as a dimension of competitiveness. It is important to note here that much of the amount spent on telecommunications by firms is for equipment and other costs that do not vary significantly by location. For example, the 1988 survey found that less than 40 percent of a typical telecommunications budget of a financial services company is accounted for by line charges.[48] Since only a portion of telecommunications expenditures can be attributed to installation and monthly service charges by local telephone utility companies, locational differences only partially influence the telecommunications component of business costs.

As with energy, the availability, quality, and reliability of telecommunications service in a locality are at least as important as price in determining the relative attractiveness of a potential area. In fact, concern for reliability and availability, as well as for cost and control, has motivated the large financial services firms to partially "bypass" public networks local and long distance telephone companies provide by installing private networks. For example, Citibank has its own fiber optic network in New York City, and is developing its own extensive satellite network. Similarly, both Merrill Lynch and Prudential-Bache are installing VSATs (very small aperture terminal satellite systems) to create bypass networks.[49]

The cost motivations driving bypass systems are twofold. First, many firms believe that despite substantial upfront installation costs, there is a favorable payback of private networks versus telephone company circuits. Second, bypass systems enable companies to better plan and control their own telecommunications costs, sheltering firms from uncertain rate and tariff charges by regulated telephone companies, and making cost increases from incremental traffic growth more predictable.

Labor costs are the final major component of business costs. Information on relative wage levels for office workers in different metropolitan areas reveals substantial variation. For example, the average 1987 pay of clerical workers in nonmanufacturing industries in the Los Angeles area was nearly 20 percent higher than that of clericals in Pittsburgh.[50] Employee compensation and benefits usually account for at least half of all non-interest, pre-tax expenses of financial firms,[51] and wage and salary cost differentials, tied in part to housing and other costs of living, are an important influence on firms' location decisions.

As with the other variable cost factors of energy, telecommunications, and taxes, the influence of labor costs on location interacts with, and sometimes can be overshadowed by, a concern for quality. In this case, firms are more interested in comparing productivity to wages in different areas rather than wages alone. A firm will not be attracted to a low-wage area if the local labor supply cannot provide the level and types of skills it needs.

A final cost influence on location decisions is an indirect one, affecting both cost and availability of labor. This is the local cost of living, including the food, clothing, housing, transportation, and other costs facing residents. In conjunction with non-cost factors such as transportation, crime, school quality, and housing availability, local costs of living help determine the quality of life available to a firm's employees, professional and clerical alike. In its survey of 400 firms, Cushman and Wakefield reported that 74 percent termed "good quality of life for employees" an "absolutely essential" or "very important" criterion for headquarters location.[52]

In localities where the cost of living is high, and/or other non-cost aspects of the quality of life are less desirable, firms may find it difficult to attract and hold qualified skilled labor and professional employees unless they offer higher wages and salaries. High living costs, particularly for housing, may be prohibitive for clerical and even some middle management staff. And non-cost factors of a locality, such as weather, poor transportation, and crime, may make it difficult for a firm to attract and retain its labor force, avoid operational disruption, and maintain productivity by reducing absenteeism or labor turnover.

Labor Force and Human Resources

Human resources are central to the operations of financial services. Firms require sophisticated professionals to structure complex deals, gauge and manage credit and market risk, keep abreast of industry trends and innovations, execute business strategies, and control costs. Skilled data processing and other technical staff are vital to the development, maintenance, and exploitation of the increasingly costly, complicated, but indispensible telecommunications infrastructure of a financial firm. Financial firms also are dependent upon large numbers of office workers who deal directly with the public, who use advanced computer technologies to perform non-routine clerical tasks, and who provide support for professional talent.

In the new, dynamic, and competitive context, a quality workforce is a major competitive advantage. The importance of the quality of local human resources as a dimension of competitiveness for financial firms cannot be underestimated. A firm wishing to establish a new operation or relocate an existing one will not consider a locality if it cannot find the labor supply it needs there, or induce its current employees to relocate, no matter how attractive the proposed site is with respect to other dimensions of competitiveness.

When considering the attractiveness of a locality with respect to human resources, it is necessary to distinguish between the different functions of a financial firm. While skilled clerical employees are an important part of a firm's front office, a sophisticated professional staff is the essential component. Successful back office operations rely heavily upon the skills and productivity of clerical workers and are less dependent upon large numbers and diverse types of professional staff. Finally, data processing centers need skilled technical workers to function. Of course, an area with an abundance of high-quality professional, clerical, and technical staff is very attractive for all operations of financial firms. But other areas whose only human resource quality is a skilled clerical labor supply may be highly suitable for the location of a firm's back office.

The attractiveness of different areas with respect to human resources varies within the United States, but often in contradictory ways. Major financial centers, such as New York and Los Angeles have by far the strongest agglomerations of professional talent. But they are also among the most expensive places to live, and increasingly do not have strong labor forces for many entry-level positions. In contrast, the quality of the labor force in other areas is highly desirable for back office activities, but labor markets in these areas often are too tight to ensure a steady supply of employees.

Skills for all types of financial services jobs have been changing in recent years. With the development, use, and sale of a greater range of products and financial instruments due to convergence, and the increased emphasis by firms on sales and customer relations, personnel in both the front and back office must have a broader knowledge of financial services products and markets. For example, tellers in many major commercial banks are expected to market new products and services to customers, reflecting a merging of clerical and sales functions. Similarly, insurance agents must be knowledgable of a variety of financial service products, as well as traditional insurance products, in order to offer customers specialized services. Skills in customer assistance, sales, group interaction, and communication have become highly valued attributes of financial services employees.

The increased application of computer technology in both the front and back office generally has motivated a work organization that features a greater integration of different processes and has broadened the span of tasks performed by any one employee. In turn, the skills needed are increasingly higher and more varied than before, especially by clericals. A study prepared for the Private Industry Council of New York City by The Labor Institute on the impact of computer technology on clerical worker skills in banking, insurance, and law concluded,

"Computer-mediated work requires skills which are more conceptual, abstract and interactive. This is true for the entry-level computer jobs as well as for the new, more highly skilled computer-related clerical positions that are being created."[53]

Taken together, both convergence and technologically-induced work reorganization have radically altered the nature of skills required in today's financial services work environment. Table 2.6 presents a summary of one analysis of the changing nature of skills needed by workers in banks and insurance companies. For all levels of personnel, there has been a general broadening of responsibilities, necessitating a greater capacity to deal with non-routine tasks in an ever-changing environment.

Upper-tier professionals not only have developed and distributed a widening array of more complex financial products, but they also have become more involved in setting strategic goals as well as in managing. For middle-level personnel, the importance of specialized skills has been eclipsed by an increased need for a more flexible, system-wide understanding of the firm's operations and a greater capacity to take initiatives. For example, account representatives in brokerage houses trade in a far greater number of markets than ever before. Finally, lower-skilled jobs involving routine clerical, data entry, and data processing tasks are beginning to shrink or disappear in the financial services industry. In some cases, this is due to the mechanization of certain tasks, such as envelope opening of credit card payments. But in others it is due to work reorganization. An example of the latter can be seen in insurance claims processing. When processing is reorganized to integrate formerly discrete, sequential tasks into continuous processing, clerical workers need a broader knowledge of the entire process.[54] Low-skilled jobs that featured simple clerical tasks and were highly repetitive no longer exist in the reorganized work environment.

Thus, increased computer use by front and back office employees creates a need to hire individuals who are either already proficient or trainable in computer use and who have the attributes that enable them to adapt to new information systems and changing work environments. This general upskilling of financial services jobs is reflected in the

TABLE 2.6 The Changing Nature of Skills in Banks and Insurance Companies

	Old Competencies	New Competencies
	General Competencies Among All Workers	
1.	Ability to operate in well-defined and stable environment	Ability to operate in ill-defined and ever-changing environment
2.	Capacity to deal with repetitive, straightforward and concrete work process	Capacity to deal with non-routine and abstract work process
3.	Ability to operate in a supervised work environment	Ability to handle decisions and responsibilities
4.	Isolated work	Group work; interactive work
5.	Ability to operate within narrow geographical and time horizons	Ability to operate within expanding geographical and time horizons
	Specific Competencies Among Upper-Tier Workers	
1.	Broad, largely unspecialized knowledge; focus on operating managerial skills	Focus on high level specialized knowledge in well-defined expert areas needed to develop and distribute complex products
2.	Old Leadership Skills: routine administration; top-down, carrot-and-stick personnel management approach; ability to carry out orders from senior management	Capacity not only to manage but also set strategic goals; to share information with subordinates; capacity to listen and to motivate individuals by treating them as equals
	Among Middle-Tier Workers	
1.	Specialized skills focused on established clerical procedures	Broader and less specialized skills focused on system-wide understanding
	Among Lower-Tier Workers	
1.	Specialized skills focused on data entry and data processing	Disappearance of low skill jobs

Source: Oliver Bertrand and Thierry Noyelle, *Human Resources and Corporate Strategy: Technological Change in Banks and Insurance Companies* (Paris: OECD, 1988), p. 41.

rising proportion of college graduates in the financial services workforce. As Figure 2.1 indicates, from 1970 to 1985 the percentage of the financial services workforce that was college-educated nearly doubled nationwide, from 15.5 percent to 29.6 percent nationwide. It more than doubled in New York State, from 16.4 to 33.6 percent. While these increases echoed similar increases in the college-educated segment of the total workforce, a much greater proportion of the financial services workforce was college-educated — 29.6 percent in 1985 compared to 17.9 percent of the entire workforce.

Upskilling of jobs has created problems for many firms in recruiting qualified individuals. Slower growth of the labor force in recent years has contributed to these problems. And in many urban areas, at the very same time that requisite skill levels have increased, the quality of applicants is believed to have declined or not kept pace with changing needs.

Many firms report marked increases in recent years in the number of job applicants that they have to screen in order to fill a position. They also report increased turnover rates for newly-hired entry-level personnel. Particularly for filling entry-level positions, firms report difficulty finding people who are either skilled or trainable. In one representative case, a major bank screens 12 high school graduates for every one accepted for a two-week teller training program. Some of those admitted then fail a drug test. Of those who begin working as tellers, over 30 percent are lost in the first year.[55] Other companies report similar or worse recruitment and turnover rates.

Many executives blame a deterioration of basic education in the U.S. for the disappointing pool of applicants. This deterioration is believed to be particularly severe in some urban areas. In New York City, for example, in the last four years only about 40 percent of the City's 300,000 high school students received a diploma after four years of study.[56]

While labor shortages are most acute for entry-level positions, some firms with front office operations in smaller cities have trouble finding highly knowledgable professionals or attracting such professionals to relocate into their area, particularly when they seek

FIGURE 2.1 Share of College Graduates in Total Workforce and Financial Services Workforce, U.S. and New York State, 1970 and 1985

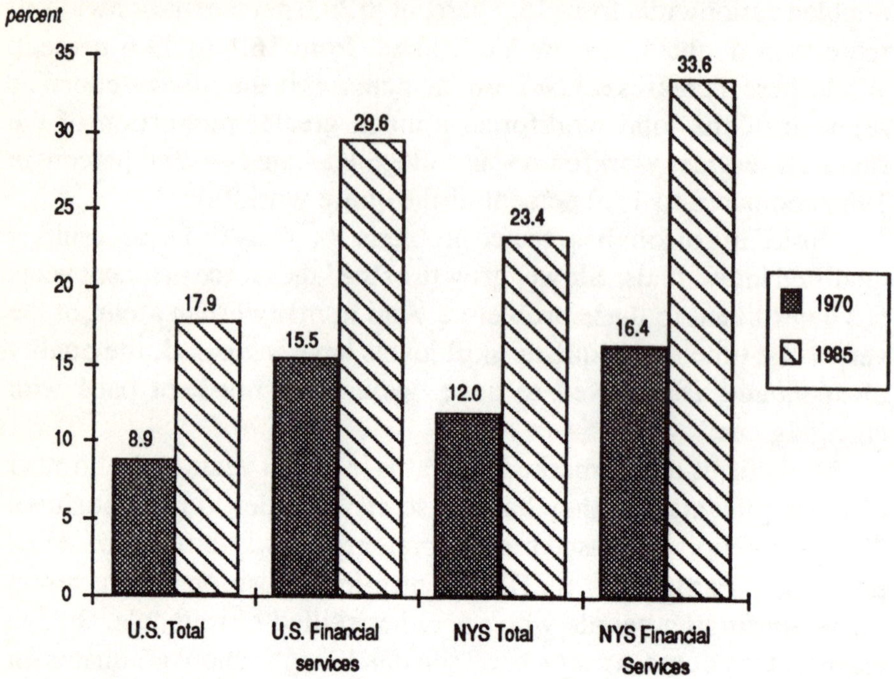

Source: Edward McDougal, Jr., and Jeffrey Zornitsky, "Labor Force Quality Issues in New York's Financial Service Sector," Urban Research Center, New York University, New York, August 1988, Table 4.

to expand activities into a new line of business. Such locations may be viewed as a corporate backwater, not the headquarters "where the action is." Other firms have encountered difficulties in their attempts to relocate data processing facilities because of a local area's shortage of skilled technical personnel.

Finally, the high cost of living and quality of life problems in some areas makes it difficult for firms to attract and retain top quality employees. Merrill Lynch Realty's report on firms' relocation policies found in 1987 that 41 percent of the 613 companies surveyed reported difficulty getting employees to accept a transfer to a high-cost area.[57] Similarly, in Runzheimer International's survey of 143 corporate relocation officers, 83 percent reported resistance to transfers to high-cost localities and that the higher the local housing prices were, the likelier employees would resist. Seventy-three percent of the companies cited the New York metropolitan region, the area with the nation's highest housing costs, as the one where employees most frequently resist moving, with high housing costs also accounting for significant employee resistance to moving to Boston, San Francisco, and Washington.[58]

Given the increasing challenge facing financial services firms to secure a well-trained and sophisticated workforce, localities whose labor supply is skilled, educated, and stable will be at a great advantage as locations for financial services firms. The quality of an area's basic education, vocational programs, and ongoing training and education programs aimed at keeping individuals abreast of changes in the industry contributes greatly to its competitiveness in the area of human resources. In a number of locations, such as Greensboro, N.C., firms work with community colleges in order to customize curricula to meet ever-changing needs of local financial services employers. The responsiveness of local educational institutions to the needs of the financial services industry in some instances may weigh decisively when firms make location decisions for their operations.

Telecommunications and Technology

The growth of financial services has been made possible and encouraged by advances in telecommunications and computer technology. The banking and brokerage sectors of financial services are perhaps more dependant upon telecommunications than any other industry, with many functions now completely automated. The automation of stock exchanges and securities firms has led to unprecedented trading volumes.

Although a strong telecommunications infrastructure within a firm does not spell success in and of itself, a weak telecommunications infrastructure can mean failure. Similarly, a high-quality and reliable telecommunications infrastructure in an area can improve the competitiveness of locally-based financial institutions, while an unreliable infrastructure can be disastrous. Thus, while the cost of telecommunications services in an area is a relatively less important factor in locational decisions, the quality and reliability of these services is increasingly critical. A brief delay in receiving ticker updates or the failure to settle on an electronic funds transfer transaction can mean the loss of millions of dollars to a firm.

The telecommunications infrastructure can be defined as all equipment and networks that facilitate the transfer of voice and data information. The strategic importance of telecommunications for financial services firms is indicated by the vast amounts of money being spent. U.S. commercial banks spent $10 billion in 1987 on information technology,[59] up from $4.2 billion in 1981.[60] Securities Industry Association figures indicate that 400 major brokerage firms spent over $2.5 billion on telecommunications in 1987.[61] Another survey found that the average annual telecommunications budget of banking and finance organizations was at least 29 percent higher than that of firms in any other industry group.[62]

As Fauerbach emphasizes, "the point of the telecommunications network is to have the flexibility and capacity needed to respond to business opportunities inherent in the network already."[63] Peter Keen details three strategic uses of telecommunications by financial firms:

> 1. Get an edge within the existing marketplace and product base by using telecommunications to redefine the quality and the nature of customer service.
> 2. Run the business better than is possible when coordination, communication and timeliness of key information are constrained by time and geography.
> 3. Reposition the firm by exploiting ownership of a large-scale delivery capability plus the advantage of lead time to change products and move outside the existing markets and product boundaries.[64]

One example of the use of telecommunications to create a market edge is the development of computer software allowing bank customers to transfer funds, trade services, and check their account balances and status of letters of credit from a personal computer terminal. For example, the IBM PC-based package Micro/Cash Register, offered to customers of Irving Trust Company of New York, is believed to handle about 2 percent of the dollar transfers worldwide, approximately half of Irving's 4 percent share of such transfers. This shows both the strength of the product and its importance for Irving's market share.[65] The benefit of this type of product and delivery system goes beyond the individual product itself. Once in place, the system can be used to deliver an expanded range of products and services, and can establish a relationship with the firm that is hard to displace, offering the potential for future business expansion.[66]

In the world of wholesale financial services, the development of screen-based trading has been dependent upon telecommunications advances. For example, Globex, a joint venture of Reuters and the Chicago Mercantile Exchange, will link major futures and options markets around the world in a completely automated auction that will reduce the trading costs for subscribing institutions to the service.

Telecommunications advances also have integrated a variety of office functions to improve banking services to corporate clients. For example, Wells Fargo's Integrated Office Support System helps bankers specialize wholesale services, such as arranging customized loans and mergers and acquisitions. By bringing together reports from credit bureaus, wire services, commodity price projections, and other information, one Wells official commented, "What used to take a day — studying things in a deal like cash flow and the sensitivity of figures to changes in interest rates — can be done in 15 minutes."[67]

The vast amounts that brokerage houses have spent to modernize their trading shows how financial firms use telecommunications to improve the speed and coordination of key information in order to compete effectively. One vendor estimates that "on average it costs $75 million to $80 million to build a new trading room, including telephones, key boards, screens, information sources, desks and back office support."[68] Industry analyst Gerald Lowe estimates that an individual trader/broker workstation costs anywhere from $10,000 to $50,000 each.[69]

Major features of the internal telecommunications infrastructure of brokerage firms include a variety of sophisticated tools. Private telephone systems called PBXs (private branch exchanges) often rival the size of the telephone company's own central office system. Personal telephone consoles, called "turrets," bring to the trader as many as 140 individual private lines and telephone system extensions. Open audio telephone circuits, known as "hoot-and-hollers," broadcast information simultaneously to the trading floors and branches of major trading firms. And trader terminals and accompanying screen switching systems allow traders instantaneous access to information from as many as 150 vendor services.

Major exchanges such as the New York Stock Exchange and the American Stock Exchange (AMEX) also are developing their telecommunications networks to further automate the execution of trading orders and thereby permit the expansion of trading volume. NASDAQ (National Association of Securities Dealers Automated Quotations) activity increased 39 percent in 1986, while AMEX increased 43 percent.[70] Similarly, telecommunications development has led to an unprecedented volume of electronic fund transfers, both over large wire services such as Fedwire and CHIPS, and through ATM (automatic teller machine) networks.

These vast expenditures on and technological advances in telecommunications make financial firms and markets rely upon the quality, sophistication, and dependability of a location's telecommunications infrastructure in order to realize the potential benefits of their own investments. For example, Pacific Bell's upgrading of public switching networks in California served 2,000 of Wells Fargo's credit card authorization terminals in Los Angeles and certain other California locations. But Wells Fargo has not been able to bring on line terminals in other parts of the state because Pacific Bell has not yet upgraded its facilities statewide.[71]

There are several important quality aspects of an area's telecommunications infrastructure. First, the degree to which modern technology is utilized within the infrastructure is an important attribute.

This includes the extent of digital facilities, percent of cable that is fiber optic, connections within the infrastructure, and the number of protocols supported. The level of investment used to upgrade the existing infrastructure also is important, as this provides some indication of future technology. Investment dollars per access line, investment dollars as a percent of sales, and telecommunications investment as a percent of overall gross national product are all ways to gauge this aspect of telecommunications quality. All of these factors are in turn tied to regulatory policies on service and incentives for investments.

The degree to which the local telecommunications company responds to business needs is another key factor. Responsiveness includes the ability of a telecommunications company to provide specialized solutions, and to offer contract pricing for services. Additionally, the timeliness of installing new facilities, particularly high-capacity fiber lines, and the ability to repair and service customers also are important aspects of responsiveness.

The attitudes of local, state, and federal regulators toward the telecommunications industry, particularly with regard to encouraging network investment, also influence the quality of the public telecommunications infrastructure. Tax policy, depreciation allowances, and the availability of tax credits are important in this regard, along with the overall regulatory climate of an area. Features of the regulatory environment that affect the quality of an area's telecommunications infrastructure include regulatory responsiveness to proposed changes in tariffed services, residential versus business bias of rates, and the degree to which regulations provide incentives for innovation and upgrading service.

The quality of an area's telecommunications infrastructure also is determined by the local availability of vendor support for the equipment and technologies being used by firms. Some companies which have relocated major facilities have had to bring vendor technicians with them to ensure support, as did Merrill Lynch when it opened a data processing facility in central New Jersey.[72] Sometimes, vendors will agree to support large clients by opening offices near them. In other instances, especially in suburban and rural areas, technical support may be provided on a dispatch basis. For some financial institutions, this sort of arrangement cannot be tolerated. A three-hour response time is not acceptable when a trader's terminal is down. Unless spare parts and high-level engineering backup are readily available, moving too far from a city is not possible for such firms.

Finally, the spatial requirements of firms' telecommunications equipment means that the quality of a locale's office buildings should be considered as an attribute of the telecommunications infrastructure. Buildings which utilize new engineering and architectural concepts to meet emerging office space demands often are called "smart buildings." One important feature of these buildings is high ceilings (often 20 to 24 feet) to accommodate under raised floors the proliferation of telephone and electrical wires that accompanies the intensive use of computer and telecommunications equipment. Provisions to distribute cables laterally in the building and on the floors are also important, as is dual penetration of outside cables into the building.

Another feature is the capacity for heavy floor loads. While a normal office building is engineered for 100-125 pounds per square foot, a floor load capacity of 250 pounds per square foot is needed to support video switching equipment, with 450 pounds per square foot needed for battery plant and other electrical equipment.[73] Smart buildings also feature enormous, column-free rooms of 20,000 to 80,000 square feet or more to accommodate trading floors, equipment rooms for telephone systems, turret systems, and the like.[74] To accommodate this internal telecommunications infrastructure, smart buildings also must be wired to meet substantial power requirements, be built of fireproof materials, and contain adequate standby power systems in case of emergency.

The features of smart office buildings usually are not found in the traditional narrow office towers within the central business district (CBD) of many urban areas, putting older cities at a potential disadvantage with respect to telecommunications infrastructure. However, these cities often have industrial, warehouse, or retail buildings located outside the CBD that can be converted into sites suitable for back office and data processing operations. For example, Manufacturers Hanover Trust Company and Citicorp utilize more than 400,000 square feet of a renovated industrial space on West 33rd Street in Manhattan for data processing facilities.[75]

As the need for sophisticated, reliable telecommunications and the size of investment in telecommunications infrastructure grow, the relative attractiveness of different areas' infrastructures increasingly will influence firms' or markets' location decisions. For some wholesale financial activities, there can be an international as well as domestic aspect to this dimension of competitiveness. If a major international financial center has an edge over others in the quality of its telecommunications infrastructure, it may become a more attractive place for trading to occur in certain markets, particularly if high trading volumes depend on the sophistication and reliability of telecommunications over time. The growth of the markets causes financial firms to expand activities and shift employment to that area.

The degree to which financial firms depend upon the quality of the telecommunications infrastructure in their location is reflected in the vast sums of money they have spent to install private telecommunications networks in order to bypass public systems. The movement to bypass is a major one among nonfinancial as well as financial services firms. It has been estimated that approximately half of the Fortune 500 companies use some form of bypass today, and that an equivalent of 10 million voice circuits could move from the public network to bypass by 1991.[76]

While the movement to bypass reflects the cost consideration discussed above, it also reflects the desire of firms to obtain the most sophisticated technologies, more effectively control their telecommunications networks, and better ensure the reliability of service. Regulatory or other policy barriers sometimes inhibit the public network from providing these services.

Availability of technologies is a major factor affecting bypass decisions. As noted earlier, firms such as Citibank and Merrill Lynch were ready to try new technologies long before they were available from the telephone company or long distance carriers. Companies also may want to install sophisticated networks in areas where the telephone company has outmoded equipment, or where their upgrade plans are out of synch with the company's time frame. Another key factor is control. Financial firms want to be able to monitor network performance automatically, to reconfigure the network as traffic patterns dictate, and to route traffic around a troublesome portion of the network before failures occur, not after.

Finally, the movement to bypass is part of a larger effort to establish backup telecommunications networks in order to safeguard against disruptions of service. The mid-1970s fire at a New York Telephone Company facility that knocked out service for over a month in a large portion of lower Manhattan and the May 1988 fire in a telephone company central office in suburban Chicago have prompted firms to build several layers of redundancy into their telecommunications networks. Bypass networks provide insurance against telephone company disruptions, though for some companies the reverse also is true: telephone company lines serve as a backup to bypass networks.

Other backup strategies of firms to protect against costly disruptions include obtaining telephone company service through two or more different central offices, securing geographically diverse alternative routings of fiber optic lines (e.g., cables running down different streets or running up different shafts to floors within a building), and having standby electricity generators in place should the main power source fail.

Despite the movement to bypass, the quality of an area's public telecommunications infrastructure remains an important concern for firms. Many firms engaged in bypass use local telephone company lines as well. The vast sums of money being spent by firms on their telecommunications facilities, whether or not they are engaged in bypass, also raises the costs of moving a firm's facilities to a staggering amount. Following the assumptions of 2,800 terminals and lines and $7,500 to $10,000 cost per employee, consultant Gerald Lowe estimates that the cost of relocating the headquarters of a financial firm to be anywhere from $35-57 million.[77] Thus, while the quality of a locality's telecommunications infrastructure has become all the more important as a dimension of competitiveness, the readiness of firms to relocate on the basis of this dimension has decreased, at least in the short run.

Regulation and Taxation

A final dimension of competitiveness is the area of governmental policy concerning taxation and regulation. Both taxation and regulation are key aspects of the quality of "business climate" of a location.

Regulation is one important element of a good business climate as a dimension of competitiveness. International regulatory differences relating to depository interest rate ceilings and to permissible activities have in the past greatly affected financial flows and thus the location of financial firms and employment. Similarly, within the U.S., regulatory differences have influenced location decisions and regulatory policy has become a means by which areas attempt to attract financial services activity. For example, much of the recent growth of Delaware's financial services activity is attributed to the removal of interest rate ceilings on credit cards. (Delaware's overall strategy is highlighted below in Chapter 6.)

The increasing importance of regulation as a dimension of competitiveness has occurred in the context of regulatory liberalization both within the U.S. and abroad. As will be discussed more fully in the next chapter, regulatory reform often has been a consequence of the successful attempts by financial firms and other financial actors, such as large corporations and institutional investors, to circumvent existing regulatory controls.

Because of this, it is tempting to conclude that the localities with the fewest regulations are the most attractive for financial services firms. For example, several British commentators view public policy concerns to ensure the smooth functioning of financial markets as contrary to the competitive interests of financial firms, arguing that "regulation has to tread a careful line so that it imposes effective control over the market but is not so restrictive that it encourages the market to move to another (unregulated) location."[78]

But it is also clear that total deregulation is not desirable. As some industry representatives have stressed, adequate regulation is needed to keep markets orderly and maintain public confidence. The recent crisis among savings and loan institutions has increased the awareness and concern for adequate regulation of financial markets, and this may in part counteract the deregulatory trend in recent years.

Nonetheless, the variations of financial services regulations across locations can make some areas more attractive than others as a place to do business. The issue of regulatory differences within the U.S. is complicated by the historical development of a dual regulatory structure involving both federal and state oversight. Whereas the regulation of the insurance industry is the sole domain of individual states, banks are regulated by both state and federal governments. Regulation of the securities industry is federal, for the most part, through the oversight authority of the Securities and Exchange Commission.

The general trend toward loosening of regulatory constraints on permissible business activities will be considered in greater detail in Chapter 3. This trend has proceeded unevenly due to the varying regulatory structure of different sectors within the industry despite the marked convergence of these sectors. Whereas securities firms increasingly have been allowed to conduct banking-like activities, banks have been more constrained in their domestic securities activities. Those localities whose regulations on permissible activities and products better reflect the realities of convergence are generally more attractive places for financial firms to do business.

Financial institutions also are concerned about regulations that affect the kinds and quality of investments they are permitted to make. For example, the investment portfolios of insurance companies in many states are subject to more restrictive regulatory controls than those of banks and securities firms. While firms generally are attracted to states whose regulations place few constraints on their choice of investments, the troublesome real estate and other investments of savings and loan institutions may underscore the desirable aspects of such regulations.

The speed with which regulatory authorities approve new products also has become an important quality of the regulatory climate. Competition among financial services firms has increased dramatically the volume of new products being made available by financial services firms. For example, while less than ten years ago insurers turned over their entire product portfolio every three years, today the turnover time is 12 months.[79] While regulators caution that these products may involve more risk to the consumer and therefore require greater scrutiny, financial services firms will be attracted to those locations whose regulatory apparatus is most responsive to industry change and innovation.

Interest rate ceilings are a form of price regulation that is of special concern to financial services firms. As highlighted below, differences in regulations affecting interest rates across countries led to the development of Eurodollar markets outside of the U.S. Within the U.S., differences in the regulation of credit card interest rates have influenced locations of credit card operations of many commercial banks. Bank operations located in Delaware and South Dakota, states which were among the first to remove all interest rate ceilings on credit cards, have captured a disproportionate share of this and other lending activities by financial institutions.

Another area of regulation that affects the attractiveness of a location for financial services activity is the set of regulations concerning the keeping of important records and books of account. These include regulations that mandate extensive record-keeping, that dictate in-state storage of administrative and investment records, and that affect the use of new technologies.

For example, financial services industry advocates were greatly concerned about recent proposals in both Delaware and New York to require in-state insurance companies to keep and maintain all books of account, such as accounting records, underwriting and claims files, policy loan applications, cancelled checks, drafts, bank statements, and evidence of asset ownership (stock and bond certificates, deeds, etc.) in the firm's central headquarters in the state. One insurance industry spokesman testified that "for reasons of responsiveness and economy, it may be more appropriate for the personnel responsible for such functions to not be physically located in New York. To require relocation into the state would not improve performance and would certainly impose burdensome costs."[80]

As the state of microfilm, data-reduction techniques, computer transmission and storage capabilities, facsimile signature, and other types of records maintenance technology develops, the necessity to retain original paper records in one central location becomes increasingly archaic and costly. As many in the industry believe, "It would be detrimental to most insurers if the originals were not able to be kept elsewhere, particularly where desirable for normal business operations, with copies to be kept at the principal office."[81]

Those states whose regulations facilitate and encourage electronic storage of records and the use of other record-keeping technology will be particularly attractive for financial services firms. Similarly, because large numbers of transactions can take place electronically or on-screen, state regulations should not impede screen trading.

Finally, as noted in the discussion of telecommunications as a dimension of competitiveness, several features of the regulatory environment affect the desirability of a location with respect to telecommunications. Historically, the monopoly environment in which telecommunications providers operated required substantial governmental regulation to assure fair treatment of all customers and promote the principle of universal telephone service. Now, competition in telecommunications in terms of the number of service providers is rapidly increasing, but regulation often constrains the ability of public service providers to compete in terms of price. This can adversely affect the range and quality of services offered by public network providers.

To the extent that increased price competition among telecommunications service providers fosters product innovation, areas whose regulations allow public network providers to compete with unregulated providers in terms of price will develop a more attractive telecommunications infrastructure. Similarly, the speed with which regulatory authorities respond to proposed changes in service and product approval also will influence the quality of the telecommunications infrastructure.

Taxes are the other important key to a competitive business climate, although their impact on location decisions is often exaggerated. The degree to which taxes influence location decisions is uncertain, but because these are cost factors that state and municipal governments can more readily alter, taxes are considered a dimension of competitiveness. As Moss and Dunau summarize, "Although taxes, like any other factor, do not by themselves have the power to induce firms to relocate, many cities and states see them as holding the potential to tip a relocation decision in their favor."[82]

While traditional financial centers have used tax abatements and policies as a means to retain firms and employment in their area, other areas are attempting to lure firms with favorable tax policies toward financial service firms. Delaware is a prime example of a locality successfully using a tax policy favorable to the financial services industry, the regressive bank franchise tax, as a means to enhance its attractiveness to financial services firms.

The limited importance of taxes as a dimension of competitiveness for firms' headquarters location is indicated by Cushman and Wakefield's 1987 survey. While "a good business climate in terms of state and local taxes and regulation" ranks sixth of 13 criteria, with half of the 400 firms deeming this criterion as either "absolutely essential" or "very important," only 10 percent of the firms claimed it was a factor in their decision to relocate.[83] Similarly, only 10 percent of the respondents in a study of San Francisco relocations cited high local taxes as a factor influencing their decision to relocate.[84]

Despite the limited importance of taxes in motivating a firm to relocate an existing operation, financial services firms do gauge the relative tax burdens of different localities once a decision to relocate or expand operations has been made. In addition to evaluating effective corporate income tax burdens, firms also are concerned with personal income taxes, sales and use taxes, property taxes, and others. Utility taxes are of particular concern to financial services firms given their intensive use of energy and telecommunications.

Proper comparison of the effective corporate income tax burdens of different areas is difficult, as one cannot simply compare tax rates. The comparison must consider and measure tax bases, credits, deductions, attribution rules, and other special features, along with tax rates. Rules on the allocation of income from out-of-state customers are one feature of state tax laws that is of particular concern to financial services firms, increasingly so as deregulation allows firms to further expand across state borders. Similarly, rules on filing for parent and subsidiary companies, rules on the apportionment of service income, and tax policy for financial firms with corporate links to nonfinancial firms also are important to financial services firms, yet these complicate comparisons of tax burdens.

Despite these difficulties, in some instances the difference in tax burdens between localities can be a significant factor in location decisions, particularly where special local business taxes exist, such as the occupancy tax on commercial rents in New York City. However, some experts have suggested that firms considering relocation of an existing operation are more influenced by their perception of the direction of change in tax burden rather than the actual level of taxes. Thus, a locality with high yet decreasing taxes might not be considered unfavorable, especially to firms already conducting business there.

Particular sectors of the financial services industry have highly specific tax concerns. For example, life insurance companies are sensitive to taxation on premiums received while banks are concerned with features of the tax law relating to debt reserve deductions. Specific taxes also affect particular financial markets, such as taxes on trading in gold bullion and other precious metals.

Many of the tax issues affecting the financial services industry concern possible inequities in the taxation of financial and nonfinancial firms, and of the various sectors within the industry. For example, in New York State, these different sectors are taxed under different parts of the tax code despite a marked convergence in recent years of the activities of banking, securities, and insurance companies. Life insurance companies in New York have argued that the dual taxation of both income and premiums has put them at a competitive disadvantage with respect to other New York financial services firms as well as out-of-state insurers. A variety of reforms have been proposed to harmonize tax burdens between financial and nonfinancial firms, and some believe a uniform taxation for all three sectors of the financial services industry would rationalize the industry's tax burden.

Financial services firms also are concerned with the level of personal income taxes in their area as an aspect of the cost of living of their employees. Cushman and Wakefield found that 88 percent of 297 executives surveyed labeled "state and local taxes that aren't burdensome to employees" as either "absolutely essential" or "important but not essential" for the quality of life of their office employees.[85] Promotional literature produced by states seeking to attract financial services firms to their areas often highlights personal income tax rates as well as those pertaining to corporate income.

NOTES

1. See Charles P. Kindleberger, "The Formation of Financial Centers: A Study in Comparative Economic History," *Princeton Studies in International Finance*, Paper No. 36, Princeton, N.J., 1974, for a useful summary of some of the literature.

2. Sidney M. Robbins and Nestor E. Terleckyj, *Money Metropolis* (Cambridge, Mass.: Harvard University Press, 1960), ch. 1.

3. Kindleberger, "The Formation of Financial Centers," p. 6.

4. Ibid.

5. Ibid., p. 7.

6. Robbins and Terleckyj, *Money Metropolis*, p. 34.

7. Ibid., p. 37.

8. See Kindleberger, "The Formation of Financial Centers," for a comparative account of the emergence of financial centers in several nations, emphasizing the relationship between financial centers and governmental capitals.

9. Robbins and Terleckyj, *Money Metropolis*, pp. 6-7.

10. Dennis Weatherstone, "A U.S. Perspective on Europe 1992," in Thierry Noyelle (ed.), *New York's Financial Markets: The Challenges of Globalization* (Boulder, Colo.: Westview Press, 1988), p. 116.

11. As argued in Jerry Coakley and Laurence Harris, *The City of Capital* (London: Basil Blackwell, 1983), London's financial institutions have always had a dual function of, on the one hand, serving the internationally-oriented firms of the British industrial economy and, on the other hand, of serving international capital in general. In recent years, the authors argue, the relative importance of the latter orientation has increased.

12. See especially Regina B. Armstrong and N. David Milder, "Employment in the Manhattan CBD and Back-Office Locational Decisions" *City Almanac*, June-

August 1984, and Mitchell L. Moss and Andrew Dunau, "The Location of the Back Offices: Emerging Trends and Development Patterns," Sylvan Lawrence Research and Data Center, New York University, New York, 1986.

13. Moss and Dunau, "The Location of Back Offices," p. 9. It has been estimated that as many as 15,000 LANs were installed in 1985.

14. Ibid., p. 8.

15. Ibid., p. 15.

16. Ibid., p. 11.

17. See Lowell C. Bryan and Paul Allen, "Geographic Strategies for the 1990s," *The McKinsey Quarterly*, Winter 1988.

18. This difference of opinion was reflected in discussion among members of the Governor Cuomo's Advisory Panel on Financial Services.

19. Moss and Dunau, "The Location of Back Offices," p. 27.

20. Mitchell L. Moss and Joanne G. Brion, "Back Office and Data Processing Facilities of Securities Firms and Commercial Banks in New York State," Urban Research Center, New York University, New York, August 1988, p. 9.

21. Moss and Dunau, "The Location of Back Offices," p. 52.

22. *American Banker Top Numbers 1989* (New York: American Banker/Bond Buyer, 1989), p. 24.

23. Moss and Dunau, "The Location of Back Offices," p. 39.

24. Moss and Brion, "Back Office and Data Processing Facilities," p. 13.

25. Ibid., Table 2.

26. Ibid., p. 15.

27. Ibid.

28. Moss and Dunau, "The Location of Back Offices," p. 44.

29. Thierry Noyelle, *Beyond Industrial Dualism* (Boulder, Colo.: Westview Press, 1987), p. 79.

30. Ibid., p. 82.

31. Ibid., p. 83.

32. State of New York Insurance Department, inter-office correspondence provided to Governor Cuomo's Financial Services Study.

33. Moss and Dunau, "The Location of Back Offices," p. 46.

34. Noyelle, *Beyond Industrial Dualism*, p. 82.

35. Moss and Dunau, "The Location of Back Offices," p. 47, and Exhibit IV.

36. Steve Lohr, "The Growth of the Global Office," *New York Times*, October 18, 1988, p. D1.

37. Eileen Appelbaum, "The Growth in the U.S. Contingent Labor Force" in Robert Drago and Richard Perelman (eds.), *Microeconomic Issues in Labor Economics: New Approaches* (Sussex, U.K.: Wheatsheaf Books, 1988).

38. "Headquarters Relocation," *Business America Real Estate Monitor*, Study No. 871014, Cushman and Wakefield, Inc., New York, October-November 1987, pp. 20 and 24.

39. Cushman and Wakefield, Inc., Market Research Department, New York.

40. Ibid.

41. Moss and Dunau, "The Location of Back Offices," p. 21.

42. "Business Relocations Out of San Francisco," Mayor's Office of Housing and Economic Development, City and County of San Francisco, June 1986, p. 9.

43. "Ranking of Electricity Prices to Commercial Users," *Energy User News*, April 18, 1988, p. 6.

44. Moss and Dunau, "The Location of Back Offices," p. 17.

45. Ibid., pp. 18-19.

46. John M. Lusa, "The Fourth Annual *TPT* User Budget Survey: Users Splurge for Carrier Services, Capital Items," *Networking Management* (formerly *Telecommunications Products and Technology*), March 1988, p. 24.

47. "State Policy and the Telecommunications Economy in New York," New York State Office of Economic Development, 1987, p. I-52.

48. Lusa, "User Budget Survey," p. 20.

49. Kenneth M. Fauerbach, "The Role of Telecommunications in the Brokerage and Banking Industries in New York," Urban Research Center, New York University, New York, August 1988, pp. 34 and 36.

50. "Wage Differences Among Metropolitan Areas, 1987," U.S. Department of Labor, Bureau of Labor Statistics, July 1988.

51. For example, in 1987 almost 46 percent of Chemical New York Corporation's non-interest, non-tax expenses were for salaries and employee benefits (*The Year in Review Annual Report 1987*, New York, p. 53). For J.P. Morgan & Co., salaries and benefits in 1988 accounted for over 60 percent of non-interest, non-tax expenses (*1988 Annual Report*, New York, p. 33).

52. "Headquarters Relocation," p. 20.

53. Cydney Pullman and Sharon Szymanski, "The Impact of Office Technology on Clerical Worker Skills in the Banking, Insurance and Legal Industries in New York City: Implications for Training," The Labor Institute, New York, August 1986, p. 6.

54. Heidi I. Hartmann, Robert E. Kraut, and Louise A. Tilly (eds.), *Computer Chips and Paper Clips* (Washington, D.C.: National Academy Press, 1986), p. 41.

55. This bank was anonymously profiled by Governor Cuomo's Financial Services Study.

56. "The Cohort Report: Four-Year Results for the Class of 1988 and Follow-Ups of the Classes of 1986 and 1987," New York City Board of Education, Office of Research, Evaluation, and Assessment, April 1989, p. i.

57. Iver Petersen, "More Resisting Transfers to New York," *New York Times*, Sunday, May 29, 1988, sec. 10, p. 5.

58. Ibid.

59. Brian Tracey, "Third Annual State of Automation in Banking Report," *Computers in Banking* (reprint), September 1987, p. 2.

60. Thomas H. Hanley et al., "Technology and Banking: The Implications of Strategic Expenditures" Salomon Brothers, New York, 1987, p. 1.

61. Gerald Lowe, "Financial Industry Relocations — Telecommunications Impact," presentation at the Conference on Financial Services in New York State, Urban Research Center, New York University, New York, June 8, 1988.

62. Lusa, "User Budget Survey," p. 24.

63. Fauerbach, "The Role of Telecommunications," p. 10.

64. Peter G.W. Keen, *Competing in Time* (Cambridge: Ballinger Publishing Co., 1988), p. 42.

65. Sheila A. O'Henry, "Irving Trust Stands Its Ground," *Computers in Banking*, December 1987, p. 74.

66. Fauerbach, "The Role of Telecommunications," p. 11.

67. Barnaby J. Feder, "Getting the Electronics Just Right," *New York Times*, Sunday, June 4, 1989, sec. 3, p. 8.

68. Pavan Sahgal and Ivy Schmerken, "The New Wave in Trading Technology," *Wall Street Computer Review*, January 1988, p. 29.

69. Lowe, "Financial Industry Relocations."

70. *NYSE Fact Book* (New York: New York Stock Exchange, 1987), p. 3.

71. Chris Roeckl, "PacBell Network 'Switches' Wells Fargo Credit Terminal," *Communications Week*, May 9, 1988, p. 24.

72. Fauerbach, "The Role of Telecommunications," p. 44.

73. Lowe, "Financial Industry Relocations."

74. Ibid.; Moss and Dunau, "The Location of Back Offices," p. 15.

75. Moss and Dunau, "The Location of Back Offices," p. 16.

76. Donald F. Burnside, "Last-Mile Communications Alternatives," *Networking Management* (formerly *Telecommunications Products & Technology*), April 1988, p. 59.

77. Lowe, "Financial Industry Relocations."

78. Andrew Leyshon, Nigel Thrift, and Peter Daniels, "The Urban and Regional Consequences of the Restructuring of World Financial Markets: The Case of the City of London," *Working Papers on Producer Services*, No. 4, University of Bristol, Bristol, and University of Liverpool, Liverpool, July 1987, p. 3.

79. State of New York Insurance Department, inter-office correspondence.

80. Peter J. Flanagan, President, Life Insurance Council of New York, Inc., "Maintenance of Books of Account and Policyholder Service Functions in New York," statement at Public Hearing on Proposed Regulation 122, State of New York Insurance Department, April 13, 1988, p. 19.

81. Ibid., p. 28.

82. Moss and Dunau, "The Location of Back Offices," pp. 24-25.

83. "Headquarters Relocation," pp. 20 and 24-5.

84. "Business Relocations Out of San Francisco," p. 9.

85. "The Second Survey," *Business America Real Estate Monitor*, Study No. 871010, Cushman and Wakefield, Inc., New York, May 1987, p. 13.

[7]

Excerpt from Jeffrey Henderson and Manuel Castells (eds), *Global Restructuring and Territorial Development*, 203–33

IV
THE URBAN DIMENSION OF GLOBAL RESTRUCTURING

9
The Fixers: the Urban Geography of International Commercial Capital

Nigel Thrift

> In the final analysis, a world paper money of obligatory usage presupposes a world state, a world government, that is, the disappearance of inter-imperialist competition, that is, superimperialism. We are further from that than ever. (Mandel, 1975: 14)

In this chapter I shall make a number of points in a preliminary fashion about the present phase of the internationalization of capital. In particular, my concern is with the internationalization of what might be called the 'intermediary economy', not banking or industrial capital but rather commercial capital (in its broadest sense). The function of this international intermediary economy is to organize and adjudicate all manner of international economic exchanges — for a fee. Its territory is the 'international financial centre'. I shall concentrate on the changing geography of one such centre, the City of London, through consideration of the recent activities of a number of its larger denizens.

International Commercial Capital

At the Most General Level

Until quite recently most interest has focused on the internationalization of industrial (or productive) capital and the internationalization of banking (or interest-bearing) capital (Thrift, 1985a). Clearly these are both important tendencies with highly visible effects, whether these be export processing zones or the eurodollar market, 'developed' country deindustrialization or 'developing' country debt. But the role of commercial capital has tended to be forgotten.

The reasons for this state of affairs are difficult to divine, particularly because, as I shall argue below, it has been commercial capital that has been responsible for much of the growth of international financial centres. One reason may be that there has been a general tendency in Marxist and Marxist-related theory, from Marx onwards, to downgrade the importance of commercial capital within capitalism by seeing it as a 'parasitic', or even 'relict' form to be relegated to the sidelines of capitalist production (see Ingham, 1984, for a critique). Another reason may be that banking and commercial capital are often occluded, especially in accounts that draw on the concept of finance capital (see Minns, 1981, for a critique).

What, then, is commercial capital?[1] Briefly, commercial capital mediates in the circulation of commodities for a fee. It does not retain any direct or long-term ownership or control of these commodities. Commercial capital can be subdivided into merchant capital which mediates the circulation of commodity capital of various kinds, and money-dealing capital which mediates the circulation of money capital of various kinds (and especially credit money having 'fictitious value'; see Harvey, 1982: chapter 9).

Certainly, given this description, commercial capital can be seen as 'parasitic' within capitalist production. As Harvey (1982: 71–72) puts it, 'On the one hand, the relationship is parasitic, in the sense that the merchant creates no value but merely appropriates it . . . On the other hand, merchants' capital can expand the surplus value realised by the producer through accelerating the turnover of capital and reducing the necessary costs of circulation'. Commercial capital, in other words, performs a vital enabling function within the capitalist productive system. The costs of circulation can also be benefits.

Just as certainly, commercial capital cannot be described as a relict form, although it is possible to find such a scenario in Marx, a scenario in which commercial capital dies out as the barriers to capitalist production are removed by its internationalization. But in reality, the role of commercial capital has become more, not less, important as capitalism has internationalized. Partly this is the result of the ingenuity which commercial capitalists have brought to bear in inventing new markets for commodities of all kinds, and most especially those which mobilize credit money. Even more importantly, a complex and wayward system of nation-states has grown up round the world with each state in economic competition with the others, necessitating the raising of all kinds of barriers to trade such as laws, and central bank regulations, and with each state founding its own national money with its record of stability and trust (Giddens, 1985). Thus

> International commercial capital is not merely based on the existence of the 'simple circulation of commodities and money'. The political system of nation states creates a set of conditions which renders international trade quite distinct from 'trade in general'. (Ingham, 1984: 94–95)

The four main reasons why commercial capital continues to thrive are as follows. First, it performs a vital function oiling the wheels of capitalist production. This function, in many cases, because of economies of scale, is performed more cheaply than could be achieved by internalizing its functions within industrial or banking capital. Second, it has ceaselessly created new markets for its services, especially in the burgeoning international credit system. Third, it has been able to take advantage of the barriers to trade implicit in the international capitalist economy. And, fourth, it provides much of the wherewithal for speculation. Thus, commercial capital forms a vast intermediary economy between industrial capital, banking capital and the state.

In spite of the above, commercial capital is still continually under threat from banking capital and industrial capital. There is no reason, in principle, why many of its functions — from making markets to accounting to information gathering to underwriting — cannot be performed internally by banking and industrial corporations. Indeed many are, to a point, and the boundary is continually shifting back and forth. There are two reasons why these functions have not been entirely absorbed by industrial and banking capital. The first reason relies upon the fact that considerable economies can be gained from subcontracting specialist services, not just because particular services can be carried out on a larger scale and therefore more cheaply by commercial capital, but also because, as the social and technical division of labour has increased in complexity, so specialist information can be pooled more easily by specialist firms, certain specialists can only be employed full-time within such firms, and so on. Of late, evidence seems to be mounting that modern banking and industrial capital is actually referring a number of previously internalized functions to commercial capital in a 'decentralization of administration' that parallels the 'decentralization of production'.

The second reason why commercial capital has not been absorbed is that it has raised numerous barriers that permit only selective access to participation in markets. Thus a constant element of the structure of commercial capital is the fencing off of markets by means of associations of various kinds. These associations are often backed up by the power of the state and by being linked to various criteria of social acceptability. Thereby, the forces of state and civil society are harnessed to the economic survival of a part of capital as a distinctive entity.

Of course, throughout history, commercial capital has had to deal with the problem of technological change. In the constant bidding to cut the circulation time of money capital, enormous technological strides have been made which have threatened the integrity of commercial capital as a separate entity. Of late, for example, pressure has been put on commercial capital by the converging technologies of computers, communications and information vending. But, so far, the evidence is that commercial capital has been able to capitalize on its extant expertise, mobilize its forms of association in new ways and move into new areas of expertise in such a way that it has been able to keep particular markets more or less to itself.

More Particularly . . .

What, then, are the different kinds of organizations and practices that go to make up commercial capital? There are four main clusters. The most ancient of these clusters of organizations are those that are concerned with mediating the exchange of commodities of various kinds, from agricultural produce (e.g. cocoa, coffee, sugar, rubber, wool, soya meal) to metals (copper, lead, tin, zinc, nickel, aluminium) to bullion (gold, silver). Merchant capital still exists, arranging the buying and selling, insurance, shipping and finance of raw materials exchange, usually within a fixed marketplace. However upon the raw materials market has been built an extensive money capital market, especially through the use of fixed-time, fixed-price bills of exchange known as futures which can be used by corporations to insure against commodity price rises and falls, or for speculation. Futures markets expanded considerably in the 1970s, especially as a result of the founding of new exchanges. In the late 1970s and early 1980s futures markets were given a further boost when they finally became fully integrated into the credit system with the establishment of markets in purely financial investments like eurodollars, municipal bonds, stock market indices, even interest rates. In the United States the number of contracts drawn on the futures markets increased from less than 20 million in 1970 to 150 million in 1984.

A special case of the market in commodities is the market in real estate. Clearly not all of this market is of concern to the subject matter of this paper since much of it is to do with the simple shifting of revenues. But certain kinds of real estate, especially office property but also large retail units, large industrial units and the like, are now traded as commodity money (Feagin, 1983). This development has only been bolstered by the appearance of institutions like property trusts and the development of secondary mortgage markets. The chief elements of commercial capital active in this property market are real estate agents (who are essentially brokers) and merchant banks.

A second cluster of commercial capital organizations is concerned with mediating monetary exchange. In the money markets commercial capital acts as a wholesaler. The grandparent of these markets is the discount market (Coakley and Harris, 1983). But, as capitalism expanded from the mid-1950s onwards it ran into a series of national rules and regulations on borrowing and lending which had to be surmounted. The new markets that resulted were co-ordinated by various 'fixers', especially the merchant banks. Of these markets the most important is the eurocurrency market, which is essentially a short-term interbank market. The eurocurrency market has grown dramatically since 1970 (for a dated but still useful account see Mendelsohn, 1980).

The foreign exchange markets have also grown rapidly. They are simply markets that shuffle foreign exchange about the world at the request of customer corporations and for purposes of speculation. In 1984 these markets had a daily turnover of $150 billion (*Economist*, 1985a). Again, the chief organizations that run these money markets are various merchant banks, acting as brokers, as well as other kinds of broker and dealer. These organizations act as processors and organizers of foreign exchange for a fee. Until recently, they have generally had little to do with lending.[2]

The third main cluster of commercial capital organizations deals in securities (stocks and shares) issued to raise capital by companies or governments (the primary market) then bought and sold in a speculative fashion (the secondary market). The organizations act as the mediators of exchange in a series of fixed marketplaces to which there is restricted access (stock and government bond exchanges).

A final important cluster of commercial capital organizations is focused on the selling of corporate services. The most important of these services is non-life insurance and reinsurance (in which insurance is reinsured to spread the risk) with its insurance companies, brokers and underwriters. This market has over time become more centralized around fixed exchange points.

Further important parts of the cluster of service organizations are as crucial to commercial capital as they are to banking and industrial capital. Since they charge a fee and are intimately involved in the process of exchange they are included in this paper as commercial capital. The profession of *accountancy*, which dates from the 1940s in its modern form, is pivotal to the capitalist system (Tinker, 1984). Accountants adjudicate the process of exchange. Through a series of historically evolved rules they define what is profit and what is not. They apply these rules to a sample of the exchanges that a corporation makes and then derive a statement of what the corporation is worth. *Advertising agencies* charge a fee for publicizing the availability of commodities for exchange. They help to create and sustain markets. Advertising agencies date from the 1820s, but it was not until the 1880s that agencies came into their own, spurred on by the growth of mass consumption of goods and the establishment of popular newspapers which gained much of their revenue from advertising (Fraser, 1981). *Legal services* have become increasingly concerned with defining and adjudicating contracts for the exchange of commodities in the presence of legal systems from many nation- states. *Tax consultants* provide the expertise for minimizing different nation-states' tolls on exchange. *Information services* provide all kinds of commercial information from analysis of transactions in markets (e.g. spot prices of currencies and securities) to analysis of competitors in particular markets. Whatever the cause it is becoming increasingly the case that information about money is money. The list of service firms goes on almost endlessly. These firms are the 'fixers' of capitalism.

International Financial Centres

The natural habitat of commercial capital is the 'financial' centre. For three interrelated reasons the organizations of commercial capital tend to group together in these centres. The first reason is to be near clients, especially the headquarters offices of banking and industrial corporations, but also major state departments and other commercial capital firms. (Commercial capital is a social as well as an economic network.) The second reason is to be in close proximity to relevant markets, many of which operate from fixed exchanges and all of which operate under quite severe spatial constraints. The third reason is to tap into information on markets and the operations of banking and industrial corporations and the state rapidly and efficiently. It is no surprise, then, to see most concentrations of commercial capital in selected cities.

Until recently most of these concentrations have served domestic national markets. Commercial capital in cities like Chicago and Tokyo is still essentially oriented to exchange within their domestic economies. With a few notable exceptions like the City of London, New York and Paris, these concentrations were not internationally oriented. In the 1970s, this all began to change. Nearly every key activity of commercial capital began to internationalize for three interrelated reasons. Partly this was a response to the internationalization of key customers amongst banking and industrial capital. This imperative required the setting up of office networks mirroring the multinational networks of plants and offices of banking and industrial capital in order to retain custom. Partly it was a consequence of the internationalization of the markets themselves, which was linked to the internationalization of banking and industrial capital and to new market opportunities afforded by developments in a number of countries. And partly it was the result of technological changes which were initially an enabling factor but which have now become a determinant in the markets.

There therefore came into being a worldwide network of *international 'financial' centres*, trading posts serving the international market (Figure 1).[3] The main activities of these international financial

FIGURE 1
The hierarchy of international financial centres in 1980[1]

First order Supranational Centres				
London	New York			
Second order Supranational Centres				
Amsterdam	Frankfurt	Paris		
Tokyo	Zurich			
First order International Financial Centres				
Basel	Bombay	Brussels	Chicago	Dusseldorf
Hamburg	Hong Kong	Madrid	Melbourne	
Mexico City	Rio de Janeiro	Rome	San Francisco	
Sao Paulo	Singapore	Sydney		
Toronto	Vienna			
Second order International Financial Centres				
Bahrain	Buenos Aires	Kobe	Los Angeles	
Luxemburg	Milan	Montreal	Osaka	
Panama City	Seoul	Tapei		

[1]Derived from hierarchical cluster analysis and stepwise multiple discriminant analysis performed on sixteen variables.
Source: Reed (1983: 227).

centres are similar, in some ways, to those carried on in domestic financial centres but they are arranged in a hierarchy that spans the globe. These activities are as follows.

International commodity exchange. Every significant international financial centre has a whole battery of commodity exchanges. Currently, the important growth area is in futures exchanges. Some of these are now being linked together to enable 24-hour futures trading to take place eventually. For example, since January 1985 the Chicago Mercantile Exchange (CME) has been linked to the Singapore International Monetary Exchange (SIMEX) for trading in a range of futures including eurodollars, eurodeutschmarks and interest rates. Another important element of international commodity exchange is the international property market. It is over the last 15 years that a truly international property market has come into being, one that relies on the activities of a select band of international real estate brokers to form a commodity market (Bateman, 1985; Thrift, 1984a, 1985b). This property market is mainly concerned with office buildings, although selected retail and industrial buildings and some expensive residential buildings can also be included. An irony of this market is that it is to a great extent concentrated on international and domestic financial centres. Thus the activities of commercial capital can form both supply and demand.

International monetary exchange (including the arrangement of eurocurrency loans). International currency clearing is one of the very important monetary exchange activities of commercial capital in international financial centres and access to clearing is an equally important determinant of location in international financial centres by offices of banking and industrial corporations. In 1982 New York cleared approximately $160 billion every day, followed by London ($17 billion), Frankfurt and Paris ($12 billion each), Tokyo ($7 billion), Zurich ($4 billion) and Amsterdam ($2 billion) (Reed, 1983).

International securities dealing. Until the last two or three years trading in foreign stocks and shares was an unusual activity. But now high-volume trading is taking off. There is considerable interest in the promotion of an international securities market, boosted by the attention of institutional investors like pension funds intent on internationalizing their portfolios. Thus, there are now 16 US globally oriented national funds. In turn, overseas institutions now own about 3.8 percent of US stocks. The New York Stock Exchange is now a major trader of the shares of British companies and there are 200 US companies listed on the London Stock Exchange. The current ambition is to link a series of stock exchanges round the world in such a way as to enable 24-hour trading. The New York Stock Exchange is linked with the Pacific Exchange in San Francisco. The Boston and Montreal Exchanges are linked. There is a task force investigating the linkage of the New York and London Exchanges (Pagano, 1985).

International services. International insurance broking used to be confined to the City of London. Now it is spreading round the globe. In North America exchanges in New York, Miami, Toronto and Chicago are taking some of London's international business and there are plans for a further exchange in Atlanta. The New York Exchange has experienced a remarkable growth since its opening in March 1980, from a premium volume of $72.5 million in 1981 to $450 million in 1984. But as yet these exchanges are still struggling to find international business (Manser, 1985). Other international services like accountancy and legal services also form important clusters of commercial capital within international financial centres.

The formation of international financial centres has been boosted by two developments. The first of these is the multinationalization of commercial capital. The result is that the ownership of commercial capital in international financial centres has become more and more cosmopolitan. In the City of London, for example, there are more

TABLE 1
Foreign banks in London and New York[1]

	London	*New York*	*Difference*
1970	163	75	88
1971	176	81	95
1972	215	85	130
1973	232	98	134
1974	264	114	150
1975	263	127	136
1976	265	144	121
1977	300	177	123
1978	313	208	105
1979	330	244	86
1980	353	253	100
1981	353	255	98
1982	379	285	94
1983	391	294	97
1984	403	307	96

[1]Includes only foreign banks directly represented through a representative office, a branch office or a subsidiary.
Source: The Banker, 1984.

foreign banks than British banks. The same goes for New York (Table 1). Similarly, there are many foreign insurers in London. For example, the present membership of the Institute of London Underwriters is 40 percent foreign. In New York, there are 70 foreign insurers operating.

The second development has been the role of the converging technologies of communications, computing and information gathering. Reed (1983: 230) sums up the importance of this convergence:

> Jet travel has made it possible to move important people and documents from one location to another, anywhere in the world, within 24 hours. This quick and relatively inexpensive means of moving highly skilled people is perhaps the single most important factor in diminishing the need for (all) financial centres to be expert in a number of ancillary activities (i.e. accountancy, advertising, law, printing, etc.). The international financial centres can export much of the needed ancillary services to other centres at substantially lower costs than would be incurred if each centre had to generate these skills internally.
>
> The non-personal form of communication may involve airmail or telephone, telex or sea mail. Important documents such as letters of credit, trade bills, term loan agreements and cheques can now be moved overnight by air courier. This has improved the operating efficiency of centres and their clients in those matters that require the movement of a physical document. Telephone, telex and other types of transmission make it possible to send and receive instructions almost simultaneously.

Indeed the rapid development of completely automated systems of exchange and information on exchange, whether for commodity, share, currency or insurance dealing, further boosts the role of the international financial centres (Langdale, 1985; *Economist*, 1985b). These systems further reduce the turnover time of capital through better co-ordination and distribution of information about exchange, as well as exchange itself:

> Better, more reliable communication links have encouraged round-the clock, round-the-world trading in what is becoming, as the cliche correctly has it, a global market place. Bonds have been following foreign exchange down that route; now the elite of world class equities are on the move as well. Better, easier-to-use computers have given firms the ability to process millions of transactions a day, investors the intelligence to track dozens of variables in scores of places. Both have made possible higher volumes and greater velocity, and allowed a wider range of more complicated instruments. They have also contributed to the rapid growth and sophistication of electronic and screen-based telephone markets. (*Economist*, 1985b: 10)

The result is that international financial centres are becoming more and more important and their importance is undoubtedly synergic: 'influence of the centres is far greater than the total reach, scope, and influence of their various institutions when measured separately' (Reed, 1983: 234).

The City of London

The doyenne of the international financial centres is still the City of London. The City has reigned supreme amongst centres of international commercial capital since the eighteenth century (McRae and Cairncross, 1984). By 1832 the City had already taken on much of its present form with, for example, the discount houses in place and several of the 'classical' fixed markets. Already in that year Nathan Rothschild could observe that

> this country in general is the Bank for the whole world . . . all transactions in India, in China, in Germany, in Russia, and in the whole world, are guided here and settled through this country. (cited in Ingham, 1984: 93)

Already, the City's international role meant that it was becoming divorced from the British domestic economy and indeed it had little to do with the industrial revolution or subsequent developments. By the turn of the century this divorce was almost complete. From 1865 to 1913,

> income from interest and dividends on foreign investments, from shipping credits, insurance, banking and the financing of foreign trade increased from a total of around $80 million to $340 million. (Ingham, 1984: 41)

This moved the UK's balance of payments into surplus. The City's earnings declined relatively before World War II, mainly because of the worldwide depression, then increased again after the war was over. The form of the City's institutions is not immutable but Figure 2 attempts to summarize its present state. Numerous introductions to the City exist which would make a longer summary superfluous (e.g. Wilson Committee, 1980; Coakley and Harris, 1983; McRae and Cairncross, 1984; Harris, 1985).

FIGURE 2
The structure of the City of London: basic commercial practices and institutions

Commodity	*Practices*	*Institutional structure*	*Organizations*
Money	Arranging loans, clearing	Wholesale money markets; foreign exchange markets	Overseas banks; Discount houses; Merchant banks (including accepting houses); arms of clearing banks; foreign exchange dealers
Securities	Issuing, broking, jobbing	Stock Exchange	Issuing houses; stockbrokers and jobbers
Commodities	Merchanting, broking	Various commodity markets and exchanges (e.g. LIFFE, LME) and other more diffuse markets	Brokers associates; Merchant banks, etc.
Services			
(a) Insurance	Underwriting, broking	Lloyds and other more diffuse markets	Lloyds, insurance companies
(b) Freight	Chartering	Baltic Exchange, Lloyds Shipping Register, etc.	Chartering companies
(c) Accountancy, legal services, advertising, public relations, tax consultants and advisers, management consultants, etc.	Adjudicating, publicizing, minimizing costs of exchange, etc.	Diffuse markets	Relevant companies

Source: Ingham (1984: 16).

By 1983 the total overseas earnings of the City stood at $5,378 million, with $2,754 million of this amount coming directly from the fee-earning activities of commercial services. The City-controlled assets double the size of Britain's GDP (Harris, 1985). Arguably, the City is still the world's leading international financial centre, despite a strong challenge from New York in the 1970s and 1980s. Specifically, the City has been able to retain its supremacy as the chief nexus of a number of markets, including:

1. *The insurance market.* London is still the major international insurance centre in the world, despite a strong challenge from New York (which is still mainly concerned with domestic insurance). It has retained its position by actively developing the world reinsurance market and encouraging, to a limited degree, foreign names and insurance companies (Manser, 1985). Already by 1978, the City's annual premium income had overtaken the gross domestic product of New Zealand (McRae and Cairncross, 1984).

TABLE 2
The growth of London as a merchant banking and broking centre, 1970–84

	1970	*1975*	*1980*	*1984*
Number of foreign banks directly represented through a representative office, a branch office or a subsidiary	163	263	353	403
Number of foreign banks, indirectly represented through a share in a joint venture or a consortium bank	—	72	50	67
Total number of foreign banks directly or indirectly represented	163	335	403	470
Number of foreign securities houses (dealers in bonds and securities)	—	—	—	96
Numbers employed by foreign banks and foreign securities houses in London	11,813	20,881	31,132	39,175

Source: The Banker, various issues.

2. *The money market.* London is one of the largest of the foreign exchange markets. It is also the major node of the eurocurrency markets. Of the $2,000 billion of eurocurrency extant in the world at the end of 1982, one-third was on the books of London merchant banks (McRae and Cairncross, 1984), many of them from overseas (Table 2). Because of the shadow of developing country indebtedness

it seems sensible to assume that the City will not see a boom through the 1980s comparable to that of the second half of the 1970s. It is quite possible too that London may shrink vis-a-vis New York, which at the end of 1981 set up offshore banking legislation to permit US banks to book loans in New York without going over the hurdle of US tax and domestic monetary controls. Within a year these International Banking Facilities, as they are called, accounted for 8 percent of the total euromarket deposits, as against London's share which was held steady at around the 35 percent mark. In bank loans booked through the different centres, London's lead was narrower: 27 percent against 14.5 percent for New York.

It is a useful warning that London can be challenged. For the time being, to be sure, London may not have much to fear. Not only do the Americans and other foreign banks already have an enormous investment in the City which will tend to keep the business here, but New York has not proved as efficient a place to raise euromarket deposits as London, and most of the loans being booked through New York have to be funded by dollars bought in established euromarket dealing centres, of which London is by far the largest. (McRae and Cairncross, 1984: 71–72)

3. *The commodity markets.* London still leads the other international financial centres in a number of commodity markets such as gold bullion. However the largest commodities markets now are futures markets. Of these futures markets, the largest is the Chicago Mercantile Exchange but this is still mainly a domestic market, although its International Monetary Market, dealing in financial futures, has had enormous influence. The largest international futures markets are in New York and London. London has the edge in cocoa, sugar and coffee futures but New York has taken the lead in many other futures. For example, COMEX in New York is easily the largest market in the world for gold futures. In the early 1980s, however, London responded to the challenge of Chicago and New York by setting up a range of new futures exchanges including the London Gold Futures Market and the London International Financial Futures Exchange (LIFFE).

TABLE 3
Employment in the City of London, 1976

Sector	*Employment ('000s)*	*Percent*
Banking	76	24
Insurance	40	12
Stockmarket and other financial	20	6
Exchange markets	22	7
Accountants and lawyers	17	5
Subtotal	175	54
City total	321	100

Source: Jones, Lang and Wootton, 1980.

4. *The service centre.* As a centre of services, and especially accountancy and legal services, the City of London is still pre-eminent.

The fortunes of many people in Britain now rely on the continuing success of the commercial activities of the City of London (Table 3) (King, 1985). The judicious use of social exclusion, the constant creation of new credit money markets (such as eurocurrency markets) and allowing the selective entry of foreign institutions have so far enabled the City to retain its position as the leading international financial centre, unbolstered by any significant national market. As Manser (1985: 115) points out with respect to the London insurance markets:

> it is important to distinguish between the 'UK market' and the 'London market'. The UK market is no more than a market of national insurers.... The London market is much more than a geographical expression. It is an international insurance centre which, apart from certain advantages of language and communications, is based in London largely by historical accident.... The speciality of London is (international) finance, where that of Detroit is motor manufacture and that of Dusseldorf is steel.

But as some of the examples above make clear, London is feeling the chill winds of competition which have, for example, already forced it to review many of its traditional barriers to integration of elements of commercial capital. It can never expect to be again unambiguously the world's major international financial centre. It is no surprise, then, that just as foreign firms based in other international financial centres have moved their operations into the City or bought into City firms in order to capture business, so City-based firms are moving their operations into other international financial centres abroad or buying into them to ensure that they are not left behind in the race for these centres' business. The City firms are trying to make sure that they are represented in every significant international financial centre. The next section examines this process of internationalization.

The Internationalization of the City of London

The City's major commercial firms have been internationalizing since the turn of the century. But it has been in the 1970s and 1980s that they have seriously moved overseas. The impact of this movement on other international financial centres has been quite substantial and has actually rebounded on London. New York, for example, owes much of its success as a foreign exchange trading centre to an influx of British-owned broking firms, with their expertise and contacts, into the city in the 1970s. Another example: London's major corporate lawyers (43 in the City, 101 in London as a whole)[4] (Investors Chronicle, 1984) have extensively internationalized in the last 15 years with a resultant concentration of their offices in particular international financial centres. For example, Stone James Stephen Jaques now has offices in New York, Sydney, Perth and Canberra, while Linklaters and Paines has offices in New York, Paris, Brussels and Hong Kong. Twenty-three foreign law firms now have offices in Singapore. Nine of these firms are based in the City of London. Thus pockets of the City of London can now be found in all the major international financial centres.

Clearly, however, there is a need for more detailed case studies of particular forms of internationalization and the next two subsections of the paper provide a survey of the internationalization of two key sectors of the City — accountants and real estate agents — via case studies of two of the largest firms in each sector.

Accountancy

The accountancy profession adjudicates exchange for which it receives a fee. It informs shareholders of an industrial or banking company what they have received in exchange for their investment. It allows creditors to assess the security of their claims. It helps the state to decide whether the revenues it received from the company are sufficient. And so on. The profession of chartered or public accounting is relatively recent. Originally, it came into being in Great Britain in the 1850s as a result of state action: the introduction of the companies acts and the bankruptcy acts. In the decades following the US Civil War, British chartered accountants crossed the Atlantic to monitor British capital investment in the United States:

> By protecting shareholders and maintaining investor confidence, accountants performed the primary service of stimulating capital accumulation in the United States in the early twentieth century. The (British) firm of Marwick Mitchell helped J.P. Morgan avert a bank collapse and restore investor confidence in the Knickerbocker Trust Co., thereby ending the panic of 1907. The State's ratification of an income tax constitutional amendment in 1913 led to a substantially increased demand for professional accountancy services, as did the call for official accounting standards and guidelines by the Federal Trade Commission and the Federal Reserve Board. But it was the stock market crash of 1929 and the Securities Acts of 1933 and 1934 that produced the largest growth in the demand for accountants. Peat, Marwick, Mitchell's experience provides some indication of the magnitude of this growth. In 1947, the firm's revenues stood at less than $10 million; by 1981 revenues had reached $979 million. British accounting experienced a comparable growth as a result of the 1948 Companies Act; Britain today (with some 100,000 chartered and certified accountants) has more accountants per head than any other advanced capitalist country. (Tinker, 1984: xvi)

The core of the accountancy business is still the audit. An audit is a summary of economic transactions. Typically, a large corporation makes millions of transactions in any year, so audits are concerned with designing a sample frame that captures the significant features of these transactions. This requires a three-phase exercise. The first phase involves the assessment of the quality of the internal controls of corporations to check if the corporation can be audited. The second phase consists of tests for errors in the corporation's recording of transactions (e.g. matching shipping documents to invoices). In the final phase additional testing is carried out (Stevens, 1982).

Recently, three trends have touched the accountant's world. The first trend has been computerization. Now auditing programs are a vital part of any audit. Many of these programs are copyrighted and have become a business in themselves. The second trend is diversification out of auditing into other services. Tax consultancy was an early favourite. Management consultancy and related business services (e.g. insolvency) are the current major areas of expansion. Accountants are also heavily involved in services to central and local government, in development consultancy, in charity consultancy, and so on. The third trend is litigation. Most accountancy firms are run as partnerships but this form of organization is now coming under considerable strain as they become subject to more and more law suits from creditors alleging careless auditing practice after companies go bust. In the United States suits against accountants are running at one a day. But even in less litigious countries accountants are now being sued. The result is that insurance cover is becoming increasingly hard to obtain and increasingly expensive. It is quite possible that, as a result of this pressure, the larger accountants may become limited companies, so protecting the partners from personal bankruptcy.

The accountancy profession is dominated worldwide by the 'big nine' firms (Tables 4 and 5), all of which are sizeable multinationals. In 1981, these nine firms between them audited 493 out of the *Fortune 500*

TABLE 4
The nine largest multinational accountancy firms, 1984, by number of audits

	USA Fortune 500 major audits	*Rest of world Fortune 500 major audits*	*Total*
Price Waterhouse	151	72	223
Peat Marwick Mitchell	156	37	193
Arthur Anderson	159	17	176
Ernst and Whinney	136	37	173
Coopers and Lybrand	98	52	150
Deloitte Haskins and Sells	116	31	147
Arthur Young	83	48	131
Touche Ross	71	25	96
Klynveld Main Goerdeler	12	48	60

Source: Price Waterhouse, 1985.

TABLE 5
The nine largest accountancy firms in the UK, 1983, by number of audits

	UK Times 500 major audits	*UK Times 1000 major audits*
Price Waterhouse	88	145
Peat Marwick Mitchell	60	133
Deloitte Haskins and Sells	62	102
Coopers and Lybrand	51	80
Ernst and Whinney	38	66
Arthur Young	34	58
Arthur Anderson	28	55
Touche Ross	20	45
Thomson McLintock	19	41

Source: Price Waterhouse, 1985.

firms. (This can be an extensive commitment: Deloitte Haskins and Sells employs 1,400 people full-time just to audit General Motors). In 1981 the big nine employed 170,000 people worldwide in some 2000 offices in more than 100 countries. In the United States alone the big nine had over 15,000 partners and employed 30,000 Certified Public Accountants. The firms employ enough lawyers to be regarded as some of the largest law firms in the world and enough management consultants to be regarded as amongst the world's largest management consultancy firms (Clairmonte and Cavanagh, 1984; Stevens, 1982; Tinker, 1984).

Of the top nine firms six are nominally City headquartered firms. There is, however, some difficulty in judging the nationality of ownership of partnerships. Historically, City accountancy firms have tended to expand overseas in part by linking with other accountancy firms to form a loose alliance of country partners all operating under the same name. Since in each of these firms the United States practices are much larger in terms of number of partners than any other and partners have, nominally at least, equal voting rights, ownership and control of these City firms is problematic. Whatever the case, currently there are 30 major accountants based in the City of London and 63 in London as a whole (Investors Chronicle, 1985).

Of these firms, one which still regards itself as a 'true blue' City firm is Price Waterhouse which, on a range of measures, is the largest of the big nine. The firm was founded in the City of London in 1849 by S.H. Price and Edwin Waterhouse. It was able to attract distinguished partners, including Knights of the Realm, and with this social background was quickly able to find impressive accounts. It has used social networks for economic gain ever since.[5]

The firm went multinational early on in its history. At the turn of the century it joined with the New York firm, Jones, Caesar and Co. By the mid-1930s it already had 57 branch offices around the world and 2,500 employees in all (Stevens, 1982). By 1984 its complement had grown to 26,500 employees (including 1,854 partners) working from 354 offices in 95 countries. In 1984 Price Waterhouse as a whole earned $1,150 million in fees (Price Waterhouse, 1985). Price Waterhouse's main activities continue to be in audit. In both the United States and the UK, for example, about 70 percent of its chargeable hours has come from this course. However taxation services are growing fast (18 percent of chargeable hours in the United States, 16 percent in the UK), as is management consultancy (about 10 percent of chargeable hours in both the United States and the UK). The firm is also involved in businesses like insolvency, business services to small firms and services to central and local government. The movement into new services has come about partly through organic growth and partly through merger. For example in 1983 Price Waterhouse UK merged with Urwick Orr and Partners, one of the City of London's major management consultancy firms. The firm has tried to merge on a larger scale than this with other accountancy firms. For example, in 1983 it tried to merge with another of the big nine, Deloitte Haskins and Sells, but partners in the two firms threw the proposal out (a problem of the partnership form).

Over time, the company has tried to act more and more like a centralized multinational corporation by adding a world tier of administration — the 'world firm' based in the City of London. The world firm co-ordinates the operations of each of the country partnerships (which was organized as 20 member firms responsible for major markets like the United States, Canada, Australia, South Africa, Asia and so on) at the world scale. It is run by a nine-member Policy Committee, a 20-member Council of Firms and a Council of Partners. The world firm is responsible for international marketing, promotion of a world image, the development of computerized auditing and other systems which can be used by each of the member firms. It would certainly be an exaggeration to say that the company is entirely run from the City, but it is subject to centralized control of a sort.

The firm has become international for two main reasons. The first is a constant search for new country markets offering profit opportunities for accountancy. The second is the fact that its clients became international and in order to continue to obtain work it was necessary to be able to display an international office network likely to match their own locational pattern. This is also vital in obtaining new audits.[6] On a worldwide basis 40 percent of all clients audited by the firm have international operations. The result of these factors is that Price Waterhouse has an employment structure which matches closely to the pattern of international financial centres (see Table 6), for that is where

TABLE 6
Price Waterhouse employment structure, 1984

(a) *Employment by chief geographic area*

Area	*Employment ('000s)*
UK	3.1
North America	12.1
Pacific and Far East	4.1
Europe	2.7
South America	2.2
Africa, Middle East and Asia	2.3
Total	26.5

(b) *Employment in largest offices*

Office	*Employment*	*No. of partners*
London (less National HQ)	1,695	87
New York (less National HQ)	1,252	73
Hong Kong	807	29
Toronto	635	43
Sydney	567	43
Buenos Aires	405	26
Kuala Lumpur	404	12
Sao Paulo	402	26
Dublin	400	29
Calcutta	388	13

Source: Price Waterhouse, 1984.

custom is to be found and that is where the existing clients are. 'More and more, bidders with the strongest presence in all the world's commercial centres win the multinational accounts. For this reason there is great pressure . . . to expand internationally by passing money and talent into overseas offices or by merging with established firms in Europe, Asia and the Americas' (Stevens, 1982: 70).

Another example of a City-based accountancy firm is Touche Ross. The firm was founded in the City in the 1880s. It reached across the Atlantic to form a United States partnership in 1905 and has linked with many other firms round the world since. By 1984 its employment had grown to 22,000 personnel operating out of 380 offices in 87 countries (Touche Ross, 1984). As with Price Waterhouse, the firm's main activities are in audit. Again, taxation consultancy, management consultancy, insolvency and services to small business are growing fast. In addition, the firm is involved in services to the voluntary sector and computer security. Like Price Waterhouse, the constituent firms of

Touche Ross are co-ordinated worldwide by a central body, Touche Ross International. Touche Ross International

> has adopted the policy of linking in each country with well established professional local firms. These practices are run by nationals of the country who have an in-depth knowledge of local business and conditions.... Clients have all the advantages of dealing with a national firm backed by the strength of a coordinated international organisation. (Touche Ross, 1984: 7)

Real Estate Agents

There are 101 major estate agents in the City of London, and 153 in London as a whole (Investors Chronicle, 1984). City of London-based international real estate agents, or international real estate consultancies as they now prefer to be called, head the international real estate consultancies of the world. Their eminence has come about because of the early existence in Britain of chartered surveying as a

TABLE 7
Equivalent net rents and occupation costs for a suite of 10,000 square feet of air-conditioned offices in a central location, May 1985

City	*Equivalent net rent sq.ft. p.a. (£)*	*Total occupation cost sq.ft. p.a. (£)*
London — City	33.00	56.20
London — West End	25.00	37.70
Manchester	7.00	13.30
Glasgow	7.50	15.70
Brussels	5.42	7.95
Paris	19.92	24.49
Amsterdam	6.39	7.77
Frankfurt	9.25	11.65
Madrid	9.12	11.57
Barcelona	5.70	7.12
New York — Mid Town	38.75	52.84
New York — Down Town	27.17	40.25
Chicago	17.07	27.30
Los Angeles	20.65	27.53
San Francisco	25.35	33.15
Sao Paulo	6.52	9.05
Singapore	15.10	23.55
Hong Kong	21.68	25.59
Tokyo	37.19	44.98
Johannesburg	5.58	6.97
Melbourne	13.22	16.81
Syney	16.56	19.93
Perth	6.48	9.90

Source: Richard Ellis, 1985.

profession. The Institute of Chartered Surveyors was founded in 1868. Its Royal Charter was granted in 1881. As with accountancy, this body of expertise was then exported, though at a much slower rate.

These consultancies are essentially commodity brokers dealing in four variants of the same commodity — office buildings, retail buildings, industrial buildings and expensive residential real estate. Over the last 15 years the market for commodities of this kind has become truly international under pressure from institutional investors wanting to internationalize their property portfolios and corporations rationalizing extant portfolios and building new ones. The market is divided amongst the international financial centres since it is here that the highest returns are possible (Table 7) and the judicious construction of a portfolio for a client means that, at any one time, buildings can be bought or developed, rented or sold in such a way that the worst vagaries of land price and rental downturns can be avoided. Other developments have also spurred the creation of an international property market. New forms of (mainly) institutional investment like property unit trusts have appeared on the scene. New forms of finance such as property leasing and other forms of forward funding have been made available by banking capital, often with merchant banks acting as fixers. In addition there is now a substantial secondary mortgage market, handled by elements of commercial capital like brokers and merchant banks, which trades mortgages (Daly, 1982; Feagin, 1983). The net result is that the international property market is a market where buildings are increasingly treated as money commodities in a context which can be divorced from the rest of the economy. For example,

> property prices in Central London have risen by an average of just over 15.7% compound since 1974. In 1984 the index rose 16.9%. The prices are no longer dependent on Britain's economic performance as *Central London is now part of the international property map. (Far Eastern Economic Review*, 1985, my emphasis)

International real estate consultancies have grown rapidly under the impetus provided by this market, helped by a number of trends, of which two are particularly significant. The first of these trends is computerization. In particular, the building up of computer data banks of properties allows clients to pick up international property portfolios more easily and, at the extreme, without even sighting them. The second trend is diversification. Over time, the functions of real estate consultancies have been added to. Clearly the firms are still involved in the traditional functions of chartered surveyors — agency, estate management, surveying, valuation, rating consultancy and the like. But increasingly they have also moved into services with which they have not been traditionally associated, including advice on and management of property portfolios, location consultancy and, taking on some of the functions of merchant banks, arrangment of finance, especially forward funding.

Like accountancy firms, real estate agents are partnerships and this organizational form has influenced the way they have internationalized. A range of options has been taken up including organic growth through branch offices, merger with extant firms in other countries, and alliances with several overseas firms. In many cases a partner from the UK has been seconded to a branch office as the representative of the City firm. The problems of co-ordination of the international network have undoubtedly become greater over time. Some firms have solved these problems by appointing partners from accountancy firms to deal with administrative and financial matters!

TABLE 8
Direct representation of major British real estate agents in international financial centres

First order Supranational Centres				
London 27	New York 7			
Second order Supranational Centres				
Amsterdam 4	Frankfurt 3	Paris 5		
Tokyo 1	Zurich 1			
First order International Centres				
Basel 0	Bombay 0	Brussels 3	Chicago 3	Dusseldorf 1
Hamburg 1	Kong Kong 4	Madrid 3	Melbourne 2	
Mexico City 0	Rio de Janeiro 1	Rome 0	San Francisco 2	
Sao Paulo 1	Singapore 4	Sydney 3		
Toronto 0	Vienna 0			
Second order International Centres				
Bahrain 0	Buenos Aires 0	Kobe 0	Los Angeles 2	
Luxembourg 0	Milan 0	Montreal 0	Osaka 0	
Panama City 0	Seoul 0	Taipei 0		
Others				
Antwerp 1	Barcelona 1	Dallas 1	Dover 1	
The Hague 1	Houston 2	Miami 1	Rotterdam 1	
Vancouver 1				

Direct representation refers to a branch, representative or joint office and the offices of a firm in which an estate agent has a shareholding. Associate firm office networks (e.g. Hillier Parker's European Commercial Property Associates) are *not* included. The estate agents are Goddard and Smith; Gooch and Wagstaff; Healey and Baker; Hillier Parker, May and Rowden; Jones Lang Wootton; Knight, Frank and Rutley, Pepper Angliss; Richard Ellis; St. Quintin; Savills; Weatherall, Green and Smith.

Whatever the case, the net spatial result of all these developments has been a concentration of the offices of British international real estate consultants in international financial centres. Table 8 shows the pattern of office location of some of the major British international real estate consultancies.

Jones Lang Wootton and Richard Ellis are two of the premier British real estate consultancies. Jones Lang Wootton was founded in the City of London as early as 1783, and has developed steadily since. From 1945 onwards it has grown particularly fast and now employs 1,500 people (including 150 partners) round the world working from 40 offices in 17 countries. It is now the largest real estate consultancy in the world, as well as the largest (with 500 employees and 80 partners) in the UK. Its international commitment is bolstered by modern communications and information systems linked up worldwide, including the COMPUTON system, a worldwide property data base system, and PPAS (Property Performance Analysis System), a suite of computer programs aimed at carrying out automatic analysis of the performance of property portfolios. In addition, in 1985 an international research department was set up in Brussels which will augment the sizeable research departments in other cities (for example, the London research department employs 20). These research departments can earn considerable income by providing information on the international property market, carrying out consultancy and issuing publications.

Richard Ellis was founded in the City of London in 1773. The firm grew steadily until 1960, when it had 80 staff worldwide. By 1972 there were 200 staff, including 35 partners. The firm's present complement of just over 1,000 employees worldwide (including 100 partners), works from 32 offices in 14 different countries, illustrating how rapidly it has grown in the 1970s and 1980s. It is the second largest real estate company in the world and one of the largest agencies in the UK (with 375 staff and 78 partners). Like Jones Lang Wootton, the firm has well established research departments.

The pattern of internationalization of Jones Lang Wootton and Richard Ellis is shown in Table 9 and Table 10. From these tables it is possible to see how in the 1970s and 1980s the two firms have moved out from the old Commonwealth countries like Australia, in which their international activities had been concentrated (and in which considerable activity still takes place; Jones Lang Wootton has a staff of 230 in Australia) to other areas of the world. Jones Lang Wootton now has offices in Europe, the Far East, and the United States. Richard Ellis has offices in Europe, the Far East, Africa, South America and the United States. Quite clearly the opening of these new offices has corresponded with the activities of particular clients in the manufacturing and financial spheres coupled with the attractions of serving particular real estate markets. For example, in Europe:

> The nature of the firm's business dealings in the various European countries has tended to vary from market to market. In some the emphasis was more on

TABLE 9
The office network of Jones Lang and Wootton, 1984[1]

Number of offices in:		*Opening of first office in:*	*Number of partners, associates and directors in:*
London	4	1939	97
Glasgow	1	1962	6
Edinburgh	1	1970	4
Jersey	1	1970	1
UK total	7		108
Dublin	1	1965	6
Paris	1	1971	7
Amsterdam	1	1972 }	
Rotterdam	1	1970 }	5
The Hague	1	—	
Frankfurt	1	1973	
Hamburg	1	1974	
Dusseldorf	1	1974	4
Brussels	1	1965	
Antwerp	1	1973	—
Europe total	10		
Sydney	3	1958	18
Melbourne	1	1958	6
Perth	1	1958	6
Brisbane	1	1958	7
Adelaide	1	1958	4
Canberra	1	1958	1
Auckland[2]	1	—	0
Christchurch[2]	1	—	0
Australia and New Zealand total	10		42
Hong Kong	2	1973	14
Singapore	1	1973	10
Kuala Lumpur	1	1973 }	
Penang	1	1973 }	4
Jakarta	1	1980	2
Tokyo[2]	1	1984	1
Far East total	7		31
New York	2	1975	11
Los Angeles	1	1978	1
Houston	1	1980	2
San Francisco	1	1982	1
Washington DC	1	1982	—
USA total	6		15
Overall total	40		224

[1]Date of opening of first office only is given; offices have subsequently been moved within city.
[2]Representative or associate office only.

TABLE 10
The office network of Richard Ellis, 1984[1]

Number of offices in:		Opening of first office in:
London	2	1973/1960
Manchester	1	1978
Glasgow	1	1965
UK total	4	
Paris	1	1969
Amsterdam	1	1973
Brussels	1	1973
Geneva	1	
Madrid	1	1974
Barcelona	1	
Europe total	6	
Sydney	1	1965/1981
Melbourne	1	
Perth	1	1966/82
Brisbane		
Adelaide	1	1969
Australia total	5	
Hong Kong	1	1978
Singapore	1	1976
Jakarta[2]	1	1982
Far East total	3	
Johannesburg	1	1969
Cape Town	1	1969
Durban	1	1969
Pretoria	1	1969
Harare	1	1978
Africa total	5	
Rio de Janeiro[2]	1	1979
Sao Paulo	1	1980
South America total	2	
New York	1	1982
Chicago	1	1976
Atlanta	1	1978
Houston	1	1981
Dallas[2]	1	1982
San Francisco[2]	1	1980
Los Angeles	1	1982
United States total	7	
Overall total	32	

[1]Date of opening of first office only is given; offices have subsequently been moved within city.
[2]Representative or associate office only.

> providing a service to British companies — perhaps associated with one of the major pension funds — that had overseas interests and were seeking suitable property for investment purposes in a country where they were operating, although the firm has always aimed to build up a local clientele as quickly as possible. In others the firm has found itself more consistently involved with local clients engaged in property investment or development, or who simply required in a local context the agency, appraisal or management services that Richard Ellis specialises in. (Richard Ellis, 1982: 27)

Sometimes the movement into Europe has had effects on the UK market. Thus, 'occasionally, the firm has been able to assist EEC clients with an eye on expanding in Britain to acquire either property or property investments in the UK' (Richard Ellis, 1982: 27).

In South America, by contrast, the emphasis has been very much on serving British corporate interests, like Unilever:

> Here, the firm has moved in mainly as advisers to the many long-established British trading houses that have built up strong business connections in the South American markets, and in the process have acquired substantial property holdings throughout the subcontinent. Now many of the firms, in line with current practice in the UK, feel the time is ripe to ensure that these holdings represent a positive asset to their organisation or, if they do not, to obtain professional advice on the steps that need to be taken to make the most of their value. (Richard Ellis, 1982: 28)

The very recent expansion of both firms into the United States is particularly interesting because it is so clearly a long-term strategic move, planned in advance. The expansion clearly coincides with the increased activity by British multinational corporations like Dixons in the United States in the 1970s and 1980s but, more importantly, stems from the lifting of exchange controls in 1979 and the consequent internationalization of the investment portfolios of British pension funds, insurance companies and marketing companies (current practice being that 33 percent of such portfolios should be in property). Take, for example, the case of Richard Ellis:

> It was in January 1975 that the firm, attracted by the potential of the vast American real estate market, but as yet quite unversed in the intricacies of operating within it, undertook an extensive study of the possibilities. The results of the research operation were sufficiently encouraging to justify the opening of the first Richard Ellis office in the United States — in Chicago, Illinois in October 1976. The firm decided from the start on judiciously combining the traditional expertise of the British chartered surveyor with local real estate know-how, and the staff were consequently drawn partly from the firm's London investment department and partly from Americans knowledgeable in real estate operations. (Richard Ellis, 1982: 28)

Richard Ellis now manages the powerful American Property Trust.

> The American Property Trust was set up in 1974 with eleven unitholders, amongst whom were the British Steel Pension Fund, South Yorkshire County Council Staff Superannuation Fund, South of Scotland Electricity Board Fund, British Rail Fund, and the Electricity Supply Nominees.... Between 1974 and 1979, the American Property Trust raised $11.5 million for direct property investment in the USA. By 1984, the trust had assets of $250 million and its participants had grown in number to forty-nine, including major concerns such as Imperial Chemical Industries, Rank Xerox and Reed International. Its geographical distribution of ownership had shifted from a concentration in the south-east of the USA to include properties in Atlanta, Dallas, Houston, Washington, Chicago, Denver, Los Angeles and Kansas City.... [Its activities] are sufficiently powerful to compete directly with domestic US investors. (Bateman, 1985: 117)

The other major area of expansion of offices by Jones Lang Wootton and Richard Ellis has been in the Far East, coincident with the Pacific Basin's rapid economic growth and the elevation of a number of cities, like Hong Kong, Singapore and Tokyo, to international financial centre status, and therefore to inclusion in the international property market. Most recently, both firms have tried to engage with the elusive Japanese property market, a market that is difficult because of its state restrictions, its ownership by a few large Japanese land companies and the tendency of Japanese corporations to internalize property buying. But it is also a market which promises long-term dividends both because of the possibility of investment in Japanese real estate and, more importantly, because of potential to direct Japanese investment into real estate around the world. Most real estate agents continue to operate in this market via, at best, a Japanese national based in London acting as link-person. On 1 May, 1984, however, Jones Lang Wootton opened the first British real estate agent's office in Tokyo:

> According to [the] Chairman of JLW's London partnership, 'the opening underlines our continued evolution as a truly worldwide integrated operation'. Japan has been seen as perhaps the last of the international property markets for UK surveyors to try to enter and JLW are first in. Initially the Tokyo office will be a representative one, setting out to help JLW provide an improved service to JLW clients who require property advice and service in the UK and Europe, USA, Australia, Hong Kong, Singapore, Indonesia, Malaysia and New Zealand. They will also be giving on-the-spot professional advice on the domestic property market to both existing clients and to non-local Japanese firms. (*Estates Gazette*, 1984)

Conclusions

This brief foray into the urban geography of commercial capital leads to at least three conclusions. First, and most obviously, commercial capital is still thriving. It still plays a role in national economies, insofar as it is still possible to talk about a national economy (Radice, 1984; Thrift, 1985a). More importantly, commercial capital has played a vital part in the most recent internationalization of capital (the so-called 'new international division of labour'). The new international system of credit money that has come about, with its multiple, piggybacked financial markets intended to spread risk and maximize short-term investment profit, would never have succeeded without the ability of commercial capital both to create new markets and, in large part, manage the system. It remains to be seen, of course, whether the improvisatory powers of commercial capital can finally surmount the current crisis (Harvey, 1982; Brett, 1983).

Second, it has become clear that the tendency *within* the organizational structure of commercial capital is towards large multinational service corporations offering a veritable supermarket of commercial services. Thus, management of the international credit money system is being centralized into the hands of fewer and fewer decision-makers.

Third, international commercial capital has had an important impact on selected cities like London and is now in the process of exporting the social relations involved to a number of other cities around the world. In the new system of international financial enclaves, commercial capital intervenes in quite forcible ways. Thus, it provides an important and growing component of demand for office accommodation, specialized labour, particular services (like telecommunications), particular types of housing and so on (see Thrift, 1985b on Hong Kong). And, it has the social power — especially through its extended social- political networks — to enforce what it demands. In turn, the results of the demands it makes change the social make-up of these cities, making parts of them the preserve of a professional middle class, of gentrified housing (Hamnett, 1984), and a whole host of other effects, quite out of proportion to the numbers of people involved. Thus, the internationalization of commercial capital poses a considerable economic, social and political challenge to a number of cities which shows no signs of abating (Coakley and Harris, 1983; GLC, 1985).

Notes

1. I have followed Ingham's usage here, rather than that of Marx. Marx refers to merchant capital in general and then distinguishes commercial and money-dealing capital. Ingham (1984: 256, fn. 9) uses 'commercial capital as the general form of profit-making through the repeated and continuous buying and selling of commodities (including money)... rather that the archaic merchant capital of Marx's work'.

2. Merchant banks are now obtaining their own capital base, usually coincident with their takeover by banking capital interested in retailing a whole series of financial services

to corporations. This is a classic case of how the integrity of commercial capital is constantly threatened and must be constantly fought for.

3. Clearly, international financial centres link to the 'world city' literature, but this paper is an attempt to unpack the world city literature by pointing to commercial capital functions only (see Cohen, 1981; Friedmann and Wolff, 1982; Noyelle, 1983; Thrift, 1985a).

4. Numbers noted here and for accountants relate only to firms that serve one or more of the *Times 500* companies.

5. Members of the firm are expected to cultivate contacts at all opportunities. These may well be functional to the business. Thus accountants in general, and all members of commercial capital, tend to have an above-average representation in any community.

6. Thus Stevens (1982: 72) discusses a Peat Marwick Mitchell bid for the Caltex audit:

> The proposal was designed in fourteen sections. Key segments covered the greater glory of Peat, Marwick International, the firm's oil industry experience, an overlay map of Peat and Caltex locations worldwide, a review of the audit scope, and a description of PMM's consulting and tax services.

References

Annual Investment File (1985) 'Chartered Surveyors Survey', *Annual Investment File*: 51–68.

Bateman, M. (1985) *Office Development: A Geographical Analysis*. London: Croom Helm.

Brett, E.A. (1983) *International Money & Capitalist Crisis: The Anatomy of Global Disintegration*. London: Heinemann.

Central Statistical Office (1984) *UK Balance of Payments 1983*. London: Her Majesty's Stationery Office.

Clairmonte, F. and J. Cavanagh (1984) 'Transnational Corporations and Services: The Final Frontier', *Trade and Development*, 5: 215–273.

Coakley, J. (1984) 'The Internationalisation of Bank Capital', *Capital and Class*, 23: 107–120.

Coakley, J. and L. Harris (1983) *The City of Capital*. Oxford: Blackwell.

Cohen, R.B. (1981) 'The New International Division of Labour, Multinational Corporations and Urban Hierarchy', in M.J. Dear and A.J. Scott (eds.), *Urbanisation and Urban Planning in Capitalist Society*, pp. 287–318. London: Methuen.

Cowell, C.K. (1983) 'The International Marketing of Services', *The Service Industries Journal*, 3: 308–328.

Crawfords (1984) *Crawfords Directory of City Connections*. London: Economist Publications.

Daly, M.T. (1982) *Sydney Boom, Sydney Bust*. Sydney: Allen and Unwin.

Darling, J. (1984) 'The Role of Financial Intermediaries in Australian Urban Investment', in C. Adrian (ed.), *Urban Impacts and Local Investment in Australia*. Canberra: Australian Institute of Urban Studies.

Economist, The (1985a) 'Round the World on $150 Billion a Day', *The Economist*, 30 November.

Economist, The (1985b) 'The Other Dimension. Technology and the City of London', *The Economist*, 6 July.

Estates Gazette (1984) 'JLW Open in Tokyo', *Estates Gazette*, 28 April: 260.

Far Eastern Economic Review (1985a) 'Property '85', *Far Eastern Economic Review*, 28 February: 45–74.

Far Eastern Economic Review (1985b) 'Banking '85', *Far Eastern Economic Review*, 25 April: 53–110.

Feagin J.R. (1983) *Playing Monopoly in Real Money*. Englewood Cliffs: Prentice-Hall.

Fraser, W.H. (1981) *The Coming of the Mass Market 1850–1914*. London: Macmillan.

Friedmann, J. and G. Wolff (1982) 'World City Formation: An Agenda for Research and Action', *International Journal of Urban and Regional Research*, 6(3): 309–394.

Gaedeke, R.M. (1973) 'Selected US Multinational Service Firms in Comparative Perspective', *Journal of International Business Studies*, Spring: 61–66.

Giddens, A. (1985) *The Nation State and Violence*. Cambridge: Polity Press.

GLC (1985) *GLC Financial Strategy*. London: Greater London Council.

Hamnett, C. (1984) 'Gentrification and Residential Location Theory: A Review and Assessment', in D.T. Herbert and R.J. Johnston (eds.), *Geography and the Urban Environment*, Vol. 6, pp. 283–329. Chichester: Wiley.

Harris, L. (1985) 'British Capital: Manufacturing, Finance and Multinational Corporations', in D. Coates, G. Johnston and R. Bush (eds.), *A Socialist Anatomy of Britain*, pp. 7–28. Cambridge: Polity Press.

Harvey, D. (1982) *The Limits to Capital*. Oxford: Blackwell.

Ingham, G. (1984) *Capitalism Divided? The City and Industry in British Social Development*. London: Macmillan.

Investors Chronicle (1984) *The City Directory 1984–85*. Cambridge: Woodhead Faulkner.

Jones Lang Wootton (1980) *Offices in the City of London*. London: Jones Lang Wootton.

Jones Lang Wootton (1982, 1983, 1984) *International Property Review*. London: Jones Lang Wootton.

Kindleberger, C.P. (1979) *The Formation of Financial Centres*. Princeton: Princeton University Press.

King, A.D. (1985) 'Capital City: Physical and Social Aspects of London's Role in the World Economy', *Development and Change*, 16.

Langdale, J. (1985) 'Electronic Funds Transfer and the Internationalisation of the Banking and Finance Industry', *Geoforum*, 16: 1–13.

Longstreth, F. (1979) 'The City, Industry and the State', in C. Crouch (ed.), *State and Economy in Contemporary Capitalism*. London: Croom Helm.

McRae, H. and F. Cairncross (1984) *Capital City. London as a Financial Centre*. London: Methuen.

Mandel, E. (1975) *The Generalised Recession of the International Capitalist Economy*. Brussels: Imprecor.

Manser, W.A.P. (1985) *The International Insurance Market. A View from London*. Economist Intelligence Unit Special Report 193 London: Economist Publications.

Mendelsohn, M.S. (1980) *Money on the Move*. London: McGraw Hill.

Minns, R. (1980) *Pension Funds and British Capitalism*. London: Heinemann.

Minns, R. (1981) 'A Comment on Finance Capital and the Crisis in Britain', *Capital and Class*, 14: 98–110.

Noyelle, T.J. (1983) 'The Implications of Industry Restructuring for Spatial Organisation in the United States', in F. Moulaert and P.M. Salinas, (eds.), *Regional Analysis in the New International Division of Labour*, pp. 113–133. Boston: Kluwer Nijhoff.

Noyelle, T.J. and T.M. Stanback (1985) *The Economic Transformation of American Cities*. Totowa: Rowman and Allanheld.

Pagano, M. (1985) 'Does 24-hour Trading Mean More Business or the Same Amount Spread Thinly?' *The Guardian*, 1 July: 19.

Price Waterhouse (1984) *An Introduction to the UK Firm of Price Waterhouse*. London: Price Waterhouse.

Price Waterhouse (1985) *Annual Review 1983–4*. London: Price Waterhouse.

Radice, H. (1984) 'The National Economy — a Keynesian Myth?', *Capital and Class*, 22: 111–190.

Reed, H.C. (1981) *The Pre-eminence of International Finance Centres*. New York: Praeger.

Reed, H.C. (1983) 'Appraising Corporate Investment Policy: A Financial Centre Theory of Foreign Direct Investment', in C.P. Kindleberger and D.B. Audretsch (eds.), *The Multinational Corporation in the 1980s*, pp. 219–244. Cambridge, Mass.: MIT Press.

Richard Ellis (1982) *Two Centuries of Service*. London: Richard Ellis.

Richard Ellis (1982, 1983, 1984) *International Property*. London: Richard Ellis.

Richard Ellis (1985) *World Rental Levels*. London: Richard Ellis.

Sargent, J.R. (1979) 'UK Performance in Services', in F. Blackaby (ed.), *Deindustrialisation*, pp.102–123. London: Heinemann.

Spence, M. (1985) 'Imperialism and Decline: Britain in the 1980s', *Capital and Class*, 25: 117–139.

Stevens, M. (1982) *The Big Eight*. New York: Macmillan.

Taylor, M.J. and N.J. Thrift (eds.) (1982) *The Geography of Multinationals*. London: Croom Helm.

Thrift, N.J. (1984a) 'The Internationalisation of Producer Services and the Genesis of the World City Property Market', *UNIDO CRP*, 36.

Thrift, N.J. (1984b) 'Taking the Rest of the World Seriously? The State of British Urban and Regional Research in a Time of Crisis', *Environment and Planning A*, 17: 7–24.

Thrift, N.J. (1985a) 'All Change: The Geography of International Economic Disorder', in R.J. Johnston and P.J. Taylor (eds.), *World in Crisis*. Oxford: Blackwell.

Thrift, N.J. (1985b) 'The Internationalisation of Producer Services and the Integration of the Pacific Basin Property Market', in M.J. Taylor and N.J. Thrift (eds.), *Multinationals and the Restructing of the World Economy*. London: Croom Helm.

Tinker, T. (1984) *Paper Prophets. A Social Critique of Accounting*. Eastbourne: Holt Rinehart and Winston.

Touche Ross (1984) *Touche Ross and Co*. London: Touche Ross.

Wilson Committee (Committee to Review the Functioning of Financial Institutions) (1980) *Report and Appendices*, Command 7939. London: Her Majesty's Stationery Office.

Part II
Historical Development

[8]

Excerpt from Charles P. Kindleberger, ***The Formation of Financial Centers: A Study in Comparative Economic History***, 1–78

I. INTRODUCTION

It is a curious fact that the formation of financial centers is no longer studied in economics, perhaps because it falls between two stools. Urban and regional economics, which concern themselves with cities, discuss the location of commerce, industry, and housing but rarely that of finance. [An exception should perhaps be made for Canada (Kerr, 1965, 1967) and for France (Labasse, 1955).] Pred's (1966) study of urban growth in the United States deals exclusively with commerce and industry, making no mention of banking or financial markets. A recent U.S. survey of urban economics mentioned finance only once in the text and referred to no work on the subject in a bibliography of 438 items (Goldstein and Moses, 1973). Only the study of the New York metropolitan area led by Vernon (1960) devotes attention to it. At the same time, a vigorous new literature on money and capital markets and their role in economic development takes no interest in geographical location or the relationships among financial centers (Goldsmith, 1969; McKinnon, 1973; Sametz, 1972; Shaw, 1973). Apart from a sentence or two, one would think that the money and capital market was spread evenly throughout a given country.

The "geography of finance," to borrow Kerr's phrase, is relevant to contemporary issues as well as being of considerable historical interest. Contemporary relevance is provided partly by the tasks of building money and capital markets in developing countries, which McKinnon (1973) and Shaw (1973) regard as vital to economic development, more important, indeed, than foreign aid or export expansion. Among developed countries, there is the issue of which center, if any, will emerge as the leading money and capital market of the European Economic Community if it achieves monetary integration. Economic analysis may not be equal to the task of predicting the answer to this question, or of recommending the policy measures a government or intergovernmental body should follow if it wishes to affect the outcome of the market process.[1]

Historically, an explanation is needed as to why money and capital markets were centered at the capital in Great Britain, France, and

[1] An up-to-date report on the subject is Interbank Research Organisation (1973). There are, moreover, indications that the U.S. government is interested in contemplating the steps that would be required to restore the supremacy of New York as the leading world financial center.

Germany but not in Italy, Switzerland, Canada, the United States, or Australia. One can formulate an aspect of the issue as a riddle: What do the Midlands Bank, the *Crédit Lyonnais,* the *Dresdner Bank,* the *Banca Tiberina,* the Bank of Nova Scotia, and the First Boston Corporation have in common? The answer: Their executive offices are located in a different place from that implied by their name—the Midlands Bank in London, the *Crédit Lyonnais* in Paris, the *Dresdner Bank* in Berlin (from 1892 to 1945), the *Banca Tiberina* (after 1879) in Turin, not along the Tiber, the Bank of Nova Scotia in Toronto, and the First Boston Corporation in New York. The two historical curiosities can be combined. A year after the Midlands Bank transferred its headquarters from Birmingham to London in 1891, there was a simultaneous movement of the *Schaffhausen'schen Bankverein* from Cologne to Berlin (i.e., from a provincial city to the capital) and of the *Eidgenössische Bank* from Bern, the capital, to Zurich. The affinity of finance and locations is underlined by the fact that so many banks have places rather than functions (Merchants, Farmers, etc.) in their names. (Private banks, where confidence is all-important, are named for people.)

An historical approach is also called for because, if modern analysts have little interest in spatial finance, the same cannot be said of their grandfathers. Two generations ago, before and after World War I, economics displayed an interest in the functions of and relations among financial centers that is rare in current research. Fanno (1913, Chap. III) had a chapter on the centralization process in banking and money markets, including geographic centralization. In his *Evolution of the Money Market,* Powell (1915) presented a detailed account of the processes by which congeries of isolated banks were formed into a financial structure centered on London, with many physiological analogies, including "natural selection" and "survival of the fittest." The most highly developed analysis, however, was provided by Gras (1922, Chaps. V, VI), the economic historian, who described the stages of development from village and town to metropolitan economy, specifying the development of specialized financial institutions as a metropolitan function.

In the pages that follow, a comparative analysis is presented in literary rather than statistical or econometric form. It is perhaps unnecessary to defend the comparative method after having shown that the administrative capital sometimes serves as the financial center and sometimes does not. I go further, however, and suggest that the study of single cases, valuable as it is, frequently tempts the economic historian to rely too heavily on single analytical models and that the comparative method, for limited problems at least, is of value in showing what is general and what special in historic process. The qualification that the comparative method is most effective with limited problems—as a rule, of a partial-equilibrium sort—reflects concern that, as the analyst moves from one to another country, society, polity, or economy, general-equilibrium issues like business cycles, stages of growth, and backwardness embody too many degrees of freedom to enable him to generalize with confidence.

That the comparative historical account is qualitative rather than quantitative derives from the limitations of the writer, the great size of the task of rendering comparable data from a wide number of countries, and an interest more in process than in the detailed outcome. Even such an impressive study as Goldsmith's *Financial Structure and Development* (1969), which shows conclusively that financial machinery becomes more elaborate as a country grows in productive process, does not examine the detailed processes, particularly the spatial ones. Extending this study to measure the process described would make it unduly long.

Chapter II briefly reviews the literature on the location of cities and their functions, the roles of money and capital markets in the development process, and the evolution of banks and banking. Its main purpose is to identify the economies inherent in a central organization of financial markets and banking machinery, and to show why financial centers tend to be organized spatially in a hierarchy, with a single center as the keystone of the arch. The description is largely limited to banks and banking, with little explicit attention to other elements of money and capital markets. Some reference is made to clearinghouses, stock exchanges, government and private security markets, mortgages, foreign bonds, and insurance, though none to factoring, consumer finance, or pension funds. As economic growth proceeds, the importance of banks as financial intermediaries diminishes relative to other institutions, but it is always strategic.

Chapter II, which concentrates on the why of a single financial center, is followed by seven case studies designed to show the processes by which a given locality is chosen. Chapters III, IV, and V deal with England, France, and Germany, where the political capital became the financial center as well. The contrast between the English and French centers, on the one hand, and the German, on the other, is provided by their respective political histories, especially the late unification of Germany in 1870, which furnishes a sort of "instant replay" of the process. Chapters VI and VII deal with the Italian and Swiss examples, each with late unification, in 1860 and 1848 respectively, but different from the German example because the financial center turns out to be a different city from the political capital. Canada and the United States, in Chapters VIII and IX, furnish cases of financial centers emerging in countries developed from the wilderness; here, again, the political and financial leadership chose different sites. The Canadian experience is of particular interest. The country felt obliged to free itself successively from money- and capital-market reliance on London and New York, experienced two shifts of the financial center, from Halifax to Montreal, then—long-drawn out and still incomplete—from Montreal to Toronto. Lately, moreover, a relatively independent market has begun to develop in Vancouver.

Chapter X deals in summary fashion with the question of a world financial center, arching over and connecting indirectly national money and capital markets. London held the position during most of the nineteenth century, though with challenges from France and Germany. In the twentieth century, a shift to New York occurred, and a second shift is now in progress from New York to the Eurodollar market. That market is spread all over the world but its heart, to use a well-worn image, beats in the American and British banks in London. A concluding Chapter XI seeks to use the lessons derived from the historical studies to throw light on the question of whether a financial center for the European Economic Community will emerge, and if so where.

II. BANKING DEVELOPMENT AND THE METROPOLIS

A recent spate of books has focused anew on the role of banking in economic development. Two of the earliest writers in the field were Hoselitz (1956) and Gerschenkron (1952), who emphasized especially the role of the *Crédit Mobilier*, founded in 1852, in stimulating rapid industrial expansion in France. German banking was said to be as powerful as the steam engine (Gerschenkron, 1962, p. 137). These leads were followed up and developed by Cameron (1961, 1967, 1972), in his own book on France and in the case studies he edited. Some of these cases, particularly Austria, Italy, and Spain, suggested that banking may or may not make a positive contribution to economic development, depending not on the personal qualities of the bankers but on the "structural characteristics of the system, and the laws, regulations and customs" (Cameron, 1972, p. 8). The contribution of the *Crédit Mobilier* to the industrial development of France has also been downgraded (Fohlen, 1972, p. 37); its interests, and those of many of its imitators, lay in speculation, not in industrial growth.

Much of this historical literature, however, focused on banking as an agent of growth through stimulation of demand. By contrast, the analytical contributions of Goldsmith, McKinnon, and Shaw emphasize the role of banking in mobilizing and allocating liquid resources. Goldsmith (1969, p. 400) points out that the development of financial intermediaries "accelerates economic growth and improves economic performance to the extent that it facilitates the migration of funds to the best user, i.e. to the place in the economic system where the funds will find the highest social return." Shaw equates "deep" with liberalized finance, which opens the way to superior allocations of savings by widening and diversifying the financial markets in which investment opportunities compete for the savings flow. In his only reference to space, he goes on: "The market for savings is extended. . . . Local capital markets can be integrated into a common market, and new opportunities for pooling savings and specializing in investment are created" (Shaw, 1973, p. 10). McKinnon's (1973) emphasis is on raising the rate of interest on financial capital to equality with the rate of interest on real capital. This makes it worthwhile for entrepreneurs to save in money form for later investment and increases the availability of external finance, enabling entrepreneurs, who would otherwise be limited to their own savings, to start businesses sooner and on a larger scale. Financing trade and production at a rate of interest equal to the return on real assets is a shot in the arm to development. Integration of capital markets eliminates local and sectoral monopoly and monopsony, but especially stimulates the formation of savings and its pooling (Shaw, 1973). Here is an echo of Powell's (1915, p. 274) reference to banking as a "magnet which pulls out hoards."

As noted, these discussions of banking innovation and financial intermediation or deepening lack a spatial dimension. Financial centers are needed not only to balance through time the savings and investments of individual entrepreneurs and to transfer financial capital from savers to investors, but also to effect payments and to transfer savings between places. Banking and financial centers perform a medium-of-exchange function and an interspatial store-of-value function. Single payments between separate points in a country are made most efficiently through a center, and both seasonal and long-run surpluses and deficits of financial savings are best matched in a center. Furthermore, the specialized functions of international payments and foreign lending or borrowing are typically best performed at one central place that is also the specialized center for domestic interregional payments. (This is not always the case. For twenty years after Berlin became the undisputed center for German domestic finance, Hamburg continued its role as the leading city for foreign-trade finance.)

To limit ourselves again to domestic interregional payments, the efficiency of a single center is akin to the contribution to utility of a single numeraire. Each locality deals not with each other locality in making and receiving payments, but with a single center; $n-1$ conduits are needed instead of $n(n-1)/2$. Small localities are typically clustered about a provincial financial center but are linked to others through the central financial market. When country clearing was established in London in 1858, the National Provincial Bank thought it "preposterous" for a bank at Manchester to collect a check on Newcastle-on-Tyne through London (Taylor, 1964, p. 229). At that time, the National Provincial Bank had offices in Manchester and Newcastle, whereas its banking office in London was opened only in 1866. Later, however, the National Provincial Bank must have cleared among its branches through a central point such as London. French centralization of distribution through Paris has been much criticized; the efficiency of central clearing for such purposes as moving artichokes from Dijon to Bordeaux obviously declines as costs of transport rise. But for money payments there can be no doubt of the efficiency of a central financial market as the apex of a national system, and of a single international market as the apex of national financial centers. An African student once complained to me that Latin-American payments to a country such as Kenya were made in dollar checks on New York; he was persuaded that the system was devised to enable imperialist extortionists to exploit the periphery. He found incredible the truth that the centralization of payments and use of a vehicle currency are efficient.

As an efficient system of payment develops, utilizing the medium-of-exchange function of banking, firms find themselves able to economize on working balances by centralizing them at the metropolitan pivot. Companies above a certain size tend to establish financial offices in the metropolis to deal in financial markets as well as to finance a larger flow of payments with smaller working balances. Increasingly competitive security markets provide larger and cheaper security issues for those who need capital, as well as more liquid investments for lenders. Economies of scale are found not only in the medium-of-exchange and store-of-value functions of money, but also in the standard-of-deferred-payment function insofar as it relates to loans, discounts, and bond issues.[1]

The origins of banking are diverse. Elementary textbooks imply that they can be traced mainly to the storage function of goldsmiths, but this is oversimplification. The goldsmiths in England, congregated in London, were an important source of private banking but by no means as important as merchant houses. Other bankers originated as scriveners or notaries, tax receivers or tax farmers who lent out funds being held for remittance to the Treasury, court bankers who provided advances and personal services to profligate princes, and industrial companies that paid wages in tokens, moving a stage beyond the truck system (payments in commodities), and found that the tokens remained in circulation. Some manufacturers lent out business profits rather than plowing them back in industrial expansion. But the bulk of bankers started as merchants, gradually becoming specialized in the financial side of commerce. Ten of fourteen private bankers in Liverpool—a commercial city, to be sure—sprang from wholesale houses (Pressnell, 1956, p. 49). Often a merchant devised a system for making or collecting payments at a distance and was asked to perform such services for others. The Bank of England was started during the Nine Years' War by wine merchants who found themselves with liquid capital as they sold their stocks and had no opportunity to replace them.

[1] I can scarcely refrain from pointing out that these economies tend to be lost in the international system when there are fluctuating exchange rates, no international money, and a disintegrated international capital market.

Beer also involved capital accumulation that in a number of instances led the brewer into banking.

Both banking and commerce involve the overcoming of distance, and the geographical pattern of banking was linked to commerce. Cities are typically located at a break in transport, and such a break must lie across a trade route (Duncan *et al.*, 1960, p. 39). London, Paris, Cologne, Rome, and Montreal lie on major rivers at the first ford or shallow part up from the sea. Berlin lies at the point of transshipment for bulk cargoes moving from the Oder to the Elbe (Henning, 1971). Lyons and Frankfurt were historic fair towns on international caravan trails, and the *furt* in Frankfurt stands for ford—the ford of the Franks on the river Main. As we shall see, the coming of the railroad, a major innovation in transport in the nineteenth century, changed the character of banking and the location of some financial centers, and only timely action by communities to influence the shape of the railroad network prevented other changes adverse to them.

Not all commodities are identical in their impact on transport or the location of financial activity. It is possible to construct a "staple theory" of finance, at least for the early stages of banking development, to explain the particular impact of different commodities on the size and pattern of financial flows. Seasonality of financial requirements is one aspect; unique production processes, a need for bought inputs, and time needed to consume outputs are others. Ports are dominated by particular commodities financed in certain ways, and this affects their financial development: Liverpool by cotton and wheat, Glasgow by sugar and tobacco, Cherbourg by cotton, Bremen by cotton and coffee (financed in London), etc.

The mechanism by which the location of a city, the transport network, and the economic characteristics of the goods and services in which an area specialized determined the financial pattern was partly Darwinian and partly the result of deliberate action by government or private individuals. The Darwinian evolution of the banking pattern is illustrated by depressions that wiped out both badly located banks and bankers and those who were well-located but incautious. State policy is reflected by the centralizing policies of the Bank of France and French government, which in 1848 wiped out the provincial banks established during the 1830s, and by the decentralizing pressures in Canada and the United States. The strength of regional banking in France in the period before World War I was in spite of, not owing to, state action, which typically operated at that time to discourage regional autonomy. At the private level, local action fostered means of transport and opposed rival financial centers. Of great interest, banks, bankers, corporation head offices, and the like deliberately changed locations, often saving face by professing loyalty to their birthplace. Goldstein and Moses (1973, p. 485, note 40) describe Webber's game-theoretic model of location decisions under uncertainty with the assumption that "once the firm is located, it is impossible to relocate." For banks, as will be evident later, such an assumption lacks historical validity.

Some allowance must also be made for pure accident. I am informed by Juan Linz that Bilbao flourishes in Spain as the second financial center outside of Madrid because Prieto, the Socialist Finance Minister in the 1930s, came from that region and saved its banks while allowing those of Barcelona to fail. The history of European and North American banking is filled with accounts of bankers' quarrels based on personal, social, political, and religious differences, which may or may not be superficial rationalizations of deep-seated economic forces.

On a staple-theory showing, banking starts out to serve the needs of sovereigns and nobles; develops in connection with commerce; then less personally with governmental finance; next with transport, including shipping, canals, turnpikes, and railroads; then with industry; and finally with intermediation in insurance, mortgages, consumer finance, factoring, pension funds, and the like. In a highly developed setting like New York or London, the money market in a broad sense includes (1) a money market with many specialized segments for commercial paper, acceptances, collateral loans, Treasury bills, federal funds (in New York), certificates of indebtedness, etc., and (2) a capital market, both private and governmental, dealing in new issues and secondary distribution, together with (3) trading in commodities, foreign exchange, bullion (in London, Paris, and Zurich), and, to a lesser degree, ships and ship charters, and insurance (Madden and Nadler, 1935, p. 110). The borrowing and lending pattern starts locally and extends to a national center, with perhaps intermediate regional stops, finally becoming international. Specialization grows in instruments and functions and by hierarchical market. Inflations, depressions, wars, and the like distort or intensify the pattern.

The hierarchical character of financial specialization was originally discussed by an economic historian, N. S. B. Gras (1922), who developed a theory of stages of metropolitan development in which finance was the apex. There is a national credit market in a country, but it is spatially concentrated in a hierarchical pattern. As summarized by Duncan (1960, p. 84), Gras traces through four phases the growth of the metropolis to serve a hinterland: (1) commerce, (2) industry, (3) transport, (4) finance. Finance is more concentrated than commerce, industry, or residence. In 1929, 4 counties had one-quarter of the savings deposits in the United States—a poor measure of financial concentration—whereas 11 counties shared one-quarter of retail sales, and 27 counties shared one-fourth of the population (McKenzie, 1933, p. 62). In 1955, New York had \$4.4 billion of nonlocal loans, compared with \$1.2 billion for Chicago and \$490 million for San Francisco—another measure of metropolitan character (Duncan *et al.*, 1960, p. 117). Similar data for Canada in the 1960s are given in Chapter VIII.

Cities, according to Vernon (1960, pp. 70, 73), attract industries or services in which there is great uncertainty and need for face-to-face contact, those in which speed of interaction is a requisite. Unstandardized outputs lead to agglomeration as a convenience for the shopper. The port of New York attracted the wholesalers, who pulled in the financial institutions, which attracted the central offices of national corporations (Vernon, 1960, p. 80). A detailed study of New York's financial functions (Robbins and Terleckyj, 1960, p. 38) supports this view and discusses the external economies arising from specialization, joint facilities, and the services of other industries such as printing. Shopping convenience is mentioned, but perhaps too little is made of the fact that the broader the financial market, the greater the liquidity of security issues, with the result that lenders and borrowers from other regions will transfer to that market their gross demands and supplies, not just net excess demand or supply. The borrower pays a lower rate of interest and/or is able to issue a larger loan. The lender acquires a qualitatively different investment because it is traded on a broader secondary market, which is why he is willing and often eager to accept a lower interest rate (Kindleberger, 1963, pp. 191–192). Insurance companies are less centralized than most other segments of the money and capital market because of a pronounced preference by consumers in the United States for locally issued insurance policies (Robbins and Terleckyj, 1960, Chap. VI).

In addition to economies, there are diseconomies which work against centralization and favor regional markets. The foremost is cost of information, which gives local credit markets an advantage in dealing with small firms in an area. Unfamiliarity with local personalities and character may discourage central money and capital markets from lending locally. The difference in time is another diseconomy of centralization that has supported the growth of North American markets as against European, the Eurocurrency market as against New York, and the West Coast of North America as against Toronto-Montreal and New York. Direct communication by telephone or telex must be simultaneous; when it spans many time zones, it involves a dislocation of the working day for at least one party. This is another specific illustration of the cost of dealing in finance at a distance; the foremost is the loss of information obtainable only with face-to-face contact. Still a third diseconomy of centralization is crowding, which made for the building of hundreds of offices in midtown Manhattan after World War II and induced one bank, the First National City Bank, to move its head office from downtown to midtown Manhattan. The same phenomenon had been evident in London, with a banking community in the West End of London, separate from the City, for the convenience of rich clients in Mayfair. The London and Westminster Bank, formed in 1836, communicated through its name that it was one of the few banks which operated in both the City and the West End.

Not a diseconomy so much as a discrimination is the tendency of governments and private persons to favor their compatriots over foreigners, even at the expense of higher cost or lower profit—an implicit or explicit mercantilist attitude.

Up to a certain high degree of concentration, positive externalities and economies of scale appear to outweigh diseconomies, favoring centralization. The continuous reduction in the costs and difficulties of transport and communication over the last two hundred years has favored the formation of a single world financial market.

III. LONDON AS THE FINANCIAL CENTER OF ENGLAND

Prior to about 1750, there was little country banking in England. Substantial incorporated banks existed in Scotland, and the Bank of England was established in London in 1694; there were also many private bankers there. The Bank of England had a monopoly of joint-stock banking in England; private banks were allowed to issue notes, but their size was limited by the fact that they could have no more than six partners.

Beginning about 1750, there was an upsurge of banks in the country. The dozen or so existing in 1750 doubled by 1772 and reached 400 by 1800 (Bisschop, 1896, pp. 150, 163). Bankers with large families or trusted relatives tended to establish a separate firm in the City in addition to one in the country. The father of the four Baring brothers had come to Exeter from Germany as a wool and serge merchant and had gone into banking in 1717; fifty years later the brothers divided up—two in London and two in Exeter (Wechsberg, 1966, p. 102). And Abel Smith II, the son of the tax receiver Thomas Smith who remitted funds to London through his connections as a mercer with goldsmith bankers, started a Nottinghamshire bank in 1757, a London bank in 1758, a Lincoln bank in 1775, and a bank at Hull for the Russian trade in 1784 (Leighton-Boyce, 1958, p. 20). Much of the activity of these banks was remittance. Landlords living in London received their rent twice a year in May and November, so that the banks were called upon at these times for London bills (Bisschop, 1896, p. 156). The West End banks, which served the landed interests, were particularly involved in government securities (Anderson, 1972, p. 251). In addition, in prosperous times country banks accumulated deposits which they remitted to London for investment. Testifying before the Bullion Committee in 1810, Mr. Richardson, a bill broker, said:

> In some parts of the country there is little circulation of bills drawn on London, as in Norfolk, Essex, Sussex, etc. . . . . I receive bills to a considerable extent from Lancashire in particular, and remit them to Norfolk &c where the bankers have large lodgments and much money to advance on bills of discount (Bagehot, 1873, p. 138).

Bagehot added in 1873 (p. 140) that the distribution of the bill brokers' customers remained much the same after sixty years, and his text speaks of funds from agricultural counties such as Somersetshire and

Hampshire, with good land but no manufactures or trade, being invested in the discount of bills from Yorkshire and Lancashire (p. 6).

The numerous country banks, hard hit by the deflation following the Napoleonic War, generated a campaign, largely led by Thomas Joplin, a timber merchant from Newcastle, for adoption of the Scottish system of joint-stock (incorporated) banking with branches. The panic of 1825, in which many small country banks disappeared, brought the adoption of joint-stock banking in 1826, but within a radius of 65 miles from London the privilege of issuing notes was reserved to the Bank of England. (The Bank sought to provide an element of stability for the country banks by opening branches outside the 65-mile area.) With the renewal of the Bank's charter in 1833, further legislation was required. This was interpreted, against the wishes of the Bank of England, as permitting joint-stock banks of deposit, if not joint-stock banks of note issue, within 65 miles of London. The result was the establishment outside the radius of many banks with the right of note issue. Inside the area, only a few banks were started, as the issuing of notes was deemed the principal source of profit. The outstanding one, which survives today, is the London and Westminster.

The other four of the five great joint-stock banks of 1967 (reduced to four by the merger of the National Provincial with the London and Westminster in 1968) were originally provincial. Lloyds was started as a private bank in 1765 in Birmingham by a successful Quaker metal trader. Members of the family set up a London firm in 1770; the last partner of both the London and Birmingham houses died in 1807. The Birmingham bank remained private until 1865, when it began a series of mergers and amalgamations which converted it from a provincial to a City and national institution. Mergers of 1884 with two private banks (Messrs Barnett, Hoares, Hambury and Lloyd, and Bosanquet, Salt and Co.) brought the bank effectively to London. The head office remained in Birmingham, but the center of gravity rapidly shifted to London (Sayers, 1957, p. 35).[1] The need to acquire branches and to establish the bank in London came from difficulties in balancing the demand and supply for investments. In 1866, a shareholder was opposed to branching, but the chairman pointed to the need to attract funds (p. 237). Then, as the branch movement grew and banks were acquired

[1] The general manager from 1871 to 1902, Howard Lloyd, went to London from Birmingham once a week; his successor made it his business to concentrate all the head office in London (Sayers, 1957, p. 50). From 1899 the Board met alternately in Birmingham and London, and by 1910, the Board met only in London (p. 272).

in areas of surplus funds, the opposite necessity to find an outlet for funds in London became imperative—a process of unbalanced growth. According to Sayers (1957, p. 269), "A main attraction for joining Lombard Street was the prospect for fuller and more remunerative employment of surplus cash." Integration of the national capital market can be seen in the tension caused by the original practice of paying 2½ per cent on deposits in Birmingham, while in Lombard Street the rate varied with the bank rate. When the bank rate rose above 4 per cent, some depositors were tempted to move cash to London. This tendency existed before amalgamation with the London banks but became accentuated thereafter. Only much later, in 1920, when a 7 per cent bank rate had made the London rate apply far out into the country, was the problem resolved by establishing a single deposit rate for the entire bank (pp. 165, 270).[2]

The history of Midlands Bank is similar to that of Lloyds. It started early as a joint-stock bank, in 1836, but moved slowly, acquiring only six branches in the next fifty years, all near Birmingham. By 1889, it had absorbed eight provincial banks, including substantial ones in Lancashire and Wales. At this point, the Birmingham Banking Company, another smaller rival of Lloyds, followed Lloyds's example in acquiring a London connection (Crick and Wadsworth, 1936, p. 311). Like modern multinational corporations, which invest defensively, following the leader to prevent it from stealing a march, the Midlands Bank merged with the Central Bank of London in the same year. So as not to offend Birmingham, it was stated that the London bank had imposed among its conditions "a sine qua non that the head office must be in London, and half-yearly meetings of stockholders in January in Birmingham and July in London." The Baring crisis of 1890 sped the process of amalgamation when Lord Goschen, the Chancellor of the Exchequer, shocked the banks by calling their reserves inadequate. By October 1898, the business of the Midlands was judged ill-balanced: "Our country business is out of all proportion to our Metropolitan business," and the head office was too small. This was corrected by merging with the City Bank of London (Crick and Wadsworth, 1936, pp. 312, 316). The bank's biographers regard the process as the outcome of an irresistible trend in English banking; Surrey and Kent and the suburbs of London—not the agricultural counties this time—were

[2] References to the ability and willingness of depositors to move funds between the provinces and London are found elsewhere in Sayers's (1957, p. 110) account of Lloyds for Birmingham, and Leighton-Boyce's (1958, p. 36) account of Nottingham.

lending surplus funds to the industrial areas of the Midlands and the West Riding (Yorkshire). The head office was the channel through which resources flowed far more efficiently than under the old agency and bill system (pp. 329, 342). There was danger for local banks which became too heavily involved in separate industries: Bradford in wool, Oldham in cotton, Sheffield in steel (p. 345).

On occasion, however, there was safety in being off by oneself. Prior to its merger with the Midlands, the Bank of Wales had little trouble in the crises of 1857 and 1866, largely because its business was predominantly Welsh (Crick and Wadsworth, 1936, p. 188). On the other hand, the Northumberland and Durham Bank failed in 1857, whether, as one story has it (Gregory, 1936, p. 184), because the bank had loaned almost £1 million of its £2.5 million assets to a single company, Derwent & Co., which was working mineral rights owned by the bank's Jonathan Ricardson, or because £250,000 of small bills on Newcastle shopkeepers, probably good in themselves, were not discountable outside of Newcastle (Powell, 1915, p. 286). Integration is good in good times; in bad times, it is good if you have the trouble and the rest of the world helps, bad if the trouble originates outside and is communicated inward.

The National Provincial Bank and Barclays developed differently. The National Provincial was organized as a joint-stock company in 1833, with £1 million of capital, a board in London, but banking operations in a series of branches outside the 65-mile limit. Some existing banks were taken over; many new ones were created. The geographical spread was wide: Gloucester, Stockton, Darlington, Kingsbridge, Manchester, Ramsgate, Newcastle, Emlyn, etc. As Withers (1933, pp. 61, 62) notes, "In those days of slow communication and transport, it must have required no ordinary courage . . . in an era of political and industrial unrest and wild speculative fever, to open for business, and to establish liabilities in places as remote as Darlington in the north and Exeter in the west." The provincial banks were given a certain amount of local autonomy but were under the general management of London. In 1866, when the bank had 122 offices, it opened for business in London. This involved giving up the right to issue notes.

The calculations which led to this decision—to exchange the right of note issue amounting to nearly £450,000 for banking operations in London—have not been made explicit. The rise of railroad communication, development of London clearing and, after the Bank Act of 1844, spread of payment by check rather than by notes, plus the development of limited liability for bank as well as other shareholders in 1857 and 1862, may all have played a role. In 1858, the National Provincial was opposed to clearing in London and the substitution of checks for country banker drafts and notes (Taylor, 1964, p. 229). By 1865 it found the trends irresistible. If the testimony of other banking histories is applicable, the London agency banks were probably earning profits on a surplus of funds generated in the branch network; the branch banks could appropriate the profit by investing the funds themselves. It would be interesting to know whether the decision was influenced by the possibility of improving intrabank settlements in London.

The last of the giant joint-stock banks, Barclays, was created in 1896 from an amalgamation of twenty private banks then doing business in various parts of England, with histories stretching back many generations. The three largest were Barclay, Bevan, Tritton, Ransom, Bouverie & Co. of London, itself a merger of a City and a West End bank; Gurney and Co. of Norwich; and Jonathan Backhouse of Darlington. Seven of the twenty original banks were firms in which there were Gurney interests. The merger combined a valuable London business with strong connections in the Eastern counties, the Southwest, and the Northwest (Matthews and Tuke, 1926, pp. 1–9). Amalgamation reflected the view that the day of the private general banker was ending and that national networks both made for efficiency in payments and protected the banker from undue dependence on other banks for funds or outlets. In particular, country banks with considerable surpluses of funds to invest required assured outlets, partly in the industrial counties but partly abroad. The necessary division of surplus funds could be made only in a central capital market, with the net excess of each branch-banking network made available for lending abroad through the discount market and the stock exchange.

In concluding the discussion of England, it is hardly necessary to explain how London became the metropolitan apex of the financial network. Whether with the correspondent system, the Bank of England branches in the provinces, or the nationally spread joint-stock banks with their head offices also in the provinces, the system had no choice but to center in London. London had an ancient banking tradition and it was a major port, the capital seat, and the hub of the railroad network; all forces were brought to bear on this locality, which was itself somewhat divided between the City and the West End. The different banking systems in Ireland and Scotland reached across their boundaries and linked up with London.

After the railroad was built in 1830, London was accessible from all parts of the country. Howard Lloyd went to London from Birmingham one day a week from 1884 to 1902, and, after his retirement in that year, attended a weekly board meeting from his country place until his death in 1920 (Sayers, 1957, p. 50). In 1899, one partner of Smiths spent three days a week at Nottingham and one each at London, Newark, and Mansfield (Leighton-Boyce, 1958, p. 279).

London was not the only port; much foreign banking business had been conducted through Liverpool, the cotton and grain port, and through Glasgow and Dundee, which specialized respectively in tobacco and jute. The centralization process occurred through failure, merger, or a change of headquarters. Three American banks, the so-called "W-banks"—Wiggins, Wildes, and Wilson—failed in the crisis of 1837 (Hidy, 1939, p. 84), and the Bank of Liverpool did not survive the crisis of 1857; the Royal Bank of Liverpool failed in 1847 and stopped payment a second time in 1867. W. & J. Brown & Co., which remained afloat in 1837, added British capital and opened a London branch during the Civil War, when cotton was scarce; it closed down the Liverpool operation in 1889. Other Liverpool banks were absorbed at the end of the century, like the Liverpool Union Bank, which was taken over by Lloyds in 1900. The takeover required courage, Sayers (1957, p. 261) states, as Liverpool valued its independence. When Lloyds tried to absorb the Manchester and Liverpool District Bank in 1903, there was an outcry. The *Manchester Guardian* protested that the "strongest, best conducted and most prosperous of the so-called country banks should not lose its identity" (Sayers, 1957, p. 263). Financing was separated from the handling of commodities and concentrated away from the port of entry. Henry Bell, who became general manager of Lloyds in 1913, had started his banking career in a private bank in Liverpool. He worked for a time with the Liverpool Union Bank, where he gained experience in the financing of cotton, corn, timber, and provisions. When the Liverpool Union was taken over by Lloyds, he was soon transferred to the Head Office in Birmingham, and in 1903 was transferred again to manage the City Office in Lombard Street. There he turned his Liverpool experience in commodity finance to such good account that he ended up as General Manager of the entire Lloyds Bank (Sayers, 1957, pp. 79–80). Successful men, management, and techniques all converge upon the center.

Two of the smaller national joint-stock banks survived into the 1960s, with head offices in Lancashire but large London branches. The Manchester and Liverpool District Bank kept its identity until 1962, despite amalgamations, but it changed its name to District Bank in 1924 when it achieved national status. By the same token, the Bank of Liverpool grew through merger to national scope, permitting its acquisitions to retain their original London agents, until in 1918 it was dealing with five private bankers. It then merged with Martin's Limited, with a head office in Liverpool but a separate board in London. In due course, after a death, the parochial name was altered to Martin's Bank (Chandler, 1964, Vol. I, pp. 420 ff.).

As they became national, banks experimented with various degrees of uniformity of practice and decentralization (Sayers, 1957, pp. 58, 232; Leighton-Boyce, 1958, p. 279). In the end, "the principal characteristic of the British money market is the decentralization of granting credit, while at the same time the various banking institutions are closely connected by the placing of their actual reserve in the hands of one note-issuing bank" (Bisschop, 1896, p. 217).

That coiner of physical images, Powell (1915, pp. 370, 372), quoted the 1858 Select Committee on the tendency of deposits to gravitate to London, the center of commercial activity, adding, "The expression 'gravitates' is singularly felicitous, though it is possible that the Committee did not realize how rapidly the mechanism of the Money Market was being modelled on the lines of the Solar system."

IV. PARIS IN FRANCE

The development of banking in France differed sharply from that in England. Centralization had been a feature of French life since the time of Louis XIV, but the French Revolution scattered banking back to its origins in Geneva or Germany, or overseas. With peace, these merchant banks returned to Paris; they began to slough off speculation in merchandise and to open subsidiaries in ports such as Le Havre to finance imports of cotton (Lévy-Leboyer, 1964, pp. 436–437). Apart from the ports, however, the development of credit markets was slow and they were poorly integrated. Emile Pereire wrote in 1834 that there were no banks outside of Paris, in contrast with England, which had five or six hundred (Bigo, 1947, p. 21). The disconnected character of money and capital markets is illustrated by the fact that Dijon paid 9 or 10 per cent for discounts, while Paris paid 4 per cent and Lyons as little as 3 per cent (Gille, 1970, pp. 57, 77). Lyons, however, found money tight each spring when it paid for silk from Italy. The seasonal tightness applied to all of rural France, which shipped funds to Paris in the first half of the year and got them back with the harvest after August (Bigo, 1947, p. 101).

Napoleon, who established the Bank of France at the turn of the century, sought to unify the national credit system by establishing subsidiaries of the Bank in the provinces to improve the circulation of specie and drafts. With the Restoration, the Bank of France abandoned this policy on two grounds, the difficulty of finding the local buyers for Bank of France stock needed to qualify as regents of the provincial *comptoirs,* and the scarcity of three-name paper, which was all the Bank would rediscount. The alternative was to establish regional banks to mobilize local savings more effectively. Such banks got off to a good start in Rouen, Nantes, and Bordeaux—all ports—and others were begun in the 1830s in Le Havre, Lille, Lyons, Marseilles, and Dijon, but under restrictions. The Bank of France decided that it needed a monopoly of the note issue and limited the regional banks as to the paper they could discount, the size of the notes they could issue, and the ability to redeem notes in Paris (Gille, 1970, pp. 1–101). In the financial crisis of 1848, the Bank of France allowed the regional banks to fail, so as to take over the note issue, and returned to a program of *comptoirs.*

One of the fundamental reasons for developing local institutions was the fear that the Bank of France would order the provinces to restrict credit in a crisis without regard for local conditions (Gille, 1970, p. 24). As we have seen in the case of England, however, integration and separation can each be a help or a hindrance in periods of stress, depending upon where the liquidity squeeze strikes.

With a fractured national market, some localities experienced unique conditions owing to specialized foreign relations. While Paris served as an intermediary between sources of capital such as Vienna, Frankfurt, Strasbourg, and Basel and outlets such as Rouen, Saint-Quentin, and Ghent, Lyons had its special connection with Geneva, and Mulhouse with Basel (Lévy-Leboyer, 1964, p. 429). Marseilles was continuously bled for specie by Spain, Corsica, Algiers, and the Black Sea (Gille, 1970, pp. 67–68).

In contrast with these cities, which were linked into two or more banking networks, the countryside went its own way. Bankers were often landed proprietors rather than merchants, with an interest in lending to agriculture and in equipping large estates, but they were dominated by security, prudence, tradition, and routine. The banking leadership was in Paris, and the small country banks chose not to follow it (Thuillier, 1955, p. 512).

With the foundation of the *Crédit Mobilier* and the large credit banks—the *Crédit Lyonnais, Société Générale, Comptoir d'Escompte*, etc.—in the 1850s and 1860s, the money and capital market of France became better interconnected but no less centralized with the passage of time. The *Crédit Mobilier* and the *Société Générale* started in Paris and undertook large-scale lending for railroads, ports, and other public works, but did not finance local industrial activity. Established in the silk capital at the entrepôt for foreign trade to Switzerland and Italy, the *Crédit Lyonnais* spread out a network of branches—first in the Languedoc and then throughout the country—to draw funds not to Lyons but to Paris. The history of the bank is discussed in detail in two books, an account of the years from 1863 to 1882 by Bouvier (1961), and one of the few studies of credit networks by a geographer, Labasse (1955).

Bouvier follows with great precision the move of the bank from Lyons to Paris. Started by Henri Germain, son of a silk manufacturer, who received a substantial dowry from his wife, daughter of another silk family, its early investments were industrial and regional. Most were in difficulty by 1870. In some cases, such as the widely discussed firm, *La Fuchsine*, manufacturers of a synthetic dye, the difficulties of the firm were intensified by the greed of the bank in seeking quick profit rather than careful development. Mme. Germain died in 1867, and M. Germain was remarried in 1869 to a Parisian. He was elected to the Chamber of Deputies, and this required his presence in Paris. Bit by bit, he spent a greater proportion of his time in Paris. He did not visit the head office in Lyons even once during 1881, and the head office was actually shifted to Paris in 1882. Even in 1879, the head of the subagency at Béziers asked whether he could not deal directly with Paris rather than going through Lyons.

In 1871, the bank made very large profits in the Thiers rente. From then on, its task was to collect savings from all France, but especially from the Lyons hinterland, to funnel to Paris for investment in foreign bonds. "Drainage" (with a French pronunciation) was the function of the branch network, the accumulation of deposits. Towns like Grenoble, Annecy, and Creusot, which had thriving industry and building and needed loans, were to be avoided. Loans were provided to commerce, the fruitgrower, the cattle feeder, and the abbatoir, but not to industrialists. The Minister of Finance made the same objection in relation to Lille in 1835: "It is rare that banks adapt to and prosper in cities of factories. There is little hope of keeping the notes of the bank in circulation for very long" (Gille, 1970, p. 36).

The change in the personal interests of Henri Germain from Lyons to Paris are of course symptomatic rather than causal. The decline in silk manufacturing in the Lyons area reduced the demand for finance and left Lyons "a gold mine for savings." Germain and the *hauts banquiers* of Paris, Geneva, and Italy who started the bank with him were interested only in lending to large and established industry, as was true of Paris banking generally. Where such loans were not available, foreign loans served instead.

Little change in this process was produced by the rise of the so-called "industrial banks," or *banques d'affaires,* founded in the 1870s. Most disappeared in the Great Depression or in the crash of 1882, which also engulfed the *Union Générale.* Those that survived did so by hoarding their profits on the Thiers rente. With recovery, from 1896 on, moreover, their investments were highly similar to those of the deposit banks, in foreign bonds and established companies.

Under these circumstances, the demand for local credit had to be filled locally in regional credit markets, which sprang up in competition with the national market. In 1910, and again in 1929, small regional banks that had not merged with or been driven under by the large Paris-led firms organized to resist the domination of the center. In 1910, the 400-member *Syndicat Central des Banques de Province* met at

Bordeaux (Brocard, 1912, p. 106). In 1929, the *Crédit Industriel et Commercial,* in cooperation with several other institutions, organized the *Union des Banques Régionales pour le Crédit Industriel* (Madden and Nadler, 1935, p. 327). The movement flourished particularly in the North, in Lorraine, and in Haute Savoie.

In the North, the *Crédit du Nord* emerged as one of the strongest of the regional banks in France. With its head office in Lille in 1848, it established a few branches—Armentières in 1878, Tourcoing in 1884, and Paris in 1889, before expanding more rapidly after 1894 (*Crédit du Nord Centenaire,* 1948). It is of particular interest that it remained a regional bank and did not move its head office to Paris. Other vital regional capital markets in Lorraine and Haute Savoie undertook to finance the expansion of Bricy iron ore after 1870 and the development of hydroelectric power generation, aluminum, and other electric metallurgical and electric chemical industry (Buffet, 1917; Charpenay, 1935). The Charpenay bank failed in 1931, receiving no assistance from the Bank of France. A well-known writer on French banking (Dauphin-Meunier, 1936, pp. 165–166) has accused the Bank of France of fostering greater centralization in the twentieth century by actively competing with the regional banks for local paper. The small regional banks were able to compete with the national institutions because their deposits were mostly at term, as opposed to sight, and they were able to maintain much lower reserve ratios, in some cases as low as 3 to 4 per cent, against 12 per cent or so for the larger banks (Fanno, 1913, p. 74).

Beyond the private and deposit banks, centralization of the capital market in France was accentuated by government institutions, not only the Bank of France but also such national institutions as the *Crédit Foncier* (1852), *Crédit Agricole* (1860), and *Caisses d'Epargne* (1881, later merged with the *Caisse de Dépôts et de Consignations*). To this day, savings banks do not invest locally, as is generally the case in the United States, but pour their funds to Paris, where they are administered by a single decision-making unit, most recently as an adjunct to the planning process.

The choice of Paris over other central locations need not be explained. Tradition, administrative centralization, the communication network laid out in a star with Paris as the center, all attest to the pull of the capital. Apart from the regional banks, there was no resistance to the centripetal force. By 1900 the Lyons bourse had been left behind and was characterized as a museum piece, despite some revival during the German occupation of France in 1940–42, when it was in the unoccupied zone (Labasse, 1955, p. 446). After World War II, the movement continued, with the transfer to Paris in the single year 1950 of the head offices of three major Lyons companies, including the *Comptoir de Textile Artificiel*, whose president continued to live in Lyons but worked in Paris during the week (Labasse, 1955, pp. 493, 500). The movement of international, largely American companies to France in the 1950s and 1960s accentuated the trend and finally elicited a program to move industry and head offices out of Paris to the provinces.

V. BERLIN IN GERMANY

The emergence of a single financial center in Germany has taken place twice, on both occasions in connection with war: first, in the rise to dominance of Berlin over Cologne, Frankfurt, Darmstadt, Dresden, Leipzig, and Hamburg after the victory of Prussia over France in 1871; and, second, in the gradual emergence of Frankfurt as the financial capital of West Germany, following the isolation of Berlin at the end of World War II. In both instances, the process was partly political and partly economic.

Prior to 1870, Germany was made up of at least thirty principalities, republics, and kingdoms, varying in size from cities like Frankfurt and Hamburg to the large state of Prussia, which encompassed a wide area from Frankfurt north to the sea and then east—including East Prussia and Silesia—with its capital at Berlin. Prior to the reduction of internal barriers in 1818, the establishment of the *Zollverein* in 1834, and the construction of the railroad in the 1840s, the constituent elements of Prussia often pursued separate policies because of physical separation. Private banks were local—the Rothschilds in Frankfurt, the Oppenheims in Cologne, Bleichröder and Mendelssohn in Berlin, Heine and Warburg in Hamburg. Beginning with the creation of the *Schaffhausen'schen Bankverein* in 1848 on the ruins of Schaffhausen & Co., which had failed, two waves of bank formation took place, from 1850 to 1857 and from 1866 to 1873, from the victory of Prussia over Austria to the onset of the Great Depression, with hardly any pause for the Franco-Prussian War in 1870 (Helfferich, 1956, p. 30).

In a passing moment of absent-mindedness, the Prussian government in 1848 granted the *Schaffhausen'schen Bankverein* permission to create an incorporated bank. But when the bank sought to grow by adding to its capital and moving to Berlin in 1853, it was refused permission (Riesser, 1911, p. 509). Its by-laws did not specifically provide for branches. Tilly (1966, p. 115) states that Berlin in the 1850s was the ideal place to start a bank, presumably because of its security activity in the finance of railroads, although he fails to say why. To get around the refusal of the Prussian government to permit further incorporated banks, Cologne financiers, led by the Oppenheims and Gustav Mevissen, and with French financial support, started the *Bank für Handel und Industrie*, known as the *Darmstädter Bank*, in Darmstadt, Hesse, a few miles from Frankfurt-am-Main and outside Prussian jurisdiction, where money was plentiful. The statutes were for the most part copied from those of the *Schaffhausen'schen Bankverein* charter of 1848, but they went beyond these to include provisions patterned after the *Crédit Mobilier* of 1852, permitting loans and participations for own account, underwriting, issuance of bonds, and powers to effect mergers and consolidations of various companies (Riesser, 1911, pp. 56–57; Cameron, 1956). The bank quickly opened an agency in Frankfurt and followed that by agencies in Mainz, Berlin, Heilbronn, Mannheim, Breslau, and Leipzig, and, considerably later, in Hamburg and Stuttgart (Benaerts, 1933, p. 275). The Frankfurt agency was converted into a branch in 1864.

In 1856 another way was found around the Prussian refusal to grant bank charters, by using the form of *Kommanditgesellschaft auf Aktien*, a limited partnership with transferable shares.[1] Scores of banks were created, among them the conversion of the private bank of Hansemann, founded in 1851, into the *Diskontogesellschaft*, the *Berliner Handelsgesellschaft* (both of them in Berlin and both with Cologne money), the *Norddeutsche Bank*, and the *Deutsche Vereinsbank* at Hamburg (Tilly, 1966, p. 115).

The participation of Cologne bankers in operations in Darmstadt and Berlin, and through them throughout the German states, raises the question whether there was a national German or at least a Prussian-Saxon money and capital market as early as the 1850s. Cologne had no security market of its own, finding it easier to use Berlin and Frankfurt, or even Brussels and Paris (Tilly, 1966, p. 118). At this stage, Frankfurt and Berlin specialized in security markets: Frankfurt loaned to princes, towns, and foreign states, but not to industry or for railroads (Böhme, 1968, pp. 151–153; 1966, p. 219).[2] The thesis of Tilly's study of the Rhineland banks is that German industrialization of the period was achieved not through the careful planning of an efficient state bureaucracy but in "thousands of profit-oriented decisions made by capitalist entrepreneurs operating throughout Prussia"—and especially in the Rhineland (Tilly, 1966, p. 138). The implication is that the decisions were decentralized. Karl Marx said of Germany that there was "no Isaac Pereire but hundreds of Mevissens on the top of more *Crédit Mobiliers* than Germany has princes" (quoted by Blumberg,

[1] Compare the British episode of 1833, when joint-stock banks were created in England within 65 miles of London, over the objection of the Bank of England, through the discovery of a loophole in the 1826 law (see Chap. III).

[2] For a discussion of the Frankfurt money and capital market more generally, see Heyn (1969).

1960, p. 171). But Mevissen was himself the president of the *Darmstädter Bank, Luxemburg Bank, Schaffhausen'schen Bankverein, Bank für Suddeutschland, Kölner Privatbank,* and the *Berlin Handelsgesellschaft,* in addition to being president of a railroad, and he sat on the boards of six mines and two industrial companies, typically as chairman of the executive committee (Blumberg, 1960, pp. 199–200). Other Cologne bankers like Hansemann, Camphausen, and Oppenheim moved freely between banking in Berlin and Cologne and business operations in the Ruhr. Eichborn was a banker in Berlin and an industrialist in Silesia. Private bankers such as Bleichröder and Mendelssohn in Berlin worked alongside the joint-stock banks and corporations, especially in the issuance of securities (Landes, 1960, p. 206). For Prussia, at least, and for Germany as a whole, excluding Bavaria, Wurtemburg, Baden in the South, and the Hansa cities in the North, the banking network solidified rapidly in the 1850s.

Hamburg was different. It clung longer to merchant banking and was slower to specialize than other parts of Germany. Its interests lay in foreign trade, in shipping, and in overseas finance rather than in domestic railroads and coal and steel. Regarded by the rest of Germany as the "English city," and itself disdainful of Prussian leadership until the successes of 1870, its banking was more closely tied to London than to Berlin. In 1857 this foreign connection almost led to disaster. The speculative excess in grain produced a crisis which spread from New York to Liverpool to London to Scandinavia to Hamburg, where a number of private houses could not meet their obligations and ship captains were unwilling to discharge their freight for fear of not being paid. Appeals for a silver loan were made to Rothschild, Baring, and Hambro in London; to Fould and Napoleon III in Paris; and to Amsterdam, Copenhagen, Brussels, Dresden, Hanover, and Berlin (Böhme, 1968, p. 254). Fould, who was the father-in-law of Heine, the Hamburg banker, telegraphed back: "Your dispatch is not sufficiently clear." The Berlin ambassador indicated that Brück and the Kaiser would not help. At the last minute, as an anti-Berlin gesture, the Austrian government sent a train with 12 million talers of silver, known as the *Silberzug,* which saved the private banks of Merck, Godeffroy, Donner, John, Berenberg, and Gossler & Co. after the discount rate had reached 10 per cent (Böhme, 1968, pp. 266–270; Rosenberg, 1934, pp. 128ff.). Shortly thereafter, Hamburg moved to specialized banking and the foundation of joint-stock banks, the *Norddeutscher Bank* and the *Commerz- und Diskontobank.*

With Prussian successes in the 1860s, German banking became

increasingly concentrated in Berlin. The defeat of Austria deprived Frankfurt of its counterweight against the power of Prussia; from having been an imperial city and a free city, it became, in Böhme's expression, a Prussian provincial city. The functions of the Frankfurter bourse in dealing with state loans passed to Berlin (Böhme, 1968, p. 236). Among private banks, Bleichröder, Mendelssohn, and Warshauer in Berlin flourished in their security dealings, while Bethmann, Erlanger, and Rothschild in Frankfurt found their clientele shrinking (Böhme, 1966, p. 219). It seems evident that the ascendency of Berlin over Frankfurt was political, but there are other explanations—the nimbleness and skill of the Berlin bankers (Helfferich, 1956, p. 27) and the greater importance of railroad issues over those of state entities (Brockhage, 1910, p. 56). Each has a portion of the truth. But Berlin had not made its start by specializing exclusively in railroad securities. The Prussian State Bank and the affiliated *Seehandlung* had undertaken some industrial development finance well before 1840. Nor had Frankfurt monopolized state issues. After the fire of 1842, Hamburg floated a loan of 34.4 million Mark banco through two Berlin and one Hamburg houses. Issued in Berlin, much of the original amount was bought in Hamburg, and all had been repatriated by 1846 (Brockhage, 1910, pp. 208–209). Berlin was thus a capital market far more than Prussia before 1850.

When the Reich was founded by unifying Prussia and the other German states, the several monies in circulation were consolidated by the adoption of the Mark; the several banks of issue were absorbed into the *Preussische Staatsbank,* which emerged in 1875 as the *Reichsbank.* In the boom that immediately followed victory, however, there was a splurge of bank creation, the most important new banks being the *Deutsche Bank* in Berlin and the *Dresdner Bank* in Dresden, both in 1872. The *Deutsche Bank* was started by a group including Adalbert Delbrück and Ludwig Bamberger, the former a private banker, the latter a member of the *Zollverein* Parliament, an economic expert who had worked in Paris banks during an exile after 1848. The bank's founders wrote to Bismarck in February 1870 indicating their intention to devote the bank to foreign trade. Outside the United States, the finance of world trade was at that time in the hands of the French and British. Georg von Siemens, a cousin of the electrical-equipment manufacturer, was the general manager of the *Deutsche Bank.* He was completely persuaded of the high national purpose of making German trade independent of British credit and filling "the gap in finance of external trade" (Helfferich, 1956, pp. 31, 38, 41). The bank was located in Berlin, "the importance of which is indicated by the eagerness with which the Frankfurt capital market comes to meet it" (Helfferich, 1956, p. 34). It also enlisted some Hamburg capital (Wiskemann, 1929, p. 206).

In the event, the *Deutsche Bank* had little success in foreign finance and found it impossible to operate in that field from Berlin. Its first step was to open a branch in London, in cooperation with two Frankfurt banks, in March 1871. It then established branches in Bremen and Hamburg in 1871 and 1872, respectively, "because of the difference in foreign exchange in inland and coastal towns, and the rather sharp differences in inner and coastal trading practices" (Helfferich, 1956, p. 43). Von Siemens's biographer insists that the requirements of overseas trade were decisive for the foundation of the *Deutsche Bank* but notes that business was not limited to foreign trade; he justifies expansion on the domestic front by the need to have the bank's acceptance signature widely recognized (p. 58). In the crisis of 1873, a number of banks failed and the *Deutsche Bank* took over several of them. In the beginning, it restricted itself to state loans, communal loans, and railroad securities, holding back from founding industries and issuing securities. Gradually, however, it built a syndicate of banks to move into industrial finance and underwriting. The finance of foreign trade was forgotten or put aside because of the need to build domestic roots (Helfferich, 1956, p. 111); lending to foreign borrowers, but not finance of German foreign trade, was undertaken in the 1890s. Foreign-trade finance remained the province of the Hansa cities, and particularly Hamburg, with its strong ties to London.

Victory in 1871 brought to the capital the *Darmstädter Bank* from Hesse and the *Mitteldeutsche Creditbank* from Frankfurt. The crash of 1873 produced a lull in the movement, and then came the *Dresdner Bank* in 1882, the *Schaffhausen'schen Bankverein* in 1892, the *Commerz- und Diskonto Bank* from Hamburg in 1892. Whale (1930, pp. 27–28) comments that these Berlin offices were at first only branches but soon grew to be coordinate head offices that rather eclipsed the original head offices. The process is set forth in more detail in the centennial volume of the *Commerz Bank* (1956). The *Mitteldeutsche Creditbank*, which had started in Sachische Meiningen in 1856 because it had been refused permission to locate in Frankfurt, opened its Berlin office, as noted, in 1871. From 1889, it began a policy of building local branches both in Frankfurt and in Berlin. By 1905, there were six such offices in Frankfurt, including Hoechst and Offenbach-am-Main, and seventeen in Berlin. These numbers reflect "the gradual shift of weight to the capital and the squeezing out of Frankfurt from its leading position as bank and stock exchange city" (*Hundert Jahre*, 1956, p. 42). When Anton Gustav Wittekind retired in 1912 after forty years of leadership, two successors were appointed, one in Berlin and one in Frankfurt.

The move of the *Commerz Bank* from Hamburg to Berlin was more complex, as befitted a surrender by the possessor of a proud heritage. Founded in Hamburg in 1870, the *Commerz Bank* saw its early hopes dashed by the crisis of 1873. Deciding to follow the fashion of the times and found a subsidiary in Berlin, it absorbed the private banking house J. Dreyfus and Co. of Frankfurt-am-Main, which had acquired a Berlin subsidiary in 1891. The merger gave rise to some competition in Frankfurt, but the *Commerz Bank's* chief interest from the first had been in Berlin. In 1899, it embarked on a policy of branch offices in Berlin, followed by more branches in Hamburg. The Frankfurt office of J. Dreyfus was given up in 1897 in favor of a *commandite* with the reconstituted firm. Even this was ended in 1908. In 1905, the *Commerz Bank* merged with the *Berlin Handelsbank*, bringing it a head office for its subsidiary and fourteen deposit branches. By 1914, the bank had eighteen branches in Hamburg and forty-four in Berlin (*Hundert Jahre*, 1956, p. 48).

Riesser (1911, p. 654) attacks a statement that banks in Germany differed from those in Britain in that the British banks moved from the provinces to London, whereas those in Germany moved from the capital to the provinces. The latter process started only after 1897, when the big banks had finished moving to Berlin. Then came the filling out of the national system in directions and areas hitherto neglected, exactly as individual British banks had done.[3]

German experience differed from that of the rest of the Continent and North America in that the metropolitan financial center for the country did not also serve for intermetropolitan dealings. Berlin had borrowed and lent abroad in the first half of the century, when the German capital market was fragmented, just as did Frankfurt, Cologne, Hamburg, and Augsburg (Brockhage, 1910). With the unification of the German capital market after 1871, domestic functions focused on Berlin and finance of foreign trade on Hamburg. The *Diskontogesellschaft* had worked closely with the *Norddeutsche Bank* of Hamburg since the early 1860s. As noted, the *Deutsche Bank* established a Hamburg subsidiary in 1872, but it became effectively interested in overseas opera-

[3] In 1900, for example, the Midlands Bank, finding itself with few branches south of a London–Bath line, created a network in the area (Crick and Wadsworth, 1936, p. 341).

tions only in 1886 (Wiskemann, 1929, p. 237). The *Darmstädter Bank* opened a subsidiary in Hamburg in 1890, the *Dresdner* in 1892, and the *Mitteldeutsche* in 1896. Wiskemann (p. 238) observes that Bismarck's interest in capital exports was not exclusively political. The "imperialistic phase" of German capital lending began after his dismissal. However much it might rival Britain in shipping and in direct rather than entrepôt purchasing, Hamburg did not challenge London in finance, whether from inability or disinclination.

The position of Berlin as a transfer point for transport between the Elbe and the Oder Rivers and its subsequent development as a railroad center have been mentioned. Friedrich List characterized it as an important communications center as early as 1833 (Baar, 1968, p. 531). Two scholars, one an economic historian, the other a social historian, have recently suggested that part of Berlin's importance lay in the fact that it was midway between the Ruhr and Upper Silesia (Borchardt, 1972, p. 152; Böhme, 1966, p. 333). Borchardt's other reasons seem more compelling—the concentration there of the Prussian authorities, the German imperial authorities, and the central bank, and the preference of associations and other organizations for that city, its easy access to Hamburg, and the like. The German geographer, W. Christaller, developed a theory that a central location tends to be chosen as a metropolis, but this view has since been discredited by the abundance of counterexamples, such as New York and London (Duncan, 1960, p. 81). Even to the extent that the central-place theory retains validity, there is no reason why it should be central between heavy industries that are competitive rather than complementary. The break-in-transport theory of metropolitan location requires connections between intercommunicating portions of a common hinterland, not a point on the ridge of equal delivered prices between competitive suppliers.

The Postwar Emergence of Frankfurt

After World War II, with the isolation of Berlin and the formation of zones of occupation, the major banks were broken up. In 1945 the *Deutsche Bank*, for example, was divided into ten branch institutes in the three Western zones of occupation. With the relaxation of Allied control in 1952, these were amalgamated into three regional banks, the *Süddeutsche Bank* in Frankfurt, the *Rheinische-Westfälische Bank* (later *Deutsche Bank West*) in Düsseldorf, and the *Norddeutsche Bank* in Hamburg. When permission was granted in 1957, these three parts were reunited into the *Deutsche Bank AG* with a legal seat at Frankfurt, but three "central offices" remained in the three cities indicated, each of which had several members on the common management committee. In the mid-1960s the central office in Hamburg was reduced in status. In 1974 Frankfurt dominates Düsseldorf on the Board of Directors, with eight directors to Düsseldorf's five, and weekly board meetings are held mainly in Frankfurt. The General Secretary of the *Deutsche Bank* explains that Frankfurt has become the main focus of the *Deutsche Bank* because the city is the most important financial center of postwar Germany. The *Bundesbank* is there, the Frankfurt bourse has the greatest turnover of all the exchanges in the German Republic, and both of the other so-called *"Grossbanken"* have their head offices in Frankfurt (*Deutsche Bank,* letter of Jan. 25, 1973; Seidenzahl, 1970, pp. 375ff.; Wechsberg, 1966, pp. 260ff.).

In the same fashion, the *Commerz Bank* of Hamburg was divided into ten successors, reassembled into three in 1952, and into one in 1958. Various directories in the 1960s gave the location of its head office as Düsseldorf. In 1974, the head office is in Frankfurt.

It is of some interest that Cologne, which is the city nearest to Bonn, the postwar capital of the German Republic, was never in contention. Düsseldorf, which gave Frankfurt the greatest competition, is the trading and financial city of the Ruhr, with its heavy industry. Hamburg and Frankfurt were chosen by the British and American authorities respectively as the seats of their occupation forces in Germany. After the moratorium on foreign investment in Germany was removed, the head offices of American-owned multinational corporations gravitated to Frankfurt, perhaps partly because of its large and efficient international airport and partly because of the American governmental presence there, although the decisive element in that presence was shortly moved to Bonn.

The fragmentation of German financial (and political) areas and their reunification in West Germany reflect the U.S. political preoccupation with decentralization and the reality of the forces pushing in the direction of a single financial center. In the initial stages, U.S. policy harbored, or at least fostered, the illusion that each of the ten *Länder* might have a central bank and a separate monetary policy. When the occupation forces were withdrawn, *Land* banks were quickly unified in a *Bank Deutsche Länder,* later transformed into the *Bundesbank.* The American effort at decentralization represented an idealistic (ideological?), interesting, but futile experiment.

VI. ITALY—TURIN, FLORENCE, ROME, OR MILAN?

In her account of the rise of the New York money market, Myers (1931, p. 6) states: ". . . there occurred a separation between the political and financial capitals which is peculiar to America. In Europe the two are generally the same: London, Paris, Berlin are the seats both of government and of the money market." Milan, Zurich, and Amsterdam attest to the fact that this is not always the case. As we shall see, moreover, the formation of the Italian financial center was more complex than this statement implies.

Italy, of course, had an ancient tradition in banking. Venice and Florence were banking centers in the Renaissance; Lombard Street in London was named after immigrant bankers from Milan and its surrounding area. In the late eighteenth century, when port cities were banking centers, Genoa, the capital of Liguria, was a flourishing trading town with a developed financial community. There was a smaller financial community down the coast at Leghorn. With its magnificent port, Naples was the commercial and financial center of the Kingdom of Two Sicilies, with the whole south of Italy as its hinterland. Its importance is indicated by the fact that the Rothschilds established a branch of their house there after the Napoleonic War.

As the northern city-states lacked a substantial hinterland (Luzzatto, 1960, p. 160), the small city-states declined, and Italy reached the middle of the nineteenth century without a substantial banking center in the North outside of Genoa. As late as 1844, Genovese were convinced that Turin could not become a banking center (Cavour, in Romani, 1968, p. 591). Attempts to create banks in Milan failed between 1821 and 1847, and Lombardy had to rely on capital imports from France during the period of seasonal financial stringency caused by silk (Greenfield, 1965, p. 142). With the unification of Italy in 1860 under the leadership of Count Cavour of Piedmont, Turin became the capital of Italy, and the banking center as well. Lombardy, which had been liberated by the Kingdom of Sardinia in the course of the unification struggle with Austria, held back from wholehearted support of "Italy" and insisted on local autonomy. Rome and the Papal States were not to be acquired until 1870.

The financial difficulties of the regime led to foreign borrowing and to the selling off of royal and Church land. Rivalry developed in France between the Pereires and the Rothschilds as to which could stake out a dominant position in Italy. Both were interested in banking and the finance of state and public works, largely railroads. Speculative fever in Paris stimulated the *Crédit Mobilier* to found the *Società Generale di Credito Mobiliare,* and the *Société de Crédit Industriel et Commerical* to start the *Banca di Credito Italiano.* The English ambassador joined the Ricasoli family of Florence to found the *Banca Anglo-Italiana,* again in Turin. In all, thirteen banks of ordinary credit (roughly equivalent to joint-stock banks in Britain or commercial banks in the United States) were founded in Turin from 1860 to 1866, including the notorious *Banco Sconto e Sete* (Bank of Discount and Silk). Elsewhere in the North, there were three leading private banks in Genoa, four in Milan, and one in Leghorn. In 1865, Florence became the capital. In 1866, de Boullay of Paris started a new bank in Florence which sold American mortgages and shares in the tax collections of Lecce. It quickly suspended payments. The *Credito Mobiliare,* which for thirty years was to be the most important bank in Italy after the *Banca Nazionale,* the predecessor of the Bank of Italy, transferred its head office to Florence in 1865 (Luzzatto, 1963, pp. 63ff.).

Gerschenkron (1968, p. 88) has ascribed the development of Italy after 1896 to the industrial investments of the *Banca Commerciale Italiana* and the *Credito Italiano,* which were founded with largely German funds. The question inevitably arises why the *Credito Mobiliare* and the *Banca di Credito Italiano* did not produce the same result thirty years earlier. Cameron (1972, p. 18) indicates that, if a banking system is to be effective, government must assure minimal conditions of both financial and political order and refrain from random ad hoc interference. Cohen (1967), who supports the Gerschenkron thesis for the end of the century, explains the earlier failure by the poor development of financial institutions, their geographic limitation to the North and Central parts of the country, and their general inefficiency (1972, p. 60).

The banks of the 1860s were supported in 1871 and 1872 by a new wave of foreign banks, including the *Banca Italo-Germanica,* which started in Florence, moved to Rome, and developed branches in Naples, Milan, and later Trieste and Leghorn. This bank speculated unwisely and collapsed in 1874. Another with a similar experience was the *Banca Austro-Italiana.* Both names indicate that nationality was not a critical factor at this stage and that German banks could fail as well as French banks. Somewhat longer lived was the *Banca Generale,* founded in Rome in 1871 with Milanese and foreign capital (Clough, 1964, p. 125). Luzzatto (1963, p. 105) comments that these bank failures were unimportant in an economy which was four-fifths agricultural and not integrated through cheap transport. Losses were mainly suffered by foreign speculators, plus some Italians in Turin and Genoa, and, in minor measure, in Florence, Milan, and Leghorn.

Despite the abortive attempts to shift the financial center to Florence when it became the capital in 1865 and to Rome when the capital was finally established there in 1870, Piedmont and its capital, Turin, remained the financial center of the country from 1860 to 1890. The *Banca Tiberina,* which had close associations with the *Banco Sconto e Sete,* moved north from Rome in 1879 and maintained its legal seat in Turin until 1889 (Clough, 1964, p. 12). Its purpose was to enlarge its capital for speculation in Roman real estate, and it sought capital not only from the *Banco Sconto e Sete* but also from the *Banca Nazionale.* In 1884, the *Banca Napoletana* was transformed with the help of the *Banca Nazionale* and new Genovese, Turin, and Swiss capital into the *Banca di Credito Meridionale* for the purpose of investing in Neapolitan real estate under the regulations of a law of the same year (Luzzatto, 1963, pp. 211–212). The *Credito Mobiliare* seems to have moved back from Florence to Turin to be in the action, although I find no explicit mention of a date, and to have participated alongside the *Banca Generale* in lending to the steel and shipbuilding complex at Terni, to railroads, and for housing, especially in Rome. One of the six banks of issue, the *Banca Romana,* was also deeply involved in the financing of Roman expansion. The note circulation of the *Banca Nazionale* reached its limit in 1866 and the limit was raised (Smith, 1959, p. 163). The *Banca Tiberina* began to fail and it was saved. Two matters caused crisis to erupt—the tariff war with France in 1887, which provoked the withdrawal of French capital, and the revelation that the *Banca Romana* had violated its statutory note-issue limit, leading to a political scandal. The result was the failure of the *Credito Mobiliare* and the *Banca Generale,* the forced amalgamation of the seven banks of note issue (including the *Banca Nazionale* and the *Banca Romana*) into the Bank of Italy, and the collapse of Turin as the financial capital of Italy. The failure of the *Credito Mobiliare* is sometimes ascribed to the death in 1885 of its leader, Balduino. While he was alive, the bank's speculations were happy. In his contemporary annual articles on Italian financial affairs, Pareto (1894, p. 59) blamed the failures on the fact that the banks engaged in affairs patronized by the government and advised the *Banca Commerciale Italiana* and the *Credito Italiano* to refrain from such activity. Under Balduino's successor, Bassi, the *Credito Mobiliare* entered into building speculation in Rome and Naples (Luzzatto, 1963, p. 266). The *Banca Generale* lost heavily in Terni, in railroads (the *Ferrovie Meridionale*), in Milan, and in foreign investment. Luzzatto (1963, p. 250) notes that its *Crédit-Mobilier*-type operations were pursued from the Rome head office, and that the Milan branch went in for strictly commercial banking.[1]

The wave of liquidation from 1887 to 1893 removed Turin from leadership and put Milan and Genoa ahead. The larger Lombard and Ligurian banks built branches in Piedmont, including its capital, Turin, and Piedmont's depositors shifted their funds to them (Fanno, 1913, p. 92n). In the mid-nineties the *Banca Commerciale Italiana* was established in Milan; the *Credito Italiano* started with its head office in Genoa and ultimately moved it to Milan (Luzzatto, 1960, p. 465). The former was purely German in origin, started by Bleichröder and the *Deutsche Bank*. The latter took over the Milan remnant of the *Banca Generale* and had German, Belgian, and Swiss stockholders. In 1898, a *Società Bancaria Milanese* was started, was transformed into the firm Weill-Schott Brothers and Co., and absorbed another private bank in Milan. It expanded rapidly in boom conditions, acquired the *Banco Sconto e Sete* in 1904, kept on expanding, and in 1907 was dominated by its Genovese group. The Bank of Italy supported it, being interested in developing a third large bank in Lombardy, in Liguria, and above all in Genoa. Bonelli (1971, pp. 29-37) notes that the bank lacked central direction, with its Milan office entirely unaware of the risks taken in Genoa. When the international money market tightened in the crisis of 1907, the *Società Bancaria Italiana*, as it was now known, collapsed, despite the efforts of Stringher of the Bank of Italy to save it. This left Milan as the undisputed financial center *in* Italy. The more interesting question is whether it was the financial center *of* Italy, that is, whether the Italian financial system was still unintegrated or had coalesced into a unified structure.

The critical questions in this abbreviated account of the geography of Italian banking from 1860 to the First World War are: Why was Rome not the financial center? If not Rome, why did Turin lose out to Milan? What role in the choice between Turin and Milan was played by the nationality of the foreign sources of capital and direction?

The reasons for the rejection of Rome seem evident. It became the capital late, it was badly located in relation to the productive parts of Italy, and its transport connections were poor. In no sense could it be called a metropolis with an economic hinterland for which it provided

[1] An earlier failure of the *Banca di Milano* was the result of the failure in 1882 of the *Union Générale* of Paris, which had created it.

service. Rome, in fact, was a parasitical city. The Church sucked income from the rest of Italy and the world, and the services it rendered in return were spiritual, and economically elusive. Savings were limited, the demand for capital for investment in housing very large. It was a sinkhole for capital, not a functioning pivot for allocating capital throughout the country.

The rise of Milan to preeminence over Turin has been attributed to the excesses and scandals of 1887 to 1893, the loss of prestige of France relative to Germany after 1871, the deep cleavage between France and Italy over the tariff agreement of 1887, and the political banking of Germany, with its Lombard connections. In my judgment, more cause should be attributed to the locational aspects. Turin got the jump on Milan with the Fréjus pass and the Mt. Cenis tunnel in 1870, the latter projected under Cavour in 1859 before unification. Cavour's policies concerning railroads, canals, and economic development generally gave the Kingdom of Sardinia (Piedmont and Sardinia) a headstart in economic development, but easy access to France was a vital aspect of it. When the Gotthard tunnel was finished in 1882, the position of Piedmont was weakened and that of Milan strengthened;[2] the completion of the Simplon tunnel in 1906 intensified the central character of Milan and the increasingly peripheral character of Piedmont.

A hypothesis emerging from this review is that Italian financial integration did not take place until 1893 and that it had an important role in the economic ursurge which occurred between then and World War I, much along the lines predicted by Shaw and McKinnon. Prior to that time, the capital market was fragmented, despite a certain amount of branch banking, the active roles of the *Banca Nazionale* and the government, and the close connections of banks in Turin and Rome on a few investments (largely housing and such railroads as were left over by foreign investors). Such a hypothesis would explain why German *Crédit-Mobilier*-type banks succeeded in stimulating the Italian economy when French banks of the same character could not. Turin industry grew rapidly after 1893, but it was financed by the *Banca Commerciale Italiano* and the *Credito Italiano,* except for the automobile industry, which used the Turin bourse (Castronovo, 1969, pp. 200ff., 215ff., 243). From 1860 to 1885, Italy, even Central and Northern Italy, was not an integrated financial market. When it became one, economic development spurted.

[2] There is irony in the fact that the *Banca di Torino* helped finance the Gotthard route (the *Società delle Ferrovie del Gottardo*) (Castronovo, 1969, p. 116).

VII. A SINGLE CENTER IN SWITZERLAND?

Almost forty years ago, Schwarzenbach (1935, pp. 482–483) made the case that Switzerland differed from France, England, and Holland in not having a single financial center but, rather, three: Zurich, Basel, and Geneva:

> In contrast to other financial centers . . . the money market in Switzerland is not concentrated in any one city. This fact is chiefly due to the political organization of Switzerland as a confederation of twenty-five states (cantons) which have wide powers of local government. As an outgrowth of territorial and historical factors, a strong individualism exists which is responsible for the lack of uniformity in the social and economic structure of the various states. Consequently there has developed no single preponderant business or financial center such as Paris in France, London in England, or Amsterdam in Holland.

This statement was hardly true. Of the seven large commercial banks in being forty years ago, five had their largest office, if not the nominal head office, in Zurich and two in Basel (Schwarzenbach, 1935, p. 497); of the seven stock exchanges, only Zurich, Basel, and Geneva were of any importance, and the Zurich turnover was from two to four times greater than that of Basel, with Geneva an also-ran (Schwarzenbach, 1935, p. 519). Switzerland provides a classic case of the formation of a single financial center, since it started with many, of which Zurich was originally not particularly important as compared with Geneva, Basel, Bern, or Winterthur. Zurich emerged as the financial center at the end of the nineteenth century, despite the connections and traditions of Geneva and Basel and the fact that the governmental seat was at Bern after confederation in 1848. Zurich's success can be ascribed to its focal location in the railroad age, especially after the building of the Gotthard tunnel, and to the pushiness of its bankers.

Geneva and Basel were old banking communities with long-established connections. Geneva's lines ran to Lyons, which had a great Swiss colony, the so-called "*Nation Suisse*" (Iklé, 1972, p. 10) and to Paris, where its Protestants mingled freely with the Huguenots and Jews of the *hautes banques* and the Bank of France. Many Parisian bankers had spent the Revolution and especially the Terror in Geneva, although others installed themselves in Zurich, Neuchâtel, Lausanne, or Winterthur (Lévy-Leboyer, 1964, pp. 425, 431). With the return of peace, fifteen out of twenty-two *hautes banques* in Paris were said to be of Genevese origin (Lévy-Leboyer, 1964, p. 432n). The traditional names of Burchardt, Iselin, and Stahelin were long associated with Basel banking, lending to Switzerland generally, but principally to Baden, as far north as Karlsruhe and Stuttgart, and to eastern France in competition with Paris, especially to Besançon, Mulhouse, Strasbourg, and Nancy (Iklé, 1972, p. 14). Mulhouse was even called the daughter of Basel finance (Gille, 1970, p. 88).

Zurich had some tradition in foreign banking going back to 1750, but it was hardly a significant town one hundred years later. It was less important than Geneva or Basel and about on a par as an economic center with Winterthur, when it started its meteoric rise in 1850. Its population increased elevenfold between 1850 and 1910 (Union Bank, 1962, p. 55). In World War I its position in the interior of the country, away from the belligerents' borders, resulted in the concentration there of international transactions.

Zurich's development can be illustrated by an account of the Union Bank of Switzerland, which was formed from an amalgamation in 1912 of the Bank of Winterthur, established in 1862, and the *Toggenburger Bank*, originally of Lichtensteig and later of St. Gall in eastern Switzerland. The Bank of Winterthur started out bravely as a *banque d'affaires* in the boom of the 1860s, in discounts, industrial-security issuance, and railroad promotion. From the 1850s, Winterthur was connected by railroad with Zurich, Frauenfeld, Schaffhausen, and St. Gall. The town fathers, proposing to make the city a center for storage and transshipment of goods, built a weighing house, a municipal granary, and a storage warehouse at the time they formed the Bank of Winterthur. By 1872, the Bank was a solid affair with a flourishing business throughout German Switzerland.

In 1873, the city embarked on a foolhardy scheme to build a "Swiss National Railway" in order to make Winterthur a link in the network running from Lake Constance to Lake Geneva, bypassing Zurich, Bern, and Lausanne. Part of the inspiration was pique against Zurich, the capital of the canton in which Winterthur was situated, and against Alfred Escher, "the strongest personality in economic and political life at the time" (Iklé, 1972, p. 18), president of the *Schweizerische Kreditanstalt*, which he founded in 1856, president of the Northeastern Railroad, and later promoter of the Gotthard tunnel. The threat of Winterthur to Zurich and Escher was met by prompt and effective action by the Northeastern and Central Railroads. The Swiss National Railway went bankrupt in 1878, and the city had to issue debt to make good its share of the loss when assets of the company in which 31 million Swiss francs had been invested were sold at auction to the Northeastern Railroad for less than 4 million (Union Bank, 1962, pp. 38–39).

"If you can't lick them, join them." Already in the 1870s, there had been a demand for the Bank of Winterthur to establish a foothold in the business center of Zurich. As Winterthur stagnated and Zurich flourished, the bank moved at the very end of the century to shift its center of gravity. In 1897, it acquired a participation in a Zurich banking and stockbrokerage firm, but this proved to be unsatisfactory and was given up in 1901. The bank then strove to overcome its prejudice against branches and in 1906 acquired the Bank of Baden's Zurich office, which had been established in the 1890s. Part of the stimulus was the rising strength of Escher's creation, the Swiss Credit Bank, growing with the city of Zurich, his success in railroading, and the threat of the Swiss Banking Corporation. This latter, started in midcentury as a syndicate of private bankers calling itself the Bank Corporation, formed into a bank, the *Basler Bankverein,* in 1870. In 1895, it merged with the *Zürcher Bankverein* to form the Swiss Bank Corporation (Iklé, 1972, p. 15). The Swiss Credit Bank and the Swiss Bank Corporation belonged to the "cartel of Swiss banks" formed in 1897 to place the loans of municipalities and cantons. The cartel excluded the Bank of Winterthur, which then formed a rival group. The Bank of Winterthur merged with the *Toggensburger Bank* of eastern Switzerland in 1912, started branching into French Switzerland in 1916, and went into Italian Switzerland in 1920. Its last penetrations into Basel and Bern occurred in 1920 and 1923.

A history of the bank, *Union Bank of Switzerland,* asserts that it was inevitable after the formation of the Zurich office that Zurich should become the heart and center of the institution. The "administrative offices" were kept in Winterthur and St. Gall, and annual meetings of stockholders alternated between them from 1912 to 1945. There was one managing director for Winterthur and Zurich and one for Lichtensteig and St. Gall; they acted alternately as chairman of the annual meeting. "Gradually the Toggensburger chairman for Lichtensteig and St. Gall gave precedence to Winterthur, and after his death in 1921, the two-consul system fell into desuetude" (Union Bank, 1962, p. 74). In World War I, the foreign-exchange business of Zurich grew, and this encouraged the concentration of the Union Bank's commercial business in Zurich. Even before the war, that branch had been making rapid progress in the handling of its stock-market and credit operations. A new building was completed in Zurich in 1917, and a year later the accounting department was moved there from Winterthur. From then on, the board of directors held all its regular meetings in the Zurich building. In 1912, the management had consisted of two ex-Winterthurers and two ex-Toggensburgers. One retired, and three new managers from Zurich were brought in, including the head manager, Paul Jaberg. Another death left the Zurich preponderance at three of five (*Union Bank*, 1962, pp. 86–88, 132).

Of further interest, the Swiss National Bank (the central bank, created in 1905 after a legislative proposal for its establishment had been rejected by referendum in 1894) has been domiciled in Bern since 1935, but effectively it is divided between Bern and Zurich. The seat of management is Zurich, and two of three departments are located there—discounts, foreign exchange, and secured loans in one, giro and auditing in the other. The third department in Bern deals with note issue, cash reserves, administration, and the fiscal agencies for the federal government and the federal railways (Schwarzenbach, 1935, pp. 484–486). This division of functions brings to Zurich all subjects that involve uncertainty and need for face-to-face communication, except those involving the federal government, leaving routine questions—except possibly cash reserves—for another location.

There is a question today whether telex and the telephone have made Basel, Geneva, and Zurich one financial center, with no real distinction among them. Are the distances between Zurich and Basel and the language barrier, if one adds Geneva, so slight as to be negligible? I think not. Some American corporations, such as Investors Overseas Service, may have chosen Geneva because it has been a more international community than Zurich ever since the location there of the League of Nations in 1919. Moreover, the French-speaking atmosphere may be more attractive to international corporations than *Schweiz'sche Deutsch* or even *schriften Deutsch*. But Zurich clearly dominates. The gnomes are the gnomes of Zurich, not of Switzerland. The location in Basel of the Bank for International Settlements—a 1930 decision dictated by the route of the railroad—and in Geneva of the League and its successors, the Economic Commission for Europe and the European offices of the United Nations, keep those cities alive administratively and as banking centers. But Zurich is the focus.

Even had it not been for its traditional banking relations to France, Geneva would have held on to some (most?) of its role as a distinct financial center because of the cultural differences between French- and German-speaking Switzerland. It is of interest to contemplate whether Geneva would have outstripped Zurich if *Suisse romande* had been larger and wealthier than the German-speaking parts. Lugano in a small way remains a separate financial community, linked to Italy by ease of communication as well as language and separated from the rest of Switzerland by the Alps, however much tunneled. But Ticino is a very small proportion of total Switzerland. Geneva, the Vaud, Neuchâtel, and the other Francophone portions are substantial both in numbers and economically. It is likely but not certain that cultural differences make for separation of financial functions.

Switzerland, I conclude, is not very different in financial agglomeration from other European cases. Tradition, the federal form of government, the seat of government in Bern, the international roles of Basel and Geneva, and the financial relations of those cities with particular hinterlands abroad, at least historically, were overwhelmed by the central location of Zurich at a crossroads. The crossroads was partly arbitrary and man-made, if we accept the Union Bank's account of the role of Escher, which I have not pursued in depth. Zurich benefited from the accident of World War I, which inhibited development of the two financial markets on the border; Geneva, with its relations with France, and Basel, connected to Germany exclusively after the loss by France of Alsace-Lorraine, may to some extent have neutralized each other. While there can be no doubt that Geneva and Basel are today closely connected with Zurich and with each other, Zurich is the financial capital of Switzerland, and an international money and capital market, though not the political capital, which is in Bern.

A final point: Measured by total assets, Zurich would stand out, but not so much as when measured by the assets of commercial or private banks. This is because of the large role of the cantonal banks, the first of which was established in Bern in 1834. Restricted to particular cantons, they do not move. Their total assets rose ahead of those of "Discount banks" and "Other banks" in the 1870s and by 1910 constituted four-fifths of the banking total (Johr, 1915, p. 457). But the cantonal banks put half their funds into mortgages, where the national market is less perfect than in bills of exchange, commercial loans, or stock-exchange securities. (In the 1960s, it took a difference of almost 2 full percentage points in savings-bank interest rates to move savings-bank funds from the East to the West Coast of the United States, indicating that in this capital market integration proceeds slowly.) The cantonal banks do not constitute so much an exception to these remarks as a different story.

VIII. TORONTO vs. MONTREAL IN CANADA

Initially, I intended to limit this exercise in comparative economic history to Europe, and thus to countries at broadly the same stage of development and with similar factor proportions. The more I considered Canada, however, the more I observed certain interesting and perhaps unique features. I therefore deal here with Canada, and, in the next chapter, as a companion piece, briefly with the United States.

Chartered banking in Canada began after the Napoleonic War. The Bank of Montreal opened its doors in 1817 without a charter. The first chartered bank, according to Neufeld (1972, p. 39) was the Bank of New Brunswick, opened in 1820. The centenary volume of the Bank of Montreal claims 1821 as the date for its charter, but royal assent was not received until 1822, putting it two years behind its New Brunswick neighbor (Bank of Montreal, 1917, p. 14). Then quickly followed the formation of the Quebec Bank, the Bank of Canada (not the central bank started in 1936, but a Montreal bank established by American citizens), and the Bank of Upper Canada.

With a large Scottish population, initial Canadian practice followed the Scottish tradition of branch banking rather than the English, and the Bank of Montreal opened agencies in Quebec, Kingston, and York in the first year, 1817. Kingston and York (now Toronto) were in Upper Canada (now Ontario), so that the tension between Montreal and Toronto, or between the Provinces of Quebec and Ontario, may be said to have started early. In the same year, the Bank of Canada founded an agency in Kingston. The Bank of Montreal opened an agency in New York in 1853, the first such agency, and one of only two as late as 1870 (Neufeld, 1972, p. 123). The Bank of British North America was organized in London in 1836 and within a year opened branches in Toronto, Montreal, Quebec, St. John, Halifax, and St. John, Newfoundland (Ross, 1920, p. 22).

While Montreal handled the export of furs and the import of general merchandise, Nova Scotia throve on shipbuilding from as early as 1761 to 1874, when wooden ships lost out to ironclads. The major banks in Nova Scotia were the Halifax Banking Company, formed in 1825 from Collins, an earlier private bank; the Bank of Nova Scotia, organized in 1832 as a counterweight to the monopoly of the former; and Merchants Bank of Halifax (later the Royal Bank of Canada), proposed during the Civil War, when shipbuilding had its last expansion. The two largest firms, heavily indebted to the Merchants Bank, passed into receivership in 1885. The Merchants Bank "now realized that if enterprises of national importance were to be financed, the bank must become national in scope, with [sufficient] capital and reserves that its position could not be shaken by local losses" (*Royal Bank of Canada,* 1920, p. 17). The bank resolved in that year to extend its operations to Montreal and, after establishing a branch there, opened agencies in the east and west of the city.[1] In twelve years, the focus of the bank had shifted from Halifax to Montreal. In 1898, Duncan of the Halifax branch ceased to be in sole command of the bank, though he remained for one more year in charge of the head office in Halifax and the branches in the Maritimes and Newfoundland. With the upsurge of business, the Montreal manager, Pease, was made general manager; the name was changed from the Merchants Bank of Halifax to the Royal Bank of Canada; branches were opened as far away as Vancouver; and some 5,000 new shares of $250 par were sold to prominent Americans. At the annual meeting of 1906, it was proposed to change the head office from Halifax to Montreal, "the natural center for expansion." This was accomplished the following year (Jamieson, 1953, pp. 17–24).

The decision of the Bank of Nova Scotia took place more slowly. Again, a personnel change was the occasion.

> One of the first important decisions made by the new general manager —a title which replaced the old Scotch form of "cashier" in 1898—was the removal of the Bank's executive office from Halifax to Toronto in March, 1900. The change was a natural outcome of the westward turn of events which followed closely on the linking of far-flung provinces by the Canadian Pacific and other railway systems and was a necessary step if the Bank were to play a leading role in the new prosperity and economy of the twentieth century. Many of its Maritime customers had already become dominion-wide concerns, and important connections which it had established in Ontario, Quebec and Winnipeg, necessitated banking facilities free from the delay attendant upon correspondence between these points and Halifax. It is a matter of pride to the citizens of Nova Scotia that the Bank still retains its head office in Halifax, and that year by year the shareholders meet on the fourth Wednesday in January in the Maritime home of their institution—now a splendid new building completed last year and fittingly used for the first time by the directors and share-

[1] It is of some interest to observe that, in the same year, poised on the brink of decline, Halifax established the first clearinghouse in Canada, but this example was quickly followed by Montreal (1889), Toronto and Hamilton (1891), and Winnipeg (Jamieson, 1953, p. 25).

holders at the hundredth annual meeting in January, 1932 (*Bank of Nova Scotia*, 1932, pp. 81, 83).

At almost exactly the same time, in 1899, Max Aitken, later Lord Beaverbrook, became secretary to a Halifax firm at the age of twenty. He arranged a merger between the Commercial Bank of Windsor and the Union Bank of Halifax, which presumably transferred the focus of that bank's operations from Nova Scotia to Ontario. Later, he formed an investment concern, Royal Securities, in Halifax, which operated in new ventures, mergers, reorganizations, and the like. This was moved from Halifax to Montreal in 1906 (Neufeld, 1972, pp. 488–489).

Puzzling in the foregoing is the lack of a single magnet: Montreal, Toronto, Windsor, and again Montreal. There is temptation to say that Montreal was the attraction in 1887 when the Merchants Bank of Halifax (Royal Bank of Canada) made its decision, and delay in the case of the Bank of Nova Scotia produced a different choice because of developments between 1887 and 1900. Moreover, the choice of Windsor in 1899 is odd unless the Commercial Bank was Aitken's second or third choice for merger with the Union Bank. But then why Montreal again in 1906? And why, once the Royal Bank had established itself in Montreal and Toronto outstripped it—a supposition we are about to examine—why did not the Royal Bank or the Bank of Montreal move to Toronto? The Bank of Montreal declined relative to the Canadian Imperial Bank of Commerce, located in Toronto (Neufeld, 1972, p. 573), but presumably not enough to warrant the expense and wrench of transferring to the livelier site.

The decline of Halifax as an early financial center needs no further explanation, but the drawn-out resolution of the competition between Toronto and Montreal is perplexing. Toronto started to compete with Montreal in the 1850s, was beaten back in the 1860s when a financial crisis followed the end of the Civil War in the United States, and then began a long rise to rival status. With the Western boom and the wave of British investment in Canada after 1896, Toronto gained further, even though much of the capital from London was handled through Montreal. After World War I, there were still further gains for Toronto but no clear-cut ascendency. Toronto continued to gain and ultimately surpassed Montreal as a financial center, but the latter did not give way, as had Cologne, nineteenth-century Frankfurt, Lyons, Turin, Philadelphia, Baltimore, and Boston. The money market in Canada is said to be centered in "Toronto and Montreal," or reference is made to the interest differential between New York and "Montreal-Toronto"

(Botha, 1972, pp. 138, 143). The Royal Commission on Banking and Finance (1964, pp. 294–315) refers to foreign-exchange brokers of Montreal and Toronto, or to the dealer inventories of the secondary security market as "concentrated in Montreal and Toronto." The Bank of Montreal and the Royal Bank retain their head offices in Montreal, whereas the three smaller but faster-growing (till 1960) chartered banks, the Canadian Imperial Bank of Commerce, the Bank of Nova Scotia, and the Toronto-Dominion Bank are headquartered in Toronto (for size in selected years from 1870 to 1970, see Neufeld, 1972, Table 4.6, p. 98). Since 1960, the Bank of Montreal and the Royal Bank have grown in total assets relative to the Toronto three, but, in regard to security deals, the Royal Commission in 1964 (p. 343) observed:

> The main volume of business has remained concentrated in Montreal and Toronto with the latter tending to grow in relative importance in response to the westward shift of Canadian economic activity and the replacement of overseas countries by the United States as the primary source of external capital.

Yet Montreal is as close to New York as is Toronto, and should not have suffered when New York replaced London as the source of overseas investment in stocks and bonds issued by Canadian entities.

But let us leave aside the question of whether Montreal or Toronto is the more important money and capital market for this or that financial instrument. The more interesting question is whether Toronto is emerging as the single financial center of Canada by a process drawn out at much greater length than in other countries or whether the two centers have been stabilized in an exceptional cooperative relationship. In 1947, Masters (p. 211) wrote, "Rivals, their capital structures became and remained closely linked." This has been the standard view until very recently. It now appears, however, that Toronto has overtaken and surpassed Montreal. So drawn out is the process, however, that Montreal banks seem to be under no pressure to move their head offices or their major money-market or foreign-exchange activities to the Ontario financial capital. The diseconomies of disarticulation are, in some inexplicable way, not very pressing.[2]

[2] As this study was being prepared for publication, Dr. Irving Silver of the Canadian Ministry of State for Urban Affairs kindly called my attention to an article that appeared in the *Montreal Gazette* on May 28, 1974. It reported that a study by Professor André Ryba of the University of Montreal established that stock-market, money-market, bond-market, and banking activities are all gradually shifting to Toronto. In particular, both the Royal Bank of Canada and the Bank of Montreal have shifted their "vital money market 'trading desks' to Toronto."

Gras (1922) distinguishes four stages—commerce, industry, transport, and finance—through which a town must pass en route to becoming a metropolis. For the early period during which Toronto came out from under the shadow of Montreal, we are fortunate in having a history that explicitly uses Gras's model. Masters's (1947) study is focused on the period from 1850 to 1890, when Toronto triumphed over its other Ontario rivals and emerged as the dominant financial center of that province. Along the way, there was a continuous struggle with Montreal, a struggle marked by the desire to avoid financial domination by New York (Glazebrook, 1971, pp. 193–194). The major episodes in that struggle were the construction of the Grand Trunk railroad and early Welland and St. Lawrence canals; the transfer of the government account from the Bank of Upper Canada in Kingston to the Bank of Montreal in 1864; the failure of the former in 1866; the determination of E. H. King, the general manager of the Bank of Montreal, to pattern banking legislation after the National Bank Act in the United States, shifting from branch to unit banking to keep ahead of challenging banks and requiring banks of issue to hold government debt, thus relieving the Bank of Montreal; and the struggle over the Canadian Pacific Railway terminus in the 1870s. The details are too complex perhaps for a non-Canadian readership. The central point is that in the 1860s Ontario was alarmed at the growing strength and dominance of the Bank of Montreal, which it believed to be draining loanable capital from Ontario to Montreal (Masters, 1947, p. 59). Determined to resist this development, Ontario made political efforts to bring transportation routes to and through Toronto, created and fostered banks such as the Bank of Commerce in 1866 and the Dominion Bank in 1870, and influenced banking legislation (Masters, 1947, p. 97). Toronto's population rose from 45,000 in 1861 to 210,000 by 1901, while Montreal's grew from 90,000 to 270,000. Thereafter, as money and migrants poured Westward, Toronto continued to gain on Montreal, but not so much as to crush it as a financial center.

Several factors account for the rise of Toronto as a rival of Montreal in addition to the transport system, the development of the West, and policy initiatives by Torontonians. One is the shift of investment from railroads to mining. St. James Street in Montreal specialized in railroad securities, while Toronto specialized in mining stocks. In manufacturing, moreover, Montreal tends to have older industries: clothing, textiles, food and tobacco products, and railway equipment, as well as machinery and aircraft, whereas the Golden Horseshoe from Niagara to Toronto and around the western end of Lake Erie, the Torontonian hinterland, specializes in flour milling (old), steel, automobiles, and agricultural implements, and electrochemical and electrometallurgical industries based on Niagara power (Ray, 1967, pp. 40, 41). Casual empiricism suggests that the income elasticity of Ontario's industry outweighs that of Quebec.

Another factor is the change in the source of external capital from Britain to the United States. Britain's gateway to Canada was naturally Montreal. New York had the choice of going up the Hudson all the way or turning west via the Erie Canal. Direct investment, however, strongly favored Toronto. Table 1, showing employment percentages in Canadian-, U.S.- and U.K.-owned firms in Canada indicates sharp differences by province. There is, of course, no assurance that the location of production facilities governs the location of head offices of investing companies, which have an effect on the location of financial facilities. United States corporations could locate production facilities in Ontario but have Canadian corporate headquarters in Montreal, in communication with the U.S. head office in New York, but this pattern is unlikely. With New York virtually equidistant from Montreal and Toronto, it makes sense for companies such as General Motors, whose production facilities are in the Middle West and whose finance is in New York, to choose Toronto over Montreal in the interest of efficient communication between U.S. headquarters and Canadian production. Where a U.S. company has only a single factory in Canada, moreover, head office and plant are probably located together. Toronto may also be favored by U.S. businessmen because of the identity of language and the similarity of culture.

But what must be explained is less the rise of Toronto than the lack of greater decline in Montreal until the 1970s. Part of the explanation may lie in governmental policy, urging the two main banks to keep their

TABLE 1

MANUFACTURING EMPLOYMENT IN SELECTED PROVINCES IN CANADA, BY NATIONALITY OF CONTROL OF FIRMS, 1961

(in per cent of total)

	Canadian	*United States*	*United Kingdom*
Atlantic provinces	78.67	6.05	15.15
Quebec	75.95	16.84	6.35
Ontario	62.39	30.71	6.10
Canada	70.48	22.54	6.16

SOURCE: Ray (1967, p. 49).

head offices in Montreal. Unlike the central bank's position in England, France, Germany, or Switzerland, but similar to that of the Bank of Italy in Rome, the Bank of Canada remains in the capital, Ottawa, where it was established in 1935. Ottawa is located in Ontario but on the Quebec border. The Porter Commission notes that until recently the Bank's senior personnel "have made only infrequent visits to the financial centers of Toronto and Montreal," and that visits of financial people to Ottawa, while always welcome, are made only for some specific purpose or complaint and do not provide the "frequency of contact needed" (Royal Commission, 1964, pp. 322–323). The remark is addressed to the question of the efficient functioning of Canadian financial machinery, which requires frequent face-to-face contact among governmental and private financial decision-makers. There are recent indications that the diffidence between central and commercial bankers noted by the Porter Commission has diminished or disappeared. It is perhaps going too far to read into the discussion a hint that the Bank of Canada remains in Ottawa because it is unable or unwilling (given the bicultural nature of the Dominion) to choose between Toronto and Montreal.

Canada is one of the few countries where geographers, as well as historians, have studied metropolitan development, using the Gras model. Geographers, along with economists, are surprised that relations between Toronto and Montreal have for so long been complementary rather than competitive, and that the country fails to conform to the model of metropolitan primacy. In population, the ratio of the largest to the next largest city is 1.2 in Canada, as compared with 2.3 in the United States and 7.5 in France (Kerr, 1967, p. 538). Almost 350 miles apart, Toronto and Montreal overwhelm the rest of Canada but not each other, as Table 2 shows. Financial concentration reaches more than 90 per cent in the two cities in stock-market activity, and here Toronto is far ahead. In all else, it has been a draw.

Geographic analysis throws more light on the separate claims of Toronto and Montreal to metropolitan supremacy by comparing the inbound and outbound passenger traffic of the two cities with that of other major Canadian cities. The nul hypothesis is that such traffic will conform to the gravity model, in which predicted traffic between any two cities is some constant times the product of the two populations divided by the square of the distance between them. The model predicts well for most pairs (Kerr, 1967, p. 545), but high residuals—positive and negative—have significance (see Table 3). The residuals suggest that Toronto has particularly close relations with distant cities,

TABLE 2

SELECTED DATA FOR INDICATED METROPOLITAN CENTERS[a] IN CANADA, ABOUT 1961
(*in per cent of Canadian total*)

	Montreal	*Toronto*	*Vancouver*	*Next Ranking City*
Population (1961)	11.6	10.0	4.3	2.6 (Winnipeg)
Population (1966)	12.2	10.7	4.4	2.5 (Winnipeg)
Service receipts and retail sales	13.4	13.8	5.4	3.1 (Winnipeg)
Value added in manufacturing	17.9	19.8	4.0	5.3 (Hamilton)
Checks cleared at clearinghouses	26.8	37.3	6.0	7.1 (Winnipeg)
Income tax paid	12.7	19.0	6.1	3.6 (Winnipeg)
Assets of leading corporations	38.1	36.7	6.3	5.0 (Calgary)
Value of stock-market transactions	26.3	67.1	6.3	0.2 (Calgary)
Domestic airline passenger traffic[b]	17.6	23.3	10.9	6.6 (Edmonton)

[a] Metropolitan census areas.
[b] Leading airports outbound plus inbound 1965.

SOURCE: Kerr (1965, Tables 16-1–16-6, 16-8).

and that Sudbury, a large mining town, has limited relations with the cities about it, presumably because it is specialized and because it deals with the world through Toronto. It is equally of interest that St. Johns and Halifax have heavy interaction in the provinces, presumably because they are so removed from other centers, whereas London and Windsor, both important manufacturing towns, deal little with each other, presumably because their relations go through Toronto. Airplane traffic is not as useful an index of financial interaction as check clearings would be, but it throws an oblique light on the phenomenon.

The centripetal tendencies in Canada, then, go less far and much more slowly than those observed in Europe.[3] Canada first detached its

[3] Note that in Australia there are two main money markets, an old one, Melbourne, and a new, Sydney, with "Sydney tending to become the more important of the two, partly because the Head Office of the Reserve Bank is there" (Wilson, 1973, p. 49). This case is worth comparing with Canada and may help determine the role in the slow rise of Toronto played by the cultural differences between French Montreal and British Toronto.

TABLE 3

PAIRS OF CITIES WITH HIGH POSITIVE AND NEGATIVE RESIDUALS[a]

High Positive Residuals in Descending Order of Importance	*High Negative Residuals in Descending Order of Importance*
Toronto–Vancouver	London–Windsor
St. Johns–Halifax	Sudbury–Quebec
Toronto–Winnipeg	Sudbury–St. Johns
Toronto–Calgary . .	Sudbury–Fort William
Toronto–Edmonton	Sudbury–Regina
Toronto–Halifax	Sudbury–Ottawa
Toronto–St. Johns	Sudbury–Montreal
Vancouver–Winnipeg	Sudbury–Edmonton
Vancouver–Montreal	Ottawa–Montreal
Vancouver–Ottawa	Moncton–St. Johns

[a] Calculated by relating airline passenger traffic to the product of their populations divided by the square of the distance between them.

SOURCE: Kerr (1967, Table 16-11, p. 545).

monetary and capital relations from London and turned them toward New York. Montreal balanced between London and New York. Toronto then rose to assert independence from Montreal, with some duality: "One group of finance capitalists were to continue to shuttle back and forth between Toronto and Montreal, while others, including mining men, were to be just as solicitous in cultivating the New York market" (Masters, 1947, p. 212). The Dominion built up "Toronto-Montreal" as a counterweight to New York, fostering a market in Treasury bills in the 1950s and a day-loan market, which enabled the Bank of Canada to control the money supply by internal operations rather than resort to New York funds.

In the same fashion, under the leadership of the Bank of British Columbia, Vancouver has set out to build its own money and capital market; in its foreign-exchange operations, it deals in U.S. dollars directly with banks in Seattle, San Francisco, and Los Angeles, rather than through Toronto-Montreal (Botha, 1972, pp. 138–143; Eaton and Bond, 1970, p. 15). One reason, of course, is the difference in time zone, and distance (i.e., the cost of wire services) may be another. It is paradoxical, except perhaps in terms of differences in rates of growth, that Canadian banks should abandon one coast—Nova Scotia—and cultivate the other.

The arguments for and against regional financial independence are summed up in a sentence from the Porter report *à propos* of stock markets, but applicable in general to money and capital markets:

> While a single national exchange would concentrate all trading, cause the markets to be broader and more resilient and might reduce trading costs per unit, it would fail to take account of the country's significant regional variety and of the need of local exchanges to provide a center for the shares of smaller and less nationally-known companies" (Royal Commission, 1964, p. 344).

Contrast this with the remark quoted earlier from the Royal Bank's fiftieth anniversary celebration volume (1920, p. 17) that if "enterprises of national importance were to be financed, the bank must become national in scope, with [sufficient] capital and reserves that its position could not be shaken by local losses."

IX. NEW YORK AS THE FINANCIAL CENTER OF THE UNITED STATES

The rise of New York as the financial center of the United States, winning out initially over Boston, Philadelphia, and Baltimore in the first quarter of the nineteenth century, and beating back, so to speak, later challenges from Chicago and St. Louis, is sufficiently familiar that it need not occupy us for long. It is, moreover, well chronicled in Albion (1939), Gras (1922), and Myers (1931), and has an up-to-date analysis in Robbins and Terleckyj (1960). Of the financial dominance of New York since 1825 there is no doubt. The remarkable feature is that it was maintained despite persistent attempts to defeat it, from the early efforts of rival cities, the Second Bank of the United States in Philadelphia, and the National Bank Act of 1863 to the attempt embodied in the Federal Reserve Act of 1913. Economies of scale in money and finance proved stronger than the institutional enactments against them.

Prior to the end of the Napoleonic War, there was no clear ascendancy of one North Atlantic American port over the others. Each had its hinterland. After 1815, well before the completion of the Erie Canal, New York took steps to pull ahead. British supplies accumulated during the war were dumped there. When commission merchants threatened to hold them back for higher prices, New York enacted an auction law that made all sales final and forbade withdrawing goods once offered for sale. Jobbers, wholesalers, and country merchants flocked to the port. In 1818, a New York merchant started the first liner service, by sailing packet to Liverpool; a ship left promptly on schedule whether it had a full cargo or not. These actions created a demand for sterling. To provide a supply, merchants, shippers, and bankers—at that time indistinguishable from one another—sought the financing of cotton and grain. Planters, always needing to buy more land and slaves, were continuously in debt. New York bankers advanced them funds to ensure that cotton bound for Liverpool from New Orleans, Mobile, Savannah, or Charleston would be shipped coastwise to New York and then across, a diversion of 200 miles which after 1850 proved physically unnecessary. The Erie Canal, projected in 1818, was finished in 1825. That same year, New York bankers advanced a large loan to the state of Ohio to divert the grain trade from the Ohio and Mississippi Rivers to the canal and New York (Albion, 1939, pp. 1–93).

Baltimore was slow in building the Chesapeake and Ohio Canal. It was still under construction when the opportunity came to build the Baltimore and Ohio Railroad. Philadelphia tried to meet the competition with the Main Line Railroad, built between 1827 and 1837. But this route was clumsy and inefficient. It ran by rail from the city to the Susquehanna River and by boat to the Alleghanies, with produce hauled over the mountains by stationary engine. By 1842, Boston had tunneled the Berkshires with the Boston and Albany Railroad but still had to rely on the Erie Canal for western produce. Supplementing the canal by the New York Central on a waterlevel route, New York stayed ahead (Albion, 1939, pp. 378–381). When Andrew Jackson destroyed Philadelphia's Second Bank of the United States in 1836, New York's position was assured.

A good illustration is the experience of Alexander Brown and Sons of Baltimore. The father came to the United States from Ulster in 1800, opened an Irish-linen warehouse in Baltimore in that year, and distributed bulky goods through Maryland and Virginia. He took William, one of his four sons, into partnership in Baltimore in 1805, sought to open a branch in Philadelphia in 1806 and again in 1809, but succeeded through his son John only in 1818. By this time, William was in Liverpool, and Liverpool and Philadelphia had outstripped Baltimore. By 1825, it was clear that New York was the most interesting center, and in that year son James opened Brown Brothers & Co., primarily to promote the interests of the Liverpool house, William and James Brown & Co. While Baltimore remained the head of the family enterprises until Alexander's death in 1834, for the last years of his life the backbone of the commission business was the sale in New York or shipment to Liverpool of the cotton sent by Southern correspondents. The first New York circular of Brown Brothers and Co. in 1825 indicated correspondents in New Orleans, Mobile, Charleston, Savannah, and Huntsville (Kouwenhoven, 1968, pp. 20–31).

Others to desert Baltimore were George W. Peabody, Elisha Riggs, and William W. Corcoran. Peabody, originally from Boston, was teamed up with Riggs, serving as London commission agent. The American end of Peabody and Riggs moved to New York in the late 1830s and subsequently broke up, with Peabody founding in London the firm that later developed into J. P. Morgan & Co. (Hidy, 1939, pp. 15, 95, 136, 237). Riggs then went into the securities business with Corcoran and, at some stage, probably at the time of the Mexican War, both moved to Washington to deal in U.S. securities. Here is the direct pull of the capital. Note, however, that neither made an optimal choice in terms of maximizing wealth, as the Riggs Bank and the Corcoran securities business, while profitable, remained small compared with New York operations.

New York attracted people as well as goods and money. Most came from Connecticut and Massachusetts (south of the Cape and west of Worcester, beyond which the pull of Boston dominated), with few, apart from the Stevens family, from New Jersey. New Englanders captured the New York port about 1820 and dominated its business until after the Civil War (Albion, 1939, pp. 238–242). The analogue is with the Scots in banking and accounting in London. While I have no definitive explanation for the divergent behavior of New Jersey and Connecticut, the answer is likely to be found in the different character of the soil, flat and relatively rich, on the one hand, hilly and rocky, on the other.

As New York became the financial center of the country, the practice developed of maintaining bankers' balances in the city. A substantial seasonal movement had to be handled. New York funds were built up during the harvest and movement of crops and drawn down during the rest of the year. New York funds bore a premium exchange rate over those in Philadelphia and other centers, which was resented by other parts of the country. Measures were taken by states to prevent the drain of funds to New York; for example, Connecticut required in 1848 a minimum reserve of 10 per cent in vault cash, prohibited in 1854 lending out of state more than one-quarter of a bank's capital and surplus, and required that loans must be made within the state up to the amount of capital and surplus before any could be loaned outside. None of these devices proved effective. Country banks found New York paper and deposits among the safest and most reliable investments. As in England, provision was made in New York State for the redemption of notes issued by country banks either at their seat or in New York, Troy, or Albany, a further incentive to build up New York balances (Myers, 1931, Chap. VI). The city served as an intermediary between Europe and the South and West, and balanced the country movement of cash on a seasonal basis as well.

The National Bank Act of 1863 furnished legal recognition of the New York banks' role as the ultimate banking reserve of the country. The original legislation provided that country banks could keep as little as two-fifths of the mandatory 25 per cent reserve in vault cash and deposit the remainder in a national bank in one of nine cities: Boston, Providence, New York, Philadelphia, Cincinnati, New Orleans, Chicago, and St. Louis. Banks in the nine cities had to hold their entire reserve in currency. This was hard on the reserve cities outside New York; they normally kept funds in New York but now had to hold only currency reserves. Revision of the law in 1864 provided for eighteen "redemption cities," enlarged from the previous list, and allowed banks in those cities to keep half their 25 per cent reserve in New York. "Country banks" were permitted to maintain two-fifths in deposits in a national bank in any redemption city. In effect, New York was a central reserve city and the other seventeen were reserve cities (Myers, 1931, Chap. XI).

In 1887, the legislation was amended again to permit any city of more than 200,000 inhabitants to become a central reserve city. Chicago and St. Louis accepted, "determined to wrest from New York its prestige and financial preeminence" (Myers, 1931, p. 240). St. Louis complained to little avail that merchants making payments to other cities bought drafts on New York rather than sending checks on St. Louis banks (Gras, 1922, p. 266). Bank balances rose rapidly in the two cities, but those in New York did not slow down. Chicago and St. Louis attracted deposits from their areas, but cities even further West and further South kept correspondent balances in New York.

The Federal Reserve Act of 1913 represented an extension of resistance to the financial domination of New York. Gras, in 1922 (p. 266), said it "struck a heavy but not a death blow." The statement seems exaggerated even for its time. New York remained the leading financial center, unchallenged by the eleven places chosen as regional centers for the other districts. Because branch banking was permitted in California, individual institutions like the Bank of America grew to be among the largest in the country, though the New York State requirement of unit banking failed to prevent New York banks from dominating the country in size and number.

The Federal Reserve Act was based on the theory that regional money and capital markets would develop around the locations of the twelve district banks. The Act implicitly contemplated separate monetary policies for the twelve districts. A structure of rates developed, the lowest rates being charged customers in New York, for example, with higher rates as size of city decreased and as one moved from North and East to South and West (Riefler, 1930, pp. 65, 72; Lösch, 1954, pp. 461ff.). Fluctuations in the rate were wider in New York than in the outlying portions of the market (Riefler, 1930, p. 74). But there was only one money market and only one monetary policy, focused on New York. Discount and open-market policies were unified. New York's facilities were more specialized, more competitive, and more available to other regions. Half the loans of New York City's banks were for borrowers outside the city, as contrasted with 8.2 per cent for Chicago, 7.8 per cent for Dallas, and 6.3 per cent for San Francisco—the three nearest competitors (Robbins and Terleckyj, 1960, p. 85). New York was also the center for international finance.

Here is a clear example of economies of scale. The financial center was a port, but the connection of finance to ports had diminished. It was neither an administrative capital nor a central location. Its dominance continued in spite of the strong resistance implicit in Populism, in spite of political steps to reduce its role, in spite of New York's own insistence on unit rather than branch banking, and in spite of efforts to create other financial centers by legislation.

The 1959 move of the head office of the First National City Bank from Wall Street to a midtown location on Park Avenue raises a series of new questions. Have the economies of centralization been exaggerated, or is modern communication reducing them? Is propinquity to corporate head offices for bank decision-makers more important than ready access to other banks, law offices, and financial markets for Treasury bills, foreign exchange, commercial paper, stocks, bonds, and the like? The bank left the bulk of its check handling in downtown Manhattan, close to the other banks and the clearinghouse but far from headquarters. It is understood that this creates some problems. In London, City banks acquired West End banks (by merger rather than by building new branches in competition with existing institutions) to serve the convenience of nonfinancial clients. Now, in New York, the same forces threaten to reverse the centralization process.

X. INTERNATIONAL FINANCIAL CENTERS

The same concentration that produces a single dominant financial center within a country (with the possible exception of Canada) tends to result in the emergence of a single worldwide center with the highly specialized functions of lending abroad and serving as a clearinghouse for payments among countries. Banks, brokers, security dealers, and the like establish branches in such centers. The process is similar to that which takes place within a country, although the barriers of exchange risk and higher transactions costs prevent it from being carried as far.

Court, merchant, and security banking spread internationally, as it did within countries, by the process of branching. Originally, these functions were usually performed by large families of male members. The court banking performed by the five Rothschild brothers moved out after the Napoleonic War to Vienna, Frankfurt, Naples, Paris, and London. Alexander Brown used his four sons to extend his merchant banking business from Baltimore to Philadelphia, New York, Boston, and Liverpool. [It has been suggested that one of the reasons for extending Alexander Brown and Sons in space, apart from efficiency, was that Alexander found it difficult to live near his most dynamic son, William (Brown, 1909)]. Early American bankers in France, such as Welles and Greene, who were associated with Welles cousins in Boston, went to Paris and Le Havre in 1817, and Fitch and Co. of New York established a branch with a brother in Marseilles in the 1830s (Redlich, 1951, Part II, p. 60). In the early 1860s, the eight Seligmann brothers went from New York and San Francisco to Frankfurt, Paris, and London (the central financial capitals rather than the ports) and to Amsterdam and New Orleans, largely to sell U.S. securities (Seligmann, 1894, p. 115). The Philadelphia banker, Drexel, who had moved there in 1837 after dealing in foreign exchange in Louisville, Kentucky, had three sons. One of them, Joseph William Drexel, set up an allied firm in Paris in 1867. He teamed up with J. P. Morgan in New York in 1871 to provide a network for selling U.S. securities in Europe in close cooperation with his brothers in Philadelphia (Hopkinson, 1952).

It is not entirely clear that there was a dominant financial center in Europe prior to 1870. It seems doubtful that the economies of scale had extended far enough that one center existed. American banks went to London, Liverpool, Paris, and Marseilles. London bankers established themselves in Paris, and Baring Brothers teamed up with Hope and Co. of Amsterdam. Prussia placed loans abroad in Hamburg, Frankfurt, Kassel, Leipzig, Amsterdam, and Genoa in the 1790s (Brockhage, 1910, pp. 34–35). By 1820, it was borrowing in Amsterdam on foreign issues, and in Frankfurt on domestic; Amsterdam was the first trading city on the Continent for public loans—Prussian, Austrian, and Russian. Interest rates differed widely among financial centers (Brockhage, 1910, p. 54).

British foreign lending at short term was stimulated by the usury laws of 1571, which limited interest charged to a stipulated rate that successively declined from an original 10 per cent to 8 per cent in 1623, 6 per cent in 1660, and finally 5 per cent in 1713, until their repeal in 1854. Akin to the interest ceilings of Regulation Q in the United States (which did not apply to foreign time deposits, allowed foreign banks to earn high interest rates in New York, and enabled them to bid for dollar deposits, stimulating the movement of funds to the Eurodollar market in the late 1950s), acceptances on foreign bills permitted charging commissions as well as interest, thereby avoiding the usury laws, as some domestic borrowers complained (Leighton-Boyce, 1958, pp. 10, 61, 205). By the time the usury laws were eliminated, this man-made distortion no longer had importance in stimulating the flow of British capital abroad, inasmuch as British savings exceeded domestic demand at going rates of interest and the efficiency of the London market kept transactions costs low.

By the mid-1820s, Britain was a substantial exporter of capital on long-term account. In one view, Britain had a monopoly of capital exports until 1850, when France moved in, largely for *la gloire* (i.e., capital exports in the service of national policies) (Rosenberg, 1934, p. 38). This view is not universally shared. Crick and Wadsworth (1936, p. 307) express an opopsite opinion:

> During the early years of the 19th century, Paris had held pride of place as the principal international banking center, but subsequently London steadily overtook her. . . . After suspension of specie payments by the Bank of France in 1848, London banks became busier in international affairs, with more and more bills domiciled in London.

Both statements seem insufficiently qualified. As Cameron (1961) has shown, French bankers experimented with international lending in the 1830s and 1840s but came into their own in foreign issues in the 1850s and 1860s, led by the *Crédit Mobilier* and the Rothschild Paris house, which transferred their intense domestic rivalry to the international arena. Whether London or Paris was the leader in the second quarter of the century, the role was contested during the twenty years after 1850, and Paris finally lost out:

> All great communities have at times to pay large sums in cash, and of that cash a great store must be kept somewhere. Formerly there were two great stores in Europe, one was the Bank of France and one was the Bank of England. But since the suspension of specie payments by the Bank of France [in the war of 1870] its use as a reservoir of specie is at an end. . . . Accordingly London has become the sole great settling house of exchange transactions in Europe, instead of being formerly one of two. And this preeminence London will probably retain for it is a natural pre-eminence. The number of mercantile bills incalculably surpasses those drawn on any other city. . . . The pre-eminence of Paris partly rose from a distribution of political power (Bagehot, 1873, p. 16).

Even this statement, written immediately after the events of 1871 and 1872, is put too strongly. London emerged as the undisputed leader in international finance after 1873, especially outside the Continent, but Paris was by no means cast completely in the shadow.

The pivotal role of London was enhanced by the part it played in transferring the Franco-Prussian indemnity. The new German government ended up with substantial claims in sterling, which, along with the Vienna stock-market crash, helped to precipitate the Great Depression (Newbold, 1932, p. 438).

Whether London focused so heavily on foreign lending that it neglected the provision of finance to domestic industry is a familiar issue incapable of clearcut answer. The presumption is that it did not. Numerous industries required large amounts of capital: for a long time, railroads; then shipping, iron and steel, cotton, banking, and finance; and, later, coal, public utilities, and communications. The London Stock Exchange was responsive to the capital needs of these industries (Jeffrys, 1938, pp. 62, 121). In addition, private companies went public in manufacturing and such profitable enterprises as brewing. Investors wanting trustee securities lost their taste for industrial shares and preferred foreign railroad and government bonds (Kindleberger, 1964, pp. 61–64). On the whole, however, domestic and foreign lending are complements, not substitutes, even though, in the British case, they were cyclically opposed.

After 1870, France did not contest British financial leadership. On the contrary, on such occasions as the Baring crisis of 1890, it supported London with a gold loan from the Bank of France to the Bank of England. While the apex of the financial system of the world was

London, foreign balances were also maintained by central banks in Paris and Berlin, like provincial cities in a national system.

Germany's attempt at resistance, led by the *Deutsche Bank*, and its failure were detailed in Chapter V. Hamburg was prepared to challenge London's preeminence in shipping and to support the German program of naval construction (Cecil, 1967) but not to contest the financial position of London. It had a special place in financing German trade and in providing a market for Northern securities (Wiskemann, 1929, p. 273), but it was too provincial vis-à-vis Berlin in domestic matters and vis-à-vis London in international ones. The *Deutsche Bank*, with a few others, opened a branch in London, but it contested British financial hegemony mainly in the narrow arena of the Ottoman Empire, or took on the Italian clients of the weakened French.

New York's challenge to the dominance of London has been traced back to 1900. In his report for 1904, the U.S. Comptroller of the Currency recommended that national banks with more than $1 million of capital be allowed to accept bills of exchange and establish foreign branches. In the panic of 1907, American banks borrowed more than $500 million from Europe to overcome the inelasticity of the money supply. As a result, Abrahams (1967, p. 10) states, it became clear that the American economy had grown too large to be carried by Europe and that an American solution was necessary.

As in 1870, however, it was war which turned positions sharply. J. P. Morgan & Co. provided an early credit to the French government against gold deposited in the vault of the Morgan, Harjes bank in Paris. In 1916, three leading American banks, the Guaranty Trust, the Bankers Trust, and J. P. Morgan, organized a syndicate under which 175 American banks made loans under acceptance credits to 75 French firms. During World War I, a number of commercial-bank branches that had been opened in France and Britain in the early years of the century were expanded and new ones were established, to serve both governmental finance and industry, but especially to handle monies for the U.S. Army.

Further branches were organized after the war in a massive expansion, which subsided after the 1920 boom. H. Parker Willis, in his Introduction to Phelps (1927, p. iii), spoke of the "unfavorable experience gained by some American banks which went hastily into foreign countries during the years 1919 and 1920." Substantial foreign lending by Wall Street began with the success of the Dawes loan in 1924, but it declined after June 1928 when the stock-market rise diverted attention to that outlet and tight money hit the domestic and foreign bond markets. Foreign, and especially German, borrowing shifted to the short-term market and finance paper, slowed down in 1930, and stopped completely after the Standstill Agreement of July 1931.

From 1914 on, London had difficulty maintaining its role as a center for foreign reserves and a source of short- and long-term credit. The rise of New York produced two reactions—anguish at the loss of leadership and relief at the shifting of responsibility. The head of the London City and Midland Bank (as it was known then) "publicly wept" over the passing of sterling supremacy, while the head of the Hong Kong and Shanghai Bank was enthusiastic about the rise of New York credits, telling Benjamin Strong—"and most English bankers agreed with him"—that New York must carry some of the load for financing the world's commerce (Abrahams, 1967, p. 53).

I have dealt elsewhere (Kindleberger, 1973) with the hiatus created in the interwar period by British inability to serve as a lender of last resort for Europe and U.S. unwillingness, at least until the Tripartite Monetary Agreement of September 26, 1936, to take over the task. In this view, the 1929 Depression was the consequence of an ineffective transition of the financial center from London to New York. No new center rose to challenge the old ones and to wrest financial supremacy or responsibility from them. Instead, in this instance an old center lost the capacity to serve as the center of the world financial system, and the most promising candidate for the position was unwilling or unable to fulfill the responsibilities.

From 1936 on, and especially during World War II, the United States increasingly accepted world financial leadership. The first steps were governmental. The Anglo-American Financial Agreement of 1946 represented a "key currency" approach in which, first, sterling would be restored to health as a means of rebuilding the financial system, so that the sterling area could play an important, and possibly even coequal, role with the dollar. In the first Marshall Plan discussions, however, in July 1947, Clayton and Douglas rejected the suggestion of Bevin and Dalton that the United States undertake a new program of assistance to Britain, after which they would approach Europe in "financial partnership" (State Department, 1972, pp. 269, 272). Gradually, the New York market recovered its interest in lending abroad, at long term and short. New York was the world financial center from the early 1950s until the end of the decade, when the Eurodollar market began to develop.

As the emphasis in this paper is historical, little will be said of the transition from New York as the leading financial center back to

London as the principal location of the Eurodollar market, or of the breakdown of the Eurodollar market with the events of August 1971, the Smithsonian devaluation, and the floating period begun in February 1973. Several points about the process should be made, however. First, U.S. banks and security dealers increased the number and size of their European branches in the 1960s. Early in the decade, the major efforts abroad of New York banks in London were as dealers in dollars seeking to escape first Regulation Q and later capital controls. In the crunch of 1966 and 1969–70, however, a number of banks throughout the United States went to London not to lend but to be in position to borrow dollars to add to their reserve balances in the United States. Second, much of the foreign branching was defensive investment. Banks went abroad not so much to earn profits as to avoid losing clients; as American corporations moved abroad, their bankers went with them. Third, with the forced devaluation of the dollar in August 1971, the Smithsonian Agreement of December 1971, and the period of floating in response to adverse speculation beginning in February 1973, the Eurodollar bond market substantially dried up.

After the second devaluation, trade payments and long-term contracts came to be denominated in currencies other than dollars. While borrowers were willing to go short of dollars, private parties outside the United States were less willing to go long. In Eurocurrency and Eurobond markets, the dollar was less widely used. No single currency took its place, however; the Deutschemark, Swiss franc, Japanese yen, and, to a lesser extent, guilder and Belgian franc severally replaced the dollar as international money. As the dollar declined in world financial use, no other currency or center, for the time being at least, rose to take its place. The international payments mechanism thereby lost the efficiency that comes from centralizing payments.

One possibility is that the European Economic Community may develop as a money and capital market to replace the Eurodollar market in the world financial system.

XI. A FINANCIAL CENTER FOR EUROPE?

Will European economic integration, and especially the formation of the European Economic Community, result, sooner or later, in geographical financial centralization? To pose the question is to review the forces which in the past have led to the formation of financial centers.

A European currency. Is a European currency neecssary to the development of an efficient money and capital market? The answer is almost certainly yes. The Segré report (1967) proposed to achieve an integrated money and capital market—presumably concentrated in space, although the issue was not addressed—by removing national restrictions on lending and harmonizing regulations. The resultant market, however, would still have been divided by currency. The Werner report (1970) recognizes that integration of financial institutions implies development of a single money, although currencies having permanently fixed exchange rates, by the Hicks theorem, are a single money in all but the trouble and expense of exchange transactions. In some views, it is necessary to go further and develop common long-term assets that are included in the portfolios of participating nations.

The London capital market operates in sterling, while New York and the Eurodollar markets operate in dollars. The movement toward world financial integration has been set back by currency realignments and floating. The development of a European capital market serving world as well as European needs probably requires a European currency.

History suggests that this is conveniently accomplished by taking an existing money and converting others into it. In Germany, the Prussian thaler was adopted after conversion from silver to gold, but it was called the "mark" after the currency used in Hamburg. In Italy, the process was more complex, involving reduction of ten separate currencies to four and then to one, the one being the new lira of Piedmont, which had taken the leadership during the political unification. The process took a decade (De Mattia, 1959; Luzzatto, 1963, pp. 60ff.). If a national currency is chosen as the basis for the new currency—say, the Deutschemark but called the "*ecu*" (both an acronym for European Currency Unit and an ancient French coin)—it might confer an advantage on the established financial center associated with the chosen currency, in this case Frankfurt. It is likely that Berlin benefited from the choice of the Prussian thaler and Turin from that of the Piedmont lira.

An attempt to create an entirely new currency would presumably not affect the ultimate choice of a particular financial center, assuming that the currency was successfully established and the agglomeration process envisaged actually took place. Some unexpected side effects would probably occur. There is, of course, a question whether the public would in fact go over to the synthetic currency. The 1958 conversion of the old to the new franc by dividing by 100 affected children and tourists more than it did the French population, which continued for a number of years to use the old franc as a unit of account. On the other hand, the conversion of sterling to the decimal system in 1970 was relatively painless. Money is established not by fiat but by public acceptance, and public acceptance in nine countries of a synthetic new money cannot be guaranteed. Such acceptance is neecssary, however, to the creation of a single financial center.

Central bank. The development of a European money ultimately requires a European central bank, and meanwhile a pooling of foreign-exchange reserves. It is not evident that the latter must have a physical embodiment and staff; the former will. If a single central bank—the Bank of England, the Bank of France, the Bundesbank, or any other—were chosen as the European central bank and other central banks were merged into it, its existing location might well have an effect on the ultimate choice by the market of a physical center. The example of the Bank of Italy in Rome, far from the financial center in Milan, makes this uncertain, however.

In any case, history suggests that the choice of one among a number of competing centers is normally evaded in the process of merging banks. The new European central bank would probably begin as a "federal reserve" system in which the various central banks started as separate units but ultimately became fully articulated subordinate parts. The managing board might be located in a nonfinancial center comparable to Washington, Ottawa, or Bern. With the passage of time, one regional bank would come to dominate the others, as New York dominates Boston, Philadelphia, or Richmond. The board in a place like Strasbourg, for instance, would probably have little attractive force.

Administrative capital. If the administrative machinery of the European Economic Community, including the European central bank, were located in an existing financial center, it would be likely to serve as a magnet to other financial institutions and to attract them into a single primary location. The creation of a new capital would surely not, as Rome, Bern, Washington, Ottawa, Canberra, and a host of other examples testify. Presumably, other factors would have to be at least neutral—with enough tradition, savings available for investment throughout the Community, and the like. This suggests an interesting question: If France persuaded the EEC to choose Paris over Brussels as its capital, would France's strong postwar tradition against foreign lending stand in the way of financial concentration?

Tradition. Tradition and skill favor London as the financial center, but it is doubtful that these are enough. Savings are also necessary, so that dealers can make a market, lend when the rest of the market is borrowing, and sell out of inventory when the rest of the market is buying. London's success in capturing the lion's share of the Euro-money market arose from the presence there of major branches of U.S. banks, which provided savings. British savings are limited in amount; are concentrated in institutionalized form, such as insurance and pension funds that no longer flow into foreign investment; and are, in any case, held at home by investment controls. It is conceivable but unlikely that skill and tradition are enough to bring the European financial center to London on the basis of brokerage, with the British participants not taking a position. The Inter-Bank Research Organisation (1973, pp. 1–8), studying the future of London as an international financial center, recognizes that Britain is unlikely to be a major exporter of capital but proposes that it operate as an entrepôt, with Europe as its hinterland. The picture is not persuasive.

Economies of scale. Clustering develops when the high risks of an activity can be reduced by continuous interchange of information (Robbins and Terleckyj, 1960, p. 35). It is possible but expensive to communicate by telephone and telex, and many financial functions involving uncertainty are better performed face-to-face. Robbins and Terleckyj (1960, p. 35) note that the central financial district of lower Manhattan minimizes communications costs. In 1960, a financial house with 120 lines to New York houses would pay $420 monthly rental if located in New York, $230,000 if in Chicago, and $640,000 if in Los Angeles. While presumably communications costs have declined in the last fifteen years (costs are not so high as to prevent the head offices of a limited number of banks from being located in Toronto and Montreal in Canada, or Basel and Zurich in Switzerland), they are not likely to be so low as to eliminate all tendency to clustering. A network of banks located in all the financial capitals of Europe—London, Paris, Frankfurt, Amsterdam, Brussels, Milan, and Zurich—would not be cheap.

Note the unimportance of clustering for new security issues. Syndicates in new issues consist of firms located virtually everywhere. But secondary markets must be concentrated so as to eliminate the need to search over wide distances for price information or to maintain continuous interchange. While long-distance arbitrage does take place in some securities, such as kaffirs (gold-mining stocks) between London and Johannesberg and between major European markets and New York, the number of securities handled in this arbitrage is limited; efficiency in handling a large number of issues is sacrificed to efficiency in handling a diffuse market through arbitrage.

Robinson (1964, pp. 19, 202) has said that the secondary market is unimportant for corporate bonds, as most investors keep them until they mature or are otherwise retired. This does not seem to be borne out for the Eurobond market, if one can judge by the number of articles devoted to "the major weakness of the Euro-bond market . . . trading rather than issuing" (Yassukovich, 1971; see also Low, 1972b; Lutz, 1973). In addition, costs of exchanging price information continuously among traders must be covered. The six leading traders—three of them American firms—were located in London, Brussels, Geneva, and Zurich in 1969; today the leaders are in Frankfurt, Paris, Luxemburg, and some centers in Canada and the United States (Low, 1972b, pp. 1157–1158). In addition, there are problems of delays in payment and delivery of bonds. To meet these, the Morgan Guaranty Trust Company organized "Euroclear" in Brussels in 1968, Barclays Bank International founded Eurobond Clearing House in London in 1969, and a group of Luxemburg banks organized a Center of Delivery of Euro-Securities in Luxemburg (CEDEL) in 1971. That such arrangements were unsatisfactory is indicated by these events: (1) Barclays Bank International abandoned the Eurobond Clearing House and substituted a different system of Registered Depository Receipts (McRae, 1972); (2) Euroclear and CEDEL agreed to collaboration after long negotiations sponsored by the Association of International Bond Dealers; and (3) the Morgan Guaranty Trust Company decided to sell Euroclear while making an agreement to render it banking services for five years. This last step represents an improvement by eliminating the control of the clearinghouse by a single bank. At the time, it was stated that the number of participants in Euroclear had risen from 74 in 1968 to 376 in 1972 (Low, 1972a, p. 31).

In 1971, Kohn (1971, p. 70) suggested that there was no need for a single center for the secondary market—"the true marketplace." While "in any particular time one locale is more attractive than another," he said (p. 68), the market really has no center at all—not London or

Luxembourg, Frankfurt or Brussels, Paris or Geneva, etc.; it is a mistake to expect all market makers to buy or sell freely in all circumstances. This verdict seems appropriate only for a period of transition or flux before an efficient centralized system has been developed. Another possibility is that the secondary market for securities could be linked up among widely separate centers by a computer-based system of bid and asked prices, supported by a regional system of security depositories. In the United States, the National Association of Security Dealers started the first of these in 1971, and the Depository Trust Company of New York, with eight regional depositories in six states, provided the second in 1973. Although it is far from clear what volume of security dealings would be necessary to cover the capital expense of establishing such a system in Europe, it seems likely that in time there will be no need for a central location for secondary markets in securities.

Other centripetal forces remain, especially the need for face-to-face communication with bankers, lawyers, security dealers, and borrowers and lenders. Telephone and telex have moderated these centralizing tendencies but have not destroyed them. Nor is the picture telephone likely to provide a substitute for face-to-face communication in the flesh.

The achievement of economies of scale in a concentrated center—an evolutionary and time-consuming process, as the historical record shows—has been disrupted by the 1971–74 currency realignments and floating. When and if a European currency is established or the Eurodollar recovers strength and is reestablished as international money, the need for scale economies is likely to lead ultimately to agglomeration. Present participants in the Eurocurrency and Eurobond markets may be content to remain where they are and deal with one another by telex and telephone (this is more likely for the Eurocurrency market and for new issues than for the secondary market), but new entrants will be drawn to optimal locations, probably a single place. Banks and security dealers located in many centers will cut down on the less efficient locations in periods of recession and expand the efficient ones when recovery comes, in spite of the decline in cost of communication. The experience of Euroclear, CEDEL, and Barclay's suggests that the choice lies between Brussels and London, but the outcome is likely to depend on other factors. Economies of scale predict one center but not which one.

Central location. The Christaller view that the metropolis chosen as the financial center must be centrally located (Duncan, 1960) probably holds at the extremes: Edinburgh, Copenhagen, Rome need not apply. It cannot count for much in Europe among London, Paris, Frankfurt, Brussels, or Amsterdam (or Geneva or Zurich if Switzerland were to join the European Economic Community). Probably even Hamburg or Munich would not be ruled out for failing to stand at the epicenter.

But need the European financial center be in Europe? Could it again be New York, with London, Paris, Frankfurt, *et al.* linked to each other by means of their connections with Wall Street? Can Europe be integrated financially by an outside center, as it is to some degree integrated in the field of labor by Mediterranean workers who have no roots in any one place, and in industry by American corporations that are more mobile than their European counterparts? The outcome is possible and, as indicated, there is some interest in the United States in developing policies to restore New York to world financial leadership. The immediate outlook is not propitious, given the dim view the world takes of the dollar. Over a longer view, moreover, the time differences round the world make a European center, rather than one in North America or Asia, more efficient in integrating European financial markets.

Transport. While metropolitan centers have grown at breaks in transport, it is usually possible today to adjust transport to function. A few communities, like Wellington, New Zealand, are so hemmed in between mountains and sea that a major airport can be developed only at exorbitant expense. Small cities may have difficulty supporting the lumpy transport facilities necessary for effective communication. Existing facilities are likely to be taken into account to avoid undertaking new ones. On the whole, however, there are few limits among European cities.

Headquarters of multinational corporations. Might banks, perhaps starting with U.S. banks, drift into a single center or build up their offices in such a center, perhaps putting those offices in charge of European branches, if a number of multinational corporations, particularly those of U.S. ownership, were to congregate? The reason for attributing particular behavior to foreign corporations and foreign banks is that, in the context of European integration, they are more mobile than "native" corporations and banks. American corporations in Canada are likely to be located in a more economic pattern than Canadian corporations, since the latter will resist leaving the place in which they started. In Canada, however, the location of the U.S. parent corporation may cast an economic shadow across the border, as Ray (1971) has suggested. The location of U.S. subsidiaries in Europe is likely to reflect no such influence. French corporations, by contrast, may move their headquarters from Lyons to Paris, but they are unlikely to continue further to London, Brussels, or Frankfurt.

What governs the choice of location for the headquarters of an American firm in Europe? Initially, investment was often made in Britain on the basis of similarity of language and culture; in a particular country from which forebears of the firm's decision-makers had migrated to the United States; or in centers thought to be agreeable, especially Paris. Later, but before the Common Market, it was frequently judged necessary to produce in each country in which the firm wanted to sell: "To sell in France, produce in France." The advent of the Common Market, and the conversion of the Six into the Nine, has changed this less than had been anticipated. With time, however, and as the European Economic Community seems more solid and less ephemeral, other firms may follow the pattern of IBM, which is said to have rationalized its production to take advantage of the elimination of tariffs, or of Ford, whose major facilities exchange parts between Antwerp and Cologne.

What is relevant, however, is not the location of production facilities but of company headquarters. In Germany, companies were attracted after World War II to the American military headquarters in Frankfurt. Today, more and more American companies seem to develop an affinity for the headquarters of the Commission of the European Communities in Brussels.[1] Sales headquarters may be divided culturally between Latin and Germanic countries, in some cases splitting Switzerland between two European headquarters. Financial headquarters of some companies have been located in London. Where companies have one headquarters, and it was not established in the last fifteen years in Brussels, it has typically been where it has its largest production facilities, or in London or Paris. If there is a trend, it is probably to Brussels.

With one exception, major American banks in Europe have not designated any one branch to head up their European network. London, Brussels, Paris, Frankfurt, Zurich, Geneva, and Rome report separately to the head office, and coordination among them is directed from New York. It is not evident that this is efficient. It is likely, rather, that

[1] "In all, some 450 international companies have their main European offices in Brussels, a total rivalled only by Paris" (Interbank Research Organisation, 1973, pp. 2–22). And, following them, two American banks—the Chase Manhattan and the Security Pacific—have put their European headquarters in Brussels rather than London.

the matter will be allowed to continue unresolved, pending the emergence of a particular location as the dominant center.

Culture. For cultural reasons, a single financial center may not emerge. Cultural factors perhaps contributed to the stalemate between Toronto and Montreal and, according to some authors, to the survival of Basel and Geneva as financial centers in spite of the competition from Zurich. French corporations stay in Paris, Belgian in Brussels, Dutch in Amsterdam, and German in Düsseldorf, Hamburg and Frankfurt. International cooperation among such banks as the *Crédit Lyonnais*, the *Banca Commerciale Italiana*, the *Deutsche Bank*, and Morgan Guaranty Trust remains voluntary for separate deals; there is no true merger, with unified decision-making. Historical evidence predicts that the emergence of a true financial center would be preceded by takeovers, mergers, and amalgamations, but in the last fifteen years these have been few.

This is perhaps the crux. If there is no integration beyond tariff removal and collaboration in international economic negotiation, there will be no single European financial center apart from the world system. Like the banks in the hinterland of St. Louis and Chicago that kept correspondent balances in New York, European financial institutions will deal partly with the Community and partly outside. During the period of the Eurodollar, the separate financial markets of the Six were more effectively joined with the Eurodollar market than they were with each other. If a European center emerges as the apex of the world hierarchical system and Europe does not achieve effective integration, sections of the capital market in Europe may even be linked to the center through outside connections, as part of the world feeder system.

Policy. Governmental policy can accelerate or slow down the emergence of a given city as the primary financial center, but it can probably not change the outcome. Pushing too hard for centralization will create resistance, while strong efforts at decentralization can be overcome by private forces. It is uncertain whether the United States could recreate in New York a financial center for the world after its maladroit handling of the troubles of the dollar. Whether the Swiss or German authorities can prevent their financial capitals from being developed to serve as a world center is less uncertain. It is difficult to use exchange control to prevent inflows of hot money, but governments can forbid the development of the positive institutions that will effectively employ foreign monies in domestic and foreign lending.

Policy requires more than governmental agreement. The Segré report

(1967) on the unification of the European capital market was widely praised, but nothing happened. No European country was deeply committed to building a well-functioning European capital market. Accordingly, I predict, very tentatively, that Brussels will emerge as the financial center of the European Economic Community, for the following reasons: It serves as headquarters for the Commission; it attracts foreign corporations and will ultimately attract foreign and European banks; it tolerates the world intellectual medium of exchange, the English language. The process will be long and drawn out, for commitment to European integration does not go deep. France will push the advantages of Paris as the federal administrative center, and incidentally the center for financial institutions, but with little likelihood of consent from the other members. Sterling is too weak, and British savings too unavailable, to advance London's claim for consideration. While the advantages of centralization are less compelling than they were in the middle of the nineteenth century, they still exist. Thus I predict that, despite cultural resistance and only with difficulty, centralization will take place, but not before the late 1980s.

REFERENCES[1]

I. AND II. INTRODUCTION AND ANALYTICAL FRAMEWORK

Cameron, Rondo, ed., *Banking in the Early Stages of Industrialization: A Study in Comparative Economic History*, New York, Oxford University Press, 1967.

———, *Banking and Economic Development*, New York, Oxford University Press, 1972.

Duncan, O. D., *et al.*, *Metropolis and Region*, Baltimore, The Johns Hopkins Press, 1960 (Resources for the Future Regional Study).

Gerschenkron, Alexander, "Economic Backwardness in Historical Perspective," in B. F. Hoselitz, ed., *The Progress of Underdeveloped Areas*, Chicago, University of Chicago Press, 1952, pp. 3–29.

———, *Economic Backwardness in Historical Perspective*, Cambridge, Mass., Harvard University Press, 1962.

Goldsmith, Raymond W., *Financial Structure and Development*, New Haven, Yale University Press, 1969.

Goldstein, Gerald S., and Leon N. Moses, "A Survey of Urban Economics," *Journal of Economic Literature*, 11 (June 1973), pp. 471–515.

Gras, N. S. B., *An Introduction to Economic History*, New York, Harper, 1922.

Hoselitz, Bert F., "Entrepreneurship and Capital Formation in France and Britain since 1700," in *Capital Formation and Economic Growth*, Princeton, Princeton University Press for National Bureau of Economic Research, 1956.

Kindleberger, C. P., "European Integration and the Development of a Single Financial Center for Long-Term Capital," *Weltwirtschaftliches Archiv*, 90 (1963), pp. 189–210.

Lösch, August, *The Economics of Location*, New Haven, Yale University Press, 1954.

McKenzie, R. D., *The Metropolitan Community*, New York, McGraw-Hill, 1933.

McKinnon, Ronald I., *Money and Capital in Economic Development*, Washington, D.C., The Brookings Institution, 1973.

Madden, John T., and Marcus Nadler, *The International Money Markets*, New York, Prentice-Hall, 1935.

Pred, Allan R., *The Spatial Dynamics of U.S. Urban-Industrial Growth, 1800–1914: Interpretive and Theoretical Essays*, Cambridge, Mass., M.I.T. Press, 1966.

[1] References are assembled by chapter in order to furnish concise bibliographies on the banking history of each country. Where a reference in one chapter is to be found in the bibliography of another, a cross reference is provided at the end of the list for the first.

Sametz, Arnold W., ed., *Financial Development and Economic Growth*, New York, New York University Press, 1972.

Shaw, Edward S., *Financial Deepening in Economic Development*, New York, Oxford University Press, 1973.

Vernon, Raymond, *Metropolis, 1985*, Cambridge, Mass., Harvard University Press, 1960.

For Cameron (1961), see France; Fanno, Italy; Fohlen, France; Henning, Germany; Interbank Research Organisation, A Financial Center for Europe?; Kerr, Canada; Labasse, France; Powell, England; Pressnell, England; Robbins and Terleckyj, United States; Taylor, England.

III. England

Anderson, B. L., "The Attorney and the Early Capital Market in Lancashire," in François Crouzet, ed., *Capital Formation in the Industrial Revolution*, London, Methuen, 1972.

Bagehot, Walter, *Lombard Street: A Description of the Money Market*, New York, Scribner, Armstrong, 1873 (reprinted by Irwin, 1966).

Bisschop, W. R., *The Rise of the London Money Market, 1640–1826*, London, Frank Cass, 1968 (first Dutch edition, 1896, first English translation, 1910).

Chandler, George, *Four Centuries of Banking* (Martin's Bank), London, Batsford, Vol. I, 1964; Vol. II, 1968.

Crick, W. F., and J. E. Wadsworth, *A Hundred Years of Joint Stock Banking* (Midlands Bank), London, Hodder & Stoughton, 1936.

Gregory, T. E., *The Westminster Bank through a Century*, London, Westminster Bank, Vols. I, II, 1936.

Jeffrys, J. B., "Trends in Business Organisation in Great Britain since 1856, with special reference to the financial structure of the companies, the mechanism of investment, and the relations between shareholder and the company," unpublished thesis, London School of Economics, 1938.

Leighton-Boyce, J.A.S.L., *Smiths, the Bankers, 1658–1958*, London, National Provincial Bank, 1958.

Matthews, P. W., and Anthony W. Tuke, *History of Barclay's Bank, Ltd.*, London, Blades, East and Blades, 1926.

Powell, Ellis T., *The Evolution of the Money Market (1384–1915): An Historical and Analytical Study of the Rise and Development of Finance as a Central, Coordinated Force*, London, 1915 (reprinted by Kelley, New York, 1966).

Pressnell, L. S., *Country Banking in the Industrial Revolution*, Oxford, Clarendon, 1956.

Sayers, R. S., *Lloyds Bank in the History of English Banking*, Oxford, Clarendon, 1957.

Taylor, Audrey M., *Gilletts, Bankers at Banbury and Oxford: A Study in Local Economic History*, Oxford, Clarendon, 1964.

Wechsberg, Joseph, *The Merchant Bankers*, Boston, Little, Brown, 1966.

Withers, Hartly, *National Provincial Bank, 1833–1933*, London, privately printed, 1933.

For Hidy, see United States.

IV. France

Bigo, Robert, *Les banques françaises au cours du XIXe siècle*, Paris, Sirey, 1947.

Bouvier, Jean, *Le Crédit Lyonnais de 1863 à 1882, Les années de formation d'une banque de dépots*, Paris, SEVPEN, 1961.

Brocard, Lucien, "Les marchés financiers du province," in A. Aupetit *et al.*, *Les grands marchés financiers*, Paris, Alcan, 1912.

Buffet, Jean, *Du régionalisme au nationalisme financier*, Paris, Berger-Levrault, 1917.

Cameron, Rondo, *France and the Economic Development of Europe, 1800–1914*, Princeton, Princeton University Press, 1961.

Charpenay, Georges, *Les banques régionalistes*, Paris, Nouvelle Revue Critique, 1939.

Crédit du Nord centenaire, Lille, privately printed, 1948.

Dauphin-Meunier, A., *La Banque de France*, Gallimard, 1936.

Fohlen, Claude, "France, 1700–1914," in Carlo M. Cipolla, ed., *The Fontana Economic History of Europe*, Vol. 4, *The Emergence of Industrial Societies*, Part I, no place, Collins/Fontana Books, 1972 (?), pp. 7–75.

Gille, Bertrand, *La banque en France au XIXe siècle, Recherches historiques*, Geneva, Librairie Droz, 1970.

Labasse, Jean, *Les capitaux et la région, Etude géographique, Essai sur le commerce et la circulation des capitaux dans la région lyonnaise*, Paris, Colin, 1955.

Lévy-Leboyer, Maurice, *Les banques européenes et l'industrialization internationale dans la première moitié du XIXe siècle*, Paris, Presses Universitaires de France, 1964.

Thuillier, Guy, "Pour une histoire bancaire régionale: En Nivernais de 1800 à 1880," *Annales*, 10 (October–December, 1955), pp. 494–512.

For Fanno, see Italy; Madden and Nadler, I and II.

V. Germany

Baar, Lothar, "Probleme der industriellen Revolution in grosstädtischen Industriezentren: Das Berliner Beispiel," in W. Fischer, ed., *Wirtschafts- und sozialgeschichtliche Probleme der frühen Industrialisierung*, Berlin, Colloquium, 1968, pp. 529–542.

Benaerts, Pierre, *Les origines de la grande industrie allemande*, Paris, Editions Turot, 1933.

Blumberg, Horst, "Die Finanzierung der Neugründungen und Erweiterungen von Industriebetrieben in Form der Aktiengesellschaften während der fünfziger Jahrhunderts in Deutschlands, am Beispiel der preussischen Verhältnisse erläutert," in Hans Mottek, ed., *Studien zur Geschichte der industriellen Revolution, Berlin, Akademie-Verlag*, 1960, pp. 165–208.

Böhme, Helmut, *Deutschlands Weg zur Grossmacht, Studien zum Verhältnis von Wirtschaft und Staat während der Reichsgründerzeit, 1848–1881*, Cologne, Kiepenheuer & Witsch, 1966.

———, *Frankfurt und Hamburg, Des Deutsches Reiches Silber- und Goldloch und die allerenglishste Stade des Kontinents*, Frankfurt-am-Main, Europäische Verlaganstalt, 1968.

Borchardt, Knut, "The Industrial Revolution in Germany, 1700–1914," in C. M. Cipolla, ed., *The Fontana Economic History of Europe: The Emergence of Industrial Societies,* Part 1, no place, Collins-Fontana Books, (1972?), pp. 76–160.

Brockhage, Bernhard, *Zur Entwicklung des preussisch-deutschen Kapitalexports, Erster Teil, Der Berliner Markt für auslandische Staatspapiere, 1816 bis zum 1840,* Leipzig, Duncker und Humbolt, 1910.

Cameron, Rondo E., "Founding the Bank of Darmstadt," *Explorations in Entrepreneurial History,* 13 (February 1956), pp. 113–130.

Cecil, Lamar, *Albert Ballin: Business and Politics in Imperial Germany, 1888–1918,* Princeton, Princeton University Press, 1967.

Helfferich, Karl, *Georg von Siemens, Ein Lebensbild aus Deutschlands grosser Zeit,* revised and shortened edition of the 1921–23 three-volume work, Krefeld, Serpe, 1956.

Henning, Friedrich-Wilhelm, "Standorte und Spezialisierung des Handels und des Transportwesens in der Mark Brandenburg um 1800," *Scripta Mercaturae,* 1/1971, pp. 1–44.

Heyn, Udo E., "Private Banking and Industrialization: The Case of Frankfurt am Main, 1825–1875," unpublished dissertation, University of Wisconsin, 1969.

Hundert Jahre im Dienste der Deutschen Wirtschaft, Ein Rückblick zur Erinnerung an die Gründung der Mitteldeutschen Creditbank, Frankfurt-am-Main, privately printed, 1956.

Landes, David S., "The Bleichröder Bank: An Interim Report," Publications of the Leo Baeck Institute, *Yearbook V,* London, East and West Library, 1960, pp. 201–220.

Riesser, Jacob, *The Great German Banks and Their Concentration in Connection with the Economic Development of Germany,* Washington, National Monetary Commission, 1911 (translation of the 3rd German ed., revised and enlarged).

Rosenberg, Hans, *Die Weltwirtschaftskrise von 1857–1859,* Stuttgart-Berlin, Verlag von W. Kohlhammer, 1934.

Seidenzahl, Fritz, *100 Jahre Deutsche Bank 1870–1970,* Frankfurt am Main, printed by the Deutsche Bank, 1970.

Tilly, Richard, *Financial Institutions and Industrialization in the Rhineland, 1815–1870,* Madison, University of Wisconsin Press, 1966.

Whale, F. Barrett, *Joint Stock Banking in Germany: A Study of German Credit-Banks Before and After the War,* London, Cass, 1930 (reprinted by Kelley, New York, 1068)

Wiskemann, Erwin, *Hamburg und die Welthandelspolitik von den Anfängen bis zur Gegenwart,* Hamburg, de Gruter, 1929.

For Crick and Wadsworth, see England; Duncan, I and II; Wechsberg, England.

VI. Italy

Bonelli, Franco, *La crisi del 1907: una tappa dello sviluppo industriale in Italia,* Turin, Fondazione Luigi Einaudi, 1971.

Castronovo, Valerio, *Economia e società in Piemonte dall'unita al 1914*, Milan, Banca Commerciale Italiana, 1969.
Clough, Shepard B., *The Economic History of Modern Italy*, New York, Columbia University Press, 1964.
Cohen, Jon S., "Financing Industrialization in Italy, 1894–1914: The Partial Transformation of a Late Comer," *Journal of Economic History*, 27 (September 1967), pp. 363–382.
———, in Cameron, ed. (1972), pp. 58–90.
De Mattia, Renato, *L'unificazione monetaria italiana*, Turin, Industria Libraria Tipografica, 1959.
Fanno, Marco, *Le banche e il mercato monetario*, Rome, Athenaeum, 1913.
Gerschenkron, Alexander, *Continuity in History and Other Essays*, Cambridge, Mass., Harvard University Press, 1968.
Greenfield, Kent Roberts, *Economics and Liberalism in the Risorgimento: A Study in Nationalism in Lombardy, 1814–1848*, rev. ed., Baltimore, The Johns Hopkins Press, 1965.
Luzzatto, Gino, *Storia economica dell'eta moderna e contemporanea*, Part II: *L'eta contemporanea*, Padua, CEDAM, 1960.
———, *L'economia italiana dal 1861 al 1914*, Vol. I (1861–1894), Milan, Banca Commerciale Italiana, 1963.
Pareto, Vilfredo, *Le marché financier italien*, 1891–1899 (annual articles reprinted in Geneva by Droz, 1965).
Romani, Mario, *Storia economica d'Italia nel secolo XIX, 1815–1914 con scelta di testi e documenti*, Vol. I, Milan, Giuffre, 1968.
Smith, Dennis Mack, *Italy, a Modern History*, Ann Arbor, University of Michigan Press, 1959.

For Cameron, see I and II; Myers, United States.

VII. SWITZERLAND

Iklé, Max, *Switzerland: An International Banking and Finance Center*, Stroudsburg, Pa., Dowden, Hutchinson & Ross, 1972.
Jöhr, Adolf, *Die schweizerischen Notenbanken, 1826–1913*, Zurich, Orell Fussli, 1915.
Schwarzenbach, Ernst, "The Swiss Money Market," in Madden and Nadler (1935), pp. 481–523.
Union Bank of Switzerland, 1862, 1912, 1962, Zurich, privately printed, 1962.

For Gille, see France; Levy-Leboyer, France; Madden and Nadler, I and II.

VIII. CANADA

Bank of Montreal, *The Centenary of the Bank of Montreal, 1817–1917*, Montreal, privately printed, 1917.
Bank of Nova Scotia, 1832–1932, Toronto, privately printed, 1932.
Botha, D. J. J., "The Canadian Money Market I: Institutional Developments," *South African Journal of Economics*, 40 (June 1972), pp. 119–143.
Eaton, G. Howard, and David E. Bond, "Canada's Newest Money Market—Vancouver," *The Canadian Banker*, 77 (November-December 1970), pp. 14–15.

Glazebrook, G. P. deT., *The Story of Toronto*, Toronto, University of Toronto, 1971.

Jamieson, A. B., *Chartered Banking in Canada*, Toronto, Ryerson, 1953.

Kerr, Donald P., "Some Aspects of the Geography of Finance in Canada," *The Canadian Geographer*, 9 (1965), pp. 175–192. Also in Robert M. Irving, ed., *Readings in Canadian Geography*, Toronto, Holt, Rinehart & Winston, 1965.

———, "Metropolitan Dominance in Canada," in John Warkentin, ed., *A Geographical Interpretation of Canada*, Toronto, Methuen, 1967, pp. 531–555.

Masters, D. C., *The Rise of Toronto, 1850–1890*, Toronto, University of Toronto Press, 1947.

Neufeld, E. P., *The Financial System of Canada, Its Growth and Development*, New York, St. Martin's, 1972.

Ray, D. Michael, "Regional Aspects of Foreign Ownership of Manufacturing in Canada," Waterloo, Canada, unpublished paper prepared for the Task Force on the Structure of Canadian Industry (Watkins Committee), 1967.

———, "The Location of United States Manufacturing Subsidiaries in Canada," *Economic Geography*, 47 (July 1971), pp. 389–400.

Ross, Victor, *A History of the Canadian Bank of Commerce*, Toronto, Oxford University Press, Vol. I, 1920; Vol. II, 1922.

Royal Bank of Canada, Fiftieth Anniversary, 1869–1919, Montreal, privately printed, 1920.

Royal Commission on Banking and Finance, 1964, *Report* (Porter report) Ottawa, Queen's Printer, 1964.

Wilson, J. S. G., "The Australian Money Market," Banca Nazionale del Lavoro, *Quarterly Review*, 104 (March 1973), pp. 46–49.

IX. The United States

Albion, Robert Greenhalgh, *The Rise of New York Port (1815–1860)*, New York, Scribners, 1939.

Hidy, Muriel E., "George Peabody, Merchant and Financier, 1829–1854," Radcliffe College doctoral dissertation, 1939.

Kouwenhoven, John A., *Partners in Banking: An Historical Portrait of a Great Private Bank, Brown Brothers, Harriman & Company, 1818–1968*, New York, Doubleday, 1968.

Myers, Margaret G., *The New York Money Market*, Vol. I, *Origins and Development*, New York, Columbia University Press, 1931 (reprinted 1971).

Riefler, W. W., *Money Rates and Money Markets in the United States*, New York, Harper, 1930.

Robbins, Sidney M., and Nestor S. Terleckyj, *Money Metropolis: A Locational Study of the Financial Activities in the New York Region*, Cambridge, Mass., Harvard University Press, 1960.

For Gras, see I & II; Lösch, I & II.

X. International Financial Centers

Abrahams, Paul P., "The Foreign Expansion of American Finance and Its Relationship to the Foreign Economic Policies of the United States, 1907–1921," unpublished dissertation in history, University of Wisconsin, 1967.

Brown, John Crosby, *A Hundred Years of Merchant Banking: A History of Brown Brothers and Co.*, New York, privately printed, 1909.
Hopkinson, Edward, Jr., *Drexel & Co. Over a Century of History*, New York, Newcomen Society of North America, 1952.
Kindleberger, Charles P., *Economic Growth in France and Britain, 1851–1950*, Cambridge, Mass., Harvard University Press, 1964.
———, *The World in Depression, 1929–1939*, Berkeley, University of California Press, 1973.
Newbold, J. T. W., "The Beginnings of the World Crisis, 1873–1896," *Economic History*, 2 (January 1932), pp. 425–431.
Phelps, Clyde William, *The Foreign Expansion of American Banks: American Branch Banking Abroad*, New York, Ronald, 1927.
Redlich, Fritz, *The Molding of American Banking, Men and Ideas*, New York, Hafner, Parts I, II, 1951.
In Memoriam, Jesse Seligmann, New York, privately printed, 1894.
State Department, *Foreign Relations of the United States, 1947*, Vol. III, *The British Commonwealth; Europe*, Washington, U.S. Government Printing Office, 1972.

For Bagehot, see England; Brockhage, Germany; Cameron, France; Cecil, Germany; Crick and Wadsworth, England; Jeffrys, England; Leighton-Boyce, England; Rosenberg, Germany; Wiskemann, Germany.

XI. A Financial Center for Europe?

Interbank Research Organisation, *The Future of London as an International Financial Centre*, London, Her Majesty's Stationery Office, 1973.
Kohn, Eric D., "Eurobonds—What Sort of Market?" *Euromoney*, 3 (October 1971), pp. 68–70.
Low, William F., "Euroclear Opens Up," *Euromoney*, 4 (August 1972a), pp. 31, 33.
———, "Improving the Secondary Market," *The Banker* (September 1972b), pp. 1157–1159.
Lutz, Alfred, "Problems of the Secondary Market—Has It Really 'Come of Age'?" *Euromoney*, 5 (April 1973), pp. 19, 21.
McRae, Hamish, "Barclay's Euro-clearing System—Mark II," *Euromoney*, 4 (September 1972), p. 33.
Robinson, Roland I., *Money and Capital Markets*, New York, McGraw-Hill, 1964.
(Segré report), *The Development of a European Capital Market, Brussels*, European Economic Community, 1967.
(Werner report), "Report to the Council and the Commission on the Realization by Stages of Economic and Monetary Union," European Communities *Bulletin*, Supplement 11, 1970.
Yassukovich, Stanislas M., "The Development of the International Capital Market," *Euromoney*, 2 (January 1971), pp. 16, 18–20.

For De Mattia, see Italy; Duncan, I and II; Luzzatto, Italy; Ray, Canada; Robbins and Terleckyj, United States.

[9]

The Function of Commercial Centers in the Modernization of European Capitalism: Amsterdam as an Information Exchange in the Seventeenth Century

WOODRUFF D. SMITH

During Amsterdam's development as the commercial center of Europe in the seventeenth century, an informal "information exchange" appeared among the economic and political institutions of the city. Informational economies of the types discussed by Stigler, North, and Pred led to the emergence of Amsterdam as the focal point of information flows throughout Europe. They also encouraged a high level of innovation within all functional areas of Amsterdam's information exchange—especially in long-term data analysis—which contributed to the general modernization of capitalism.

ONE of the commonplaces of early modern economic history is the dominance of Amsterdam over European international commerce in the seventeenth century. Amsterdam was the apex of several different regional hierarchies of trade and finance. According to Fernand Braudel it succeeded Venice, Antwerp, and Genoa in this role and preceded London and New York. Amsterdam's commercial dominance, closely linked to the economic preeminence of the Netherlands as a whole, is regarded by Immanuel Wallerstein as one of the key features of the "world system" in the seventeenth century. Although there is considerable disagreement about the nature of Amsterdam's commercial hegemony, historical opinion lines up solidly behind the picture of Amsterdam as the most important of Europe's commercial centers.[1]

Journal of Economic History, Vol. XLIV, No. 4 (Dec. 1984) ISSN 0022-0507.

The author is Professor of History, University of Texas at San Antonio, San Antonio, Texas 78285. He has received valuable comments from Paul Hohenberg, Donald McCloskey, and two anonymous reviewers. The following abbreviations are used in the notes:

ARA *Algemeen Rijksarchief* (Netherlands National Archives, The Hague)
CCM Ethel Bruce Sainsbury, *A Calendar of the Court Minutes etc. of the East India Company 1635–79*, 11 vols. (Oxford, 1907–1938).
GA *Gemeente Archief Amsterdam* (Amsterdam Municipal Archives)
VOC *Vereenigde Oostindische Compagnie* (Dutch East India Company)
WIC *West-Indische Compagnie* (Dutch West India Company)

[1] Fernand Braudel, *Afterthoughts on Material Civilization and Capitalism* (Baltimore, 1977), pp. 39–75; Immanuel Wallerstein, *The Modern World-System II: Mercantilism and the Consolidation of the European World Economy, 1600–1750* (New York, 1980), pp. 57–61; Jean-Claude Boyer, "Le capitalisme hollandais et l'organisation de l'espace dans les Provinces-Unies," *Dutch Capitalism and World Capitalism*, ed. Maurice Aymard (Cambridge and Paris, 1982), pp. 13–22.

But what did it really matter that Amsterdam or any other single city functioned as the commercial center of Western Europe? Was there anything that Amsterdam provided to the international economy that was not, or could not have been, provided also by a number of other, lesser centers? Was Amsterdam actually unique in any functional sense, and if so, what significance did that uniqueness have? Equally important is the question of economic change. Did Amsterdam play a unique role in preindustrial economic modernization, other than simply being the place where many economic decisions were made?

The economic functions of Amsterdam as a commercial center have been approached in several ways, often as part of attempts to deal with the peripheral issue of Amsterdam's "rise." Some historians have emphasized the fact that Amsterdam in its heyday was Europe's financial center and a major generator of investment capital. It is, however, difficult to identify anything unique in the long run about the capital assembly functions located there. It is far from clear that these could not have been as easily performed by the lesser centers in northwestern Europe that also engaged in capital formation.[2] Other historians, including Braudel, have treated the large early-modern commercial centers as unprecedentedly large markets that aggregated and transferred pressures for economic change.[3] But again, the growth of markets was a general phenomenon. What was different or significant about Amsterdam other than its large size? In what ways was a single, dominant marketing center functionally superior to an array of lesser centers? Put differently, what economies of scale prevailed in Amsterdam and not elsewhere, and what difference did they make?

P. W. Klein, following the line of analysis first laid down by T. P. van der Kooy, comes close to an answer. He argues that Amsterdam's economic paramountcy was due to its emergence as an international warehousing center connecting several different regional economies.[4] Amsterdam merchants, by linking control of warehousing to finance, manufacturing, overseas trade, and distribution, could create monopolistic conditions in commodities markets. It can be argued that a single, strategically located warehousing center can regulate the rate of commodity flow from one region to another, reducing transaction costs

[2] Wallerstein, *Modern World-System II*, pp. 57–61; J. G. van Dillen, *Van Rijkdom en Regenten. Handboek tot de economische en sociale geschiedenis van Nederland tijdens de republiek* (The Hague, 1970), pp. 30–35; Charles Wilson, *Anglo-Dutch Commerce and Finance in the Eighteenth Century* (Cambridge, 1941). Charles Carrière, "Image du capitalisme hollandais au xviiie siècle. Le miroir marseillais," in *Dutch Capitalism*, ed. Aymard, pp. 171–96, points out that for Marseilles, Amsterdam was a useful payments center but not a major source of investment capital.

[3] Braudel, *Afterthoughts*, pp. 39–75; Fernand Braudel, *Civilisation matérielle, économie et capitalisme, xve–xviiie siècle*, 3 vols. (Paris, 1979), vol. 3, pp. 17–24, 71–234; Jan de Vries, *The Economy of Europe in an Age of Crisis* (Cambridge, 1976), pp. 147–75.

[4] P. W. Klein, *De Trippen in de 17e Eeuw: een studie over het ondernemersgedrag op de Hollandse Stapelmarkt* (Assen, 1965), pp. 1–17; T. P. van der Kooy, *Hollands Stapelmarkt en haar Verfall* (Amsterdam, 1931).

within the trading system as a whole. What relation warehousing may bear to long-term economic change is, however, unclear.[5]

I shall focus here on another function: the handling of *information*. Economic historians have long stressed that the assembly and exchange of business information are important parts of the operation of a commercial center. Relatively little comprehensive research has been done on information systems in late preindustrial economies. It is clear, however, that one byproduct of markets in the period was the creation of institutions and business contacts through which large amounts of information passed.[6] While earlier commercial centers such as Venice were similar, none could match the reputation of seventeenth-century Amsterdam as a source of information.[7]

It is unlikely that Amsterdam possessed any particular advantage in information-handling before the city's rise to economic prominence in the late sixteenth century, and therefore we must see her informational role as a product rather than a cause of her commercial paramountcy. As Allan Pred has argued with respect to nineteenth-century New York, however, dominance of an informational network by an urban center, once achieved, tends to reinforce itself.[8] This may explain why Amsterdam continued to be regarded as the fulcrum of European commerce well into the eighteenth century, long after London and Rotterdam had surpassed her in volume of trade.

The main concern here is not, however, the question of Amsterdam's rise and the maintenance of her paramountcy. It is the structure of information-handling in early modern Amsterdam and its role in the modernization of capitalism. I shall argue that the nature of information as a commodity and as a byproduct of the operations of trade networks led in the seventeenth century to the evolution in Amsterdam of a central information exchange for all of Europe. I shall also argue that Amsterdam's information functions, unlike most of the others that she performed, were necessarily unique. Finally, I shall argue that innovations in information-processing at Amsterdam contributed to the modernization of the European economy.

[5] It might also be objected that since warehousing capacity is largely a function of direct investment, one would expect the reign of a prime commercial center resting its hegemony on warehousing to be a short one in the face of a determined rival (of which Amsterdam had many) willing to build up its own facilities.

[6] See, for example, Braudel, *Civilisation matérielle*, vol. 2, pp. 353–82, and Violet Barbour, *Capitalism in Amsterdam in the 17th Century* (Ann Arbor, 1963), p. 53.

[7] De Vries, *Economy of Europe*, pp. 116, 121. In the mid-seventeenth century the intelligence systems of the major European states consisted to a large extent of agents stationed in the Netherlands. See Herbert H. Rowen, *John de Witt, Grand Pensionary of Holland, 1625–1672* (Princeton, 1978), pp. 356–61. Amsterdam was a center of the nascent newspaper business. When the directors of the English East India Company wanted quick and reliable information about what was going on in their *own* factories in Asia, they consulted their correspondent in Amsterdam. See CCM, 1664–1667, pp. 417–18 (Court of Committees, 18 Dec. 1667).

[8] Allan R. Pred, *Urban Growth and the Circulation of Information: The United States System of Cities, 1790–1840* (Cambridge, Massachusetts, 1973), pp. 186–238.

COMMERCIAL CENTERS AND THE THEORY OF INFORMATIONAL ECONOMIES

It is possible to derive from Douglass North's concept of transaction costs and from George Stigler's classic discussion of informational economies an explanation for the concentration of information-gathering activities in a single center.[9] According to North, as the complexity of a system of production or exchange increases, the aggregate cost of transactions within the system also increases. Participants in the system will seek to reduce transaction costs. In the seventeenth century they did so by internalizing costs within large organizations (the East India companies, for example) and by attempting to concentrate as many transactions as possible in one place. Since acquiring information is a major transaction cost, information-handling functions also tended to concentrate in that place—Amsterdam—and to become to some extent a function of the large, cost-internalizing organizations.

Stigler's analysis of search in dispersed markets explains why information-handling tends to become organized into a system with a unique center. In dispersed markets such as those of the early modern international economy, he says, search for the lowest price will constitute an important part of a buyer's costs. Search for buyers will be part of a seller's costs. Buyers and sellers will conduct their searches up to the point at which the expected marginal return from searching equals the marginal cost. In the longer run they may try to change the structure of transactions to reduce the unit cost of searches, increase the efficiency of search, and realize economies of scale. When, as in the seventeenth century, mass advertising is not effectively available as a means of identifying buyers, sellers, and prices, growth of market size will be a "powerful inducement to localize transactions" and will encourage the emergence of "specialized traders whose chief service . . . is implicitly to provide a meeting place for potential buyers and sellers."[10] Scale economics will be realized through an increase in the experience levels of repetitive buyers in a central market. They will wish to pool information. Stigler also predicts that there will be a strong tendency toward monopoly in the provision of information, because the cost of collecting information is independent of its use by any particular market participant.

The dispersed markets in the sixteenth and seventeenth centuries confirm some of Stigler's predictions, such as specialized traders and a convergence of prices. But it is hard to get further. A slightly different approach proves useful—the notion of an *information exchange* contained within a commercial center.

[9] Douglass C. North, *Structure and Change in Economic History* (New York, 1981), pp. 33–44; George J. Stigler, *The Organization of Industry* (Homewood, Illinois, 1968), pp. 171–90.

[10] Stigler, *Organization of Industry*, p. 176.

TABLE 1
INFORMATION EXCHANGE

General Functions	Examples of Structures Performing Functions in Seventeenth/Eighteenth-Century Amsterdam
1. Acquisition of Information	See Figure 1
2. Transfer	Bourse, merchant houses, local correspondence networks, East India Company, Bank, municipal government, *information market*
3. Aggregation/short-term analysis	Bourse, other markets, municipal government, East India Company, larger merchant houses
4. Dissemination	See Figure 1; also newspapers, merchant handbooks, occasional printed materials and advertising, price listings
5. Long-Term Accumulation	Municipal government, East India Company, merchant houses
6. Long-Term Analysis	Municipal government, East India Company, merchant houses

Source: See footnote 11.

THE COMMERCIAL CENTER AS INFORMATION EXCHANGE

I have chosen the term "information exchange" to denote the information-handling structure of early-modern commercial centers because of two connotations of "exchange": its general connotation of a system of trading; and a narrower one of an actual place for trading. The same abstraction from the actual handling of commodities that resulted in the appearance of the Amsterdam Bourse and the Royal Exchange of London also produced information exchanges. As we shall see, the Amsterdam information exchange conformed to many of the characteristics of the market structure to which it was attached. It consisted in part of institutions (the Bourse, the East India Company, and so forth) that developed information-handling as a secondary purpose.

Table 1 indicates the functions performed by an information exchange. The functions can be identified in the operations of practically any modern information exchange, whether it be part of a commercial center such as New York City, or a government, a corporate headquarters, or an intelligence agency.[11] There will always be a certain amount of overlap between functions. Table 1 shows the order in which a piece of information passes through the system. In many cases, of course, the order will not be followed. The dissemination function, for instance, usually is fourth in the flow of short-term information; but it must necessarily come elsewhere in long-term analysis. Moreover, the functions involving long-term analysis were not important in the information exchanges until well into the seventeenth century. Their appearance, in fact, constituted one of the most significant steps taken toward the modernization of capitalism in preindustrial commerce.

[11] The specific categories are the author's. For various approaches to informational structure, see Alfred Rappaport, ed., *Information in Decision Making: Quantitative and Behavioral Dimensions* (Englewood Cliffs, New Jersey, 1970).

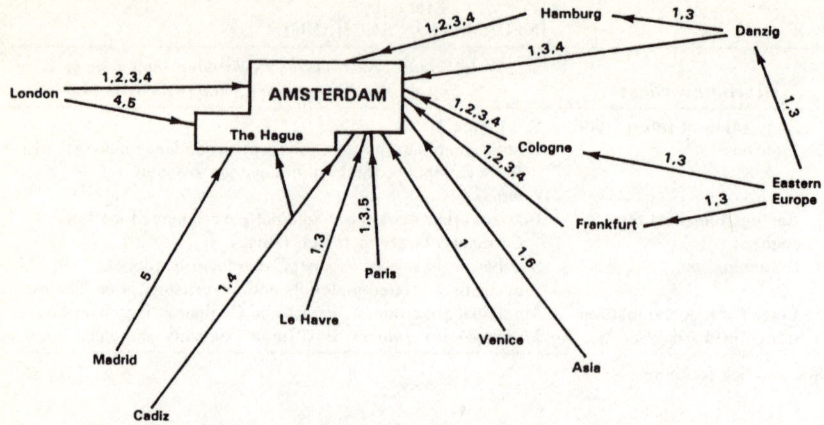

FIGURE 1
EXTERNAL INFORMATION ACQUISITION IN AMSTERDAM:
EXAMPLES OF CHANNELS

1. Private merchant correspondence
2. Institutional correspondence
3. Movement of businessmen
4. Consular reports
5. Diplomatic reports
6. Special channels

Sources: GA: Burlamachi papers (P.A. 1); Brants papers (P.A. 88); De Graeff papers (P.A. 76); Velters papers (P.A. 2); consular and ambassadorial reports cataloged under Cadix, Cork, Danzig, Hamburg, Keulen, London, Lübeck, Stockholm, and Warschau. ARA: VOC, WIC, and Levantse Handel.

THE ACQUISITION FUNCTION IN THE AMSTERDAM INFORMATION EXCHANGE

The physical channels through which business data flowed into the Amsterdam information exchange in the seventeenth and eighteenth centuries are represented schematically in Figure 1. Most of the channels shown are examples of types rather than sole instances. There were, roughly speaking, six types: the correspondence of private merchants, the correspondence of business institutions, the actual movement of businessmen to and from Amsterdam, the reports of Dutch consuls in other trading centers, the reports of Dutch diplomatic representatives in political capitals, and special channels of communication set up by particular organizations (such as that between the East India Company and its agencies in Asia).

The correspondence of individual Amsterdam merchants and their houses with businessmen in other cities represented an ancient means of conveying business information. Taken together it probably constituted the largest input into the Amsterdam exchange. Early modern postal services primarily served businessmen's needs; the expansion and improvement of the Dutch post in the seventeenth century were due largely to the demand placed on it by business.[12] By the second half of the century, mail could be passed between Amsterdam and Paris in six days by the "ordinary" post, and in two days by more expensive express service. Even when France and the Netherlands were at war, it seldom took more than a week for mail to get between businessmen in the two countries. Most correspondence with London depended on twice-weekly packets, but express communication could also be bought. Within the central and southern Netherlands, most mail service required one to two days.[13] In other words, the speed of postal communication (although not the price) was reasonably close to that of modern mail services, especially at shorter distances.

Although business correspondence had been an essential part of international trade for centuries, the amount, diversity, and degree of systematization of private correspondence increased markedly in Amsterdam in the seventeenth century, as did the importance of such correspondence in business operations.[14] This probably resulted from the vast expansion of Amsterdam's participation in regular trading networks and from the growth of postal services. Whatever the reason, the possibility of entering into regular correspondence with businessmen in other European cities opened up opportunities in the seventeenth century for a large number of small operators to enter long-distance trade. At the beginning of the century, for success in foreign trade a merchant had to have agents in his main markets, or else family ties there.[15] Otherwise, he was usually limited by the distance that he himself could traverse—for example, from Amsterdam to the annual fairs of the western German cities. Improved postal services made it possible for smaller Amsterdam businessmen to find reliable correspondents through whom sales and financing arrangements could be made.[16]

[12] See Jan de Vries, *The Dutch Rural Economy in the Golden Age, 1500–1700* (New Haven, 1974), pp. 202–9, and George T. Matthews, ed., *The Fugger Newsletter* (New York, 1970), pp. 13–27.

[13] GA: Burlamachi papers, no. 495 (correspondence with Morand, Paris), esp. letter Morand to Burlamachi, 8 May 1687; Velters papers, no. 2/8, pp. 531–32 (letter R. Ferret, Paris, to J. Velters, 8 Oct. 1676); p. 556 (letter Ferret to Velters, 29 Oct. 1676); De Graeff papers, no. 200 (a printed commercial diary, 1680, with schedules for Dutch postal services).

[14] Evidence for this assertion comes from an examination of the inventories of family papers maintained in GA and from samples of the papers listed in the note to Figure 1.

[15] Other factors were of course involved as well, but long-distance trade conformed well to the pattern outlined here. See for example the well-documented business affairs of Lionel Cranfield, discussed in Menna Prestwich, *Cranfield. Politics and Profit under the Early Stuarts. The Career of Lionel Cranfield, First Earl of Middlesex* (Oxford, 1966), pp. 49–106. See also Cranfield's correspondence for the period 1597–1607 in Historical Manuscripts Commission, *Calendar of the Manuscripts of Major-General Lord Sackville Preserved at Knole, Sevenoaks, Kent*, vol. 2, ed. F. J. Fisher (London, 1966), pp. 2–178.

[16] Examples of the ways such links of correspondence were established and maintained are contained in GA: Velters papers, no. 1, p. 137 (letter Velters to A. de Cuijper, 1 July 1670); Brants papers, no. 902 (correspondence between D. Leeuw and T. and H. Boursse, Middelburg, 1713–1725).

This, and the extensive development of brokerage functions in Amsterdam, greatly expanded the amount of business correspondence passing into the city. It therefore expanded the total pool of information. The amount of information entering Amsterdam is unlikely to have increased at the same rate as the volume of correspondence, of course, because of duplication. But there were compensations: duplication provided opportunities for checking reliability.

The growing importance of information can be seen in the standard formats of business letters. In the sixteenth century it had become customary for correspondents to note on their letters the rates of currency exchange. In the seventeenth century it became standard procedure—a matter of politeness and form—to include in business letters general economic and political information and prices of major commodities.[17] From these sources the printers would collect the data they used to issue periodical price lists for the major trading cities and tables of exchange rates. In the seventeenth century Amsterdam was the acknowledged center for the publication of such lists, and the information they contained was generally considered to be the most accurate available in Europe.[18]

Correspondence went in all directions and led to the accumulation of information everywhere that commerce existed—the pooling of information predicted by Stigler. Like international commercial relations in general, the flow of information through private correspondence acquired a hierarchical structure. Regional centers such as Cologne and Frankfurt, serving as markets for much of Central Europe and depending increasingly on Amsterdam as a distribution and warehousing center, tended over time to become secondary information exchanges also. Regional information, assembled in the course of a local merchant's operations (for example, at the annual Frankfurt fairs) would be passed by correspondence to Amsterdam. That so many channels of private correspondence culminated in Amsterdam made it important for businessmen in certain key trades (textiles, Asian goods, grain) to maintain correspondence with Amsterdam even if their actual commerce there was limited.[19] Although the Amsterdam information exchange was built on prior commercial connections, it expanded beyond them in the course of the seventeenth century. It was convenient to

[17] Braudel, *Civilisation matérielle*, vol. 2, p. 361. The format can be seen in most surviving sets of business correspondence, as for example in GA: Velters papers, no. 2/8 (correspondence with P. Macaré, 1676).

[18] See the assessment of Dutch price information in Michel Morineau, "Or brésilien et gazettes hollandaises," *Revue d'Histoire Moderne et Contemporaine*, 25 (Jan. 1978), 3–60.

[19] The relationship between central and regional information exchanges can be traced in correspondence series to be found in GA: Burlamachi papers, nos. 288 (correspondence with Frankfurt), 362 (Cologne), 481–502 (Paris), and 701–22 (Vienna). The interim maintenance of correspondence links can be seen in GA: Velters papers, no. 2/4, p. 76 (letter Velters to M. Fletcher, 16 Aug. 1675) and no. 2/6, p. 188 (letter Velters to G. Minviele, New York, 26 Nov. 1675).

merchants in regional centers that there be one central information exchange tying the regions together. In turn the growth of the Amsterdam information exchange attracted additional business to Amsterdam and reinforced the predominance of the city.

Closely related to the private correspondence of merchant houses was the correspondence of business institutions. Most of Amsterdam's local and European business up to the eighteenth century was done by family firms whose heads supervised their own correspondence. In the course of the seventeenth century, however, some of the larger firms developed into extensive commercial and financial institutions with bureaucratic structures.[20] The range and regularity of the information flowing into such houses were much greater than in the smaller firms. The state-chartered commercial institutions—the East and West India companies, for example, and the Directorate of the Levant Trade—all developed their own lines of external communication in Europe, often employing agents and paid correspondents in major cities who could report systematically and could be queried on matters of particular interest.[21] Institutional information was nothing new in Europe—witness the Florentine banks, the Fuggers, the Venetian state. What was different in Amsterdam was the proliferation of connected institutions within the same information exchange and the immense variety of channels that they brought together.

The large number of businessmen who passed in and out of Amsterdam brought information with them, although the relative importance of this ancient mode of transmission was probably declining. Yet the linking together of the western Dutch cities by canal and road in the first half of the century made movement so cheap that businessmen traveled frequently between Amsterdam, The Hague, Middelburg, and Rotterdam. This effectively made these part of the same expanded information exchange—a matter of some importance in view of the political information available in The Hague and Rotterdam's close connections with England.[22]

The state also brought information into the Amsterdam exchange, primarily through diplomatic reports. The Dutch in this were neither

[20] The process can be seen most clearly in the voluminous records of the Burlamachi house. Of particular interest is GA: Burlamachi papers, no. 6, which is a kind of guidebook to the operations of the house, with examples of real transactions drawn from the years 1663–1665, apparently intended for the training of junior clerks.

[21] See Pieter van Dam, *Beschryvinge van de Oostindische Compagnie*, ed. F. W. Stapel; R. G. P. Grote Serie, vols. 63, 68, 74, 76, 83, 87, 96 (The Hague, 1927–1954), vol. 63, pp. 410–11, for the VOC's use of correspondents. Van Dam's *Beschryvinge* is a massive description of the operation of the VOC, written for internal company use at the end of the seventeenth century and not published until the twentieth. Also: ARA: WIC, no. 812 (foreign correspondence book, 1688–1711); VOC, no. 4464 (letter J. Beekmans, agent in Hamburg, to VOC Amsterdam chamber, 29 Nov. 1678).

[22] The linking of Dutch cities together into a single interurban system is one of the subjects of Jan de Vries, *Barges and Capitalism: Passenger Transportation in the Dutch Economy (1632–1839)* (Utrecht, 1981). See also Boyer, "Capitalisme hollandais," pp. 13–22.

innovators nor models. The state intelligence services of several other countries—Venice, England, France, Spain—were older and apparently much more efficient than those of the politically fragmented Netherlands.[23]

On the other hand it could be argued that from the standpoint of commerce there were advantages in the Dutch system. The information generated by state sources was probably disseminated more widely and rapidly outside the government than it was elsewhere, because of the central role in Dutch politics played by the mercantile upper class. The commercial oligarchy of Amsterdam provided a large proportion of the state's personnel, and the distinction between their public and private capacities was sufficiently vague to allow them to use for business purposes information acquired by the state.[24] Moreover, in such a commercially oriented country, much of the state's information-gathering capacity was organized to provide business information. In the seventeenth century the Dutch organized their consuls (the senior members of the Dutch merchant communities in foreign towns) into a quasi-diplomatic information-gathering system. The repository of consular reports was the municipal government of Amsterdam. During periods of peace between Spain and the Netherlands, for example, the Dutch consul in Cadiz was responsible for summarizing intelligence about the annual American trading fleet and estimating the demand for imported goods that would be generated by the fleet's preparation. This information was then made available to the leading Amsterdam merchants, from whom it would rapidly pass to the rest of the business community.[25] Diplomatic channels were theoretically a matter of greater secrecy, but in fact Dutch diplomacy was notoriously public and its security something of a joke. Moreover, both private merchants and organizations such as the East India Company regularly bribed Dutch and foreign diplomats to get first-hand information about matters likely to affect their interests.[26]

There were, too, specialized channels of information. The best example is the East India Company (VOC—*Vereenigde Oostindische Compagnie*), which maintained some correspondents in Europe and a

[23] Donald E. Queller, "The Development of the Ambassadorial Relazione," in *Renaissance Venice*, ed. J. R. Hale (Totowa, New Jersey, 1973), pp. 174–96; Rowen, *De Witt*, pp. 731–80. See also Herbert H. Rowen, *The Ambassador Prepares for War. The Dutch Embassy of Arnauld de Pomponne, 1669–1671* (The Hague, 1957).

[24] On the commercial oligarchy in general, see Johan E. Elias, *De Vroedschap van Amsterdam, 1578–1795*, 2 vols. (Amsterdam, 1963; orig. ed. 1903, 1905), and C. R. Boxer, *The Dutch Seaborne Empire: 1600–1800* (New York, 1970), pp. 31–54. An example of the private use of state and VOC information can be found in GA: Velters papers, no. 2/7, pp. 514–16 (letter Velters to Macaré, 25 Sept. 1676).

[25] ARA: Levantse Handel, no. 173, contains reports of this sort from Cadiz. See esp. letters of 14 Sept. 1691 and 8 July 1696.

[26] Van Dam, *Beschryvinge*, vol. 68, pp. 334–37, discusses the VOC's "gratuities."

vast system of communication with its offices in Asia. The voluminous reports of the Company's stations in the East, supplemented by summaries prepared at the Dutch headquarters at Batavia in Java, traveled with the Company's return fleets. The VOC also employed special rapid-communication routes overland for passing information vital to ordering and marketing.[27]

INFORMATION TRANSFER

The heart of the Amsterdam information exchange, at least as far as short-term information was concerned, lay in the transfer of information. The majority of actual exchanges of information followed a pattern that, with allowances for the introduction of the telephone, still persists in commercial centers: face-to-face encounters among businessmen and interchange of short-distance correspondence within Amsterdam. The exchange was, of course, largely incidental to the conduct of commerce and of upper- and middle-class life; its volume was essentially a result of the high volume of commercial transactions in the city. Through his regular business dealings a merchant of even middling means could acquire an impressive fund of economic and political information, much of it relevant to his work, which he could pass on to his more distant correspondents.[28]

Somewhat apart from the general interchange of information in Amsterdam was a more privileged level among members of the city's merchant elite, frequently involving elite-dominated institutions such as the city government, the VOC, and the Exchange Bank. Information about the imminence of war or peace in Europe obtained through the government, or about the size of pepper cargoes coming from Asia acquired from the VOC, tended to circulate first among the heads of the major commercial houses. Although leakage into the information exchange as a whole tended to be quite rapid, first access gave the bigger businessmen a decided advantage.[29] Interchange between institutions and the state was also sometimes vital to the institutions. The VOC, for example, needed information about impending war among the Atlantic states as rapidly as possible so that it could arrange to protect return fleets already at sea.[30]

[27] The reports of the Asian stations are maintained in ARA: VOC, Overgekommene Brieven en Papieren. See also W. Ph. Coolhaas, ed., *Generale Missiven van Gouverneurs-General en Raden aan Heren XVII der Verenigde Oostindische Compagnie*, R. G. P. Grote Serie, vols. 104, 112, 125, 134, 150, 159, 164 (The Hague, 1960–1979), and Kristof Glamann, *Dutch Asiatic Trade, 1620–1740* (Copenhagen and The Hague, 1958), pp. 25–26.

[28] ARA: Hudde papers, no. 5 (exchanges of notes, Hudde and others, 1687–1689); CCM, 1668–1670, p. 120 (letter East India Co. to Hampson, agent in Amsterdam, 20 Nov. 1668).

[29] For an instance of advantages expected from early access to VOC information, see GA: Velters papers, no. 14 (letter Velters to Bornezee, 12 May 1694). See also ARA: Hudde papers, no. 5 (letter C. van Beuningen to Hudde, 5 May 1688).

[30] Van Dam, *Beschryvinge*, vol. 68, pp. 555–605.

The expanding role of institutions in transfer is one of the most important characteristics of the Amsterdam information exchange. Most earlier commercial centers had possessed public institutions or locations at which the physical process of information exchange was focused: the Rialto in Venice, for example, or the Antwerp Exchange.[31] Amsterdam had its own equivalents, in its Bourse and in periodic events such as the VOC's public auctions, where multitudes of Dutch and foreign businessmen gathered. But Amsterdam also possessed an increasing number of other permanent institutions (the VOC's Amsterdam chamber, the Exchange Bank, the other trading companies) with particular sources of information. In the boardrooms of these institutions, the pulling together of data from the companies' special sources was combined with the exchange of information within the city's elite. Considerable evidence attests to the importance of this kind of exchange in the commercial life of Amsterdam, an exchange that took place in an environment in which it was possible to check rumors systematically and to act immediately, through the institutions themselves, on the basis of information transferred.[32]

Another, somewhat bizarre innovation in information transfer was the appearance by at least 1650 of a literal market in political and economic information from all over Europe. The key figures were a number of specialized information brokers, of whom the best-known in the 1650s and 1660s was the transplanted German Leo van Aitzema.[33] Both governments and commercial enterprises—especially non-Dutch ones wanting to tap the Amsterdam information exchange—relied heavily on Aitzema and his competitors, who collected information by bribing government officials, maintaining contacts in all of the institutions involved in information handling, and collating gossip. Cromwell and Charles II both acquired much of their intelligence in the Dutch information market, in which the English East India Company also regularly purchased the secret schedules and ladings of VOC ships before their arrival from Asia.[34] The market in secrets was certainly not a central feature of the Amsterdam information exchange, but its appearance is another indication of the growing complexity and specialization—in short, the tendency towards modernization—of information handling.

[31] Braudel, *Civilisation matérielle*, vol. 2, pp. 78–92; vol. 3, p. 106.

[32] Van Dillen, *Van Rijkdom en Regenten*, pp. 108–37; Glamann, *Dutch Asiatic Trade*, pp. 29–34; GA: De Graeff papers, no. 200, esp. entry for 30 July 1680.

[33] Aitzema's compilations of data were later published as a current history, which is our main source for the way he worked. See Lieuw van Aitzema, *Saken van Staat en Oorlogh*, 6 vols. in 7 (The Hague, 1669 ff.). In vol. 5, pp. 193–99, Aitzema includes a verbatim transcript of a secret 1664 VOC internal report on conditions in Asia. The best modern discussion of Aitzema is in Rowen, *De Witt*, pp. 356–61, 373.

[34] CCM, 1664–1667, pp. 420–21 (letter East India Co. to Hampson, 20 Dec. 1667); CCM, 1668–1670, p. 120 (letter East India Co. to Hampson, 20 Nov. 1668).

AGGREGATION AND SHORT-TERM ANALYSIS

The assembly of information, and the drawing of short-term conclusions from it, are closely related to transfer. Commercial centers have long provided the physical location for the formation of rumors and consensus among merchants. Market consensus was a recordable entity regularly reported by businessmen to their correspondents and considered by governments to be a major item of current intelligence.[35]

This sort of thing occurred in Amsterdam as well, primarily as a byproduct of the operation of open institutions such as the Bourse. Market opinion and rumor, however, have obvious limitations: they can be manipulated relatively easily, and they cannot be readily evaluated. The appearance of institutions within the Amsterdam commercial center that were more restricted and more highly structured than open markets, employing systematic procedures to acquire and compare information, made improvements possible. These institutions (the VOC and the expanded Amsterdam municipal government, for example) also tended to be the ones that underwent substantial bureaucratization in the course of the century. In theory, at least, the systematic culling of sources to obtain greater accuracy should have reduced the risks of poor business decisions and lowered transaction costs for all of the participants in the Amsterdam information exchange, both in the Netherlands and abroad.[36]

Several examples can be cited of developments in short-term analysis. The Directorate of the Levant Trade, a government-chartered body overseeing trade with the eastern Mediterranean, assembled information useful to merchants from consular reports and from the correspondence of cooperating businessmen.[37] In the VOC the rapid growth of bureaucratic capacity was accompanied in the middle of the seventeenth century by a conscious employment of the company's machinery to collect European information from as wide a variety of sources as possible, and to develop marketing policy accordingly. Using committees of directors assisted by salaried clerks, the Amsterdam chamber of the VOC assumed these responsibilities for the Company as a whole. Correspondence and reports from Europe and Asia were examined by the chamber's secretariat under the leadership of the Company Advocate, who would then present summaries to the directors. Other committees, formally established to undertake purchasing, sales, and the operation of the Company's warehouse, collected and examined

[35] See HMC, *Calendar* (Cranfield papers), vol. 2, pp. 4–5, 31, 32, 35, for examples of rumor and consensus-building in early seventeenth-century markets.

[36] Institutional aggregation of business information was not new in the seventeenth century, but earlier examples, such as the Fugger "newsletters," were very primitive compared with the instances discussed here. See Matthews, ed., *Fugger Newsletter*.

[37] ARA: Levantse Handel (for example, 173, consular letters from Cadiz, 1657–1765).

trade statistics, formed estimates of changing demand patterns in Europe, and canvassed Amsterdam merchants about their experiences with certain goods. The results were brought together by a general committee, which would annually make recommendations to the chamber and through the chamber to the directors of the entire Company concerning orders from Asia, pricing, and marketing strategy.[38]

Although most of these processes were intended ostensibly to benefit the companies, in fact the large companies acted in many respects as instruments of their directors and the merchant oligarchy to which the directors belonged. In the last quarter of the century, for instance, the Company's estimates of the extent of the European pepper market were regularly exploited by its directors and their friends for private business—often to the detriment of the Company as an institution. By this means VOC estimates rapidly became common knowledge.[39]

DISSEMINATION

Any information exchange must incorporate some means of disseminating the data that it assembles. Although the Dutch did not pioneer the use of the printing press in distributing business information, in the seventeenth century they adopted and greatly extended most of the important innovations in the field. As we have seen, enterprising publishers consulted major Amsterdam merchant houses about commodity prices and rates of exchange reported by their correspondents in other places and printed lists for cities throughout Europe. Companies such as the VOC had advertisements printed and distributed throughout Europe listing the general contents of cargoes from abroad and the types of goods to be offered for sale at auctions. Examples can be multiplied.[40]

The culmination was the introduction of the newspaper and the

[38] Woodruff Smith, "The European-Asian Trade of the Seventeenth Century and the Modernization of Commercial Capitalism," *Itinerario*, 6, no. 2 (1982), 68–90. Van Dam, *Beschryvinge*, vol. 63, pp. 270–84, describes the work of the Advocate (Van Dam himself) as examiner of correspondence. The early composition and operation of the key Amsterdam committees—the committee of receivers and the committee on sales—are noted in ARA: VOC no. 230 (resolutions of Amsterdam chamber, 23 March 1623), and 231 (resolutions of Amsterdam chamber, 23 Oct. 1636). VOC no. 237 (resolutions of Amsterdam chamber, 29 March 1663) notes the establishment of a special committee to make up the order from Asia; no. 241 (resolutions of Amsterdam chamber, 16 Feb. 1682) includes recommendations on pricing to be presented to the board of the whole VOC; no. 243 (resolutions of Amsterdam chamber, 23 March 1688, 7 Feb. 1692) contains recommendations on pricing based on analyses of price trends in pepper.

[39] GA: Velters papers, no. 2/7, pp. 514–16 (Velters to Macaré, 25 Sept. 1676, enticing the latter into speculation in Indian wares based on "inside" VOC information); Glamann, *Dutch Asiatic Trade*, pp. 73–90; Van Dillen, *Van Rijkdom en Regenten*, pp. 37–68; Klein, *De Trippen*, pp. 163–83, 236–40.

[40] ARA: Hudde papers, no. 17 (collection of printed price lists, exchange rates, announcements of sales, etc.); Van Vredenburch papers, no. 11 (collection of VOC publications); VOC, no. 237 (resolutions of Amsterdam chamber, 18 Oct. 1663); no. 6985 (printed sales announcements).

merchant's handbook. Although "newspapers" as party political weapons had appeared earlier, the seventeenth century in the Netherlands saw the development of the newspaper as a regular bearer of general information: a compilation of political and economic news, largely culled from the Amsterdam information exchange, often printed in several languages and intended for sale throughout Europe.[41] Advertising as we understand it was not an important feature of Dutch newspapers until the eighteenth century; in the seventeenth, newspapers functioned primarily as links between the Amsterdam information exchange and the information networks of commercial Europe. Merchants' handbooks, although again not entirely new in the seventeenth century, achieved a mass market when printed in several languages and when their scope and accuracy improved through drawing on the data pool in Amsterdam.[42] They usually contained information about business procedures, taxes, laws, banking facilities, and major products available in various trading centers.

LONG-TERM ACCUMULATION

Short-term information was obtained directly from evidence about the immediate past useful for making decisions about the immediate future. The short-run orientation of Amsterdam's information functions was nothing new. Innovations in short-term information, though modifying the operations of commercial capitalism, did not amount by themselves to modernization. Innovations in long-term information did.

Files are the prerequisite for long-term analysis. Governments, merchant houses, and economic organizations, of course, kept records before the seventeenth century. From earlier times, however, few examples exist of files maintained systematically over long periods and containing quantitative information needed to make forecasts. Nor are there indications in Amsterdam or elsewhere that much thought was given to using records for such purposes.[43] Account books and contracts were kept to maintain control over current business operations and to record past agreements. Governments, in their roles as taxing

[41] For example, *Hollantsche Mercurius*, vol. 1, p. 26 (July 1650), contains, along with international political news likely to affect trade, an announcement of the arrival of the VOC return fleet from Batavia. *Amsterdamze Mercurius* (Feb.–July 1689) also concentrates on political news, mostly from England. On early newspapers, see Anthony Smith, *The Newspaper: An International History* (London, 1979), pp. 17–45.

[42] Lucas Jansen, *"De Koophandel van Amsterdam." Een critische studie over het koopmanshandboek van Jacques Le Moine de l'Espine en Isaac Le Long* (Amsterdam, 1946), esp. pp. 1–7.

[43] See Richard Brown, ed., *A History of Accounting and Accountants* (Frankfurt am Main, 1968), pp. 41–180. Records of agricultural estates had of course long been kept for planning purposes. The whole question of the influence of agricultural planning on business practices is worth investigating but has not yet, to my knowledge, been studied.

agencies and economic regulators, tended to keep more elaborate records, but hardly ever for purposes of economic prediction.

There is evidence that during the early and middle years of the seventeenth century, information was being employed in the Netherlands in new ways. Attempts were made in the 1620s, for example, to use past data on the prices of staple goods (apparently kept by the Amsterdam municipal government) to identify cyclical price movements and to anticipate rates of recovery from periods of food scarcity.[44] In the 1650s, Johan de Witt used data on mortality to devise a state annuity system.[45]

For the most part the keeping of records suitable for analysis and the first steps toward their utilization appear to have been connected with bureaucratization in government and business. In the seventeenth and early eighteenth centuries, firms such as the VOC, the semipublic joint-stock and regulatory corporations, and the largest of the private merchant houses, developed recognizable business bureaucracies; it was these organizations that began to keep systematic files.[46] In the VOC a functional division of administrative labor and the establishment of hierarchies, career patterns, training systems, and performance review were all reactions to the pressures to organize a complete long-distance trade, run an overseas empire, and coordinate marketing on an international scale—mostly functions that it had not originally been intended to perform. Bureaucratization in other companies and in the large merchant houses also appears to have been the result of having to respond to an expanded scope of business activity. The systematic keeping of business records arose mainly from the requirements of bureaucratic operation. Only after extensive files had been maintained for some time did businessmen, company directors, and bureaucrats realize that they could be used for prediction. Since organizations such as the VOC possessed a dual character as firms in their own rights and instruments of the commercial oligarchy, the capabilities that they developed through exploiting their bureaucratic and record-keeping potential were made available fairly readily to at least the upper levels of the Amsterdam business community. They became assets of the Amsterdam information exchange as a whole.

Examples of the growth of record keeping in response to bureaucratization can be found throughout the history of the VOC in the seven-

[44] *Klare Ende waerachtige Vertooninghe, van eenige merckelijke Veranderinghen van goede ende duyre tijden* (Amsterdam, 1624).

[45] Rowen, *De Witt*, p. 184.

[46] On bureaucratization in the VOC, see Glamann, *Dutch Asiatic Trade*, pp. 2–49; Van Dam, *Beschryvinge*, vol. 63, pp. 230–43, 270–84, 309–43, 369–416, 554–619; vol. 68, pp. 304–7; ARA: VOC, no. 360 (operating regulations for East India House, late seventeenth century); Van Vredenburch papers, no. 15 (collection of VOC regulations). A process of bureaucratization can be inferred from the files of the Burlamachi house, especially GA: Burlamachi papers, no. 6 (handbook for employees).

teenth century. Within the VOC's Amsterdam chamber the increasing reference to files arising simply from the Company's expansion led after about 1640 to a systematic organization of records according to the functional divisions of the Company. Inventories were constructed to assist in file-searches, and clerks specializing in file maintenance were added to the central administration. Most importantly, the information-handling function in the VOC was standardized in such a way that the final action taken with a document containing commercial data was to place it in its proper place in a sequential file.[47] Other firms and the Amsterdam municipal government similarly established systematic files of their commercial papers.[48] The collection of such files in major Amsterdam institutions created a potential for important changes in the functioning of the Amsterdam information exchange and of the commercial economy as a whole. By the second half of the century the potential was beginning to be realized.

LONG-TERM ANALYSIS

The growth of an awareness of the possibilities of long-term analysis based on systematic filing can be followed again most readily in the records of the VOC. As the Company turned increasingly to the use of fixed-price sales in small lots and then to open auctions to dispose of its major products, it began to keep careful records of the amounts of goods sold and the prices they fetched.[49] Originally, these appear to have been used merely as means of inventory control and as a check on sales contracts. After mid-century, however, the directors of the Company's dominant Amsterdam chamber began to use the records more imaginatively, for planning purposes. In February 1668, for example, a committee consisting of the Company Advocate and the directors in charge of the warehouse (and therefore of marketing) filed a report with the chamber recommending a company-wide strategy for marketing pepper the following year. The recommendations (to sell a set quantity of pepper in fixed-price lots and to retain a reserve in the warehouse) were based on estimates of the amount of pepper likely to be on the market in Europe and on an examination of what had previously happened to sales under similar conditions of supply. At about the same time the Compa-

[47] Van Dam, *Beschryvinge*, vol. 63, pp. 369–416; ARA: VOC, no. 241 (resolutions of Amsterdam chamber, 22 Jan. 1682, on the appointment of VOC librarians); no. 221 (index of resolutions of Heeren 17); no. 307 (register of resolutions of Amsterdam chamber); Hudde papers, no. 6 (standard filing procedures and formats, with data for 1672–1681).

[48] The remnants of such files can be found in GA, especially the consular reports series and the Burlamachi papers, and ARA: WIC.

[49] For example ARA: VOC, no. 14,532 (records of sales in Hoorn chamber, 1669–1685); *Lyste Vande Gedenckwaerdige Teyckininghe op de Peper* . . . (Haarlem, 1639), a list of purchasers of VOC pepper and the amounts they bought.

ny's secretariat, under the direction of the Advocate, began regularly surveying the VOC's historical files to find precedents for current situations requiring decisions about investment and marketing—which eventually resulted in Advocate Pieter van Dam's massive historical description of the VOC.[50]

Perhaps more importantly, the VOC directors began to draw up time-series of data on the Company's costs and sales in order to plan business strategies and limit wasteful expenditures. In 1692 an elaborate set of time-series was used to identify cycles of overstocking and to plot an exact pepper marketing strategy for the next few years.[51] Past precedents, including time-series of prices, were used to plan the introduction of new products. Time-series were also drawn up to identify changes over time in the VOC's overhead expenses and to explore the effects of different kinds of dividend distribution on the Company's performance.[52] Expectations based on such analyses were not always borne out by reality, but Company directors appear to have been convinced that time-series analysis improved performance; it was incorporated into the standard procedures of the Company throughout the eighteenth century.[53]

Many of these innovations in long-term analysis appeared as a result of a reform movement within the VOC, led by some of the Company's Amsterdam directors between the late 1670s and about 1700.[54] The most important leader, the merchant and mathematician Johannes Hudde, was primarily interested in increasing the directors' control over the VOC's far-flung operations and in reducing overhead. While the movement did not achieve all of its objectives, it did have a permanent effect on the Company's handling and analysis of information. Hudde, working with other directors and senior employees, developed standard techniques for constructing and analyzing time-series and for deriving forecasts from them. It was he who conducted the 1692 analysis of trends in the pepper market; his explanation of how he did so was printed and used as a model for market research by the VOC well into

[50] ARA: VOC, no. 238 (report of committee on sales and pricing, 11 Feb. 1668); no. 6988 (price estimate report, 1680); Van Dam, *Beschryvinge*, vol. 68, pp. 104–10, 144–299. "It is to be hoped," writes Van Dam after describing earlier cases of excessive reliance on Indian loan capital for covering purchases in Asia, "that the foregoing will make us wiser on that score" (vol. 68, p. 109).

[51] ARA: Hudde papers, no. 3, item 52; no. 9, item 3 (time-series and analyses, about 1692).

[52] ARA: Hudde papers, no. 3, items 2–19 (data on costs, 1614–1682); item 43 (summaries of dividends, 1612–1682); no. 5 (papers on overhead appended to file); no. 18 (summary of sales); VOC, no. 243 (resolutions of Amsterdam chamber, 23 March 1688); Van Dam, *Beschryvinge*, vol. 63, pp. 416–36.

[53] ARA: Van Vredenburch papers, no. 11 (collection of forms and procedures); Radermacher papers, no. 116 (summary of VOC returns, 1700–1733, with 1732 prediction of prices).

[54] On the reform movement, see F. W. Stapel, "Johannes Hudde over de balansen van de Oostindische Compagnie," *Economisch Historisch Jaarboek*, 13 (1927), 215–39. Unpublished material is collected in ARA: Hudde papers, nos. 2, 3, 5, 6, 9. See also Stapel's introduction to Van Dam's *Beschryvinge*, vol. 63, pp. ix–xxxix.

the eighteenth century.[55] Hudde also introduced an elaborate system of tabular, standardized formats through which the branches of the Company were supposed to report to the chambers on all aspects of their activities. The formats were specifically designed to provide the data required for Hudde's analytical techniques; the sample formats sent out to Asia were accompanied by clear descriptions of the items to be recorded.[56] While there was certainly a difference between stating a requirement for precise information and actually getting it, the VOC was sufficiently satisfied with Hudde's system to adopt it permanently.

The VOC was, of course, an unusual institution for its time. The appearance within it of modern techniques is hardly evidence of a general revolution in capitalism. On the other hand, there are substantial indications that similar techniques were coming to be used elsewhere in the Amsterdam information exchange—to some extent as a result of diffusion from the VOC. The Dutch West India Company, for example, seems to have imitated the VOC's data handling.[57] Some individual businessmen employed Hudde's formats for their own purposes.[58] The diffusion is readily explained by the overlapping directorates of the VOC and the West India Company and by the VOC's role as an instrument of the Dutch commercial elite. The diffusion was not widespread, at least by the early eighteenth century, but there is no indication that the advances pioneered by the VOC were later lost. They remained part of the apparatus of the information exchange into the later eighteenth century.[59]

There is also evidence of changes in economic consciousness connected with the emergence of long-term information analysis in Amsterdam. For instance, Hudde, in attempting to analyze his time-series, was led to recognize the planning problems created by inflation and cross-elasticities of demand.[60] Although his treatment of these factors was primitive—little more than a statement of their existence—they were nonetheless formally taken into account by the directors of the VOC from the 1690s onward when placing their annual Asian orders and when deciding on pricing policy.[61]

[55] A copy of the printed essay is contained in ARA: Van Vredenburch papers, no. 11, item 2.

[56] The formats and descriptions of data items are contained in ARA: Hudde papers, no. 3, items 22, 27–30, 45, 49, 52.

[57] ARA: WIC, no. 1232 (sales book of the Zeeland chamber of the WIC).

[58] For example, the 1730s estimates of anticipated income from the sale of Indian goods in the files of S. Radermacher, a VOC director (ARA: Radermacher papers, no. 116).

[59] It should be noted that the English East India Company, even after it drew ahead of the VOC in sales in the eighteenth century, did not for many years follow the VOC's lead in developing means of market research. Instead, the English company remained dependent on information emanating from Amsterdam. The English company's forté was active demand creation. K. N. Chaudhuri, *The Trading World of Asia and the English East India Company, 1660–1760* (Cambridge, 1978), pp. 79–81.

[60] ARA: Hudde papers, no. 9, item 3.

[61] For example, the general letter of instructions sent from the VOC to Batavia on 21 Nov. 1720 (ARA: VOC, no. 236, especially entries under Banda, Maccaser, Jambij, and Ceylon).

INFORMATION AND MODERNIZATION

A complex structure for handling business information evolved from the regular operations of Amsterdam as a center of commerce, following in general the pattern of responses to perceived informational economies discussed in Stigler's theory. The nature of these economies under conditions of market expansion led to the linking of regional and international information networks at one central location and to the specialization of institutions there. Unlike most other elements of Amsterdam's commercial operations, the role of central information exchange was necessarily a unique one, a role that only one city could perform if the larger system of which it was a part was to function at something like optimal effectiveness. It *did* make a difference, therefore, that Amsterdam acted as Europe's main information exchange.

There remains the question of the historical significance of Amsterdam's information exchange in economic modernization. At least two sources of significance can be identified. In the first place, an effective, centralized information-handling system may have lowered transaction costs and risks in the European world economy, thus indirectly contributing to economic expansion and ultimately to industrialization in northwestern Europe.

More readily demonstrated is the contribution to the modernization of capitalism—capitalism regarded in its broadest sense. The long-term analysis of information, distinctly foreshadowing the procedures of modern organizations, emerged in the larger Amsterdam businesses in the course of the seventeenth century. Market research and forecasting had historical significance beyond any immediate improvement in efficiency.

It could be argued, for example, that the reforms in the VOC sponsored by Hudde were failures. The VOC continued in some senses to decline. Its directors never solved the management problems that the reform movement had addressed; their accounting methods never gave them a complete picture of the VOC's profit situation.[62] One might, of course, respond that Hudde's innovations kept the unwieldy giant from collapsing altogether. But in a larger sense the argument is irrelevant. What matters is that businessmen *believed* that forecasting, like other functions of the Amsterdam information center, was efficacious and that they adopted some of the actions that follow from such a belief. The orientation of marketing and investment planning around the systematic collection and analysis of long-range information is one of the central

[62] The argument about the relative modernity and effectiveness of the VOC is summarized in Glamann, *Dutch Asiatic Trade*, pp. 244–65, which comes down on the side of the VOC as an effective trading organization with a reasonable amount of internal control throughout the seventeenth and eighteenth centuries.

characteristics of modern capitalism. It appeared first on a substantial scale and in a recognizably modern form in seventeenth-century Amsterdam. In other words, it appeared first in a commercial center that persisted into the industrial era, and could therefore carry this new characteristic with it into the modern economic world.

[10]

Excerpt from Economists Advisory Group, *City 2000: The Future of London as an International Financial Centre*, 7–17

CHAPTER 2 THE EVOLUTION OF LONDON AS AN INTERNATIONAL FINANCIAL CENTRE

2.1 Introduction

Although the position of the City of London is now radically different from what it was before 1914, its present role derives from its historical predominance. A modern financial centre, however, performs a different function from the "classical" centre. The City has been able to adapt to the demand for new services at least partly because its size and experience gave it strength and flexibility. These characteristics may be loosely summed up under the heading of economies of scale, where London still has an outstanding advantage over all other international financial centres except New York.

In this chapter we look at the sources of London's early predominance, the breakdown of the classical system, and the functions of a modern international centre. Finally, we consider the role of economies of scale in international financial transactions.

2.2 London as the "Classical" International Financial Centre

The classical model of an international financial centre is London in the forty years prior to World War I. The City's position was based on the UK's central role in the world economy - on the role of sterling in international trade and on the export of capital from Britain to the rest of the world.

The major currencies of the world were then fixed in value in terms of gold, and legally convertible into gold. However, some central banks placed obstacles in the way of gold payments, so that the Bank of England was the readiest day-to-day source of gold for anyone anywhere who held sterling. (The London gold market was also the centre through which newly-mined gold was distributed). It was convenient to use sterling, rather than gold, so that more than half of the world's international trade was invoiced in sterling and financed by sterling bills of exchange, many of them drawn on and accepted by London merchant banks and discounted in the London discount market. In the words of David Lloyd George, "The crackle of a bill on London was as good as the ring of gold in any port in the civilised world."

Britain was also by far the largest and most regular exporter of capital. Some of this took the form of direct investment by British companies developing overseas activities, mainly in the British Empire. London played little part in financing industry either at home or abroad. New manufacturing enterprises depended on domestic financial resources. Most of the City's lending was by loans and share issues floated in London. Issues were made on behalf of foreign governments, railways, public utilities, mines and plantations. They were denominated in sterling, arranged by London merchant banks, bought predominantly out of the savings of the Victorian middle classes and traded on the London stock exchange. Loans were not normally tied to any particular project and there were no "strings" attached to how or where the borrower spent his money.

For practical purposes sterling was "as good as gold" to a foreign holder and with the advantage that it could be invested at interest in highly liquid markets. Hence both governments and commercial enterprises overseas came increasingly to hold balances in sterling. Although Britain had a large current account surplus and a large short-term creditor position vis a vis the rest of the world, sterling was a reserve currency. This was a sharp contrast with the reserve position of the dollar in the post-war world, where since the 1960s the growth of reserves in the rest of the world has depended on the US deficit.

The fact that so much of the world's business was done in sterling reduced the need for foreign exchange transactions but also led to London becoming the principal market for such transactions when they did take place.

The dominant position of London in world trade and its financing encouraged the development of other activities. Lloyds became the world's leading international insurance market; British insurance companies, besides transacting international business in London, established branches and subsidiaries in many parts of the world; and London became an important, and in some cases dominant, market for many commodities.

Depending on, but at the same time providing support for, these major activities were a host of others - brokers and agents of many different kinds; import and export merchants; confirming houses; lawyers and accountants with special knowledge of international business; and a technical press supplying information and comment on all these manifold activities.

2.3 The Breakdown of Classical International Financial Centres

No financial centre has achieved or seems likely to achieve so great a predominance in such a wide range of activities as did London in the late nineteenth century. Since then many changes have taken place that together make the role of a modern financial centre very different from that of the classical model.

Attempts to restore the international gold standard after World War I broke down in the crisis of 1931 and were not repeated. For a while, after World War II, the Bretton Woods system provided reasonably stable exchange rates but that, too, broke down in the 'seventies. Since then, there have been regional arrangements, notably the European Monetary System, but prospects for a general system of fixed rates seem remote.

During the 'sixties and 'seventies the UK authorities were doing their best to shed what was left of the pound's role as a reserve currency. The dollar has become the predominant reserve currency but it suffers from the defect that, since its supply depends largely on the US deficit, it tends to be most plentiful at times when the world least wants it. That the supply of dollars is excessive may be temporarily obscured by other factors, as it was in 1983 when the dollar rose despite the widening US payments deficit because of very high US interest rates. In the longer run, however, so long as the dollar is not tied to gold or some international currency unit, the US must run an overall payments deficit if the rest of the world is to acquire more dollars.

Sterling has lost most of its predominance as an international unit of account and no other currency has entirely replaced it. Air and shipping charges and the prices of oil and some other commodities are normally set in dollars; but many transactions are now invoiced in the currency of either the exporter or the importer, some in other currencies including the deutschemark mark, the Swiss franc and the yen, and some in the new international units of account, the SDR and the ECU.

In the past, invoicing in sterling was closely linked to financing in sterling, but this is no longer so. During the 'sixties, the Bank of England tightened exchange control restrictions so as to reduce sterling finance of third-country trade. London responded by arranging "currency" finance. This was one of the factors in the growth of eurocurrency markets, and it also means that far more trade is now financed through London than is invoiced in sterling.

World War I put an end to the long run of large current account surpluses which had been the foundation of London's long-term international capital market and no other country has fully assumed that role. The United States, Germany, Japan and the major oil-exporting countries have all been capital exporters at times but not regularly for decade after decade. The role of the market has thus become less a matter of mobilising local resources for export and more a matter of seeking capital wherever it can be found as different countries pass through recurrent periods of surplus and deficit.

The effect of this change has been magnified by the extension to long-term securities of the changes already noted in the finance of trade flows. In the classical model securities issued in London were denominated in sterling and, though there was no bar against foreign ownership, the great majority of them were bought by British citizens. The growth of the eurobond market means that securities may now be denominated in the currency of one country, sold in another, and held in yet others. Only for corporate equity is the link still close. The shares of a company need to be denominated in the currency of the country where it is registered and under whose laws it operates, but even this can be overcome to some extent by the establishment of foreign subsidiaries.

2.4 The Role of a Modern Financial Centre

The effect of these and other changes is to make the role of a modern financial centre very different from that of the classical model.

One function of the classical financial centre noted above was to act as a kind of "super central bank". Gold was the legally recognised means of international payments but sterling was widely used as a substitute both for actual payments and as a reserve and, when gold was needed, London was the readiest source. Though textbooks have made much of this, it was probably the least important of the functions described above and it has now virtually disappeared.

There is nothing that now takes the place formerly held by gold as both a universally accepted means of payment and an ultimate reserve. The dollar is widely used for both purposes but, if a country runs short of dollars, it does not necessarily turn to New York. If the monetary authorities abstain from intervention, all that happens is that the exchange rate falls to a point at which the shortage disappears. If, as is more usually the case, the monetary authorities decide at some point to support the exchange, they will need dollars but they are more likely to get them in the euromarkets of London, from other monetary authorities or from the IMF than in New York. The change is important, for it means that the use of the US dollar as an international means of payment and as a reserve currency has little relevance to the prospects of New York as a financial centre. Even should more borrowers turn to New York in future, which they may well do, it will still not be the only or even the prime source of dollar finance.

- 12 -

In the primary markets, where financial centres act as suppliers of new finance to borrowers, the range of instruments - traditionally bills of exchange and bonds - has been broadened. We now have export credits in a variety of forms: "project finance" tailored to the special needs of large construction works; "sovereign" lending by banks to governments; and medium-term bank lending to international companies; while bonds can be issued at fixed or floating rates and denominated in various currencies. Some of this, for example "project finance" heavily insured and supported by government subsidies, is semi-political in character; but mostly it represents the development of "new products" to meet the changing pattern of demand.

Even more important, the fact that no country can now be relied on year in, year out to be a large exporter of capital has led to the growth of an entrepot trade. Just as banks and other financial institutions within a country collect the savings of individuals and companies that have a financial surplus and lend them to these that have a deficit, so international institutions collect the savings of surplus countries and lend them to deficit countries.

Of course, it is an over-simplification to talk of surplus and deficit countries in this way. The total transactions of any country in international markets will be made up of a host of individual deals, some one way, some another. But it is part of the function of financial markets to bring about a pattern of exchange rates and relative interest rates such that residents of surplus countries will, in total, be net lenders, and those of deficit countries net borrowers.

The growth of the entrepot trade has seen a growth in the number and variety of foreign institutions operating in major international centres; a growth of consortia arrangements; and the development of markets such as the interbank, CD, and eurocurrency markets in which institutions can borrow from, and lend to, one another. Again the change is important for the future of London, since the fact that Britain may not have a regular balance-of-payments surplus need not affect London's participation in the entrepot trade.

It is not only primary markets that provide channels for the flow of capital between countries. Transactions in secondary markets also give rise to capital flows insofar as residents in any country are net buyers or net sellers of existing assets, and at times flows through the secondary markets may be substantially larger then those through primary markets.

The other main functions of secondary markets are to enable investors to diversify their portfolios, and to switch their holdings when they expect that this would be advantageous. This kind of international investment is relatively new. As noted above, the foreign securities issued in London in the 19th century were mainly owned and traded by British citizens; international trade in them was small. There was some foreign investment in "Consols" but again it was small and such international flows as took place were mainly bank deposits.

The growth of international trading on secondary markets is being stimulated by the increasing importance of institutional funds, the growing sophistication of investment managers, continuous pressure on them to secure the highest possible yield on their funds; and improvements in information technology.

Dealing in financial assets denominated in a currency other than ones own obviously involves an exchange risk. The risk is related to the currency of the security, which may or may not be that of the country in which dealing takes place. The existence of an exchange risk is, however, an addition to the normal reasons why investors value the ability to get into and out of a market quickly and at minimal cost. The financial centres that will be most attractive to international investors in the future are those that offer a wide range of markets with low dealing costs and in which large transactions can be made quickly and with the minimum disturbance to prices.

Besides these basic financial services, London was and still is a major market for insurance, commodities, and shipping as well as providing a wide range of related professional activities. The linkage between these services and the financial markets is not peculiar to London but is stronger than in other financial centres. Historically, the development of London's insurance and commodity markets was always linked with the role of the port in world trade. When communication over long distances was slow and expensive, there was an obvious advantage in having finance, shipping, insurance and marketing at places within a few minutes walk of one another. As time went on fewer goods actually passed through the City, commodity markets came to trade in claims on goods rather than physical products, and the activities of insurers spread far beyond the actual trade of London. The improvement of communications also weakened the linkages between different activities and will doubtless continue to do so.

It is, therefore, quite possible to conceive of a flourishing set of financial markets in a centre that does not provide major markets in insurance or commodities. Nevertheless there is still convenience in having these related activities close together and also in having close contacts between all of them and specialist professional advisers.

2.5 Economies of Scale

Financial centres grow only slowly but, once established, they show remarkable powers of survival. This may be partly due to force of habit, customer loyalty or plain inertia, but it arises largely from the advantages enjoyed by established centres from various kinds of economies of scale. Outside engineering, economies of scale are notoriously hard to pin down. Even in manufacturing they can be very difficult to measure because of the inter-relationship between scale and competiton. Moreover, many scale economies are a function of technology; as it changes, so will the optimum scale of operations. Technological change is separately examined in Chapter 4, and the size of firms and markets operating in London in the relevant chapters in Part 2. Here we shall only briefly describe the various kinds of scale economies to provide a background for subsequent discussion.

Economies of scale operate at three levels, the individual undertaking, the particular market and the centre as a whole. Scale economies that may accrue to the individual undertaking include the spreading of risks; access to capital; advertising and marketing; specialisation among personnel, and the employment of expensive mechanical and electronic equipment. In some activities, eg most forms of brokerage, information services, and computer software, these economies are unimportant and financial centres contain large numbers of small firms. In other areas, eg banking, insurance and security dealing (as distinct from brokerage) they are very important and individual undertakings are often very large.

The value of a market to its users lies in establishing prices that reflect all the relevant information affecting the value of the assets traded, and so are fair to all; and in providing conditions in which transactions can be made quickly at low cost and with little disturbance to prices. These functions can only be performed with a high degree of efficiency when there is a substantial volume of business. For example, unless there is a regular flow of business, prices will be uncertain and a would-be buyer may have to wait a long time before he finds a seller at an acceptable price, and vice versa. The larger the volume of business, the larger the transactions that can be made at or near the current price. A large volume of business may also make it worthwhile for firms to establish themselves as "market makers", giving the public the opportunity of dealing immediately, and smoothing random price variations. The same is true of information; where an asset is rarely traded, information about it is hard to come by but where there is a regular and substantial flow of business, brokers, journalists and others find it worthwhile to conduct research. Equally, a substantial flow of business tends to narrow the gap between buying and selling prices and minimise dealing costs.

In the past, any centre that established a market in any financial asset that was bigger than those existing elsewhere enjoyed some of these advantages and so was able to attract business from its rivals, increase the scale of its operations, secure more scale economies, and attract yet more business. In this way a cummulative process was created that tended to concentrate financial markets in a small number of centres and to make it difficult for new centres to become established. Even though large organisations often have extensive branch networks, a centre that houses the headquarters of several of them tends to have a "pull" over its rivals. An important question for the future is how far these centripetal forces will be weakened by developments in information technology, and this is discussed in Chapter 4.

Economies that operate at centre level include the advantages of having a number of markets in close proximity to one another; the development of specialised ancillary services; and the creation of a pool of special skills that can be drawn upon both by existing undertakings and by new firms entering the market.

In some cases groups of markets are so closely inter-related that it is hardly conceivable that they should operate other than in one place. An obvious example is the money market, the Treasury bill market, the commercial bill market, the interbank market and the CD market in London. The location of these short-term financial markets is closely linked to the operations of the central bank but, even where central banks have a regional organisation, money market operations tend to concentrate in one centre, eg New York and Frankfurt.

Other financial markets, eg in government bonds, company securities and commodities, are less closely linked both with one another and with the short-term markets, but there are still advantages in proximity. To a large and growing extent the same institutions deal in all financial markets; price movements in any one of them have an impact on others, and information relevant to one is often also relevant to others. Again, these advantages may be reduced by technological change but it is hard to imagine their being wholly eliminated. In the future, business negotiations may be conducted not between people gathered together in rooms ('smoke-filled' or not) but in offices or homes in different cities or different countries linked together by television, but it will be a long time before face to face contacts lose their value altogether.

The advantages derived by financial centres from specialised ancillary services and the development of special skills have already been mentioned. They are the most difficult of all economies of scale to evaluate but economists and geographers are unanimous in regarding them as important reasons why particular kinds of economic activity - industrial and commercial as well as financial - tend to congregate in particular centres. A more subtle but very important matter is the way in which skills are acquired and passed on; a fund of expertise is built up; and innovation is stimulated among a group of people with similar occupations and interests whose work brings them into close personal contact with one another. It is hard to see how even the most sophisticated information technology could provide a complete substitute for this.

[11]

Excerpt from Youssef Cassis (ed.), *Finance and Financiers in European History, 1880–1960*, 405–28

21 International financial centres in Asia, the Middle East and Australia: a historical perspective[1]

GEOFFREY JONES

Emergence and growth

Financial centres are much discussed but rarely defined. A major difficulty is that the products of the financial sector are diverse, and include markets for capital, money, debt, insurance and other financial services, and gold, silver and other precious metals. A 'financial centre' might include some or all of these markets. The twentieth-century financial services industry has also seen very rapid product innovation, especially since the emergence of a global capital market from the late 1950s. The upshot is that the identification – and ranking – of financial centres is a subjective matter, and a 'financial centre' in one time period may look very different from one in another period.

There are also marked differences in the geographical areas served by financial centres. Almost every modern economy has some kind of 'centre' where there is a clustering of financial services serving the requirements of the rest of the country. Bangkok has served this role in Thailand over the last one hundred years. Such 'national financial centres' are beyond the concern of this chapter however which focuses on centres which provide financial services for an area outside their own political boundaries: a location where there is a concentration of activity engaged in the international trade of capital and financial services.[2]

There is general agreement that there has usually existed a hierarchy of international financial centres. Howard Curtis Reed's pioneering attempt to rank financial centres over time both surveys the variety of names given to different types of centre and develops a hierarchy of his own.[3] In the present context, a simpler typology seems more appropriate, in which centres can be divided into three types. Type A are *sub-regional* – international financial activities are clustered in such places, but often their focus is on bilateral trade between the centre's host economy and other economies. Type B are *regional* – these centres supply financial services to an entire region, which might be very large ('Asia' or the 'Pacific Rim'). Finally, type C are *global centres* – supplying a broad range of financial services to the entire world, a role London pioneered in the nineteenth century, and which it shares with New York and Tokyo in the contemporary period.[1]

Table 21.1 attempts to identify the leading international financial centres of the Middle East, Asia and Australasia from the First World War onwards, dividing the centres into types A, B and C. Japan is not included in this analysis. Tokyo, Osaka and Yokohama were all international financial centres of sorts in the 1920s, but the era of nationalism and war in the 1930s and 1940s greatly curbed this role. By the time the Japanese economic miracle was underway in the 1960s, Tokyo had sufficient international banking activity to qualify as an international financial centre (probably type B), but regulation and other factors constrained its role until the 1980s, when a full-blown global centre emerged.

This identification of international financial centres is crude and subjective compared to Reed's statistical analysis, which investigates the role, as financial centres, of seventy-six cities between 1900 and 1975 (and eighty cities in 1980) using a large number of variables. However, there is probably little fundamental conflict between the identification and hierarchical positions suggested here and the Reed analysis. In Reed's ranking of 'international banking centres' for five yearly intervals between 1900 and 1980, Hong Kong appears in the 'top ten' every year except 1970 and 1980, and Shanghai was also ranked highly before the Revolution. Hong Kong also featured in Reed's lists of 'international financial centres' between 1955 and 1980. Singapore appears less important than suggested in this paper, but Reed himself cites evidence that he might have underestimated its significance. Reed does not identify a Middle Eastern centre that was more important than Beirut until 1980, when he adds Bahrain to his sample of cities. Reed also places these centres in about the same position in the hierarchy of financial centres as suggested here.[5]

Reverting to the typology suggested here, during the interwar years Shanghai, Singapore and Hong Kong have the greatest claims to be type A international financial centres. The number of banks with representation in a city provides one proxy of financial activity. In 1919 Shanghai had twenty-three modern banks represented there, Hong Kong fourteen, and Singapore twelve: in all cases these were largely foreign institutions. As civil disorder spread through China in the 1920s, Shanghai developed as the Republic's monetary and banking centre. The city experienced a trebling of population between 1914 and 1936, leaving it nearly four times

Table 21.1 *Financial centres in Asia, the Middle East and Australasia since 1919*

1919–39			1945–65			1965–75			1975–present		
A	B	C	A	B	C	A	B	C	A	B	C
Shanghai Sing- apore Hong Kong			Hong Kong Sing- apore	Beirut			Beirut Sing- apore Hong Kong			Bahrain Sing- apore Hong Kong Sydney	

as large as the British Colony of Hong Kong in that year, which was essentially a smaller version of Shanghai throughout the interwar years. By 1936, thirty-three foreign banks had branches in Shanghai, including British, American, German, Belgian, Dutch, Portuguese and Japanese institutions, all of which were actively engaged in foreign trade finance and exchange operations, utilizing the free exchange market existing at Shanghai. There were seventy-four Chinese commercial banks in the City, linking Shanghai with the rest of China. In addition there were branches of the major banks established by the Overseas Chinese community, including four from Hong Kong, three from the Straits Settlements and one from the Philippines, which specialized in handling the remittances flowing between the various Chinese settlements in Asia.[6]

Other financial activities were also well-represented in Shanghai. The city had a Stock Exchange, on occasion which, for example, companies developing Malaya tin or rubber were floated.[7] Shanghai was 'the pivot of British business in China'.[8] British merchant houses which operated in Shanghai, such as Dodwell's, Gibb Livingston's and Gilman's, provided a range of trading, shipping and insurances services.[9]

Singapore, the major city of the British Colony of the Straits Settlements, had grown over the nineteenth century as a major regional trading centre. Western traders and bankers flourished in a complementary relationship with their Chinese and other Asian counterparts.[10] Between the late nineteenth century and the interwar years, for example, most of south-east Asia's rice trade was organized and financed through Singapore by means of a system of barter conducted by Singaporean Chinese merchants, in turn linked to European merchants trading in tin and tropical produce.[11] International banking activity developed early: the rulers of Thailand and other neighbouring states kept their accounts in Singapore banks in the second half of the nineteenth century, before their own states had modern banks. Modern banking grew in interwar Singapore (there were twenty-two banks represented there by 1941) and the Singapore branch often acted as a regional head office overseeing other branches in neighbouring Malaya and sometimes elsewhere, a role still very common in the 1980s. Traditional Asian credit institutions were well represented in Singapore, not only Chinese but also Indian, such as Chetty bankers, and these were all engaged in interregional trade and exchange operations. In 1932 a powerful modern Chinese bank, the Overseas Chinese Banking Corporation, was established at Singapore. Singapore, like Shanghai, had its own Stock Exchange, on which many Malayan tin and rubber companies were quoted, and a substantial number of diversified western trading companies, such as Borneo Company performing shipping, trading and insurance functions. The slump in the prices of commodities such as tin, rubber and palm oil from the late 1920s left south-east Asia in a depressed economic condition before the Second World War, but Singapore retained its position as the leading financial centre.

The limitation of type A status to Shanghai, Singapore and Hong Kong is arbitrary. There were other cities where financial services were clustered, though their 'sub-regional' roles were less extensive. In British India, Bombay and Calcutta had large numbers of banks (many foreign owned) and their own Stock Exchanges. However, the Indian capital and money markets were severely fragmented, and primarily focused in British India, especially in the 1930s as India entered its 'relative disengagement from the international economy'.[12] It would be extremely difficult to identify any sub-regional financial centres in the interwar Middle East. Cairo came closest. It had a number of branches of banks, and other financial institutions, and a Stock Exchange established in 1903, but even in the interwar years most of this activity was built around the finance of Egypt's cotton trade with the rest of the world.

In the two decades after the Second World War, the most significant event was the advent of Beirut as a regional financial centre. Beirut had been a centre of banking activity in the old Ottoman Empire. During the interwar years, under French control, the city had supplied financial services to its Syrian hinterland. After the war, and now the capital of an independent Lebanon, Beirut became a leading banking centre, overwhelmingly concerned with short-term capital. By 1965 nearly ninety banks were active in Beirut, many of them foreign. Aided by a banking secrecy law in 1956 (modelled on that of Switzerland), Beirut became a depository for flight capital from all over the Middle East, much of which was channelled via Beirut to Europe and the United States.[13] An early feature of the Beirut money market was the large percentage of deposits in foreign currency. As early as 1953 a branch of a British bank in Beirut had 40 per cent of its deposits in foreign currency, mostly US dollars: this was some years before the conventional starting date for the Eurodollar market.[14] From the late 1950s foreign currency deposits in Lebanon grew very rapidly: in 1964 they comprised 35 per cent of total commercial bank deposits, and ten years later 68 per cent.[15] Despite Beirut's very important role as a short-term money market between the 1940s and the mid 1970s, its other financial activities were minimal. The Beirut Stock Exchange, for example, was established in 1920, but never grew to any significance.[16]

The advent and growth of the Euro-currency loan and bond markets at the end of the 1950s and in the 1960s, already pre-figured by developments in Beirut, brought fundamental changes to international banking and finance, and an enormous stimulus to their growth. These supranational markets, outside national regulatory control, also provided new opportunities for places such as Beirut, Hong Kong and Singapore, for they enabled international banks to settle 'offshore' to raise and supply capital on a world-wide basis.[17]

After 1965 the availability of IMF statistics on the foreign assets held by banks enables a more quantitative picture to be presented of the location of international financial activity, although it must be stressed that these statistics measure only one type of business conducted at financial centres.[18] Table 21.2 gives this measure of international banking activity by country between 1965 and 1987.

As table 21.2 suggests, until the mid 1960s Lebanon was the leading centre for international banking activity in Asia, the Middle East and Australasia, once again excluding Japan. Singapore continued to function as a 'centre' of sorts, but probably less so than in the interwar years because it suffered from political and other uncertainties until the mid 1960s, when it withdrew from Malaysia, and abandoned its attempt at import substitution in favour of an export-oriented industrialization strategy. As part of this new strategy the government established an Asian currency market. The development of the Euro-currency markets found no echo in Asia until 1968, when the Singapore government permitted the Bank of America to establish an operation dealing in foreign currency (an Asian currency unit as such institutions became known), designed to collect dollars circulating in Asia for on-lending to their Asian customers. The interest earned from non-resident deposits was made tax-exempt. Singapore thus acquired first-mover advantages in the new Asia dollar market, and it was well-placed to take advantage of the flood of petro-dollars following the 1973–4 crisis. The number of Asian currency units in Singapore grew from one in 1968 to fifty in 1974 to 115 in 1980. Over the same period, the total assets of these Asian Currency Units expanded from US$ 30.5 million to US$ 199.9 million to US$2,438 million. In addition to this development, the Singapore government encouraged the

Table 21.2 *International banking activity 1965–1987; percentage share by leading countries*

	1965	1970	1975	1980	1985	1987
UK	17.1	25.0	22.2	19.6	19.9	18.5
US	23.7	8.6	9.7	11.2	15.1	11.6
Japan	5.7	4.4	3.6	3.6	6.6	12.2
France	4.3	6.8	7.3	8.1	5.8	5.6
Germany	7.7	9.5	6.8	4.7	3.8	4.9
Switzerland	8.3	9.4	8.4	7.7	6.9	7.0
Luxembourg	0.9	2.5	5.3	5.7	4.4	4.8
Bahamas	—	4.8	9.7	6.9	4.8	3.3
Lebanon	1.3	0.4	0.4	0.2	0.1	n.a.
Bahrain	—	0.04	0.4	1.7	1.7	1.3
Singapore	—	0.3	1.9	2.4	4.1	4.4
Hong Kong	1.1	0.8	1.6	2.1	3.4	5.6
Australia	—	—	0.05	0.02	0.04	n.a.
Others	29.9	27.46	22.65	28.08	23.36	20.8
Total amount of all countries (US $ billion)	44.8	149.4	565.9	1,821.4	2,964	4,725.3

Source: IMF, *International Financial Statistics Yearbook*, 1981 and 1988. The data give the foreign assets held by deposit banks in each country at year end.

growth of an Asian bond market through the issue of loans in the early 1970s, and this market took off around 1976.[19]

By 1975 Singapore was well-established as the leading Asian centre for short-term loans and borrowings in a range of convertible currencies, and also as an international market for the issue of medium- and long-term bonds in convertible currencies. By that year there were seventy commercial banks with banking operations in Singapore (and another thirty-eight representative offices), twenty-one merchant banks, four discount houses, thirty-six finance companies, sixty-nine insurance companies and five 'international money brokers'.[20] However, Singapore had comparatively little expertise in certain areas of financial activity, such as fund management and loan syndication.

The Communist Revolution in China in 1949 ended Shanghai's role as an international financial centre. Hong Kong was the direct inheritor of the mantle: indeed, many of the Colony's industries of the 1950s were founded and prospered under Shanghaese entrepreneurs. It had a growing number of banks and was the headquarters of a major regional bank, the Hong Kong and Shanghai Banking Corporation. Hong Kong attracted substantial 'hot' or 'funk' money in the 1950s, especially from the Overseas Chinese community in south-east Asia. Table 21.2 suggests that international banking activity there in 1965 nearly approached the level of Lebanon. However in the decade after 1965 Hong Kong allowed Singapore to take advantage of the new opportunities offered by the global capital markets. The Bank of America expressed an interest in establishing an Asian Currency Unit in Hong Kong rather than Singapore, but the colonial government declined to grant exemption from a 15 per cent withholding tax on offshore currency transactions, a policy which was not changed until 1982. Hong Kong also failed to develop as a centre for the Asian Bond Market to rival Singapore. One handicap was that the Hong Kong government traditionally worked on the basis of balanced budgets and rarely needed to issue debt.

Hong Kong's 'take off' as a type B financial centre came several years later than that of Singapore, and all through the 1970s it was Singapore, rather than Hong Kong, which had a greater claim to be Asia's leading financial centre. The 1970s, however, saw growing internationalization of Hong Kong's financial activities. Between 1969 and 1979 total bank credit rose six fold, while the relative share of offshore loans in total bank credit rose from 2.6 per cent to 26 per cent. There was a similar trend towards internationalization in the financial markets. Short-term money market activities ceased to be confined to inter-bank dealings in Hong Kong dollars. After 1974, when a ban on import and export of gold was removed, Hong Kong developed a large gold market, and in 1977 a Commodities Exchange was established. Hong Kong developed expertise in areas such as fund management and loan syndication, in which Singapore lagged.[21]

Hong Kong and Singapore functioned, to some extent, as complementary financial centres in the 1970s and early 1980s, each specializing in various activities. There was little duplication and funds flowed between the two centres to take maximum advantage of their respective regulatory, fiscal and other advantages. As one writer described the process,

> shrewd bankers and businessmen find it most advantageous to have investment operations at Hong Kong and to collect ADM deposits at Singapore... Singapore is primarily a funding centre, whilst Hong Kong is a 'booking' centre for lending. Funds are banked together in Singapore and this is rechannelled to Hong Kong for on-lending to non-bank borrowers.[22]

The period after 1975 saw the rapid emergence of Bahrain as a regional (type B) financial centre. Bahrain had a tradition of acting as a banking centre to the economically backward Gulf. The first modern bank on the Arab side of the Gulf was established there in 1920 by the Eastern Bank, a British-owned bank.[23] During the 1950s and 1960s it began to serve as a regional base for British banks and other companies.[24] Yet Bahrain's role as a financial centre remained modest – the country even used the Indian Rupee as its currency until 1965 – until shortly after the 1973–4 oil crises. The catalyst was the Bahrain government's decision in 1975 to allow Offshore Banking Units (OBUs – modelled on Singapore's Asian Currency Unit's) to be established, which were exempted from all corporate profits tax.

After 1975 Bahrain's offshore banking units grew very rapidly. There were two OBUs in 1975, fifty-eight in 1980 and seventy-five in 1983. Their total assets expanded over the same period from US$ 1,687 million to US$ 37,466 million to US$ 62,741 million. Bahrain's function, at least initially, was as a collecting centre for the surplus savings of oil-rich Saudi Arabia and Kuwait, which were recycled to the outside world. Business transactions were largely of a short-term nature. Between 1976 and 1986 87 per cent of OBU assets and 97 per cent of OBU liabilities had a maturity of one year or less, with some tendency for borrowing to be on a shorter-term basis than lending. Most of the currency dealings in Bahrain were in US dollars, although there was some use of regional currencies. In 1980 22 per cent of assets were denominated in regional currencies such as Saudi riyals, Kuwaiti dinars, UAE dirhams and Qatar riyals, although this percentage tended to fall in the 1980s. It was 14.4 per cent in 1986.[25]

Bahrain replaced Beirut as the regional financial centre of the Middle East. The Lebanese financial system began to show signs of strain in the mid 1960s, notably with the collapse of the largest bank in the country, Intra Bank, in 1966. The Arab-Israeli War in 1967 caused further difficulties for the financial system.[26] Nevertheless Lebanese banking proved very resilient until the outbreak of the Civil War in 1975, when funds began to by-pass Beirut and banks began to withdraw or reduce their operations. Beirut's role as a regional financial centre was further damaged by the Israeli invasion of 1982, which caused enormous physical destruction and the withdrawal of practically all remaining foreign personnel. The Israeli's completed the elimination of any remaining confidence in Beirut's ability to act as a financial centre by overriding Lebanese banking secrecy laws by forcing banks to reveal the accounts of wealthy Palestinians.[27]

The post-1975 period saw the advent of Sydney as a fledgling regional financial centre. Twentieth-century Australia had a well-developed financial system and capital markets. Before 1939, however, the Australian economy was heavily tied to that of Britain and the country had little international activity. 'Melbourne and London were then Australia's financial centres', as one writer has recently observed.[28] Links with Britain weakened after the Second World War, but the Australian financial system was highly cartelized and regulated within a framework of exchange controls. Foreign institutions were not allowed to undertake commercial banking in the country, apart from the descendants of British banks established in the nineteenth century. The last of these, the ANZ Group, migrated from Britain in 1976 and became an entirely Australian institution.[29] There was, however, substantial foreign activity in merchant banks and a variety of non-banking financial intermediaries, usually in the form of joint-ventures with Australian interests.[30]

Australia, therefore, offered unpromising soil for an international financial centre until the late 1970s, when a process of liberalization began. The big change came in 1983 when the newly elected Labour government lifted exchange controls and floated the Australian dollar. In 1985, fifteen foreign banks were granted full banking licences. The full consequences of Australia's extremely fast and comprehensive financial and banking deregulation for the development of Sydney's role as a financial centre remain to be seen.

Apart from the entry of Sydney and the exit of Beirut as regional financial centres, the fifteen years after 1975 showed some diversification of functions by the centres and also a tendency towards instability. After 1975 Singapore developed more business in fund management and loan syndication, while Hong Kong sought to expand its role in Asia currency and Asia bonds by, for example, abolishing the 15 per cent withholding tax on foreign currency deposits in 1982. Both developed markets in financial futures. Hong Kong's growth was particularly spectacular; by October 1987 Hong Kong claimed to have the second largest stock index market in the world, with as many as 30,000 contracts changing hands each day. Unfortunately the collapse of world stock markets in that month revealed the growth to have been based on reckless and corrupt speculation, and the Hong Kong futures market collapsed. A year later, in October 1988, daily turnover rarely exceeded 600 contracts.[31] Bahrain, in the 1980s, suffered from the decline of oil revenues from the oil-exporting Gulf states, the Iran/Iraq war and the Third World debt crisis, for many of Bahrain's offshore banks had been heavy lenders to developing countries. The assets of Bahrain's OBUs fell continuously from US$ 62,741 million in 1983 to US$ 55,680 in 1986.[32] One consequence of this trend was a growth in the regional dimension of Bahrain's offshore banking sector. In 1980 36 per cent of OBUs in Bahrain originated from western Europe, 17 per cent from North America and 21 per cent from the Arab world. In 1986 the proportions were 32 per cent, 12 per cent and 32 per cent.[33]

In the late 1980s it remained a hazardous exercise to rank financial centres in any more than the most general terms. Using the proxy of the amount of foreign assets held by deposit banks, it can be seen from Table 21.2 that the international banking activity of Hong Kong grew substantially in the 1980s, and by 1987 the volume of foreign assets there was greater than in Singapore, which grew rather more slowly between 1980 and 1987. International banking activity in Lebanon has been in absolute decline since 1980, while Bahrain has failed to maintain its rapid growth of the 1970s. Australia's share of international banking activity remained, in 1987, very small. Singapore and Hong Kong rivalled in size the international financial centres of Continental Europe, but remain far less important than 'the three key financial centres of the world' – London, New York and Tokyo.[34] Other measures confirm such a view. In 1988 probably around 85 per cent of all equity trading took place in the United States, London and Tokyo.[35]

A number of features emerge from this brief survey of the emergence of financial centres in Asia (outside Japan), the Middle East and Australasia since the First World War. First, financial centres come and go. Shanghai went in 1949. Beirut came after 1945 and went after 1975. Sydney began to emerge as a financial centre in the 1980s. Only Singapore and Hong Kong showed continuity over the whole period, with a considerable rise in their importance from the late 1960s.

Secondly, while the financial centres of London, New York and – later – Tokyo developed within large advanced industrialized economies, the centres that grew in Asia and the Middle East were often located in small economies and indeed, physically small countries. Shanghai and Sydney provide exceptions, though it is arguable if interwar Shanghai can be regarded as an integrated part of the national Chinese economy, while Australia is an extremely thinly populated country compared to ASEAN neighbours such as Indonesia. Within the general problem of why international financial activity is not randomly scattered around the world, there is a more specific problem of why financial centres have tended to flourish – especially over the last thirty years – in these small economies.

Thirdly, no Asian, Australian or Middle Eastern financial centre – once more apart from Japan in the 1980s – has achieved global status. By 1990 London, New York and Tokyo offered capital markets, money markets and a range of financial services on a world-wide basis. The centres discussed have remained regional financial centres, integrated into global financial markets (as the rapid fallout from the October 1987 stock market crash indicated) but not primary centres. None of the centres have offered the full range of financial markets available in London or New York, and indeed centres have tended to specialize, and to operate in niches in the markets.

An explanatory framework

This section offers some reasons for the growth of the Asian, Middle Eastern and Australasian financial centres. Why did Beirut, Bahrain, Singapore and Hong Kong emerge as centres, rather than (say) Damascus, Kuwait, Seoul and Taipai? Unfortunately, there is no theory of financial centres, or even of international service centres, which can be readily applied to answer such a question. 'It is a curious fact', Charles Kindleberger observed in a seminal study in 1974, 'that the formation of financial centres is no longer studied in economics'.[36] Urban and regional economists focused on the location of commerce and industry rather than financial services, while the literature on the money and capital markets showed little interest in the physical location of these markets. Since 1974 there have been more studies of financial centres, but this work has resulted in the accumulation of valuable data and insights rather than the formulation of any rigorous model.[37]

A straight application of traditional models of comparative advantage is unhelpful. Such a factor endowments approach might suggest that international financial centres developed in economies with abundant or 'surplus' capital. This helps to explain the growth of London in the nineteenth century, and the subsequent emergence of New York and Tokyo. However, this model does not explain London's continued primacy when Britain ceased to be a capital exporter, nor New York's when the United States became a net debtor. Although Bahrain's geographical and cultural proximity to the major Arab Gulf oil producers was an important permissive determinant of its development, along with Singapore and Hong Kong it grew and functioned essentially as an entrepôt. The rapid growth of Tokyo in the 1980s does indicate, however, that capital abundance enables barriers to entry to becoming an international financial centre to be rapidly overcome.

It is helpful to make a preliminary distinction between the original and the subsequent growth of financial centres, although this will need to be qualified subsequently. In explaining the origins of our particular financial centres, three general factors seem to be important:— reputation, willingness to act as a haven, and accessibility.

A variety of features make up the reputation of a financial centre. In general, it can be suggested that bankers, financiers and investors will be attracted to a location which has a reputation for stability, integrity, impartiality and confidentiality. Different types of financial activity will weigh certain of these features more heavily than other types. Depositors, for example, might put heavy emphasis on the integrity and business ethics of a financial centre, while certain firms of speculative trading might flourish if the integrity level is somewhat lower.

Confidence in political stability was an essential pre-requisite for the emergence – and maintenance – of a financial centre. Investors seek an assurance that their funds will be safe and, at all times, accessible and mobile. It is significant that the majority of financial centres in Asia and the Middle East often developed in areas which had a legacy of British political institutions. Twentieth-century Britain, although lacking in many business management and entrepreneurial skills, excelled at creating stable governance structures with due respect for the process of law. Hong Kong has been a British colony throughout the century. Australia inherited the political structures of its British colonists. Singapore was a British colony until 1959, and Bahrain was under British 'protection' until 1971. The British inheritance gave these places stable administrative structures, and familiar legal systems for British and American financial institutions. Shanghai and Beirut lacked a British political inheritance, but at both there were special factors which enhanced political confidence in them. Shanghai was one of China's nineteenth-century Treaty Ports and home of a large international settlement: a foreign community which was self-governing. Beirut flourished as a rare instance of stability in the Arab World in the 1950s and 1960s. Its unique constitution, which shared power between assorted religious groups, apparently guaranteed political stability, providing a contrast with the revolutionary and anti-western governments which took power in Egypt, Iraq and Syria in the 1950s, and in Libya in 1969. With the Communist victory in China and the outbreak of the Lebanese civil war, political confidence evaporated and with it Shanghai and Beirut's role as financial centres. Hong Kong's future as a financial centre rests heavily on the maintenance of political confidence in the post-1997 situation, as evidenced by the fluctuations in the Hong Kong markets because of political events within the People's Republic of China. In the 1984 Joint Declaration on the future of Hong Kong, the British and Chinese governments emphasized their commitment that Hong Kong 'shall retain the status of an international financial centre'.[38]

It is widely agreed that regulatory activities of governments have played an important part in the emergence of financial centres. They are crucial to the integrity, impartiality and confidentiality elements of a centre's reputation. A variety of government-imposed barriers to trade in financial services have influenced the location of financial activity, probably more than trade barriers have influenced the location of foreign direct investment in manufacturing. Regulatory measures and exchange controls in western Europe and the United States after the Second World War provided a major stimulus to the development of offshore financial centres. The role of the Federal Reserve's Regulation Q, which imposed a ceiling on the level of interest paid on bank deposits, in the development of the Eurodollar, and later Asiadollar, markets is perhaps the most dramatic example of this point.[39]

Conversely, regulatory regimes in host economies attracted – or hindered – the emergence of financial centres. Extensive regulation can substantially raise costs, and, if the regulatory authorities are unpredictable or corrupt, generate an unacceptable degree of concern about integrity and impartiality. However some regulation to provide consumer protection can stimulate the growth of a financial centre by, for example, reducing the cost of funds. Some regulation, but not too much, appears to provide the ideal institutional structure.

A fully fledged central bank was certainly not essential for the emergence of a financial centre.[40] European commercial banks often performed quasi-central banking functions in the initial stages of a centre's development, and, indeed, the absence of a central bank could make a location attractive. 'Whilst I realise what a great boon Central Banks are to Commercial Banks generally', the General Manager of one British exchange bank wrote to his manager in Singapore in 1949, 'it would certainly not suit any of the British Banks at the moment for a Central Bank to be established in Malaya. You would find it would cut into your business very considerably.'[41] Singapore had no central bank before the establishment of the Monetary Authority of Singapore in 1971, and Bahrain before the formation of the Bahrain Monetary Authority in 1973 (although the Bahrain Currency Authority created in the mid 1960s performed some central bank functions). In Lebanon there was no central bank until 1964: some central banking functions were performed by the French-owned Banque de Syrie et du Liban, which also acted as a commercial bank.[42] Hong Kong remains (in 1990) without a central bank. The British-managed Hongkong and Shanghai Banking Corporation (Hongkong Bank for short) performed some regulatory and central bank roles in addition to its position as the Colony's largest commercial bank. It shared with another British overseas bank the issue of bank notes in the Colony, acted as the banking system's clearing bank, and, sometimes, served as banker of last resort at times of banking crisis.[43]

While the initial growth of a financial centre benefits from little regulation and, perhaps, the absence of a central bank, as the centre grows in complexity more regulation may be required to maintain a desirable reputation. Hong Kong has been the most reluctant of the centres discussed here to move in this direction. The Colony's First Banking Ordinance was passed in 1948, but this had almost no regulatory content. A banking crisis in 1961 finally led to the establishment of a Banking Commissioner's Office in 1964 to enforce minimum capital and liquidity requirements. A major stock-market collapse in 1973–4 led to regulatory controls on deposit-taking companies. The 1980s saw further regulatory measures. Stock-market scandals in 1987, which threatened the Colony's reputation, led to much greater regulation of financial markets, with banks in Hong Kong being obliged to meet the capital adequacy rules set by the Basle agreement two years ahead of the agreed international timetable. Before 1987, however, the general pattern had been that the government responded to a crisis with more controls, rather than tried to pre-empt problems. 'Hong Kong's financial liberalism', Lee and Yao observed in 1982, 'has tended at times to border on permissiveness'.[44]

Permissiveness was a visibly more potent stimulus to the emergence of financial centres than prudence. Excessive regulation has provided infertile ground for the growth of international financial centres. Tokyo was hindered from becoming such a centre until its highly regulated financial markets began to be de-regulated in the 1980s. Post-independence India provided an even more unpromising regulatory framework for the emergence of a financial centre. During the 1950s and 1960s, the central bank, the Reserve Bank of India, was highly interventionist, enforced strict controls of banking ratios, sought to influence bank lending portfolios and pressured foreign financial institutions to hire Indian staff. In 1969 the government nationalized most of the domestic banking system, creating uncertainty about future intentions towards foreign institutions.[45] The impact of these policies on the British-owned Grindlays Bank was evident in 1971 when that bank began planning its world-wide business strategies: 'In the sub-continent, high tax rates and uncertain attitudes of governments towards foreign banks will make it necessary to scrutinise very carefully the likely earnings of any new investment. Our guiding principle must again be rationalisation and consolidation of existing business.'[46]

If reputation was one important factor in the emergence of these financial centres, the willingness to act as a haven for foreign enterprise and capital was another crucial factor. Shanghai, Beirut, Hong Kong, Singapore and Bahrain (and perhaps even Sydney since the mid 1980s) developed as financial centres not because of indigenous strengths in their capital markets or in their systems of management education, but through their willingness to permit foreign financial institutions to operate with considerable freedom in their territories, Like reputation, the haven dimension had several aspects.

At the most basic level, international financial centres did not develop in countries such as India, Australia and Japan while they excluded or very closely regulated foreign banks. Beirut, Bahrain, Singapore and Hong Kong were all characterized by a great willingness to allow foreign financial institutions to operate, just as nineteenth-century London had been willing to let foreign 'merchant bankers' locate and flourish there. After 1950 oil-rich Kuwait provided a more obvious home for an international financial centre than neighbouring Bahrain, but only one foreign institution – the British Bank of the Middle East – was ever allowed to operate in the country, and this bank was localized at the expiry of its concession in 1971.[47] 'There is little doubt', Rodney Wilson concludes, 'that the absence of nationalistic pressures has aided Bahrain's emergence as a leading banking centre, as foreign banks which were unable to establish themselves in Saudi Arabia or Kuwait found Bahrain the most conveniently placed alternative'.[48]

The degree of international 'openness' was always an important factor encouraging international banks to locate at a particular site. In 1971, for example, a director of Grindlays Bank isolated the Pacific Basin as an area of major economic development in the future, and his discussion of the 'four contenders' for the Basin's 'financial centres' – Tokyo, Sydney, Singapore and Hong Kong – provides a valuable insight on the factors which made a centre attractive to the western banking community:

> The first two (i.e. Tokyo and Sydney) should dominate the area, yet may not do so. The latter two (i.e. Singapore and Hong Kong) show all the signs of doing so and I believe they will. Tokyo will be a necessary base for most international banks, but their freedom will remain controlled. Sydney, too, remains remarkably insular. As for Hong Kong and Singapore, both benefit from Chinese commercial acumen, both have an international outlook, both are dependent on international trade, and both have competent monetary authorities guiding them.[49]

A willingness to let foreign firms operate provided financial centres with required skills. Hong Kong's liberal employment rules and willingness to let international law and accounting firms operate in the Colony provided the legal and accounting skills which facilitated the development of the loan syndication business there.[50]

Fiscal regimes were an element of the haven factor. None of the financial centres discussed here can be regarded as 'tax havens' in the strictest sense. They should be distinguished from the 'tax havens' which flourished in the western Hemisphere from the late 1960s, such as the Bahamas (whose importance can be seen in table 21.2), Cayman Islands, Anguilla, the New Hebrides and the Netherlands Antilles. Financial institutions usually established a token presence at those places through which business could be recorded as a device to avoid tax.[51] In Lebanon, Bahrain, Singapore and Hong Kong taxes were usually light rather than non-existent. Yao stresses the simplicity of Hong Kong's tax structure as a favourable factor in its growth as a financial centre.[52]

Variations in tax laws often explain why particular activities developed at one place rather than another. As already noted, it was Singapore's exemption from tax on interest earned from non-resident deposits which gave it the advantage over Hong Kong in the Asia Dollar Market. Conversely, international banks favoured Hong Kong as a 'lending' centre because of a tax system which – before 1978 – did not subject income generated outside the Colony to tax, while in Singapore offshore income earned by banks was still subject to income tax.[53]

An absence of exchange controls was an important part of the haven element in the growth of financial centres. London did flourish as a centre despite the existence of British exchange controls before 1979, although it functioned as an entrepôt in non-sterling currencies. Certainly, given the development of the Asian and Middle Eastern centres as financial entrepôts, the absence of free convertibility would have been a formidable handicap. Arguably the existence of exchange controls was one factor hindering the development of financial centres in South Korea and Taiwan, the two Asian NICs apart from Hong Kong and Singapore. Post-war Lebanon was distinguished from all its Arab neighbours by free convertibility and a liberal foreign exchange policy.[54] Singapore began reducing its exchange controls from the mid 1960s and in 1978 all remaining controls were abolished.[55] Although post-war Hong Kong was in the sterling area, the colonial authorities tolerated in the 1950s and 1960s an open market in foreign exchange to coexist alongside a market dealing with foreign exchange at official rates subject to sterling area constraints. Formal exchange controls ended altogether when Hong Kong left the sterling area in 1972. Singapore and the Arab Gulf States were also allowed open exchange markets within the sterling area.[56]

Accessibility was the third factor which stimulated the emergence of financial centres. International financial centres require good communications. Beirut in the 1950s and 1960s was distinguished by efficient post and telephone systems. It was the first centre in the Middle East to have telex equipment installed, and Lebanon even had its own airline, Middle Eastern Airlines.[57] In the era of jet airlines, the correlation between excellent air communications and status as an international financial centre was striking. Bahrain was the headquarters for Gulf Air, which it partly owned. Singapore and Hong Kong were the homes of Singapore Airlines and Cathay Pacific respectively, two of the most dynamic Asian airlines in the 1970s and 1980s.

The widespread use of English among the local labour force was another dimension of accessibility, certainly from the 1950s. The high level of international activity by American and British banks meant that a centre where English was little spoken would have problems in attracting a large foreign bank presence. British colonial rule or protection in Singapore, Hong Kong and Bahrain left a legacy of an English speaking labour force, while the British banks which were active in those places provided training (usually 'on the job') for nationals in English and basic banking principles.[58]

Accessibility to business customers was also important. Singapore began growing as a banking centre in the late nineteenth century because it was there that the heads of the British agency houses and trading firms operating in south-east Asia were usually found. Hong Kong in the second half of the nineteenth century was the headquarters of important expatriate merchant houses, such as Jardine Matheson. Bahrain performed a similar role, on a greatly reduced scale, in the Arabian Gulf.

Advantages of accessibility were also derived from time zone positions. 'Singapore's offshore currency market owes its existence in part', Arndt observes, 'to Singapore's time zone advantage, the fact that its business hours overlap with those on the US West Coast and Tokyo and for an hour or two with London'.[59] Beirut and later Bahrain had time zone advantages which enabled them to operate after Singapore closed but before the western European centres opened. Technological advantages in the 1980s, however, reduced such advantages in certain markets because it became possible to conduct financial operations without the physical presence of people.

Reputation, accessibility and willingness to act as a haven for foreign enterprise, therefore, stimulated the emergence of particular financial centres in Asia, the Middle East and Australasia. The retention or loss of this status is, naturally, also explained in part by such factors. However the subsequent growth of such centres also raises the matter of economies of agglomeration.

As Kindleberger observed in his 1974 article, the concentration of banking and financial activities at a given point leads to positive externalities and economies of scale.[60] Firms become linked in organized markets where liquidity and efficiency increases with the number of participants. Unless there is a regular flow of business, prices will be uncertain. There are advantages of having a number of markets in close proximity to one another, including the development of specialized ancillary services and the creation of a pool of skills. Professional services such as lawyers and accountants accumulate at centres. A supply of skilled labour is available for new entrants. Networks of personal contacts develop. The result is a momentum towards further growth and a reluctance to exit from such a centre unless there is a major change of circumstances, such as the Communist Revolution in China or the outbreak of Civil War in Lebanon. It follows that departure on a large scale – as with Beirut in 1975 – will produce a rapid downward spiral of activity at a financial centre, as external economies fall.[61]

The European connection

Many of the links between Europe and the financial centres discussed in this chapter will already be apparent. It is immediately evident that they have not played a large role in the loss of Europe's position as a 'world banker'. New York from the late nineteenth century, and Tokyo in the 1980s, challenged London and other European financial centres. Hong

Kong, Singapore and Bahrain have competed with London for certain types of business, but only in specialized areas. Bahrain in the 1980s, for example, was said to be 'competing with any major financial centre in Europe not only in the recycling of petrodollars but also in all international banking business relating to trade and industrial links with the Middle East'.[62] However, in the typology developed in the first section, no Asian (apart from Japan), Australasian and Middle Eastern country has developed a type C, or global financial centre. Only regional financial centres have emerged and these have not offered the wide range of markets available in London, New York or Tokyo.

Any threat posed by the Asian and Middle Eastern centres to these centres, including London, was reduced by their volatility, in contrast to the longevity (despite the changing circumstances of their domestic economies) of London and New York. Shanghai and Beirut disappeared as financial centres. In the 1980s Bahrain's future was clouded by warfare and political upheavals in its proximity, and by the world debt crisis. After 1982, when the 1997 handover of sovereignty to China first became an issue, Hong Kong's markets fluctuated violently with political events in China. The reasons for the volatility of these financial centres is evident. The Asian and Middle Eastern centres were not located in large economies with (at least originally) surplus capital and domestic currencies used widely in international transactions. They developed as entrepôts, dealing in others' currencies, and their attractiveness as havens and locations with a desirable reputation was vulnerable to – for example – political changes outside their control. Shanghai, Hong Kong, Beirut, Bahrain were points of stability in unstable and changing regions; safe havens for money to flow through, if not linger.

The origins of the Asian and Middle Eastern financial centres were closely tied to European business and trading enterprise. The initial clustering of western banks and other financial institutions at Shanghai, Singapore and Hong Kong was the result of flows of trade, capital and people between Europe, especially Britain, and east and south-east Asia. Foreign trade finance and the related exchange business were the principle concerns of the western banks which established branches at these places. Many of the companies initially quoted on the Stock Exchanges of Shanghai, Singapore and Hong Kong were established by Europeans to exploit regional trading and commodity opportunities.[63]

Over time, these trading and financial links between Europe and Asia declined, but the rise of global capital markets provided new links. The Eurodollar and Asian dollar markets were in essence the same market, and funds moved between the European, Asian and Middle Eastern financial centres. Table 21.3, which provides a snapshot of the geographical distribution of assets and liabilities of Offshore Banking

Table 21.3 *Assets and liabilities of Bahrain OBUs and Singapore ACUs in 1979 (per cent)*

	Assets				Liabilities			
	Europe	Asia	Arab	Other	Europe	Asia	Arab	Other
Bahrain	25	n.a.	53	22	28	n.a.	58	14
Singapore	15	73	n.a.	12	29	52	n.a.	19

Source: G. Germidis and Charles-Albert Michalet, *International Banks and Financial Markets* (Development Centre Studies, OECD, Paris, 1984) pp. 71, 77.

Units in Bahrain and the Asian Currency Units (ACUs) in Singapore for the single year of 1979 brings out this point.

As Table 21.3 shows, in 1979 Europe provided virtually 30 per cent of the funds in both the Singapore and Bahrain offshore banking sectors, while a quarter of the Bahrain funds, and 15 per cent of the Singapore funds, were employed in Europe in that year.

The European role in the emergence of these non-western financial centres was considerable. Shanghai flourished as an international settlement of the western powers. Singapore, Hong Kong, Bahrain and Sydney all had British colonial or settler pasts, as did many tax havens elsewhere in the world, such as the Bahamas, Cayman Islands, Gibraltar and the Channel Islands. Stable government structures and legal systems and the English language were among the more important British legacies. European trading companies and banks played a leading role in the initial accumulation of financial institutions and skills at these centres. In Beirut until the mid 1960s, and in Hong Kong until the present day, French and British managed commercial banks performed quasi-central banking functions. Western financial institutions provided training which created a pool of skills.

It would be misleading, of course, to imply that the Asian and Middle Eastern financial centres were entirely the legacy of European colonialism or business. India experienced both British imperial rule and considerable activity by British banks without developing a major financial centre. Interaction between western enterprise and a dynamic local business community was important. In Shanghai, Hong Kong and Singapore, British and other western bankers were joined with Chinese business communities with their own powerful commercial and financial traditions and institutions. In the Middle East, the Lebanese had a strong mercantile tradition in the Arabian Gulf, while Bahraini's were noted for their trading and outward-looking perspective compared to their neighbours. It was as sovereign states in the 1960s and 1970s that Singapore and Bahrain took decisions about tax and regulations which led to their growth as regional financial centres.

Conclusion

This chapter has examined international financial centres in the Middle East, Australasia and Asia, excluding Japan, from the First World War to the present day, adopting a crude typology which distinguishes a hierarchy of such centres by their geographical activity. Type A are sub-regional international centres, type B are regional and type C are global. In the interwar years, Shanghai, Hong Kong and Singapore were identified as type A centres. In the two decades after the Second World War, Shanghai disappeared as a financial centre because of the Communist Revolution in China, Hong Kong and Singapore retained their type A status, and Beirut emerged as a type B centre. Between 1965 and 1975 Singapore and Hong Kong joined Beirut in this category, a development related to the growth of the Euro-currency markets. After 1975 political problems destroyed Beirut's role as an international financial centre, but Bahrain and, later and to a much lesser extent, Sydney became type B centres.

We have suggested an explanatory framework for the emergence and growth of type A and type B financial centres (this framework may also apply to global, type C, centres but other factors are also involved). Their emergence rested on reputations for stability, integrity, impartiality and confidentiality, on their haven status, and on accessibility. It is thus highly appropriate that, of the three leading Asian and Middle Eastern financial centres at the end of the 1980s, two (Singapore and Bahrain) are islands while the third (Hong Kong) has most of its international financial activities located on Hong Kong island rather than its small foothold on mainland China. These financial centres grew as islands of hospitality to western banks and business. They are, as Shanghai and Beirut were, places where the financial transactions of western capitalism can be safely, efficiently and profitably conducted, in English. Once started, further growth was encouraged by economies of scale and agglomeration. Such was the size of these economies, that only a major change in a centre's reputation, haven status or accessibility could, by prompting a large number of exits, lead to its decline and disappearance.

Notes

1 This chapter has benefited enormously from comments on an earlier draft by Mark Casson, Paul Campayne, Frances Moss and Brian Quinn, and from comments by Mira Wilkins and other participants at the Geneva Conference. I would like to thank Grindlays Bank and

the Hongkong Bank Group for permission to cite material from their confidential archives.

2 Many economists are critical of, or dubious about, the concept of international trade in services. See, for example, H. G. Grubel, 'There is no direct international trade in services', *American Economic Review*, Papers and Proceedings (1987). For a contrary view, which defines trade in financial services 'in terms of value added created using the factors of production of one country and then sold to residents of another country', see Ingo Walter, *Global competition in financial services* (Cambridge, Mass, 1988), especially chapter 5.

3 Howard Curtis Reed, *The preeminence of international financial centers* (New York, 1981), pp. 3–7.

4 Paul Campayne suggests that, using this typology, a type D should be introduced, consisting of specialized global centres, such as Chicago (futures markets) and Zurich (fund management).

5 Reed, *Preeminence, passim.* For contradictory evidence on Singapore's importance, see p. 41. Reed sees five types of international and financial centres by 1980: host international financial centres, international financial centres (including Bahrain, Beirut, Singapore and Sydney in 1980), supranational financial centres of the second order (including Hong Kong in 1980), supranational financial centres of the first order (New York and Tokyo in 1980); and the supranational financial centre (London).

6 F. H. H. King, *The history of the Hong Kong and Shanghai Banking Corporation* (Cambridge, 1988) III, pp. 368–71.

7 F. H. H. King, *The History of the Hong Kong and Shanghai Banking Corporation* (Cambridge, 1988), II, pp. 457–8.

8 Jurgen Osterhammel, 'British business in China, 1860–1950s', in R. P. T. Davenport-Hines and Geoffrey Jones (eds.), *British business in Asia since 1860* (Cambridge, 1989), p. 202.

9 Stephanie Jones, *Two centuries of overseas trading* (London, 1986), chapter 6.

10 Wong Lin Ken, 'Singapore: its growth as an entrepot port, 1819–1941', *Journal of Southeast Asian Studies*, 26 (1978); J. J. van Helten and Geoffrey Jones, 'British business in Malaysia and Singapore since the 1870s', in Davenport-Hines and Jones, *British business*, pp. 160–1.

11 W. G. Huff, 'Book keeping barter, money, credit and Singapore's international rice trade, 1870–1939', *Explorations in Economic History* (1989).

12 B. R. Tomlinson, *The political economy of the Raj* (London, 1979), p. 44; A. G. Chandavarkar, 'Money and credit', in D. Kumar (ed.), *The Cambridge economic history of India* (Cambridge, 1983); Reed, *Preeminence*, includes Bombay and Calcutta as one of his top ten 'international banking centres' in 1925, but they subsequently disappear from his lists until after the Second World War.

13 Rodney Wilson, *Banking and finance in the Arab Middle East* (London, 1983), pp. 57–60; Abdul-Amir Badrud-Din, *The Bank of Lebanon. Central banking in a financial centre and entrepôt* (London, 1984), pp. 141ff.

14 Geoffrey Jones, *Banking and oil* (Cambridge, 1987), pp. 190–1.

15 Wilson, *Banking*, p. 59.

16 Badrun-Din, *Bank of Lebanon*, 161–2.

17 There is an enormous literature on the growth of the Euromarkets. For links between this and the growth of 'offshore' centres, see J. Sengupta, 'Internationalization of banking and the relationship between foreign and domestic banks in the developing countries', *International Journal of Development Banking*, 16 (1988); Sarah Bartlett, 'Transnational banking: A case of transfer parking with money', in R. Murray (ed.), *Multinationals beyond the market* (Brighton, 1981); Reed, *Preeminence*, p. 53.

18 S. R. Choi, A. E. Tschoegl and C. M. Yu, 'Banks and the world's major financial centers, 1970–1980', *Weltwirtschaftliches Archiv* (1986) ranks financial centres on the basis of the number of the world's Top 300 banks with an office in the centre in question. Singapore was ranked the eleventh largest international financial centre in 1970 and sixth in 1980. Hong Kong eighth in 1970 and fifth in 1980.

19 S. Y. Lee, 'The Asian dollar market, Asian bond market, and the Hongkong Bank Group', in F. H. H. King (ed.), *Eastern banking* (London, 1983); S. Y. Lee and Y. C. Yao, *Financial structures and monetary policies in Southeast Asia* (London, 1982).

20 Hafiz Mirza, *Multinationals and the growth of the Singapore economy* (London, 1986), p. 127.

21 Y. C. Yao, 'The rise of Hong Kong as a financial centre', *Asian Survey*, 19 (July 1979).

22 Lee, 'Asian dollar market', p. 578.

23 R. Wilson, 'Financial development in the Arab Gulf: The Eastern Bank experience 1917–50', *Business History*, 29 (1987).

24 Jones, *Banking and oil*, p. 172.

25 Wilson, *Banking*, pp. 110–19; Talal Shoker, 'Offshore financial centres in the Middle East', Institute of European Finance, Research Papers in Banking and Finance RP 88/21 (1988), University College of North Wales, Bangor; Arab Banking Survey, *Financial Times*, 25 November 1987.

26 Jones, *Banking and oil*, pp. 198–204.

27 Shoker, 'Offshore financial centres', pp. 3–4.

28 Michael T. Skully, 'Financial institutions and markets in Australia', in M. T. Skully (ed.), *Financial institutions and markets in the South-west Pacific* (London, 1985), p. 4.

29 D. T. Merrett, *ANZ Bank* (Sydney, 1985), pp. 295–301.

30 There was a surge of foreign investment in Australian financial institutions in the late 1960s and early 1970s. 'Overseas participation

in Australian investment banking and financial institutions', *Financial Review* (1970); 'Big London banks forge links with Australia', *The Australian*, 9 July 1971.
31 'Hong Kong as a Financial Centre', *Financial Times*, 26 October 1988.
32 Arab Banking Survey, *Financial Times*, 15 November 1987.
33 Shoker, 'Offshore financial centres', p. 13.
34 Derek F. Channon, *Global banking strategy* (Chichester, 1988), p. 56.
35 *Far Eastern Economic Review*, 14 April 1988, p. 65.
36 C. P. Kindleberger, 'The formation of financial centers; A study in comparative economic history', *Princeton Studies in International Finance*, No. 36 (1974) p. 1.
37 Reed, *Preeminence*; H. W. Arndt, 'Comparative advantage in trade in financial services', *Banca nazionale del lavoro* (1988). In addition to the empirical literature cited above, see also D. Germidis and Charles-Albert Michalet, *International banks and financial markets in developing countries* (Development Centre Studies, OECD, Paris, 1984), chapter 3 on offshore financial centres.
38 'Hong Kong as a Financial Centre', *Financial Times*, 26 October 1988; 'Hong Kong shows political nature', *Financial Times*, 26 May 1989.
39 Channon, *Global banking strategy*, p. 4.
40 For the theoretical debate on the merits of 'free banking' versus having a central bank, see B. Klein, 'The competitive supply of money', *Journal of Money, Credit and Banking*, 6 (1974); R. G. King, 'On the economics of private money', *Journal of Monetary Economies*, 12 (1983); Charles Goodhart, *The evolution of central banks* (Cambridge, Mass. 1988).
41 R. N. Drake to C. R. Wardle, 14 April 1949, Mercantile Bank Archives MB 970, Hongkong Bank Group Archives.
42 Badrun-Din, *Bank of Lebanon*, pp. 27–35.
43 Lee and Yao, *Financial structures*, pp. 224–5.
44 Ibid., p. 47; Yao, 'Rise', pp. 690–1. 'Hong Kong as a business and trading centre' *Financial Times*, 8 November 1989.
45 Jones, *Banking and oil*, pp. 243–9; information on the Indian business of Mercantile Bank of India and National and Grindlays Bank from Hongkong Bank Group Archives, and Grindlays Bank Archives respectively.
46 Draft Strategic Concept, 14 December 1971, Office of the Chairman, Grindlays Bank Archives.
47 Jones, *Banking and oil*, pp. 135–149.
48 Wilson, *Banking*, p. 111.
49 'Economic Prospects. The Next Five to Ten Years', report by William M. Clarke, July 1971, Office of the Chairman, Grindlays Bank Archives.
50 Yao, *Rise*, p. 686.

51 Germidis and Michalet, *International banks*, p. 78 dub such havens as 'fictitious offshore financial centres'. Walter, *Global competition*, p. 161, distinguishes places such as Hong Kong and Singapore from countries 'like the Bahamas and the Cayman Islands, which represent "booking" rather than "functional" centers (the actual transactions are done elsewhere)'. For information on the Caribbean tax havens, see *Euromoney* (May 1989) supplement on 'Treasure Islands'.
52 Yao, *Rise*, p. 685.
53 Lee and Yao, *Financial structures*, p. 225.
54 Wilson, *Banking*, p. 57.
55 Mirza, *Multinationals*, p. 125.
56 F. H. H. King, 'The Hong Kong open market, 1954', in F. H. H. King (ed.), *Asian policy, history and development* (Hong Kong, 1979): F. H. H. King, *The history of the Hong Kong and Shanghai Banking Corporation*, IV (Cambridge 1991), pp. 345–7. On the 'Kuwait Gap', see Jones, *Banking and oil*, pp. 137–8.
57 Wilson, *Banking*, p. 58.
58 For the case of the Middle East, see Jones, *Banking and oil*, p. 288.
59 Arndt, 'Comparative advantage', p. 72; Channon, *Global banking strategy*, p. 72; Mirza, *Multinationals*, p. 123.
60 Kindleberger, 'Formation', p. 11.
61 The importance of external economies of scale is stressed in an unpublished Bank of England report on London's position as a financial centre cited in 'The City finds its head start under attack', *Financial Times*, 1 June 1989. See also Economists Advisory Group, *City 2000, The future of London as an international financial centre* (London, 1984), chapter 2.
62 Sengupta, 'Internationalization of banking', p. 42.
63 R. P. T. Davenport-Hines and Geoffrey Jones, 'British business in Asia since 1860', in Davenport-Hines and Jones, *British business*, p. 10.

Part III
International Finance and International Financial Centres in the 1980s and 1990s

[12]

Excerpt from Richard O'Brien and Sarah Hewin (eds), *Finance and the International Economy 4*, 143–68

8

Reconfiguration of Global Financial Markets in the 1990s

ROY C. SMITH AND INGO WALTER

Introduction

During the 1980s world financial markets experienced change as never before. These were years of explosive growth in all types of financial transactions. The US bond and stock markets entered a boom period early in the decade that continued until nearly its end, alongside a torrent of financial innovations and aggressive trading operations, the fourth wave of mergers and acquisitions of the twentieth century, and a new focus on international investment management. The decade also saw extraordinary growth in the issuance and trading of Euromarket securities, radical deregulation of financial markets in the UK and several other countries, a flurry of privatization share issues by governments, as well as the EC 1992 initiatives and the launching of the first great mergers wave to envelop the whole of Europe—where industrial restructuring more or less along American lines was seen to be necessary and unavoidable. Meanwhile, Japan emerged during the period as the world's most solvent nation, pumping its excess savings into foreign securities, real estate, and control of corporations.

Although propelled by a certain degree of serendipity, these developments were hardly accidental. They were the result of more or less simultaneous policy shifts toward the free market on the part of governments of the OECD countries, shifts that reflected sharply different philosophies of economic governance than had prevailed before. This policy redirection also reflected a broad realization that global economic forces cannot be ignored or resisted, and indeed must be accommodated.

The further evolution of world financial markets will continue to be highly sensitive to such basic policy developments, and can be discussed in terms of the implications for each of the three principal regional market-places—Europe, the United States, and Japan. Just as the oil price rise which so affected international finance in the 1970s was unforeseeable at the beginning of that decade, or as the impact of 'Reaganomics' and the changing role of Japan were unforeseeable at the beginning of the 1980s, the full consequences for financial markets of new developments such as the political and economic reforms in Eastern Europe or events in the Middle East remain unforeseeable today. Some probable directions, however, can be identified based on an assessment of underlying policy vectors and the changing capabilities of the markets themselves.

Europe

The key development in Europe will be a convergence between the use of bank finance and capital market finance in corporate restructurings. In the UK banks are likely to play a larger role, while on the Continent the single market in financial services in the 1992 programme will encourage greater use of capital markets for industrial restructuring. The rapid growth in mergers and acquisitions throughout Europe is set to continue.

The European financial and industrial deregulation and privatization already underway, and those additional developments associated with the EC single market initiatives, will help sustain a long overdue restructuring of industry in Europe. This restructuring is occurring through mergers, corporate recapitalizations, strategic alliances and minority investments, leveraged management buyouts, and other free-market responses. In addition, the restructuring has been aided by the availability of financial resources, somewhat more aggressive attitudes about business takeovers that have accompanied capital market liberalization, and the availability in Continental Europe of US and UK takeover knowhow (Walter and Smith, 1989). Nevertheless, there are persistent differences in how industrial restructuring is carried out through the market for corporate control as between the Anglo-Saxon and Continental European traditions. This in turn has a great deal to do with the structure of relationships between business firms and their investors and creditors.

1. Changing Banking Relationships

The differences between corporate restructuring in Continental Europe and the Anglo-American experience reflect the fundamental differences that have existed in national financial systems. In much of Continental Europe, corporate finance traditionally has been heavily bank-oriented. Universal banking institutions are dominant in corporate lending as well as securities issuance. The banks also make equity investments for their own and fiduciary accounts, and retain voting rights on shares held in trust. Such practices provide banks with both non-public information and (indirectly and through external board memberships) considerable influence over management decisions involving corporate restructuring activities. Firms that do not meet bank performance expectations find themselves under pressure to restructure (Rybczynski, 1989). When such restructuring is to be accomplished, it is usual for the company's main bank (*Hausbank*) to carry it out. Historically, Continental European banks have periodically been called upon to push through industrial restructurings in the absence of well-functioning capital markets, especially following periods of war or economic collapse, and so are accustomed to this role.

In the United States and the United Kingdom, on the other hand, banks have not had a comparable tradition since the early 1930s, and capital markets have played a large role in industrial finance for most of this century. Corporate debt financing has relied much more heavily on the securities markets, with bondholders exerting limited influence on managerial decisions. Nor have shareholders exerted much influence over management in recent years. Neither US nor UK banks have been able to effectively exercise surveillance and influence on management even remotely comparable to that of some of their Continental European counterparts.

Consequently, changes in corporate control have been effected through the capital markets, frequently contested by incumbent management and justified by a need to replace that management so as to improve the performance of the company. Even when such efforts are unsuccessful, management may choose to carry out its own restructuring of the company, often resulting in changes not dissimilar from those sought by the challenger. Some observers of the US and UK merger scene over the past several years believe that self-restructurings to escape or avoid takeovers have been more numerous than the takeover attempts themselves, arguably enhancing corporate profitability and efficiency (Jensen and Ruback 1983).

Others worry about the impact of increased leverage on the stability and competitive viability of firms (especially in times of recession), redistribution of wealth to shareholders from bondholders, employees, and other interest groups, and the sort of managerial short-termism and distraction from conduct of the underlying business that takeover activity may entail. They point to the lack of empirical evidence that companies and countries exposed to intensive takeover activity outperform those exempt from such pressures over the long term, for example UAL Inc. (United Airlines) versus AMR Corp. (American Airlines) or the United Kingdom versus Germany. Definitive conclusions, of course, remain elusive given the impossibility of running the world twice, i.e. how things went as against how they might have gone under different takeover market conditions.

The merits and demerits of the two systems have been widely debated. Bank-oriented systems are said to be less crisis-prone, to favour long-term as opposed to short-term views in corporate decision-making, and to provide superior continuous monitoring of corporate performance leading to pre-emptive structural adjustment. Market-oriented systems are credited with greater efficiency, financial innovation, and dynamism, superior resistance to inherent conflicts of interests among the various stakeholders involved, and (through better transparency) less susceptibility to major uncorrected industrial blunders.

In the 1990s there is likely to be some degree of convergence between the two approaches. Financial liberalization and wider use of the securities markets by Continental European corporations—together with increasingly performance-oriented portfolio management on the part of European mutual funds, insurance companies, and other institutional investors—is leading to a gradual shift away from bank finance, and the introduction of unwanted takeover attempts through acquisition of shareholdings by unaffiliated (perhaps foreign-based) investors. At the same time, easing restrictions on bank activities in the United Kingdom and the United States is beginning to allow them to play a larger role in industrial restructuring transactions, and to exploit some of the information and relationship advantages they have as lenders.

2. *The Unfolding European Merger Wave*

Of the $329 billion of non-US merger and acquisitions recorded between 1985 and 1989, $196 billion, or 60 per cent, were intra-European (Smith and Walter, 1990). An additional $156 billion (80 per cent of the intra-European total) involved Europe–non-Europe transactions. European corporations were entering the M&A field more aggressively, with transaction volume growing far more rapidly than anywhere else in the world during the 1985–9 period. This expansion was occurring simultaneously on two fronts—within Europe and in other regions of global importance to European corporations, mainly the United States. Intra-European transactions increased by a factor of nine during the five-year period, and Europe–non-Europe deals (in which 73 per cent of the transactions by volume involved European acquisitions of non-European corporations) grew 5.4 times, as shown in Table 8.2. Overall, European transactions rose from 8 per cent of the world M&A volume in 1985 to 32 per cent in 1989 and made further gains in 1990.

Although it is difficult to predict how long the growth in European M&A volume will continue, it appears that—barring any unexpected reversal of government policies affecting market-driven transactions or a substantial deterioration of economic prospects in Europe—there remains a great deal more to be done. Most of the M&A activity in Europe during the period 1985–9 (about 58 per cent by volume) has involved United Kingdom corporations, which have a long history and familiarity with such transactions. French and Italian corporations (together accounting for 22 per cent of intra-European transaction volume) have been the next most active M&A participants, followed by German corporations which—despite the size of the German economy—accounted for only 5 per cent of intra-European transaction volume during 1985–9.

Table 8.1. Volume of completed international merger and corporate transactions,[a,b] United States (1985–9) (millions of US dollars)[c]

			Cross-border US									
	Domestic US		Buyer from US		Seller from US		Total cross-border		Outside US		Global totals	
Year	(#)	($M)	(#)	($M)	(#)	($M)	(#)	($M)	(#)	($M)	(#)	($M)
1985	778	181.544.6	28	4.799.1	72	9.732.6	100	14.531.7	82	16.296.5	960	212.372.8
	[d](852)		(60)		(104)		(164)		(90)		(1.106)	
1986	1.145	201.745.8	35	2.905.4	147	27.280.1	182	30.185.5	132	28.728.5	1.459	260.659.8
	(1.253)		(59)		(138)		(197)		(161)		(1.611)	
1987	1.273	199.878.2	46	7.669.4	172	35.481.7	218	43.151.1	310	70.706.7	1.801	313.736.0
	(1.267)		(102)		(123)		(225)		(279)		(1.771)	
1988	1.510	286.918.8	72	5.886.6	226	60.915.9	298	66.802.5	1.115	97.798.4	2.923	451.519.7
	(1.178)		(135)		(168)		(303)		(789)		(2.270)	
1989	1.489	200.330.6	124	17.500.0	324	44.615.5	448	62.115.5	1.459	115.306.5	3.396	377.752.6
	(1.331)		(184)		(183)		(367)		(1.275)		(2.973)	
Totals 1985–9	6.195	1,070,418.0	305	38,760.5	941	178.025.8	1.246	216,786.3	3.098	328.836.6	10.539	1,616,040.9
	(5.881)		(540)		(716)		(1.256)		(2.594)		(9.731)	

Data: Securities Data Corporation, Mergers and Corporate Transactions database.

[a] Completed transactions include: mergers, tender-mergers, tender offers, purchases of stakes, divestitures, recapitalizations, exchange offers, and LBOs.

[b] The volume data are classified according to the announcement date of a transaction—not taking into consideration when a transaction is completed.

[c] Million dollars of purchase price—excluding fees and expenses—at current exchange rates. The dollar value includes the amount paid for all common stock, common stock equivalents, preferred stock, debt, options, assets, warrants, and stake purchases made within six months of the announcement date of the transaction. Liabilities assumed are included if they are disclosed in press releases or newspaper articles.

[d] Number of completed transactions with undisclosed dollar values.

Table 8.2. Volume of completed international merger and corporate transactions,[a,b] Europe (1985–9)[c] (millions of US dollars)[d]

	Intra-European transactions		Europe/non-Europe transactions: Buyer from Europe		Seller from Europe		Total cross-border	
Year	(#)	($M)	(#)	($M)	(#)	($M)	(#)	($M)
1985	31	8,326.0	40	6,083.2	22	2,441.0	62	8,524.2
	[e](32)		(44)		(40)		(84)	
1986	59	11,911.4	85	17,752.0	34	3,523.2	119	21,275.2
	(75)		(54)		(33)		(87)	
1987	189	38,335.0	111	27,825.9	45	8,307.5	156	36,133.4
	(161)		(67)		(72)		(139)	
1988	835	63,431.6	179	35,978.9	104	8,433.6	283	44,412.5
	(559)		(134)		(125)		(259)	
1989	1,090	74,432.9	255	33,367.1	180	12,671.0	435	46,038.1
	(874)		(134)		(211)		(345)	
Totals 1985–9	2,204	196,436.9	670	121,007.1	385	35,376.3	1,055	156,383.4
	(1,702)		(433)		(481)		(914)	

Data: Securities Data Corporation, Mergers and Corporate Transactions database.

[a] Completed transactions include: mergers, tender-mergers, tender offers, purchases of stakes, divestitures, recapitalizations, exchange offers, and LBOs.

[b] The volume data are classified according to the announcement date of a transaction—not taking into consideration when a transaction is completed.

[c] The region includes Eastern European countries.

[d] Million dollars of purchase price—excluding fees and expenses—at current exchange rates. The dollar value includes the amount paid for all common stock, common stock equivalents, preferred stock, debt, options, assets, warrants, and stake purchases made within six months of the announcement date of the transaction. Liabilities assumed are included if they are disclosed in press releases or newspaper articles.

[e] Number of completed transactions with undisclosed dollar values.

Most of the Continental European countries do not have a tradition of, or substantial experience with, market-driven domestic M&A activity. As a result, only a comparatively small percentage of enterprises in Continental European countries have so far participated in such transactions. As more of them become involved, and the benefits of doing so become more visible (such as utilizing an efficient market for corporate control to dispose of shares in family-owned or closely held businesses that have limited liquidity), participation in M&A activity should continue to penetrate further.

The patterns of intra-European M&A volume for the 1985–9 period can be observed by sorting transactions by the nationality of buyers and sellers—see Table 8.3. The average annual rate of growth of all intra-European M&A volume was 120 per cent, an exceptionally high growth rate. UK activity in the European merger market-place was by far the greatest—64 per cent of all reported intra-European transactions involved British seller companies. British seller volume grew at an average annual rate of 66 per cent, consistent with the overall intra-European growth rates. Transactions involving British sellers to British buyers grew at a somewhat slower rate of 60 per cent during the period.

French and Italian companies, however, were acquiring other European companies (including British companies) at a much more rapid rate of increase. Especially active on the buy-side in the intra-European market, French buyer-transactions grew at a rate of 465 per cent per annum, and purchases by Italian companies grew at 111 per cent annually during the same period. French buyers acquiring French companies totalled $13.7 billion (out of a total of $26.7 billion of French intra-European acquisitions) during the five-year period, and reflected an annual growth rate of 373 per cent. Italian companies acquired other Italian companies worth $13.9 billion during the period, a growth rate of 112 per cent.

Although much less active in intra-European volume terms during the period ($9.7 billion) German companies, whose rate of growth in intra-European buyer transactions was 50.8 per cent annually during 1985–9, substantially lagged British, French, and Italian acquirers. German sell-side activity grew even more slowly, only 19 per cent per annum. It has evidently become much easier for French and Italian companies to use the merger market for seller-initiated transactions than it has been for German companies, which are the least accustomed to domestic M&A activity among all those engaging in European mergers and acquisitions. Sellers from these four countries made up about 86 per cent of aggregate intra-European transaction volume during the period, although German sellers accounted for only 2.7 per cent of all seller activity.

Assuming Eastern Europe's political and economic changes maintain direction and momentum, further and perhaps more extensive and entirely different restructuring patterns may lie ahead. These include the need to carry out large-scale privatizations and the development of new debt and equity markets in an environment where valuation of enterprises is exceedingly difficult, where property rights and legal business structures are yet to be fully defined, and where the role of foreign investment remains highly uncertain—in national economic settings subject to high levels of macro-risk.

3. Capital Market Integration

European industrial restructuring will require impressive amounts of financing. This should be available primarily, if not entirely, from European sources. European corporations should no longer find it necessary to rely largely on bank lending or to arrange their capital market financings in non-European currencies or in non-European markets. Domestic financial markets in Europe have benefited considerably from increased transaction volumes, greater liquidity, and more competition in recent years, although the percentage of such financings arranged by non-financial (i.e. industrial) borrowers remains far lower than in either the United States or Japan—see Table 8.4.

With the elimination of all barriers to cross-border transactions going into effect for both issuers and investors (as well as financial intermediaries) in the coming years, it can be expected that a large, single European capital market will emerge. This integrated market will reflect the consolidation of previously separate domestic capital markets, serviced mainly by local banking institutions, with the existing Eurobond and European 'foreign bond' market structures.

Table 8.3. Volume of completed intra-European M&A transactions by country (1985–9) (millions of US dollars)

Country of buyer company		Country of seller company: UK	France	Italy	Germany	Other European	Totals buyer
UK	1985	6,747.4	0.0	0.0	0.0	12.2	6,759.6
	1986	7,713.7	0.0	0.0	0.0	60.0	7,773.7
	1987	21,671.3	4.3	100.0	0.0	236.6	22,012.2
	1988	27,391.7	1,085.0	149.9	139.8	741.7	29,508.1
	1989	44,035.9	1,163.7	257.1	293.5	2,048.3	47,798.5
	Total	107,560.0	2,253.0	507.0	433.3	3,098.8	113,852.1
	CGR	59.8%					63.1%
France	1985	0.0	10.7	0.0	0.0	0.0	10.7
	1986	0.0	176.0	520.9	0.0	0.0	696.9
	1987	316.7	1,324.2	0.0	0.0	0.0	1,640.9
	1988	2,897.6	6,860.5	98.7	310.2	3,253.7	13,420.7
	1989	4,896.5	5,344.0	392.4	0.0	248.3	10,881.2
	Total	8,110.8	13,715.4	1,012.0	310.2	3,502.0	26,650.4
	CGR		372.7%				464.7%
Italy	1985	16.8	0.0	165.0	0.0	0.0	181.8
	1986	0.0	0.0	1,199.4	71.0	0.0	1,270.4
	1987	0.0	20.4	7,876.3	0.0	1,050.8	8,947.5
	1988	0.0	710.0	1,292.7	0.0	887.7	2,890.4
	1989	99.9	90.9	3,344.3	63.1	0.0	3,598.2
	Total	116.7	821.3	13,877.7	134.1	1,938.5	16,888.3
	CGR			112.2%			110.9%

Germany	1985	0.0	0.0	0.0	898.5	0.0	898.5
	1986	425.0	0.0	887.4	0.0	0.0	1,312.4
	1987	159.6	330.6	0.0	251.0	0.0	741.2
	1988	59.2	154.0	627.4	1,231.8	44.8	2,117.2
	1989	170.0	1,176.1	37.5	1,803.0	1,457.4	4,644.0
	Total	813.8	1,660.7	1,552.3	4,184.3	1,502.2	9,713.3
	CGR				19.0%		50.8%
Other European	1985	0.0	0.0	0.0	0.0	475.4	475.4
	1986	563.9	0.0	0.0	0.0	294.1	858.0
	1987	382.0	153.4	0.0	239.0	4,218.8	4,993.2
	1988	6,673.8	0.0	1,759.5	0.0	7,061.9	15,495.2
	1989	1,729.0	20.3	305.9	149.7	5,306.1	7,511.0
	Total	9,348.7	173.7	2,065.4	388.7	17,356.3	29,332.8
	CGR					82.8%	99.4%
Totals seller	1985	6,764.2	10.7	165.0	898.5	487.6	8,326.0
	1986	8,702.6	176.0	2.607.7	71.0	354.1	11,911.4
	1987	22,529.6	1,832.9	7.976.3	490.0	5,506.2	38,335.0
	1988	37,022.3	8,809.5	3.928.2	1,681.8	11,989.8	63,431.6
	1989	50,931.3	7,795.0	4,337.2	2,309.3	9,060.1	74,432.9
	Total	125,950.0	18,624.1	19,014.4	5,450.6	27,397.8	196,436.9
	CGR	65.7%	419.5%	126.4%	26.6%	107.6%	72.9%

Data: Securities Data Corporation. Mergers and Corporate Transactions database.

Table 8.4. Volume of corporate sector capital market financing by regional corporations in their respective home markets (1988)
($ billions of proceeds at average exchange rates)

	USA			Europe			Japan		
	Financial	Non-financial	Total	Financial	Non-financial	Total	Financial	Non-financial	Total
Equities	28.8	13.6	42.4	9.5	42.3	63.0	25.1	40.8	65.9
Bonds	141.1	221.9	363	155.2	26.3	181.4	287.7	137.9	425.6
Total	169.9	235.5	405.4	164.7	68.6	244.4	312.8	178.7	491.5
GNP ($ tlns)			4.88			5.27			2.9
Financing per dollar of GNP	$0.03	$0.05	$0.08	$0.03	$0.01	$0.05	$0.11	$0.06	$0.17

Notes:

Source: OECD Financial Statistics Monthly Domestic Markets December 1989 (earlier months where not updated).

Equities include public and private enterprise issues (lines A.1.a + b for non-financial; lines A.1.c for financial).

Non-financial corporate bonds include public issues for private and public non-financial corporations plus private placements where reported (lines B.1.1 c + d + private placements).

Financial corporate bonds are taken from line B.1.1.e (or lines B.1.1.e.1 + e.2).

Because the US 1989 equities' breakdown into financial and non-financial corporations is only given for first 2 quarters the breakdown given above was estimated from proportions evident in those quarters:

Total 22.7 NF 7.3

Issues by domestic firms outside of their home country are excluded.

European figures are aggregated from Germany, France, Greece, Italy, Norway, Netherlands, UK, Switzerland, Finland, Spain, Belgium, Portugal, and Luxembourg.

In essence, the new market will derive from the integration of financial competition in Europe. Under the EC Second Banking Directive a German bank, for example, may open branches or buy local banks in France and in Italy. In Germany, however, the bank will itself be subject to new competition for the business of its traditional clients from German branches of French and Italian banks. The German bank may propose an ordinary, traditional *Hausbank* financing for an old customer, only to discover that better terms under a more imaginative structure are offered by a German branch of a foreign bank, or by a US investment bank operating out of London.

The German bank may match the terms to keep the client's business. The financing could then become a capital market operation, because the cheapest financing for borrowers tends to emanate from the issuance of securities rather than from bank loans, especially in those situations in which the rates have to be sharpened to fully competitive levels. The German bank would take the client to the market for the necessary funds, perhaps using the domestic bond market structure and prospectus, if this is convenient. If it is not—for example if it involves translating the prospectus into all EC languages—the bank could instead offer a Eurobond structure, even though the ultimate investors may in either case be the same—partly local nationals who know the issuer well, partly other Europeans who will be offered the new paper through the bank's branches or affiliates throughout the EC. Some French investors may subscribe to a German domestic issue, just as they might to a Eurobond issue, and German investors may subscribe just as they might to a domestic private placement. Before long, all such issues will be structured to find the most receptive investors, wherever they may be located in Europe, or outside Europe.

4. The Stimulating Effects of Competition

The simultaneous activities of financial market competitors throughout Europe—by banks and securities firms from EC member countries, as well as from Switzerland, Japan, and the United States—will force the markets to conform to the most efficient transactions structure possible. The result should be similar to the introduction of the 'bought deal' to the Eurobond market in the early 1980s, which opened all clients to the competitive offerings of capable securities houses with whom no prior relationship existed. Indeed, the competition-enhancing influence of the bought deal was so strong that the Securities and Exchange Commission took it into account when proposing and later adopting Rule 415 ('shelf registration') in the United States, which likewise led to a marked increase in competition for the new issue business involving corporate debt securities.

The emerging, consolidated European market will be characterized by comparably free-wheeling competition, pressure for financial innovation, and proliferation of sophisticated financial services. The large European issuers will be the first to benefit from these changes, but certainly not the last. Soon US and Japanese issuers will likewise be attracted to a large and more efficient pan-European financial market. And financial firms marketing these services will certainly attempt to reach beyond large blue-chip companies, to capture as well the business of middle-market companies that previously did not think themselves capable of capital market access.

United States

In remedying a structure of financial regulation that has become increasingly obsolete and uncompetitive, major changes in US banking laws—especially in the Glass–Steagall separation of banking and securities activities, and restrictions on interstate banking—can be anticipated early in the 1990s. These will result in far-reaching, possibly radical restructuring of the US commercial and investment banking industries.

1. Market Interpenetration

A dozen or so large banks will enter the domestic securities business as important competitors, particularly in the underwriting of new debt and equity issues. Few in number but including some of the premier money centre and regional banking entities, they will attempt to introduce a version of universal banking to the United

States. Some of these institutions view investment banking as the preferred vehicle for escaping the destiny of large, unwieldy, and bureaucratic institutions trapped in an overcrowded industry with depressingly low margins and questionable credits. They expect that universal banking will be a business they can assimilate—in the manner of the large German or Swiss banks, for example—more easily than they could assimilate the aggressive, free-wheeling business of a Morgan Stanley or a Shearson Lehman. Other banks will prefer to pursue opportunities in interstate banking and/or possibly insurance. These efforts will be focused on middle-market lending and retail financial services, as the viability of classic wholesale banking activities continues to erode.

The choice of direction is not an easy one, and both offering universal banking services and establishing a universal banking network will be expensive. Nationwide financial services offer much appeal to banks hemmed in by regulatory geography. But the cost of putting together a first-rate nationwide banking network may well exceed the $1 billion or so that many observers think is the minimum needed for a comparable investment banking commitment.

These challenges will arrive at a time when bank capital has been depleted by various ldc charge-offs, bond ratings have been lowered throughout the banking industry, share prices are at historic lows, and tough new capital adequacy standards have been adopted by the Federal Reserve and the other bank regulators. Banks also enter the 1990s with problems in their HLT (highly leveraged transactions) portfolios and troublesome prospects for real estate loans in a market likely to remain soft throughout the savings and loan workout and a macroeconomic slowdown.

It none the less seems probable that among the US banks most adept at money market, government securities, and foreign exchange dealing, there will emerge several that will attempt to become leaders in global securities markets. Initially at least, these banks could be expected to concentrate on all types of debt financing, in all of the major currencies, using all of the latest swapping and synthetic securities techniques.

Foreign banks operating in the United States will find these market developments ideal—they can continue to attempt to increase their penetration of the traditional commercial banking businesses (where their superior credit standing has provided a decided advantage over many US banks), and they can improve their international securities business by placing US issues in their home markets or in other foreign markets.

2. Globalizing the US Bond Market

Bond market operators will be taking advantage of the opportunities presented by SEC Rule 144A, which became effective in April 1990 and offers a safe haven to any issuer (domestic or foreign) offering securities to qualified institutional investors on an unregistered basis. Whereas SEC Rule 415 earlier permitted qualified issuers to sell securities under a shelf-registration procedure, Rule 144A omits registration requirements altogether, thereby greatly simplifying new-issue procedures for international borrowers unwilling to submit to the trouble and cost of preparing a registration statement (SEC, 1988). By eliminating the two-year holding period for qualified investors in privately placed securities, it adds significantly to the liquidity of these securities and therefore reduces the yield penalty to borrowers as against public issues—even as it significantly cuts issuing costs—and for the first time qualified such securities for purchase by mutual funds whose shares are sold to the public. For all practical purposes, Rule 144A has transformed the US institutional market for debt securities into an equivalent of the self-regulated and highly innovative Eurobond market.

Rule 144A contemplates a substantial increase in the number of non-US debt and equity financings done in the American capital market, many of which will be offered not only to domestic investors but also, simultaneously, to investors in Europe and Japan. Figure 8.1 illustrates the market overlaps that are expected as a result. Debt issues brought to European and Japanese markets—whether by US or other corporate issuers—may also be offered to institutional investors in the United States under Rule 144A. From a regulatory viewpoint, it has eliminated virtually all remaining obstacles to full international market integration. Issuers will, as always, choose the lowest-cost market for the securities they wish to offer—which may or may not be in the United States—regardless of regulatory considerations.

Rule 144A also permits banks to broaden and perfect their

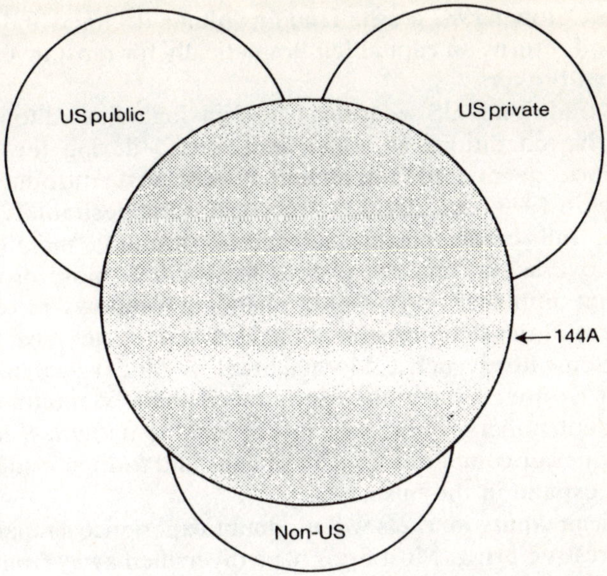

Figure 8.1. Potential market structure after the adoption of Rule 144A

distribution of loans. During the 1980s, many US banks adopted the practice of 'selling down' loan participations to other banks. This process could be made more efficient by securitizing the loans through Rule 144A provisions that would permit liquid markets to develop and extend the group of investors to whom they are offered to encompass non-bank financial institutions as well. Should such practices become widespread, the market for bank loans would come to be substantially integrated with the bond market, thereby facilitating the development of meaningful placing power by banks in the securities field—and raising questions as to how such loans/securities should be treated for accounting and regulatory purposes.

3. Adjusting to Overcapacity

Competition in the securities market from the banking industry is occurring just as the US securities industry is recovering painfully slowly from a substantial overcapacity problem that developed after the October 1987 crash. Trading volume declined and profitability and returns on capital fell dramatically for most investment banks and brokers.

Many traditional US securities firms, having adjusted to intense competitive conditions at home and abroad during the fifteen years since negotiated commissions were first introduced on 'Mayday' in 1975, may decide to reconsider the desirability of life as large, full-service players subject to shrinking margins and growing overheads, and opt instead for smaller, more profitable niches that offer the sort of rapidly changing 'windows' of rewards and opportunities that investment bankers as a species have always sought. Some firms, such as Morgan Stanley, Kidder Peabody, and Salomon Brothers, have already reduced their commitments to certain debt underwriting and market making activities, leaving room for newer competitors such as banks and foreign institutions eager to expand in the business.

American equity markets will no doubt experience similar competitive restructuring. Most firms have diversified away from plain institutional block trading or retail sales activities in search of more profitable areas, such as money management, programme trading, and foreign securities brokerage. The equities markets in general, however, should be buoyed by greater international involvement in the 1990s as overseas portfolio investors—especially those from Japan—develop professionally and become more active. Greater volume will not, of course, relieve the pressures on margins caused by new domestic and foreign-based market entrants.

4. Growing Foreign Presence

Foreign corporations, attracted by strategic requirements and relatively low stock prices in the US, have continued to be active as acquirers of US companies. This continuing foreign investment volume could offset somewhat the downward pressure on equity prices that the ending of the US merger boom and adverse environmental developments might be expected to have on the market. Permanent foreign participation in US portfolio investments and acquisitions will become more welcome and should, by the end of the 1990s (perhaps much sooner), begin to alleviate

American anxieties over 'excessive' foreign ownership. It will become clear that foreign capital injections are beneficial and that foreign shareholders are no more threatening to Americans than American stockholdings, now long in place, have been in European and other foreign companies.

US and foreign equity trading may also become integrated on an expanded NASDAQ/SEAQ electronically linked system, which could result in a substantial increase of American institutional ownership and trading of foreign equities. Such linkages could, by the end of the 1990s, offer lower trading costs, simpler clearing systems, and ultimately lead toward a greater standardization of accounting, disclosure, and regulatory procedures, all of which tend to encourage still greater international financial market activity.

Japan

Japanese financial markets are likely to experience substantial additional deregulation in the 1990s, which in turn should lead to major changes in the competitive dominance of capital markets by Japanese banks and brokers.

The basic business of the Japanese banks has changed rapidly—the surplus cash of Japanese companies has substantially paid down all but the barest minimum of bank debt owed by manufacturing companies. Table 8.5 shows the dramatic decline of net interest costs as a percentage of Japanese corporate operating profits. The traditional influence and power of the banks over their industrial customers is becoming a thing of the past. Banks, however, continue to have large balance sheets, which are partly inflated by cosmetic loans maintained for the sake of appearances (i.e. loan proceeds that are subsequently redeposited in the same bank). Increasingly, however, loans and other new business are coming from banking transactions outside Japan.

1. Pressures on Article 65

As in the United States, Japanese banks need to find a new domestic business, and many believe the greatest promise resides

Table 8.5. Net financial costs (interest charges) as a percentage of operating profits, Tokyo Stock Exchange first-section companies, fiscal 1975–88E (parent-company basis)

Year	All companies (%)	Manufacturing sector (%)
1975	62.8	69.0
1976	39.6	44.4
1977	41.5	42.3
1978	44.7	30.8
1979	36.7	23.9
1980	33.3	30.0
1981	35.5	28.6
1982	35.8	28.0
1983	35.9	24.5
1984	28.6	16.1
1985	27.0	13.3
1986	26.5	11.8
1987	18.9	4.4
1988	0.0	0.9
		(0.6)*

* net financial *receipts*—i.e. investment income—exceeded interest charges in manufacturing.

Source: Tokyo Stock Exchange.

in securities activities. Similarly, Japanese brokers want to be able to move into lucrative areas that have traditionally been set aside for banks, if possible without giving up their exclusive hold on their extremely profitable securities business. The question of reforming Article 65 (the Japanese law which closely resembles the US Glass–Steagall provisions), however controversial and locked into immovable opposition it may appear, will have to be resolved during the 1990s—presumably soon after, or perhaps even leading, any legislative changes to the US Glass–Steagall Act. Otherwise, the Japanese market will be entirely out of alignment with markets in Europe and the United States. American and European banks and securities firms will use every opportunity (as they have over matters of Tokyo Stock Exchange membership) to force roughly equivalent Japanese deregulation and substantial equality of market access. Failure to change Article 65 sets up the question in both the EC and in the US of imposing sanctions under existing or proposed reciprocity provisions.

Repeal of Article 65 will dramatically alter the competitive structure of financial intermediation in Japan. In the United States there are a dozen or so large securities firms preparing to face competition from a handful of large and adequately capitalized banks with the demise of Glass–Steagall. In Japan four large securities firms face sixteen large City banks, three long-term credit banks, and a dozen trust banks and co-operative banks with major aspirations in the securities field. Certainly, the coming battle between the traditionally well-capitalized and well-connected banks and the big securities firms will have a number of important competitive consequences for Japanese and non-Japanese players alike.

2. Negotiating Commissions

Fixed commission rates in Japan are required by the Tokyo Stock Exchange—virtually the last major exchange in the world that does not mandate negotiated commissions between customer and broker—although in recent years there have been a number of authorized institutional discounts from standard rates for large orders. It is inevitable in the 1990s that the Japanese commission structure will collapse, after which competition for securities transactions will—as in the case of Mayday in the United States, Big Bang in Great Britain, and virtually everywhere else negotiated rates have been introduced—become very bloody indeed. This will be true especially if the big banks are allowed into the game at the same time, as was the case in the United Kingdom.

Japanese brokers trace virtually all of their profitability to domestic brokerage commissions. They are reluctant block traders, offer little else in the way of service beyond taking orders against the latest stock ideas, and are heavily overstaffed for what they do. Profit pressure could be exceedingly tough for these firms for some time, especially if competent, smaller-sized foreign brokers are nicking off their clients with block trading and research services. Several foreign firms operating in Tokyo have been able to demonstrate their ability to do this, and a few have introduced US programme trading techniques and other derivatives-related business into Tokyo and have become very profitable in the process. It is certainly not unthinkable for foreign firms to develop a significant share of securities activities in Japan, assuming a fully level playing field and large commitments of time and resources.

3. *New-Issue Market Reforms*

Japan must also bring its domestic new-issue capital market access conditions into line with those of the United States and Europe. This has not been the case in the past, new securities issues being subject to substantial regulations that have limited market usage to a comparatively small number of blue-chip companies, queuing delays, interest rate controls, collateralization requirements, and approval of 'commission banks' (City banks acting as trustees for bondholders). Accordingly, most Japanese corporations have preferred to utilize the Eurobond market, where none of these obstacles exist, even when the investors in their securities are overwhelmingly Japanese. During 1987–9, for example, in excess of $100 billion of Japanese debt issues with equity purchase warrants attached were offered to Euromarket investors, although most of these securities (perhaps 70–80 per cent) were ultimately sold back to investors in Japan. The round-tripping to escape confining new-issue conditions in the domestic market was motivated almost entirely by financial arbitrage on the part of the issuers.

The authorities finally began to act in 1989 to bring this business back to Japan by liberalizing the standards to be met by Japanese companies seeking to use the domestic public bond markets, by introducing shelf-registration procedures to provide quicker access to markets, and by proposing that securities issued abroad bought predominantly by Japanese investors be registered in Japan. These steps, along with fewer opportunities for gain in financial arbitrage, should substantially curtail the use of the Euromarket for the purposes of Japanese round-tripping. An important result of recapturing this business for Japan, however, would be the continued liberalization of market-access rules, in turn increasing further the volume of corporate new issues in the Japanese market. Many of these issues, like Rule 144A issues in the United

States and Euromarket issues, could well be sold on a global basis to foreign investors.

Market Realignments in the 1990s

Most capital market issues, wherever they originate, will be capable of being offered simultaneously to investors worldwide by the middle of the 1990s. Those investors will continue to differ significantly as to their preferences for names of issuers, for the form of the issue (e.g. bearer form, as opposed to registered form), for maturities, and for currencies—although the latter can be easily and cheaply accommodated through currency swaps and hedging instruments. Institutional investors will emerge as the dominant buyers, even in Europe, as more individuals switch to performance-oriented investment funds. Issuers shopping for the lowest-cost financing opportunities will find substantial investing capacity in the emerging integrated European market, the post-144A US market, and in a newly unrestricted Japanese domestic bond market.

The development of a global, 'seamless' fixed-income securities market may begin to resemble the global, 'seamless' market in foreign exchange and certain commodities. The resemblance will be greater as the volume and spread characteristics of the bond markets fall into line with those of the foreign exchange market. Competitive skills in the foreign exchange markets, with related activities in swaps and hedging, may indeed become a model for what it takes to succeed as leaders in the debt markets of the 1990s. Such changes in world bond markets will substantially alter the character of the market-place for debt securities and those competing in it.

The markets for equity securities have never been the same as debt markets; the volume of activity is much less, and each individual stock is different from all the others. But as volume increases, as electronic trading and settlement takes over from the traditional pit-based markets, as commission rates become very low (as in the US and London), and as technology encroaches on individual trading skills, the market in equities too will change along the same lines as the bond markets. Banks will see opportunities to move in alongside securities firms and competition will be intensified greatly, particularly in Continental Europe and in Japan.

There should thus develop during the 1990s powerful capital market centres in the United States, Europe, and Japan that are predominantly regional but none the less global in operation. These markets will be extremely competitive, internally and with each other, forcing some well-known players to retire to other pursuits or to market niches. The three principal hubs will adopt essentially similar principles of market governance: (*a*) Universal banking will be permitted; (*b*) commission rates will be negotiated; (*c*) foreign banks and brokers will gradually approach market access equal to locals although in some environments it will require a long, sustained effort; (*d*) cross-border investment demand will become a major factor in all securities trading; and (*e*) similar, if not standardized, trading rules, disclosure requirements, settlement procedures, and capital requirements will apply to securities firms (as they will to banks).

Changes in government policies, of course, could once again substantially alter these conclusions. Protectionism could undo much of the real-sector market integration already achieved. The Middle East crisis of 1990 could have unforeseen and long-lasting repercussions. The 1992 initiatives in Europe could give way to internal squabbling and foot-dragging, or be derailed by developments in Eastern Europe, or by disputes over alignment of monetary and tax policies. Japan or the United States could further delay the deregulation needed to assure all markets and competitors a level playing field. Capital controls could be reimposed. Policies affecting savings rates and capital formation, mergers and acquisitions, leveraged transactions, enforcement of securities laws, foreign direct investment, and competition could likewise force reversals in market evolution.

Barring such developments, however, the configuration of the financial markets at the end of the 1990s could in many ways constitute a global modernization of financial capacity, which in turn could help to lower the cost of capital, including all of its agency costs, and provide a basis for sustained world economic growth during the next century. As such, the financial markets of the future will not be government dependent. They will constitute independent sources of funds provided by the private sector, and the role of the market itself will dominate. Thus, it may resemble the global financial market of the period prior to the First World War, when the role of governments was slight as against that of the private sector, and the market played the dominant role in allocating capital. In that context, perhaps the world of finance will exit this century much as it entered it.

References

Arthur Andersen & Co. (1989), *European Capital Markets: A Strategic Forecast* (London: Economist Publications).

Bank for International Settlements (1986), *Recent Innovations in International Banking* (Basle: Bank for International Settlements).

Bloch, Ernest (1989), *Inside Investment Banking* (2nd edn.) (Homewood, Ill.: Dow Jones Irwin).

Dermine, Jean (ed.) (1990), *European Banking in the 1990s* (Oxford: Basil Blackwell).

Hayes, Samuel, III, Spence, A. M. and Marks, D. V. P. (1983), *Competition in the Investment Banking Industry* (Cambridge, Mass.: Harvard University Press).

Jensen, Michael C., and Ruback, Richard S. (1983), 'The Market for Corporate Control: The Scientific Evidence', *Journal of Financial Economics*, Vol. 2.

Kallberg, Jarl S., and Saunders, Anthony (1986), *Direct Sources of Competitiveness in Banking Services* (New York University: Salomon Center) (mimeo).

Levich, Richard M. (1988), 'Financial Innovation in International Financial Markets', in M. Feldstein (ed.), *The United States in the World Economy* (Chicago: University of Chicago Press).

Office of Technology Assessment, US Congress (1986), *International Competition in Banking and Financial Services* (Washington, DC: OTA) (July) (mimeo).

Organization for Economic Cooperation and Development (1983), *Trade in Services in Banking* (Paris: OECD).

Pastré, Olivier (1981), 'International Bank-Industry Relations: An Empirical Assessment', *Journal of Banking and Finance* (March).

Rybczynski, T. N. (1989), 'Corporate Restructuring', *National Westminster Bank Review* (August).

Securities and Exchange Commission. Securities Act of 1933, Rule 144A and Amendments to Rule 144 and 145 (1988), *Federal Register*, 53 FR 44016 (1 November).

Smith, Roy C., and Walter, Ingo (1991), 'European Industrial Restructuring and the Market for Corporate Control', in Karel Cool, Damien Neven, and Ingo Walter (eds.), *Economic Restructuring in Europe* (London: Macmillan).

Walter, Ingo (ed.) (1985), *Deregulating Wall Street* (New York: John Wiley & Sons).

—— (1988), *Global Competition in Financial Services* (Cambridge, Mass.: Ballinger–Harper & Row).

—— and Smith, Roy C. (1989), *Investment Banking in Europe: Restructuring for the 1990s* (Oxford: Basil Blackwell).

[13]

The changing world of banking

The globalization of financial markets

Joel A. Bleeke and Lowell L. Bryan

If there were any justification needed for understanding the globalization of the world's capital markets, the "crash" of October 19, 1987 certainly provided it. What was happening in London, Tokyo, Hong Kong and Zurich was suddenly as important to American investors as the news from Wall Street itself, and the same urgent interest in multimarket information gripped their counterparts overseas.

Though October's abrupt and simultaneous decline in world stock prices surprised nearly everybody, the fact that capital markets have become increasingly linked is not in itself surprising, especially to members of the professional financial community. But what, in fact, is the nature of the linkages? Are the linkages cyclical or a new, permanent reality? And what are the strategic implications of the global relationships for various players in this new kind of marketplace?

In the following article, Joel Bleeke and Lowell Bryan tackle such questions, and offer both valuable insights and occasionally surprising answers. In distinguishing a "global" from an "international" perspective, the authors argue for the need to think beyond cross-border flows of capital to a broadly integrated, large but single marketplace.

Rolando Polli
McKinsey & Company

In the tumultuous weeks of mid-October, new questions were on the minds of many Americans: not only "What was the Dow yesterday?" but "What was the Tokyo close?" and "Where's London at now?" Traders and investors in New York, Tokyo, London and bourses around the world paid unprecedented attention to what was happening in each others' markets. A weak morning in Lon-

Exhibit I **Fall of world stock markets, October 1987**

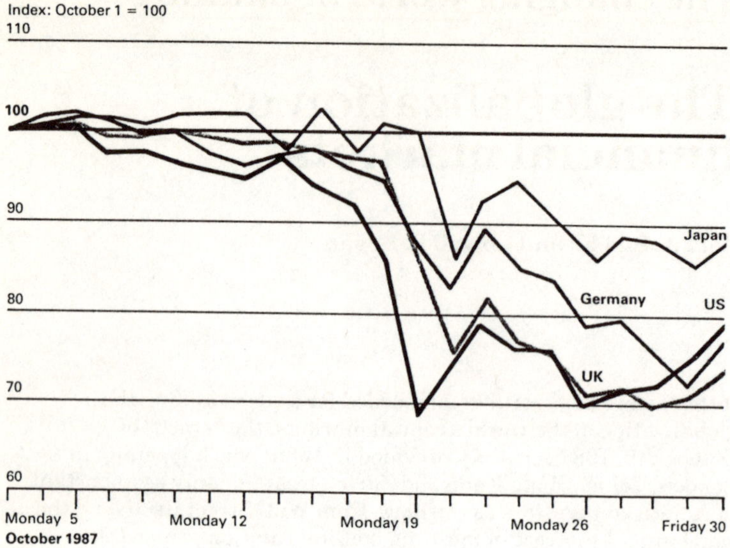

Source: *Financial Times*

don often spelled a poor open in New York. An uptick in Tokyo was welcome solace for London and New York. By the close of the month, all major world markets were down significantly (Exhibit I).

Globalization is not, of course, limited to the equities market; trading volumes of all financial instruments have also soared worldwide. Indeed, linkages in the foreign exchange and bond markets are stronger and longer established than in the equity markets. Traders in London, New York, Tokyo, Frankfurt and Zurich, among others, are increasingly making markets and exchanging instruments in currencies other than their own. Such trading has been done in modest amounts for a long time; what is distinctive today is the enormity of the cross-border business. For example, foreign exchange trading is now running at $65 trillion per year – while the total annual amount of world trade in goods is closer to $4 trillion.

In the primary markets, too, corporations, banks and sovereign governments have borrowed massive amounts – often in innova-

Exhibit II **Growth of international vs. domestic bonds outstanding, 1980-85**

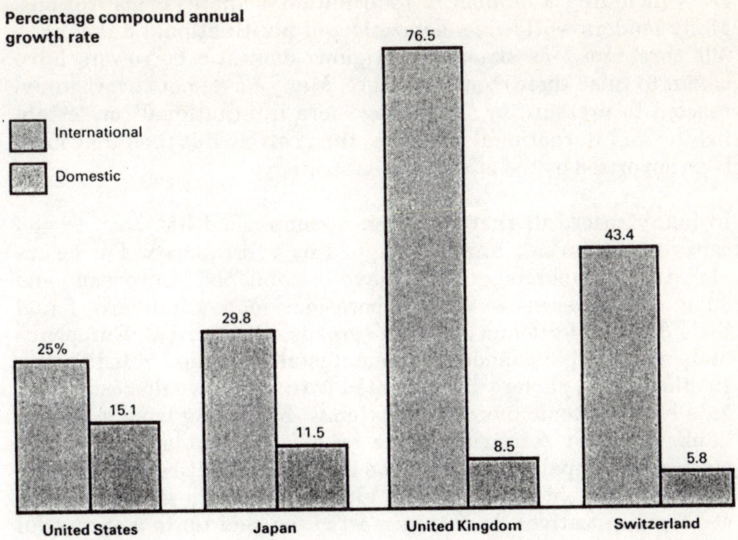

Source: Salomon Brothers

tive multicurrency offerings – in the Eurobond market over the last several years, and the growth of international bonds outstanding has outstripped the growth of most national markets (Exhibit II). Meanwhile, huge volumes of funds have also been raised, cross-border, in various domestic markets (e.g., European commercial banks raise commercial paper in the United States, US corporations raise money in the Japanese bond market).

Global vs. international thinking

Clearly, something is having a profound, global effect on financial institutions, corporations and investors. But, so far, most participants are not sure what to do about it – and, in fact, many are probably acting against their own best interests because they are thinking internationally, rather than globally. What is the difference? An international thinker sees the world as a series of national markets. A global thinker sees it as an interconnected, integrated marketplace. The two mind-sets result in very different programs of action.

International thinkers

Among financial institutions, there are many international thinkers – including a number of multinational financial institutions. Many lenders worldwide, domestic and multinational alike, have felt threatened as strong, prestigious domestic borrowers have begun to raise their money offshore. Many have, not surprisingly, reacted to pressure by "becoming more international" or "establishing an international presence" themselves. But then they have been surprised by the effects of this strategy.

In many cases, all that has been accomplished has been to add capacity in markets already plagued by overcapacity. For example, US commercial banks have established European and Japanese presences to lend corporations money but have found little demand for loans and thin spreads upon arrival. Europeans and Japanese have made the same mistakes in the United States. In other cases, players disenchanted with their own domestic markets have "become more international" by buying troubled retail banks in other countries. Since as a rule troubled banks lack strong local capabilities, let alone global capabilities, these banks have not brought their aquirers global success. In short, multiple strategic initiatives do not, in most cases, add up to a successful global strategy.

To a large extent, financial institutions are victims of globalization, since the entire process of global finance is being driven by domestic borrowers, who are seeking to take advantage of a global marketplace to raise money more cheaply than through domestic sources, and by domestic investors seeking higher returns than are available locally. To the extent they succeed, financial institutions, often domestic commercial banks, wind up with lower profits. Foreign participants, trying to crack into formerly domestic markets which are already awash with capacity, add little value by trying to compete.

And the increased volatility for which globalization may in part be responsible has magnified the risk faced by institutions, as many recent trading losses demonstrate.

Global drivers' problems

At the same time, the drivers of globalization – domestically or even multinationally oriented corporations – are having their own problems. True, they are finding that they can use global corporate finance to lower their costs of raising capital. But they are also finding that in their main business, the production of goods, they are being exposed to unbelievable risks due to currency movements that are, in turn – at least partially – being driven by the globalization of the world's financial markets. German and Japanese manufacturers have had to face a 40 percent decrease in the value of the dollar against their currencies over the last year and a half. This has both made their domestically produced goods less competitive and lowered the worth of their international investments in the United States.

The same thing happened to US manufacturers between 1981 and 1985, and many have yet to recover from the loss of competitiveness they suffered at that time. Still reeling from this experience, corporations in the United States spent enormously in 1985 and 1986 on operating and financial strategies to protect themselves from a strengthening dollar just when the dollar began its rapid descent, thus negating many of the benefits of a depreciating currency. In the process, it has made it harder for the US trade deficit to turn around (i.e., the J-curve has taken a long time to take effect).

We believe that such strategies are also the result of thinking internationally rather than globally. For example, international thinking leads to assessing currency risk as bilateral when in fact it is multilateral. The interplay and linkages between operating and financial strategies are far more complex in a global world than in an international world.

Finally, investors have fallen into the trap of thinking internationally. For example, last July Japanese life insurance companies wrote off $14 billion of the stated value of their holdings of US Treasuries due to the depreciation of the dollar against the yen. Simply making international cross-border investments in bonds is clearly not a sufficient response. Similarly, an exclusive focus on international equity investments would have proven disastrous given October's declines in world stock markets. Again, a global portfolio perspective is needed which takes into account how the instruments of investment are affected by global financial linkages.

The global players

If going "international" is not an effective response to a globalizing marketplace, what is? The fact is that, while everyone is talking about "globalization," most admit they do not really understand what is happening. However, a few of the leading banks, securities firms, industrial companies and institutional investors appear to be playing an effective global game.

What insights are the leading players basing their strategies on? From what we have seen, they are not just thinking about the "globalization of financial markets" purely in terms of the increasingly large cross-border flow of capital and the related increase in cross-border corporate finance (e.g., Eurobond finance, purchases of US Treasury bonds by Japanese investors). Rather, they – and we – define "globalization" as the process by which the world's various national financial marketplaces are beginning to act as if they were one single, integrated marketplace.

Global finance is one important element of this move to globalization, to be sure, and most of our discussion with issuers, intermediaries and investors in 12 countries earlier in 1987 focused on the issues of global capital flows and global corporate finance. But more important, we believe, are the pricing linkages being forged across national borders. The remarkably similar falls in the equity markets last October demonstrate the critical effect of these price linkages.

Our objective in this article is simple. We want to encourage the adoption of a global, rather than an international, financial mind-set – a mind-set that centers on the linked financial markets, rather than on cross-border flows of funds. To support our proposition that this is the right course, we will:

¶ Describe the linkages that are developing worldwide

¶ Demonstrate that these represent permanent, irreversible change despite recent events in the stock market

¶ Suggest how participants in the global financial marketplace should develop the mind-set they need to play their new, successful roles – whether those roles are played out in the global arena or a purely domestic one.

Linkages are increasing

Thinking of "globalization" in terms of market linkages, rather than cross-border flows of funds, forces us to view the globalization phenomenon differently. Financial flows will wax and wane, driven by cyclical factors which may or may not be sustainable in

Exhibit III **Linkages between instruments**

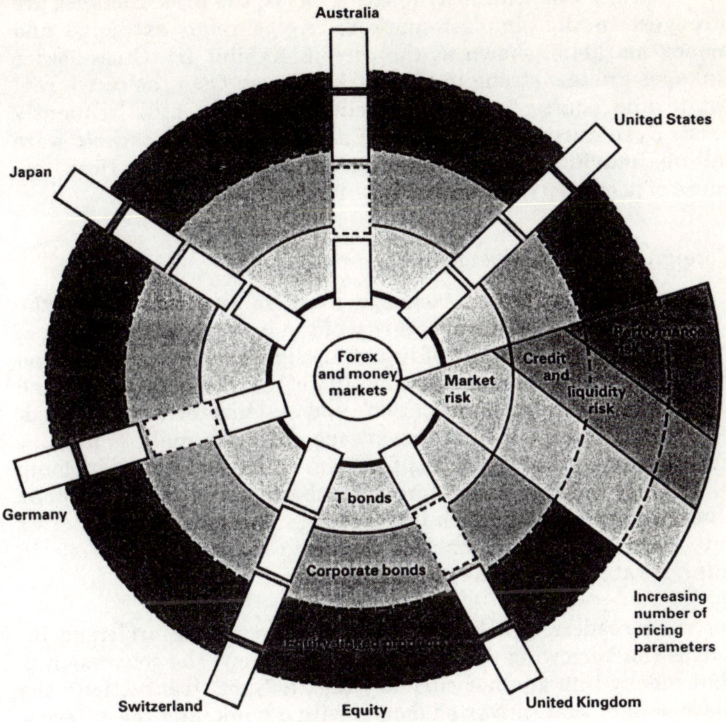

the long run. If that were the extent of globalization, it too could be just a cyclical phenomenon.

On the other hand, if globalization of financial markets is the process by which domestic financial markets are becoming more closely linked together, so that the price of financial instruments in one market is significantly affected by supply and demand of funds in other markets, then that represents a structural, not cyclical, change – for reasons we will explain in the next section. Even in Europe, where this change occurred years earlier, the financial linkages within Europe and between Europe, the United States and Japan have become much stronger. Let us now look at the linkages in question.

The strength of global pricing linkages appears to depend significantly on the number and the complexity of the risks influencing the price of a financial instrument. That is, the price linkages are strongest in the simplest markets (e.g., foreign exchange and money markets), shown at the core in Exhibit III. Cross-border linkages are less strong in the markets away from the core – real estate and equities – where pricing anomalies still frequently exist. Even during October, while all major equity markets were falling, individual cross-border equities were still "mispriced" because of poor information and imperfect market linkages.

Foreign exchange market linkages strongest

Linkages in the foreign exchange markets are tight due to the simplicity and short-term maturity of the instruments, the lack of restrictions, the existence of liquid foreign exchange forward and futures markets, the ready availability of market information, and the low cost of telecommunications and systems technology. Traders and arbitrageurs take advantage of even small, transitory misalignments in the prices of financial instruments and, in doing so, tightly link the world's foreign exchange and money markets. One major process by which this occurs is through covered interest rate arbitrage, which enables traders to exploit differentials in interest rate and foreign exchange prices.

As most readers will know, covered interest rate arbitrage involves the borrowing of money in one currency, the conversion of that money into another currency (i.e., a "spot" transaction), the placement of that converted money with a bank, and the entering into an agreement (e.g., a forward foreign exchange contract) to reconvert that money at the end of the placement period back into the original currency. This money is then used to repay the borrowing in the original currency and the participant is left with a risk-free profit. There are opportunities for such profits whenever the interest differential between the borrowing and placement exceeds the differential between the spot rate and the forward rate less the costs of doing the transaction. There are also similar opportunities for such profit whenever the rate between the spot and forward exchange rates exceeds the interest rate differential between the borrowing and placing rates less the transaction costs (Exhibit IV).

After a decade of technological advancement and continuous structural investment by participants, most of the physical barriers that used to preserve these pricing anomalies between mar-

Exhibit IV **Structure of a covered interest arbitrage transaction between US dollar and deutsche Mark**

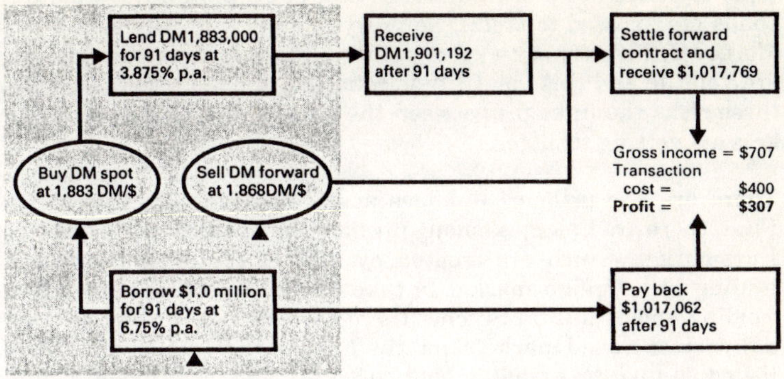

Source: McKinsey analysis

kets have been removed. For example, global telecommunications systems for both voice and data transmission are now far more effective and far more efficient (i.e., the cost per message unit has fallen sharply). Most of the major participants have automated systems that continuously search for arbitrage opportunities through the simultaneous analysis of data for multiple markets. Some participants are even planning systems that can complete arbitrage transactions without human intervention.

All of this has led to huge surges in volumes. To put this in perspective, the number of money market and foreign exchange payments settled annually just through the New York Bank Clearinghouse CHIPS system expanded from 13.2 million to 31.3 million between 1980 and 1987. The volume of dollars settled per day increased from $147.9 billion to $533.7 billion during the same period.

Today, covered interest rate arbitrage opportunities persist for only moments before they disappear, but because of the enormous trading volumes involved, the profits for the leading players (e.g., major commercial and investment banks) are still frequently large, although the margins are minuscule. In the process, the foreign exchange and money markets of the major industrial countries have become quite tightly linked and changes in the price of any one instrument in one currency affect the price of other instruments in other currencies almost simultaneously.

Bond market linkages are developing

Linkages in the bond market are somewhat weaker, because the risks of bonds are more numerous and more complex. Corporate bonds are exposed to credit, liquidity and often prepayment risk. Moreover, inflationary expectations relative to future inflations are volatile and this volatility is reflected in bond prices. Despite these risks the linkages between the various domestic bond markets are getting stronger.

There are two primary linkages across domestic bond markets. First, there are linkages among primary domestic markets and the Euromarket, which are created by mainly corporate borrowers issuing in a foreign market to take advantage of less expensive funding opportunities. Second, there are linkages among secondary domestic bond markets and the Euromarket, which are established by investors trading both corporate and government bonds outside their home market.

In the primary markets, issuers forge linkages when they take advantage of pricing discrepancies across markets to secure a lower-cost source of funding. These pricing discrepancies are created by differences in accounting standards, access to information, regulatory constraints, taxation, financial services industry structure, cultural patterns and investor attitudes.

For example, enormous foreign investment assets have been built up in Switzerland – partly because tax evasion is not a criminal offense there and partly because of Switzerland's tough privacy laws which enable investors who avoid their local national laws (i.e., "flight capital") to be protected from detection. These assets create a huge demand for "bearer" instruments – i.e., unregistered instruments that do not identify the owner, even to tax authorities. Eurodollar bonds by US issuers are in "bearer" form; in the United States, corporate bonds and equities are registered. US issuers who place their bonds in the Eurobond market, with private banking clients of Swiss banks, are often able to issue at better rates than they can get in the United States because the banks making portfolio decisions for private investors care more about privacy for their clients than obtaining the absolutely highest yield.

Certain issuers can also take advantage of another discrepancy between the markets to obtain lower-cost funding: Eurobond issues are priced largely upon the "name" recognition of the issuer. This is because US investors have historically been more sensitive to nuances of credit risk than offshore Eurobond investors, who are less used to evaluating credit risk on the basis of ratings and who have only recently begun to use them. Therefore, a US single-A company with a good, well-recognized name can raise money in the Eurobond market at AA or AAA rates, thus saving a quarter to a half percent on their borrowing rates.

Bond market linkages have been greatly strengthened in recent years by the development of interest rate and currency swaps, which allow a low-cost transformation of the interest rate type (e.g., floating to fixed) and the currency of the financing. After the skyrocketing interest rates of the early 1980s, the 1982 liberalization of deposit rates in the United States led to a dramatic increase in the floating rate liabilities of US commercial and savings banks.

These institutions in turn sought matching floating rate assets, which led to a collapse of floating rate lending spreads in the United States. This created a situation where BBB US corporations could borrow far more cheaply on a floating rate basis (e.g., 0.25 percent over what AAA borrowers would pay) than they could in the fixed-rate market (e.g., 1.50 percent over what AAA borrowers would pay). Therefore, AAA borrowers from all nations were able to raise fixed-rate dollars (where they had a significant competitive advantage) and BBB borrowers were able to raise floating rate dollars (where they had a relative comparative advantage) and use interest rate swaps to exchange interest exposers.

This enabled AAA borrowers to raise floating rate money at a lower cost than they would otherwise have had to borrow at. It also enabled BBB borrowers to borrow fixed-rate money at a lower rate than they would otherwise have had to pay. Finally, it also enabled an intermediary to earn a fee for arranging the swap and for arranging the bond issue.

In the secondary markets, national bond markets are also becoming far more closely linked. Bonds and notes, once issued, remain outstanding until they are redeemed, are called, or default. With maturities, upon issuance, ranging from 2 years to 20 years or more, the only way for an investor to get his money back before the issue is redeemed is to sell it in the secondary market.

Historically, domestic secondary markets are self-contained, but they have become increasingly linked through the same technology changes that have enabled the foreign exchange and money markets to be linked. There is even a trading practice equivalent

Exhibit V **Yields on US long-term bonds by quality of issue, June 30, 1986**

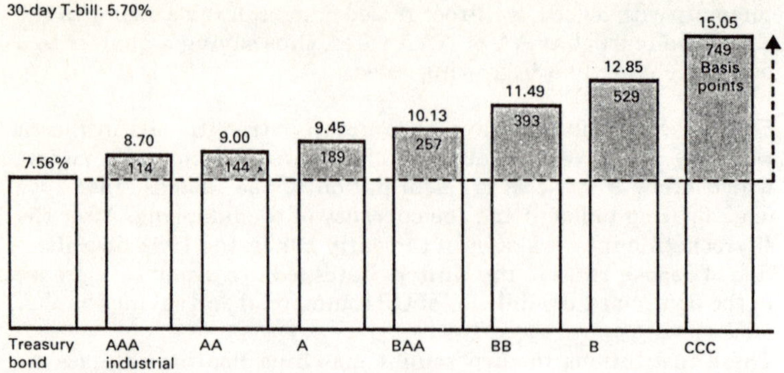

Source: Salomon Brothers

to covered interest rate arbitrage that uses bonds and currency swaps rather than money and foreign exchange market instruments. There are some arbitrage differences, however. For one, because the linkages among markets are looser, owing to the complexity of the risks involved, arbitrage opportunities with bonds last longer. For another, because the markets are imperfectly linked and the instruments have longer durations, the spreads are larger. And finally, because of the complexity of the instrument, the arbitrageur cannot factor out all risk, as he can in the money and foreign exchange markets.

In addition to direct arbitrage linkages, the prices of all bonds are linked through investors searching for the best risk-adjusted yield. Such linkages have long existed in national markets. Local investors are always trading off the risks and returns of money market instruments with medium- and long-term corporate and government bonds, thereby moving up and down the yield curve and trading off various credit, liquidity and prepayment risks against differences in yield. In the process, pricing relationships between instruments change continuously. For example, in the United States the differences between the yield on the highest quality corporate bond and a "speculative" grade (i.e., "junk") bond of similar maturity can be over 4 percent (Exhibit V), which reflects the premiums buyers require before they will take the higher credit and liquidity risks represented by junk bonds.

Exhibit VI **Yield volatility* of 10-year government bonds, 1982-86**

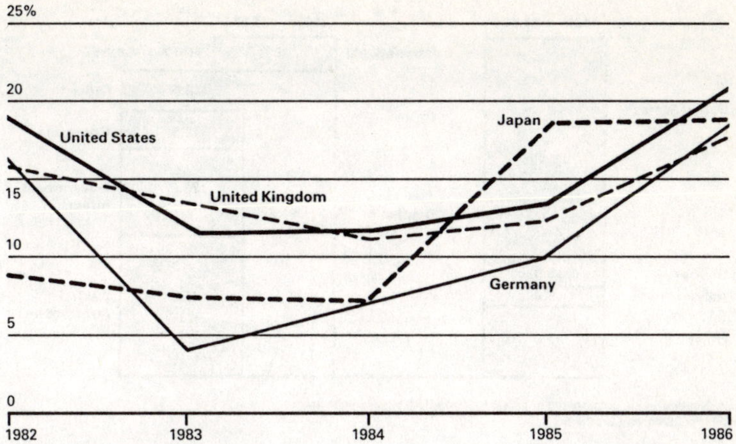

* Annualized rates based on daily data

Source: Salomon Brothers

Increasingly, investors are making such pricing tradeoffs between the Eurobond secondary market and national secondary markets. As a result, Eurobonds sold by Japanese corporations are increasingly winding up in the portfolios of Japanese investors, while Eurobonds sold by American corporations are winding up in the portfolios of American investors. This led to some embarrassment for US regulators just last summer, when the US Treasury invalidated the Netherlands Antilles tax treaty exempting Eurobonds issued before 1984 from US withholding taxes. In fact, they were surprised to discover that 20 percent of the holders were Americans – none of whom were allowed to purchase the bonds until their primary placement was completed.

Even more fundamentally, investors are now trading off more and more the yields between bonds issued in their own currency with yields issued in other countries' currencies. One of the reasons why Japanese investors, such as the large life insurance companies, have been willing to take the currency risk implicit in investment in US Treasury bonds is the low nominal yield available to them in domestic 10-year Japanese government issues (i.e., 5 percent) relative to the nominal yield in 10-year US Treasury issues (i.e., 8 percent).

Exhibit VII **World bond markets by country and type of issue, year-end 1986***

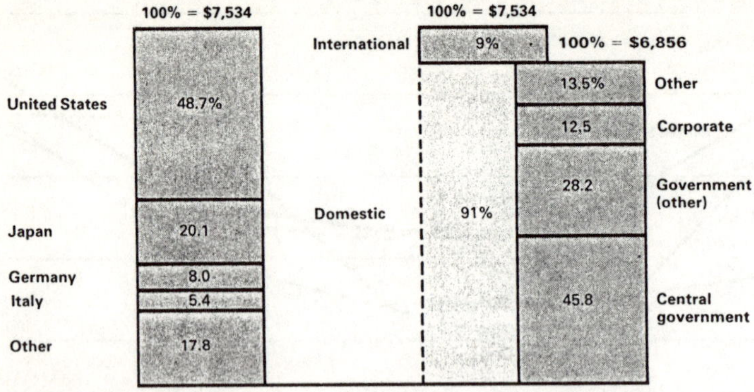

* Nominal value outstanding of public issues in US $ billions equivalent
Source: Salomon Brothers

The combination of this increasing interdependence due to trading arbitrage and cross-border, cross-instrument and cross-currency trading is leading to a convergence in bond volatility across the world (Exhibit VI). In some countries, like the United States, bond yields have become highly correlated with changes in the value of the dollar against other currencies.

While most observers' attention has been focused on the volume of new cross-border issues in the Eurobond market, the increase of pricing linkages in the world's existing total stock of bonds (approaching $7.5 trillion by the end of 1986, of which $3.7 trillion were issued in the United States and $1.5 trillion were issued in Japan, as Exhibit VII shows) is perhaps a more important trend. Increasingly, bond prices in all markets are being affected directly by global events, as more and more bond instruments issued in different markets get more and more closely linked by traders – although the linkages will probably never be as strong as in the foreign exchange and money markets, because of the complexity of the bonds themselves.

Equity markets less linked by arbitrage mechanisms

Pricing linkages are weakest among equity markets, where significant differences in price/earnings ratios exist across different markets, even for comparable companies in the same industry. In the primary equity markets, no simple product technology is currently available that would allow multinational corporations to take advantage in their equity issues of the different price/earnings ratios available in different markets. In the secondary market, cross-border equity investments require very sophisticated analytical skills and research capabilities, given the greater complexity of equity pricing which involves assessment of credit, liquidity and performance risk.

But the remarkably similar rise and fall of the world's equities markets demonstrates that, despite the hurdles, cross-border equity markets too are becoming more closely linked, in large part by investor psychology. Selling pressure during October last year was fueled by nervous foreign investors who began beating a retreat from unfamiliar markets. Foreigners on the Tokyo stock exchange sold a record 1.12 trillion yen worth of equities in the week of October 19.

We believe that the linkage of equity markets is likely to be much less perfect than linkages in bond and foreign exchange markets for the medium-term future. Cross-border equity markets entail many complex, difficult-to-evaluate risks and the trend has been for equity markets to be only loosely correlated. Indeed, many studies have shown this weak correlation makes international equity portfolios less risky than purely domestic portfolios. But equity linkages are clearly developing and will continue to develop as cross-border information on management quality, hidden reserves, cash flows, and so on, improves.

Linkages represent permanent structural change

We believe pricing linkages in all types of financial assets will continue to grow stronger because we believe the underlying forces at work are structural rather than cyclical. The evolutions in telecommunications, systems and new product technology mentioned earlier have significantly reduced the transaction costs of global financial operations and expanded cross-country financial flow volumes in the same way that a reduction in transportation costs opened the way for international trade to flow in response to patterns of comparative advantage. This is a structural change, which has permanently broadened access to global financial markets. Supply and demand forces that were previously confined to national borders (e.g., the liberalization of deposit ceilings in the United States or the savings rate in Japan) are now spilling over and affecting prices of financial instruments worldwide.

There are three other reasons why the linkages among financial markets are likely to endure:

¶ Many players have already invested heavily in the infrastructure of globalization.

¶ Many players are reaping enormous benefits from globalization, which they will resist giving up.

¶ Regulatory bodies could be powerless to re-erect national barriers, given the size of the existing linkages.

Let us look at each of these in turn.

Investments already made

The players making the investments in technology and infrastructure that are allowing all of this to happen are former domestic players who are becoming committed to fundamentally different global roles. The most committed participants are the global banks and global securities companies that have made enormous investments in systems, telecommunications, staff and premises in London, New York, Tokyo and elsewhere. Even recent 10 percent staff layoffs by two large investment banking and securities firms in London have left their foreign capital markets presence well above the levels of a year or two ago.

Similarly, some global industrial companies all over the world have made huge commitments and have built up advanced inhouse banks. Indeed, the investments of some of the global trading companies which capitalize on their telecommunications systems and their trading-oriented corporate culture rival the investments of the major global banks and securities firms.

Not far behind are institutional investors. In most countries, nonbank institutional investors are becoming a more important channel for the flow of financial assets (Exhibit VIII). In Japan, for example, pension fund and life insurance company assets have grown at compounded annual rates of 25 and 16 percent, respectively, over the last 6 years as annual GDP has grown at a 5.3 percent compounded rate. Similar trends are taking place in Switzerland, Germany, Britain and the United States.

As they grow in size and sophistication, these institutions are becoming increasingly interested in exploring opportunities from

Exhibit VIII **Evolution of US and German personal financial assets, 1980-85**

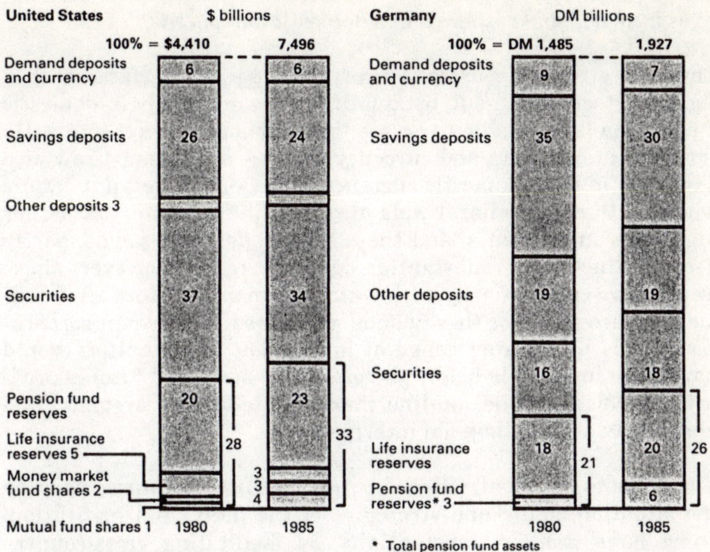

Source: Federal Reserve Bank; Deutsche Bundesbank; Salomon Brothers

global investment – particularly in Germany, Switzerland and Japan, where their domestic investment alternatives are limited and where they continue to have enormous inflows of money to invest. Indeed, many of them already hold enormous cross-border investments, and this makes them structurally committed to the global financial marketplace.

Despite the events of October, there is little indication that institutional investors are abandoning their global sights long-term. Two weeks after "Black Monday" Baring Brothers, a London merchant bank, held an international investment conference. The keynote speaker extolled the virtues of the South Korean stock market, which had hit new highs while other world markets fell.

Benefits will not be given up

The structural commitment of the major players is one reason why we believe the linkages among markets are permanent; a second is that virtually all players are likely to be reluctant to give up the benefits of globalization. By strengthening links across domestic financial markets, globalization has created better funding options and investment opportunities for those who assess their alternatives from a global rather than a domestic perspective.

Thus, for example, Australian corporate *borrowers,* faced with a significant crowding-out by public borrowers in their domestic market, have been able to access the Eurobond market indirectly through interest rate and currency swaps – and thus borrow at a fixed rate in their domestic currency. The German retail *investors* who buy the Australian bonds also benefit. They are starved for high-yield investments, and these bonds offer high yields, partly because they carry substantial currency risks. However, these issues have credit quality with which German investors are familiar, because many of these bonds are issued by German corporations. This broadening range of investment opportunities would have been impossible before the era of the swap and futures product technology, global on-line market intelligence systems, and global networks of financial intermediaries.

The benefits of globalization for *financial intermediaries* vary by the situation, skills and strategies of the individual institution. Some have profited substantially by facilitating cross-country flows and leveraging product innovation skills, product niches and global networks; others with strong protected domestic franchises have been hurt by the increased level of competition and are searching for alternatives to confront competitive threats and for new opportunities created by the changing environment.

Globalization has thus significantly changed the rules of the financial world. It has created new opportunities for all players, and new threats to intermediaries who fail to adjust to a global environment. We believe that, to the extent that there are persistent benefits for borrowers and investors, globalization will proceed largely unabated and will be irreversible. As history shows, economic agents seldom surrender newly won opportunities voluntarily, and market forces, once unleashed, can rarely be successfully reined in. The alternative to globalization is self-containment, but the main costs of self-containment are borne by the citizens of the country – the domestic borrowers and investors.

Reregulation infeasible

It is not surprising that the worldwide tumult in equity markets has led to calls for reregulation of financial markets. But we

Exhibit IX **Evolution of US current account balance and net international debt, 1978-87**

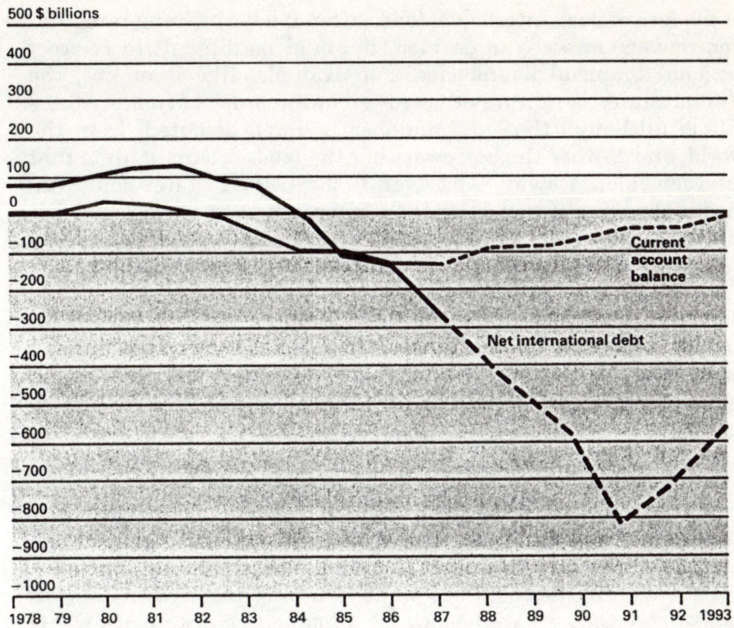

Source: Department of Commerce

question the ability of regulators to overcome the amount of financial interdependence that already exists between the nations of the world. Indeed, it is the enormous volume of cross-border instruments already outstanding that creates the greatest structural interdependence.

Even if each nation were able, miraculously, to run a balanced current account from now on and there were no new cross-border capital flows, the existing stock of cross-border financial instruments already outstanding would still remain, and the prices of those financial instruments would need to continue to adjust to all the differences in the various domestic economies (e.g., differentials in investment rates, savings rates, inflation rates). Since the opposite is likely to be true – that is, since cross-border capital flows are likely to continue to grow and current account surpluses and deficits seem likely to remain – we can expect to see the structural interdependence of the various national financial markets increase, rather than decrease.

In the face of such interdependence, even if a very strong reregulation movement were to develop, it would be difficult to re-erect national financial boundaries. For example, like it or not, the United States is now a net borrower in the order of roughly $250 billion (although the exact number is much disputed) from the world, and neither the borrowers nor the lenders can regulate that interdependence away. And even if the United States could immediately convert to a constantly improving current account balance, it will likely take into the year 2000 to get back to the degree of self-containment it had in the early 1980s (Exhibit IX).

Finally, regulation is a weak force compared to the marketplace under the best of circumstances. History has shown that financial innovation can overcome almost any regulatory barriers. In fact, much of the globalization existing today is the result of regulatory barriers.

Adopting a global mind-set

We are moving rapidly to a fully integrated, global financial marketplace. We are the first to admit that no one, including ourselves, fully understands what is taking place. But it seems undeniable that we are headed for a financial marketplace where the price of all financial instruments in all domestic markets is heavily affected, not just by the domestic supply and demand for that instrument, but by the supply and demand for all other financial instruments in other countries (excluding countries which still maintain exchange controls).

Yet most corporations, financial institutions and investors think about finance in national terms, even when they are internationally oriented. In the United States or Japan and – to a slightly lesser degree – in Europe, the overwhelming bulk of even informed participants operates on purely national models. People, worldwide, know intellectually that national economies have become more interdependent, but they lack the information flows, the decision frameworks, and the mind-set to act on that intellectual understanding.

What, then, should managers do? What does adopting a global mind-set mean? To us it means assuming that the marketplace is global rather than national. It means expecting opportunities to result from obtaining superior information about multiple markets, mobilizing that information across markets, and building decision frameworks which integrate that information. It means looking for anomalies between national markets and finding means to exploit them.

In other words, we believe that adopting a global mind-set means making decisions from an integrated, global perspective that assumes the interdependence of financial markets rather than the independence of those markets. Bearing this in mind, there is no requirement that a player must participate through having extensive international operations or physical facilities. To the contrary, we expect that many of the successful players in the global financial marketplace will cultivate domestic franchises – but with a global perspective.

For a *financial institution,* a global mind-set will prompt such questions as: What are our sources of profit, and to what extent are they built on real skills rather than market shelters which are not likely to survive in a fully integrated global financial marketplace? Which of our local markets are underserved and are likely to create an opportunity for an innovative foreign player? How will the prices for the domestic financial instruments we use to invest, trade and raise money be affected by the global marketplace? How should this affect our financial strategies? What global products can be profitably delivered to our own customer base (before a global competitor offers them first)? Where are our foreign competitors taking advantage of their customers? What opportunities does this provide for us?

For an *industrial corporation,* a global mind-set will prompt such questions as: How can global financial strategies help us compete better in the production of goods? Where are there opportunities to exploit market anomalies between national financial markets to raise funds more cheaply? How are operating risks and currency risks linked? How can global operating and global financial strategies be better linked? How should our operating and financial strategies change to reflect the instability of exchange rates? Should we build up our global in-house banking capabilities?

For an *institutional investor,* a global mind-set will prompt such questions as: Where are there opportunities to exploit market anomalies between national financial markets to increase returns relative to the risks taken? What mix of investments provides the best global diversification – i.e., how risky is it to keep 100 percent invested in domestic financial instruments? How can risks be taken in pure form, that we understand, as opposed to bundled, global risks (e.g., currency, credit, market, interest, liquidity) that we do not understand? What are the real risk/return tradeoffs of various different investments in different instruments in different currencies?

Joel Bleeke is a Principal in the Chicago office and has worked extensively with financial institutions. *Lowell Bryan* is a Director in the New York office and a leader of the Firm's North American Financial Institutions Group (FIG) practice. This article is adapted from a research report issued by the McKinsey Globalization Project, an eight-month, worldwide practice development effort sponsored by the FIG practice and co-headed by the two authors. *Rolando Polli*, Managing Director of the Milan office, heads up the Firm's work on banking.

[14]

Excerpt from Yoon S. Park and Musa Essayyad (eds), *International Banking and Financial Centers*, 235–46

15. RECENT FUNCTIONAL CHANGES IN INTERNATIONAL FINANCE AND THEIR IMPLICATIONS FOR INTERNATIONAL FINANCIAL CENTERS

Yoon S. Park
George Washington University

INTRODUCTION

It is well known that the State of Alaska has experienced severe economic difficulties in recent years. The adverse economic impact on the people of Alaska is exacerbated by the fact that the state used to enjoy bountiful economic growth in the 1970s riding on the crest of the Alaskan oil boom.

The current economic difficulty poses a new challenge for Alaska. In this context, one can easily recognize the importance of international partnership for the future of Alaska's economic development, given the state's abundantly endowed natural resources and geographic and locational advantages. The relatively small population base of the state also requires the economies of scale made possible through external economic linkages. Therefore, international business should be a key part of the state's overall economic strategy, as Alaska needs foreign markets and international capital. Fortunately for Alaska, the state is strategically located within easy reach of the dynamic economies of the Asia-Pacific region.

Alaska can greatly benefit from diversification of its economic base, turning away from overdependence on a single resource industry. International business linkages will promote the process of economic diversification through foreign trade, foreign direct investments and the influx of entrepreneurial stimulus from the dynamic Asia-Pacific region. Foreign trade will not only provide the markets for Alaska's abundant natural resources such as fishery, timber, mining and energy, but also make it possible for Alaska's manufacturing industry to construct and operate optimum-size facilities, taking advantage of the economies of scale.

Alaska's geographic proximity to the Asia-Pacific region allows it a strategic advantage in accessing the region's countries, which can become attractive markets for Alaska's abundant natural resource products. Especially, the fast-growing countries such as Japan and the Asian NICs (the so-called "little Japans") lack the natural resources that are richly endowed in Alaska. Thus, Alaska and these Asia-Pacific countries are ideal partners in foreign trade and economic development.

Of course, development of Alaska's natural resources requires both capital and management. In addition to foreign trade, therefore, Alaska should also encourage foreign direct investments in the state. In recent years, the world debt crisis has led to increasing reluctance of both the international banking community and multinational corporations to make further financial commitments in most developing countries, which are suffering from heavy foreign debt burden. Since the world debt crisis emerged to the surface in 1982, the debt problems of developing countries have become worse rather than getting better. The total foreign debt of developing countries has increased from about $600 billion in 1982 to over $1 trillion in 1987. And there is still no prospect in sight for an early resolution of this world debt crisis.

Consequently, both international banks and multinational corporations will become extremely reluctant to transfer their capital resources to many developing countries, and instead they are likely to channel both capital and other business resources increasingly to politically stable, Western developed countries in search of investment opportunities. Alaska can greatly benefit in the coming years from the redirected flow of capital away from Third World countries. By developing a coherent strategy to attract this flow of capital, Alaska can become an important recipient of foreign direct investments, especially for many natural resource sectors.

RECENT DEVELOPMENTS IN INTERNATIONAL BANKING AND FINANCE

International trade and foreign direct investments go hand in hand with international finance. An international financial center in Alaska can attract and mobilize the needed international capital for the state's economic development. It can also boost foreign trade through both abundant trade financing opportunities and collection of worldwide commercial and economic intelligence. A successful international financial center expands employment in financial and ancillary services such as legal and accounting professions and also promotes development of such infrastructure as office buildings, hotels, restaurants, and other businesses.

During the past decade and a half, the international banking and financial markets have experienced phenomenal growth. The size of the Eurocurrency market grew from $110 billion in 1970 to over $4,000 billion by 1987, while the total international assets of all banking institutions rose from $130 billion to $4,800 billion during the same period. The development of international financial centers has also accompanied the rapid expansion of international banking and Eurocurrency activities. Some of the better known offshore financial centers are playing a major role in international financial markets, as demonstrated by the size of their international banking assets: Bahamas ($144 billion), Hong Kong ($130 billion), Bahrain ($46 billion), and Panama ($32 billion).

Not only has the scale of international banking and finance grown tremendously over the years, but also the market environment and financial institutions have undergone a marked change in recent years. This change can be characterized by: deregulation, internationalization, securitization, and financial innovations.[1] Major factors for deregulation were the substantial increases in inflation and interest rates in the 1970s and early 1980s. For the seven major industrial countries, inflation reached a peak in 1980, when the increase in the GNP deflator for these seven countries was 9.2 percent from the previous year, and the increase in consumer prices was 12.1 percent. Short-term interest rates in these seven countries reached a peak of 13.2 percent in 1981. Interest rate controls were in existence in several of the industrial countries as inflation and interest rates began spiraling upward in the 1970s. The United States was one of these countries. As interest rates rose, the institutions--most notably, banks--that were subject to interest rate controls in these countries came under competitive pressure from institutions that were not. The situation became particularly acute in the United States, where money market funds enjoyed exponential growth in the late 1970s at the expense of commercial bank deposits. The response of the U.S. government was to provide for the gradual phasing out of interest rate controls. This was done in the Depository Institutions Deregulation and Monetary Control Act of 1980, and the phase-out was completed in March of 1986.

The relaxation of interest rate controls was probably the major but certainly not the only aspect of deregulation. Functional distinction between different types of institutions has been breaking down, in part in response to the increasingly volatile economic environment. As financial institutions sought to expand the range of their products and services, they ran up against hostile laws, regulations, supervisory attitudes, and competitors. Although not always successful, those financial institutions seeking to overcome these impediments did so with sufficient frequency to cause a number of changes in the roles and relative importance of the different types of players in the financial arena.

Depository institutions are not the only financial institutions that have been caught up in deregulation. The securities industries in a number of countries, most notably the United States and the United Kingdom, have had to contend with changes in the rules of the game. In the United States, deregulatory measures in the 1970s increased competition by, among other things, ending the fixed rate structure for securities trades and lessening the power of the Big Board, the New York Stock Exchange. In the United Kingdom, the securities industry is undergoing more far-reaching alterations. Not only are rates and fees being deregulated; restrictions are also being dropped on divisions of functions between different types of securities firms and on the ownership of securities firms by banking organizations.

The global integration of financial markets is also a trend that has been underway for some time. The rise of the Eurocurrency and Eurobond markets in the 1960s was an important milestone in the development of this trend. International linkages increased in the 1970s and have accelerated in the 1980s. Internationalization is a commonly used term for the global integration of financial markets that is occurring. Neatness is not a characteristic of internationalization. The hodgepodge of institutions, financial instruments, flow of funds channels, and supervisory entities that make up domestic financial systems is reflected, and amplified, in the emerging international financial system.

Securitization is another feature of the current financial environment. Securitization is not a term that has achieved a generally accepted precise definition. Rather, it refers to what appears to be a move away from traditional bank lending and deposit-taking activities toward financial intermediation involving various kinds of negotiable financial instruments. The manifestations of securitization are numerous and varied. In the U.S. domestic market, loan-backed securities have achieved a significant presence. These are securities whose underlying assets are loans. Mortgage loans are the most common collateralization. In 1985, approximately one-fourth, or $366 billion, of one- to four-family residential mortgage loans ended up in mortgage-backed securities. In 1980, the dollar amount had been $114 billion, or only 13 percent of all one- to four-family residential mortgage loans.

Although mortgages are the predominant type of loans finding their way into loan-backed securities, a number of other types of assets have also been used. Among these are car loans, credit card receivables, computer leases, and Small Business Administration loans. The securitization of assets is limited only by the ingenuity of the packagers. The easiest assets to securitize, however, are those that are homogeneous, that is, that have similar terms and credit characteristics. To date, securitizing non-homogeneous assets, such as commercial and industrial loans, has not met with much success.

Both the richness and complexity of international funding sources and investment outlets bear a testimony to the robust spirit of financial innovations that has pervaded the international financial markets in recent years. Some of the innovations turned out to be faddish, but others have gained wide acceptance and made valuable contributions to the growth of international financial markets known as the Euromarkets. Both the development of markets for new financial instruments and the expansion

TABLE 1

Borrowings In The International Capital Markets (U.S. dollars, in billions)

	1983	1984	1985	1987
Floating-rate bond issues	19.5	38.2	58.4	10.7
Other bond offerings	57.6	73.3	109.3	184.8
Syndicated loans	67.2	57.0	42.0	88.8
NIFs and other back-up facilities	9.5	28.8	46.8	29.9
Non-underwritten facilities and Euro-commercial paper programs	-	-	18.3	69.6
Total	153.8	197.3	274.8	383.8

Source: Organization for Economic Co-operation and Development, *Financial Market Trends*, June 1986 and May 1988, p. 5.

and deepening of markets for the pre-existing instruments are the results of the innovative spirit in the Euromarkets. Viewed in this way, the emergence of various Euromarket instruments since the early 1960s has been the result of financial innovation designed to meet the special needs of long-term international borrowers and investors.

The recent rapid expansion of Euromarkets has been promoted by further institutional innovations. The private use of both the European Currency Unit (ECU) and the Special Drawing Right (SDR) was first practiced for Eurobonds well before their use in bank deposits and Eurocredits. New clearing house mechanisms for international bonds and Euro CDs have greatly facilitated secondary market trading of these instruments. Gray market trading was pioneered in the Eurobond market and it still remains a unique feature of a Eurobond issue. Development of floating-rate notes (FRNs) in the 1970s is another example of Euromarket innovation.

Financial innovation involves more than development and diversification of new borrowing sources. It affects the entire range of financial intermediation, both domestic and international. In fact, the variety of services offered by financial intermediaries has been equally impressive on the liability side of their balance sheets. Liability management of modern financial institutions has become an important part of their integrated approach to financial intermediation. Innovations on the liability side have significant policy implications for monetary authorities.

CAUSES OF FINANCIAL MARKET CHANGES

The rapid pace of financial market changes in recent years is due to several factors. The first of these is the high level of interest rates worldwide since 1965 and especially since the late 1960s. High interest rates have reflected the serious inflation that the world economy has experienced over the years since the late 1960s. Rising inflation has led to anticipation of high future inflation, and lenders have sought higher interest rates as compensation for the depreciating purchasing power of their savings. Not only the high level of interest rates but also the greater fluctuation of interest rates increased significantly the risk exposure of most market participants. Savers and investment managers have been exposed to larger capital losses, as well as capital gains, on their financial portfolios due to widely fluctuating interest rates, since the market price of debt instruments moves inversely with interest rates. Also, banking institutions that have traditionally engaged in maturity transformation by funding medium to long-term loans with short-term liabilities are subject to greater uncertainty over their funding costs due to widely fluctuating money market rates.

Financial institutions have devised various counter measures to cope with this increased risk. On the one hand, the interest rates on medium to long-term loans have shifted increasingly from fixed rates to floating ones tied to certain short-term base rates such as three- or six-month LIBOR or the prime rate. Floating-rate loans significantly reduce the funding cost risk for financial intermediaries. Floating rates have been adopted not just for bank loans in the form of Eurocredits but also for long-term debt securities such as floating-rate notes, floating rate CDs and medium-term notes. On the other side of their balance sheet, financial institutions have also diversified their liabilities and lengthened their maturities. The trend toward liability diversification in terms of both instruments and maturities has intensified recently concomitant with the general deregulatory movement in the financial sector. In addition to traditional domestic CDs, banks now offer Eurodollar CDs as well as longer-term floating-rate CDs in various Euromarket centers. Medium- to long-term FRNs have been an important source of funds for banking institutions since the mid-1970s. Repurchase agreements (RPs) and Negotiable Order of Withdrawal (NOW) accounts have been extensively used by both thrift institutions and commercial banks in the United States. Interest rate swaps and currency swaps have been utilized by banks to tap longer-term funds at substantially reduced interest costs, while being hedged against foreign exchange risks.

High interest rates increase the opportunity cost of holding noninterest-bearing assets and encourage the economizing of such assets. Thus, high interest rates provide incentives for savers to shift out of demand deposits and into high-yield alternatives provided by new types of money market instruments. In order to slow down the disintermediation process, banks have had to devise new types of bank liabilities. Banks, forced to pay increasingly market-related rates in order to attract deposits, started to use actively a variety of new instruments for raising interest-sensitive funds, and they have also contributed to the creation of new secondary markets in which these assets are traded actively.

Variable-rate financing such as FRNs and floating-rate CDs enabled banks to raise medium- and long-term funds at a time when fluctuating interest rates continued to act as a major disincentive for savers to purchasing and holding long-term investment assets. The fast-growing interest rate futures market also serves as an example of continuing efforts to reduce risk exposure created by high and volatile interest rates. The Eurobond market has created new types of bonds designed to deal with the high and volatile interest rates. In addition to interest rate swaps and the FRNs, they include index-linked bonds, rolling rate notes (RRNs), extendable-maturity notes, medium-term notes (MTNs), zero coupon bonds, deep discount bonds, etc.

The floating exchange rate regime, that has been in force since early 1973 with the breakdown of the Bretton Woods system, greatly increased the volatility of exchange rate movements, increasing the level of financial risk exposure for market participants similar to widely fluctuating interest rates. Before 1973, many economists expected exchange rates to be fairly stable under the flexible exchange rate system. Because most market-determined prices are not volatile, it was believed that the market-determined price of foreign exchange would not be volatile either.[2] Instead of being stable, however, exchange rates have been highly volatile under the floating exchange rate regime. According to a study, the absolute percentage changes in the U.S.-German spot exchange rate between 1973 and early 1984 were 29.8 percent on a monthly basis and 107.4 percent on a daily basis.[3]

When spot exchange rates are volatile, the differences between forward exchange rates and future spot rates tend to be amplified,[4] thus lessening the degree of accuracy of the forward exchange rate as a predictor of the actual spot rate on a particular future date. Widening divergences between forward exchange rates and the subsequently observed spot rates for corresponding dates increase the degree of risk present in the financial

242

market. Innovations such as currency swaps, currency options and currency futures contracts reflect the attempt by market participants to mitigate or even circumvent the heightened exchange risk perceived during the past decade and a half of floating exchange rates. A number of innovations in the Eurobond market have been designed specifically to lessen the foreign exchange risk exposure for international investors. They include currency option bonds, commodity-linked bonds, and bonds denominated in SDRs and European Currency Units (ECUs).

As the volume of outstanding loans to developing and Eastern European countries increased rapidly in the 1970s, international credit risk became a critical issue for financial intermediaries in the Euromarket. The recent world debt crisis accentuated the need for devising new ways to deal with the mounting international credit risk in general. In an attempt to supplement or even substitute the traditional Eurocredit mechanism (which was in itself a major financial innovation in the early 1970s), the Euromarket has experimented with a variety of new financing techniques such as bought deals, club loans, loan swaps, participation certificates, FRNs, and Euronotes with a revolving underwriting facility (RUF), note issuance facility (NIF), primary underwriting facility (PUF), etc. These new instruments are intended for certain specific needs perceived in this era of heightened international credit risk. Both NIFs and RUFs are designed to encourage continuing participation by U.S. and other banks in international banking activities despite the general decline of the traditional Eurocredit lending mechanism. To the contrary, club loans do away with the traditional loan syndicate structure with open invitations to banks for participation, and instead package the loans among a small number of pre-selected banks participating on an equal basis. Both loan swaps and participation certificates are designed to diversify the credit exposure of banking institutions among as many borrowing countries as desirable.

Another reason for rapid financial changes was the rise of computer and communications technology, which has provided financial institutions with the capacity to process massive amounts of data and to make financial transfers rapidly and economically. The introduction of new technology contributes to greater transactional efficiency and a higher degree of integration of world financial markets. The impact of new information processing techniques has been most visible in such new financial services as automated teller machines (ATMs), home banking systems and point-of-sale (POS) terminals. Corporate and individual depositors are now able to carry out significant portfolio shifts in order to economize on cash balances and low-yielding transactions accounts by quickly investing their liquid resources in various money market instruments.

Cash flow management has been enhanced significantly by such electronic fund transfer systems as the U.S. Federal Reserve System's Fed

Wire and the New York's Clearing House Interbank Payments System (CHIPS), which have made it possible to clear millions of transactions both efficiently and rapidly. London's new Clearing House Automated Payments System (CHAPS) plays a similar role, significantly reducing transactions costs. Automated international message transfer services such as the Society for Worldwide Interbank Financial Telecommunications (SWIFT) contributes to integration of world financial markets through efficient and almost instantaneous sharing of messages and information worldwide on a secure base. In many instances, sophisticated new equipment has resulted in sizable amounts of excess capacity, thereby creating incentives for expanding existing financial services and offering new kinds of services. New electronic banking technology has also produced significant structural changes in the organization of financial markets. For example, automated payment systems have facilitated the entry of non-banking institutions into the retail deposit business since ATMs have made it possible to avoid the heavy expense of building extensive branch networks.

Also, the regulatory environment for international financial transactions has been conducive to the kind of competitive and creative spirit needed in financial innovations. Regulatory authorities have traditionally allowed a greater operational leeway for "Euro" or foreign currency banking. In fact, this regulatory asymmetry was originally responsible for the creation of the Euromarket itself in the first place. For example, the absence of reserve requirements and interest rate ceilings encouraged the development of the Eurodollar market by providing the competitive advantage to banking institutions in Eurodollar funding operations. The Eurobond market was promoted in the absence of such strict securities regulations in domestic markets as registration requirements and disclosure rules.

Consequently, the Euromarket has provided a relatively fertile field for new financial experimentation free of stifling regulatory constraints. Even in the domestic financial markets of most Western industrial countries the process of financial deregulation has been at work during the past decade or so. In general, deregulation tended to follow rather than precede the introduction of new financial products and services which first would transform the financial market environment substantially enough to force the change in the traditional regulatory outlook. Deregulation would then accelerate further financial innovations, triggering more deregulation and so on in a self-reinforcing manner.

Between the Great Depression in the early 1930s and the expansion of Eurobanking in the 1960s, bank regulatory philosophy in major Western industrialized countries was dominated by a preoccupation with the soundness of individual institutions, mindful of the great financial crash in the late 1920s and early 1930s. Competition in banking was viewed as a double-edged sword, incorporating notable deficiencies as well as some generally recognized advantages in improving the quality of banking services to the public. However, recent regulatory changes were designed to promote competition not only among banks but also between commercial banks and other financial institutions, encouraging a rapid pace of financial innovations in the Euromarkets.

REQUIREMENTS FOR AN INTERNATIONAL FINANCIAL CENTER

Development of international financial centers has been a natural response by banking institutions to benefit from economies of scale in their international operations. Modern international financial centers require sophisticated and costly infrastructure, such as telecommunications, air transportation, and accounting and legal services. It would be cost inefficient to establish an elaborate infrastructure in each country to service just one national market. By locating most international banking and financial infrastructure in one central place, banks can spread their overhead costs in servicing clients in various countries.

Additionally, a sufficient number of banking and financial institutions must be located in one financial center to provide the critical mass needed to service international clientele effectively and efficiently. International banking requires both sophisticated financial expertise and up-to-date market information. Such knowledge cannot be generated in a vacuum; it needs constant innovation and cross-fertilization of ideas among bankers and other finance professionals. An accurate and up-to-date sense of financial markets can be obtained only through active market participation in the financial center.

Further, modern international banking frequently requires teamwork among many banks in loan syndication and other credit transactions. The amount of money involved is often huge and no one bank can prudently handle such transactions alone. International banking syndication necessitates close coordination and smooth working relationships among banks. Familiarity with each other's strengths facilitates such coordination and teamwork. A financial center provides the environment for frequent interaction among bankers and other finance professionals.

Apart from syndication and risk sharing, a cluster of international banking institutions in one place is helpful for funding and investment operations. The existence of active interbank money markets leads to efficient channeling of financial resources. Banks invest surplus funds in the interbank market from which other banks obtain funding to finance their international operations. Such a market is possible only where a large number of banking institutions are clustered together in one place. Attractive international financial centers serve not only as locations for international financial communities serving clients in various countries but also as havens for international savings and pools of liquidity seeking profitable investments free from monetary and exchange control restrictions. Efficient interbank markets provide the opportunity to invest these surplus funds easily and with minimal risk.

Location economics is important for international banking. Financial centers should be easily accessible in terms of geography and time zone to both investors and borrowers. Contact with potential borrowers is essential to bankers for marketing purposes and for packaging and negotiating customer loans. Location economics in international banking implies that a financial center should be in or near countries whose economies are dynamic and industrializing quickly, and thus requiring extensive borrowing. The development stage of these economies should also be high enough to assure reasonable credit risk for banks.

The availability of good air transportation to neighboring countries as well as telephone and telex communication links is essential for a financial center. It also needs liberal government regulation of banking and foreign exchange transactions, taxation, securities dealings, and work permits for expatriate staffs functioning in an environment of political and economic stability. Locally available internationally-oriented personnel in the legal, accounting, and clerical professions is also useful.

Anchorage possesses many advantages as a potential international financial center, such as political stability, convenient air transportation links with major cities in North America, Europe and the Asia-Pacific region, well-developed telecommunication facilities, and competent legal and accounting personnel. Another important advantage of Anchorage is its time zone, being conveniently linked during business hours to New York and Chicago on the one hand, and when these markets close, then to Tokyo, Hong Kong and Singapore on the other. As international financial markets are developed into one global market place with 24-hour trading, the Anchorage financial center could play a crucial trade linkage role by taking over the trading positions of New York and Chicago at the close of their business hours and off-loading them unto Tokyo, Hong Kong and Singapore as these markets open up.

Thus, the Anchorage financial center could provide valuable services in international trading of foreign currencies, domestic and international bonds and stock, Eurocurrency deposits, financial futures and options, currency swaps and interest swaps, etc. As Anchorage develops its international financial expertise and reputation, it will also attract offshore Eurocurrency deposits, insurance and reinsurance business for the Asia-Pacific region, investment and financial counselling, commodity broking, precious metals trading, and other related business.

246

CONCLUSION

Some might be skeptical at this point over the possibility of ever developing an international financial center in Anchorage, but the recent history of international financial centers gives us encouragement in this regard. About ten years ago in 1975, a tiny Middle East country, called Bahrain, boldly proclaimed to the international banking community its intention to become an international financial center. At that time, the odds seemed to run heavily against Bahrain, which is located in the middle of almost nowhere literally on the sea of desert sand, with no oil, no name recognition, no industry, no international financial experience or expertise, no trained personnel, no infrastructure, and, above all, no money. It only had a dream, a hope. Ten years later today, Bahrain is an important international financial center, with close to 200 financial institutions located there and almost $50 billion deposits, and lively financial trading activities in all sorts of financial instruments for Middle Eastern, European, and Asian customers.

Of course, it is erroneous to say that it will be easy to develop an international financial center in Alaska. But it is equally erroneous to conclude that it will be impossible for Alaska to do so. With both judicious planning and the cooperation between government officials and the private sector in the state, a viable international financial center can be established in Anchorage.

NOTES

1. The following discussion benefits heavily from an excellent treatment of the topic by David Holland. 1988. *Off-Balance Sheet Activities of Commercial Banks*, Ph.D. dissertation, George Washington University, Washington, D.C., 1988.

2. For example, see Harry G. Johnson, 1969. The Case of Flexible Exchange Rates. *Federal Reserve Bank of St. Louis Review*, June.

3. Craig S. Hakkio. 1984. Exchange Rate Volatility and Federal Reserve Policy. Federal Reserve Bank of Kansas City *Economic Review*, July-August.

4. See, for example, International Monetary Fund, *Annual Report 1982*, Washington, D.C. 1982, pp. 42-45.

[15]

Excerpt from Economists Advisory Group, *City 2000: The Future of London as an International Financial Centre*, 37–55

CHAPTER 4 REGULATION, COMPETITION AND TECHNOLOGY IN THE SUPPLY OF FINANCIAL SERVICES

In this chapter, we consider changes in the supply of international financial services. The two dominant influences are likely to be the nature and extent of government regulation and the revolution in information technology.

4.1 Regulation and Competition

Relative freedom from official regulation is often claimed as one of the big advantages enjoyed by London as an international financial centre. There is a fear that this advantage may diminish, or even be lost altogether, as London becomes more regulated while other centres, notably New York and Tokyo, become less so. However, this is an over-simplification; there are different kinds of regulation imposed for different reasons and, both in London and elsewhere, some are increasing while others are being reduced.

The nature of regulation

Though it is impossible to draw hard and fast lines, it is useful to distinguish between regulations whose primary effect is on competition (even though they may have originally been introduced for some other reason) and those whose primary impact is on consumer protection (even though they may have incidental effects on competition).

Among the first category are:

- Restrictions on the areas within which particular institutions may operate. Some of these have been imposed by self-regulatory organisations to protect their own interests, eg the Stock Exchange membership restrictions in London, and some have been imposed by government in the belief that they were in the public interest, eg the Glass-Steagall Act in the US.

- Regulation of prices or interest rates that may be charged, eg minimum commission rules on stock exchanges, the former interest-rate cartel of the London clearing banks, Regulation Q in New York and official regulation of interest rates in Japan.
- Restrictions on entry to a particular occupation, where these exceed what is necessary to ensure that entrants have the experience and resources required to protect the public interest. An important example in our present context is the discrimination applied by some countries against the entry of foreign institutions.
- Restrictions on the use of funds, including quantative "ceilings" on bank lending, investment direction, and exchange control.

The second category consists mainly of:

- Restrictions on entry designed to ensure that practitioners have adequate qualifications and experience.
- Rules on capital adequacy, liquidity and solvency margins designed to reduce the risk of insolvency.
- Disclosure rules and codes of dealing conduct designed to protect the public against fraud.
- Compensation funds to protect the public from loss due to insolvency or fraud.

There is a widespread tendency, both in Britain and elsewhere, for regulations in the first category to be relaxed or dismantled, and for those in the second category to be imposed or reinforced.

Another important distinction is between self-regulation and regulation by governments or public agencies. Self-regulation has the obvious advantage that the regulators are drawn from practitioners in the activity concerned, and so are more familiar with their markets than public officials can ever hope to be. Hence, their rules should be more flexible, less liable to avoidance and less onerous to business. On the other hand, self-regulation tends to be uneven in its incidence, since some activities develop better regulatory systems than others; conflicts of interest can arise between those who provide financial services and those who use them; and self-regulatory organisations may be tempted to impose anti-competitive rules to protect the interests of their members.

Regulation in London

London's rise to pre-eminence as an international financial centre occurred in a climate of extreme "laissez-faire". Subject to the general law on such matters as fraud, contract and limited liability, individuals and institutions were allowed to go their own way and to organise their activities, or not, as they saw fit. Early organisations had one or more of three objectives:

- to provide the infra-structure (eg trading floors and clearing arrangements) for organised markets;
- to protect honest dealers (who were assumed to be the great majority) against rogues in their own line of business;
- and (somewhat later) to represent the general interests of those engaged in particular activities.

It was assumed that the principle of "caveat emptor" combined with generally high standards of morality and the power of competition would ensure adequate protection for the public.

The result was a system that allowed great flexibility and scope for innovation and where, on the whole, standards of user protection were surprisingly high. In particular, the role of the Bank of England has been greatly admired in other financial centres. However, the growth of associations with some self-regulatory functions was haphazard. For example, there are at least five organisations representing dealers in securities who are not members of the Stock Exchange, but there is no effective regulation of investment managers and advisers, as distinct from dealers.

Moreover, self-regulatory organisations did not always resist the temptation to restrict competition. Some restrictions were also imposed by the government and/or the Bank of England in the interests of monetary policy or the balance of payments. By the late 1960s there was a formidable body of anti-competitive restrictions, most of which have been or are being removed. Among the most important are:

- the abandonment of the clearing banks' interest rate cartel in 1971;
- the withdrawal by the Bank of England of its objection to mergers between deposit banks and merchant banks;
- the abandonment of quantative "ceilings" on bank lending to the domestic private sector in 1971;
- the abandonment of mandatory reserve ratios in domestic banking in 1982;
- the removal of exchange control in 1979;
- the pending abolition of minimum commissions on the Stock Exchange;
- the pending removal of restrictions on Stock Exchange membership by banks and other outside financial institutions.

We have not had any great public debate about "deregulation" but we have already gone further than any other major country in removing restrictions that inhibit competition in financial services.

In the field of consumer protection governments have long ago abandoned the extreme "laissez-faire" attitudes of the nineteenth century. The first Prevention of Fraud (Investment) Act was passed in 1939 and regulation of insurance and unit trusts has an even longer history. These regulations have been tightened in some respects, but the major piece of recent legislation has been the 1979 Banking Act. Prior to 1979 there was no general legal definition of a bank. The Bank of England had some authority under the Exchange Control Act and the Prevention of Fraud (Investment) Acts, but its main power rested on voluntary compliance together with certain privileges (eg rediscount facilities; the recognition of a bank's bills for re-discounting; and special facilities for dealing in government securities) that it was able to give or withhold. The Banking Act, 1979, required institutions accepting deposits, with some exceptions, to be recognised by the Bank of England as either banks or "licensed deposit-taking institutions", and gave the Bank considerable discretion over criteria for recognition. The Bank has used these powers to negotiate standards of liquidity, capital adequacy and foreign exchange exposure. So far, the Bank has exercised its enhanced authority in close co-operation with the institutions concerned, and with careful regard to the different circumstances affecting different types of bank.

In July 1981, the Secretary of State for Trade commissioned Professor L.C.B. Gower to undertake a wide-ranging review of investor protection and to advise on the need for new legislation. The preliminary results of Professor Gower's work were published as a consultative document in 1982 (1) and a final report(2) appeared in 1984. It seems likely that the main recommendations of the report will be embodied in a new and wide-ranging Investor Protection Act.

Professor Gower describes his "basic philosophy" as that regulation should be "no greater than is necessary to protect reasonable people from being made fools of." He recognises that government should not attempt "the impossible task of protecting fools from their own folly"; that it is necessary to strike a balance between cost and efficiency; and that "it would be detrimental to the national interest if controls were disproportionately strict in comparison with those of other financial centres to which the business could move"(3).

The proposed legislation would have a broad scope, covering not only security dealing but also financial futures and options, commodity futures (though not actuals) and investment management and advice related to any of these activities. All professional operators in areas covered by the Act would be required to register either as members of a recognised self-regulatory organisation or directly with the Department of Trade or a specially-created Commission.

Professor Gower believes that self-regulation is both less costly and more efficient than regulation by a Department or Commission, and expects that the great majority of registrations would be through self-regulatory

---

(1) Review of Investor Protection HMSO Jan 1982
(2) Review of Investor Protection Report Cmnd 9125. HMSO Jan 1984 Hereafter referred to as the Gower Report. The second part, a draft Investor Protection Bill, is forthcoming.
(3) Gower Report. Paras. 1.15 and 1.16.

organisations. These organisations would be either "investment exchanges" or associations of dealers, managers and/or advisers. Recognition would depend on approval by the Department or Commission of their rules and their machinery for enforcing them. In return, their rules would not be subject to the Restrictive Trade Practices Acts and they would gain certain other legal privileges. In some areas it would be necessary to form new organisations or to extend the powers of existing ones; in others, it would be desirable to avoid overlapping. A suggested way of achieving this is by smaller organisations becoming corporate members of larger ones. Those who registered directly rather than through recognised organisations would be subject to rules drawn up and policed by the Department or Commission.

The question of whether the government agency should be the Department of Trade or a special Commission depends, in Gower's view, on the amount of direct registration. If this is small, so that that the role of government is mainly surveillance of self-regulation, he would favour the Department. If it is large, so that a lot of detailed monitoring would be needed, he would favour a Commission.

Many of those affected by these proposals will be concerned only with supplying financial services to British residents, but there are several ways in which legislation might impinge on the international competitiveness of London. An obvious example is the eurobond market. Though London is the largest single dealing centre, the self-regulatory organisation is the Association of International Bond Dealers (AIBD) which has its headquarters in Zurich and operates under the Swiss Civil Code. Professor Gower sees this as no obstacle to the recognition of AIBD but, if we are too insular for this, he suggests that UK members might form a branch, with similar rules to those of the parent organisation.

A more general set of problems arises from differences in regulation between different countries. These range all the way from the sale of insurance-linked bonds of companies operating in foreign tax-havens that have no effective regulation, to the achievement of freedom of establishment and of service within the EC. Again, the Gower approach is liberal. We can control the activities of companies subject to no effective regulation only by regulating their branches or agents here. We should not seek to duplicate the rules of countries where regulation is already effective, and we should not discriminate against overseas institutions. We should work towards harmonisation, on a basis of minimum effective regulation within the EC, and we should seek to negotiate reciprocal arrangements with countries outside the Community.

Regulation in the US

In some respects the process headlined as "deregulation" in the US is similar to that which has happened without hitting any headlines in the UK, but there are three important differences. The US started from a more restrictive position than the UK, eg the Federal Reserve imposed interest rate ceilings and reserve requirements on both domestic and foreign business, and banks' participation in the securities industry was limited by the Glass Steagall Act. The US has a multiplicity of regulatory agencies; banking regulation is shared between the Federal Reserve System, the Federal Deposit Insurance Corporation and the Controller of the Currency, and banks are also subject to state laws; issues of and dealings in securities are regulated by the Securities and Exchange Commission (SEC); commodity markets are subject to the Commodity Futures Trading Commission (CFTC); and insurance is regulated by state insurance commissions. Finally, though the stock exchanges and commodity markets have important self-regulatory powers, the US system depends much more than the British on official surveillance.

Regulations affecting particular activities are discussed further in the relevant chapters of Part 2. The main steps towards deregulation that have been taken are:

- the enforcement by the SEC of negotiated commissions on stock exchange deals from "Mayday" 1975;
- the Depository Institutions and Monetary Control Act, 1980, which required the abolition of all interest rate ceilings within six years;

- the creation of IBFs, which in effect set up a self-contained offshore banking centre free from interest rate controls, reserve requirements and insurance requirements (see Chapter 6).

The expansion of banks into securities dealing and of securities houses into banking has so far occurred within the framework of existing law though in some respects the legal position is uncertain. A financial Institutions Deregulation Act, now before Congress, would amend the Glass-Steagall Act to give the banks more freedom of action and also reduce the regulatory powers of "the Fed". The Act has the support of the FDIC but has run into strenuous opposition from the Federal Reserve. This conflict is one example of the difficulties that can arise from multiplicity of agencies. Another has arisen from banks' involvement in discount broking, over which the SEC has staked a claim to jurisdiction.

So far deregulation in the US has taken the form of an attack on restrictions that either never existed, have been abolished or are in course of abolition in the UK. In the field of solvency and consumer protection, the trend is similar to that in the UK. The SEC is tightening its surveillance over new issues and securities dealing; the CFTC was set up to oversee commodity markets in 1975; and the banking authorities are hardening their attitude on provisions against doubtful debts. Further moves in the latter direction are likely as a result of a sharp increase in failures among small banks and the recent troubles of Continental Illinois.

Finally, we should note, though it is not strictly a matter of regulation, the proposal now before Congress to repeal the 30 per cent withholding tax on interest on US securities paid to foreigners. The possible effects of this on the eurobond market are discussed in Chapter 9.

Regulation in Japan

The Japanese financial system in the early post-war years was designed to insulate the domestic capital market from the rest of the world so as to provide cheap finance for industry and government. Foreign exchange transactions were tightly controlled, and foreign borrowing in the

Japanese market was not allowed; the interest paid and charged by banks was regulated, and these were no markets in money or short-term paper; the banks were obliged to buy government debt from the Bank of Japan on a low yield basis, and the market in these securities was restricted.

Since the early 'seventies some big steps towards liberalisation have been taken. Foreign banks have been admitted to the country in substantial numbers and can deal in the local money market, in the foreign exchange market, and in a market for dollar deposits. Japanese banks are active in international lending and in the eurobond market, and Tokyo is already third in the world, after London and New York, as a centre for international bank lending. Foreign security issues on the Tokyo market have also been permitted in substantial volume. But controls remain on foreign exchanges, foreign security issues, trading in government securities and domestic interest rates, and there is still no market either in bank bills or Treasury bills.

The Japanese interest rate structure has come under pressure as a result of the government having to re-finance large amounts of maturing debt, and other countries, especially the US are constantly urging more liberalisation.

In May 1984, Japanese and US officials were reported to have agreed on a new package including:

- creating a bankers' acceptances market;
- relaxation of regulations governing the issue of yen CDs;
- liberalisation of trading in government securities;
- moves for the establishment of a treasury bill market;
- relaxation of foreign exchange controls; and
- relaxation of the "guidelines" given by the Bank of Japan on rates of interest payable on wholesale deposits.

However, no timetable was laid down for these measures and Japanese officials stressed that progress would be gradual. In announcing the agreement, the head of the Bank of Japan's foreign department, Mr. Ohta, is reported to have said, "Our goal is to make Tokyo like the City of

London, so we need a completely liberalised on-shore market". Clearly there is still a long way to go before that goal is attained. There has also been discussion of the creation of an offshore yen market on the lines of the offshore dollar market created by IBFs in New York, but it is uncertain what, if anything, will come of this.

Regulation elsewhere

A detailed discussion of other centre is beyond the scope of this study and we note only a few salient points. In one important respect European countries have always been less restricted than the US or even the UK; demarcation lines between deposit banks, investment banks and savings banks have never been very strong and the major institutions are all "universal banks". In other areas, however, a lot of restrictions remain and there is little sign of a "deregulation movement". For example most countries, apart from Switzerland, still have mandatory reserve ratios; a number still retain exchange controls; fixed commissions are still the general rule on European stock exchanges, though they have been abolished in Canada and Australia; and insurance companies are subject to regulations affecting premiums, the investment of funds and the ability of residents to purchase insurance from abroad.

Deregulation and London

The brief description given above should make it clear that deregulation is not a simple one way change that will be either good or bad for London. Its effects are far reaching and complex, and some are likely to be beneficial and others harmful. Specific issues affecting particular activities are discussed in Part 2, and our general conclusions may be summarised as follows:

- The relaxation or removal of restrictions affecting competition will make the financial services industry, both domestic and international, more competitive and will stimulate innovation both in the attraction of savings and the provision of loans.

- Until the 1970s London had more of this type of restriction than is generally realised, but Britain has been among the leaders of the deregulation movement and, when the Stock Exchange rules are amended, London will have less restrictions than any other centre.

- Insofar as competition promotes efficiency, this should give London a competitive edge over it rivals.

- Deregulation will permit changes in structure including the development of large institutions covering a wide range of activities. This should be to the advantage of London, though it could lead to greater penetration by overseas institutions, especially in the securities industry.

- As other centres catch up in deregulation, London's competitive advantage will diminish. In particular the liberalisation of the Japanese market is likely to lead to a big expansion of Tokyo, though complete liberalisation is still some way ahead.

- The creation of IBFs in the US has increased the market share of New York in international bank lending, but not at the expense of London. (See Chapter 6).

- If the US withholding tax were removed there would probably be some adverse effects on the eurobond market in London and elsewhere, but we should not expect these to be very severe. (See Chapter 9).

- Restrictions on the participation of international insurance companies in national markets are likely to continue and curtail the growth of London as an international market. (See Chapter 11).

- Regulations that improve consumer protection benefit financial centres insofar as they increase public confidence, but damage them insofar as they raise the costs of providing financial services.

- There are uncertainties as to what will follow from changes in the Stock Exchange and from the Gower Report, but Britain will probably continue to rely on self-regulation more than most other countries. In particular, British regulation is likely to remain more flexible and less onerous that that of the US.

4.2 Technology

A second major influence on the structure of financial institutions and financial markets will be the developments in what is loosely called "information technology". That phrase has been much abused, and it is well to remember that there have been many "breakthroughs" in information technology since man first wrote on a wall. Nevertheless we are in the early stages of what promise to be remarkable changes. The following paragraphs look at the essential economic, as distinct from technical, nature of these changes and at their main applications to financial services. We then consider their impact on financial institutions, financial markets and financial centres.

The nature of technological change

The economic impact of the changes we are considering will follow from two characteristics. First, there is the ability to store, sort, analyse and retrieve very large quantities of information, and to perform complicated calculations very quickly.

Secondly, and linked with the first, is the ability to transmit very quickly information either in great detail or in summarised form. For example, each transaction on a securities or commodities market can be fed into a computer which can then either transmit the whole lot to screens in subscribers' offices, as with the NYSE tape, or use it to calculate index numbers that can be similarly displayed.

Applications in financial services

This technology has a great many applications, and the following list is not exhaustive but covers only those that seem to us most important:

- "Back-office" operations, eg the sending out of contract notes, bills, bank statements, etc., and keeping the appropriate accounts.

This was one of the earliest applications of computers and is now highly developed in all financial centres.

- Clearing services for banking systems and for markets. Examples in London are the Clearing House Automated Payments System (CHAPS), and Talisman on the Stock Exchange. International clearing for eurobonds is provided by Euroclear and CEDEL, and there are the related international message transmission services of the Society for Worldwide Interbank Financial Telecommunications (SWIFT).

- Registration and transfer of securities. The procedures differ between registered and bearer securities. Euroclear and CEDEL provide facilities for eurobonds (bearer) and both the London and Tokyo stock exchanges are developing electronic book transfer systems for registered securities.

- A rather specialised application is the use of cash dispensers in retail banking and the probable development of systems by which members of the public can have access to their bank accounts through terminals in shops or in their homes. Such developments are relevant in the present context only insofar as they affect competition for savings.

- Price information. Information about the prices at which deals have been done on financial markets can be distributed almost immediately not only to market members, but to members of the public who subscribe to the service. The NYSE consolidated tape gives price and volume for all deals in listed securities on eight exchanges and by members of the National Association of Securities Dealers. London lags well behind in this kind of information about stock exchange deals, for reasons explained in Chapter 8, but information on commodity prices is available through Reuters, Telerate and other services.

- Other market information. Relevant information, other than individual deals, includes price index numbers, company news, crop reports, and general economic statistics and forecasts. Again an increasing volume of information is being distributed by a growing number of organisations both in London and in other centres.

- 50 -

- Organisation of trading. An example is the Opening Automated Report Service (OARS) of NYSE. A feature of NYSE trading is the large number of orders, at stated or limit prices, received before opening. These orders are analysed by computer so that the specialist in each security can see the number of buying and selling orders at each of a series of prices, but the actual fixing of an opening price is left to the specialist. This system would only be appropriate where there are a large number of pre-opening orders. Other systems will, no doubt, develop to meet other special circumstances of particular markets.

- Automated quotations. Bids and offers for securities, commodities or futures can be displayed on screens in the same way as other information described above. Among the largest and best known systems is NASDAQ (National Association of Security Dealers Automated Quotations) in the US. In London such systems are widely used in the eurobond and foreign exchange markets, ARIEL offers similar facilities on a small scales for UK equities, and the McGraw-Hill EMIS system provides facilities for petroleum related commodities. Such systems are often described as automated dealing, but this is highly misleading. Dealers get information about bids and offers, but actual negotiation takes place on the telephone or, in some cases, by entering counter bids or offers on the screen. The ultimate decision still rests with the dealer.

- Automated dealing. True automated dealing would remove all discretion from the dealer once he had put a bid or offer into the system. The computer would simply match orders according to given rules and all parties would be bound by the results. Such a system operates on a limited scale on the Toronto stock exchange but, in general, dealers are very reluctant to give up their discretion.

- Audit trails. The publication of price information, even in the detail provided by the NYSE tape, gives only limited consumer protection. In order to detect the more sophisticated abuses, exchange authorities would need to be able to recall details of a series of transactions (including price, volume and names of brokers and the parties for whom they were acting) in the order in which they occurred. This is known in the US as an "audit trail". Both the London and New York stock exchanges already record much of the relevant information, and both are working on systems that will give a complete audit trail.

This check list should demonstrate the variety of applications of information technology to financial services and also the breadth of their inpact on individual institutions, individual markets, financial centres and links between centres.

<u>The impact on institutions</u>

At the level of the individual firm, changing technology will change the structure of costs, though in a complex way. We have not attempted to examine these relationships in detail but a few general points are clear. The initial cost of developing and installing systems is high, but marginal operating costs are low. This may give increased economies of scale in high volume/low value transactions, eg retail banking, but markets are already developing ways of spreading costs. Companies that acquire expensive systems may spread the cost by selling computer time or computer services, as do some of the banks; specialised information services distribute a variety of information relatively cheaply to large numbers of clients; other services are also being provided by specialist organisations, eg portfolio valuations by Datastream and clearing services by ICCH; and firms may "club together" to provide services, eg a well-known London gilt-edged list is produced by a consortium of leading brokers.

The ability to acquire and handle up-to-date information in large quantities and to summarise it quickly should improve the quality of decision-making of both large and small operators, and the developments described in the last paragraph may give small and medium-sized firms access to information formerly available, if at all, only to their larger competitors. Moreover, new opportunities for small firms are being created in computer software, and in specialised research and advisory services. Thus, while new technology may increase the size of some financial institutions, it is unlikely to enhance the dominance of large firms in the financial services industry as a whole. Insofar as this happens it will due more to other factors than to technology.

It has been suggested that technology will change cost structures in a way which would lead to "round the clock" shift working and so remove the advantages enjoyed by different centres from different time zones, but this seems to us unlikely. However, further computerisation of, for example, back office systems will reduce the level of employment as firms seek to become more efficient.

The impact on markets

An obvious question is what effect technological changes will have on the operation of financial markets. Clearly there is no longer an absolute need for transactions all to take place on the trading floor of an exchange. Money markets and foreign exchange markets have operated for a long time past over the telephone, but dealing in securities and commodities is mainly on trading floors, though a lot of telephone dealing is done out of hours, and many deals are arranged in brokers offices and "crossed" on the trading floor. It is probable that such deals will increase in number but trading floors are likely to remain well beyond the end of the century.

It is one thing to make and respond to bids and offers over the telephone or electronically on a screen, and quite another to remove the human element altogether and match bids and offers on a fully computerised system. There is strong resistance to recent developments in this area both from market operators and their clients. This is more than just a conservative attitude towards an established way of life or a desire to preserve jobs. Dealers feel that, except possibly in the most routine transactions, they are likely to get a better price for their clients by personal negotiation. Clients apparently agree and regard it as poor service if their orders are simply fed into a system. It is sometimes alleged that these views are held mainly by old-fashioned operators in protected markets, but they have been put to us, among others, by one of the largest and most aggressively competitive of New York securities firms. Though it may come eventually, fully automated dealing on a large scale is still a long way off.

The impact on London

There is no doubt that financial centres will become ever more closely linked. Financial information will be available even more readily and quickly than it is now, and markets will be connected with one another by automated quotation systems and mutual clearing arrangements. Business will become even more competitive, but there seems no reason to fear that new technology, in itself, will be disadvantageous to London. We are in no position to judge the technical merits of the systems used in different centre, but the brief survey given above suggests that London has advanced systems operating or developing in all the main applications except price information on securities deals; for that there are special reasons discussed in Chapter 8, and the situation is likely to change rapidly. Moreover the companies distributing financial information are international; of the two leaders, Exco/Telerate is London-based, and Reuters is has been floated jointly in London and New York.

4.3 Future Developments in Structure and Competition

Besides adapting to changes in regulation and technology, financial centres will have to respond to the demand-side changes discussed in Chapter 3. The size of individual financial transactions has increased in real terms, apart form the nominal increase brought about by inflation. Governments have incurred larger deficits in real terms; companies have increased in size; technological progress has created large and expensive units - steel plants, motor and aircraft factories, oil rigs, jumbo jets and supertankers - which have to be financed and insured; and the growing dominance of institutional funds has increased the size of security deals. Financial business is also becoming more international. Disequilibria in the payments balances of individual countries have increased the size of capital flows; and the growth of multinational companies has created a demand for global financial services.

The financial services industries are meeting these challenges in several ways. The size of undertakings is increasing both by natural growth and through mergers, eg among banks, insurance companies, insurance brokers and security dealers. All these institutions are increasing their international activities by establishing foreign branches and subsidiaries, by acquiring established institutions in foreign countries, and by forming consortia.

At the same time, traditional lines of demarcation between financial activities are breaking down. For example, in the UK, the Bank of England has withdrawn its long-standing objection to mergers between banks and merchant banks; though only one such merger has yet occurred, all the clearing banks now have merchant banking arms. Both banks and merchant banks have developed and are expanding their interests in insurance, leasing and factoring. Banks are competing with building societies and savings banks for personal savings, and these institutions are retaliating by offering chequing facilities and credit cards; and recent changes in Stock Exchange rules are inducing other financial institutions to buy into broking and jobbing firms.

In the United States, banks are finding ways round the Glass-Steagall Act and taking a growing part in the securities business. Security firms are dealing in other markets, including commodities, and are offering insurance, banking and credit card services to their customers; and American Express and Prudential Insurance have each acquired a major New York securities firm.

There have also been a few cases where an industrial or commercial company (sometimes a conglomerate in itself) has acquired all or part of a financial undertaking. Examples are Sears Roebuck/Dean Witter and Phibro/ Salomon Bros. in the USA and BAT/Eagle Star and Charter Consolidated/Rowe and Pitman in Britain.

These changes are likely to lead to some of the largest institutions becoming "financial supermarkets", offering a wide range of financial services both to industrial and commercial companies and to the general public. Business customers would be offered cash management and borrowing facilities of various kinds; advice on corporate financial planning, mergers and takeovers; foreign exchange transactions; the handling of security issues both at home and abroad; and probably insurance. The general public would be offered traditional retail banking services, together with a growing range of savings plans linked to insurance, share ownership and commodities, advice on financial planning, and facilities for "over the counter" security dealing. The personal savings gathered in the course of retail operations would be an important source of finance for lending to industry and commerce. Institutions of this kind would establish themselves in more than one financial centre both to serve their multinational clients and to gain access to personal savings wherever they were to be had on the most advantageous terms.

What will be the long-term effect of all this on international financial centres? Will one centre come to dominate the world? Will there be a substantial number of roughly equal centres? Or will technology go to the point where it is possible to deal from anywhere with everywhere and the need for centres disappears?

The first and last of these suggestions seem far fetched. The centripetal forces that draw financial transactions to a centre are still very strong, but there are enough differences between countries and between national financial centres to prevent any one from devouring all the others. What seems much more likely is that a small group of centres - probably New York, London and Tokyo - will share a large part of international business, but that some will also be transacted alongside domestic business in the main national centres of industrial and commercial countries. What seems certain is that, except on a very pessimistic scenario of world economic development, the volume of international business will increase; that financial centres will become more cosmopolitan; and that business will become more mobile between centres. The centres that are most successful will be those that can best combine low transactions costs; breadth and depth of markets; high standards of service and consumer protection; and a capacity for innovation. Apart from the specific instances mentioned in Section 4.1 above, we see no reason why London should be less competitive in these respects than it has been in the past.

Part IV
Communications and Financial Centres

[16]

Excerpt from Richard O'Brien, *Global Financial Integration: The End of Geography*, 73–82

8

EVERYBODY HAS TO BE SOMEWHERE: THE NEW DETERMINANTS OF LOCATION

In theory, the end of geography should mean that location no longer matters. Yet, 'Everybody has to be somewhere,' as Spike Milligan once put it so eloquently in response to the standard question: 'What are you doing here?'. Location still exists, even though electronic markets make that location more difficult to identify in traditional geographical ways. Firms, individuals, markets, even products, have to have a sense of place. This chapter examines the question of location from two perspectives: that of financial centres, and that of the financial firm.

Financial centres

The most lively debate as to location focuses on the role and location of financial centres, especially those with international pretensions. Studies abound on the rival attractions of London, Frankfurt, Paris, Hong Kong and Singapore, New York and Chicago, Beirut and Bahrain, Tokyo and Osaka, with very strong public and private interest groups supporting such studies. Financial centres mean jobs for the city in question (finance is like the Olympic Games in this regard: it tends to be the city not the nation that competes for the activity). There is also expected to be some benefit for the economy and companies of the country in which the financial centre is located, although London has long been criticized for paying insufficient attention to UK interests, and its contribution to the invisibles line on the balance of payments tends to be the main apparent benefit to the nation. Centres compete not only internationally but also with other cities and regional centres in each economy.

Everybody has to be somewhere

Quite clearly, financial centres develop in order to bring together in one convenient location the wide range of talents and knowledge needed to develop financial markets. Strength in breadth and depth has always been important. London, to take the pre-eminent international example, drew strength from the fact that so many markets were located in a small area: commodity markets, precious metals markets, the stock market, currency markets (especially when based on sterling as a reserve currency) and the world's biggest insurance market. No other centre could boast such a collection. Since markets thrive on the rapid interchange of information, so a marketplace such as London developed, and the location of the world's leading news services in London has been an additional key factor. The same principles apply to all markets, from the smallest street-market to the London Stock Exchange (itself founded where people met, for coffee). As the markets developed, so they attracted the necessary ancillary services, notably legal services, accounting and auditing skills, and, in today's world, public relations and advertising expertise. Geography has traditionally had a lot to do with the location of financial centres and, indeed, as the label the Square Mile bore witness, has even defined the limits of the financial centre. Elsewhere we have seen expertise confined to very specific locations, as in the Jewish areas of European cities in the past, or in the entrepôt islands of Hong Kong and Singapore, or in the islands of the Caribbean (where the true location of the service was perhaps more questionable: a brass plate is the legal, not the actual, location).

What happens under end-of-geography conditions? There are two counterforces: on one side it can be argued that financial centres are no longer needed, since communications allow experts to work together on the telephone, over the fax and through computer-linked trading. For every example of integration there exists a counterbalancing example of growing specialization and fragmentation in markets. Even London is no longer confined to the Square Mile. The other side of the argument suggests that there should be more concentration of expertise in centres: thanks to communications, there are even greater possibilities to develop economies of scale through concentrating markets in one location, selling the same product from one centre across an even greater area. Perhaps we need only three major centres, one to cover each of the three main time zones (despite the attempts to make even time zones irrelevant through 24-hour trading).

The divergent forces are both consistent with the end of geography and with each other, reflecting an important tension in the dynamics of change. Confusion arises only if we confuse production with marketing and delivery, back-office with front-office services and if we forget the laws of comparative advantage. As free trade literature and experience demonstrates, free trade leads to specialization and product differentiation, as competing firms hone their competitive edge. Removal of barriers increases the tradability of financial products and increases the volume of trade. (For a discussion of the trade and tradability aspects, see Hoekman and Sauvé, 1991). Level playing-fields make the competition keener, not duller. The more nearly equal each producer's competitive position becomes, the more sensitive are the markets to small differences in production costs and consumer tastes, and the more important it is that comparative advantages are recognized and exploited.

In practice this means that pools of specialist expertise will continue in some financial centres, with technology making it easier to link those pools with others outside the financial centre, often closer to the market. At times this outreach will be important because of the remaining geography, involving different tastes and languages, etc., in different marketplaces. As British companies have already shown, selling insurance to the Italian market is easier said than done, even if the laws are making it more and more possible. At the same time, certain markets will not be able to stop other centres competing for their own business, as we see in stock markets, in the competition for different bond, futures and option contracts. Centres will compete, and in fact are likely to proliferate in terms of the delivery and selling functions, as players compete to get as close as possible to the client, even if the products are developed elsewhere. The increased volume of trading means that financial centres are not competing for a fixed amount of business: the volume of business is likely to increase as more players (investors included) have access to more markets and as companies can be brought to market in more countries.

A market is, of course, one of the primary expressions of geography, being the meeting-place for buyers and sellers, for producers and consumers, and being the location of the middlemen, the traders. Furthermore, and very relevant for the end-of-geography challenge, regulations are focused on markets. The idea that conduct-of-business patterns alter from market to market implies different conduct according to geography. Markets develop a close affinity with other aspects of their location, from nationality issues (or regional issues) to other local characteristics and customs. Firms have to operate in markets. The Big Bangs were all about the opening-up of specific markets, located in previously restricted areas, to outsiders.

Everybody has to be somewhere

Certain activities will still be transacted within a relatively limited physical area, in which a collection of expertise is valuable: corporate finance, for example, requires close negotiation involving a number of experts, such as bankers and lawyers. The communications between the principals can be conducted a great deal over the telephone, but they are not trading a simple product, and the sharing of information is not always easily done outside the personal contact, however sophisticated the technology. Where deals require the personal touch, and where charisma is important (for deal-making and, of course, marketing), location of the players will still matter. It is often eyeball-to-eyeball stuff, all night if need be. Such 24-hour business is not an alien concept to those who have put loan documentation together over the years. However, even these deals bring with them additional services that can be provided through non-personal means.

Retail markets will retain a strong local aspect, for obvious reasons, although in this area more ATM-based communication can be expected to develop between the customer and the service provider. Mail-order selling of financial products may well increase, especially in Europe as the regional retail market opens up, and perhaps in the United States as nationwide banking emerges. In Japan, also, the securities houses fear that it is the extensive branch networks of the larger banks that threaten their business if banks obtain a strong foothold in the retail securities business. There are, of course, some global retail products, such as travellers cheques and credit cards, which are of added value to the customer because the regular payments system, which is provided through normal cheque payments, does not always work outside the nation (or the even narrower state/region in the United States). These payments products would be under threat in a truly global payments system.

Many wholesale markets of course have already gone global, especially where the product is global. Derivative markets are a direct challenge to existing ideas of geography and to the idea of independent stock markets. The European scene seems set for a more integrated European stock market, despite efforts to maintain local powers. But the process is not just regional, although Globex is at present being used as a communications tool for separate futures and options markets to trade together, eventually there will be greater integration, and markets on both sides of the Atlantic will be brought together.

The future of the stock and other trading markets will ultimately be decided by the attitudes of the member firms of the exchanges, and by the location preferences of these firms. Stock exchanges are generally owned by their member firms, and their principal aim is to make a profit as an exchange and to enable members to make trading profits. Profit in trading is heavily dependent on trading volumes, so growth maximization is a key factor in profit maximization and also creates the necessary depth to markets themselves. In practice, every stock exchange has developed a business niche (large or small), but, like all marketplaces, it is always possible for the trading to move elsewhere. The same analogy would apply for a financial centre. Exchanges try to preserve geography, to ensure that their business does not move elsewhere. But the member firms can move. Thus, if all trading moved from New York to Chicago, that would be bad news for New York itself, but the firms would gradually build up their presence in Chicago.

Yet in an end-of-geography world, in which location is not supposed to matter, why would a market move at all? Markets and traders can, after all, be linked up wherever the necessary technology is installed. The answer, it seems, is that there is still a strong incentive for stock exchanges to be close to the location of the operations of the companies whose shares are traded on the exchange, since research has remained localized (unlike currency research, as discussed earlier). The less global the company, the less 'commodity-like' the product, and the more geography is likely to be retained.

Given that corporate equities have local characteristics, the easiest way for them to develop as global products is as part of the indexed products on the market (i.e., investors believe that they can make a judgment about the Australian economy and buy or sell the Australian stock markets accordingly, but would not make individual stock-picking choices quite so readily). Sometimes there are formal restrictions that require foreign investors to buy the market, not the stock (the rationale for a number of emerging country funds). In addition there will be a local nucleus of investors interested in the local companies. In the longer run, part of the key to the true globalization of stock markets will lie in the globalization of the companies themselves that trade on the exchanges, which will be a slow process.

The decision over the appropriate location also depends upon the development of global systems. A heavy investment in technology is needed before systems reach global proportions. Progress has to be made in several areas: clearing and settlements systems, trading systems, global custody systems, clearing for retail transactions, in-house computerization, and reducing the flow of paper, from cheques to stock certificates.

Everybody has to be somewhere

The London Stock Exchange's TAURUS system, which will put all stock records onto computer and eliminate stock certificates, the so-called 'de-materialization', has taken far longer to put on line than anticipated. In retail markets, ATM networks have to be expanded through new investment. It is in the area of systems that barriers can be put up to prevent the end of geography and to preserve a degree of proprietorial control. Globex-traded products will all be cleared in the 'home' exchange, giving the exchange control over the product even though over time it will be the trading activity, not the clearing, that will count. And there is no reason why networks cannot be developed to provide effective cartels.

Towards the global firm

Financial firms have been among the most enthusiastic supporters of globalism, investing in the new technology to improve their global operations. Those observers that foresee the demise of globalism cite the over-capacity in the major markets and the pulling-back of many firms from the attempt to have a global presence. The truth is, such firms have begun to understand more closely the costs of global presence and the demand for such services. As the barriers between sectors in the financial services industry are taken away, so firms can restructure themselves according to existing and potential markets. There is a great deal of room for different strategies somewhere between that of the super-global universal banking financial firm and the niche/specialist/boutique approach.

Both growth and profit maximization remain the driving forces of firms' behaviour. Only experience can tell us what is the best route to the optimal mix. The optimal strategy also changes according to market conditions and perceived strategic priorities. At times the objectives translate into survival and protection against takeover, at other times into more aggressive expansionism, with profits being in the future, reinforced at the time by rising price/earnings ratios as shareholders second-guess management.

Alongside these geographical issues, financial firms face ongoing business-restructuring questions. Which will be the most profitable financial services business, in terms of the rate of return on capital (the question that shareholders ask)? Where will these businesses be profitable? The same questions then have to be asked in line with growth ambitions. Finally, the firm has to decide on the best way to operate in those markets/businesses, as a global player or as a niche player. Allied to all location issues will be tax considerations, affecting in many cases the location of incorporation rather than of business activities (where such divergences are permitted).

It seems very likely that there will be only a few players in each broad segment of financial services who will be able to call themselves (in all honesty) global businesses. And global business means being able to deliver services across the globe, not necessarily in every corner of the globe, but certainly in the major financial capitals. Delivery means delivery in a timely and competitive way. Gaps in global coverage can still be filled either by network arrangements with other suppliers, or by accepting that the service may not be comprehensive, accepting that some clients will go elsewhere for part of the service. Ultimately, the cost of being non-global will be influenced by the extent to which clients themselves need global delivery, or whether clients themselves, in reality, have less than global needs.

A degree of specialization is likely to persist, with global banks, securities houses, insurance companies and other financial services companies. For each group, the 'global' structure is likely to be tailored to that appropriate for the sector. The global/multinational bank tries to be in as many places as possible. To some extent this is more of a multinational approach than a global, integrated one. The bank offers its customers its services everywhere, and trades on its name and brand worldwide. Its services are likely to be more global in nature in the wholesale business than in the retail sector.

Global securities firms aim at a presence in each of the major securities markets – London, New York and Tokyo – offering 24-hour support and the ability to trade in all the important markets and to raise funds for clients everywhere. Again, at present this is more of a multimarket than an integrated global market approach. However, in so far as clients are trading global portfolios (i.e. the clients themselves are global) then the activity in each market will be linked. However, despite the efforts to develop 24-hour trading in New York and elsewhere, the sheer physical obstacles suggest that, in an end-of-geography world, with the right technology in place, the idea of having to provide a 24-hour service from one physical location is outdated.

The increasingly international and global role of the insurance business is moving into prominence in the financial industry, both in retail markets (in the sale of savings products) and in wholesale markets (driving investment strategies on to the global plane, alongside the world's big pension funds). In the present climate of deregulation and

Everybody has to be somewhere

giving the customer greater control over his/her own financial assets and affairs, the consumer is demanding more financial (often savings) products. Insurance, pension and unit-trust-related products account for a high percentage of the financial assets of the consumers. Insurance firms deal in the savings of the consumer, while banks handle transactions, which are the payments services of the consumer. Insurance (and pension) companies are already among the biggest financial services companies and are the biggest institutional investors. Their end of geography is related to the increasing ability to invest in all markets, in the absence of exchange controls and other restrictions, in whatever market offers the best price and liquidity.

Finally, the global reach of companies selling global payments services, such as American Express, depends on being able to service clients everywhere. The product needs to penetrate as many markets as possible, so that it can be used worldwide, and, as already noted, services such as delivery of travellers cheques and use of credit and charge cards has to be global. This does require a presence in markets in the form of a licence to do business. It also requires a global payments systems network, operating through local payments systems.

In addition, there is the possibility of the global conglomerate, of a global firm that combines one or more of the above sectors. For the moment, the global conglomerate has to work within the structure, country by country, sector by sector, specializing in some markets, playing several roles in others. It will be tough to be a truly global conglomerate. At present, of course, many firms are already tempering ambitious global growth plans, whether on the part of banks reducing their international networks, or securities firms withdrawing from markets and locations. The withdrawal of players does not necessarily reduce globalization; rather, it indicates that only a few firms will be able to play the global game and be a force in all major locations.

Alongside these global firms will be the powerful local players, who in the local market may be as strong as the global players, and will be price-setters. Some of these will have tried the global route and withdrawn to reinforce their domestic base. Given that there will still be markets and needs that we can call domestic, this strategy should be workable. Then there will be the smaller players, some offering a degree of global service through a network, without being price-setters in any major market, others being small players in local markets. There are many possible permutations. In fact each firm will be looking for its own special permutation of the general formula.

Undoubtedly the greatest progress towards building the global firm will be in the wholesale and corporate markets. It is unlikely that many, if any, firms can realistically entertain ambitions to be major competitors in all retail markets, although this is more feasible on a regional basis, for which there are likely to be regional economies of scale and scope. It will still be very tough for the 'foreign' player to obtain high-quality access to local retail markets or even to local corporate customers: credit assessment and wooing the best customers cannot be done overnight. The majority of the world's financial firms still have a strong domestic base with a widely varying degree of international operations or of operations outside the home base (which can often be branch or subsidiary business in other local markets). The principal advantage that a foreign firm has over local firms is that the parent of the branch or subsidiary is foreign, and can therefore bring a new dimension into negotiations with the client.

Where a firm attempts to have a large retail presence abroad, that presence is, on the whole, aimed at emulating and outperforming the local financial firms. Competitiveness depends on efficiency (e.g., use of technology that might not be fully available to local competitors, notably in poorer countries) or often on regulations (which may handicap the foreign entrant). One of the key measures of globalization, integration and the end of geography comes where inroads into local retail markets are made by foreign firms, which then lend to local businesses and, less frequently, trade on local markets. The 1980s have seen advances in this direction as foreign firms (especially banks) have operated more widely in the United States, and in Europe some of the largest battles will take place in the retail banking field. Frequently, where these advances take place through acquisition (e.g. the Australian takeover of the Yorkshire Bank), the retail customer is less aware of the change, which at the beginning is primarily one of ownership rather than having any other impact.

If there is a slight shift away from the global approach that was so fashionable in the 1980s it may be because of a re-emphasis on the firm's status within regional markets, where regions represent expanding 'single', integrated markets. Positioning in Europe, in the US market or in Japan is quite likely to be the clearest point of focus for management. Many of the important strategic decisions may still apply to local business. In the United States, the long-awaited reform of the whole financial system offers tremendous rewards for those who get the business mix right, buy/sell the right businesses at the right time and price, and use greater opportunities to develop nationwide banking profitably. In Japan,

Everybody has to be somewhere

the key rivalry will be between the securities firms and the banks and between different parts of the segmented banking system: the foreign challenge will be of less importance. The European protagonists will certainly have other European firms in focus. Meanwhile, the forces of globalization, integration and securitization will tend to open the closed systems, assisted by the influence of foreign competition gaining access to domestic markets.

Reference

Hoekman, Bernard, and Sauvé, Pierre (1991). 'Integration and Interdependence: Information Technology and the Transformation of Financial Markets', part of an ATWATER Institute project on 'The Impact of Telecommunication and Data Services on Commercial Activity and Economic Development', mimeo.

[17]

Excerpt from *Information and Behaviour*, **3**, 239–52

13

Telecommunications and International Financial Centers

Mitchell L. Moss

Communications technologies are often regarded as space-extending phenomena; specifically, they allow individuals and firms to function within a geographically larger set of boundaries (Kellerman, 1984). For most observers, the ability to overcome traditional spatial limits implies a weakening of the city (Abler, 1975). New technologies, it is argued, allow people to exchange information and ideas without interpersonal contact; thus, the comparative advantage of cities, whose existence has been traditionally based on their role as centers for face-to-face contact, is no longer necessary (Gottman, 1977). This article argues that advances in communications technologies are not leading to the demise of cities; rather, they are strengthening a handful of principal world cities (Hall, 1984). Three critical issues are examined, to demonstrate the way in which technological change is influencing the pattern of urban development and the emergence of global finance and legal centers: (1) How has the emergence of a global economy led to the creation of major financial centers, and what role do these centers play? (2) How will the emerging telecommunications infrastructure influence future patterns of urban development? (3) What types of cities will benefit from telecommunications deregulation, and why?

Cities in a Global Economy

Telecommunication systems, by allowing firms to overcome the traditional limits of distance, permit what were once separate economic activities to become highly integrated functions. Multinational firms, for example, although headquartered in one location, produce and sell a diversity of goods and services in numerous countries. More precisely, information and computer systems enable a relatively small number of people to control and coordinate production, marketing, and financing from geographically remote points. Because of the widespread decentralization of manufacturing and assembly operations, there has actually been an increased need for a central headquarters responsible for the policies and financial decision making that allow such dispersion to occur. Noyelle and Stanbach (1984) have shown that such corporate headquarters rely extensively on "advanced producer services," (e.g., finance, law, accounting, management consulting, and advertising) which are predominantly situated in the central business districts of large cities; the city provides the sophisticated financial and information services that allow a firm to operate globally. As a result, according to Cohen (1981), cities that specialize in international finance and producer services have witnessed considerable growth in their economic activity.

This emergence of the internationally oriented financial capital represents a considerable departure from the traditional role of certain large cities as centers for a nation's international trade and commerce. In a report by *The Economist Publications* analyzing changes in London's financial markets, the authors highlight London's transformation into a global financial capital:

> The City of London has always been an international financial centre, or at least since the late Middle Ages. However, until recently its cosmopolitanism merely reflected the international scope of *British* trade and financial interests. British merchant banks . . . traditionally engaged in the finance of British trade, while the 'colonial and foreign banks' . . . provided a banking network throughout the Empire and British trading enclaves elsewhere. The international horizons of these institutions were essentially the global horizons of the British political and economic interests which they served. However, the recent globalization of the City's interests, occurring at a time of economic recession and stagnation in the UK, is a different phenomenon from the internationalization that occurred in the 19th century, when the City financed British trade and economic influence. The central feature of many recent changes has been the development of the City as a centre for an emerging world capital market, as opposed to its more traditional role as a financial base for cosmopolitan interests. (Hewlett & Toporowski, 1985, p. 43)

The rise of the multinational firm has been intimately connected to the globalization of banking and finance activities. Facilitated by the advent of communications technology, these activities grew for reasons that extend beyond responding to the finance demands created by the rise of the multinational firm. Specifically, the rapid rise and fluctuation of inflation and interest rates, which began in the early 1970s, created conditions of far greater uncertainty and risk. This, in conjunction with an influx of petro dollars, increased nation-state budget deficits, and the lowering of capital barriers between countries has led to the internationalization of finance activities and the proliferation of new finance-related services and products. Most important, "Technological change, particularly the advance in computer technology, has altered the environment of financial markets. . . . The increased speed and lower cost of communication have been important to the development and expansion of international markets" (Germany & Morton, 1985).

As a recent report by the *Group of Thirty* stated, "Improved telecommunications and the presence of the larger banks in several time zones have created a continuous, round-the-clock market which responds instantaneously to new developments" (Group of Thirty, 1985). This is one of the reasons given for London's continued prominence as an international financial capital. "London's position in between the U.S. and Far Eastern Time Zones make[s] it a useful centre for arbitrage between financial markets in those zones (chiefly the markets of the USA, Japan and Hong Kong); dealings on all those markets can be orchestrated from London in the course of one deal day" (Hewlett and Toporowski, 1985.) In addition, telecommunications systems are now being used to link geographically separate stock and commodity exchanges, leading to considerably longer trading days. For example, the Chicago Mercantile Exchange is linked to a futures exchange in Singapore, the Sydney Stock Exchange has agreed to do joint trading with the New York Commodity Exchange, and the London Stock Exchange and the National Association of Securities Dealers share price information on actively traded British, American, and international stocks (Lohr, 1985a; 1985b).

As Charles Kindleberger (1978) has wisely noted: "The continuous reduction in the costs and difficulties of transport and communication over the last two hundred years has favored the formation of a single world financial market" (p. 130). The emergence of international finance centers has facilitated the emergence of this global market; however, it has also weakened the role of the small- and medium-size city. The headquarters of the independent firms that once thrived in smaller cities are now subsidiaries of large, multinational companies. As a result, their headquarters have been consolidated within larger financial centers. Thus, communications and information technologies are strengthening a small number of world cities while weakening the traditional autonomy of many smaller cities.

In the Pacific Rim, Tokyo, Hong Kong, Singapore, and (to a lesser extent) Sydney have emerged as major financial centers. Tokyo's emergence as a particularly powerful financial center is closely linked to Japan's large capital base and its preeminence in the Pacific Rim economy. In 1981, Japan generated 69% of the Pacific Rim's gross domestic product. Japan's economic presence also extends beyond the Pacific Rim. In a recent report by the *American Banker,* Japan was shown to account for 35.5% of the total foreign-bank lending to business in the United States—the largest single source of such activity (Foreign Banking, 1986).

Tokyo has long been Japan's preeminent financial center. Despite stringent financial regulations that limit its role in offshore activities, Tokyo is the headquarters of 11 of the world's 50 largest banks. Moreover, the Tokyo Stock Exchange is the fastest growing major market in the world (McMurray & Browning, 1986). With the gradual loosening of Japan's finance regulations, and the admission of three major American securities firms as Tokyo Stock Exchange members, Tokyo is becoming an increasingly powerful world financial center. In Hong Kong and Singapore, their emergence as financial centers has been closely linked to their ability to facilitate offshore capital market activity. Hong Kong has a liberal regulatory environment, and both cities have strong historical ties to international trade and commerce. Most important, an infrastructure exists that adequately facilitates increasing demands for international communication and transport (Kirby, 1983).

In order to determine the location of international financial centers in the Pacific Rim, the ten largest U.S. banks were surveyed. Seven of these banks indicated that they had established a regional headquarter office in the Pacific Rim. Citicorp designated regional headquarters in three cities: Tokyo, Hong Kong, and Singapore. Of the remaining six, three banks established regional headquarters in Hong Kong and three in Tokyo. In addition, all banks had their largest operations in Tokyo, Hong Kong, and Singapore, while three had equivalently large operations in Sydney. The importance of these financial centers is underscored by a 1983 comparison of world rental levels, in which New York led, followed by Tokyo, London, San Francisco, Los Angeles, Hong Kong, and Singapore tied with Sydney for seventh place (Rowley, 1984).

As financial centers are drawn to areas with complementary services, the strength of these centers can also be measured by analyzing the location of branch offices of leading American law firms. Moreover, the location of these law firms underscores the concept that these areas serve as neutral settings that facilitate face-to-face contact and transactions. While many law firms rely on travel, telephone-based contact, and/or correspondent relationships with local counsel, a growing number of firms recognize the need for maintaining a physical presence in the Pacific Rim.

Such firms place a premium on being able to readily serve clients without encountering time differences whenever a meeting is necessary. As table 13.1 shows, Hong Kong houses the largest concentration of American law firms—followed by Singapore and Tokyo. Although one might expect Tokyo (due to Japan's economic predominance) to have a larger concentration of law firms, Japan's Practicing Attorneys Act of 1955 severely restricts the presence of foreign lawyers. Thus a regulatory impediment rather than a market impediment is constraining the growth of an international legal community in that country (Weber, 1983.)

Telecommunications Infrastructure and Cities

While the initial development of financial centers has been spurred by cultural, economic, and regulatory factors, a new optical fiber telecommunications infrastructure is being built that will further enhance the communications capabilities of national and international financial centers. As stated in *The Economist:* "The world's telecommunications are going on a high-fibre diet. Within two years, optical fibres will carry telephone calls beneath the Atlantic and Pacific" (Optical Fibers, 1986, p. 84). Although optical fiber systems have inherent technological advantages

TABLE 13.1
Location of Largest 15 U.S. Law Firms in the Pacific Rim

LOCATION	LOCATION OF ALL LAW FIRM OFFICES IN PACIFIC RIM	LOCATION OF FIRMS WITH ONLY ONE OFFICE IN PACIFIC RIM
HONG KONG	11	6
SINGAPORE	6	1
TOKYO	5	1
MELBOURNE	2	1
SHANGHAI	1	1
TAIPEI	1	0
SYDNEY	1	0
BANGKOK	1	0
PEKING	1	0

Source: Legal Times, "500 Largest Law Firms," vol. 8, pp. 15–17 (Washington, DC: September 15, 1985).

over copper wire, satellite, and microwave communication systems, the current state of the technology and economics of fiber favor high-volume point-to-point communications—from one hub to another. As a result, the new optical fiber systems are initially being built to serve the heavily used communication routes, typically those linking major cities (Moss, 1986). This pattern of development is in sharp contrast to communication satellites, where the economics favor traffic from one point to multiple points or vice versa.

In the United States and other nations, optical fiber systems are being installed along transportation right-of-ways, often following the railroad routes established in the nineteenth century. MCI has built its Northeast fiber system along the AMTRAK right-of-way; Cable and Wireless is using the right-of-way of the Missouri-Kansas-Texas Railroad to connect the Texas cities of Austin, San Antonio, Dallas, and Ft. Worth; and in England Mercury Communications is building a fiber system on British Rail's right-of-way. It is ironic that the choice of cities to be first served by advanced fiber systems is in part due to the decisions concerning transportation right-of-ways in the nineteenth century.

The initial comparative advantage fiber optics confers on financial centers is seen by examining New York City and Los Angeles, the United States' preeminent East and West Coast financial centers. These cities account for approximately 30% of all overseas telephony emanating from the United States. In addition, New York, with 43%, has the largest concentration of foreign bank offices in the United States, followed by Los Angeles with 11.8%, and Chicago with 8.4% (Foreign Banking, 1986). Further, advanced telecommunications systems have reinforced the comparative advantage that New York and Los Angeles have. Within each city, extensive fiber optic systems are being used to facilitate intraurban communication flows. New York Telephone has built three fiber optic networks around Manhattan and an interborough fiber network that links the counties adjacent to Manhattan. In the Los Angeles region, the fiber network built for the 1984 Olympics provides an advanced regional telecommunications infrastructure that can support the information-intensive firms in southern California. Clearly, telecommunications has not resulted in the economic decline of the largest central cities in the United States, but is being used to move information in, through, and out of such cities with greater speed and efficiency.

Telecommunications and the Pacific Rim

Just as the emergence of fiber optic networks in the United States demonstrates the way in which new technology can strengthen large cities, the fiber and analog networks being built in the Pacific Rim show similar trends. Due to the dramatic increase in trade between Pacific Rim nations and the United States, the current telecommunications infrastructure is being seriously challenged. Because the existing Hawaii-3/Transpac-2 (HAW-3/TPC-2) cable is saturated, satellite transmission is being increasingly used to meet communication needs. By the end of 1984, 70% of the transmission in the Pacific Rim was via satellite and 30% via cable. The estimate in 1986 was that by 1987 76% of transmission would be via satellite and 24% via cable (Logue, 1986).

The Federal Communications Commission considers this dependence on one medium of transmission to present risks, and has therefore supported the new Hawaii-4/Transpac-3 (HAW-4/TPC-3) fiber optic system. By 1991, this system is projected to shift the balance between satellite and cable traffic to 56% satellite and 44% cable (Federal Communications Commission, 1986). Further, the configuration of this cable provides valuable insights concerning the emerging pattern and location of economic activity. While the initial Hawaii/Transpac cables were oriented toward national security interests with direct links from Hawaii to Guam, the new HAW-4/TPC-3 cable is designed to accommodate both economic and military linkages. After stopping in Hawaii, the cable extends far into the Pacific and then branches in two directions—the national security link runs to Guam and then on to the Philippines via a branch called GP-2; the economic and trade connection extends directly from Hawaii to Japan. By 1990, other key Pacific Rim centers will be linked via a ring that will connect Guam, the Philippines, Hong Kong, Korea, and Japan. By 1994, Taiwan will also be connected.

Although the design of this network appears to favor the northern countries in the Pacific Rim, it is important to note that the ANZCAN cable connects Vancouver, Hawaii, the Fiji Islands, Sydney, and New Zealand. With both the Canadian and U.S. cables stopping in Hawaii, this will become an important point for information transfer. Further, it serves to mitigate the strong comparative advantage that the northern countries would otherwise have received.

As figure 13.1 shows, there is also an extensive amount of intraregional telecommunications systems being built. The systems shown on the map have been constructed since the early 1980s. As can be seen, these systems link areas that have both cultural and/or economic ties. For example, the Japan-Korean cable shows the important economic relationship between these countries. In the early 1980s, 28% of South Korea's trade was with Japan; and in 1980, 41% of South Korea's overseas telecommunications messages were with Japan (Kirby, 1983). In addition, the ASEAN cable shows how a new communications infrastructure can further the develop-

FIGURE 13.1
Pacific Rim Cables

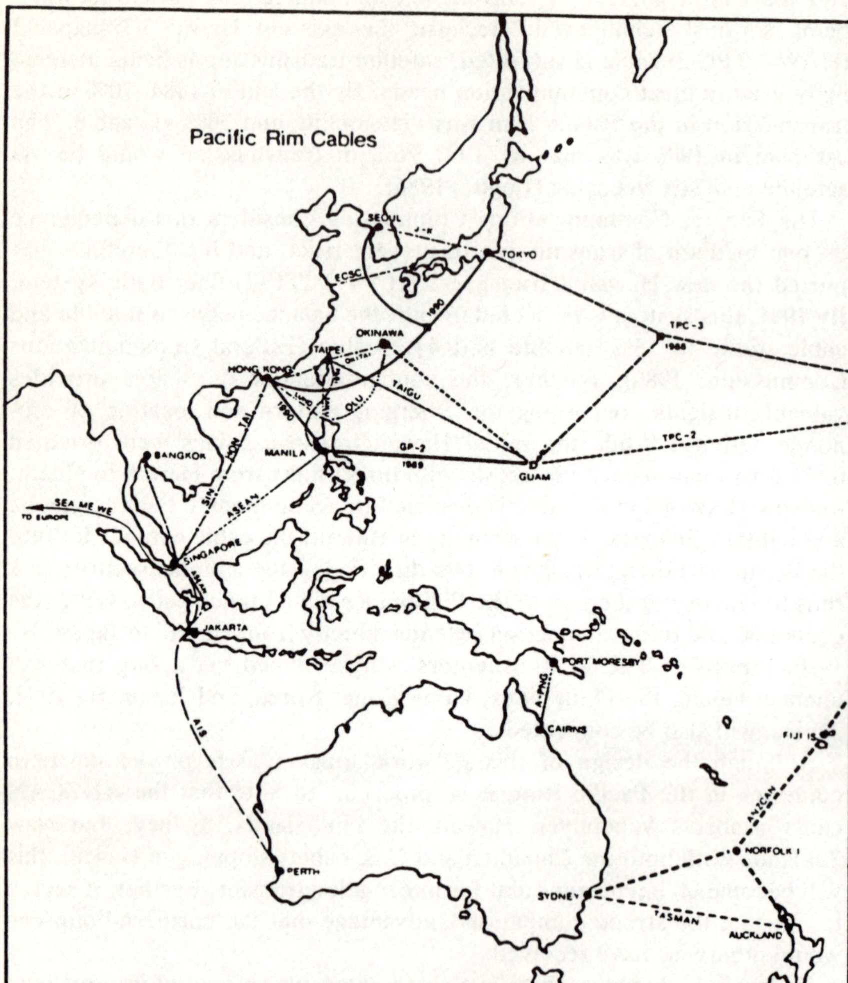

ment of a coalition whose goal is to develop stronger economic and cultural ties.

Urbanization, Trade, and Telecommunications

While the emerging web of cable systems shows that the strength of key centers with an existing comparative economic advantage will be reinforced, figure 13.2 shows that trade relationships do not completely account for international communication linkages. Although the NIC's—South Korea, Taiwan, and Hong Kong—show a strong association between trade and communication, Japan's pattern is different. Japan accounts for

FIGURE 13.2
U.S. Pacific Rim: Trade and Communication

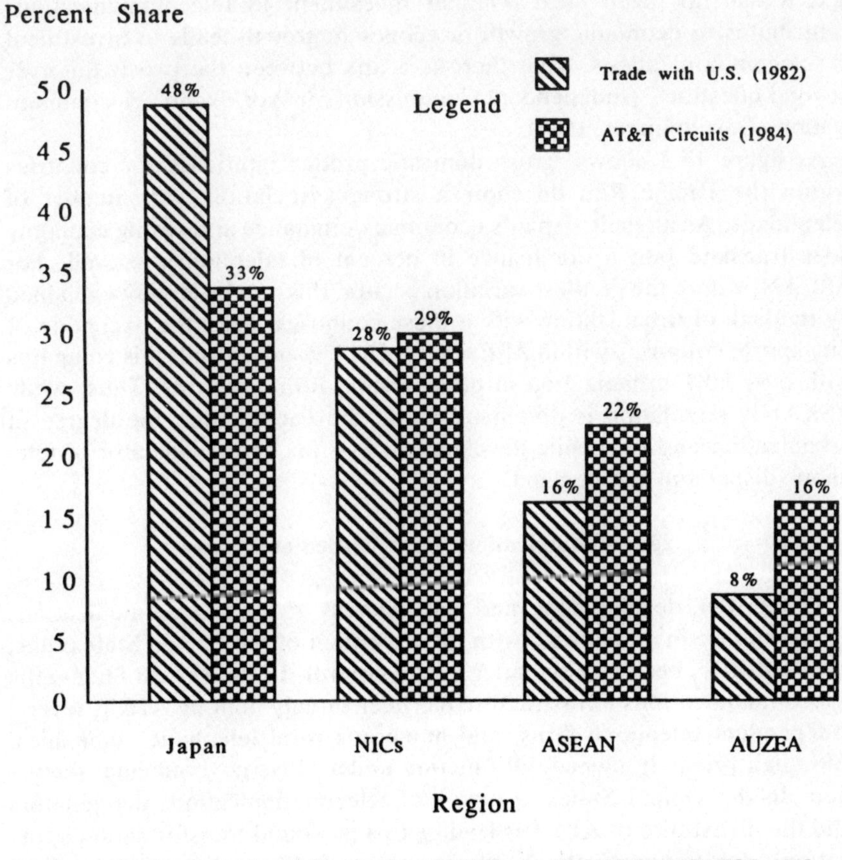

Sources: "The Pacific Arrives," *The Banker, 135* (713), pp. 16–23 (July 1985); FCC, 1985.

almost half of all Pacific Rim trade with the United States, yet it has only one-third of the AT&T circuits between the Pacific Rim and the United States. Given the strong cultural ties which also exist between the two countries, one might argue that this is an area where demand for international communications should be far higher. Conversely, while ASEAN accounts for 16% of Pacific Rim trade with the United States, 22% of AT&T's circuits link ASEAN and the United States. Such disparities demonstrate that telecommunications is a permissive factor that can contribute to locational decisions, but it is not a deterministic factor that, by itself, can generate economic activity (Mandeville, 1983). The Maitland Commission has recently highlighted this complex relationship between telecommunications and economic development when it stated, "while a strong correlation has been established between the number of telephones per capita and economic development measured by gross domestic product, it has not been clear whether investment in telecommunications contributes to economic growth or economic growth leads to investment in telecommunications. That there is a link between the two is however beyond question" (Independent Commission for Worldwide Telecommunications Development, 1984).

As figure 13.3 shows, gross domestic product statistics for countries within the Pacific Rim do show a strong association with number of telephones. As a result, Japan's economic dominance and strong economy does translate into a dominance in percent of telephones as well. For ASEAN, where the greatest variation occurs, this can be largely explained by the lack of urbanization within these countries. With the exception of Singapore, countries within ASEAN are 25–35% urbanized; this compares with over 80% urbanization in other Pacific Rim countries. Thus, while ASEAN's population is dominant within the Pacific Rim, the degree of urbanization and economic development is a far better indicator of telephone dispersion and demand.

Telecommunications Deregulation and Cities

The design, development, and management of the telecommunications infrastructure in all nations (with the exception of the United States) has, until recently, been totally under public control. In the United States, the telecommunications infrastructure has been largely built by AT&T, several independent telephone firms, and numerous rural telephone companies. Although privately owned, all function under close governmental regulation. In the United States, a policy of telecommunications deregulation and the divestiture of AT&T is leading to a profound transformation in the nation's telecommunications infrastructure. Public policy at the federal

FIGURE 13.3
Pacific Rim: Concentration of GDP, Telephones, and Population

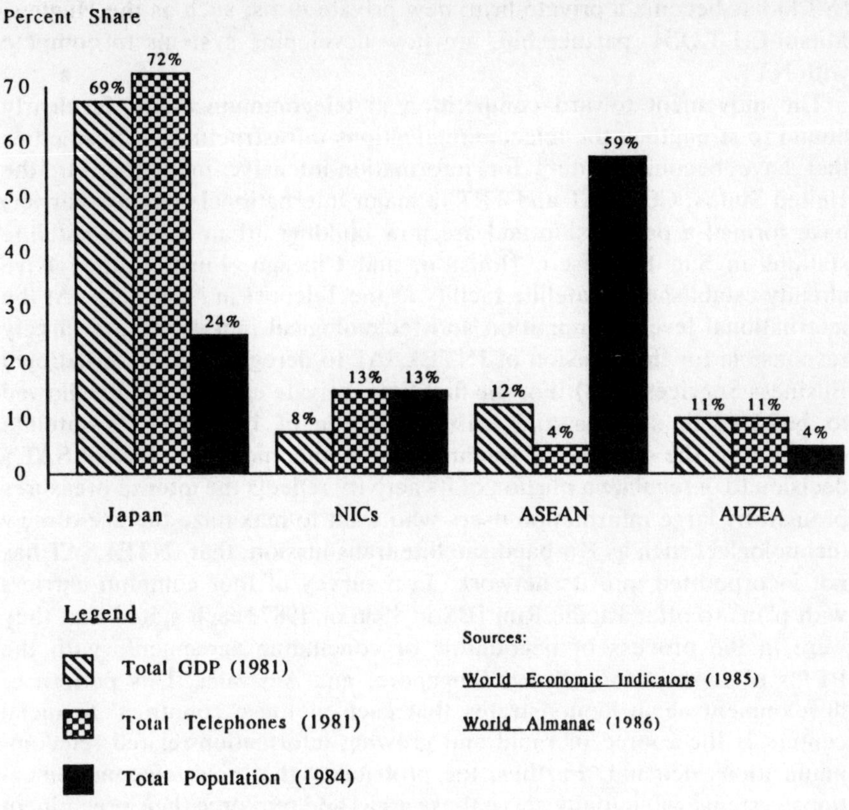

Sources: World Economic Indicators, 1985; *World Almanac*, 1986.

level is now geared toward letting market forces increasingly determine the pattern of telecommunications investment. This supplements the policy of ''universal service,'' the goal of providing everyone (regardless of location) low-cost and reliable telephone service. As a result, new telecommunications systems are being built to serve large communications users, most of whom are located in the nation's largest metropolitan areas (Moss, 1986).

A growing movement to rely on private firms to develop telecommunications systems is occurring in other nations as well. Nowhere, however, is this competitive telecommunications environment as pronounced as in the United States. In Britain, privatization has occurred with the creation of British Telecom; presently, limited competition in telecommunications infrastructure is taking place between British Telecom and Mercury Communications. In Japan, the state-owned Nippon Telegraph and Telephone (NTT) has become a private firm; new private firms, such as the Hughes-Mitsui-C.I.T.O.H. partnership, are now developing systems to compete with NTT.

The movement toward competition in telecommunications is clearly bound to strengthen the telecommunications infrastructure in those cities that have become centers for information-intensive industries. In the United States, COMSAT and TRT (a major international common carrier) have formed a partnership and are now building urban gateway satellite stations in San Francisco, Houston, and Chicago. Further, they have already established a satellite facility at the Teleport in New York. At the international level, competition and technological innovation are largely responsible for the decision of INTELSAT to deregulate its International Business Services (IBS). For the first time, private carriers will be allowed to build earth stations and lease a portion of INTELSAT's satellite capacity for the purpose of sending data communications. INTELSAT's decision to deregulate a portion of its activity reflects the intense pressures brought by large information users who want to maximize the use of new technologies, such as Ku-band satellite transmission, that INTELSAT has not incorporated into its network. In a survey of four common carriers with plans to offer Pacific Rim IBS in 1986 or 1987, each stated that they were in the process of negotiating or concluding agreements with the PTT's of Japan, Hong Kong, Singapore, and Australia. This pattern of development again demonstrates that each of these countries' financial centers is the source of rapid and growing information-related telecommunications demand. Further, the probability that new telecommunications systems will initially serve these areas and reinforce their preeminent position is underscored. As a result of these developments, planners and policymakers concerned with regional development will need to give heightened attention to the availability of telecommunications systems in cities.

Conclusion

This essay has examined the relationship between advanced communication and information technologies and the future pattern of urban development. It has sought to demonstrate that (1) telecommunications technologies are facilitating the globalization of world financial markets and increasing linkages among principal world cities; (2) the emergence of fiber optic systems for international and interurban communications is strengthening the telecommunications capacities of large metropolitan centers; and

(3) increased competition in telecommunications will require policymakers to give greater attention to the private sector's role in providing advanced telecommunications services in cities.

Note

The author would like to acknowledge the research assistance of Mr. Andrew Dunau in the preparation of this article.

References

Abler, R. (1975). Effects of space adjusting technologies on the human geography of the future. In R. Abler, D. Janelle, & A. Philbrick (Eds.), *Human geography in a shrinking world*. Scituate, MA: Duxbury Press.

Cohen, R. B. (1981). The new international division of labor, multinational corporations, and urban hierarchy. In M. Dear, & A. J. Scott (Eds.), *Urbanization and urban planning in capitalist society*. London, UK: Methuen.

Federal Communications Commission. (1986). *Memorandum opinion, order, and automation*. File No. I-T-C-85-219, (June 7), p. 9.

Foreign banking in the United States. (1986). *American Banker* (February 14), p. 1A.

Germany, J. D., & Morton, J. E. (1985). Financial innovation and deregulation in foreign industrial countries. *Federal Reserve Bulletin* (October), p. 743.

Gottman, J. (1977). Megalopolis and Antipolis: The telephone and the structure of the city. In I. de Sola Pool (Ed.), *The social impact of the telephone*. Cambridge, MA: MIT Press.

Group of Thirty. (1985). *The foreign exchange market in the 1890s*. New York.

Hall, P. (1984). *The world cities*. London, UK: Weidenfeld & Nicolson.

Hewlett, N., & Toporowski, J. (1985). *All change in the City*. London, UK: Economist Publications. Special Report, No. 222.

Independent Commission for Worldwide Telecommunications Development. (1984). *The missing link* (December). Geneva, Switzerland.

Kellerman, A. (1984). Telecommunications and the geography of metropolitan areas. *Progress in Human Geography*, *8*(2), 232.

Kindleberger, C. P. (1978). *Economic response: Comparative studies in trade, finance, and growth*. Cambridge, MA: Harvard University Press.

Kirby, S. (1983). *Toward the Pacific century: Economic development in the Pacific Rim*. London, UK: Economist Publications. Special Report, No. 137.

Logue, T. (1986). Recent major U.S. facilities-related policy decisions: Letting a million circuits bloom. In. D. Wedemeyer, & A. Pennings (Eds.), *PTC '86 proceedings*. Hawaii: University of Hawaii Press.

Lohr, S. (1985a). Global stock trading near. *New York Times*, November 27, p. D1.

Lohr, S. (1985b). The global exchange. *Fortune*, February 4, p. 9.

Mandeville, T. (1983). The spatial effects of information technology. *Futures*, *15*(1), 67.

McMurray, S., & Browning, E. (1986). Merrill Lynch, other U.S. firms, expect big things from Tokyo exchange seats. *Wall Street Journal*, January 31, p. 24.

Moss, M. L. (1986). Telecommunications and the future of cities. *Land Development Studies*, *3*(1), 3.

Noyelle, T. J., & Stanbach, T. M. Jr. (1984). *The economic transformation of American cities*. Totowa, NJ: Towman & Allenheld.
Optical fibres straddle the globe (1986). *Economist, 289*, March 22, p. 84.
Rowley, A. (1984). Where does the market go from here? *Far East Asian Review*, March 8, p. 45.
Weber, D. (1983). The Asian connection: Lawyers in the financial centers of the Far East. *California Lawyer, 3*(11), 29.

[18]

Geoforum, Vol. 16, No. 1, pp. 1–13, 1985
Printed in Great Britain.

0016–7185/85 $3.00+00.0

Electronic Funds Transfer and the Internationalisation of the Banking and Finance Industry

JOHN LANGDALE,* Sydney, Australia

Abstract: Growth of electronics funds transfer (EFT) is examined in the context of the internationalisation of the banking and finance industry. EFT has grown in response to the internationalisation of the industry and in turn has facilitated its development. Reasons for the geographical diversification of transnational banks and other financial institutions are discussed. The growing interdependence between international financial centres of New York and London is highlighted as is the emergence of Asian financial centres of Tokyo, Hong Kong and Singapore. Various types of international EFT systems are examined including SWIFT and leased networks operated by transnational banks. In addition, entry of non-banking institutions into the international EFT area is considered. Competition between banks as well as between banks and non-banking institutions is examined in the context of these EFT developments.

Introduction

The international banking and finance industry has attracted an increasing amount of attention in recent years, partly because of the series of crises it has been faced with, but also because of the rapid pace of change in the industry. One of the major changes has been the rise of the Eurodollar market in the postwar period. This market, unlike conventional capital markets, occupies no fixed location but relies on an international telecommunications network linking financial centres throughout the world. Its growth along with a number of other changes have led to a rapid internationalisation of the banking and finance industry.

The purpose of this paper is to examine the growth of electronic funds transfer (EFT) in the context of the internationalisation of the banking and finance industry. EFT is defined as the electronic transmission of payments or other money transmittals among financial institutions, individuals and businesses. EFT encompasses a wide range of payment systems and services directed towards the substitution of paper or coin movements by electronic means (WEIL, 1982, pp. 176–177). EFT has grown in response to the internationalisation of the banking and finance industry and in turn has facilitated this development. The paper focuses on international EFT and neglects domestic EFT developments; it is, however, recognised that this distinction is artificial since many of the forces leading to the adoption of information technologies by banks and finance companies are applicable in both the international and domestic arenas. Internationalisation of the banking and finance industry is examined in terms of the new international division of labour (NIDL). COHEN (1981, p. 288) defines NIDL as consisting of:

(i) an international spread of manufacturing, with trade occurring more frequently between subsidiaries of transnational corporations (TNCs);
(ii) an international spread of corporate-related services, including transnational banks (TNBs), as well as legal, accounting and advertising firms, etc.;
(iii) a system of international financial markets.

*Senior Lecturer in Geography, School of Earth Sciences, Macquarie University, North Ryde, NSW 2113, Australia.

TNCs are increasingly integrating their operations on a global basis. While much of the geographical literature has been concerned with manufacturing, there is increasing interest in the banking and finance industry because of the key role of capital in international industrial restructuring (TAYLOR and THRIFT, 1982; HIRST *et al.*, 1982).

The emergence of NIDL has stimulated the demand from organisations for international information systems. The growing importance of large public and private transnational organisations has been a major factor in the development of sophisticated information systems, which are necessary to tie various parts of a global organisation together. In addition, rapid advances in information technologies have lowered costs of computer and office equipment as well as lowering long-distance telecommunications charges and increasing the diversity of business services which are available. The feedback effects of these demand and supply factors have, in combination, led to organisations' being able to coordinate their international operations more easily.

EFT developments are a response to the demand for rapid transfers of international capital; but in turn they have facilitated the internationalisation of the industry. The banking and finance industry, telecommunications carriers and other groups are responding to these demands by installing more sophisticated EFT services.

Internationalisation of Banking and Finance

Geographical spread of transnational banks

A UNITED NATIONS (1981, p.3) report on TNBs defined them as deposit-taking banks with branches or majority-owned subsidiaries in five or more different countries. It identified 84 in 1975 and suggested that there would be many more by the late 1970s.

The early TNBs were European based (especially from the U.K. and France) and their international operations reflected the colonial empires of European countries in Africa and Asia. The colonial banking networks were characterised by an emphasis on retail banking with little global integration of the operations of the various networks. In the post-World War II period there was a rapid decline in the number of branches of British and French TNBs as newly independent African and Asian countries forced banks to establish local subsidiaries or nationalised their operations (PAGE and SOSS, 1981, p. 148).

U.S. TNBs grew rapidly in the postwar period. By the 1960s they accounted for six of the top ten and 20 of the 50 largest banks (CRANE and HAYES, 1983, p. 42). In addition there was a rapid expansion in the number of U.S. foreign branches during the 1960s, with a total of 124 in 1960 rising to 532 in 1970 (UNITED NATIONS, 1981, p. 23).

The emergence of NIDL was an important factor in the rapid growth of TNBs. Banks, in common with other service firms, internationalised their operations in order to meet the new requirements of the TNCs. Furthermore, TNBs were able to obtain substantial transaction cost advantages over nationally based banks in the international wholesale market, which is characterised by large transactions amongst banks, governments and large firms (DAVIS and LEWIS, 1982, pp. 547–548). TNBs were able to minimise transaction costs in international financing by relying on their linkages with correspondent banks and their communication networks connecting branch offices.

Moreover, TNBs, operating in Eurodollar markets have benefited from the asymmetry between the strict regulations governing residents operating nationally and the great freedom of non-residents to operate in foreign currencies. TNBs have been important contributors to the growth of the Eurodollar market.

The rapid growth of TNBs' operations is also related to the banks' competitive strategies. This can be seen in the follow-the-leader strategy of U.S. banks. Citicorp pursued an aggressive strategy of rapid growth in foreign markets. As a result other U.S. banks, particularly the large New York banks, internationalised their operations (DAVIDSON, 1982, p. 86). The European banks' push to create international networks was in part a defensive strategy against the inroads of U.S. banks into Europe.

By the late 1970s, the dominance of U.S. TNBs was slipping, while the number of Japanese and West German banks in the top 50 rose substantially (Table 1). One reason was that international dominance of the U.S. economy slipped, while West

Geoforum/Volume 16/Number 1/1985 3

Table 1. Major corporations and banks by home country

	Corporations among the world's 300 largest			Banks among the world's 50 largest		
	1959	1969	1979	1959	1969	1979
U.S.	206	188	142	20	14	6
Japan	5	25	35	6	10	14
West Germany	19	16	26	3	4	8
U.K	30	27	26	5	4	4
France	12	14	18	3	3	4
Sub-total	272	270	247	37	35	36
Other countries	28	30	53	13	15	14
Total	300	300	300	50	50	50

Source: CRANE and HAYES (1983, p. 49).

European countries and Japan experienced rapid economic growth. This is illustrated by the growing number of large corporations headquartered in Japan and West Germany (Table 1).

U.S. banks are limited by domestic restrictions on interstate banking. While this encouraged the early internationalisation of U.S. banks, it hinders their international operations in that their standing within their home market is reduced. In contrast, banks from many other countries have a protected home market.

A large percentage of international banking is conducted by the major TNBs. In the late 1970s the largest 12 TNBs in the U.S. accounted for 67% of all foreign lending by U.S. banks. The degree of concentration is even higher in other countries, where the top three or four banks in Europe, for example, dominate foreign loans business (UNITED NATIONS, 1981, p. 5).

The truly global TNBs, with foreign branch offices in a number of different countries, tend to be restricted to banks from major industrialised countries (U.S.A., U.K., France, Japan and West Germany), although Dutch and Canadian TNBs also have significant global networks (PAGE and SOSS, 1981, p. 156). In contrast, branches of TNBs from other countries are more restricted in their range of locations: world financial centres (New York and London), selected offshore centres (Bahamas, Cayman Islands, Singapore, etc.) and particular countries within the same region. For example, the pattern of Australian banks' overseas representation is concentrated in the Southwest Pacific Region (New Zealand, Papua New Guinea and Fiji). In addition, offices have been established in New York and London, as well as in offshore banking centres (HIRST *et al.*, 1982).

Geographical spread of other financial institutions

Many financial institutions are also expanding the geographical extent of their operations so as to take advantage of the emerging internationalisation of financial markets. The nature of this diversification varies substantially but is characterised by firms from major industrial countries (principally U.S. and U.K.) merging or taking a partial or complete ownership in firms based in other industrial countries. Frequently, the head offices of the two firms are located in New York and London. Such a connection gives the new firm representation in New York and London as well as access to the U.S. and European markets. Furthermore, the new firm may diversify in terms of the services it provides.

U.S. financial institutions have been active in investing in U.K. and other countries' firms. For example, Aetna Insurance has taken a 40% share in Samuel Montagu, a London-based merchant bank. For Aetna it provides opportunities for expansion in Europe as well as the advantage of the merchant bank's offices and expertise in East and South East Asia, while for the British firm it opens up Aetna's huge customer base in the U.S. for selling financial services. Similar reasons account for other takeovers. Citicorp has purchased a 29.9% share in

Vickers da Costa, although outside the U.K. it has purchased a majority ownership of its overseas offices, including branches in Hong Kong, Singapore, Tokyo and New York (ANDERS, 1983).

While U.S. financial firms have been primarily interested in U.K. companies, they are also moving directly into the Asian region. This reflects the growing importance of Japan, Hong Kong and Singapore as international financial centres. For example, Merrill Lynch and the French group, Paribas, have invested in Sun Hung Kai Securities as well as its associated bank; the group is a Hong Kong-based firm with extensive contacts with wealthy Chinese in East and South East Asia. The aim of the merger was that Merrill Lynch would direct its U.S. clients interested in investing in East and South East Asia to Sun Hung Kai, while the Hong Kong firm in turn would direct its clients wishing to invest in the U.S. to Merrill Lynch. For Merrill Lynch the move represented a further internationalisation of its activities, complementing its operations in international capital markets of New York, London and Tokyo (COTTRELL, 1982; ANON., 1983d). Unfortunately for Merrill Lynch the Hong Kong land market collapsed in 1982 and it suffered substantial losses on the deal.

U.S. financial institutions are expanding the size of their operations in major financial centres. This is particularly true of their London operations, but is also true in the Asian-Pacific area for Tokyo, Hong Kong and Singapore. U.S. investment bankers are expanding the range of their London operations; in particular, the Eurobond market has become increasingly intertwined with the U.S. capital market and the strength of the dollar has created a demand for dollar-denominated securities on a broader basis overseas (LAMBERT, 1983).

Foreign firms are also moving into the U.S. financial services market. Increasing numbers of foreign securities firms (U.K. and Japanese in particular) are setting up operations in New York to facilitate the demand from overseas investors wishing to invest in U.S. securities.

The geographical expansion of operations reflects the desire of financial institutions to acquire information on financial opportunities throughout the world. In order to achieve this goal they need a network of branch offices in international financial centres interconnected by a communications network.

While many stockbroking firms, merchant banks and security brokerage firms traditionally have had considerable expertise in particular markets and regions, many have been unable to diversify the range of services or the geographical extent of their operations because of their limited capital base. The purpose of many of the mergers has been to integrate the large capital reserves of insurance and banking firms with the specialist information held by the smaller brokerage and other financial firms.

This internationalisation of the finance industry, however, is limited by strict rules in many countries. In London no non-stock exchange company is allowed to own more than 29.9% of a London stock exchange member. However, this rule is likely to be relaxed in the near future. Similar types of restrictions operate in other countries. Even in cases where this limitation is removed, other restrictions may limit entry. For example, while the Tokyo Stock Exchange removed barriers to entry by foreign firms in 1982, they face very high costs of opening operations. Thus only large foreign securities firms such as Merrill Lynch, Vickers da Costa and Smith Barney are likely to join the Tokyo exchange (MILLER, 1982).

Internationalisation of the finance industry has the advantage of spreading risks. This is particularly true in the insurance broking industry where natural disasters (bushfires, earthquakes, etc.) in a particular region may cause large losses for insurance companies. The international reinsurance market centred on Lloyds of London represents an important method of spreading risk throughout the world, although London's pre-eminent position is being challenged by U.S. developments (MACRITCHIE, 1983).

The desire to reduce risk by geographical diversification of investment also underlies moves towards international portfolio management, especially for U.S. firms. Recent changes in U.S. laws have compelled U.S. pension funds to seek the best global return on their funds (MAUGHAN, 1983). Of a total of approximately U.S.$700 billion invested assets of the U.S. pension fund industry, some U.S.$7 billion was invested overseas at the end of 1982 (BYLAND, 1983, p. 47). Even a small change in the level of foreign investment would result in a major influx of U.S. money onto international capital markets. The internationalisation of U.S. pension fund assets may have substantial economic implications within the U.S., since many North East states have suffered a serious erosion of their revenue base; the internationalisation of pension funds from firms in this region may further reduce the level of investment in the region (BYLAND, 1983, pp. 47–49).

Financial institutions operating in currency markets on a global basis have offices located in various regions so that the closing of operations in one market overlaps with the opening of the market in the next region. This internationalisation of financial markets has been important in the growth of Singapore, Hong Kong and Tokyo for the Asian region and Bahrain for the Middle East. Bahrain's time zone location was one factor in its establishment as an offshore banking centre: its business day starts at the closure of the Tokyo market and ends at the opening of the New York market (MONTAGNON, 1982).

While there has been a substantial development of 24-hour trading, the emergence of a global currency market should not be overemphasised since trading tends to be concentrated in European business hours. Activity in the New York market drops off after the European markets close and, apart from trading in Japanese currency, foreign exchange trading in Singapore and Hong Kong is more active after the European market opens (SYNTEC ECONOMIC SERVICES, 1982, p. 93). However, the growing economic and financial sophistication of Asian markets indicates that trading will be stronger in the future.

International Electronic Funds Transfer

The rapid growth in demand for international EFT services can be related to the growing importance of NIDL. Large multiplant and multiproduct operations require improved information on their own operations in order to deal with uncertainty from factors within the organisation and from the external environment. Firms' information systems provide them with financial information on which to make decisions. In addition, they want improved financial information from the banks they deal with in different countries. Thus rapid changes in organisations' information systems has forced banks and finance companies to improve their delivery of financial information or face the risk of losing important clients.

On the supply side, rapid changes in information technologies are increasing the range of available EFT services. The microelectronic revolution is leading to lower costs and greater capability in computers, computer terminals, automatic teller machines (ATMs) and point-of-sale (POS) terminals, as well as in telecommunications networks and attachments. In the international telecommunications field technological change is rapidly lowering transmission costs and reducing the 'friction' of distance. It is becoming much cheaper to connect branch offices into worldwide networks and transfer financial information internationally.

Growth of international EFT services should also be considered in the context of the earlier discussion of internationalisation of the banking and finance industry. Establishment of global operations by financial institutions with international networks of branch offices requires a sophisticated computer-communications network. Rapid geographical and service diversification of financial institutions can be seen as encouraging the spread of more sophisticated international EFT systems; these services in turn are facilitating this internationalisation of the industry.

Types of EFT systems

There are a number of different types of international EFT systems. The nature of each system, its ownership, its access by different users and its geographical extent are all factors which have important implications in internationalisation of the industry. Firms which control EFT systems are likely to be financially profitable in the long term because of rapid growth in traffic. More importantly, they occupy a strategic position in the emerging information economy.

Public switched services operated by the telecommunications common carriers (telephone, telex and data) are heavily used; they are relatively expensive for users but have the advantage of being connected in a worldwide network. The SWIFT (Society of Worldwide Interbank Financial Telecommunications) network provides cheaper, more reliable and more secure means for interbank transactions. It is cooperatively owned by its member banks and links 37 countries.

Leased networks are an alternative network utilised by large TNCs and TNBs primarily for intraorganisational communications; lines on these networks are leased from PTT (Postal, Telephone and Telegraph) Authorities. The networks operated by TNBs are an integral component of their competitive strategy to attract those large customers (principally TNCs) with sophisticated information transmission requirements. Thus there is a significant rivalry between these TNBs in upgrading their networks, as well as between TNBs on the one hand and SWIFT, PTTs and other financial and non-financial institutions offering EFT networks on the other.

Entry of non-banking organisations into the provision of EFT systems stems from the adoption of information technologies. Once financial information has been electronically encoded, it may be handled in the same manner as any other type of information. Thus, aside from regulatory constraints on entry of new firms, it is possible for other organisations to compete with banks and other financial institutions in the delivery of financial services.

An emerging source of competition to financial institutions is coming from TNCs. Corporate treasurers of large TNCs with sophisticated global information systems are able to handle an increasing percentage of their own financial transactions, thus bypassing the services of financial institutions. This internalisation of financial transactions has a parallel in the telecommunications area. Large firms with heavy intraorganisational communications linkages between offices are increasingly moving towards operating their own private or leased-line network (LANGDALE, 1982, 1983). Furthermore, some are using such networks as a springboard for full entry into the provision of EFT or information services.

Swift

The SWIFT network was set up to provide banks with a means of handling inter-bank transactions, including bank transfers, foreign exchange confirmations, statements and query messages. It is cooperatively owned by over 1000 banks and operates in 37 countries as of October 1983. SWIFT does not provide a payment system; the settlement process between banks is still handled through traditional correspondent banking linkages (BYLER and BAKER, 1983, p. 458).

The demand for SWIFT originated from a group of European banks who wanted a cheap and secure international message switching facility. The banks were concerned about the poor quality of postal services, which handled 80% of their international transactions, hindering their operations (REVELL, 1983, p. 158). SWIFT was originally conceived in the late 1960s as a substitute for mail. However, it was realised during the 1970s that telex and other forms of telecommunications would become more important. By the time SWIFT came into service in May 1977 it represented a distinct threat to the PTT-operated telex service; the PTTs attempted to block SWIFT's introduction but were unsuccessful. The European banks were also concerned at the competitive advantage held by large U.S. TNBs because of their sophisticated leased networks. In addition, they faced competition from the Post Office GIRO system (BYLER and BAKER, 1983, p. 460).

The pressure on U.S. banks was not as great. They were able to use several domestic electronic message transfer systems within the U.S.: FEDWIRE, a network operated by the U.S. Government's Federal Reserve System, and BANKWIRE, a cooperative computerised message transfer system owned by approximately 200 banks (VEITH, 1981, pp. 46–47). For many international transactions the large U.S. TNBs used their own leased networks and telex for other interbank transactions. However, the deficiencies of telex were also apparent to them and they were willing to adopt the SWIFT service.

SWIFT's membership was initially dominated by European banks (Table 2), although it has widened its international coverage in recent years. In February 1980 there were 710 banks that were members from 26 countries; by October 1982 there were 1017 member banks from 42 countries. Numerous banks have joined SWIFT, even though it does not directly serve the country in which they are headquartered.

The geographical distribution of traffic flows also reflects this growing internationalisation of the network, although Europe still accounted for 73% of all messages as of December 1982 (Table 3). In 1979 West German banks were the largest users with 413,000 messages per month, followed by the U.S. with 374,000 (VEITH, 1981, p. 48). By December 1982 U.S. banks received or originated 2,940,000 messages or 18.3% of the total, followed by West Germany with 14.1% and the U.K. with 8.7%. It has been estimated that in the U.K. SWIFT has

Geoforum/Volume 16/Number 1/1985 7

Table 2. Number of banks belonging to SWIFT by region

	February 1980		October 1982	
	Total	%	Total	%
Europe	511	72.0	613	60.3
North America	91	12.8	141	13.9
Central & South America	50	7.0	148	14.6
Asia	58	8.2	92	9.0
Africa	0	0	12	1.2
Oceania	0	0	11	1.1
Total	710	100.0	1017	100.1

Source: Unpublished information from SWIFT.

Table 3. Number of messages sent on SWIFT network by region, December 1982

	Total '000	%
Europe	11,784	73.3
North America	3196	19.9
Central & South America	127	0.8
Asia	771	4.8
Africa	83	0.5
Oceania	119	0.7
Total	16,080	100.0

Source: Unpublished information from SWIFT.

captured 70% of the international traffic of the 100 banks which are members with approximately 700,000 messages per month being sent in early 1983 (SNODDY, 1983).

Traffic outside Europe and North America is small. Japan is not a major user, partly because the Government delayed SWIFT's entry. In addition, Japanese banks have tended to use their leased networks as much as possible. In some cases countries have only recently been connected to the network. For example, Australia and New Zealand were connected in November 1982. In addition, the volume of traffic in peripheral regions is likely to increase as additional countries in these regions are added to the network. For example, additional Southeast and East Asian countries are scheduled to join the network in 1984–1985.

The largest category of messages sent on the network from October to December 1982 was 37% for customer transfers, 27% bank transfers and 25% special messages (confirmation of credits and debits in correspondent banking). European countries use SWIFT heavily for customer transfers (West Germany 55% of total messages, Austria 55% and Belgium 49%). Peripheral European countries are important in the bank transfer category (Greece with 48%, Ireland 47% and Italy 45%). The U.S. and U.K. dominate the special message category with 66 and 34% respectively of their total messages falling in this category. The central role of New York and London as international financial centres and their importance as clearing houses with extensive correspondent banking relationships are factors accounting for these figures.

Most countries are relatively balanced in the number of messages sent and received (Figure 1). Peripheral countries in Europe (Portugal, Spain and Greece) and in the rest of the world (Hong Kong, Australia, Canada and Chile) tend to receive more messages than they send, although several other peripheral countries have figures which reverse this situation. The trend to receive more messages could reflect an imbalance in the number of customer and bank transfers between peripheral and major industrialised countries. Within Europe, West Germany receives relatively more messages, while neighbouring Austria, Luxembourg and Belgium send more messages; this reflects West Germany's economic dominance within Europe.

Swift is interested in increasing the range of services that it offers as well as the geographical extent of its operations. This strategy is leading to conflicts with other organisations. Some of SWIFT's member banks, especially those with their own aspirations to develop international networks, would prefer to see SWIFT's range of services remain limited. While there would not be any major conflict with SWIFT extending its operations to additional countries, it is interested in carrying more telecommunications traffic for banks within countries. This strategy is likely to bring it into conflict with existing private networks such as BANKWIRE in the U.S. or with PTT's new public packet switched networks. The latter are unlikely to look favourably at any further encroachment on their area of operations.

Leased Networks

Many large organisations operate domestic and

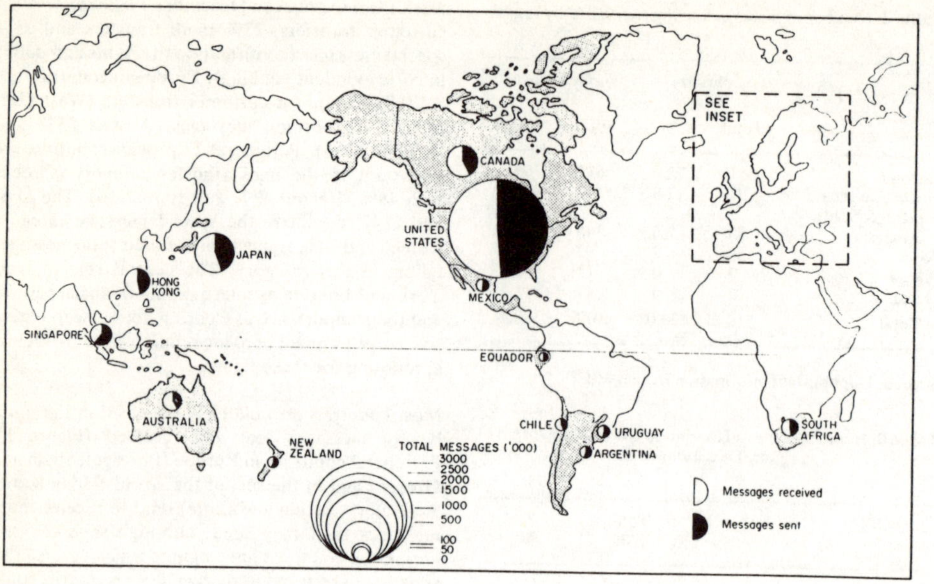

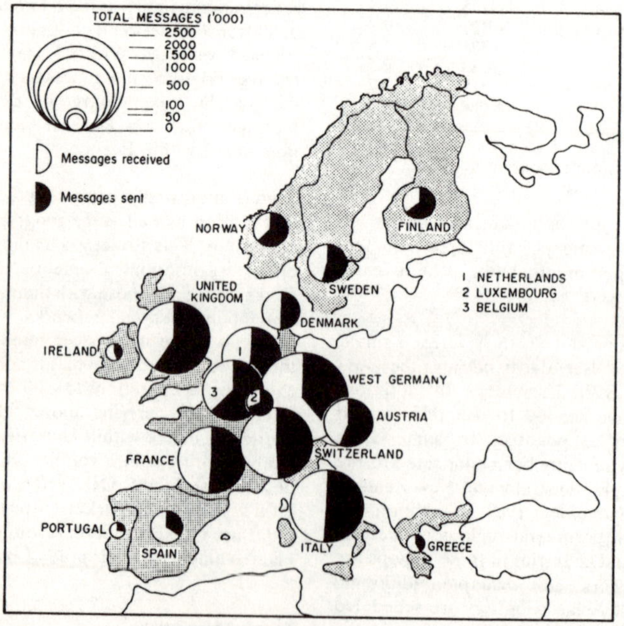

Figure 1. Number of messages sent and received on SWIFT, December 1982. *Source*: Unpublished information from SWIFT.

international leased networks, which are rented from telecommunications carriers for the organisations' internal use. They are, however, connected to the public switched network so that the organisation can decide which service it wishes to use. They are charged on a fixed rate per month, unlike the public switched services (telephone and telex) which are charged on the basis of time or volume of traffic.

Leased networks have a number of advantages for banks. They are able to send a large amount of domestic and international traffic without incurring extra charges. They often obtain economies of scale by operating high-speed lines between branch offices in major international financial centres and are able to 'piggyback' a variety of services onto their network. Leased lines may be enhanced with special features so as to be more reliable; many banks feel that they are more secure than public-switched services. A leased network allows a bank to offer services in developing countries where SWIFT is not available and where the telecommunications infrastructure is poorly developed.

The sophistication and extent of leased networks varies from bank to bank. Citicorp operates a very sophisticated and extensive worldwide network. The major switching points are at London, New York, Hong Kong and Bahrain, with high speed (56,000 bits per second) lines linking these centres. Connected to each of these centres are lower order centres with slower speed lines. Computer switches at each level in the hierarchy decide whether messages are to be carried over the leased network or routed by the public switched network or SWIFT.

Some banks operate highly centralised data processing systems and use their leased networks to feed information to head office (U.S. CONGRESS, 1980). For example, Continental Illinois' European branches enter daily computerised transaction details. At close of daily transactions the stored data are transmitted to Continental's regional communications centre in Brussels. The data are queued for high speed transmission to Chicago. Data are processed in Chicago and each unit's detailed records by customer and transaction type are updated.

Leased networks are primarily used for intraorganisational communications. Interbank transfers would be handled by telex or SWIFT; however, even in this case the leased network may be used to minimise costs. For example, a TNB sending a telex from London to a bank in Paraguay may route the message on its leased network to its branch office in Buenos Aires in Argentina and then by the public network for the last link. The leased network thus minimises telecommunications costs as well as providing the TNBs with more sophisticated services than those provided by many public networks.

A number of the large TNBs have also decentralised their administrative structure to parallel their leased network. While regional switching points on the network do not necessarily have to be in the same location as regional administrative locations, they frequently are. For example, Chase Manhattan has established regional service centres in Bahrain, New York, Singapore, Hong Kong, Tokyo and London, which coincide with many of its high level switching points (CANE, 1982). These service centres were established to reduce the delays needed to transfer money.

Detailed information on the extent of leased networks is not available. It would appear that U.S. TNBs have the most extensive networks which offer sophisticated services to customers throughout the world. Global banks such as Citibank, Chase Manhattan, Bank of America and Bank of Tokyo operate networks connecting branch offices throughout the world. However, European and Japanese TNBs are rapidly expanding their networks, although a number of the smaller TNBs rely on the services of computer services bureaux to connect their offices.

Smaller financial institutions also operate leased networks. Many merchant or investment bankers, money market and commodities brokers and other financial firms operate networks, although the number of branch locations is smaller than the major TNBs — they are generally confined to the major international financial centres. Similarly, smaller TNBs are likely to have offices only in the major international financial centres as well as countries in their region of origin.

Banks and other organisations in the U.S. are permitted to own and operate private telecommunications networks. As deregulation of the U.S. banking industry continues apace, more banks are moving into the telecommunications field either for the carriage of intraorganisational communications via private networks or to act as telecommunications carriers themselves. The move to become financial information utilities is also reflected in the development of subsidiaries handling data processing, and business and financial information, and in the shared ATM area. For example, Citicorp operates a subsidiary, Citishare, which operates primarily in the U.S. but also in some other countries to provide data processing services to financial institutions. It is also marketing an ATM system to banks which connects ATM systems into a national network (GINSBURG, 1982, pp. 94–95). In addition, it is moving into the telecommunications business by establishing a subsidiary which has purchased communication satellite transponder capacity and has built earth stations for two-way transmission of data. It is also establishing digital termination systems in major U.S. cities, which will allow it to provide sophisticated telecommunications services to business and financial subscribers (ANON., 1983, p. 74).

A number of large TNBs have entered the financial information business. Initially they offered database services to their clients and later created specialised public services. Both Chase Manhattan and Citicorp have extensive interests in this field (UNITED NATIONS, 1983, p. 39).

Entry of non-Banking Firms and EFT

The development of EFT systems is creating an opportunity for nonbanking firms such as telecommunications carriers, computer service bureaux, business and financial information providers, and retail and other service organisations to compete with financial institutions in the provision of financial services. However, a major limitation on entry of these organisations is the set of government regulations governing the banking and finance industry.

Telecommunications carriers and computer service bureaux have introduced services which provide the basic infrastructure to operate EFT services. The packet-switched networks being introduced by telecommunications carriers allow financial institutions to offer POS terminals at a relatively low cost to a wide variety of locations. Computer service bureaux such as Tymnet, Telenet and General Electric's subsidiary GEISCO offer a wide variety of computer services to business customers throughout the world. They also provide a number of specialised financial services for banks and this market is growing very rapidly in most industrialised countries. There is little to stop them from providing these services to non-bank firms if they are legally allowed to operate.

Entry of non-banking firms has, in some cases, been facilitated by developments in information technology. These firms are more easily able to enter the retail banking area because they can install ATMs and do not have to develop costly branch networks. With the prospect of videotex being used by some customers for home banking services, such as account interrogation, shifting money between accounts or paying bills, it is likely that such entry will expand in the future.

In the wholesale banking area new information technologies have lowered barriers to entry in some areas and raised them in others. They have been lowered because information equipment has become much cheaper and economies of scale in operating large computer installations have been eroded. However, while equipment may be cheaper much of the computer software necessary to automate banking operations is beyond the resources of small banks (REVELL, 1983, p. 139). Numerous computer service companies have emerged to supply small banks with software in the U.S.

Many large TNCs have international leased networks with spare capacity; some are interested in offering this capacity to users at a low cost. Aside from regulatory restrictions to entry, the barriers are not whether the firm is in the banking industry, but whether it is large enough to support a worldwide information system.

Financial information providers

The business and financial information market is a high growth area that is attracting numerous entrants. Two of the largest companies are Reuters and Telerate; the former had in early 1983 approximately 38,000 terminals worldwide, while the latter had 10,000 (ANDERLA, 1983, p. 31). Reuters has been a general news agency for newspapers around the world; in recent years most of its profits have come from the provision of business and financial information (ANON., 1983c). It operates an extensive international leased network and has been able to 'piggyback' additional business and financial information services onto its basic network. Its various services are complementary in character: for example, the business and financial services include a brief summary of general news items.

Rapid growth in the demand for financial information services from banks, financial institutions and large companies is partly a function of instability in international financial and economic conditions. The greater the fluctuations in exchange rates, the more important it is for firms to have up-to-date information on exchange rates for various currencies.

Credit card companies

Credit card companies are emerging as a major threat to banks in EFT systems. While Visa and Mastercharge are cooperatively owned by banks and American Express has a major international banking presence, many banks fear that these credit card companies have the potential to squeeze them out of highly profitable areas. In addition, there are numerous other credit-card systems operated by retailers and oil companies. Large retailers have an advantage of possessing a wide distribution network of stores and a captive market.

Credit-card companies are reorganising themselves into general delivery systems for electronic payment services. Visa's 'electron' card can operate both as a debit and a credit card and Mastercharge has set up telecommunications linkages with SWIFT for the international verification and processing of credit-card transactions. While both are owned by banks, they are willing to franchise use of their services to banks and non-banks (HOPTON, 1983, p. 52). Visa's 'electron' card can be used in ATMs throughout the world at any bank associated with Visa. However, both Visa and Mastercharge are facing considerable resistance to their proposed worldwide networks; many banks do not want to share their ATMs with competitors in their own markets.

There is growing competition on a global basis between the major international payment systems groups, all of which are U.S. based — Visa, Mastercharge, American Express and Diners Club. The international push partly reflects the saturation of the U.S. credit-card market, but also is a recognition of the growing market opportunities for global operations (FRIEDMAN, 1982). American Express is diversifying into a variety of financial services. The importance of information systems to its operations is crucial: an official of the company characterised the business as being in communications and information processing (ANON., 1983b). The worldwide communications network allows centralised credit card transaction approval, which lowers fraudulent use of cards but also provides the company with a vehicle for the delivery of new services.

Conclusions

The interrelationships between EFT and internationalisation of the banking and finance industry have parallels in other industries. The emerging internationalisation of production in many manufacturing, service and information industries is facilitated by the internationalisation of the banking and finance industry (and vice versa). Similarly, the growth of EFT should be seen both in the context of NIDL and in the emergence of the international information economy. Rapid technological change in information industries combined with growth in demand for information storage, processing and transmission, especially from large organisations, is expanding the degree of global interdependence. These changes are affecting all information service industries (advertising agencies, accounting firms, consultants, banks and financial institutions, etc.); however, banking and finance in particular is characterised by heavy information interdependencies within and between firms on a national and international basis.

The emerging internationalisation of production, especially in the information services area, has had a major impact on the growth of firms headquartered or based in the international business centres of New York and London (COHEN, 1981). This is particularly true of the influence of banking and finance. Foreign banks have established numerous branches in these cities. In addition, there have been many mergers and takeovers involving financial institutions headquartered in New York and London. Substantial growth, although at a lower level in the international financial centre hierarchy, has also occurred in such centres as Chicago, Zurich, Paris and Tokyo. In addition, the widening of the network caused by the growth of offshore cities in Bahrain, Singapore, Hong Kong and Panama has further internationalised the industry.

The rapid growth in international EFT linkages complements this international financial centre hierarchy. The majority of international EFT transactions are between major financial centres, although with the growth of economic activity elsewhere (South East and East Asia and the Middle

12 Geoforum/Volume 16/Number 1/1985

East) there is an increasing volume of transactions with these other regions.

The question arises as to whether EFT contributes to the degree of instability in the international capital market. It is impossible to fully explore this issue in this paper. Market economists have traditionally argued that competitive markets will benefit all in the long term. They point out that the introduction of EFT lowers barriers of time and distance, thus allowing international capital markets to function more effectively. Government restrictions in such areas as the entry of foreign banks and the international transmission of financial information inhibit the operation of markets.

There are a number of negative aspects to international EFT. One is that the growing internationalisation of the industry and the rapid rise in the volume of transactions has raised the level of risk in the system. With same-day settlement it is possible for a bank to fail within one or two hours (REVELL, 1983, p. 170). There is far less time for the central bank to monitor the situation. More fundamentally, internationalisation of the banking and finance industry has made it more difficult for governments to control their economies. This is clearly a matter of degree since even the Communist Bloc countries are influenced by major international political and economic events.

The national sovereignty issue has arisen in a variety of forms in various information service industries. In the banking industry a number of countries have placed very tight restrictions on the entry of foreign banks. In international telecommunications the debate over whether transborder data flows should be subject to any type of restrictions has reflected, in part, a concern about the erosion of national sovereignty by the global transmission of information.

The sovereignty issue can be clearly seen in the question of whether competition should be allowed in the provision of international telecommunications services. If competition were allowed, it is likely that U.S. carriers would dominate much of the lucrative and rapidly growing traffic of TNCs between major industrial countries (particularly between North America and Western Europe) (LANGDALE, 1982). In the international EFT situation the cooperatively owned network, SWIFT, has staked out a central position. However, its future success could be dubious in a competitive environment if several large TNBs upgraded their existing networks to carry third-party traffic. A number of large TNCs would be interested in following such a strategy.

Despite these problems, it seems clear that the internationalisation of the banking and finance industry will continue and that it will be more difficult to recognise a clearly defined banking and finance industry as service diversification occurs. The basic policy issue is likely to be the reconciliation of national goals of moving into an information economy with international forces, some of which may conflict with the national goals.

References

ANDERLA, G. (1983) *The International Data Market Revisited*. Committee on Information, Computer and Communication Policy, OECD, Paris.

ANDERS, G. (1983) Citicorp in £20m buy into UK broker, *Australian Financial Review*, 9th November, 22.

ANON, (1983a) Citicorp strives for nationwide bank net, *Data Communication*, September, 74.

ANON. (1983b) American Express plays its trump card, *Business Week*, 24th October, 70.

ANON. (1983c) Reuters' scoop in financial news, *Business Week*, 17th January, 63.

ANON. (1983d) Corporate quadrille, or excuse me? *Far Eastern Economic Review*, 1st September, 113.

BYLAND, T. (1983) How Erisa has affected US pension funds, *The Banker*, August 47–49.

BYLER, E. U. and BAKER, J. C. (1983) SWIFT: a fast method to facilitate international financial transactions, *Journal of World Trade Law*, **17**, 458–465.

CANE, A. (1982) The EFT revolution, *The Banker*, February 59–65.

COHEN, R. B. (1981) The new international division of labour, multinational corporations and urban hierarchy, In: *Urbanization and Urban Planning in Capitalist Society*, pp. 287–315, M. Dear and A. J. Scott (Eds.). Methuen, London.

COTTRELL, R. (1982) Sun Hung Kai widens its horizons, *Financial Times*, 11th May, 29.

CRANE, D. and HAYES, S. (1983) The evolution of international banking competition and its implications for regulation, *J. Bank Res.*, **14**, 39–52.

DAVIDSON, W. H. (1982) *Global Strategic Management*. Wiley, New York.

DAVIS, K. and LEWIS, M. (1982) Foreign banks and the financial system, In: *Australia, Australian Financial System Inquiry, Commissioned Studies and Selected Papers*, Part 1. Australian Government Publishing Service, Canberra.

GINSBURG, D. (1982) *Interstate Banking*, Program on Information Resources Policy P-82-4. Harvard University, Cambridge, MA.

HIRST, J., TAYLOR, M. J. and THRIFT, N. J. (1982) The geographical pattern of the Australian trading

Geoforum/Volume 16/Number 1/1985 13

banks' overseas representation, In: *The Geography of Multinationals*, pp. 117–138, M. J. Taylor and N. J. Thrift (Eds.). Croom Helm, London.

HOPTON, D. (1983) *Payment Systems: a Case for Consensus*. Bank for International Settlements, Basle.

LAMBERT, R. (1983) U.S. investment bankers make their mark in London, *Financial Times*, 25th August, 20.

LANGDALE, J. (1982) Competition in telecommunications, *Telecommun. Policy*, 283–299.

LANGDALE, J. (1983) Competition in the United States' long-distance telecommunications industry, *Regional Studies*, **17**, 393–409.

MACRITCHIE, L. (1983) Challenge from North America, *Financial Times*, Survey on Reinsurance, 5th September, VII.

MAUGHAN, R. (1983) London banks see portfolio boom, *Financial Times*, World Banking Survey, 16th May, V.

MILLER, W. (1982) Cautious response to removal of barrier to stock exchange membership, *Financial Times*, Japanese Banking and Finance Survey, 18th October, VI.

MONTAGNON, P. (1982) Investment banking has scope for development, *Financial Times*, Survey on Bahrain, 1st June, VII.

PAGE, D. and SOSS, N. M. (1981) Some evidence on transnational banking structure, In: *Foreign Acquisition of U.S. Banks*, pp. 133–189. U.S. Staff of the Office of the Comptroller of the Currency, R. F. Dame Inc., Richmond, VA.

REVELL, J. R. S. (1983) *Banking and Electronic Funds Transfer*. OECD, Paris.

SNOODY, R. (1983) New clearing system bridges UK banking gap, *Financial Times*, Survey on Electronics in Banking, 30th March, II.

SYNTEC ECONOMIC SERVICES (1982) Foreign exchange controls and forward exchange agreements in Australia, In: *Australia. Australian Financial System Inquiry, Commissioned Studies and Selected Papers*, Part 2. Australian Government Publishing Service, Canberra.

TAYLOR, M. J. and THRIFT, N. J. (1982) Introduction, In: *The Geography of Multinationals*, pp. 1–13, M. J. Taylor and N. J. Thrift (Eds.). Croom Helm, London.

UNITED NATIONS (1981) *Transnational Banks: Operations, Strategies and their Effects in Developing Countries*, Centre for Transnational Corporations, New York.

UNITED NATIONS (1983) *Transborder Data Flows: Access to the International On-Line Data Base Market*. Centre for Transnational Corporations, New York.

U.S. CONGRESS (1980) *International Data Flow*. Hearings before a House Subcommittee of the Committee on Government Operations, 96th Congress, 2nd Session, Washington, D.C.

VEITH, R. (1981) *Multinational Computer Nets: the Case of International Banking*. D. C. Heath, MA.

WEIL, U. (1982) *Information Systems in the 80's: Products Markets, and Vendors*. Prentice-Hall, Englewood Cliffs, New Jersey.

THE JOURNAL OF FINANCE · VOL. XXXIII, NO. 3 · JUNE 1978

SESSION TOPIC: MONEY AND CAPITAL MARKETS

SESSION CHAIRPERSON: ROBERT A. KAVESH

TECHNOLOGY, COMMUNICATION AND THE PERFORMANCE OF FINANCIAL MARKETS: 1840–1975

KENNETH D. GARBADE AND WILLIAM L. SILBER*

"The products of the world, which, if left free to move naturally would be attracted to the most profitable markets, are frequently impelled towards unprofitable ones because the knowledge of which are the best ones becomes known in most cases only after the product has been shipped to an unprofitable one. All this source of mercantile loss and embarrassment ceases where the telegraph is established."

Hunt's Merchant Magazine
July, 1865, p. 18

I. INTRODUCTION

MOST THEORETICAL and empirical investigations of the behavior of securities prices implicitly assume that the price at which an asset trades at any moment of time is determined by a balancing of the supplies and demands of all participants in a single integrated market. Many assets, however, trade in multiple, geographically separated, market centers. Participants in one center may be only imperfectly aware of opportunities for purchases and sales of *identical* assets in other locations. Contemporaneous asset prices may, therefore, differ between the various market places. Stigler (1961) has suggested that the analysis of markets which are not completely centralized may be viewed from the context of the economics of information.

One of the most important causes of inter-market price differentials is the existence of time delays in communicating price information between market centers. The purpose of this paper is to investigate the contribution of improvements in communication technology to the integration of decentralized markets. We consider the impact of the domestic telegraph system on the New York and Philadelphia stock markets and on the New York and New Orleans foreign exchange markets during the 1840s. In a similar vein we examine the effect of the opening of the trans-Atlantic cable in 1866 on the New York and London bond markets. Finally, we analyze the effect of the consolidated stock market ticker tape on the New York and regional stock exchanges in 1975.

Although these innovations in communications technology span more than one hundred years, they all served to speed the flow of information from one market

*The authors are Associate Professor of Economics and Finance and Professor of Economics and Finance at New York University. They wish to thank Jody Kunis for her excellent research assistance. Helpful discussions with William J. Baumol are gratefully acknowledged. Mr. James O'Donnell of the Midwest Stock Exchange was kind enough to provide us with necessary data. This project was conducted under NSF grant No. RDA75-17953.

center to another. We hypothesize that opportunities for accelerated search and order execution induced more efficient arbitrage between markets, thereby reducing inter-market price differentials and increasing market integration. While this is an apparently straightforward proposition, there are those who contend that there may be considerable lags before market participants apply new technological innovations to specific business practices. One of our objectives is to examine the timing of the economic impact of improved communications devices, thereby shedding light on the rate of diffusion of technological innovations in financial markets.

In Section 2 we outline the similarities and differences among the three innovations studied and the welfare implications of each. In Sections 3, 4 and 5 each technology is discussed and the markets to which it applied described. The hypothesis that the innovations led to greater market integration is tested by examining whether inter-market price differentials narrowed significantly after the introduction of each innovation. Section 6 summarizes the results and presents our conclusions.

Our foray into economic history is purposeful. Following McCloskey (1976), we believe history provides a useful laboratory for examining hypotheses suggested by economic theory. Diversity of institutional detail is an advantage rather than a disadvantage. Certain types of economic behavior are sufficiently powerful to transcend a particular historical framework.

II. Information Lags and Financial Markets

As an example of the impact of improved communications on market performance, consider the effect of the trans-Atlantic cable on the London and New York bond markets in the mid-1860s. English investors held a substantial volume of U.S. Treasury debt, and that debt traded in London as well as in New York. Prior to the opening of the cable participants in one market location received price information from the other center with a time delay equal to the duration of an ocean crossing, or about three weeks. Investors had to decide whether to transact in their own market at a known price, or whether to enter an order in the "foreign" market where the transaction would occur at a currently unknown price. Purchase and sale orders directed to the foreign market had to cross the Atlantic. Investors, therefore, had to estimate the price in the foreign market which would prevail three weeks hence based on information which was already three weeks old. Since the precision of this estimate was necessarily low, it took a relatively large differential between the current price in the home market and the last available price in the foreign market to induce an investor to enter an order in the foreign market.

After the opening of the trans-Atlantic cable, investors could learn of prices in the foreign market within a day, and could enter orders for execution in that market with a one day delay. They were, therefore, able to form far more precise estimates of the prices at which they would be able to transact in the foreign market, based on the latest available foreign market information. Differentials between the current price in the home market and the last available price in the foreign market which might have been ignored before the cable, now presented attractive arbitrage or investment opportunities. The greater sensitivity of market participants to prices on identical assets in foreign markets, and the ability to execute foreign market transactions faster, should have produced a narrowing of average inter-market price differentials.

This analysis of the impact of more rapid communication between market centers applies to the other cases we study, although the relative reduction in information lags are less than the reduction in the London-New York example. Prior to the introduction of telegraphic communication between New York and Philadelphia, price data from the distant market were available to local market participants with a one day delay. The telegraph made it possible for investors to obtain prices from the distant market before the close of their own market. This decrease of (at most) a day in the receipt of information is much smaller than the reduction in delays stemming from the opening of the trans-Atlantic cable. Before telegraph lines were strung between New York and New Orleans, dealers in foreign exchange in the two cities received quotes from the other city with a delay of from four days to a week. The telegraph reduced the delay to a day or less.

The introduction in 1975 of consolidated ticker tape reporting of all regional stock exchange transactions in equity issues listed on the New York Stock Exchange represents a reduction in information lags far smaller than the three examples from the nineteenth century. Prior to the introduction of the consolidated tape the price of a trade completed on a regional exchange could be learned by participants in the New York market with a five or ten minute delay. Consolidated reporting of transactions reduced this delay to one or two minutes. One peculiarity important to the analysis of the consolidated tape is that, even prior to consolidated reporting, participants on the floors of regional exchanges had rapid access to information on NYSE transactions, since the regional markets all had NYSE ticker tapes on their floors. Participants on the floor of the NYSE, however, did not have access to regional exchange ticker tapes. The effect of the consolidated tape on intermarket price differentials should reflect the fact that information flows became symmetric, that is, regional price information became available at the New York Stock Exchange as quickly as New York price information was transmitted to regional exchanges.

Delays in receiving information are not the only reason why prices for an identical asset may differ between two market centers. Even if buyers know that prices are lower in the foreign market they might prefer to transact in their home market if foreign market trades entail significantly larger transaction costs. These costs include the cost of shipping securities, the cost of making payments in distant locations or the cost of sending transaction instructions. Moreover, arbitrageurs who are likely to be most alert to relative price differentials have to pay two sets of transaction costs (when they buy and sell). Thus, price differentials can persist as long as they are less than transactions costs. Our hypothesis asserts that inter-market price differentials should narrow, but not fall to zero, as delays in the receipt of information decrease.

Welfare Implications of Faster Inter-market Communication

The gain to society from the innovation of improved communications between financial markets can be isolated theoretically through a consumer surplus argument. Since the relative prices of securities can differ between markets in the pre-innovation period, the marginal rates of substitution between securities for portfolio managers may differ. Introduction of faster communications leads to an equalization of securities prices and hence to equalization of the marginal rates of substitution between different securities. Thus, there are gains to the direct consumers of financial markets—portfolio managers.

Improved communication may also have welfare implications for real sector economic activity. If the time delays in information transfers were sufficiently great in the pre-innovation period, differences in the level of securities prices between market centers might affect real sector decisions (consumption and investment). Before the trans-Atlantic cable, a time delay of about six weeks for a roundtrip ocean voyage between New York and London might have been sufficiently long for inter-market price differentials to have had real sector implications. For the case of pre-telegraphic communication between stock exchange participants in New York and Philadelphia, where the time delay was measured in days, the real sector implications are minimal. The gains stemming from improved communication between the foreign exchange markets in New York and New Orleans might be in both the financial and real sectors.

There is a third category of welfare gains from improved communication between geographically dispersed markets. Financial markets provide liquidity services as well as influencing portfolio allocation and real sector decision-making. The cost of liquidity services can be measured by the cost of a roundtrip transaction resulting from a process of search over alternative markets (Garbade and Silber, 1976). Innovation of faster communications reduces the cost of searching for the best price in alternative markets. Introduction of the consolidated tape in 1975 provided investors with quicker access to price information on regional stock exchanges. Similarly, introduction of telegraphic communication between New York and Philadelphia in the 1840s reduced search costs. Thus, the *expected* cost of liquidity services was reduced by such innovations. This represents a gain in consumer surplus even if the time interval compressed by the new communication technology was too short to affect either portfolio allocations or real sector investment decisions.

Speed of Adoption of New Communication Technologies

In addition to the magnitude of the reduction in inter-market price differentials following the adoption of new communications technologies, there is also the question of the time delay between the commercial availability of the new technology and its use by market participants. This empirical issue is of particular interest in light of discussions surrounding the rate of diffusion of an innovation and the speed with which it alters existing institutional arrangements. There is, for example, a puzzle concerning the trans-Atlantic cable which requires clarification. While the cable was completed on July 27, 1866, Arthur Cole's (1928) oft-cited study of the evolution of the foreign exchange market notes that cable transfers of funds were not mentioned in the financial press until 1879. Davis and Hughes (1960, p. 59) confirm Cole's statements regarding the delay in the use of the cable. Furthermore, Cole cites the *Commercial and Financial Chronicle* (1882, p. 416) as the authority for his additional claim that arbitrage transactions between the London and New York markets first became important in 1882. These delays in the appearance of cable transfers and arbitrage seem unconvincingly long to us, as well as to Friedman and Schwartz (1963, p. 26). While it is possible that barriers to arbitrage existed before 1882, e.g., in the form of transactions costs and thinness of markets (inability to transact in sufficiently large volume to compensate arbitrageurs), it does not seem likely. The only proper way to test this conjecture is to examine the data.

III. The Domestic Telegraph

The practical use of the telegraph was first demonstrated in 1844 on an experimental line between Washington and Baltimore. Commercial development took place over the succeeding years. In January 1846 telegraphic communication opened between New York and Philadelphia (via Newark), but it was not until July 1848 that a connection between New York and New Orleans was completed (Thompson, 1947, pp. 33, 142). Financial market participants have been cited specifically as early users of telegraph facilities. On March 3, 1846 *The New York Herald* complained that "certain parties in New York and Philadelphia were employing the telegraph for speculating in stocks." Perkins (1975) notes that Alexander Brown & Sons and Brown Brothers & Co. used the New York-New Oreleans telegraph to set common rates for the purchase and sale of foreign exchange in the two cities (pp. 156–157). The stock markets in New York and Philadelphia and the foreign exchange markets in New York and New Orleans offer two opportunities to test the impact of the telegraph on inter-market price differentials.

One institutional detail common to both markets is the cost of making payment in a geographically distant region. Exchange rates between cities in the United States existed during the entire 19th century and the first two decades of the 20th century. As with foreign exchange, domestic exchange rates fluctuated with supply and demand, e.g., the price in New Orleans of one hundred dollars on deposit in New York could be above par ($101) or below par ($99), depending on the demands of New Orleans merchants who were making payments to, versus the supplies of those who were receiving funds from, New York. The cost of shipping the ultimate means of settlement, gold, bounded the fluctuations in domestic exchange rates. Market participants had to consider the cost of domestic exchange in deciding whether to transact in a distant market. Indeed, Perkins (1975, p. 186) notes that the "House of Brown" set foreign exchange rates in different cities at differentials which reflected prevailing domestic exchange rates. Thus, in comparing foreign exchange rates in New York versus New Orleans and securities prices in Philadelphia and New York, the prices must be adjusted by inter-city domestic exchange rates.

Integration of Foreign Exchange Markets

The institutional arrangements of the foreign exchange markets in the 1840s and 1850s are set forth in Cole (1928), Davis and Hughes (1960) and Perkins (1975). Foreign exchange transactions arose primarily in connection with bills of exchange drawn by U.S. exporters on British merchants. In the 1840s these bills were usually 60 day drafts, and quotations on foreign exchange reported in the contemporary press referred to 60 day bills. Foreign exchange dealers purchased bills of exchange from cotton exporters, mainly in the southern states, and sold them to importers, mainly in the northern states, who had to make remittances to London (Cole, 1928, p. 394; Perkins, 1975, p. 187). New York and New Orleans were the principal exchange centers in the United States. Transactions were handled by banks, but more importantly by specialized dealers such as Brown Brothers & Co. In view of our present concern, it is interesting to note that the partners in the various branches of the House of Brown "employed the telegraph...to communicate adjustments on foreign exchange rates" (Perkins, 1975, p. 45).

Our test of the impact of the telegraph on integration of the foreign exchange markets focuses on the differentials in the prices quoted on 60 day bills of exchange in New Orleans compared with New York. We recorded exchange rate quotations on or about the first day of each month from each of the market centers, making certain, of course, that the quotations were for identical dates in the two cities. The sample period extended from the beginning of 1843 through the middle of 1855 and was split in July 1848, when telegraphic communication commenced. After adjusting the New York quote by the sight domestic exchange rate in New Orleans, we compared the New Orleans equivalent of the New York rate with the actual rate prevailing in the New Orleans market.[1]

Panel A of Table 1 reports the results of the comparison. As a measure of the inter-market price differentials we computed the mean absolute difference (MAD) of contemporaneous prices on foreign exchange in the two markets in the pre-telegraph and post-telegraph periods. SDAD is the standard deviation of the absolute difference series (about the mean absolute difference), and N is the number of observations. As can be seen, the MAD was about 5.7 cents prior to the introduction of the telegraph, and fell to 3.4 cents following the opening of telegraph communication. We can reject, at a confidence level better than .01%, the null hypothesis that the MAD was the same in both periods in favor of the alternative hypothesis that it was larger in the pre-telegraph period.[2] The post-telegraph MAD did not, however, fall to a value insignificantly different from zero. The fact that a significant differential between regional rates persisted after the introduction of the telegraph may reflect the influence of transaction costs. These costs could have been sufficiently high that arbitrage between foreign exchange markets became unprofitable once the mean absolute differential narrowed to 3.4 cents.

1. A detailed description of data sources and subsequent adjustments for all of the innovations studied is available from the authors upon request.

2. The significance level was computed as follows. Let MAD_i denote the estimated mean absolute difference in prices in period i ($i=1$ before the innovation and $i=2$ following the innovation), let SDAD_i denote the sample standard deviation of the absolute difference and let N_i be the sample size. Under the null hypothesis the statistic:

$$z=(\text{MAD}_1-\text{MAD}_2)/[(\text{SDAD}_1^2/N_1)+(\text{SDAD}_2^2/N_2)]^{1/2}$$

has, asymptotically with N_1 and N_2, a standard normal distribution. We computed z and compared it to its asymptotic distribution.

TABLE 1

EFFECTS OF DOMESTIC TELEGRAPH AND TRANS-ATLANTIC CABLE

	MAD	SDAD	*N*
A. Foreign Exchange in New York and New Orleans[a]			
Pre-telegraph			
January 1843–July 1848	.057	.034	58
Post-telegraph			
August 1848–June 1855	.034	.022	65
B. Reading Railroad Stock in New York and Philadelphia[b]			
Pre-telegraph			
November 1845–January 1846	.799	.625	51
Post-telegraph			
February–April 1846	.606	.703	54
March 1847	.638	.619	10
C. Pennsylvania State Bonds in New York and Philadelphia[b]			
Pre-telegraph			
November 1845–January 1846	.551	.491	48
Post-telegraph			
February–April 1846	.387	.343	65
March 1847	.387	.292	16
D. United States 5-20 Bonds in New York and London[c]			
Pre-cable			
April–July 1866	4.118	2.265	60
Post-cable			
August–November 1866	1.272	.762	83
October–November 1867	1.097	1.221	38
October–November 1868	1.419	1.399	48
October–November 1871	1.208	.973	45

[a]Units are dollars on deposit in New Orleans.

[b]Units are dollars on deposit in Philadelphia.

[c]Units are gold dollars in New York.

Telegraph communication produced a measurable and significant improvement in the integration of the foreign exchange markets in the United States. The fact that our data reveals this improvement supports the heretofore unsubstantiated hypothesis expressed by Perkins (1975, p. 7) that the telegraph provided the communications facilities needed to forge a truly national market in foreign exchange. Similar references to the role of communication technologies by Davis and Hughes (1960, p. 59) can now be given a more concrete interpretation as well.

Integration of Domestic Stock Markets

In the 1840s several securities were listed on the stock exchanges in both Philadelphia and New York. These dually listed issues provide the opportunity to test the impact on market integration of the telegraph communication between the two cities which began on January 27, 1846 (see advertisement in the *New York Herald*, January 27, 1846).

There are two complications in evaluating the impact of the telegraph on New York-Philadelphia price differentials. First, direct inter-city telegraphic communication was not available when service was inaugurated at the end of January 1846. The line extended only from Newark, New Jersey to Philadelphia. Communications were relayed between New York and Newark by messenger. Nevertheless, telegraphic service anticipated mail service by a few hours, so prices from the distant market became available more quickly. Within a few months the telegraph line was extended to Jersey City, with messages ferried across the Hudson River to Wall Street. Second, there were many interruptions in service during the first six months of operation (Thompson, 1947, pp. 44–47). It is difficult to tell, *a priori*, to what extent these shortcomings prevented telegraphic communication from narrowing average inter-market price differentials.

To test the impact of the telegraph we collected daily price data on two securities traded in both the New York and Philadelphia markets: the common stock of Reading Railroad and the five percent bonds of the State of Pennsylvania. For the pre-telegraph period we used daily quotes from the three months prior to the telegraph: November and December 1845, and January 1846 (through the 27th). The immediate post-telegraph period is represented by daily data from February through April 1846. To test whether market integration improved over time we also collected daily data for March 1847.

Panels B and C of Table 1 record the mean absolute difference (MAD) between contemporaneous stock and bond prices in New York and Philadelphia for the periods listed. The standard deviation of the absolute difference (SDAD) and the number of observations (N) in each sample are also shown. The hypothesis that the MAD between bond prices in the two markets was the same in the pre- and post-telegraph periods can be rejected at a 2.4% confidence level. The same hypothesis for stock prices can be rejected at a 6.8% confidence level. Thus, considering the incompleteness and lapses of early telegraph service between New York and Philadelphia, its appearance is associated with a relatively significant drop in inter-market price differences. There is no evidence that the integration of the New York and Philadelphia markets improved during the year following the introduction of the telegraph.

IV. The Trans-Atlantic Cable

After several unsuccessful attempts, the first trans-Atlantic cable was completed on July 27, 1866 (*New York Evening Post*, July 30, 1866). The contemporary press immediately recognized the importance of the cable for enhancing the integration of American and European markets. On July 30, 1866 the *New York Evening Post* wrote, "The Atlantic Cable will tend to equalize prices and will eliminate from the transactions in bonds, in merchandise and in commodities, an element of uncertainty which has had the effect of...seriously damaging the commercial relations between this country and Europe." As if to foster these ends, the *Post* began to publish price quotations from the London market on the next day.

Needless to say, arbitrage of securities prices had taken place prior to the cable. These arbitrages, however, were primarily in response to extended periods of expansion or contraction in stock prices in Europe or the U.S. (see Cole, 1928, p. 416). Over shorter periods, prices on identical assets differed substantially between the markets in New York and London (compare *Hunt's Merchant Magazine*, January–June, 1866, pp. 308, 390).

To test the significance of the cable for market integration, we chose to compare the London and New York prices of the U.S. Treasury 6 percent, 20 year bonds of 1862, the so-called 5-20's. These bonds were widely held in Europe (*Hunt's Merchant Magazine*, October 1868, p. 245), and enjoyed active markets on both sides of the Atlantic. Quotations were available daily for the New York and London markets.

To represent the pre-cable period we used the four months immediately preceding the cable: April, May, June and July 1866. To represent the post-cable period we used the four months immediately after the cable: August, September, October and November 1866. Daily data were collected for each of these months. We also collected daily data for the months of October and November 1867, 1868 and 1871. With this data set we can examine the immediate impact of the cable and then, using the October–November data, determine whether market integration increased over time.

In comparing quotations from the New York and London markets a number of institutional details and quoting conventions have to be taken into account. Prices in New York were quoted in terms of legal tender (greenbacks). Since convertability of such paper currency into gold was suspended in 1862, the price of greenbacks in terms of gold dollars varied. Daily quotations for gold in terms of greenbacks appeared in the newspapers. The greenback prices of bonds have to be translated into gold dollar prices since all foreign exchange transactions were in gold dollars. In order to, say, sell a 5-20 in New York and buy the same bond in London, the transaction was as follows: sell the bond on the New York Exchange for greenbacks, sell the greenbacks for gold dollars and then buy pounds sterling with the gold dollars to pay for the purchase of the bond in London. To properly compare prices in New York and London we collected, in addition to the quoted bond prices, the price of gold in terms of greenbacks in New York and the foreign exchange rate in New York (the price of sterling in units of gold dollars). In a perfectly integrated market (without transactions costs) the greenback price of the bond in New York divided by the price of gold in terms of greenbacks, divided by the gold dollar price of sterling, should equal the London sterling price of the bond.

An investor seeking to transact in the foreign market had to complete several changes in currency. Each of these changes required the services of a gold or foreign exchange dealer, and each imposed transactions cost on the investor. These transaction costs suggest that even after the cable some price differentials ought to be observed.

Panel D of Table 1 records the mean absolute differences (MAD) between New York and London bond prices for the periods listed. The standard deviations of the absolute difference (SDAD) as well as the number of observations (N) in each period are also recorded. From the results displayed we can reject, at a confidence level better than .01%, the hypothesis that the mean absolute difference between contemporaneous New York and London bond prices was the same in the pre-cable period compared with any of the post-cable periods. There is no evidence that integration of the New York and London markets increased further during the first five years after the introduction of the cable.

The results presented in this section suggest that the cable was used to arbitrage the London and New York securities markets immediately after its opening. We also have independent evidence on the innovation of cable transfers of funds. As we mentioned earlier, Arthur Cole dates the first reference to cable transfers as November 1879. Cole correctly notes that this was the first time a cable exchange rate was listed among the money and exchange market data in the *Commercial and Financial Chronicle*. But that hardly means that cable transfers were not offered earlier. The financial advertising section of the *Commercial and Financial Chronicle* shows that two firms, Williams and Guion and August Belmont, offered cable or telegraphic transfers to London as early as 1870.[3]

V. The Consolidated Tape

The New York Stock Exchange is the principle market for transactions in the common stock of most large American corporations. For many years investors have also been able to execute transactions in NYSE-listed issues on regional stock exchanges, such as the Midwest Stock Exchange, the Pacific Stock Exchange, and the Boston Stock Exchange. Most brokerage houses, however, maintained only a ticker tape reporting NYSE transactions, and did not maintain ticker tapes reporting regional trades. Market-makers on the regional exchanges found it difficult to attract public orders to their markets since many brokerage houses simply directed all public orders to the floor of the NYSE.

In the early 1970s the Securities and Exchange Commission directed the New York and regional exchanges to develop a consolidated ticker tape which would display all transactions in NYSE listed issues, regardless of where they were executed. Consolidated reporting of transactions in fifteen equity issues started on October 18, 1974 during a test period of the new system. Beginning June 16, 1975 trades in all NYSE listed issues were reported on a single consolidated tape.

As we mentioned above in Section 2, the introduction of the consolidated tape eliminated an asymmetry in the flow of transaction price information between

3. See the *Commercial and Financial Chronicle*, March 26, 1870 (p. 385) for August Belmont's advertisement offering "telegraphic transfers of money on California, Europe and Havana." The first use of the term cable transfers appears in the advertisement by Williams and Guion in the *Commercial and Financial Chronicle*, May 14, 1870, (p. 609). The cable is mentioned in the advertising section of the *Chronicle* as early as November 17, 1866 (p. 812) when the firm L. P. Morton & Co. (80 Broad Street) offered to make "telegraphic purchases and sales of stocks and bonds in London."

exchanges. Prior to the consolidated tape, participants on the floors of regional exchanges could readily observe (via the NYSE ticker) the prices of the latest transactions on the floor of the NYSE. Before 1975, however, NYSE participants did not have a prompt source of price information on regional transactions. The consolidated tape provided faster access to information *from* regional markets. Instead of a five or ten minute delay in the dissemination of regional price information, a regional trade is now displayed within a minute or two of its execution. If the consolidated tape was successful, it should have produced a narrowing in the difference between the price of a regional trade and the price of an NYSE trade which took place at the same time or slightly after the regional trade.

To test this proposition we collected price data for every transaction in the common stock of five corporations (General Electric, General Motors, Gulf Oil, International Business Machines and Westinghouse) executed on the New York Stock Exchange and the Midwest Stock Exchange during the months of August 1973 (prior to the introduction of the consolidated tape) and September 1975 (after the introduction of the consolidated tape).[4] For *each* regional trade we computed the average price of all trades executed on the NYSE k minutes later, for $k=0$, 1, 2 and 3. We chose short time spans to minimize the likelihood of significant changes in equilibrium values of securities. The mean absolute difference (MAD) between the regional price and the average New York price, the standard deviation of the absolute difference (SDAD), and the number of observations for each of the four values of k are recorded in Table 2.

IBM is the only stock for which the average inter-market price difference appears to have narrowed significantly after the introduction of consolidated reporting. The reduction in the inter-market price difference for GM for $k=0$ and 1 minutes is significant at a 5% confidence level, as is the reduction for Westinghouse for $k=1$ minute. Otherwise, for all stocks and all values of k, we are unable to reject the hypothesis that the consolidated tape had no effect on inter-market price differences.[5]

These results lead us to conclude that, with the exception of trading in IBM, the consolidated tape did little to enhance the integration of the New York and the regional exchanges. Although our data apply only to the Midwest Stock Exchange, there is no reason to suspect that other regional exchanges would show any systematic differences. In light of the highly developed leased wire communication links between brokerage houses and their branches throughout the country which

4. We would have also liked to use Third Market data in our price comparisons. Information delays were particularly long in this market. Unfortunately, the data are simply not available for the pre-innovation period. The two months chosen for comparison both had similar volumes of trading. August 1973 was before the "test period" began and September 1975 was after the consolidated tape began full operation.

5. This analysis was repeated for negative values of k, comparing the difference between regional prices and preceding transaction prices on the NYSE. With one exception we could not reject at a 5% confidence level the hypothesis that the consolidated tape did not narrow the difference between NYSE prices and prices on slightly later regional trades. In view of the asymmetry of information flows before the consolidated tape, this result was expected. Indeed, we would have been surprised were it otherwise.

TABLE 2

EFFECT OF CONSOLIDATED TAPE ON NEW YORK STOCK EXCHANGE AND MIDWEST STOCK EXCHANGE[a]

	August, 1973			September, 1975		
	MAD	SDAD	*N*	MAD	SDAD	*N*
a) $k=0$ minutes						
General Electric	.1097	.1274	64	.1187	.0991	53
General Motors	.0866	.0870	197	.0702	.0719	184
Gulf Oil	.0709	.0695	149	.0640	.0576	54
IBM	.3989	.4315	52	.1658	.1706	45
Westinghouse	.0841	.0949	29	.0646	.0621	56
b) $k=1$ minute						
General Electric	.0882	.1004	52	.0990	.0882	48
General Motors	.0928	.0915	179	.0772	.0837	199
Gulf Oil	.0638	.0706	148	.0635	.0635	61
IBM	.4445	.3401	65	.3175	.2919	50
Westinghouse	.0969	.0872	20	.0565	.0709	61
c) $k=2$ minutes						
General Electric	.1086	.1138	68	.0952	.0978	63
General Motors	.0799	.0863	194	.0795	.0771	235
Gulf Oil	.0629	.0641	144	.0551	.0760	48
IBM	.4424	.3239	55	.2347	.1417	37
Westinghouse	.0695	.0980	18	.0703	.0643	32
d) $k=3$ minutes						
General Electric	.0927	.0967	51	.1216	.0992	43
General Motors	.0928	.0995	210	.0924	.0956	186
Gulf Oil	.0720	.0767	131	.1061	.0817	59
IBM	.5095	.4037	56	.3016	.3349	49
Westinghouse	.0804	.0865	21	.0602	.0612	53

[a] Units are dollars

existed prior to the consolidated tape, it is perhaps not that surprising that the consolidated tape contributed little to the reduction in price differentials.

VI. CONCLUSIONS

This paper examined the effect of three innovations in communications technology on the integration of geographically separated markets. The first two innovations, the domestic telegraph and the trans-Atlantic cable, led to significant and rapid narrowing of inter-market price differentials. There is no evidence that market integration improved during a learning period as market participants became more familiar with the possible uses of the technologies. Instead, we find that the effects were fully felt in the immediate post-innovation period. Contrary to earlier hypotheses market participants appear to have quickly appreciated the usefulness and profit opportunities of the new technologies for financial investment and arbitrage. Their activities led to a significant narrowing of inter-market price differences.

The statistical significance of the enhanced market integration was greatest in those applications where the information delays were largest prior to the innovation, e.g., the New York-New Orleans telegraph and the New York-London cable. The significance of the impact of the telegraph on the New York-Philadelphia stock markets was smaller, as was the reduction in information delays.

With respect to the third technological innovation, the consolidated ticker tape, we found little evidence of a significant narrowing of price differences between the New York Stock Exchange and regional exchanges (represented by the Midwest Exchange). The telegraph and the cable were innovated by the private sector, in response to perceived profit opportunities. The consolidated tape, on the other hand, owes its existence to the regulatory authority of the Securities and Exchange Commission. We conjecture that the tape would not have been innovated by private sector initiative (even if an innovator could have captured the externalities associated with the production and dissemination of information). The already advanced state of communications and the relatively short delay in information transfers made the consolidated tape unnecessary, and its measurable economic benefits minimal.

There is one important distinction between the consolidated tape and telegraphic communication that helps to explain the difference in their respective effects on market integration. Telegraphic communication, both domestic and international did two things: it speeded the flow of price information and also provided a quicker mechanism for transmitting an order to execute a trade. These are distinct processes. The consolidated tape only accelerated the flow of information. Transmission of inter-market trading instructions still relies on the telephone. The automation of the trading processes itself is the next logical step in market integration, and is currently under active consideration by the exchanges and the SEC. Will it produce significant economic benefits? Perhaps, but one of the lessons of our story is that it might be best to leave that decision to the instincts of the private sector.

REFERENCES

1. Arthur H. Cole. "Evolution of the Foreign Exchange Market of the Unites States," *Journal of Economic and Business History*, Vol. 1 (1928–29).
2. *Commercial and Financial Chronicle, A Weekly Newspaper*, William B. Dana & Co., New York, 1870, 1882.
3. Lance Davis and J. R. T. Hughes. "A Dollar-Sterling Exchange, 1803–1895" *Economic History Review*, Vol. 12, 1960.
4. Jonathan Elliot. *The Funding System of the United States and Great Britain*, Washington, 1845.
5. Milton Friedman and Anna J. Schwartz. *A Monetary History of the United States, 1867–1960*, Princeton University Press, 1963.
6. Kenneth D. Garbade and William L. Silber. "Price Dispersion in the Government Securities Market," *Journal of Political Economy*, August 1976.
7. *Hunt's Merchant Magazine* (correctly entitled *The Merchants Magazine and Commercial Review*), New York, 1845, 1848, 1865, 1866, 1868.

8. London *Times*, various issues.
9. Donald N. McCloskey. "Does the Past Have a Useful Economics," *Journal of Economic Literature* (June 1976).
10. *New Orleans Times Picayunne*, various issues.
11. *New York Evening Post*, various issues.
12. *New York Herald*, various issues.
13. Edwin J. Perkins. *Financing Anglo-American Trade: The House of Brown, 1800–1880*, Harvard University Press, 1975.
14. George J. Stigler. "The Economics of Information," *Journal of Political Economy* (June 1961).
15. Robert Luther Thompson. *Wiring a Continent: The History of the Telegraph Industry in the United States*, 1832–1866, Princeton University Press, 1947.

Part V
International Financial Services and International Financial Centres

[20]

Measuring Trade in Financial Services

There has always been trade in financial services.[1] Bankers have provided financial intermediation, foreign exchange market and other financial services across national boundaries. But the importance of such trade has increased greatly in the past two decades with the internationalisation of banking and the growth of international financial centres as the bases for offshore currency markets and other activities linking national capital markets. The question naturally arises how to measure the value and growth of this trade in financial services. The issues involved in this question are closely related to the difficulties that have been encountered in the treatment of financial enterprises in social accounts for national economies. It is best approached by going back to these issues.

Financial Services in Closed Economies

The crux of the problem was clearly explained in the 1947 memorandum by Richard Stone which laid the foundations for the original United Nations system of national accounts. "If we treated banks (and other financial intermediaries) like ordinary businesses, we should show as their sales proceeds simply their charges to customers and, as a consequence, a deficit rather than a surplus would appear on the other side of the operating account. In practice, this deficit would be so large that the property income generated in banking and even perhaps the whole income generated in banking would appear to be negative. This is clearly unsatisfactory".[2]

---

[1] This paper deals with financial services other than insurance.

[2] *Measurement of National Income and the Construction of Social Accounts*, "Appendix. Definition and Measurement of the National Income and Related Totals" by RICHARD STONE, United Nations, Geneva, 1947 (hereafter cited as "Stone Memorandum"), p. 40.

The solutions to this conundrum which have been adopted by social accountants fall into three classes corresponding to the three main functions of banks, the creation of money, the provision of a payments mechanism and related services, and financial intermediation; or, in the words of an early contributor to the debate, "loan services, clearance or transfer of circulating medium services, and the creation and maintenance of circulating medium".[3] Those who have put the emphasis on the creation of money function have regarded the services of banks as being provided to the community at large and have treated them, by analogy with government services, as final products and thus as contributing to gross domestic product (GDP). Those who have emphasised the payments mechanism function have regarded the services of banks as being rendered primarily to depositors and have divided them into those rendered to households, considered as final products and therefore included in GDP, and those rendered to enterprises, considered as intermediate products and therefore excluded from GDP. Those, finally, who have focused on the intermediation function have viewed bank services as being rendered mainly to borrowers and have therefore treated them wholly as intermediate products used as inputs by enterprises (except sometimes for those associated with consumer loans, considered as a service to households).[4]

Services to the Community. The first approach has not been widely used. But it was proposed in Australia by H.P. Brown and was employed in the Australian national accounts from 1947 until 1972.[5]

---

[3] CLARK WARBURTON, "Financial Intermediaries" in National Bureau of Economic Research, *Studies in Income and Wealth*, vol. 22, Princeton University Press, 1958, p. 511.

[4] There have also been suggestions for dealing with the problem by doing away with the distinction between factor and non-factor services. Industrial economists using an input-output approach to the study of the service sector tend to treat all non-factor service incomes as though they were factor incomes (e.g. Bureau of Industry Economics, *Features of the Australian Service Sector*, AGPS, Canberra, 1980), while there has also been a proposal, on the contrary, to treat all interest as a non-factor service income (P.T. SUNGA, "An Alternative to the Current Treatment of Interest as Transfer in the United States and Canadian System of National Accounts", IARIW 18th General Conference, Luxembourg, August 1983). This would seem to be a case of throwing out the baby with the bath water. The distinction between output of enterprises (consisting of goods or services) and the services of factors of production which constitute the ultimate inputs of such enterprises, even though it breaks down in marginal cases, seems of sufficient importance not to be lightly jettisoned.

[5] See H.P. BROWN, "Some Aspects of Social Accounting - Interest and Banks", *Economic Record*, August 1949; also B.D. HAIG, "The Treatment of Banks in the Social Accounts", *Economic Record*, December 1973 and comment by A.W. ROCHE and reply by B.D. HAIG, *Economic Record*, March 1975.

Brown argued that the function of banks was essentially similar to a major function of government, "oiling the wheels of industry and the community generally".[6] He therefore proposed that "as for governments, the contribution of banks to the national income is equal to the wages and salaries paid by banks".[7] In effect, though not in rationale, Brown's approach was similar to the "aggregation of individuals" approach originally proposed by Kuznets and used by the US Department of Commerce until 1947, except that Brown excluded bank profits on the ground that they were merely a channel through which surplus of trading enterprises was passed on to shareholder-depositors, so that their inclusion would have involved double counting.[8] The crucial feature of both versions was that the output of banks, valued at factor incomes (including or excluding profits) in banking, was included in national income without any deductions in other parts of the economy. In treating the whole output of financial enterprises as final products, this approach certainly involved double counting (though not more so than in the case of government services) and has therefore been generally discarded.

Services to Depositors. The second approach was first worked out in the US Department of Commerce and then adopted in the first United Nations system of national accounts on the recommendation of a committee chaired by Richard Stone. Its rationale was explained by Stone as follows: "Financial enterprises require special treatment in view of the different functions they perform and the method they adopt in charging for services. Consider commercial banks as a typical example. On the one hand, they provide services to their customers in the form of keeping their accounts for them and providing advice on various financial matters. For this they make a charge which, in many cases, is inadequate. On the other hand, they lend the money deposited with them, whether as a result of their own activities or not, and from this receive a net return large enough to enable them to subsidise the other aspect of their business".[9]

To overcome this difficulty, he proposed the following procedure: "An income is imputed to bank depositors for the use of their money

[6] H. P. Brown, cited B. D. HAIG, *Economic Record*, December 1973, p. 625.

[7] *Ibid.*

[8] *Ibid.*, p. 626. For references to earlier literature on the subject, see R. E. SPEAGLE & L. SILVERMAN, "The Banking Income Dilemma", *Review of Economics & Statistics*, vol. 35, 1953, pp. 139.

[9] "Stone Memorandum", p. 40.

equal to the excess of interest and dividends received by banks over interest paid out and this income is assumed to be used in 'paying' for uncharged banking services. In the case of persons, this imputed income and outlay appears on either side of the revenue account of persons, but, in the case of enterprises of all kinds, the imputed outlay is charged to operating account, thus diminishing the surplus of the enterprise, while the imputed income is credited to the appropriation account, thus restricting the effects of the adjustment to the operating surplus alone... The allocation of the total amount imputed between persons and businesses can only be based on knowledge of the bank expenses incurred in respect of, but not charged to, these two types of depositor".[10] In effect, depositors were regarded as receiving, in return for depositing their money with banks, an income in kind in the form of payments mechanism and other services, in much the same way as factory workers may receive, in addition to their cash wages, free canteen meals.

When this approach was adopted by the US Department of Commerce the allocation of the imputed bank service charge between households and enterprises, and thus between final and intermediate products, was based on deposit ownership.[11] When the same approach was adopted in the first UN system of national accounts (SNA), the same procedure was recommended, though the difficulty of inadequate statistics of deposit ownership in many countries was acknowledged. "The contribution of banks, etc. to gross domestic product is here evaluated by imputing to depositors a service charge equal to the excess of investment income accruing to these institutions and by imputing at the same time a corresponding amount of income to depositors. Thus these imputations do not change the income of banks or of other enterprises, but they result in a change in the industrial classification of domestic product (from other enterprises to banks) in so far as the imputation is made in respect of business deposits, and in an increase in the domestic product to the extent that the imputation is made in respect of the deposits of households, etc. The main problem in applying this rule is of a statistical character, but the total amount involved in most countries is small" and inaccuracies hardly serious.[12]

---

[10] *Ibid.*, p. 41.

[11] U.S. Department of Commerce, *National Income 1951 Edition*, cited R.E. Speagle & L. Silverman, *op. cit.*, p. 130.

[12] *A System of National Accounts and Supporting Tables*, United Nations, New York, 1953, [ST/STAT/SER F./No. 2], p. 32.

In the following years, the second approach came under heavy criticism, chiefly on the ground that it misconceived the functions of banks. One exposition of this view criticised the Department of Commerce interpretation of the banking function as "primarily a matter of keeping accounts for depositors, including the mechanical operation of monetary transfers... As far as these lending institutions are concerned, lending and investing functions are performed free of charge to borrowers. The creation of purchasing power through the lending process is passed over."[13] In the view of these critics, "the chief business of commercial banks... consists of two things: the expert management and investment of funds belonging to the banks' owners and creditors and, of equal importance under a fractional reserve system, the simultaneous creation of money." Since the capacity of banks to provide credit depends on their ability to maintain the convertibility of deposits, even "the expense of an elaborate clearing machinery set up expressly to keep deposit money freely convertible" should be regarded as part, indeed "a major part of lending costs".[14]

Apart from its complexity and its neglect of bank services to borrowers, the Department of Commerce (and old SNA) approach was criticised also on the ground that ownership of deposits was a very inadequate guide to the relative costs of services provided by banks to household and business depositors, if only because of economies of scale.[15]

Services to Borrowers. The third view, that bank services should be regarded as rendered primarily to borrowers rather than to depositors, because the primary function of banks is financial intermediation, prevailed in the 1960s. In 1968 it was incorporated in a revised UN system of national accounts. "The imputed service charge is to be treated as intermediate consumption of industries for a number of reasons" of which the first was that "a key service performed by banks and similar institutions is to channel the savings of other economic agents into loans to industries".[16] Or, as it was put by the Australian government stati-

---

[13] R.E. SPEAGLE & L. SILVERMAN, *op. cit.*, pp. 131f.

[14] *Ibid.*, p. 131.

[15] G. JASZI, "The Conceptual Basis of the Accounts: A Re-Examination" in NBER, *op. cit.*, p. 63.

[16] *A System of National Accounts (Rev. 3)*, UNITED NATIONS, New York, 1968. Other reasons given for the change were the statistical difficulty of allocating the imputed service charge among industries and the advantage that under the new system, unlike the old, "the value of gross domestic product... is not inflated by assigning part of the service charge to final consumption expenditure" (*ibid.* p. 97). For reasons which are not clear, it was also argued that, in principle, the imputed bank service charge should be equated to net investment income of banks arising from loans and other investments "made from the deposits they hold" but not "from their own funds" (*ibid.*).

stician who changed over to the new SNA procedure in 1973, the imputed bank service charge "measures the expenses associated with organising borrowing and lending".[17]

The Australian explanation gives a clear account of the mechanics of this approach. "Interest received is viewed as consisting of a pure interest component and a service charge for organising the funds. It is not practicable to allocate all the service charge to customers [i.e. among borrowers by industry]. The part relating to consumer loans (including hire-purchase) is treated as being paid by the customer and included in private consumption expenditure. The remainder, termed the imputed bank service charge, is not allocated to customers but treated as being paid by a 'nominal industry' which accordingly has a negative operating surplus of this amount".[18]

Thus, whereas on the second approach the output of banks (other than services explicitly charged for) is divided between final products (included in GDP) and intermediate products (excluded from GDP) in proportion to household and business ownership of deposits, on this third approach, most of the output of banks (and other financial intermediaries) is treated as consisting of intermediate products which enter into the costs of enterprises and are therefore excluded from GDP, the only exceptions being services to household depositors for which banks make explicit charges and services to household borrowers for which banks receive interest on consumer loans.

The Primacy of the Financial Intermediation Function. Two surprising facts stand out from this summary history of the treatment of financial enterprises in national accounts. One is that each school of thought focused on only one of the three major functions of banks, *either* services rendered to the community at large, such as the creation of money, *or* services to depositors, such as keeping accounts and providing payments facilities, *or* services to borrowers, such as financial intermediation. It would seem obvious that banks perform all three functions and, more particularly, provide services to both depositors and borrowers. Ideally, therefore, one would look for an allocation of the imputed bank service charge between these two main categories of bank customers and then, within each category, between services which

---

[17] *Australian National Accounts: Concepts, Sources and Methods*, AUSTRALIAN BUREAU OF STATISTICS, Canberra, p. 100.

[18] *Ibid.*, p. 109.

meet final demand and thus contribute to GDP, such as those rendered to households, and those which enter into the costs of production of enterprises (and government) and should therefore be excluded from GDP as intermediate products. If this makes unmanageable demands on statistical services, it becomes a question of which simplification is conceptually to be preferred.

The old SNA approach of treating bank services as being rendered to depositors, although usually explained by reference to the payments mechanism functions of banks (keeping accounts, cheque facilities, clearing machinery, etc.) had its original rationale in the old-fashioned notion that banks merely lend out money they have borrowed from depositors. The services rendered by banks to depositors were therefore viewed as "financed from interest received to the account of depositors but retained by the banks rather than actually credited or remitted to their customers",[19] and when an income equal to the banks' net investment income was imputed to depositors to enable them to pay the imputed bank service charge it was "for the use of *their* money".[20]

The most obvious reason why this rationale of the net investment income of banks is difficult to accept is that it is applied in the national accounts equally to banks *and other financial enterprises*, yet non-bank financial intermediaries have a net investment income without rendering any payments mechanism services to demand depositors. Clearly, at the very least, not *all* net investment of income of banks represents payment for services rendered to depositors. The rationale of the old SNA derived what plausibility it had from too exclusive concentration on deposit banks.

There is of course a difference between deposit banks and non-bank financial intermediaries (NFI) in that the former secure a large part of their deposits interest free, and thus pay a lower average rate of interest on their deposits, and instead attract demand deposits by the provision of cheque and other facilities. To this extent, deposit banks must, *cet. par.*, be assumed to have a larger net investment income per dollar of funds employed, balanced by larger administrative costs, than NFI. It is reasonable to assume that deposit banks, as profit-maximising firms, have provided services to demand depositors to the extent they have judged necessary to attract demand deposits, not least in competition with one another. Thus, there is a case for treating

[19] R.E. Speagle & L. Silverman, *op. cit.*, p. 130.
[20] "Stone Memorandum", p. 41; italics supplied.

some part of the cost of bank administration as a payment to demand depositors in lieu of interest.

However, there has been a marked tendency in recent years for deposit banks to charge explicitly for an increasing proportion of the services rendered to depositors, such as keeping accounts, providing cheque facilities, making transfers, etc., without any evident shift of depositors' funds to time deposits or currency holdings or any decline in the banks' net investment income. It is not unlikely that the payments mechanism facilities provided by banks are so valuable to demand depositors that they would be willing to pay for them in full in explicit charges. While there might be some drift of funds from demand deposits to time deposits or currency, it would probably be slight and temporary, at least in countries in which the cheque habit is well established. In that case, the rationale for an imputed bank service charge *to depositors* would disappear, yet the banks' net investment income would not diminish significantly.

The conclusion to which this argument points is that all of the net investment income of NFI and a large and increasing proportion of the net investment income of deposit banks is appropriately regarded as payment for financial intermediation rather than for payments mechanism services, in other words, for services to borrowers rather than to depositors. Since the bulk of bank credit is to enterprises rather than to households, the argument supports the new rather than the old SNA treatment of financial enterprises. There remains, however, the second surprising feature of the traditional social accounting treatment of financial enterprises. This is the assumption of a closed economy.

The Closed Economy Assumption. The assumption was made quite explicitly by Stone in his 1947 memorandum. "This example relates to a closed economy with no public authorities".[21] Others as best mentioned in passing "deposits held by governmental bodies, foreigners and individuals".[22] Generally, in all the discussions of the treatment of financial enterprises in national accounts, the assumption was implicit – international aspects of the problem were simply ignored. Yet, there is here a major difference between a closed and an open economy. For the conclusion of the preceding argument, that most services of banks and other financial intermediaries are rendered to business enterprises and

[21] *Ibid.*, p. 89. Public authorities which have also been neglected should, of course, be treated like enterprises; banking services rended to them are intermediate products.

[22] R.E. SPEAGLE & L. SILVERMAN, *op. cit.*, p. 130.

must *therefore* be treated as intermediate products, while valid for the closed economy, is clearly invalid for an open one. Services rendered to non-residents represent final products, whether the customers are business enterprises or not. They are in this respect on a par with services rendered to domestic households. The consequence is that the new SNA treatment understates GNP to the extent that financial services are exported.

This defect has not mattered very much for countries with very large finance sectors only a small proportion of whose business has been with the rest of the world, and the same still applies to the majority of countries in varying degree. But with increasing internationalisation of banking the error has become significant for a good many countries, and for some it has become very large indeed. And it is of course central to the measurement of trade in financial services, the subject of this paper.

Before examining possible ways of handling this problem, it is worth noting that the assumption of a closed economy has also led to complete neglect of another function of banks which, in countries like Australia, has provided a considerable part of bank profits. This is their role as dealers in foreign exchange. The income which banks derive from the provision of spot (and in some countries forward) exchange market services is distinct both from explicit charges and from the net investment income which finances the imputed bank service charge. It consists of trading margins (spreads between buying and selling rates) analogous to the income of shopkeepers and other traders. But, partly because much foreign exchange business takes the form of discounting usance bills where the foreign exchange trading margin enters into the discount rate, the banks' receipts from foreign exchange trading margins are not usually itemised separately in statistics for financial enterprises but included in their net investment income.

Trade in Financial Services

Table 1 shows, for all countries for which the data are available in the UN *Yearbook of National Accounts Statistics*, the imputed bank service charge as a percentage of GDP in 1970 and 1979. In 1970 the (unweighted) average percentage for the developed countries was 2.5

TABLE 1

IMPUTED BANK SERVICE CHARGE AS PERCENT OF GDP, 1970, 1979

%

	1970	1979
I .		
Australia	2.2	2.5
Austria	3.1	4.6
Belgium	0.9	1.5
Canada	0.7	0.7
Finland	1.5	2.2
France	2.8	3.5
Germany, F.R.	2.3	3.3
Italy	2.8	4.1
Japan	4.4	4.3
Luxembourg	4.6	26.7 [af]
Netherlands	2.1	3.5
UK	2.8	4.1
USA	2.2	2.5
average (unweighted)	*2.5*	*4.8*
		3.1 [d]
II.		
Ghana	1.2	1.7 [a]
Ivory Coast	1.2	2.0 [b]
Kenya	1.8	1.9
Malaysia	1.1 [c]	1.2 [a]
Mexico	1.1	1.1
Saudi Arabia	0.2	1.0 [b]
Singapore	1.9	4.3
Sri Lanka	0.3	0.3
Venezuela	2.1	6.8
average (unweighted)	*1.2*	*2.3*
		1.7 [e]

a 1977.
b 1978.
c 1972.
d Excluding Luxembourg.
e Excluding Venezuela.
f Since 1977, on revised definition, excluding exports of financial services (see text), 1977: 12.4; 1979: 8.0 (*Comptes Nationaux 1960-1980*, Luxembourg, September 1982).

Source: UN Yearbook of National Accounts Statistics 1980.

and for less developed countries 1.2. By 1979 it had risen to 3.1 for developed countries (excluding Luxembourg) and to 1.7 per cent for less developed countries (excluding Venezuela). Most striking, however, are the figures for Luxembourg and, to a less extent, for Venezuela and Singapore. For Luxembourg, the percentage, already 4.6 in 1970, had by 1977 risen to 26.7 per cent. In other words, close to a quarter of the country's GDP was omitted because of the treatment of financial services as intermediate products. In the case of Singapore, the rise was from 1.9 to 4.3 per cent in 1977; by 1981, it had reached 6.8 per cent.[23] Unfortunately, no such data are available for the pre-eminent international financial centres, Switzerland and Hong Kong. But it is worth noting that Austria, the United Kingdom and (rather surprisingly) Italy and Japan have relatively high percentages. It would be interesting to know how far these are accounted for by international financial business.

The inappropriateness of the SNA treatment of financial enterprises for countries with large international financial business has been raised for discussion in OECD and other fora by the government statistical service of Luxembourg.

Luxembourg. In a memorandum presented to an OECD conference in May 1982, the government statistical service of Luxembourg argued that the SNA treatment of financial services "is not well suited for analysing the activities of an international financial sector, whose banks export their services and so produce a 'final' output".[24] "The growing contribution of the banking sector to the economy of Luxembourg, and to economic progress in general, could not be brought out by GDP statistics compiled according to the rules of the ESA [the European version of the SNA], since the effect of these rules was to conceal the contribution from the banking sector. We were in the paradoxical position that the most prosperous branch of the economy appeared to have no effect on the structure of production".[25]

The solution adopted in Luxembourg "consisted in making a distinction between those banking services provided to residents and

---

[23] *Economic Survey of Singapore 1981*, Singapore, 1982, Table 1.2.

[24] "Imputed Bank Services", Note prepared by the Central Office of Statistics and Economic Studies of the Grand Duchy of Luxembourg (mimeo), OECD, Paris, May 1982, p. 7; French version printed in *Comptes Nationaux 1960-1980*, MINISTÈRE DE L'ECONOMIE, STATEC, Luxembourg, September 1982.

[25] *Ibid.*, p. 8.

those provided to foreigners, these latter being estimated on the basis of the percentage of [banks'] liabilities towards non-residents to total liabilities".[26] The memorandum added that "recently, other countries which find themselves in a similar situation (Singapore, Bahrein, Kuwait) have proposed that the accounting system of the United Nations... should be revised regarding the treatment of banks".[27]

The memorandum does not give reasons for the decision to allocate bank services between those rendered to residents and non-residents, or in effect between exports and production for the home market, on the basis of deposit ownership. Ideally, the allocation, as Stone pointed out in his 1947 memorandum, "can only be based on knowledge of the bank expenses incurred in respect of... these two types of" customers.[28] It seems most unlikely that the share of non-residents in the business of Luxembourg financial enterprises is correctly measured by their share in the deposits (or even total liabilities) of Luxembourg banks. If the procedure has been adopted simply on the precedent of the US Department of Commerce practice, it is even less appropriate in relation to exports of banking services than we have shown it to be in a closed economy. For in international banking business, the financial intermediation function clearly predominates over the payments mechanism function even more than in domestic banking, if only because so much of it is inter-bank business. The real explanation for the Luxembourg procedure is probably the pragmatic one that no better statistical data for distinguishing between export and home-market business of Luxembourg banks are available.

The Luxembourg memorandum also points out that the decision to include a part of the imputed bank service charge in GDP as exports of bank services requires consequential adjustments in the social accounts.[29] Three adjustments are necessary. First, in the balance of payments accounts, there has to be a transfer from factor service to non-factor service receipts (which, of course, leaves the balance on current account unaffected). Secondly, in the sector accounts for financial enterprises, there has to be a transfer from interest received to operating surplus (the increase in the latter taking the form of a reduction in the imputed bank service charge by the amount treated as

[26] *Ibid.*; the English version refers to "assets", the French to "*engagements*".
[27] *Ibid.*
[28] "Stone Memorandum", p. 41
[29] *Op. cit.*, p. 11.

receipts from exports of bank services). Thirdly, net property income received from abroad (which is added to GDP to give GNP) includes the banks' net investment income from abroad, part of which is now to be treated as receipts from export of non-factor services; if it is thought desirable to retain the whole of the banks' investment income from abroad in the total of the country's net property income received from abroad, a negative adjustment is necessary. All these adjustments are required in order to avoid an apparent increase in domestic savings as a result of the inclusion of exports of banking services in GDP. Corresponding adjustments would be needed if bank services rendered to domestic households were also treated as meeting final, not intermediate, demand.

Singapore. In international financial centres, such as Singapore, where banks and merchant banks operating in the offshore currency market as Asian Currency Units (ACUs) are required to keep separate accounts, the measurement of exports of financial services may be easier. Although ACUs provide some financial intermediation services to resident Singapore borrowers, the great bulk of their business is with non-residents. Conversely, the bulk of the business of Singapore banks, whether locally or foreign owned, is with residents. As a first approximation, therefore, it may be legitimate to equate Singapore's exports of financial services with explicit charges by Singapore financial enterprises to non-resident *plus* the net investment income of its ACUs. The latter amount (including profit from foreign exchange trading) has been estimated at about $ US 196-233 million (or 1.1-1.3 per cent of GDP) in 1979.[30] This may be compared with the imputed bank service charge for Singapore of $ US 881 million in the same year[31] and an estimated contribution of financial institutions to GDP of about $ US 1,115 million.[32] This would suggest that the services measured by the imputed bank service charge accounted for about four-fifths of the contribution of financial institutions to Singapore's GDP (the balance being due presumably to services charged for explicitly); and that about one-quarter of the imputed bank service charge was accounted for by

[30] J.R. HEWSON, "Offshore Banking in Australia" in Australian Financial System Inquiry, *Commissioned Studies and Selected Papers*, Part 2, Macroeconomic Policy: External Policy, AGPS, Canberra, 1982, p. 529.

[31] *Economic Survey of Singapore, loc. cit.*

[32] J.R. HEWSON, *op. cit.*, p. 528.

exports of financial services (i.e. the contribution of the offshore currency market).[33]

These, of course, are very rough figures. But they may serve to indicate how trade in financial services might be measured in the relatively straightforward case of offshore currency markets with separate accounts.

Australia. What of the majority of countries, such as Australia, which are not major international financial centres and not, as such, clearly net exporters of financial services?

Two of the main categories of what Australian banks would regard as their foreign business do not give rise to Australian exports of financial services. One of these is most income from foreign exchange trading margins. For the bulk of foreign exchange bought by Australian banks is bought from Australian residents (exporters) and most foreign exchange sold is sold to Australian residents (importers). None of this is business with non-residents. It is true that there were, even before the recent abolition of exchange control, certain exceptions to the general prohibition on non-resident holdings of $A balances.[34] Among them were working balances held by foreign banks and $A balances held temporarily in connection with capital (portfolio and direct investment) transactions which had received exchange control approval. Australian banks, therefore, derive some income from foreign exchange dealings with non-residents in connection with capital account transactions. But this probably accounts for only a small part of their foreign exchange business. Statistically, all bank income from foreign exchange trading, whether with residents or non-residents, appears to be included in the banks' investment income. Special returns by banks would be needed to separate it out, and even the banks themselves would have difficulty in distinguishing business with non-residents.

The second category of foreign business which does not statistically give rise to exports of financial services by Australian banks is the large proportion of such business which is handled by the Australian banks' overseas branches, whether operating as Singapore ACUs or as bran-

---

[33] It is worth mentioning that Singapore has not yet followed the example of Luxembourg in adapting its social accounts to its new role as a major international financial centre. One reason may be that Singapore is not anxious to see an upward adjustment in its per capita income which would hasten the day of its "graduation" out of the category of developing countries.

[34] Since 12 December 1983, this prohibition has been confined to foreign governments and banks.

ches in Hong Kong, London, New York and other financial centres. Such business includes net investment income of overseas branches, income from their foreign exchange trading, commissions on loan syndications, bank charges, fees, etc. Since these branches operate as financial enterprises of the countries in which they are domiciled, their output and exports of financial services enter into the national accounts of these countries. Only their net profits which accrue to the parent banks enter the Australian balance of payments and national accounts. In effect, a large part of the business of Australian banks is analogous to that of Australian manufacturing companies which, instead of exporting their products from Australia, set up subsidiaries to produce offshore. The implication is that part of the net investment income of the overseas branches would, on the SNA treatment of financial enterprises, be included in the imputed bank service charge (i.e. as income from the sale of non-factor services) of the countries in which they are located. But by the time the net profits enter the Australian statistics they have become pure factor income.

This is not to say that none of the business of Australian banks and other financial enterprises is of a character that its output would properly be regarded as exports of financial services. Such exports are of three kinds.

The first is income from explicit charges, such as bank and brokerage charges, fees and commissions, for services rendered by Australian financial enterprises (as contrasted with their overseas branches) to non-resident customers. Such income is recognised in the national accounts as explicit bank charges and in the balance of payments accounts as receipt from non-factor services among current transactions. There is, secondly, such income from foreign exchange trading margins as arises from business of Australian banks with non-residents; as we noted above, this probably constitutes a small part of the banks' foreign exchange trading income and is in the statistics lumped in with investment income. There is, thirdly, net foreign investment income of Australian banks, i.e. income received on foreign assets less interest paid out on foreign-owned deposits, which in the national accounts is at present included in the imputed bank service charge and mostly excluded from GDP. By far the largest component of this is probably the interest earned by the Reserve Bank on its foreign exchange reserves. But Australian banks also hold working balances in foreign exchange and there may be other foreign investment income by Australian financial enterprises, on some of which they earn some interest. All such deposit interest income of banks, as contrasted with loan interest, doubtfully qualifies for treatment as a return on bank (non-factor) services. A central bank, for example, hardly renders services of financial intermediation to foreign banks with which it holds its foreign exchange reserves. But since such receipts are included in the net investment income which is treated as the imputed bank service charge, they should logically be regarded, like interest on consumer loans, as payment for final (not intermediate) products.

Australia is also a large importer of capital. Some of this capital is obtained from foreign banks, and the interest paid on this external debt, by enterprises, governments or households, enters into the net investment income of these foreign banks and, under SNA procedure, into the imputed bank service charge in the national accounts of the home countries of these banks. Such interest income, which at present is included in the Australian national and balance of payments accounts as "property income to overseas", i.e. as factor income, should be regarded as imports of financial services, i.e. as payment for non-factor services of financial intermediation.

Obviously, for none of these components of Australian exports and imports of financial services are adequate statistical data available, and it is doubtful whether in Australia's case the amounts are large and significant enough to warrant the cost of collection and processing. But there may be such trade in financial services in countries which, without being major international financial centres, export or import financial services on a scale significant relative to their GDP or their current account balance of payments.

Conclusions

The conclusions of the preceding discussion of the conceptual problems of measuring trade in financial services may be summarised as follows.

First, the new SNA treatment of financial services which regards the imputed bank service charge as a charge for services of financial intermediation to borrowers is conceptually superior for a closed economy to the old SNA treatment which regarded it as a charge for payments mechanism and related services to depositors. But even on this interpretation, services to household borrowers (personal loans) should be treated as final, not as intermediate, output and therefore included in GDP.

Secondly, in an open economy, even bank services to enterprises must be regarded as final output if the enterprises are non-residents. For countries, such as Luxembourg, where exports of financial services represent a large sector of the economy, it is essential to include the value of exports of financial services in GDP. Conceptually, ownership of deposits is not a suitable criterion for allocation of this output between residents (strictly, enterprises and public authorities) and non-residents, unless there are reasons to believe that the value of financial intermediation services rendered to borrowers is roughly proportionate to their ownership of deposits. In practice, no better statistical measure may be available.

Thirdly, for countries, such as Singapore, where most exports of financial services are provided by statistically distinct units of an offshore currency market, the net investment income of these units, together with their receipts from explicit charges, may be an adequate measure of exports of financial services.

Fourthly, for all other countries, where trade in financial services is not large relative to the economy as a whole, it may not be worth going to the trouble of collecting and extracting the statistics that would be needed to measure exports and imports of financial services. But it is desirable to secure agreement, for such purposes as internationally comparable national and balance of payments accounts, on what, ideally, should be measured. Exports of financial services should be taken to include that part of the net investment income of financial enterprises which is received from abroad, together with explicit charges to non-residents by financial enterprises. Where local banks provide a significant volume of foreign exchange market services to non-residents, it would be desirable to include an appropriate part of bank receipts from foreign exchange trading margins. Imports of financial services, conversely, should consist of that part of (net) interest on external debt that is paid to foreign financial enterprises, together with payments to such enterprises in the form of explicit charges. It is unlikely that the contribution of nationals to the income of foreign banks from foreign exchange trading margins could ever be identified.

Canberra

H.W. Arndt

[21]

Comparative Advantage in Trade in Financial Services

In the past decade there has been a great increase in interest in trade in services, both in academic and official circles, largely because the comparative advantage of the United States is believed to be shifting towards service trade. But what is almost certainly the fastest growing and possibly the largest component of international trade in services, trade in financial services, has received little attention in this connection. A major reason is that the volume of trade in financial services is difficult to measure. But the very concept of international trade in financial services is elusive and subject to a good deal of confusion. An earlier article has dealt with the problem of measurement (Arndt, 1984). The object of this article is to clarify the concept and to show that the pattern of trade in financial services is as amenable to explanation, in terms of comparative advantage and distortions, as trade in manufactures.*

The concept of trade in financial Services

A country's exports of manufactures consist of that part of its manufacturing industries' output that is sold to non-residents. By analogy, a country's exports of financial services consist of that part of the output of its finance industry, in the form of financial services of all kinds, that is sold to non-residents. Among them are the payment and transfer facilities provided to depositors, including spot and forward facilities in the foreign exchange market, all the services in the long

* The author is indebted to P.J. Drake, R.E. Falvey, H.G. Grubel and C.P. Kindleberger for helpful comments on an earlier draft. The usual *caveat* applies.

chain of intermediation between ultimate lenders and final borrowers rendered by banks and non-bank financial intermediaries, as well as brokerage and advisory services and life and other insurance. These are all non-factor services, as distinct from the factor services provided by capital which generate interest or dividends. Before examining the list more closely, it will help clarify the concept if, to start with, trade in financial services is distinguished from *a)* international capital movements and property income, *b)* direct foreign investment in banks and other financial institutions and *c)* growth of international financial centres.

a) International capital movements and property income. The object of trade theory is to explain the location of industries and the pattern of trade as determined by comparative advantage, not the initial factor endowment of different countries and the way in which this may be modified by international factor movements. The theory of international trade, therefore, is concerned with trade in outputs, not inputs, in other words with trade in goods and non-factor services, not with international movements, or with earnings, of factors of production, labour and capital. It is true that, in a general equilibrium model of economic activity, the distinction between factor and non-factor services loses importance because there is little reason for distinguishing between the labour component of value added (a factor service) and labour services purchased as intermediate products from other firms (non-factor services). One can easily think of borderline cases in trade in services, such as the architect from country A who renders a factor service if he goes to country B as a consultant, but contributes to a non-factor service if he does the same work as employee of a firm in A which sells its consultancy services under a contract with its customer in B. But in the context of international trade theory the distinction is crucial. Thus, in terms of the balance of payments accounts, the theory of international trade concerns itself with activity reflected in receipts and payments on account of exports and imports of goods and non-factor services, not with the capital account or with factor income, such as interest and dividends or migrant labour remittances.

The difficulty in the case of trade in financial services is that for a considerable part of their output of non-factor services banks do not charge customers directly but recoup themselves in the form of factor income, *i.e.* net interest earned (interest received on loans less interest paid out on deposits); even their receipts from trading margins in foreign exchange business tend, in banking statistics, to be lumped in with their (gross) interest receipts. This difficulty greatly complicates measurement but does not invalidate the commonsense definition of trade in financial services.

b) Direct foreign investment in financial enterprises. What is often referred to as the "internationalisation of banking" covers two distinct though interrelated developments. One is the expansion of international business by a country's banks, that is sale of their services to non-residents. The other is the establishment by a country's banks of branches or subsidiaries abroad, for business with residents or non-residents of the host country. In relation to goods, such as manufactures, the distinction between trade and direct foreign investment (DFI) is familiar and fairly clearcut (though even here there are problems in defining "residents"). The theory of international trade seeks to explain the pattern of trade in terms of the natural comparative advantage of a country's manufacturing industries and in terms of barriers and inducements through government intervention. The theory of DFI seeks to explain why manufacturing companies establish subsidiaries to produce their products in foreign countries rather than export them to these countries.

Conceptually, the distinction is just as relevant to banking as to manufacturing, and it seems desirable to distinguish between a country's comparative advantage in trade in financial services and a bank's motives for going "multinational". In relation to banking, however, the distinction is less familiar and often blurred in the literature, and there are at least two reasons for this.

One is that in banking international trade and investment tend to be complementary rather than, as in the case of manufacturing, alternatives. In principle, given modern telecommunications technology, one could imagine all international banking services being supplied by one or more banks in a single international financial centre, dealing with customers in other countries directly or through purely domestic banks. In practice, quite apart from the diseconomies of such extreme concentration, banks have always felt the need for a more substantial presence than through "corresponding banks" in major foreign markets for their services. Even nineteenth century imperial banks, engaged in trade finance and other traditional international banking from their home bases in London, Amsterdam or Paris, set up overseas branches, whether to conduct domestic business in the absence of (or in competition with) local banks or for international business, because they felt the need for local contacts and knowledge. In the twentieth century, multinational banking has spread partly for the same reasons as multinational manufacturing, to defend markets against host or third country competition (Grubel, 1983). But in banking, distortions such as those which have given rise to the Eurodollar market and other offshore banking have probably had even more influence on the pattern of trade and DFI than in manufacturing.

The other reason relates back to the problem of measurement. The receipts from exports of financial services and the returns on international investment in financial enterprises are inextricably mixed up in the banks' own accounts and in any national statistics. If it is difficult to estimate the contributions made to British earnings of foreign exchange by exports of financial services by purely British banks trading from London, it is even more awkward for those made by a British bank operating in the Singapore offshore currency market. In principle, the situation in the latter case is exactly analogous to that of a British manufacturing subsidiary in Singapore which contributes to Singapore's export earnings but whose profits constitute an offsetting debit item in Singapore's, and credit item in the British, current account. But since the export earnings, in the case of banking services, themselves largely accrue as interest income, the distinction is harder to maintain.

c) International financial centres. There is a large literature on the growth of international financial centres (*e.g.* Kindleberger, 1974; Reid, 1981). But trade in financial services rarely receives any explicit mention in this literature, even though much of the business of international financial centres consists of such trade and the explanation of the growth of international financial centres is largely to be found in international trade theory. There are a number of reasons for this, apart from the general elusiveness and neglect of the subject.

Some of the interest in international financial centres is in the role of the single world centre, London or New York, as the key or reserve currency centre and lender of last resort of the international monetary system, analogous to the domestic role of the central bank (*e.g.* Kindleberger, 1974, pp. 61ff.). This role clearly has more to do with monetary than with trade theory.

Even when the focus is on the role of international financial centres as providers of financial services, there are differences. Centres are by definition cities, not — with obvious exceptions of city states, such as Hong Kong and Singapore — countries; their external transactions therefore are not necessarily international. In any case, much of the business of the major international financial centres, such as London, New York or Zurich, or even Singapore, is domestic business within the city which does not involve international, or even interregional, trade. More important, all countries have some international trade in financial services, but only a handful have international financial centres.

For all these reasons, the literature on international financial centres cannot be expected to give an adequate account of the nature and determinants of international trade in financial services. But there is enough overlap to make this literature a useful source.

Having decided what international trade in financial services is not, it is time to look more closely at its nature and composition.

Definitions

Our earlier preliminary definition — that a country's exports of financial services consist of that part of the output of its finance industry, in the form of financial services of all kinds, that is sold to non-residents — has several loose ends.

The bulk of financial services consists of services of financial intermediation, lending and borrowing (other than lending by ultimate savers and borrowing by ultimate investors). But international finance also involves the provision of payments and transfer facilities, in the form of drafts, travellers cheques, credit cards, etc., and the sale and purchase of foreign exchange, spot and forward, swap and hedge transactions. A broader definition, therefore, would be trade in paper assets, if this can be taken to include both currency and book entries in bank ledgers (or computers).

This definition clearly includes the international business of security brokers and money market dealers, and of leasing, factoring and other such finance companies. It is more debatable whether one should also include trade in commodity futures or the sale of life and other insurance policies which both combine financial intermediation with distinct risk-cover services. Certainly, many ancillary services provided by banks and other financial enterprises, such as safe deposit, account-keeping, travel, investment-advisory and other consultancy services, are not financial services in this sense, and such services rendered to non-residents would not properly be part of a country's trade in financial services.

For similar reasons, it is not easy to give a precise definition of financial enterprises, and familar problems attach to the precise definition of "non-residents". Do the international transactions of a country's central bank constitute part of its trade in financial services? What about a bank's transactions with its own representative offices or branches abroad, or with an overseas bank in which it has a 26 or 49 or 51 per cent equity interest? But, except for statistical purposes where these fine points have to be settled somehow, there is no need to split hairs. It seems reasonable to assume that the largest part of international trade in financial services is conducted by banks and consists of financial intermediation business. It is the pattern of this dominant component that one wants to explain. It is also for this dominant component that we can put some figures to the pattern of international trade in financial services.

Statistics

The IMF in its *International Financial Statistics* regularly publishes data on international bank lending under the headings of "cross-border interbank claims" and "cross-border bank credit to nonbanks", both by country of residence of lending bank. Table 1 shows totals outstanding at the end of 1978, 1984 and (where available) 1986 for the major lending countries. Between them, these accounted in 1984 for over 90 per cent of the world total.

At first sight, the twenty countries seem to fall readily into two categories, industrial countries with highly developed financial systems and less developed countries with offshore currency markets or surplus petro-dollars. Closer inspection, however, shows this to be an oversimplification. Table 2, which ranks the twenty countries according to the ratio of total (interbank and nonbank) cross-border bank credit (CBBC) outstandings to domestic money supply (M_1) at the end of 1984, shows that there were five distinguishable categories:

1) Industrial countries with relatively small CBBC (USA, Japan, Germany, Italy, Spain).

TABLE 1

CROSS-BORDER CREDIT BY RESIDENCE OF LENDING BANK

End of period	$US billion								
	1978			1984			1986		
	Interbank	To Non-Bank Borrowers	Total	Interbank	To Non-Bank Borrowers	Total	Interbank	To Non-Bank Borrowers	Total
United Kingdom	150	68	218	345	145	490	527	188	715
United States	97	33	130	324	119	443	397	110	507
Japan	23	11	34	90	37	127	260	85	345
Belgium-Luxembourg	61	48	109	99	74	173	177	114	291
Switzerland	68	24	92	133	28	161	205	49	254
Cayman Islands	13	6	19	83	60	143	102[a]	72[a]	174[a]
Germany	40	34	74	43	32	75	117	61	178
Singapore	22	7	29	69	36	105	131	41	172
France	69	29	98	94	56	150	n.a.	n.a.	n.a.
Bahamas	70	36	106	108	39	147	114	42	156
Hong Kong	12	8	20	60	19	79	133	23	156
Netherlands	36	11	47	43	15	58	63	28	91
Bahrain	15	6	21	38	18	56	38	14	52
Canada	17	4	21	34	8	42	42	8	50
Saudi Arabia	29	1	30	49	..	49	n.a.	3	n.a.
Italy	n.a.	n.a.	n.a.	34[b]	..	34[b]	n.a.	n.a.	n.a.
Austria	7	7	14	15	15	30	24	25	49
Spain	17	2	19	23	6	29	29	8	37
Panama	7	12	19	9	23	32	10[c]	23[c]	33[c]
United Arab Emirates	3	1	4	12	2	14	14	3	17
Netherlands Antilles	1	2	3	4	4	8	3[c]	3[c]	6[c]
Venezuela	n.a.	n.a.	n.a.	6	..	6	4	..	4
Total (excl. Comecon)	842	356	1,298	1,924	761	2,680	2,895	1,001	3,896

Notes: [a] 1985; [b] 1983; [c] 1986 (II).
Countries with total outstandings of less than $US 5 billion at end of 1984 have been omitted.
Source: IMF, *International Financial Statistics*.

TABLE 2

RATIO OF CROSS BORDER BANK CREDIT TO MONEY SUPPLY, END OF 1984

< 1		1-5	
Italy	0.23	Canada	1.06
Japan	0.37	France	1.36
USA	0.78	Saudi Arabia	2.11
Germany	0.80	Netherlands	2.42
Spain	0.88	Austria	3.75
5-100		> 100	
UAE	5.78	Bahamas	773.4
UK	8.12	Panama	839.9
Belgium-Luxembourg	10.88	Bahrain	875.0
Hong Kong	17.40	Cayman Islands	
Singapore	25.80		
Switzerland	54.89		

Source: IMF, *International Financial Statistics.*

2) Industrial countries with more substantial but moderate CBBC (Canada, France, Netherlands, Austria).

3. Industrial countries (and NICs) with very large CBBC (UK, Belgium-Luxembourg, Switzerland, Singapore, Hong Kong).

4. Booking or reporting centres (Bahamas, Bahrain, Cayman Islands, Panama).

5) Oil exporters with surplus petro-dollars (Saudi Arabia, UAE).

This suggests that, while the countries in the first two categories have been responsible for bank lending abroad more or less in proportion to the relative size of their financial systems, those in the three latter categories have, in one way or another, specialised in international bank lending.

One might suppose that CBBC by countries in the first two categories would be preponderantly to nonbank borrowers and CBBC by countries in the latter three countries interbank credit. This turns out not to be the case, as the figures in Table 3 show. The oil exporters, not surprisingly, lent their petro-dollars almost exclusively to banks. But there were countries in the first two categories with relatively high proportions of interbank lending (Canada, Spain, but also USA and

Netherlands) and countries in the third and fourth categories with surprisingly low ones (Belgium-Luxembourg, Singapore, Panama, Cayman Islands).

TABLE 3

RATIO OF INTERBANK TO TOTAL CROSS BORDER BANK CREDIT, END OF 1986

	%		%
Saudi Arabia	100[a]	Bahamas	73.0
Venezuela	100	Bahrain	73.0
Hong Kong	85.3	Netherlands	69.2
Canada	84.0	Germany	65.7
United Arab Emirates	82.4	France	62.7[a]
Switzerland	80.7	Belgium-Luxembourg	60.8
Spain	78.4	Cayman Islands	56.8
United States	78.3	Netherlands Antilles	50.0
Singapore	76.2	Austria	49.0
Japan	75.4	Panama	30.3
United Kingdom	73.7		

Note: [a] 1984.
Source: Table 1.

This is as far as available statistics take us in identifying "revealed comparative advantage" in trade in financial services and, for all the reasons given before, it is not very far.

CBBC outstandings measure assets of lending banks. Even year-to-year changes in these could be accepted as a proxy for the banks' exports of financial intermediation services only if net lending could be assumed to be proportionate to gross lending and if the latter provided a reliable indicator of the value of financial services provided by the lending banks to the foreign borrowers. This would still leave out of account the value of all other financial services provided by banks to non-residents, such as payment and foreign exchange facilities and all the other ancillary services mentioned before, as well as financial services to non-residents by non-bank financial intermediaries, insurance companies, etc. Until, if ever, the problems of measuring all these kinds of trade in financial services can be overcome, the pattern indicated by CBBC is probably as close as we can get towards identifying the major trade flows.

There is yet another complication. Any attempt to explain the pattern of trade in financial services needs to allow not only for the great variety of such services other than those of financial intermediation services captured by CBBC but also for the fact that international financial intermediation itself covers a range of activities which differ in many respects relevant to different countries' comparative advantage.

Demattè has distinguished five roles and five functions of banks in the chain of international financial intermediation, each requiring specific kinds of expertise and capacities (Demattè, 1981). At the beginning of the chain, banks perform a collecting role, collecting funds from ultimate surplus units almost on a retail scale. At the end of the chain, they perform a final lending role which requires local knowledge of borrowing areas and expertise in credit evaluation. In between, there is the interbank intermediation role which can involve maturity, risk and currency transformation, as well as a "packaging" function (raising funds in certain amounts and placing them in larger or smaller amounts) and a spatial transmission function (funding in one geographical interbank market and lending in another). This classification provides a useful guide to likely determinants of comparative advantage.[1]

Comparative advantage

What determines the pattern of international trade in financial services? In principle, the answer should be found in texbook theory of international trade. The explanations most relevant to financial services will differ from those relevant to textiles, but so will those relevant to cereals and pharmaceuticals. It is, however, important at the outset to emphasise once more that we are concerned with the determinants of trade in financial services, not with those of international capital movements or DFI in banking.

Of course, much of the international business of financial enterprises is connected with international lending and borrowing, so that one would expect important links between the two patterns. But international banks handle purely domestic business in their home and foreign

[1] Demattè also identifies a "transmission" role which, unlike the transmission function incidental to financial intermediation, is undertaken, independently of any intermediation, by financial enterprises acting merely as brokers and a "speculation" role presumably on the assumption that speculation by financial intermediaries is, on balance, stabilising (DEMATTÈ, 1981, p. 98).

countries, and the concentration of international financial centres by no means corresponds to the patterns of international capital flows. Shipping services provide an analogy. Shipping industries naturally grew first, and are still dominant, in countries with large foreign trade requiring shipping services; their large home market has provided a natural base for export of shipping services. But there are countries, such as Greece and Norway, which have specialised in shipping and have developed shipping industries far out of proportion to their own demand; and there are countries, such as Panama and Liberia, which have secured a modest foreign exchange income from the provision of flags of convenience. In finance, Britain, the USA, France and Germany correspond to the first category of maritime nations; Switzerland, Luxembourg, Hong Kong and Singapore to the second; the Bahamas and Cayman Islands to the third.

Manufacturing, as we suggested before, provides the better analogy for the distinction between trade in financial services and multinational banking. Trade in manufactures occurs when a firm in country A sells its products to residents of country B; direct foreign investment occurs when the firm decides instead to produce its product in country B, whether for the domestic market in B or for export. The same holds for financial services. The factors giving a country a comparative advantage in trade in financial services, as explained in the theory of international trade, differ from those which induce and enable individual banks to establish branches or subsidiaries abroad, as explained in the theory of direct foreign investment (Grubel, 1983). But here, too, there are links since the conditions which make a country a major exporter of financial services overlap with those which make it a major source of direct foreign investment by and in financial enterprises.

As in the theory of merchandise trade, it will be useful to divide the discussion of determinants of the pattern of trade in financial services into two parts: first, the basic determinants of comparative advantage in a free competitive market and, secondly, the effects of market power and government intervention; or, as it is sometimes put, "natural" comparative advantage and "distortions".

"Natural" comparative advantage

The standard neo-classical explanation of comparative advantage, the Heckscher-Ohlin explanation in terms of different factor endowments among countries and different factor proportions among products, has little relevance to trade in financial services. The reason why countries with abundant capital have a comparative advantage in trade in financial services is not that the banking industry is capital-intensive. It is true that a comparative advantage in financial intermediation has normally developed where there was an initial concentration of wealth, such as to give rise to a domestic banking system and capital market. In all the major financial-service exporting countries, international banking grew out of domestic banking which, in turn, had developed in rich cities — Florence, Amsterdam, Paris, London, New York, Zurich, Frankfurt (Kindleberger, 1974; Reid, 1981). But the source of comparative advantage was not a cost advantage due to abundance of capital but a large domestic market for financial services and consequent economies of scale and development of specialised skills.

Nor, rather obviously, is the extension of the factor-proportions explanation to natural resource endowment which is so important for a large part of commodity trade (Garnaut-Anderson, 1980) of much use here. But it is not entirely irrelevant. Just as a waterfront is obviously crucial to a country's comparative advantage in shipping, so location can be significant for comparative advantage in trade in financial services. Proximity is important at the retail ends of the chain of financial intermediation, both in fund-collecting and in ultimate lending (Johnson, 1976; Demattè, 1981); and Singapore's offshore currency market owes its existence in part to Singapore's time-zone advantage, the fact that its business hours overlap with those on the US West Coast and Tokyo and for an hour or two with London (Hewson, 1982).

But this is something of a *curiosum*. Much more important for a country's comparative advantage in trade in financial services is its endowment with man-made conditions and resources favourable or necessary to efficient performance of financial services. Among the conditions are political stability, including peace and effective law enforcement, economic stability and a good infrastructure of complementary services. Paris is said to have lost its pre-eminence as a financial centre to London when France suspended specie payment during the 1870/1 war (Kindleberger, 1974, p. 61); and the Philippines' efforts to develop an offshore currency market in the 1970s failed, and Hong Kong lost some of its comparative advantage in the 1980s, partly because of political uncertainties. Among aspects of economic stability sometimes mentioned as relevant to comparative advantage in international financial intermediation is exchange rate stability (Johnson, 1976, p. 2; Reid, 1981, p. 5; Kindleberger, 1974, p. 7), but this is debatable. Important elements of a good infrastructure of complementary services are, most obviously, telecommunications, but also accounting and specialised legal services. Hong Kong had an advantage over Singapore in developing loan syndication because it had the requisite legal skills (Lee, 1986, p. 216).

But however much the Heckscher-Ohlin factor-proportions explanation is stretched, it clearly cannot adequately account for comparative advantage in trade in financial services, any more than in intra-industry trade in manufactures, and for similar reasons (Grubel-Lloyd, 1975; Giersch, 1979). As Corden has pointed out, it makes little sense to say that "Switzerland has a comparative advantage in watches because she is watchmaker-intensive... Factor proportions theory refers to factors of production that are generally available to be used in the production of many different products and are (allowing for adjustment lags) available to be used in the production of many different products. It does not apply to factors specific to one activity" (Corden, 1979, pp. 5, 8).

As in the case of intra-industry trade in manufactures, the main explanation of "natural" comparative advantage in trade in financial services has to be sought elsewhere, chiefly in economies of scale combined with product differentiation (Grubel-Lloyd, 1975; Corden, 1979). In banking, the major sources of immense economies of scale are the possibility of clearing of debits and credits, and of centralised decision-making through modern telecommunications technology. Another contributing factor is the fact that international trade in financial services is largely wholesale trade (Demattè, 1981, p. 95). In addition, it reaps economies of scale from a large domestic market, *i.e.* demand by residents for banking and other financial services. Specialisation, whether or not based on product differentiation, yields further scale economies and promotes the development of a wide range of specialised skills.

Economies of scale may be offset by countervailing factors. Local knowledge is essential at the final lending end of the intermediation chain and will usually favour DFI (the establishment of local branches of foreign banks) rather than trade in financial services. For somewhat similar reasons, there may be diseconomies of centralisation in international banking, and advances in telecommunications technology may be reducing economies of scale in some respects (Kindleberger, 1974, p. 54; Reid, 1981, p. 2).

Individual banks and other financial enterprises may achieve competitive superiority through links with trading and manufacturing companies, through the provision of ancillary (payment, travel, advisory) services and through goodwill based on reputation for soundness and efficiency and on skilful marketing. If these qualities characterise the average, or leading, financial enterprises of a country, they will collectively give the country a comparative advantage in trade in financial services.

Whether product cycle theory (Vernon, 1966) is also relevant to trade in financial services is perhaps more doubtful. Innovations in financial service techniques and instruments have revolutionised international trade in financial services in recent times, but few if any are patentable. Comparative advantage based on temporary technological superiority must therefore be rare in this field.

"Distortions"

So far we have assumed a free competitive market (already somewhat qualified by references to product differentiation and patents). In the real world, the pattern of international trade, in financial services as in merchandise trade, is modified or "distorted" by private market power and government intervention. It is not easy to think of examples of open resort to private market power, in the form of cartels or restrictions on entry, in international finance. It is a highly competitive, though oligopolistic-competitive, industry. But banks are powerful and are therefore often able to invoke the help of government to protect their interests. Governments, moreover, have their own motives for intervention. Private market power is therefore a much less important influence on the pattern of trade in financial services than government intervention. Such intervention can be classified under two headings, barriers to trade and inducements to trade. Since DFI is often an alternative to trade in financial services, and both are often complementary, the distinction between government intervention, whether barriers or inducements, aimed at the one or the other is not always clearcut.

Barriers to Trade. Barriers to trade in financial services, as to trade in manufactures, are mainly protectionist in intent; but some of the protection is of a special kind.

There is, first, straightforward protection of the domestic banking industry from foreign competition. This can take the form of partial or complete prohibition of entry of foreign banks into domestic banking or into the foreign exchange market (as until recently in Australia) or into domestic banking outside the national capital (as still in Indonesia). The instruments of intervention may be licensing (equivalent to QRs) or discriminatory taxation (equivalent to tariffs). There is, secondly, protection of the national monetary authorities (or, in their view, of the national interest) from external shocks or other undesirable market developments. Examples are the use of foreign exchange controls to insulate domestic money supply and the exchange rate from volatile international capital movements or to support an overvalued currency by restrictions on capital outflow, and the often unintended effects on international trade in financial services of domestic monetary and banking policies.

The effects of such intervention on international trade in financial services may be to inhibit, to distort or even to stimulate it. Protection of domestic banks from foreign competition undoubtedly limits direct foreign investment in banking; whether it necessarily reduces the volume of international trade in financial services (*i.e.* the sale of such services to non-residents by domestic or foreign financial intermediaries) is perhaps more doubtful. The use of exchange control to prevent destabilising short-term international capital movements has generally met with limited success, being easily undermined or evaded by "leads and lags" and other devices. The effect of the emergence of grey or black markets is to distort the pattern of trade in financial services, rather than to reduce its volume. In the years preceding deregulation in Australia, the Australian trading banks were not permitted to hold foreign currency, beyond minimum working balances (so they established overseas branches which were able to participate in loan syndication); foreign banks were excluded from domestic banking business in Australia (so they established merchant bank subsidiaries which were able to do everything except to accept deposits) and from the spot and forward foreign exchange market (so, through merchant bank subsidiaries, they promoted the Australian hedge market).

More significant for the growth and pattern of international trade in financial services in recent times than either of these two kinds of deliberately restrictive intervention have been the unintended consequences of domestic monetary policy measures. The most striking example, of course, is the emergence of the Eurodollar market in the late 1950s because British banks were prohibited from lending sterling abroad (so they began to lend dollars) and because the US banks were subjected to restraints on lending abroad and to interest ceilings at home (so they set up branches in London which were free from both restraints).[2] But these are only specific instances of what McKinnon has called the more general phenomenon of "regulatory imbalance" whereby domestic lending by banks is constrained through reserve requirements and other instruments of domestic monetary policy which do not apply to foreign operations (McKinnon, 1984; also Grubel, 1983). The result has been a wholly unintended enormous increase in the volume of international trade in financial services, as well as major changes in the geographic and institutional pattern of this trade, with a much larger role for banks in long-term capital flows than in earlier times (McKinnon, 1984; Arndt-Drake, 1985).

Inducements to trade. Governments have also in some cases offered special inducements to both trade and investment in financial services. The usual method to attract foreign banks, as in the case of other direct foreign investment, has been the use of special tax concessions and exemption from controls, such as reserve requirements, applicable to domestic banks. Examples have been the efforts of many governments in small countries to foster an offshore currency market, whether as in the case of Singapore to strengthen an already considerable comparative advantage in this field (Hewson, 1982) or to conjure a tax-haven industry into existence, as in various West Indies and Pacific island booking centres. Other countries — Luxembourg and Hong Kong are outstanding examples — have successfully promoted a vigorous export-oriented finance industry by creating a congenial environment in the form of "liberal banking laws" (Johnson, 1976, p. 262).

---

[2] KINDLEBERGER (1974, p. 58) mentions that British foreign lending at short-term was stimulated by the usury laws of 1571.

Conclusion

The purpose of this and the preceding paper on trade in financial services has not been to make policy recommendations. It has been to carve a small niche in positive economics for an important but hitherto neglected component of world trade, both in balance of payments statistics and in trade theory.

As regards trade theory, it appears that the theory developed to explain the pattern of trade in terms of natural comparative advantage is as applicable to trade in financial services as to trade in goods. But because distortions of trade in financial services are frequently by-products of policies with other objectives, such as domestic monetary policy, trade in financial services, unlike trade in goods, is not necessarily reduced by such distortions but often merely diverted or even expanded.

Canberra

H.W. ARNDT

REFERENCES

ARNDT, H.W. (1984), "Measuring Trade in Financial Services", in this *Review*, June.

ARNDT, H.W. & DRAKE, P.J. (1985), "Bank Loans or Bonds: Some Lessons of Historical Experience", in this *Review*, December.

CORDEN, W.M. (1979), "Intra-Industry Trade and Factor Proportions Theory" in Giersch (1979).

DEMATTÈ, C. (1981), "International Financial Intermediation: Implications for Bankers and Regulators", in this *Review*, March.

GARNAUT, R. & ANDERSON, K. (1980), "ASEAN Export Specialisation and the Evolution of Comparative Advantage in the Western Pacific Region" in Garnaut, R. (ed.), *ASEAN in a Changing Pacific and World Economy*, Australian National University Press, Canberra.

GIERSCH, H. (ed.) (1979), *On the Economics of Intra-Industry Trade*, Mohr, Tuebingen.

GRUBEL, H.G. (1983), "The New International Banking", in this *Review*, September.

GRUBEL, H.G. & LLOYD, P.J. (1975), *Intra-Industry Trade*, Macmillan, London.

HEWSON, J.R. (1982), "Offshore Banking in Singapore — A Case Study" in *Commissioned Studies and Selected Papers*, Part 2, Macroeconomic Policy: External Policy, Australian Financial System Inquiry, AGPS, Canberra.

JOHNSON, H.G. (1976), "Panama as a Regional Financial Centre: A Preliminary Analysis of Development Contribution", *Economic Development and Cultural Change*, Vol. 24 (2), January.

KINDLEBERGER, C.P. (1974), *The Formation of Financial Centres: A Study in Comparative Economic History*, Princeton Studies in International Finance, No. 36.

LEE, S.Y. (1986), "Developing Asian Financial Centres" in Tan, H.H. & Kapur, B. (eds.), *Pacific Growth and Financial Interdependence*, Allen & Unwin, Sydney, p. 216.

MCKINNON, R.I. (1986), "Issues and Perspectives: An Overview of Banking Regulation and Monetary Control" in Tan, H.H. & Kapur, B. (eds.) *Pacific Growth and Financial Interdependence*, Allen & Unwin, Sydney.

REID, H.C. (1981), *The Preeminence of International Financial Centres*, Praeger, New York.

VERNON, R. (1966), "International Investment and International Trade in the Product Cycle", *Quarterly Journal of Economics*, Vol. 80 (2), May.

[22]

Banks and the World's Major Financial Centers, 1970–1980

By

Sang-Rim Choi, Adrian E. Tschoegl, and **Chwo-Ming Yu**

Contents: I. Introduction. – II. Data. – III. The Degree of Interconnectedness. – IV. The Determinants of Interpenetration. – V. Summary and Conclusion.

I. Introduction

In which financial centers do foreign banks establish themselves? How interconnected are the centers? Has this pattern changed in the decade 1970–1980? Why do the banks go where they go? We address these questions by examining the location pattern of offices of the world's largest banks. As such, the study contributes to the literature on financial centers, foreign direct investment in banking, and the strategic interaction of firms.

Kindleberger [1974] in his seminal study remarked that financial centers had not attracted much serious academic attention in the years following World War II. Since then there has been limited progress with work by Johnson [1976] and Reed [1980; 1981] being noteworthy examples. Grubel's [1982] work on the welfare effects of free economic zones is also germane to the theory of financial centers, though his arguments are more general.

The scholarly empirical literature on foreign direct investment (FDI) in banking has also paid little attention to financial centers. Most of the studies use aggregate data at the national level [e.g. Dean, Giddy, 1981; Goldberg, Saunders, 1981; Khoury, 1979; Terrell, 1979]. The more microeconomic study of Ball, Tschoegl [1982] deals with two locations, Japan and California, where foreign bank entry motivation might include a desire to participate in the financial center, but the authors' focus is on the extension of the activities of existing entrants.

Section II presents the basic data for the interpenetration of the centers. We begin by using the data to rank the centers in importance in 1970 and 1980, and note some changes. In Section III we introduce and apply measures of interconnectedness. We use these simple measures to see how interlinked the centers are, and whether or not they are becoming more interconnected. In Section IV, we investigate some of the determinants of the observed location pattern. In particular, we examine measures of the attractiveness of the centers, and of impediments external to the banks such as

Remark: The authors would like to thank the anonymous reviewer for his comments. Responding to his suggestions improved the paper noticeably, though of course he or she is not responsible for any remaining flaws.

distance and regulations, and variables reflecting the interaction between banks from the various centers. Section V is a summary and conclusion.

II. Data

We have identified fourteen centers by drawing on Reed's [1980] work and adding some commonly acknowledged financial centers which are major business sites of developed countries. We combined pairs of neighboring centers when these shared financial importance with each other, were located in the same country, and in our opinion were close substitutes. We did not include centers which are legal fictions where little or no actual economic activity takes place (e.g. Cayman Islands), or where the government essentially bars new foreign bank entry (e.g. Rio de Janeiro/São Paulo). The fourteen centers we chose are: London (LO), New York (NY), Paris (PA), Frankfurt/Hamburg (FH), Tokyo (TO), Singapore (SI), Hong Kong (HK), Los Angeles/SanFrancisco (LS), Zürich/Geneva (ZG), Amsterdam (AM), Brussels (BR), Panama (PN), Milan/Rome (MR), and Toronto/Montreal (TM).

The centers provide the basis for To/From matrices for 1970 and 1980 (Table 1). The diagonal elements (Y_{ii}; $i = 1,2, \ldots, 14$), are the number of banks in the world's Top 300 commercial banks with headquarters in the centers. For two centers (Panama and Singapore) with no banks in the Top 300, we used the largest bank in each. The off-diagonals (Y_{ij}; $i \neq j$), are the number of these banks which have an organizational presence (representative office, branch, subsidiary, or Edge Act subsidiary) in the other center.

While one might wish to have asset data, for most of the off-diagonal cells it is just not available. Even where available, the amounts are subject to gross error because of the frequency with which loans arranged in one center are booked elsewhere for tax avoidance or other reasons. Employment numbers would avoid the recording error problem, but the data does not exist. Moreover, one could not distinguish the employment attributable to retail banking activities from that attributable to financial center ones.

We rank the centers using the column totals. The basis for the ranking, therefore, is the number of the world's Top 300 banks from the centers comprising our study which are represented by an office in the center in question. Other measures such as size of the offshore currency market, or total number of foreign banks present regardless of size and origin, would give different results.

In both years, London, New York, and Tokyo were the three most important. All three are centers of large domestic financial systems as well as international centers. Between 1970 and 1980, New York displaced London as the most important banking center. The Far East assumed greater importance. Tokyo moved into second place, and Hong Kong and Singapore moved up in the rankings with the latter narrowing the gap between the two.

Table 1 – *Head-Offices of Major Banks and Their Representation in Other Centers, 1970 and 1980*[a]

FROM \ TO	LO	NY	PA	FH	TO	SI	HK	LS	ZG	AM	BR	PN	MR	TM	Σ
LO	14 *8*	9 *8*	8 *6*	4 *5*	4 *8*	1 *4*	1 *7*	2 *4*	1 *3*	7 *3*	2 *4*	0 *1*	2 *2*	0 *4*	55 *67*
NY	10 *9*	13 *10*	8 *8*	7 *8*	8 *8*	3 *9*	6 *8*	0 *7*	3 *5*	5 *3*	4 *4*	2 *4*	5 *7*	1 *4*	75 *94*
PA	5 *11*	3 *13*	7 *14*	3 *8*	3 *9*	1 *6*	1 *9*	1 *4*	1 *2*	4 *5*	3 *3*	1 *3*	4 *8*	0 *2*	37 *97*
FH	3 *4*	2 *6*	1 *2*	12 *12*	1 *4*	1 *3*	0 *5*	0 *1*	0 *0*	0 *0*	0 *1*	0 *1*	0 *1*	0 *2*	20 *42*
TO	8 *14*	8 *15*	2 *7*	2 *10*	17 *23*	2 *11*	2 *8*	6 *11*	1 *4*	1 *2*	1 *3*	0 *2*	1 *1*	1 *6*	52 *117*
SI	0 *1*	0 *1*	0 *0*	0 *0*	0 *1*	1 *1*	1 *1*	0 *0*	0 *0*	0 *0*	0 *0*	0 *0*	0 *0*	0 *0*	2 *5*
HK	1 *1*	1 *1*	1 *1*	1 *1*	1 *1*	1 *1*	1 *1*	1 *1*	0 *1*	0 *1*	0 *0*	0 *0*	0 *0*	0 *1*	8 *11*
LS	5 *4*	4 *4*	1 *3*	2 *4*	5 *4*	1 *4*	5 *4*	8 *4*	1 *1*	1 *1*	2 *1*	1 *1*	1 *2*	0 *2*	37 *39*
ZG	1 *3*	1 *3*	1 *2*	0 *0*	1 *3*	1 *2*	1 *3*	1 *3*	3 *5*	1 *1*	0 *0*	0 *0*	0 *0*	1 *2*	12 *27*
AM	2 *2*	2 *3*	0 *0*	0 *0*	1 *2*	0 *2*	2 *2*	1 *2*	0 *0*	3 *4*	0 *1*	0 *1*	0 *1*	0 *0*	11 *20*
BR	0 *3*	1 *3*	0 *1*	1 *1*	0 *3*	0 *3*	0 *2*	0 *0*	0 *2*	0 *0*	3 *7*	0 *0*	0 *2*	0 *0*	5 *27*
PN	0 *0*	0 *1*	0 *0*	0 *0*	0 *0*	0 *0*	0 *0*	0 *0*	0 *0*	0 *0*	0 *0*	1 *1*	0 *0*	0 *0*	1 *2*
MR	4 *7*	5 *7*	4 *4*	5 *6*	0 *5*	1 *4*	0 *3*	1 *4*	2 *0*	0 *0*	3 *4*	0 *0*	12 *10*	1 *3*	38 *57*
TM	5 *5*	5 *5*	2 *4*	2 *4*	4 *5*	0 *4*	4 *5*	4 *5*	1 *1*	1 *1*	2 *1*	0 *2*	1 *2*	7 *5*	38 *49*
Σ	58 *72*	54 *80*	35 *52*	39 *59*	45 *76*	13 *54*	24 *58*	25 *46*	13 *24*	23 *21*	20 *29*	5 *16*	26 *36*	11 *31*	391 *654*
Rank	1 *3*	2 *1*	5 *7*	4 *4*	3 *2*	11 *6*	8 *5*	7 *8*	11 *12*	9 *13*	10 *11*	14 *14*	6 *9*	13 *10*	

[a] The figures for 1980 are shown in italics below the figures for 1970. – Sum of main diagonal: 102 in 1970 and 105 in 1980.

Source: The Banker [1971; 1981]; The Bankers' Almanac and Yearbook [1970–1971; 1980–1981].

III. The Degree of Interconnectedness

We use four measures of interconnectedness. The first three measures are based on a census of nonzero off-diagonal cells (i.e., cells for which $Y_{ij} > 0$). We treat the existence of at least one office in a center from a bank in another center as establishing a direct link between the two centers. The first measure reflects the percentage of actual to potential links. The numerator is the number of nonzero cells, and the denominator is the total number (182) of off-diagonal cells. For the second measure the numerator consist of the number of cells in which *either* Y_{ij} *or* Y_{ji} is not zero. The denominator is equal to one-half the number of off-diagonal cells (91). This measure captures the percentage of pairs of centers which have a direct link in at least one direction. The third measure gives the percentage of pairs of centers which have direct links in both directions. The numerator consists of the number of cells in which *both* Y_{ij} *and* Y_{ji} are not zero, and the denominator is again 91. The fourth measure is Cohen's kappa:

$$\kappa = 1 - (\Sigma P_{ii} - \Sigma P_{i.} P_{.j}) / (1 - \Sigma P_{i.} P_{.j})$$

where $P_{ij} = Y_{ij}/\Sigma_i\Sigma_j Y_{ij}$. Kappa can take any value between one and zero. A value of one indicates complete dispersion, i.e., every bank from each center has an office in every other center. A zero signals extreme concentration on the main diagonal or no interpenetration of offices. The measure takes into account the actual cell frequencies, not just the presence or absence of a direct link.

Table 2 presents the results. Interconnectedness has increased over the decade. Not only are there more connections between centers so that the number of pairs with no direct connection has fallen, but also the links are more intensive. From Table 1 we can calculate that while the number of banks represented has increased by only 3 percent, the number of foreign offices has increased by 90 percent.

Table 2 - *Measures of Interconnectedness Between Centers*

	Percentage of links			Cohen's κ
	actual to potential	one-way	two-way	
1970	60	78	59	.82
1980	77	91	64	.92

During the decade 1969–1979, the net size of the Eurocurrency market increased 537 percent in real terms, and the number of foreign banks with direct representation in London increased 139 percent. The fastest growth in both these measures occurred in the years 1969–1973. Tschoegl [1982] suggests that there is an association between the growth in size of the international market and the number of participants in it, on the one hand, and the low levels of concentration, lack of size advantages, or persistence of advantages among the world's largest banks and among the leading Euroloan syndicators on the other. There is some evidence that the result has been to reduce prices for loans, and one may presume for other services as well.

IV. The Determinants of Interpenetration

1. Conceptual Discussion

A financial center is a marketplace for financial services. For the marketplace to function, the location must have the following characteristics: *(i)* a stable legal and regulatory environment that permits entry, operation, and ownership, and *(ii)* an adequate infrastructure, particularly for physical and electronic communication.

Because we are dealing with established financial centers, there is little variation along these dimensions between them relative to cities which are not centers. All permit entry and minimize restrictions, at least for offshore transactions. None has suffered a violent overthrow of the government since the end of World War II, or is at war with its neighbors. All have an established legal system. Almost all are major cities in developed countries and have the necessary physical infrastructure. Six of the fourteen centers are in English-speaking countries and hiring English-speaking staff is not a major problem in the others. Given these similarities then, why might the centers differ in the number of banks each can attract?

We assume profit seeking behavior and model the banks' interest in representation in a center as being positively related to indicators of the revenues to be generated by such a presence, and negatively to ones of the costs. The revenue proxies include various measures of market size. The cost variables include such considerations as the distance between home and host centers, regulatory obstacles, and the effect of the banks' actions on the competition they face.

The revenue potential of a presence in a center derives from two conceptually different sources. First, there are those activities for which the center provides a convenient location, but which are independent of the presence or absence of other banks. Second, there are the activities which are a consequence of the agglomeration of institutions. Both types require the presence of the service providers. It is the nature of services that they generally cannot be stored or transported. Instead, they must be produced in contact with the customer because production and consumption take place simultaneously. The banks can serve some of their customers' requirements via correspondent relationships, but the range is quite limited.

Although a full discussion of why banks go abroad is beyond the scope of this paper, two major motivations are to service trade [Terrell, 1979], and to follow their corporate customers [Vastrup, 1983]. The major cities which are the hosts of financial centers provide a convenient location for such activities. They are often the site for many corporate headquarters, major distribution points, and the centers of communication networks. A foreign bank may establish itself and operate profitably in such a location without being affected by whether or not there are other banks engaged in similar activities. All that the bank requires are a sufficient volume of trade or demand for credit.

However, the presence of several institutions makes possible two types of central marketplaces. First, an interbank market may develop. Foreign exchange and money market trading provide an activity in themselves. The banks can trade generally, or specialize in the currencies of their home countries and regions. Second, as Stuart [1975] points out, the presence of several sellers of similar but not identical services in one location can reduce search costs for buyers. Thus any bank that enters the center has two opposed external effects, it increases the number of competitors for the existing business, but causes an increase in the total size of the market. The latter result is a consequence of the reduction in buyers' search costs. Thus, in joining a center, a bank may be entering into any one or more of these three types of markets. In the subsection 3 below, we will discuss these considerations further in connection with the discussion of the variables we use to operationalize the revenue and cost factors.

2. Statistical Techniques

We use two statistical methods, ordinary least squares (OLS), and nonlinear weighted least squares (NLWLS). The first method is perhaps more familiar. NLWLS is an appropriate technique when, as here, the dependent variable consists of count data. We regard the two techniques as complements. If different techniques permit similar inferences the researcher can be more confident of the results as they then do not depend crucially on the distributional assumptions which each requires.

We denote the matrix of independent variables by X, vectors of parameters by β and γ, and a vector of stochastic error terms by ε which we assume meets the classical assumptions. Then the OLS models we fit have the form

$$y = X\beta + \varepsilon$$

where y_{ij} is the Box-Cox [1964] transform of Y_{ij} ($i \neq j$), with parameters $\lambda_1 = 0$ and $\lambda_2 = 0.5$. As we are taking the natural log of Y_{ij}, we first add 0.5 to all elements of the vector rather than omit zero cells from the estimations. Dropping all zero cells would make it impossible for us to check for evidence of cooperation between banks from different centers which is one of the issues we address below. Furthermore, this approach is theoretically preferable to the common but unsound practice of replacing just the zero values with the constant "1" [Young, Young, 1975]. A check at values of λ_2 of 0.1 and 1.0 indicates that the results are not very sensitive to the location shift.

The NLWLS models rest on the following assumptions:

$$E(Y) = \exp(X\gamma) = m$$
$$\mathrm{cov}(Y) = \psi^2 D(m)$$

where D(m) is an N by N diagonal matrix with the vector of expectations, m, on the main diagonal. To estimate the models we implemented a three-step procedure suggested by Marlow *et al.* [1984]. First we use maximum likelihood methods to estimate γ and m. Second, the formula

$$\hat{\psi}^2 = [\Sigma_{ij} (Y_{ij} - \hat{m}_{ij})^2/\hat{m}_{ij}]/N - K$$

yields an estimate of ψ^2. Finally, we obtain the correct asymptotic covariance matrix for $\hat{\gamma}$ from

$$\mathrm{var}(\hat{\gamma}) = \hat{\psi}^2 (X'D(\hat{m})X)^{-1}$$

The NLWLS technique assumes that the bilateral flows are independent of each other: i.e., Y_{ij} is independent of Y_{ik}, $(k \neq j)$. Our combining certain cities within countries already indicates that we are aware that this may not always be the case. For some banks at some times, Brussels and Amsterdam, or Hong Kong and Singapore, for instance, may be adequate substitutes. We assume that for the large banks which make up our object of investigation, centers in different countries or more than some distance apart (say 500 miles or one hour by airplane), are not close substitutes.

One potential problem for both methods is that Y_{ij} is bounded above and below. That is, $0 \leq Y_{ij} \leq Y_{ii}$. While fitted values of Y_{ij} below zero are not possible because of our estimation techniques, ones greater than Y_{ii} are. Even so, there are no cases of violations of the upper bound in the OLS estimations, and only two minor ones in the NLWLS estimations.

3. Models and Results

The first model we fit uses as explanatory variables two measures based on the data in Table 1, and the distance between the centers[1]. We fit the model separately for 1970 and 1980.

[1] We proxy the trade in bank services in financial center i by banks from financial center j by the maintenance of bank offices. Our approach is isomorphic to that of the gravity model, which is probably the most successful empirical trade device of the last twenty-five years [Anderson, 1979]. In the gravity model, bilateral flows are a function of potential flow and resistance variables. One can derive gravity-like models as reduced form equations in different ways [Anderson, 1979; Bergstrand,

The first explanatory variable we use is the natural logarithm of $TO_j = Y_j - Y_{ij}$. TO_j is a proxy for the attractiveness of center j. The more banks from centers other than i that are in j, the more attractive j will be to banks from i both as a central marketplace and because of the indication that this gives that there is a demand for bank services at that location. Both of these factors should be subject to diminishing returns. Thus we expect the sign of the coefficient to be positive and its magnitude in the OLS estimations should be less than one. There is a simultaneity issue in that elements of the dependent variable vector enter into the construction of the elements of TO of our independent variables. We further address this problem in subsequent models.

The variable $FROM_i$ reflects the office establishment potential at the source. $FROM_i = Y_{ii}$ and we use the natural logarithm. Given our measures, a center cannot send out more offices than it has bank headquarters. We expect the coefficients to be positive, significant, and larger in 1980 than in 1970. This last expectation is a consequence of our earlier finding that the degree of interconnectedness has increased. Here too we expect the OLS coefficient's magnitude to be less than one. The more headquarters the sending center has, the smaller the last one will be. If we assume some fixed costs to establishing and maintaining an office abroad and that the office can expect to gain business roughly proportional to its parent's size, it becomes increasingly probable that the smaller banks will not find the representation worthwhile.

$DIST_{ij}$ is the airline distance between i and j. Because a number of our centers consist of pairs of cities, this forces us to use simple average distances. The coefficient of the variable will, therefore, be biased towards zero. The sign of its coefficient is ambiguous. On the one hand, in the trade and foreign direct investment literature the notion is that the costs of overcoming geographic and cultural distance will reduce bilateral flows. Ball, Tschoegl [1982] did indeed find a negative, statistically insignificant, relationship between the probability that a bank would have a subsidiary in California or a branch in Japan and the distance between these locations and the head office. On the other hand, there may be large fixed costs to operating a foreign office but low additional costs as a function of distance, and high costs as a function of distance of providing the bank services from the home office (particularly face-to-face contact). Then the farther apart two centers are, the more likely it is that banks will serve the foreign center from an office there, all other things being equal.

Table 3 presents the results in the discussion of which statistical significance will mean at the five percent level on a one-tailed test. In both periods and across both techniques, the coefficients of the variables for the attractiveness of the destination and the potential of the source are positive as

1985; Leamer, Stern, 1970; Senior, 1979; Sheppard, 1978]. However, doing so exposes some conceptual shortcomings and limiting assumptions.

Table 3 – *Results: Model I (t-statistics in parentheses)*

	OLS		NLWLS	
	1970	1980	1970	1980
Constant	-2.60 (-5.21)*	-4.28 (-8.68)*	-4.10 (-6.69)*	-4.73 (9.49)*
*ln*TO	0.51 (6.28)*	0.76 (7.86)*	0.91 (9.63)*	0.88 (14.66)*
*ln*FROM	0.57 (10.53)*	0.76 (5.06)*	0.91 (7.80)*	0.99 (9.61)*
*ln*DIST	0.05 (1.15)	0.14 (3.41)*	-0.01 (-0.29)	0.05 (1.41)
R^2	0.43	0.60		
F	45.41	67.06		
SER	0.71	0.64		
Log-likelihood			-342.17	-362.97
Sample size	182	182	182	182

Note: R^2 is the coefficient of determination. – F is the F-statistic. – SER is the standard error of the regression. – * indicates significance at the 5 percent level on a one-tailed test.

expected, and statistically significant. In the OLS estimations, TO's coefficient is less than 1, also as expected, and statistically significantly so. The coefficient of FROM is larger in 1980 than in 1970. As expected, in the OLS estimations the magnitude is less than one, and the difference from one is statistically significant. The distance variable is positive in three of the four estimations, and statistically significant in the OLS test for 1980. These results are inconsistent with the FDI literature's assumptions about the costs of operating at a distance. We pursue below the possibility that omitted factors are affecting the results.

We augment our basic model with some new variables. These introduce another measure of the attractiveness of the destination, a regulatory effect, and considerations of some bank interactions, particularly within Europe. These possible interactions are interesting in themselves and may be affecting the results on the distance variable.

We introduce a new proxy for the attractiveness of the destination. CGNP is an estimate of each center's share of gross national product (GNP). We arrived at the estimate by multiplying the population of each center by GNP per capita and converting all dollar values to constant 1978 dollars. CGNP provides a measure of the economic size of the centers. Because we have no basis for estimating the area served by each center, we have chosen this lowest common denominator. The variable is also a proxy for trade and direct investment flows. Ideally we would like to use direct measures of these quantities. However, the relevant statistics are not maintained in terms of inter-city flows, only national ones if at all. Even so, the trade and direct investment literatures have consistently found strong correlations between such flows and the economic size of the destination.

JPN is a (0,1) dummy variable for those cases where the sending center is Tokyo. The Japanese government has pursued a policy of gradually relaxing restrictions on the establishment of offices abroad by its banks. The degree of restriction depends on the class of the bank (city, trust, long-term credit, or provincial). It frequently takes the form of a limitation on the number of foreign offices per year that the banks may establish. We expect the coefficient to be negative in both years.

We are also interested in the effect on the interconnectedness of the centers of interaction between banks in different centers. More particularly, in deciding on whether or not to establish a presence in a center, banks must consider the response of the host country banks to their presence. Possible outcomes range from reciprocal entry when implicit or explicit agreements have not developed, or have broken down, to mutual forebearance via the operation of self-reinforcing contracts [Telser, 1980].

The first bank interaction variable we introduce is Y_{ji}, the reverse flow to Y_{ij}. Graham [1976; 1978] has suggested and presented evidence for manufacturing industry that one motive for FDI is rivalrous behavior and an "exchange of threat". That is, firms from j will invest in i if firms from i invest in j to prevent the latter from gaining a decisive advantage. This is also consistent with one of Grubel's [1977] arguments for foreign direct investment in banking: a failure to follow their customers will erode the home country's banks' advantage in serving them by giving host country banks an entrée.

Using Y_{ij} as an independent variable compounds our simultaneity problem. We deal with it via a two-stage least squares (TSLS) procedure in which the elements of Y_{ji} and TO on the second pass are the fitted values of the regression of the exogenous variables on Y_{ij}.

As we discuss below, there is reason to believe that the dynamics of intra-European bank behavior are such that they reduce the degree of interpenetration. That is, there may in fact be agreements among European banks not to establish offices in each others' countries.

Many of the largest banks in Europe have joined in cross-national groups which foster cooperation in external ventures, and may result in some suppression of competition [Steuber, 1977]. To reflect this possibility we have constructed a (0,1) dummy variable EURO which only takes on a value of one if Y_{ij} represents a flow between any two of the following five centers: Paris, Brussels, Amsterdam, Frankfurt/Hamburg, or Milan/Rome.

There is a second source of resistance to flows between proximate centers based on the behavior of the Swiss banks. The major banks in that country have reportedly adopted a policy of not opening branches in other European centers [Paltzer, 1977]. Much of their international business has to do with the management of nonresident accounts, and the banks have been content to let their customers come to them. Customers seeking Swiss banking secrecy may not have found Swiss bank branches in their own countries of any great value to them. The variable SWISS, therefore, takes on a value of one if Y_{ij} represents a flow from Zürich/Geneva to any of the five other centers listed in the preceding paragraph and zero otherwise.

Finally, we create a (0,1) dummy variable (FHZG) for interpenetration between Zürich/Geneva and Frankfurt/Hamburg. There is journalistic evidence of a mutual nonaggression pact between the largest banks in these two centers [World Business Weekly, 1980]. We do not include this variable in the NLWLS esimations. In unreported estimations, inclusions of the variable rendered all coefficient estimates meaningless. The above three variables suggest the possibility that the positive coefficient on the distance variable may be due to the fact that many of the centers which are close to each other are in Continental Europe.

Before going on to discuss the results we wish to mention some omitted variables. We are aware of the importance of time zone placement of offices, especially in connection with 24-hour trading. However, two different attempts to model the phenomenon were unsuccessful. This may be due to the crudity of our approaches relative to the complexity of the issue. The second variable we tried had to do with cultural similarity between centers as proxied by the use of English as the national language. The coefficients were small and insignificant. Finally, we tried another measure of the attractiveness, the size of the Eurocurrency market in each center. However, prior to the authorization of International Banking Facilities in 1981, the size of the offshore currency market in New York and Los Angeles/San Francisco was effectively zero. This severely understates these centers' importance in international finance. As a result, the variable's coefficients were small, frequently of the wrong sign, and never significant.

Table 4 presents the results for the OLS estimations, and Table 5 the NLWLS ones for the factors and associated variables we do consider. In the discussion below we will refer to the model with $\hat{T}O$ as Model II, and that with CGNP and OFFSHR instead as Model III, with the roman numeral preceded by the year when appropriate.

Both models perform better in 1980 than in 1970. There is some collinearity between the destination variables ($\hat{T}O$ and CGNP), and $\hat{Y}_{ji}$ in 1970. When we drop $\hat{Y}_{ji}$ (Models IIA and IIIA), the significance levels of the other two coefficients improve. The collinearity problem does not arise in 1980 as the increased density of the matrix has resulted in a decline in the

Table 4 – *Results: Expanded Model (OLS) (t-statistics in parentheses)*

	1970				1980	
	II	III	IIA	IIIA	II	III
Constant	-0.11 (-0.19)	-1.42 (-1.10)	-0.52 (-0.89)	-2.53 (-3.28)*	-1.30 (-2.54)*	-3.20 (-3.94)*
$ln\hat{T}O$		0.38 (0.93)		0.80 (5.18)*		0.62 (3.36)*
*ln*CGNP	-0.12 (-1.02)		0.22 (4.19)*		0.12 (2.28)*	
*ln*FROM	0.40 (5.43)*	0.50 (5.84)*	0.54 (8.88)*	0.57 (9.47)*	0.76 (12.85)*	0.78 (13.29)*
*ln*DIST	-0.01 (-0.15)	-0.04 (-1.64)	-0.07 (-1.11)	-0.07 (-1.11)	0.06 (0.96)	0.06 (1.09)
$ln\hat{Y}_{ji}$	0.74 (3.12)*	-0.29 (-1.07)			0.22 (2.59)*	0.18 (2.34)*
JPN	-0.22 (-0.95)	-0.15 (-0.65)	-0.10 (-0.44)	-0.10 (-0.46)	-0.38 (-1.74)*	-0.31 (-1.44)
EURO	-0.21 (-0.92)	-0.35 (-1.46)	-0.44 (-1.96)*	-0.46 (-2.13)*	-0.51 (-2.60)*	-0.46 (-2.34)*
SWISS	-0.36 (-0.96)	-0.27 (-0.72)	-0.22 (-0.59)	-0.23 (-0.62)	-0.72 (-2.18)*	-0.65 (-2.00)*
FHZG	-0.24 (-0.39)	-0.83 (-1.27)	-1.17 (-2.10)*	-1.22 (-2.25)*	-1.11 (-2.19)*	-1.17 (-2.35)*
R^2	0.44	0.44	0.40	0.43	0.60	0.61
F	16.74	16.70	16.88	18.90	32.31	34.16
SER	0.72	0.72	0.74	0.72	0.65	0.64

Note: R^2 is the coefficient of determination. – F is the F-statistic. – SER is the standard error of the regression. – * indicates significance at the 5 percent level on a one-tailed test.

correlations between $\hat{T}O$ and CGNP, and $\hat{Y}_{ji}$.

In 1970 $\hat{T}O$ is positive, and significant in Model IIIA, and positive and significant in 1980. The number of banks in a center is apparently a good proxy for attractiveness. It may also be a positive characteristic in itself. We cannot test this possibility as the attractiveness variables are highly collinear, and CGNP and OFFSHR are imperfect measures of the market size.

The coefficient of CGNP is positive and significant in both 1970 IIA and 1980 II, and for both statistical methods. Clearly, the size of the economy at the center is a major factor in its attractiveness. Again, this may reflect the variable's proxying for trade and direct investment flows as well.

As expected, the coefficients of FROM for the OLS estimations are larger

Table 5 – *Results: Expanded Model (NLWLS)*
(asymptotic t-statistics in parentheses)

	1970				1980	
	II	III	IIA	IIIA	II	III
Constant	- 1.79 (- 2.29)*	- 1.62 (- 2.01)*	- 1.55 (- 2.32)*	- 5.19 (- 5.33)*	- 1.05 (- 2.25)*	- 3.30 (- 4.12)*
$\ln\hat{T}O$		0.55 (1.05)		1.44 (6.62)*		0.70 (3.83)*
lnCGNP	- 0.03 (- 0.20)		0.39 (5.38)*		0.14 (2.77)*	
lnFROM	0.70 (4.81)*	0.79 (4.85)*	0.88 (7.70)*	0.97 (7.99)*	0.83 (9.91)*	0.86 (10.57)*
lnDIST	0.04 (0.46)	- 0.02 (- 0.17)	- 0.10 (- 1.40)	- 0.11 (- 1.64)	- 0.01 (- 0.24)	0.00 (0.06)
$\ln\hat{Y}_{ji}$	1.26 (4.02)*	0.91 (2.47)*			0.24 (3.20)*	0.15 (1.94)*
JPN	- 0.35 (- 1.36)	- 0.24 (- 0.91)	- 0.07 (- 0.08)	- 0.04 (- 0.17)	- 0.28 (- 1.67)*	- 0.15 (- 0.96)
EURO	0.31 (0.94)	0.16 (0.46)	- 0.24 (- 0.88)	- 0.28 (- 1.03)	- 0.34 (- 1.81)*	- 0.28 (- 1.54)
SWISS	- 0.72 (- 0.56)	- 0.72 (- 0.68)	- 0.86 (- 0.95)	- 1.01 (- 1.02)	- 1.24 (- 2.05)*	- 1.17 (- 1.99)*
Log-likelihood	- 339.68	- 338.51	- 353.24	- 343.73	- 386.84	- 382.76
Sample size	182	182	182	182	182	182

* indicates significance at the 5 percent level on a one-tailed test.

in 1980 than in 1970, though statistically significantly smaller than one. The coefficients are significant across models, years, and methods. The implication would be that the more banks a center has, the greater the number that will establish themselves elsewhere, but at a decreasing rate.

The distance variable's coefficients are always small and not significant – negative in 1970 and positive in 1980 for the OLS estimations, and mixed in both years for the NLWLS ones. As discussed above, the coefficient of the variable is biased towards zero because of errors in variables problems. In addition, as Sheppard [1979] points out, spatial autocorrelation may cause the coefficients to be biased and inconsistent. Experiments with standardizing the variable with respect to the range of each center from all other centers as suggested by Johnston [1976, p. 75], however, had no material effect. Once one adjusts for other factors, it is not clear that physical distance has any particular net effect on the attractiveness of a center to banks from another center.

The coefficient of JPN is consistently negative but not significant in 1970. As the coefficients are larger in absolute value and significant in one estimation for 1980, government regulations may bind more in 1980 than in 1970. That is, the government policy of only permitting some banks to open another office abroad when the evidence is quite strong that the venture will be successful may be based on too conservative a set of criteria.

The coefficients of the backflow variable, $\hat{Y}_{ji}$, are positive and significant for seven of eight estimations. That is, penetration in one direction generally is associated with penetration in the other.

Clearly, there is far less interpenetration between European centers than one might otherwise expect. The coefficients of EURO are negative in ten of twelve estimations, and statistically significant in four of the OLS and one of the NLWLS tests. This is consistent with cooperative behavior between banks in the five continental European Economic Community centers. While the existence of the Swiss strategy of not penetrating European centers is not strongly supported in 1970, by 1980 the increased density of the matrix makes it quite apparent. Finally, as far as FHZG is concerned, the coefficient is negative and significant in four of six OLS estimations, and negative in the other two. This is consistent with cooperative behavior between the Swiss and German banks. We conjecture that physical proximity between different national centers is conducive to cooperative behavior, but is not sufficient to induce it as we have other proximate centers (e.g. New York-Toronto/Montreal, and London/European Centers) which are interconnected via bank interpenetration. There is emerging evidence that the Swiss-German entente is now breaking down. A replication of this study with 1990 data then may well show no such effect.

V. Summary and Conclusion

In this paper we have analyzed the interconnectedness of fourteen world financial centers by examining the location pattern of offices of some of the world's largest banks in 1970 and 1980. Over the decade, there appears to have been some shift in the relative importance of various centers with the Far East ones, in particular, having become much more important. The degree of interpenetration has increased substantially as the total size of the offshore market has grown.

The attractiveness of a center is clearly related to the size of the economy it represents, and perhaps to the amount of international financial activity there. To banks from another country, one good measure of a center's attractiveness is simply the number of banks that are already there. However, the effect is subject to diminshing returns.

Distance between centers seems neither clearly to inhibit nor encourage interconnectedness. Foreign bank presence in a bank's home center is generally associated with increased propensity to establish a presence in the foreign banks' home center, indicating some internationally rivalrous behavior.

There is also clear evidence of cooperative behavior (i.e., a failure to interpenetrate) among continental European banks. Swiss banks, moreover, appear deliberately to have chosen not to enter European centers.

Banks or countries could conceivably use the models for forecasting the consequences (in terms of the number of offices) of a country's either permitting its banks to go abroad (Model III), or permitting banks from other countries to establish themselves in one of its cities (Model II). Obviously, the models would give conservative estimates for a number of reasons. We have not included all possible sources or destinations or, in the centers we have examined, all banks with offices abroad. Second, we may not have captured some external effects such as that the more banks there are, the more attractive is a center. Third, the model will not work well for centers such as Bahrain where attractiveness may be a function of time zone and proximity to other economies, even though the center's own economy may be quite small [Gerakis, Roncesvalles, 1983].

Even so, the models provide a starting point for the analysis of proposals for foreign bank entry into India or Sweden. They may be even more interesting in the examination of cases such as Spain and Australia, where entry has recently been permitted, but is apparently rationed. Here they may permit some assessment of whether the limitations are binding, and if so, with respect to what countries. These concerns remain topics for further research.

References

Anderson, James E., "A Theoretical Foundation for the Gravity Models". *The American Economic Review,* Vol. 69, 1979, pp. 106–116.

Ball, Clifford A., Adrian E. Tschoegl, "The Decision to Establish a Foreign Bank Branch or Subsidiary: An Application of Binary Classification Procedures". *Journal of Financial and Quantitative Analysis,* Vol. 17, 1982, pp. 411–424.

The Banker, Vol. 121, No. 544, June 1971; Vol. 131, No. 664, June 1981.

The Bankers' Almanac and Yearbook, 1970–1971; 1980–1981. New York.

Bergstrand, Jeffrey H., "The Gravity Equation in International Trade: Some Microeconomic Foundations and Empirical Evidence". *Review of Economics and Statistics,* Vol. 67, 1985, pp. 474–481.

Box, George E. P., David R. Cox, "An Analysis of Transformations". *Journal of the Royal Statistical Society,* Vol. 26, 1964, pp. 211–252.

Dean, James W., Ian H. Giddy, "Strangers and Neighbors: Cross-Border Banking in North America". *Banca Nazionale del Lavoro Quarterly Review,* No. 137, 1981, pp. 191–211.

Gerakis, Andreas S., O. Roncesvalles, "Bahrain's Offshore Banking Center". *Economic Development and Cultural Change,* Vol. 31, 1983, pp. 349-364.

Goldberg, Lawrence G., Anthony Saunders, "The Growth of Organizational Forms of Foreign Banks in the U.S.". *Journal of Money, Credit and Banking,* Vol. 13, 1981, pp. 365-376.

Graham, Edward M., *Theories of Foreign Direct Investment.* MIT Working Paper, No. 847-76, 1976.

–, "Transatlantic Investment by Multinational Firms: A Rivalistic Phenomenon?" *Journal of Post Keynesian Economics,* Vol. 1, 1978, pp. 82-99.

Grubel, Herbert G., "A Theory of Multinational Banking". *Banca Nazionale del Lavoro Quarterly Review,* No. 123, 1977, pp. 349-364.

–, "Towards a Theory of Free Economic Zones". *Weltwirtschaftliches Archiv,* Vol. 118, 1982, pp. 39-61.

Johnson, Harry G., "Panama as a Regional Financial Center". *Economic Development and Cultural Change,* Vol. 24, 1976, pp. 261-286.

Johnston, Ronald J., The World Trade System. London 1976.

Khoury, Sarkis J., "International Banking: A Special Look at Foreign Banks in the U.S.". *Journal of International Business Studies,* Vol. 10, 1979, No. 3, pp. 36-52.

Kindleberger, Charles P., *The Formation of Financial Centers: A Study in Comparative Economic History.* Princeton Studies in International Finance, No. 39. Princeton, N.J., 1974.

Leamer, Edward E., Robert M. Stern, *Quantitative International Economics.* Boston 1970.

Marlow, Michael L., John P. Link, Robert B. Trost, "Market Structure and Rivalry: New Evidence with a Non-Linear Model". *Review of Economics and Statistics,* Vol. 66, 1984, pp. 578-682.

Paltzer, Edgar F., "Internationalization of Banking by Foreign Bases and Addresses". In: John E. Wadsworth, John S. G. Wilson, Henri Fournier (Eds.), *The Development of Financial Institutions in Europe, 1956-1976.* Leyden, 1977, pp. 167-174.

Reed, Howard Curtis, "The Ascent of Tokyo as an International Financial Center". *Journal of International Business Studies,* Vol. 11, 1980, No. 3, pp. 19-35.

–, *The Preeminence of International Financial Centers.* New York 1981.

Senior, Martin L., "From Gravity Modelling to Entropy Maximization: A Pedagogic Guide". *Progress in Human Geography,* Vol. 3, 1979, pp. 175-210.

Sheppard, Eric S., "Theoretical Underpinnings of the Gravity Hypothesis". *Geographical Analysis,* Vol. 10, 1978, pp. 386-402.

–, "Gravity Parameter Estimation". *Geographical Analysis,* Vol. 11, 1979, pp. 120-132.

Steuber, Ursula, "International Co-Operation and Competition among Banks in Europe". In: John E. Wadsworth, John S. G. Wilson, Henri Fournier (Eds.), *The Development of Financial Institutions in Europe, 1956-1976.* Leyden 1977, pp. 175-189.

Stuart, Charles, *Search and the Organization of Market Places.* Lund Economic Series. Malmö 1975.

Telser, Lester G., "A Theory of Self-Enforcing Agreements". *Journal of Business,* Vol. 53, 1980, pp. 27-44.

Terrell, Henry S., "U.S. Banks in Japan and Japanese Banks in the United States: An Empirical Comparison". *Federal Reserve Bank of San Francisco Economic Review*, Summer 1979, pp. 18–30.

Tschoegl, Adrian E., "Concentration among International Banks: A Note". *Journal of Banking and Finance*, Vol. 6, 1982, pp. 567–578.

Vastrup, Claus, "Economic Motives for Foreign Banking: The Danish Case". *Kredit und Kapital*, Vol. 16, 1983, pp. 117–125.

World Business Weekly, "Deutsche Bank Crosses the Border". September 15, 1980, pp. 50–51.

World Financial Markets, var. issues.

Young, Kan Hua, Lin Ying Young, "Estimation of Regressions Involving Logarithmic Transformations of Zero Values in the Dependent Variable". *The American Statistician*, Vol. 29, 1975, pp. 118–120.

* * *

[23]

Excerpt from Augustine H.H. Tan and Basant Kapur (eds), *Pacific Growth and Financial Interdependence*, 247–60, 381–2

11 Trade in financial services: its nature, causes, growth prospects and social effects

HERBERT G. GRUBEL

Three factors incite the interest of scholars and policy workers in the prospective growth of financial services in the Pacific region. First, there has been the spectacular growth of the financial sectors of Hong Kong and Singapore in recent years.[1] Can other countries replicate the success of these two centres and through financial sectoral growth enjoy a powerful stimulus for the rest of their economies?

Second, research has shown that in industrial countries the service sector has grown much more rapidly than the rest of the economy. In the United States especially, projections of this trend into the future have raised fears about a US economy without industrial production[2] and goods exports. Under these conditions, US imports have to be paid for by the export of services. Unfortunately, trade in services is hampered by many obstacles. To overcome these, the US government has taken a number of initiatives on the diplomatic front.[3] A better understanding of the nature and magnitude of trade in financial services will help policymakers in the Pacific rim countries deal effectively with these US initiatives.

Third, the growth of international banking went hand in hand with the growth of financial integration of most Pacific rim countries. This integration brought benefits through increased capital flows and financial efficiency. But it also caused a loss of national economic sovereignty. This loss of sovereignty is of great concern to policymakers and, to the extent that it is linked to trade in financial services, needs to be studied carefully.

In the first part of this paper I analyse the nature and likely magnitude of trade in financial services generally. The second part examines the nature of Hong Kong's and Singapore's financial business. Part three draws conclusions for policy from the preceding analysis, paying special attention to the trade-off between allocative efficiency and economic sovereignty.

THE NATURE AND MAGNITUDE OF TRADE IN FINANCIAL SERVICES

The financial service industry accomplishes two tasks. First, it clears payments among economic agents that arise from the production of goods and services, the activities of government and foreign economic relations. The cheque-clearing services of banks, foreign exchange and cash transactions are the main components of business accomplishing this task.

Second, it intermediates between ultimate savers and borrowers of funds. This task is accomplished by the use of a wide variety of debt instruments such as equities, bank deposits, fixed and variable interest securities with different maturities and security features including bills, certificates of deposit, mortgages, bonds and mutual funds. All of these may be the obligations of ultimate borrowers such as manufacturing corporations, governments or individuals that spend the proceeds on real assets, goods or services. Or they may be the obligiations of intermediaries such as banks and insurance companies that hold to themselves the obligations of ultimate borrowers. To meet the diverse needs of ultimate lenders and borrowers, modern financial industries have developed an almost bewildering variety of instruments, much as consumer goods industries have developed many varieties of basic goods.

It should be noted that the financial intermediation industry performs two distinctively different tasks. One consists of the initial sale and ultimate redemption of obligations. This is performed mainly by so-called merchant banking houses and commercial banks through loan consortia. The second task involves the brokerage of existing debt instruments in organised stock exchanges or informal kerbs on over-the-counter markets.

THE MAGNITUDE OF THE FINANCIAL SERVICE SECTOR

In principle, the size of the financial service sector can be measured in three ways. The first considers the stock of outstanding debt obligations at any moment in time. The second measures the flow of transactions per time period, that is, the total value of securities, cash and foreign exchange that changed hands. The third sums the amount of real resources used up in the provision of the sector's services during a given period. This measure is the value-added of national income accounting.

Each of these three measures has advantages and disadvantages. For the present purposes of analysis, the value-added is the most appropriate. Unfortunately, however, historic time series and data for different countries were available to me only at a level of aggregation known as 'Finance, Insurance and Real Estate', FIR for short and SIC 9 in standard national account nomenclature.

Table 11.1 presents data on the contribution of this sector to Gross Domestic Product (GDP) in countries of the Pacific rim. As can be seen, the first group of countries comprises the industrialised nations, the United States, Japan and Canada, where in 1980 the sector contributed 20.7 per cent, 15.7 per cent and 9.6 per cent of GDP, respectively. During the period 1970–80 the US and Japanese ratios grew by 13.7 per cent and 27.6 per cent, respectively, while the Canadian ratio remained unchanged.[4]

The second group consists of the developing countries, Malaysia and

Table 11.1 Finance, insurance and real estate as percentage of GDP: selected countries, 1970–80

	United States	*Canada*	*Japan*	*Malaysia*	*Indonesia*	*Hong Kong*	*Singapore*
1970	18.2	9.8	12.3	8.7	2.6	14.9	13.9
1971	18.4	10.1	13.5	8.7	2.8	18.3	14.2
1972	18.2	10.1	14.1	8.5	3.2	21.9	14.3
1973	18.0	9.9	14.2	8.3	3.3	19.1	14.7
1974	18.4	9.7	13.5	8.1	3.6	16.0	15.2
1975	18.2	10.4	14.2	8.4	3.9	15.5	15.5
1976	18.2	10.7	13.9	8.0	4.0	16.0	15.5
1977	18.9	10.8	14.1	8.0	4.5	18.3	15.3
1978	19.3	11.1	14.8	8.2	4.7	19.6	15.4
1979	19.8	10.0	15.1	8.2	4.9	20.8	15.8
1980	20.7	9.6	15.7	8.3	4.9		17.0

Source: UN *Yearbook of National Account Statistics* Vol. 1, Tables 1 and 10 for each country.

Indonesia. As can be seen, Malaysia's ratio was 8.3 per cent in 1980, which is much less than that of the United States and Japan, but only slightly smaller than that of Canada. Indonesia's FIR industries in 1980 contributed 4.9 per cent to GDP. Noteworthy is the fact that Indonesia's ratio nearly doubled and Malaysia's dropped slightly during the period 1970–80.

The data for Hong Kong and Singapore show that the FIR sector in these countries is comparable to that of the industrial countries. Of interest is the great volatility of the data for Hong Kong: from 14.9 per cent in 1970 the figure jumped to 22.6 per cent in 1972, dropped to 15.5 per cent in 1975 and reached 20.8 per cent again only in 1979. Singapore, on the other hand, showed a relatively steady growth from 13.9 per cent in 1970 to 17.0 per cent in 1980. This difference may well be due to the greater volatility of Hong Kong housing prices during the period.

The data in Table 11.1 confirm conventional wisdom regarding the importance of FIR in industrial countries, the sector's smaller role in developing countries and its growth and significance in Hong Kong and Singapore. We may conclude confidently that industrialisation of the LDCs in the Pacific Basin will bring relatively rapid growth in the FIR sector.

RELATION TO OTHER SECTOR GROWTH

However, Table 11.2 shows that during the 1960s in Singapore, the trade and finance sector grew only at roughly the same rate as GDP. The leading growth sectors during this period were construction, manufacturing and utilities. During the 1970s, on the other hand, trade and finance had the second largest growth rate after transportation and communications, but utilities and manufacturing grew at nearly the same pace.

It is interesting to note the similar experience of Canada. During the 1960s trade and finance grew exactly at the rate of GDP. During the 1970s this sector retained the growth rate of the preceding decade while that of GDP was lowered significantly by the reduced growth of all of the goods-producing industries.

Figure 11.1 The growth of service- and goods-producing industries in Canada, 1935–84

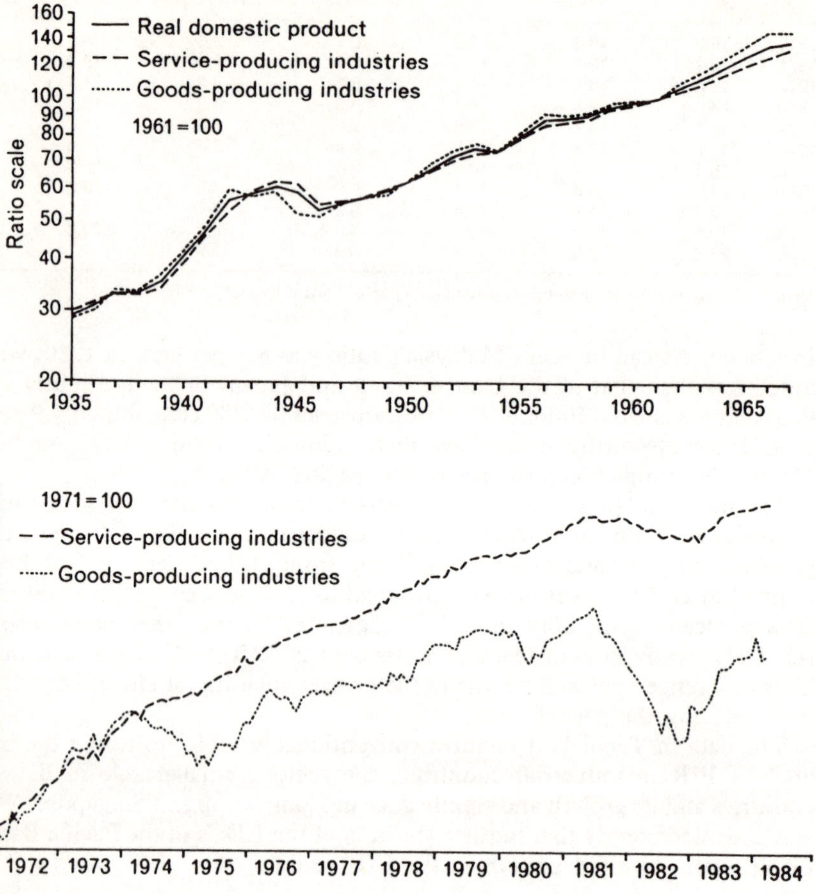

Source: Statistics Canada *Real Domestic Product by Industry* Cat. 61–213.

The data in Table 11.2 suggest that the trade and finance sectors grew in proportion to GDP during the prosperous 1960s and were a source of stability and stimulus to growth during the 1970s when the energy crisis, inflation and recessions slowed output growth in the goods-producing sectors.

FINANCE IN PERSPECTIVE TO INSURANCE AND REAL ESTATE

Table 11.3 shows the contributions to GDP which are made by the individual components of the class Finance, Insurance and Real Estate in Canada during the period 1971–81.[5]

Table 11.2 Trade and finance growth rates in perspective: Singapore and Canada

	Canada		*Singapore*	
	1960–70	*1970–81*	*1960–70*	*1970–81*
	Average annual growth rates at constant factor costs			
Agriculture	2.5	1.8	5.0	1.7
Mining	6.5	−0.2	9.0	8.8
Manufacturing	6.8	3.2	13.0	9.7
Construction	4.5	2.2	12.3	5.8
Electricity, gas and water	7.9	6.3	10.6	10.0
Transport and communications	6.6	5.3	7.8	14.0
Trade and finance	5.6	5.3	9.0	10.1
GDP at market prices	5.6	3.8	8.8	8.6

Source: IBRD *World Tables* 3rd edn, 1983.

Table 11.3 Finance compared with insurance and real estate: Canada, 1971–81 (industries as percentage of GDP)

Year	*Finance industries SIC 901*	*Insurance carriers SIC 902*	*Insurance agencies and real estate industries SIC 903*	*Imputed rent*	*Banks and other depositories SIC 701*	*Security brokers and dealers SIC 705*
1971	2.28	0.92	3.87	3.89	1.52	0.21
1972	2.34	0.86	3.64	3.71	1.53	0.23
1973	2.35	0.72	3.76	3.39	1.57	0.23
1974	2.38	0.58	3.79	3.20	1.61	0.17
1975	2.64	0.66	3.70	3.19	1.82	0.17
1976	2.57	0.90	3.77	3.27	1.78	0.16
1977	2.58	0.89	3.91	3.53	1.70	0.15
1978	2.54	0.88	4.06	3.61	1.80	0.19
1979	2.37	0.70	4.03	3.55	1.61	0.23
1980	2.44	0.60	4.10	3.69	1.57	0.34
1981	2.28	0.57	4.24	4.23	1.50	0.26

Source: Statistics Canada *Real Domestic Product by Industry* (April 1984) Cat. 61–213.

As can be seen, the Finance Industries, SIC 901, contributed only 2.28 per cent to Canadian GDP in 1971 and 1980. The contribution of insurance carriers, SIC 902, fluctuated between a high of 0.92 per cent in 1971 and a low of 0.57 per cent in 1981. In 1981, insurance agencies, the real estate industry and imputed rent made up 70.8 per cent of the total of the FIR sector. A similar relationship existed in other years.

In Table 11.3 the contributions of banks and other deposit-accepting institutions (SIC 701) and of security brokers and dealers (SIC 705) are shown separately. The data suggest that these two industries represent the bulk of the category finance industries.

We may conclude from the data in Table 11.3 that the contribution to GDP of finance industries proper is relatively small in Canada. If this relationship also holds for LDCs and Singapore and Hong Kong, the data in Table 11.3 have important implications for the future growth in trade in financial services.

TRADE IN FINANCIAL SERVICES—RETURNS ON CAPITAL

Services generally are produced as a flow from stocks of physical, human, knowledge and financial capital. For example, aeroplanes and ships yield transportation services; the human capital of physicians produces medical services; the knowledge capital of computer firms underlies the sale of computer services; security portfolios bring investment income. Financial services draw on all four types of capital brought together in financial intermediary firms.

In the analysis of trade in financial services, it is important to distinguish between the trade in capital assets and the services proper. The flow of finance capital is recorded in the capital accounts of the balance of payments. The income from foreign-asset holdings is reflected in current trade on services accounts.[6]

Income and payments on capital have attracted the attention of analysis frequently in the past, mainly as part of the study of balance-of-payments structure and trends and the welfare effects of capital flows.[7] National balance-of-payments statistics show prominently data on trade in capital services. To avoid confusion, this type of international financial service trade will here be referred to as international factor service trade. It is not the main focus of this chapter. Other chapters in this volume deal with the balance-of-payments and financial interdependence aspects of international capital and factor service flows.

TRADE IN FINANCIAL SERVICES PROPER

National balance-of-payments statistics do not routinely publish statistics on trade in services that have as their domestic counterpart the value-added of FIR noted above. The main reason for this state of affairs is that, historically, financial services have been either intermediate inputs into exportables, or they have been non-tradable.

Financial services required in the production of exported goods and services are part of the final price of these exports. As such, they are reflected in balance-of-payments statistics, but just like other intermediate inputs, they are not shown separately.

The services provided by financial intermediaries to consumers typically involve close personal relationships. Bank lending and borrowing, pension and trust management and trade in securities with private wealthholders draw heavily on personal knowledge of the creditworthiness and character of transactors. In the production and maintenance of this essential knowledge in the past, physical proximity has been so essential that for all practical purposes the sevices were non-tradable. Historically, therefore, balance-of-payments accounts on financial services have been zero or negligibly small.

However, in recent years changes in communications and transportation technologies and different regulation of financial sectors in different countries have encouraged the spread of multinational banks and enterprises and increased travel. As a by-product of these developments, financial services have ceased to be non-tradables. In the next section the nature and likely growth of this new financial trade will be analysed in detail.

Before we turn to this task it is useful to note that current practices used in the construction of national accounts are based on the assumption that bank services are non-tradable.[8] Thus, national income accountants apportion the value-added of banks and other such institutions into intermediate inputs and consumption according to the proportion of the banks' liabilities owned by firms and private individuals respectively. There is no provision for the fact that in recent times some proportion of the firms and individuals may be foreigners.

As a result of this practice the level and growth of national income and of the financial sector are biased downward. This may be seen by considering the allocation of $1 million of bank services to the domestic manufacturing sector under present practices. That sector's value-added and therefore contribution to GDP is lowered by $1 million, as financial services along with other intermediate inputs are deducted from final sales. Now assume that in fact the $1 million bank services did not go to a domestic but to a foreign firm with all its manufacturing facilities abroad. Under these conditions, the sale of financial services should be treated as an export. As such, it would raise GDP by the full $1 million and would not diminish the value-added of domestic manufacture.

The bias from the disregard of the export of financial services in national accounting practices has been negligible historically and probably still is for relatively closed economies. However, for small, open countries and especially those specialising in financial service production, like Singapore, Hong Kong and Luxembourg, the existing practices may involve a serious bias.[9]

DIRECT TRADE IN FINANCIAL SERVICES

Direct trade in financial services takes place between financial intermediaries in one country and residents of another. It is useful to distinguish four types of such financial business.

Traditional Capital Flows Intermediation

International capital flows are the end of a long chain of interregional flows mediated by the financial industry. Thus, banks in small towns attempt to bring together local lenders and borrowers. Local imbalances are passed on to regional centres and remaining imbalances reach national centres. Groups of countries often have regional supra-national centres, with New York serving as the world centre of finance. Imbalances within national centres give rise to international capital flows.[10]

Singapore and Hong Kong are regional, supra-national centres that attract loan and deposit business from within their territories and neighbouring countries. This regional business was fostered by the comparative advantage which the local communities developed during their colonial status, when English banking skills were the best in the world and dominated international capital markets. Their comparative advantage also results from the central location of these countries and the deliberate support which government policy provided for its advance. Human capital, good communications systems and a favourable regulatory environment are essential ingredients in the development of this business.

But Singapore and Hong Kong also serve as centres through which the region is linked to other parts of the world. As such, they are members of a small club of centres that includes London, New York, Tokyo, Luxembourg, Bahrain and Panama. These centres provided the expertise that put together the very large loans of the 1970s, which in the final analysis brought together as ultimate lenders and borrowers the OPEC surplus countries and the LDCs with ambitious development plans.

There is little doubt that the regional, supra-national intermediation role of Singapore and Hong Kong will continue to grow in the future along with the growth of income and wealth in the Pacific region. The intermediation business derived from OPEC surpluses has diminished and is likely to give little further stimulus. On the other hand, traditional capital flows from industrial countries to Pacific region LDCs should increase further and add to the business of the two centres as the entire region enjoys rapid development.

It is easy to overestimate the value-added that is involved in the business giving rise to international capital flows. The principal sums may be large, but value-added consists merely of the spread between lending and borrowing rates and some placement fees. The lower cost of information caused by the electronics revolution will probably put further pressure on these spreads in the future. To the extent that the spread reflects risk, increasing international diversification of lenders serves to reduce risk and therefore narrow the spreads. Growth reduction will also be caused by policies of neighbouring countries designed to develop their own financial sectors.

Diverted Trade

Analysts of Euro and Asian currency markets are in almost unanimous agreement that the growth of these markets since the mid-1960s is largely due to trade diversion caused by taxation and regulation in the industrial countries. In chapter 8, Hewson showed how the Singapore government carefully and deliberately deregulated and removed taxes on international banks in order to encourage them to take up residence there. The absence of reserve requirements on commercial bank deposits denominated in foreign currencies undoubtedly represents the greatest single stimulus for the growth of the Asian currency business of Hong Kong and Singapore.[11]

The Asian currency business basically involves lending and borrowing by firms and individuals who, in the absence of differential taxation, would do their lending and borrowing in locations more suitable to their basic business. For example, the corporate headquarters of Exxon and IBM are in New York, where they do most of their banking transactions. In the past, they would also lend and borrow short-term and meet long-term financing needs in this centre. However, because of the differential rate of taxation on intermediation business, these firms can obtain both higher rates on their deposits and lower costs on their borrowing abroad than they could in New York. Often, they do this business abroad with branches of their New York banks.

There is no doubt that a substantial part of the Singapore and Hong Kong financial business is due to this locational diversion.[12] Unfortunately, it is not possible to quantify exact amounts. However, in the assessment of the future growth of trade in financial services, it is important to note that this type of business may well cease to grow and may even shrink, as many industrial countries deregulate their financial sectors, reserve requirements are reduced and nominal interest rates drop. Lower nominal interest rates reduce the implicit effective tax rate of given reserve requirements. The withdrawal of several foreign banks from London, Singapore and Hong Kong in recent years shows the effects of recent developments in the field. Working in the opposite direction and increasing incentives for locational diversion are the expected further reductions in communications costs, which lower the costs and risks of international branch banking.

Global Money Market Business

The US federal funds market has for several decades permitted banks to lend and borrow very short-term funds. Through this market, US banks have been able to use a given high-powered money base to generate a greater money supply than was possible previously.

In recent years, a worldwide equivalent of the US federal funds market has developed. It arbitrages between very short-term national money markets and takes advantage of global time-zone differences. Singapore and Hong Kong banks participate in this business, aided by their favourable time-zone location and the existence of efficient communications and banking systems.

Unfortunately, it is not possible to document the magnitude of the value-added in these banking operations. However, it is known that all of these operations are between banks and take place at extremely thin margins. The value-added is probably very small relative to the other business under discussion, though nearly all of it represents direct trade with other countries. This trade is likely to grow with the real growth of the world economy.

Direct Financial Service and Retail Business

The electronic revolution and deregulation have permitted the financial sectors of industrial countries to expand the menu of differentiated payments and investment services. Charge cards, automated tellers, money market funds, travellers cheques, Euro-credit cheque systems and others have made it easier, more convenient or cheaper to make payments. Mutual funds, futures markets for securities, commodities and currencies, credit-card systems operated by banks and retailers have raised returns to lending and lowered the risks and cost of borrowing and lending.

It is not clear whether and by how much this product differentiation of the financial service industries has raised their value-added. On the one hand, the new services may have met some previously hidden needs and there has probably been some increased value-added through linkages with other services. An analogy may be useful here. The product differentiation in the automobile industry and the sale of built-in music systems may have induced an increased consumption of automobile services as a proportion of GDP.

On the other hand, the electronics revolution and deregulation also have lowered costs of production and raised efficiency. This could have resulted in reduced overall spending on financial services, just as the lower cost of cars can encourage less spending on transportation.

Conditions in Hong Kong and Singapore

Hong Kong's and Singapore's financial service industries have similarly expanded the menu of differentiated financial services. However, it is likely that observed growth in this field reflects primarily the income elasticity of demand for these services. In the future, this elasticity will continue to lead to growth of the industry.

International trade in financial service and retail business generally is small because all of it requires, or benefits from, the physical proximity of customers and agents. Local banks and securities dealers are infinitely more convenient for business than are their foreign counterparts, in spite of the low costs of telephone communications.

Tourist Business

There exist some financial services that are useful mostly for tourists and international business travel, such as credit cards and travellers' cheques systems. Clearly, in this field, global integration gives rise to significant economies of scale. The provision of these services to travellers and licence fees to Visa, American Express and similar firms result in international transactions on financial service accounts. Unfortunately, no data are available on the magnitude of this business. It should be noted, however, that margins in these activities cannot be large since electronics keep costs low and rents from product differentiation are limited by the relative ease of entry. Nevertheless, the value of this tourist-related trade should continue to grow together with the expected increase in international travel.

Differentiated Services and Product Cycles in the Financial Service Trade

Differentiated financial services, developed by intermediaries in the industrial countries, are unlikely to give rise to intra-industry trade[13] in the way product differentiation has in consumer goods. The reason for this is that differentiation in the service field is easy to imitate and adapt to local conditions. For example, economies of scale in providing NOW accounts are negligible relative to those encountered in the production of automobiles and video recorders. The special ingredients of success that underlie the worldwide franchising of retailers in the fast-food, hotel, clothing and car-rental business, appear to be present in the financial service business to a much smaller degree. However, even if there is a significant expansion of global branches of the American Express Company and Merill Lynch serving local consumers, the amount of international trade in financial services due to it is likely to be small. After all, most of the business is with locals and most employees are recruited locally. The essential foreign input that gives rise to foreign payments consists of some top-level managerial input, product know-how and the economies of linkage to a global information and advertising network.

In this context it is worth noting that one of the most dynamic innovators in the financial service field in the United States has been Chicago's International Money Market. This institution is the offspring of the well-known Chicago Mercantile Exchange and it pioneered successfully trade in foreign exchange futures, among other financial instruments. For some time, Asians wishing to invest in such futures had to do business with the Chicago institution. The result was trade in financial services. However, recently there was an announcement that the Singapore Money Exchange (SIMEX) would be established and offer much the same services as the Chicago IMM. While cooperation between the two centres can be expected to be high, international trade in financial services should drop, much as the US export of cars drops when General Motors opens a manufacturing plant abroad.

Vernon has shown that US manufacturing firms have been able to maintain exports in spite of foreign imitation of product differentiation. They produce a constant flow of innovations.[14] The resultant product cycle trade reflects the comparative advantage of the United States in human- and knowledge-capital endowment.

The possible existence of a similar service cycle trade in finance is potentially important for Singapore and Hong Kong. These centres appear to be at a stage of development where available skills are more suited for imitation than innovation. However, the differentiated financial services available in these centres may well serve the entire region.

THE BENEFICIAL EFFECTS OF TRADE IN FINANCIAL SERVICES: THE EXPERIENCE OF HONG KONG AND SINGAPORE

The development of human- and knowledge-capital resources rather than the availability of basic, low-cost labour provide the basis of exploitable comparative advantage in Hong Kong and Singapore. Statistics show that Hong Kong and Singapore have financial industries that are large in comparison with those of other developing countries in the region. This fact reflects the successful development of the human and knowledge capital, which is partly the outcome of historical traditions and partly the result of deliberate government policies, especially in Singapore. Because of their locations and the characteristics of the neighbouring countries, a significant proportion of the value-added in financial service industries in Hong Kong and Singapore is due to exports.

The decision to concentrate human- and knowledge-capital formation on these industries appears to be rational and intelligent, given the basic original factor endowments of these two small countries. The growth of the financial service industries has undoubtedly contributed significantly to the countries' increased productivity. Further human- and knowledge-capital formation in this industry is likely to yield similar positive results.

The development of the financial service industries of Hong Kong and Singapore has also increased the efficiency of the capital markets of these countries and of other countries in the region. This has resulted in better use of scarce capital resources, lowered transaction costs and increased capital inflows from abroad.

These benefits accrue to the two countries and the region largely in the form of externalities. They are nevertheless very important and may become even more so in the future. The entire literature on financial repression discussed in other chapters in this volume stands in support of this proposition.[15]

It is well known that the benefits of financial development and integration with world markets are acquired at the cost of reduced national economic sovereignty. The free, rapid and massive movement of capital between countries should make it impossible to have interest rates, exchange rates, or both, that are optimal for the pursuit of Keynesian employment policies, especially the choice of an optimal inflation–unemployment trade-off. However, the conventional wisdom on economic sovereignty in the Keynesian sense has been challenged by monetarist theories and empirical evidence during the 1970s. The opportunity for a longer run trade-off betweem inflation and unemployment seems largely illusory.

Instead, theory and empirical evidence have shown that the true costs of integrating nations into the global capital market is greater susceptibility to cyclical and random disturbances. The inflations and recessions of the 1970s were worldwide to an extent unknown before the integration of the world's capital markets.

The experiences of Hong Kong and Singapore during the 1970s and early 1980s are, by and large, consistent with this world wide experience. However, while most industrial countries and the LDCs of Africa and South America went through periods of absolute, real declines of GNP, Hong Kong, Singapore and their close neighbours only experienced slowdowns in growth rates.

These facts may be explained by two characteristics. Singapore and Hong Kong have always insisted on a strict separation between Asian-currency and related business on the one hand and their domestic financial development on the other. While this separation has not been entirely successful—Singapore residents can now make deposits and take out loans in the Asian currency business—it has been tight enough to prevent the excesses that caused the overexpansion and debt crisis in so many other countries during the 1970s. And, with some exceptions, governments of the region kept realistic perspectives on both the alleged energy crisis and the seemingly very low cost of foreign capital. These experiences suggest that the development of financial sectors and trade in financial services will bring potential loss of economic sovereignty and may increase economic instability. But they also show that intelligent management can deal effectively with these costs of financial development. Under these conditions, the benefits from this development in the form of capital market efficiency and higher factor productivity clearly outweigh the costs.

In preceding sections the analysis suggested that the growth of Singapore's Asian currency business owed its success largely to selective deregulation in a surrounding sea of regulation. This fact has one important social implication if deregulation becomes more general. In the extreme, it could lead to a severe shrinking of this business in Singapore. Under these conditions, office space, communications facilities and human skills employed by the industry would have to find alternative uses. The adjustment costs would be a real social burden. It remains to be seen whether and when they arise, and how large they would be, but policymakers should be aware of the potential problem.

The attribution of the growth of the Asian currency business to selective deregulation also has important implications for other countries. It is highly unlikely that other centres can repeat Singapore's success by initiative and selective deregulation. There simply is not enough business to be diverted, little to be created, and 'learning by doing' economies have given Singapore a very significant productivity advantage. This, of course, does not mean that countries cannot develop strong, productivity-increasing domestic financial sectors. The limitation concerns trade in international financial services that is based on selective deregulation.

SUMMARY AND CONCLUSIONS

International trade in financial services, as contrasted with international capital flows and Asian currency markets, is a neglected field of study. The basic reason for this state of affairs is that in the past financial services required heavy local inputs, which made the services non-tradable except as intermediate inputs into conventional traded goods and services.

The falling costs of communication, heavy regulation of the financial sector and product differentiation through the application of computers have opened the possibility of increased trade in financial services. The rapid growth of Hong Kong's and Singapore's financial sectors in recent years appears to have been strongly influenced by opportunities for international trade.

Statistics on value-added by financial intermediaries suggest that, compared with more traditional export-oriented industries, the potential for trade in financial services is quite limited. In industrial Canada, the contribution of the financial sector to GDP is only about 2 or 3 per cent.

In the future, Singapore's export of financial services is likely to continue to grow as it performs its role as a regional, supra-national centre, serving its neighbours and linking the region to the world's capital markets. The growth of the Asian-currency business is more uncertain, as the government-created stimuli for its past development diminish with deregulation and lower interest rates. Future trade in differentiated payments and investment services is uncertain. In this field, locational advantages dominate over proprietary, product-differentiation characteristics, though there is a potential for short-lived service cycle trade and international franchising.

Trade in financial services in the Pacific and elsewhere is likely to have its main social effects not through the exploitation of comparative advantage. Instead, trade in financial services has its main social effects through its influence on the efficiency of national and regional capital markets. Foreign competition is a powerful antidote to financial repression by government policies. But trade in financial services also increases the level and volatility of international capital flows, and through them reduces national economic sovereignty. The social effects of this loss of sovereignty are, to a considerable degree, dependent upon the wisdom with which governments handle the opportunities and dangers, as recent history has shown.

Chapter 11

1 See Z. Hodjera 'The Asian Currency Market: Singapore as a Regional Financial Centre' *IMF Staff Papers* 25, 2, June 1978; J.R. Hewson 'Offshore Banking in Australia' *Australian Financial System Inquiry, Commissioned Studies and Selected Papers, Part 2* Canberra: AGPS, 1981; and J. Wong 'ASEAN Economies: Growth and Adjustment' *The Studies of Business and Industry* March 1984.

2 For influential US arguments about the decline of US manufacturing, see B. Bluestone and B. Harrison *The Deindustrialization of America: Plant Closings, Community Abandonment and the Dismantling of Basic Industries* New York: Basic Books, 1982; and R.B. Reich *The Next American Frontier* New York: Times Books, 1983.

T.J. Dilorenzo criticises the deindustrialisation hypothesis in 'The Myth of America's Manufacturing Sector' *The Heritage Foundation Backgrounder* 321, January 1984.

In Figure 11.1, I present Canadian data on the growth of the services and goods-producing industries between 1935 and 1984. Until 1973, both sectors grew at practically identical rates. They did so again from 1975 to the middle of 1981 and during 1983. Sharp declines in goods production during the recessions of 1974 and 1981–82 opened up a performance gap that has been narrowed, but not closed, during the 1983 recovery. These data show that the growth of goods production tends to be cyclic, and that the relative growth of the service industries is a very recent phenomenon.

3 For a review, see F.C. Bergsten and W.R. Cline (eds) *Trade Policy in the Eighties* Washington, D.C.: Institute for International Economics, 1983, especially chapter 17.

4 As noted above, this growth in the US may well be due to the relative decline of goods-producing industries following the 1976 recession. However, it may also be due to the general deregulation of US industry, which took place simultaneously. For reasons that I have been unable to unravel, the UN statistics on FIR for Canada are smaller than those shown in Canadian Department of Finance and Statistics *Economic Review* April 1978 and April 1983, according to which Canada's FIR sector contributed the following to GDP:

Year	1950	1960	1970	1980
Percentage	12.25	12.33	11.54	12.85

5 The sum of SIC 901–903 in Table 11.3 does not add up to the value of SIC 9, as shown in the same source from which the data of Table 11.3 were taken. Adding imputed rent, which has no SIC code, results in a sum only marginally different from SIC 9. However, adding SIC 701 and 705 to SIC 901–903 plus imputed rent gives a number greater than SIC 9. Presumably, SIC 701 and 705 are components of SIC 901.

6 The following analogy may be useful. The export of US aeroplanes is recorded in the merchandise account. When US citizens use these foreign-owned planes they give rise to a US import of travel services.

7 See G. Hufbauer and M. Adler *Overseas Manufacturing Investment and the US Balance of Payments* Washinton, D.C.: US Treasury Department, 1968.

8 For a more detailed analysis of this point see H.W. Arndt 'Measuring Trade in Financial Services' Banca Nazionale del Lavoro *Quarterly Review* 1984.

9 The issue of this bias was the subject of a recent annual meeting of the Association for Research in Income and Wealth.

10 For a development of these arguments, see C.P. Kindelberger *The Formation of Financial Centers* Princeton, N.J.: Princeton University Press, 1974.

11 Consider a bank receiving a deposit of $100 on which it pays $8 interest. It lends out the full amount and earns $10. Assume that under these conditions the average $2 value added per $100 deposit is the normal return to banking in all countries.

Now consider that one small country imposes a reserve requirement of 10 per cent on deposits and that it pays no interest on these reserves. In this small country lending and borrowing rates are unchanged. The only effect of the tax is that banks can lend out $90 and earn only $9 on every $100 deposit, leaving a value-added spread of $1. The reserve requirement has in fact imposed a tax of 50 per cent on the free-market value added of banks. Under these conditions, banks have strong incentives to open branches abroad and encourage their traditional customers to do business there. For an elaboration of this point, see H.G. Grubel 'Interest Payments on Required Reserves to Control Euro-Currency Banking' in Machlup et al. *Reflections on a Troubled World Economy. Essays in Honour of Herbert Giersch* London: Macmillan, 1982.

12 It probably constitutes the main reason for the existence of branches of foreign banks in Singapore, though they also perform minor service functions for their national enterprises and for tourists. For a fuller discussion, and further references see Grubel, ibid.; 'The New International Banking' Banca Nazionale del Lavoro *Quarterly Review* 1983; and 'Towards a Theory of Free Economic Zones' *Weltwirtschaftliches Archiv* 118, 1, 1982.

13 ibid.

14 R. Vernon 'International Investment and International Trade in the Product Cycle' *Quarterly Journal of Economics* May 1966.

15 A standard reference on the subject is R.I. McKinnon *Money and Capital in Economic Development* Washington, D.C.: The Brookings Institution, 1973.

[24]

Excerpt from Yoon S. Park and Musa Essayyad (eds), *International Banking and Financial Centers*, 247–68

16. FINANCIAL CENTER HEGEMONY, INTEREST RATES, AND THE GLOBAL POLITICAL ECONOMY

Howard Curtis Reed
Managing Director and CEO
Curt Reed & Co., Little Rock, Arkansas

INTRODUCTION

In recent years, concern about the continued vitality of the world economy has led some observers to conclude that international financial institutions and markets, as they are presently structured, may not be fully capable of performing the traditional functions of providing:

(1) Large amounts of capital at relatively cheap rates for borrowers, and

(2) Safety and liquidity for savers and investors.

Since 1973, the developing countries have amassed a staggering amount of debt. At year end 1986, the total debt of developing countries was $967 billion; approximately 70 percent of this amount is owed to the large internationally active commercial banks.

Brazil, the country with the largest amount of debt ($109 billion), announced in March 1987 that it was suspending payments on $68 billion of its foreign debt, and freezing $5 billion of short-term deposits owned by foreign banks. Brazil's objective is to have these loans restructured by lengthening the maturity and lowering the interest rate. Other developing countries with large external debt positions are eagerly waiting to see the terms of Brazil's restructuring agreement. The most interested countries are Mexico with $107 billion of outstanding foreign debt; Argentina, $52 billion; Venezuela, $35 billion; Philippines, $28 billion; and Peru, $22 billion. Bankers, government officials, and politicians generally agree that the stagnant level of world trade and economic growth has virtually eliminated any possibility that most of these loans will ever be repaid.

The question then arises as to how the banks and the regulating authorities should handle the accounting for these problem loans. Should these loans be written off entirely, partially, or carried on the books as if no problem existed? Additional questions that must also be answered are: Can a sovereign country go bankrupt? Is it reasonable to expect that the central banks will (and can) act as lenders-of-last-resort in the event of a major default? What powers should creditors have to collect their debt? What changes should be made in the international financial system? Who

248

should manage the international financial system? And, how should the international system be managed?

These problems can clearly be traced to the 1973-74 quadrupling of world oil prices. In 1979-80 another major oil price increase exacerbated the situation that had developed in 1973-74. Oil prices, in 1979-80, increased to $32.50 per barrel from $14. As a result of these price increases, the OPEC countries accumulated enormous current account surpluses, while the non-OPEC developing countries and the industrialized nation were experiencing sizable current account deficits. The industrialized nations in varying degrees were able to offset their deficits. The deficits of the industrialized nations were, in a large part, offset by direct and portfolio investments from the OPEC countries.

The non-OPEC developing countries, on the other hand, did not attract OPEC capital. In addition, the non-OPEC developing countries generally discouraged direct investments from the multinational corporations apparently in the belief that these large organizations fostered dependency. Direct loans from banks, etc. were deemed, by the developing countries to be more acceptable than capital inflows coming from the multinational corporations because bank loans carried no direct financial control of an indigenous asset. The OPEC surpluses and the non-OPEC deficits for selected years is given in Table 1.

TABLE 1
Current Account Balances
(Billions of U.S. Dollars)

	1974	1980	1986
OPEC Surplus (Deficits)	$ 64	$105	$(33)
NON-OPEC Developing Country Surplus (Deficit)	(20)	(69)	(9)
NON-OPEC Bank Loans	44	195	524

Source: **World Financial Markets**, Morgan Guaranty Trust Co., various issues.

This trend, and to some extent the magnitude, of these flows was clearly seen and predicted as early as 1974. I am therefore perplexed at the behavior of interest rates since 1973. A question that remains unanswered is why interest rates did not fall precipitously (perhaps as much as 300 to 400 basis points) in the weeks and months following the oil price increase of 1973-74. At the time of the oil price increases, the international financial system was still adjusting to the consequences of the demise of the fixed exchange rate system that had been in existence since the conclusion of the Bretton Woods conference following World War II. Worry over rising unemployment land inflation and the economic health of LDCs was also being voiced.

In early 1974, the magnitude of the shift in wealth from the industrialized Western nations to the oil exporting countries was becoming quite clear. OPEC oil revenues in 1973 were $22 billion. Early estimates of 1974 OPEC oil revenues ranged from $100 to $115 billion (the actual revenues were slightly less than $90 billion). Armed with this information, it seems reasonable to have expected that London, the principal beneficiary of OPEC funds, would have bid down substantially the price it was willing to pay for new deposits. New York, the only other center capable of handling such a large influx of funds, was not receiving, directly, any of these new deposits from OPEC--for obvious political reasons.

It was clear at the time that these new liabilities, accruing to London, would be converted into assets by primarily increasing the loans made to developing countries, which were already having difficulty meeting their financial obligations. It should have been clear that rising interest rates have a destabilizing effect on the world's equity markets which make it difficult for corporations to maintain the appropriate debt/equity mix in their capital structure, which is vitally important to investor confidence. London, and the American banks which dominate the Eurocurrency market, should have realized that rising interest rates increase the general level of uncertainty, which has a tendency to slow capital investment activity in favor of shorter-term cash management actions. This puts additional upward pressure on inflation and unemployment.

This paper attempts to shed some light on interest rate behavior since 1973 by showing what happened and by arguing that the behavior has been misguided. The misguided behavior results from a theoretical framework that analyzes interest rate behavior by emphasizing financial institutions and financial markets, instead of "financial centers." In other words, interest rate behavior is a product of financial center determinants, not just the activity of the large internationally active commercial banks or the activity of the internationally active financial markets.

250

FINANCIAL CENTERS

Financial centers can be classified into three distinct groups:[1]

(1) *Host centers*. These centers enhance their own financial infrastructures and capabilities by attracting relatively large numbers of foreign financial institutions from a large number of countries.

(2) *International Centers*. These centers are headquarters for large internationally active banks which influence events that pertain to global asset and liability management.

(3) *Supranational Centers*. These centers are managers of large amounts of foreign financial assets and liabilities; net suppliers of foreign direct investment capital to the rest of the world; located close to a large number of large (measured by assets) industrial corporations; active users of global communication facilities (i.e., airplanes, telephone, telex, etc.); and management meccas that attract and generate ideas and information in ways that eventually establish the organizational and operating norms that govern internationally active organizations (private and governmental).

Financial centers are not only organized in a hierarchical structure for finance but they are also organized hierarchically for communications and management. As a result, the "supranational" centers are preeminent in finance, communications, and management. Finance centers facilitate the flow of goods, services, and capital within its own national economy and between its national economy and the other national economies of the world. Communication centers are places where interaction occurs, ideas are exchanged, and information is gathered, analyzed, and disseminated. Management centers are locations that require and subsequently attract skilled persons to organize the sourcing, reformulation, and marketing of resources in a clearly defined manner, a manner that lends itself to standardization and eventually the adoption of these practices on a wide scale.

The supranational centers, it is argued, provide the environment, the mechanism, and the competence for evaluating, on a continual basis, the policies and activities of the institutional components of the global political economy. These centers are important for:

(1) Financial sourcing and allocation

(2) Evaluating the policies, strategies, and activities of nations[2]

(3) Industrial project evaluation and pricing

(4) Monitoring the activities of the institutional components of the political economy, and

(5) Providing money and capital management services. The level of efficiency with which a center can perform these functions is dependent on its astuteness in gathering, evaluating, and utilizing information from around the world. Additionally, a center's astuteness is largely dependent upon the number (and size) of its locally headquartered banks, the management acumen of these institutions, the collective connections (to other centers) of these institutions, and the industrial power (and reach) of the nation's corporations.

The 1981 study (by Reed, Note 1) provided considerable insight into what is required to build financial center infrastructure over time (i.e., institutions, connections, markets, etc.), and into the organization, distribution, and influence of these centers. That study, however, left unexplored a whole range of factors that have emerged in the past ten to fifteen years that may have a significant influence on the building of financial center infrastructure, organization, and influence. The 1981 study uses a nine-variable analysis. The analysis in this study uses sixteen variables (six variables from the 1981 study plus ten new variables).[3]

In this sixteen-variable study, the organizational structure was determined by (in the order of their statistical significance) the amount of international currency clearings, the size of the Eurocurrency market, foreign financial assets, and headquarters for the large internationally active commercial banks (Figure 1).

As a result of the analysis, supranational centers can be characterized as centers whose principal operating currency(ies) is (are) widely used for settling international trade and capital transactions and whose financial infrastructures (primarily the large commercial banks) are developed to the extent that they are entrusted with the management of the world's foreign financial liabilities and assets. The large internationally active commercial banks have the primary responsibility for facilitating international clearings which in 1985 amounted to a U.S. equivalent of $324 billion a day. U.S. dollars accounted for approximately $225 billion of the total, and New York was clearing approximately 90 percent of these dollar transactions. In addition to the currency transactions, the clearing infrastructure is also used for coupon, dividend and interest payments on securities; and it is used to facilitate the transfers and registration of securities.

INTEREST RATE THEORY AND FINANCIAL CENTER INFRASTRUCTURE

The theories of interest rate determination and structure are based in large part on market expectations about the future. Traditional interest rate theory determines the rate of interest by intersecting the supply and demand curves for all financial assets.[4] The assumption is made that economic units:

(1) Are risk averse, and

(2) Base their utility preferences on the expected return and risk associated with a particular financial asset. It is further assumed that the principal objective of an economic unit is to maximize its total utility by selecting a diversified portfolio of financial assets that is optimal with respect to expected value of return and risk.

Theories that attempt to explain the yield-maturity relationship of financial assets argue that the behavior of interest rates is a function of the level of expected future short-term rates. The unbiased expectation theory argues that long-term interest rates are an unbiased average of current and future short-term rates. Therefore, an upward sloping yield curve implies that interest rates are expected to rise, and a downward sloping yield curve says that interest rates are expected to decline. Another theory, the expectations and liquidity preference theory, argues that investors generally prefer to lend short unless they receive a liquidity premium large enough to offset the risks associated with lending long-term. Liquidity premiums are thought to be a function of risk, where risk is a function of time (i.e., maturity schedule). The bias in this theory is toward upward sloping yield curves.

In the classic economic environment, it is perfectly legitimate to conclude that interest rates are determined by market supply and demand. For the large internationally active banks, the objective is largely traditional, i.e., maximizing total utility and optimizing income and wealth. For the supranational center (hereafter, financial center) the objective is quite different. The financial center's objective is, at the very least, to maximize the welfare of the political economy by optimally distributing financial resources throughout the world. The financial center is a synthesized infrastructure of institutions and markets whose function is to evaluate the operating efficiencies of the financial, industrial, commercial, and political organizations that utilize the center's capital, information and management resources.

The large internationally active commercial banks in addition to performing the traditional intermediary function of accepting deposits and making loans are also instrumental in gathering, analyzing, and disseminating information. These banks provide the principal direct links by which the financial centers access and disseminate information. Through the global branch networks, the internationally active banks transmit information between centers presumably at greater speeds, and at higher levels of quality and accuracy than information transmitted between center through relatively public networks. The strategic role of these banks naturally leads to the question: In international finance, is it the banks or is it the centers that are preeminent? The question is perhaps best answered by examining some aspects of the relationship between banks and centers.

In Japan, for example, the large internationally active banks headquartered in Osaka (Sumitomo, Sanwa, and Diawa), Kobe (Taiyo), Nagoya (Tokai) have their "top" international people in Tokyo and have recently split their top domestic people between their home office and Tokyo. Similar activities have taken place in California (USA). Bank of America has officially split its headquarters into a northern division in San Francisco (the original headquarters), headed by the president (chief executive officer) and a southern division in Los Angeles, headed by the chairman of the board (chief operation officer). The other large San Francisco bank, Wells Fargo, now has its chief executive officer spend 40 to 50 percent of his time in Southern California. This reflects the growth of Los Angeles as a significant financial center.

The importance of New York as a financial center is underscored by pointing out the impact of its international clearing facilities on the status and influence of international banking activity. Foreign banks have made it quite clear that having access to New York's Clearing House Interbank Payment System (CHIPS) is an important consideration when deciding on whether to open an office (or enlarge an existing office) in New York. Apparently the large U.S. banks headquartered outside of New York also feel that way. In the early years of this decade, a group of large U.S. banks headquartered outside of New York, led by Bank of America and Continental Illinois, attempted to delay and perhaps prevent New York from receiving final approval from the Federal Reserve to establish International Banking Facilities (IBFs). The support of this group was contingent upon their being given direct access to the CHIPs computer from their home offices outside of New York. It was argued that with IBFs and CHIPS at their disposal, the 12 settling banks headquartered ind New York will be able to obtain deposits at lower costs and make loans more profitably, thus giving the New York banks an unfair competitive advantage. (The ploy did

254

not work. New York's IBFs began operating on December 1, 1981 and the non-New York banks do not get direct computer access to CHIPS).

Another action which appears to clearly favor the importance of the center over the banks is the behavior of the Arab Organization of Petroleum Exporting Countries (AOPEC) in 1973-74. When AOPEC quadrupled oil prices in 1973 and 1974, its members initially chose to employ their cash reserves (billions of new dollars) in London, even though comparable deposit rates in New York were 50 to 75 basis points higher. The London branch and subsidiary offices of the New York banks were the principal recipients (receiving more than 70 percent of the total) of the funds going to London.

If the banks were preeminent, then why not take advantage of the higher yields being offered in New York, since the London affiliates of the New York banks were the principal depositories for these AOPEC funds? This example points to the significance of politics and confidence, in addition to the more quantifiable variables, as important determinants of financial centers structure, particularly the perceived willingness of a center to use economic means to achieve a political objective. As important as the banks are, the evidence appears to clearly show that the large internationally active banks are not more important than the centers. The evidence also appears to clearly show that the reach, scope, and influence of the center is far greater than the total, reach, scope, and influence of its various institutions when measured independently.

Financial markets are comprised of a wide range of intermediary institutions, including the large internationally active banks. Financial markets are the formal mechanism by which savings are efficiently allocated. The efficiencies of these markets are reflected in the economies generated in the coordination of a wide range of financial transactions, such as providing the mechanism for:

(1) Clearing checks, stock certificates, etc.

(2) Larger and cheaper security issues for those that need capital, and

(3) Greater liquidity for lenders of capital. These rationing and coordinating activities are governed largely by the cost/price relationship of the supply and demand for these activities.

The foreign exchange markets are much more representative of the financial center than are the banks and securities markets. The foreign exchange market reflects immediately that center's evaluation of a nation's political economy. In the intermediate and very near term, it is reflected in the spot rate. In the future, or long term, it is the forward rate. The exchange rate is (at least, it should be) a synthesized evaluation of a nation's overall status--its policies, strategies, and activities. Nations, including their economic organizations, are active users of the products and services of financial centers.

A shift in a nation-state's policy, strategy, or predicted activity could substantially alter the portfolio quality of the center, and, in turn, of its investors. Accurate evaluation is also essential to evaluating and pricing industrial projects that are targeted for investment in foreign countries or projects that are dependent upon cash flow emanating from that country. Industrial project evaluation is also important for the initial pricing of the borrowed capital. Monitoring the progress of the projects is necessary so that the current value of the outstanding principal can be assessed. The quality of the money and capital management services offered by the center is largely a function of how well these other functions are managed.

INTEREST RATE BEHAVIOR: A FINANCIAL CENTER PERSPECTIVE

The expectation theory looks at future interest rates from the financial market's point of view. The theory concedes (albeit implicitly) that financial markets themselves have no significant influence over the future level of interest rates. Long-term interest rates are merely the market's expectation about the level of future interest rates. A financial center view of the future level of interest rates is more explicit about what influences future rate levels. The financial markets cannot determine or significantly influence the future level of interest rates, because these markets are only the mechanism by which the center makes the results of its evaluation known. The center's evaluation then results in a future level of interest rates being established.

The large internationally active banks and other financial institutions do not independently evaluate projects, price capital, and allocate resources. They do not independently set interest rate levels. The evaluation, pricing, and allocation is the result of all of the center's institutional components acting and reacting to the environment in a predictable manner. Succinctly stated, the financial center at any given period of time has the power and the responsibility to significantly influence the future level of interest rates by determining the direction of future interest rate trends. Interest rates should not necessarily be determined or significantly influenced by the supply and demand for financial assets.

The financial center does have a set of expectations about future interest rate levels. The expectations are based on the center's forecast of inflation, savings, consumption, industrial activity, trade, money supply,

256

source(s) of funds, and so forth. Based on these predictions, the future trend (direction) of interest rate movement is initiated. Therefore, the center's expectation about future interest rate levels at any given time is a function of the accuracy of the center's forecast and its ability to speed up, slow down, or leave unchanged the forecasted trends (and levels) of inflation, savings, consumption, industrial activity, and so on. The direction of movement in the level of rates, as initiated by the center, is designed to speed up, slow down, or leave unaffected (or at least minimally so) the various environmental components (i.e., inflation, savings, etc.)

The expectations and liquidity preference argument holds that investors (lenders) require a liquidity premium sufficient to offset the risk associated with longer-term investments (loans). From the financial center's point of view, the expected future level of interest rates is a function of the accuracy of its forecasts and the extent to which it can carry out its desired purpose with respect to the environmental components. All investments that are not free of default require a liquidity (risk) premium for the investor. The center, however, has the option of determining whether the risk is initially absorbed by the saver (depositor) through lowering the interest rate paid to the saver or the borrower by increasing the interest rate charged. The center's earnings (and risk premiums) are generated from the spread between what it pays for funds and what it charges.

When focusing on earnings, the center must first take steps to ensure the success of its clientele. This means that the center is concerned foremost with the earnings and overall value of the portfolio of its clients and less concerned with its own earnings and investment portfolio. The reason for this is twofold. First, the center operates as an intermediary providing capital, information, and management products and services. And second, the center's total portfolio of clients represents the center's investment. The financial center is unlike the corporation, in that the lower the expected risk, the greater the expected return for the center. The center's primary concern at all times will be to reduce the expected risk of return on its portfolio of activities. For example, in cost of capital considerations, and where interest rates are an important determinant, the center's behavior will be to bid down the amount it pays for funds so as to minimize what it must charge for funds. The higher the capital servicing requirements for the borrowing firms, the greater the probability of problems occurring with the center's portfolio.

Figure 2 shows the financial center's risk-earnings possibility curve. The center's earnings are derived principally from fees and the spreads received between bid and ask on a wide range of intermediary activities. The negative slope of the curve suggests that, along with the benefits derived from an increase in the volume of activity, the center could widen the spread between bid and ask and increase the base rate of its fee schedules without significantly increasing risk or reducing volume of activity. By increasing the spreads and adjusting upwardly the base rate for its fees, the center adds to its reserves and capital accounts. The risk premiums required by the center varies inversely with the level of interest rates. The center wants to enhance the quality of its asset portfolio by providing capital to users at a cost that minimizes the risk of capital depreciation (e.g. being unable to service debt obligations; omitting or reducing dividend payments; etc.) and capital destruction (e.g. being unable to repay the principal from debt obligations; having the value of stockholder's equity reduced; etc.)

The large internationally active commercial banks, in most instances, respond quite differently to events. The behavioral differences between banks and the centers are primarily the results of their operating within inherently different market structures. The number of large internationally active banks competing on a global scale in a large number of product markets is considerably more than one hundred; and when regional competitors are included, the number of competitors exceeds two hundred. The number of financial centers with global capability is limited to New York and London. There are five centers with "near" global capability--Tokyo, Frankfurt, Paris, Zurich and Amsterdam. The market structure in which banks operate is considerably more competitive than the market structure in which the centers operate.

An example of the significance of the market structure constraints on banks can be seen when capital adequacy is examined. There are no absolute capital requirements for banks operating outside of their home countries, but investors, depositors and regulators impose their own standard as to what constitutes a sufficient amount of capital. A bank may also recognize that the quality of its portfolio, and the level of its earnings, will be enhanced if interest rates were lower. But when the bank lowers the interest rate it pays for deposits, it will lose future deposits as well as maturing deposits to competitor banks paying a higher interest rate. In other words, it is very unlikely that a bank will unilaterally lower the rate it pays for deposits prior to its reaching its minimal capital/deposit ratio. Even at this minimum, an interest rate reduction will not be necessary because the depositors will shift future additional funds to competitor banks (i.e., those banks with a more favorable capital/deposit ratio). Any bank moving unilaterally and precipitously to lower the interest rate it pays for deposits, exposes itself (in the short run) to the risk of having to fund its asset portfolio.

The comprehensive nature of the financial center (i.e., institutional infrastructure, investment instruments, and sophisticated clients) precludes the banks from having to move unilaterally to lower interest rates and reduce risk. The process of lowering the center's cost of capital to its clients will begin, for example, when one of the large internationally active banks reaches (or approaches) its minimum capital/deposit ratio. The depositors will direct future flows to other, better capitalized, banks. The undercapitalized bank will continue to lose deposits until the capital adequacy (in this particular situation it's the capital/deposit ratio) of all competitor banks has been minimized. Once the minimal capital/deposit ratio has been reached, the competitor banks will then lower their interest rates.

As a result of all banks now paying lower interest rates, future flows of funds to banks will be reduced. In addition, maturing deposits (in the short-run) will seek alternative investments. This will result in a net outflow of funds from the banking industry, which will result in a capital/deposit ratio that is optimal (particularly from the depositor's perspective) instead of minimal. The beneficiary of the outflow of funds from the banks will be the center's other money and capital market instruments (i.e., commercial paper, bonds, common stock, etc.). These actions will lower the overall cost of capital to all capital seekers using (and operating within) the center.

The interest rate behavior of both the large internationally active banks and the supranational financial center is illustrated in Figure 3a and 3b respectively. The interest rate paid is measured on the vertical axis and the quantity of funds supplied is measured on the horizontal axis. Figure 3a shows the behavior of the large internationally active banks operating within the center. The vertical lines labeled C_1, C_2, and C_n denotes the amount of capital in bank 1, bank 2, and bank n. The supply curve is labeled S. If the banks operating in a financial center believe that their capital resources are not being fully utilized, they take steps to increase deposits (liabilities) and, in turn, assets.

Assuming a competitive environment, price elasticity, and industry leadership, the most influential bank (perhaps C_n, if it is also the largest) will increase the rate of interest it pays for deposits. In due course, the rest of the center's banks also increase their interest rates. At interest rate I_1, the bank represented by the capital constraint line C_1 has reached its minimal capital/deposit ratio. At this point, X, bank C_1 will no longer compete with the rest of the industry for deposits on the basis of price. It will not be compelled to follow the industry in increasing its interest rates paid for future deposits because future deposits will flow to banks C_2 and C_n. At point Y, bank C_2 reaches its minimal capital/deposit ratio. Depositors will now direct all future deposits to bank C_n. At point Z, the center's banking industry will be fully utilizing its operating capital. The broken lines of the supply curve, S, represents the quantity of funds that will seek employment in the other money and capital market instruments available in the center.

There are two types of funds available to the center's banking industry:

(1) Unique Funds - capital that is made available to a financial center on the basis of that center's operating character (e.g. AOPEC funds in London during 1973-74, or clearing deposits maintained in New York).

(2) Volatile Funds - capital that continuously moves between all financial centers, usually seeking a higher return.

The cost of "unique" funds to the banking industry will not begin to decline until the capital/deposit ratio of all banks operating in that financial center falls below some minimum level. The cost of "volatile" funds to the banking industry will not begin to decline until the capital/deposit ratio of all banks, in all financial centers, falls below some minimum level. Therefore, each financial center's capital resources are classified as "unique" and "volatile". The center's influence over the future trends of interest rates is confined to its "unique" funds' portfolio. A center's "unique" funds' portfolio becomes vulnerable only when its capital/deposit ratio becomes unfavorable, when compared to other competitor centers.

Figure 3b shows the interest rate behavior of the financial center. The vertical line labeled C_* is the amount of capital supporting the center's activities. The TFS curve represents the total amount of funds available in the center (TFS = unique funds + volatile funds). The UFS curve represents the amount of unique funds available in the center. At the interest rate level I_*, the financial center is operating at its minimal capital/deposit ratio. At point A, the center will lose its volatile funds to other centers with more favorable capital positions. The supply curve for the center now shifts to UFS. The center's supply of unique funds will continue to 'increase beyond A', because of the "special" relationship between these funds and the center. After a while, the center recognizes its monopoly position with these funds, and at this time (point B) the center begins to lower the interest rate it pays for these funds. With lower interest rates being paid on deposits, the spread between interest paid for liabilities and interest earned on assets can be widened. The increased earnings permit the center to add to its reserves and increases its capital base.

The general supply curves facing the financial center is shown in Figure 4. The center has two supply curves (1) the relatively inelastic "unique" funds curve, s_u; and (2) the relatively elastic "volatile" funds curve, s_v. The center's relative influence over its "unique" funds fall somewhere in between monopoly and oligopoly. And the market structure for volatile funds is between monopolistically competitive and perfectly competitive markets.

MISGUIDED BEHAVIOR?

Developing a theoretical framework to explain behavior is not only important because it may explain the events that have already taken place, or because it may explain future events, but in this instance, a theory is also important because it is useful in identifying those factors that may be impeding the more "logical" and the more "rational" behavior of financial centers. Since the early 1970s, financial center behavior has been at odds with the theoretical framework argued for in this paper. A case in point: since the initial quadrupling of oil prices in 1973-74, the global economy has generated virtually no real growth, unemployment has more than doubled, inflation has increased threefold, corporate bankruptcies have more than doubled, and the international financial system is precariously plodding along without a clear plan for solving the problems associated with the prohibitively high costs.

Many (perhaps most, or even all) of these problems could have been avoided if London had reduced the interest rates it paid for Eurodollar deposits after the two major oil price increases: in 1973-74 and again in 1979-80. Table 2 gives the average annual Eurodollar and U.S. dollar rates (overnight and three month) for the years 1973 through 1981; and it also gives the oil price levels for the same time period.

Perhaps the theoretical framework presented in this paper will in some small way illuminate the importance and the significance of the supranational financial centers. London's view (in 1973-74 and again in 1979-80) of its supply curve with respect to AOPEC funds was, in my opinion, misguided. Apparently, London believed the AOPEC funds were unique and relatively inelastic, depicted in Figure 5b[5]. If London had lowered the price it was paying for capital, AOPEC funds would have been forced to: accept the lower rate, place substantial amounts in other European and Asian centers, accept the risk and utilize New York, or pursue a direct investment strategy.

Lower rates would have reduced OPEC's incentive to increase oil rates further, restrained inflation and enhanced the level of confidence in the global economies, and indirectly forced OPEC to absorb some of the costs associated with recycling their surplus.

In addition, the problems that the large internationally active banks are now encountering (i.e., the danger that a substantial percentage of their asset asset portfolios will become non-performing) would have been avoided.

TABLE 2

Eurodollar and U.S. Dollar Deposit Rates
(Yearly Average)

	Overnight		Three Month		Oil Prices Index
Year	Euro	U.S.	Euro	U.S.	(1974 = 100)
1973	8.80	8.73	9.35	8.49	
1974	10.40	10.49	11.23	10.28	100
1975	5.77	5.82	6.90	6.33	98
1976	5.07	5.05	5.55	5.20	106
1977	5.70	5.54	6.11	5.73	114
1978	8.09	7.90	8.97	8.41	117
1979	11.29	11.15	11.94	11.31	178
1980	13.40	13.41	14.35	13.32	306
1981	16.11	16.35	16.47	15.31	327

Surely, London realized that the developing countries would be requiring substantial amounts of capital, over and above the large amounts that they already owed, just to finance their oil imports. London must also have realized that the growth in non-oil world trade would certainly slow down, and more likely would shrink. It therefore seems reasonable to conclude that London recognized that the demand for its funds was relatively inelastic (Figure 6).

From the perspective of the theoretical framework presented in this analysis, London's behavior was clearly "misguided". But the explanations given by private (and central) bankers, multinational corporate executives, economists, etc. clearly show that London's behavior was consistent with traditional interest rate theory. The relevance and the usefulness of the framework presented here may not be fully known for some considerable

262

time into the future. At the very least, however, it is hoped that this framework will stimulate worthwhile arguments, debates, and discussions.

NOTES

1. Howard Curtis Reed, *The Preeminence of International Financial Centers*, (New York: Praeger Publishers, 1981), pp. 60-61.

2. This evaluation is reflected immediately in the foreign exchange (spot and forward) market value of currencies, and later on, in the nation's collective cost of capital.

3. The sixteen-variable measures are (asterisk indicates variables used in the 1981 study):

   * Capital/Deposit ratio of the large internationally active banks headquartered in the center.

   * Capital/Asset ratio of the large internationally active banks headquartered in the center.

   * Pre-tax Earnings/Capital ratio of the large internationally active banks headquartered in the center.

   * Pre-tax Earnings/Assets ratio of the large internationally active banks headquartered in the center.

   * Revenue/Asset ratio of the large internationally active banks headquartered in the center.

   * Total international currency clearings (daily average) of the center.

   * Size (liabilities) of the center's Eurocurrency market.

   * Total amount of international bonds issued in the center during the year.

   * Foreign financial assets held in the center.

   * Foreign financial liabilities residing in the center.

   * The daily average of the center's stock exchange activity (sales value).

* The number of large internationally active commercial banks headquartered in the center.

* The number of large internationally active foreign banks with offices (agencies, branches, or subsidiaries) in the center.

* The number of foreign financial centers with direct links to the local center and the links are provided by the foreign internationally active banks.

* The center's airline passenger traffic (yearly total).

* The center's airmail/airfreight volume (yearly total).

4. An excellent overview of interest rate theory and structure is given in James C. Van Horne, *Functions and analysis of capital market rates*, (Englewood Cliffs, New Jersey: Prentice-Hall, 1970), Chapter III, IV, and V.

5. An argument could be made that the supplies of capital, supplied after the maximal capital/deposit ratio is exceeded (Point A), would get the additional risk premium. It is highly unlikely that the suppliers of capital recognized this situation. And there is no evidence to support such an argument.

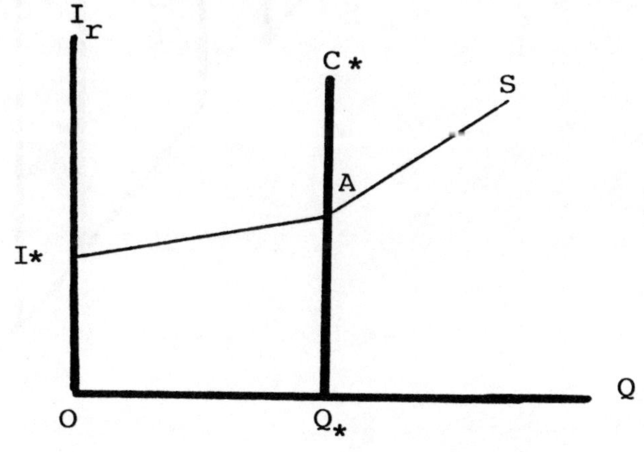

Figure 1

INTERNATIONAL FINANCIAL CENTERS
(Organization and Structures)

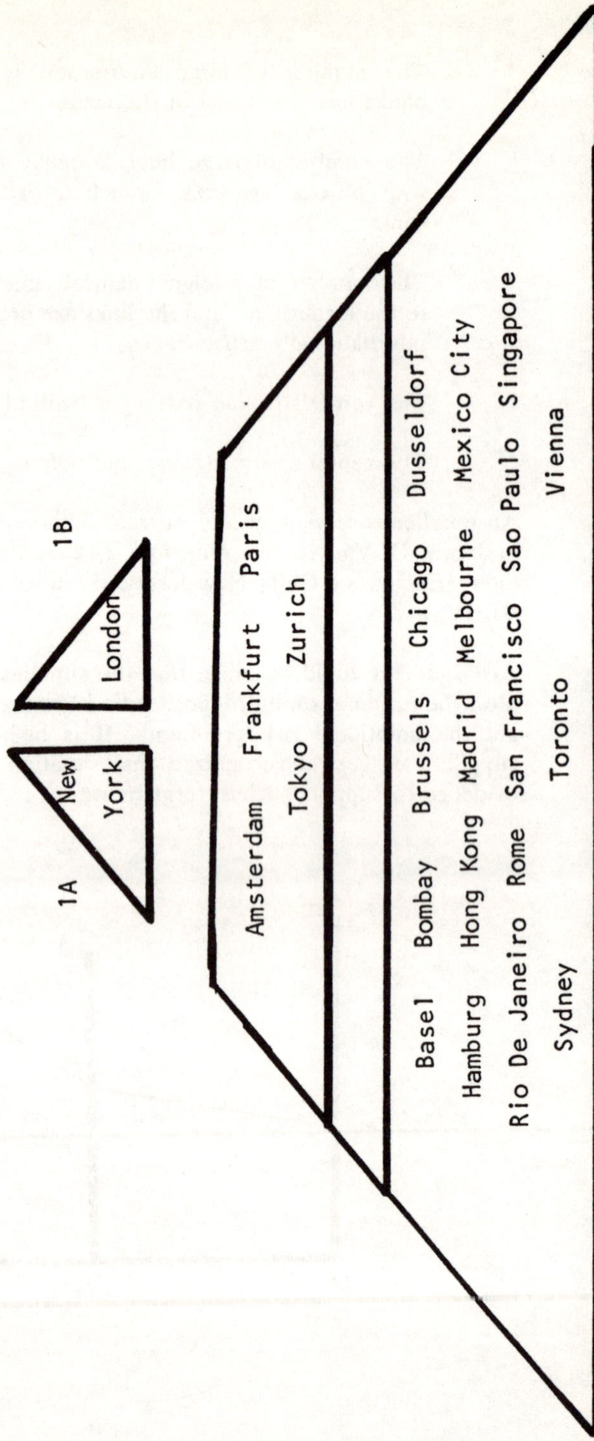

Figure 2

SUPRANATIONAL FINANCIAL CENTERS

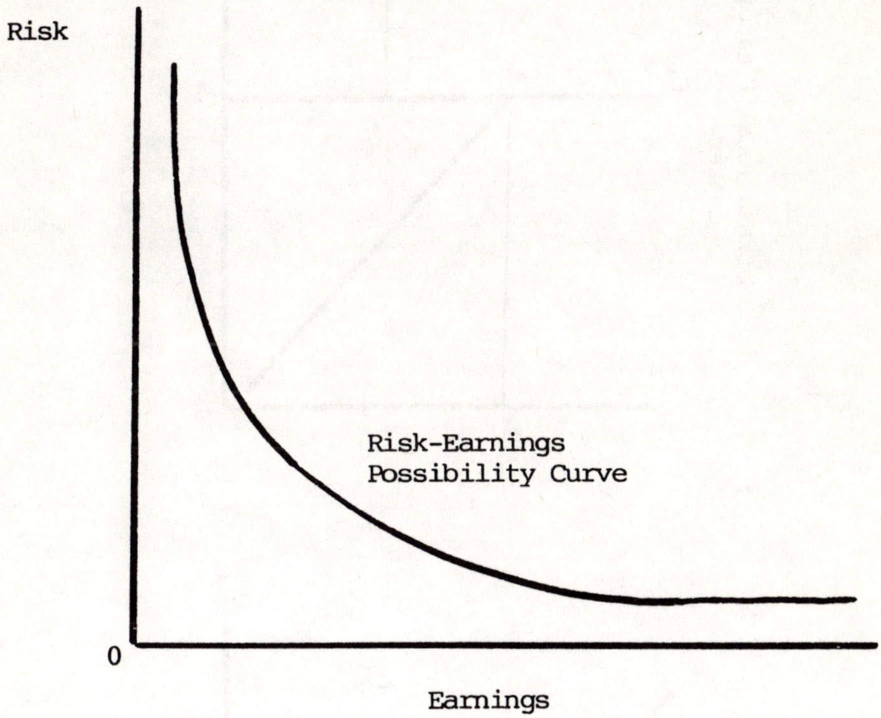

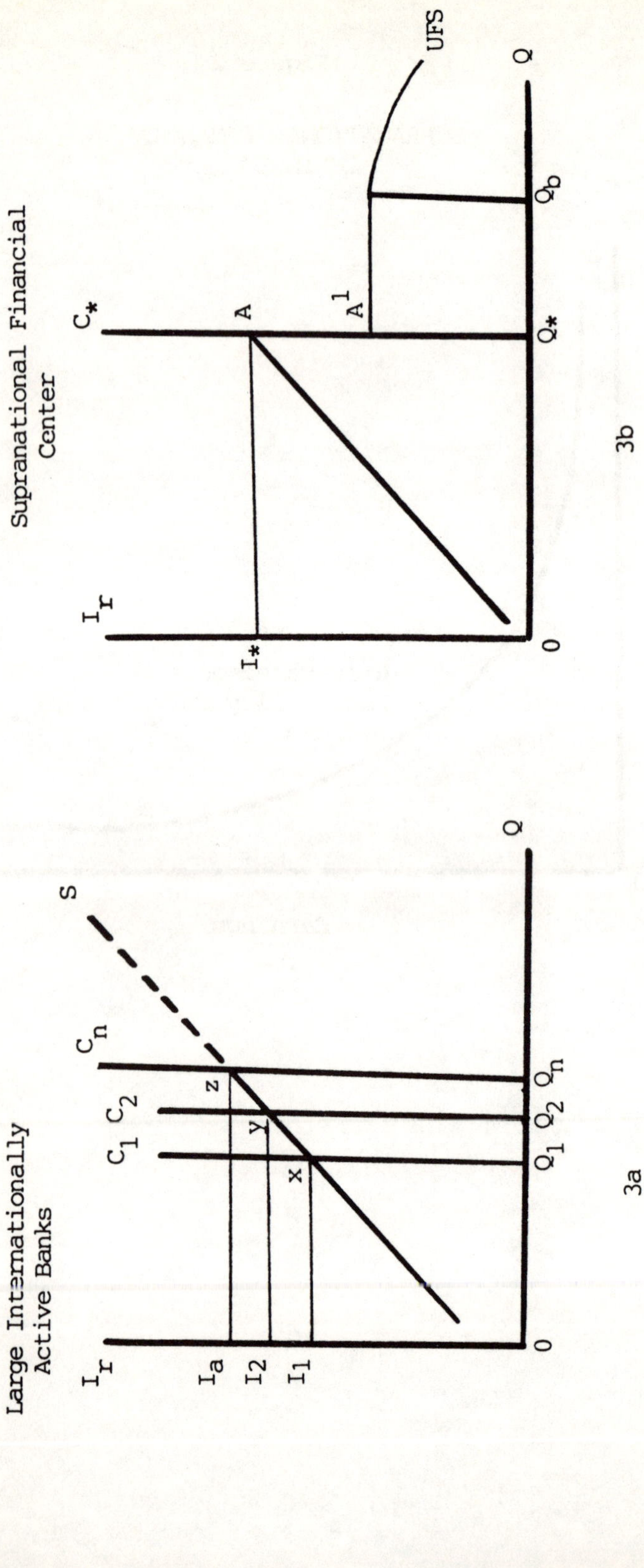
Large Internationally Active Banks
I_r
I_a
I2
I1
C_1 C_2 C_n
x
y
z
S
0
Q_1 Q_2 Q_n
Q
3a
Supranational Financial Center
I_r
I_*
C_*
A
A^1
UFS
0
Q_*
Q_b
Q
3b

Figure 4

Supranational Financial Center Supply Curves

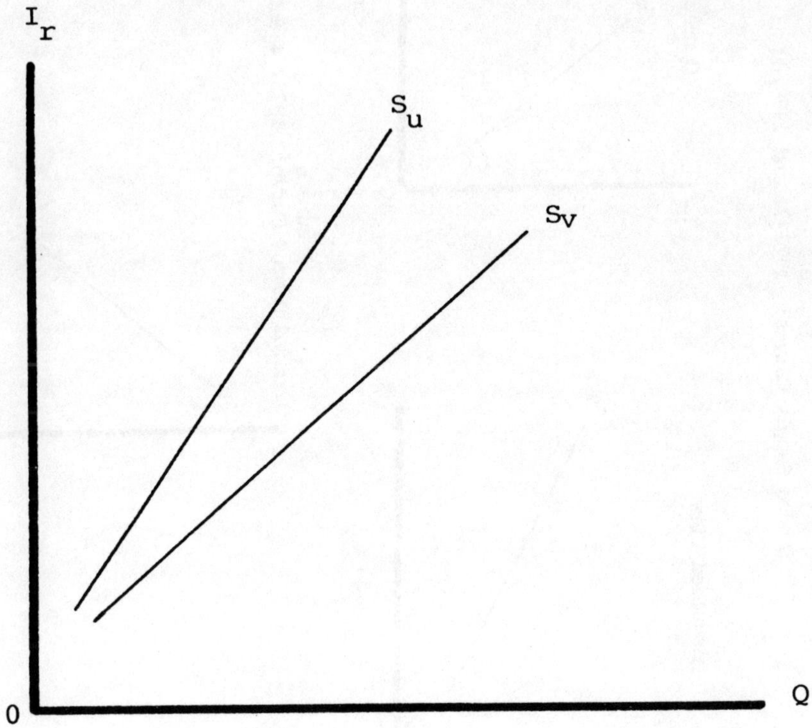

Figure 5
London Supply Curves: 1973/74 and 1979/80

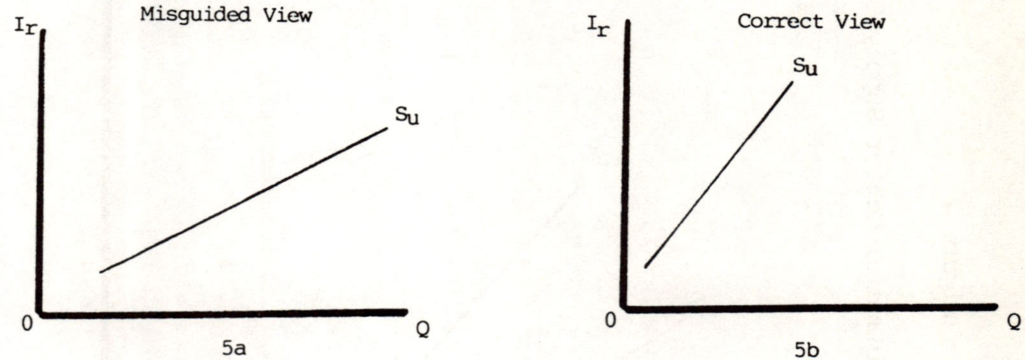

Figure 6
Londond Demand Curve: 1973/74 and 1979/80

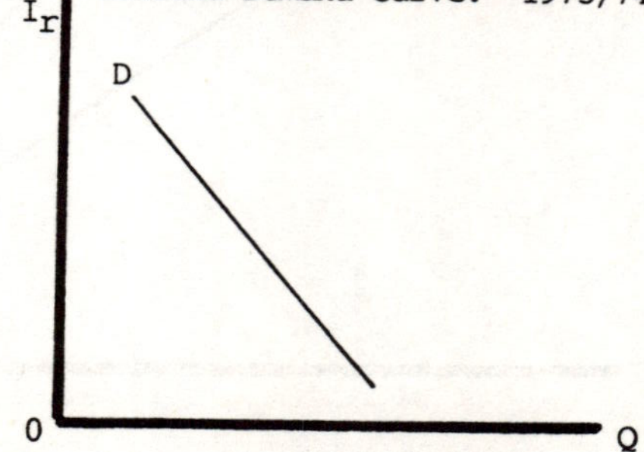

Name Index

Place Index